Everyday Mathematics®

The University of Chicago School Mathematics Project

Teacher's Lesson Guide
Volume 1

Grade 2

McGraw Hill Wright Group

The McGraw·Hill Companies

The University of Chicago School Mathematics Project (UCSMP)

Max Bell, Director, UCSMP Elementary Materials Component; Director, *Everyday Mathematics* First Edition; James McBride, Director, *Everyday Mathematics* Second Edition; Andy Isaacs, Director, *Everyday Mathematics* Third Edition; Amy Dillard, Associate Director, *Everyday Mathematics* Third Edition

Authors

Max Bell, Jean Bell, John Bretzlauf, Amy Dillard, Robert Hartfield, Andy Isaacs, James McBride, Cheryl G. Moran*, Kathleen Pitvorec, Peter Saecker

*Third Edition only

Technical Art
Diana Barrie

Editorial Assistant
John Wray

ELL Consultant
Kathryn B. Chval

Mathematics and Technology Advisor
Jim Flanders

Teachers in Residence
Kathleen Clark, Patti Satz

Photo Credits

©Tom Brakefield/Getty Images, p. xxiii, *center;* ©Cartesia/PhotoDisc Imaging/Getty Images, xxxi *top;* ©Cassy Cohen/Photo Edit, p. 92; ©Corbis, p. 376 apples and oranges, steak, milk; Courtesy NASA/JPL-Caltech, p. 460; ©2002 Dotti Enderle, p. 450; ©Getty Images, cover, *right;* pp. 443, 376 broccoli, carrots, lettuce, bowl of rice; ©JupiterImages Corporation, pp. xxiv *top,* 3, 464, ©Christina Kennedy/Alamy, p. xxi *top;* ©Linda Lewis; Frank Lane Picture Agency/CORBIS, cover, *bottom left;* ©Gerben Oppermans/Getty Images, p. 456; ©Photodisc/Getty Images, pp. xxix *top,* 376 food pyramid; ©Martin Poole/Getty Images, p. xxvii *bottom;* ©Mike Powell/Getty Images, p. xxiii *bottom;* ©Alison Shaw/VEER, p. 377; ©Ariel Skelley/CORBIS; ©Star/zefa/Corbis, cover, *center;* ©Martin Vickery/Alamy, *bottom;* ©David Michael Zimmerman/CORBIS.

Contributors

Catherine Ann Gesell, Serena Hohmann, Lisa Christine Munson, Kathleen Marie Pina, Gabriel Sheridan; Librada Acosta, Carol Arkin, Robert Balfanz, Sharlean Brooks, Jean Callahan, Anne Coglianese, Mary Ellen Dairyko, Tresea Felder, Dorothy Freedman, Rita Gronbach, Deborah Arron Leslie, William D. Pattison, LaDonna Pitts, Danette Riehle, Marie Schilling, Robert Strong, Sadako Tengan, Therese Wasik, Leeann Wille, Michael Wilson

www.WrightGroup.com

Send all inquiries to:
Wright Group/McGraw-Hill
P.O. Box 812960
Chicago, IL 60681

ISBN 0-07-603594-8

11 12 13 RMN 12 11 10

The McGraw·Hill Companies

The University of Chicago School Mathematics Project (UCSMP)

Acknowledgements

The first edition of *Everyday Mathematics* was made possible by sustained support over several years from the GTE Corporation and the National Science Foundation; additional help came from the Amoco Foundation through its support of the University of Chicago School Mathematics Project (UCSMP). Earlier projects supported by the National Science Foundation, the National Institute of Education, and the Benton Foundation provided us with insights into the surprising capabilities of young children.

Development of the second edition of *Everyday Mathematics* was funded by the Everyday Learning Corporation and the authors; development of this third edition was supported by Wright Group/McGraw-Hill, the University of Chicago, and the authors.

For all three editions, many University of Chicago and UCSMP colleagues have been helpful. For this third edition, Deborah Arron Leslie, David W. Beer, Rachel Malpass McCall, Cheryl G. Moran, Mary Ellen Dairyko, Amy Dillard, Noreen Winningham, and Ann McCarty formed a committee that provided invaluable guidance on many key issues. We also acknowledge dedicated and resourceful assistance on production and technical tasks by many people at the University of Chicago and at Wright Group/McGraw-Hill.

Over the years that UCSMP has been working in schools, feedback and advice from teachers willing to take risks in trying development versions of our materials have been essential and enormously helpful. There are too many such teachers to list, but their contributions are gratefully acknowledged.

Andy Isaacs	**James McBride**	**Max Bell**
Director, Third Edition	Director, Second Edition	Director, First Edition

Contents

A Mission to Improve School Mathematics

Everyday Mathematics

The University of Chicago School Mathematics Project

Everyday Mathematics was developed by the University of Chicago School Mathematics Project (UCSMP) in order to enable children in elementary grades to learn more mathematical content and become life-long mathematical thinkers.

◆ The National Science Foundation and Amoco, GTE, and other leading corporations supported the project through substantial, long-term funding.

◆ A strong partnership was developed among researchers, mathematics educators, classroom teachers, students, and administrators.

◆ A consistent, core author team at the University of Chicago School Mathematics Project collaborated on all grade levels to provide a cohesive and well-articulated Pre-K through Grade 6 curriculum.

> "We, our funders, and our users believe strongly that even the best curricula of decades ago are not adequate for today's youth."
>
> University of Chicago School Mathematics Project

Which Web?

Decide if the number on each spider is odd or even.
Cut out the spiders along the dotted lines and glue each one on the correct web.

ODD

EVEN

Student Page

Research Foundation

Everyday Mathematics began with the premise that students can, and must, learn more mathematics than has been expected from them in the past. This premise is based on research the UCSMP author team undertook prior to writing the curriculum. Following are some major findings of this research:

- The typical U.S. mathematics curriculum is arithmetic-driven, slow-paced with isolated instruction, and broad, without depth of content.
- International studies show that U.S. students learn much less mathematics than students in other countries.
- Children are capable of learning more mathematics in a richer curriculum.
- All children can be successful mathematical thinkers.
- Mathematics is meaningful to children when it is varied, rich, and rooted in real world problems and applications.

Instructional Design

The *Everyday Mathematics* instructional design was carefully crafted to capitalize on student interest and maximize student learning.

- High expectations for all students
- Concepts and skills developed over time and in a wide variety of contexts
- Balance among mathematical strands
- Dynamic applications
- Multiple methods and strategies for problem solving
- Concrete modeling as a pathway to abstract understanding
- Collaborative learning in partner and small-group activities
- Cross-curricular applications and connections
- Built-in professional development for teachers

"Our teachers in Grades 6-8 tell me that students using the *Everyday Mathematics* program in earlier grades are arriving in their classrooms with a deeper understanding of mathematical concepts and are ready to start the year at a much higher level."

Principal Ken Tucker,
Florence Sawyer School Pre-K to 8

Everyday Mathematics

Meeting Standards, Achieving Results

The *Everyday Mathematics* program is celebrating 20 years of research and development. The program offers schools results unmatched by any other elementary mathematics program.

Research, Validation, Results

As part of the research for *Everyday Mathematics,* the authors at the University of Chicago School Mathematics Project examined successful curricula from around the world, researched how children learn mathematics, and studied the actual use of mathematics by people in their everyday lives. The results of this research were used to establish the scope and sequence for the mathematical content of the *Everyday Mathematics* program.

Field Testing

The program was written and field tested one grade-level at a time, beginning with kindergarten. Field tests gathered information from classroom teachers and students in three main areas: teacher use of materials, student response to materials, and student achievement. Based on teacher and student feedback, the authors revised the curriculum before *Everyday Mathematics* was published.

Learner Verification

The best way to show effectiveness of a program is to study it over time. Several independent research studies have been conducted which provide evidence for the effectiveness of *Everyday Mathematics.* For example, *Everyday Mathematics* was the focus of a five-year longitudinal study conducted by researchers at Northwestern University. Reports from this study and others are available through the University of Chicago School Mathematics Project or Wright Group/ McGraw-Hill.

Everyday Mathematics Timeline of Research and Development

	Pre-1989	1989	1990	1991	1992	1993	1994	1995	1996	1997
Pre-K										
Kindergarten	PUBLISH								FEEDBACK ♦ WRITE ♦ FIELD-TEST	
Grade 1		WRITE ♦ FIELD-TEST REWRITE ♦ PUBLISH							♦	
Grade 2			WRITE ♦ FIELD-TEST ♦ REWRITE ♦ PUBLISH						♦	
Grade 3				WRITE ♦ FIELD-TEST ♦ REWRITE ♦ PUBLISH					♦	
Grade 4					WRITE ♦ FIELD-TEST ♦ REWRITE ♦ PUBLISH					
Grade 5						WRITE ♦ FIELD-TEST ♦ REWRITE ♦ PUBLISH				
Grade 6							WRITE ♦ FIELD-TEST ♦ REWRITE ♦ PUBLISH			

Tri-State Student Achievement Study

The ARC Center, a National Science Foundation (NSF) funded project, located at the Consortium for Mathematics and its Applications (COMAP), completed a study of the effects of standards-based mathematics programs on student performance on state-mandated standardized tests in Massachusetts, Illinois, and Washington.

The findings in this report are based on the records of over 78,000 students: 39,701 who had used the *Everyday Mathematics* curriculum for at least two years, and 38,481 students from comparison schools. The students were carefully matched by reading level, socioeconomic status, and other variables.

Results showed that the average scores of students in the *Everyday Mathematics* schools were consistently higher than the average scores of students in the comparison schools. The results hold across different state-mandated tests and across topics ranging from computation, measurement, and geometry to algebra, problem-solving, and making connections. (A complete report is available from COMAP or Wright Group/McGraw-Hill.)

A report based on 78,000 students showed that average standardized test scores were significantly higher for students in *Everyday Mathematics* schools than for students in comparison schools.

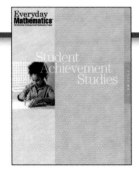

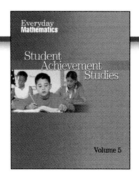

Closing the Gap

Many districts using the *Everyday Mathematics* program have helped minority students increase achievement, reducing the minority/majority achievement gap while maintaining growth for all students. This helps schools and districts meet adequate yearly progress set forth by No Child Left Behind legislation. District information is available by contacting Wright Group/McGraw-Hill.

1998	1999	2000	2001	2002	2003	2004	2005	2006	2007	2008
			FEEDBACK ♦ WRITE ♦ FIELD-TEST ♦ PUBLISH				FEEDBACK ♦ WRITE FIELD-TEST ♦ PUBLISH			
PUBLISH — 2ND EDITION					▲	FEEDBACK ♦ WRITE ♦ FIELD-TEST ♦ PUBLISH — 3RD EDITION				
FEEDBACK ♦ WRITE ♦ FIELD-TEST ♦ PUBLISH — 2ND EDITION					▲	FEEDBACK ♦ WRITE ♦ FIELD-TEST ♦ PUBLISH — 3RD EDITION				
FEEDBACK ♦ WRITE ♦ FIELD-TEST ♦ PUBLISH — 2ND EDITION					▲	FEEDBACK ♦ WRITE ♦ FIELD-TEST ♦ PUBLISH — 3RD EDITION				
FEEDBACK ♦ WRITE ♦ FIELD-TEST ♦ PUBLISH — 2ND EDITION					▲	FEEDBACK ♦ WRITE ♦ FIELD-TEST ♦ PUBLISH — 3RD EDITION				
	♦ FEEDBACK ♦ WRITE ♦ FIELD-TEST ♦ PUBLISH — 2ND EDITION				▲	FEEDBACK ♦ WRITE ♦ FIELD-TEST ♦ PUBLISH — 3RD EDITION				
	♦ FEEDBACK ♦ WRITE ♦ FIELD-TEST ♦ PUBLISH — 2ND EDITION				▲	FEEDBACK ♦ WRITE ♦ FIELD-TEST ♦ PUBLISH — 3RD EDITION				
	♦ FEEDBACK ♦ WRITE ♦ FIELD-TEST ♦ PUBLISH — 2ND EDITION				▲	FEEDBACK ♦ WRITE ♦ FIELD-TEST ♦ PUBLISH — 3RD EDITION				

♦ = 1st edition update   ▲ = 2nd edition update — electronic components added

Everyday Mathematics

Rigorous Mathematics

Program Goals and Grade-Level Goals

Everyday Mathematics structures content into Grade-Level Goals and Program Goals. Program Goals are then organized by content strand and are carefully articulated across the grades. The content in each grade provides all students with a balanced mathematics curriculum that is rich in real-world problem-solving opportunities. The success of this approach to teaching mathematics is evident in students' improved scores on standardized tests.

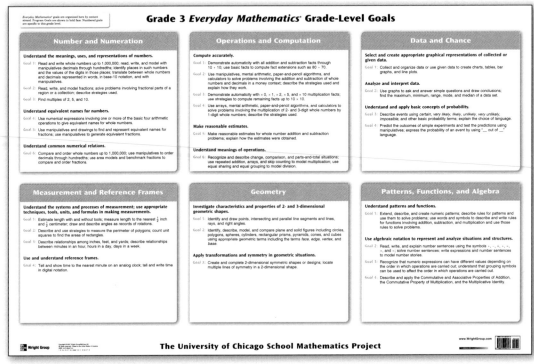

Grade 3 Grade-Level Goals Poster

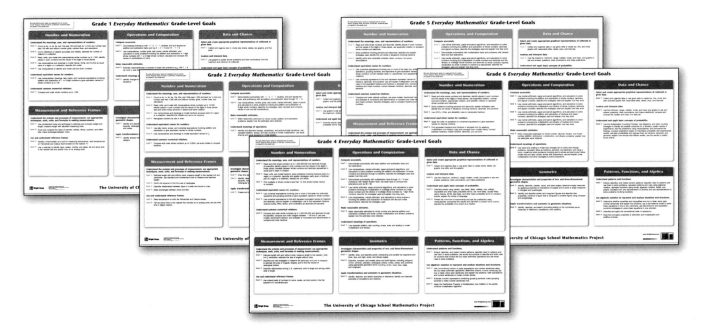

The *Everyday Mathematics* Program Goals are listed below. *Everyday Mathematics* Program Goals are organized by strand and extend across all grade levels.

Number and Numeration Strand

◆ Understand the meanings, uses, and representations of numbers

◆ Understand equivalent names for numbers

◆ Understand common numerical relations

Operations and Computation Strand

◆ Compute accurately

◆ Make reasonable estimates

◆ Understand meanings of operations

Data and Chance Strand

◆ Select and create appropriate graphical representations of collected or given data

◆ Analyze and interpret data

◆ Understand and apply basic concepts of probability

Measurement and Reference Frames Strand

◆ Understand the systems and processes of measurement; use appropriate techniques, tools, units, and formulas in making measurements

◆ Use and understand reference frames

Geometry Strand

◆ Investigate characteristics and properties of two- and three-dimensional geometric shapes

◆ Apply transformations and symmetry in geometric situations

Patterns, Functions, and Algebra Strand

◆ Understand patterns and functions

◆ Use algebraic notation to represent and analyze situations and structures

Components at a Glance

The table below shows core materials that are used on a regular basis throughout *Everyday Mathematics*.

STUDENT MATERIALS

Student Reference Book (Grades 3-6) Contains explanations of key mathematical content, along with directions for the *Everyday Mathematics* games. This hardbound book supports student learning in the classroom and at home.

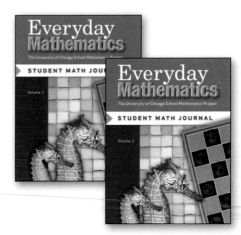

My Reference Book (Grades 1 and 2) This hardcover book is a child's first mathematical reference book. *My Reference Book* contains explanations of key concepts as well as directions for games.

Student Math Journal, Volumes 1 & 2 (Grades 1-6) These consumable books provide daily support for classroom instruction. They provide a long-term record of each student's mathematical development.

TEACHER MATERIALS

Teacher's Lesson Guide, Volumes 1 & 2 (Grades 1-6) The core of the *Everyday Mathematics* program, the *Teacher's Lesson Guide* provides teachers with easy to follow lessons organized by instructional unit, as well as built-in mathematical content support. Lessons include planning and assessment tips and multi-level differentiation strategies to support all learners.

Math Masters (Grades 1-6) Blackline masters that support daily lesson activities. Includes Home/Study Links, lesson-specific masters, game masters, and project masters.

Minute Math®+ (Grades 1-3) 5-Minute Math (Grades 4-6) Brief activities for transition time and for spare moments throughout the day.

TEACHER RESOURCES

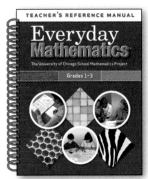

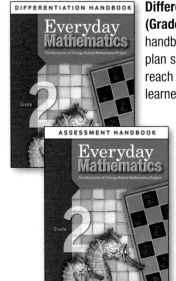

Differentiation Handbook (Grades 1-6) Grade-specific handbooks that help teachers plan strategically in order to reach the needs of diverse learners.

Assessment Handbook (Grades 1-6) Grade-specific handbooks provide explanations of key features of assessment in the *Everyday Mathematics* program. Includes all assessment masters.

Teacher's Reference Manual Contains comprehensive background information about mathematical content and program management for grades Early Childhood, 1-3, and 4-6.

Home Connection Handbook Enhances home-school communication for teachers and administrators. Includes masters for easy planning for grades Early Childhood, 1-3, and 4-6.

TECHNOLOGY COMPONENTS

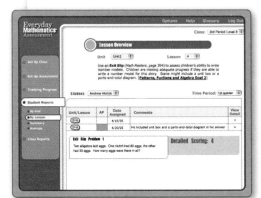

◄ **Assessment Management System (Grades K-6)** Web-based software that provides teachers with the opportunity to track student progress toward Grade-Level Goals.

Interactive Teacher's Lesson Guide ▶ (Grades K-6) Grade-level specific CD-ROM provides access to student and teacher materials. Content is searchable.

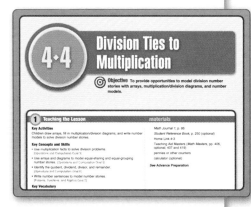

KINDERGARTEN MATERIALS

Kindergarten Teacher's Guide to Activities

Assessment Handbook

My First Math Book

Minute Math®

Resources for the Kindergarten Classroom

Everyday Mathematics®

Planning and Instructional Support

Each unit organizer provides an overview of the content for the unit. Also included is support for ongoing learning and practice, problem solving, and differentiated instruction. Detailed content support relating to the unit instruction is provided in Mathematical Background.

Overview

Describes concepts and ideas that are the focus of the unit.

Contents

Includes the objective for every lesson.

Key Concepts and Skills

Lists the Key Concepts and Skills, the important mathematical ideas that are covered in each lesson.

Learning in Perspective

Identifies connections to prior and future content both within and across grade levels.

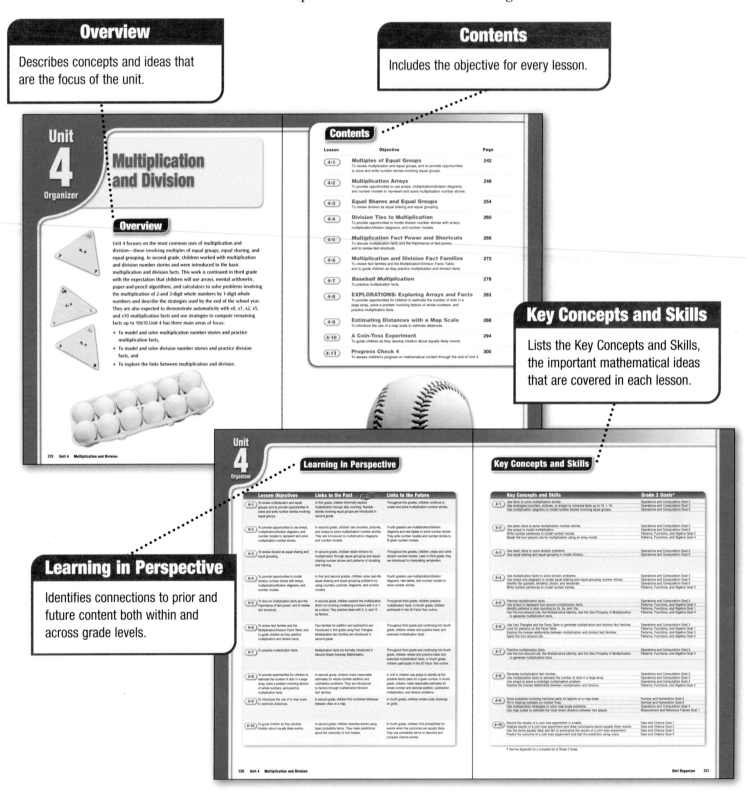

Ongoing Learning and Practice

Highlights essential activities which provide review and practice for maintaining skills. These activities include Math Boxes, Home/Study Links, games, and Extra Practice.

Ongoing Assessment

Includes the assessment opportunities in each lesson to assess progress toward Grade-Level Goals.

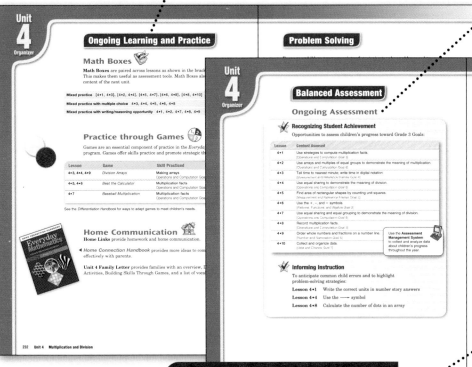

Assessment Support

Identifies useful pages in the *Assessment Handbook* for each unit.

Mathematical Background

Provides content support for important mathematical ideas in the unit.

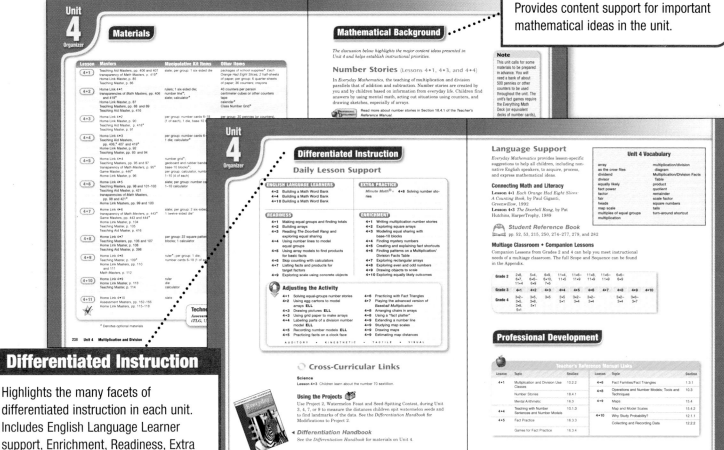

Differentiated Instruction

Highlights the many facets of differentiated instruction in each unit. Includes English Language Learner support, Enrichment, Readiness, Extra Practice, and Using the Projects.

Everyday Mathematics®

Instructional Plan

3-Part Lessons

① **Teaching the Lesson** Provides main instructional activities for the lesson.

② **Ongoing Learning and Practice** Supports previously introduced concepts and skills; essential for maintaining skills.

③ **Differentiation Options** Includes options for supporting the needs of all students; usually an extension of Part 1, Teaching the Lesson.

Getting Started

Contains quick mental math activities, Math Message (an independent warm-up), and follow-up suggestions for Home/Study Links.

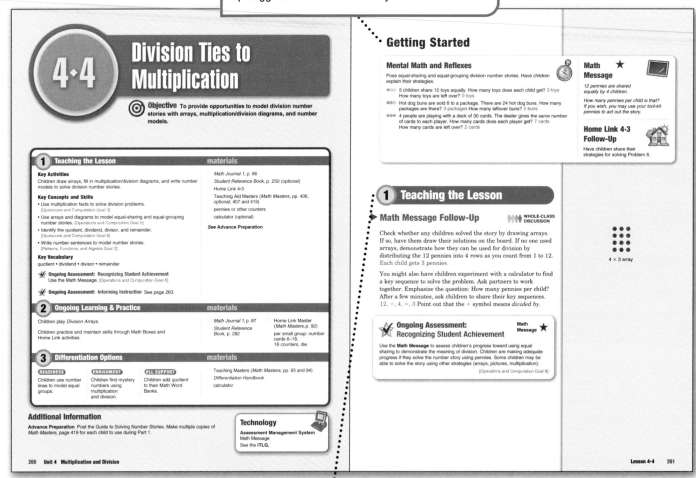

Teaching the Lesson

Main instructional activities for the lesson which introduce new content.

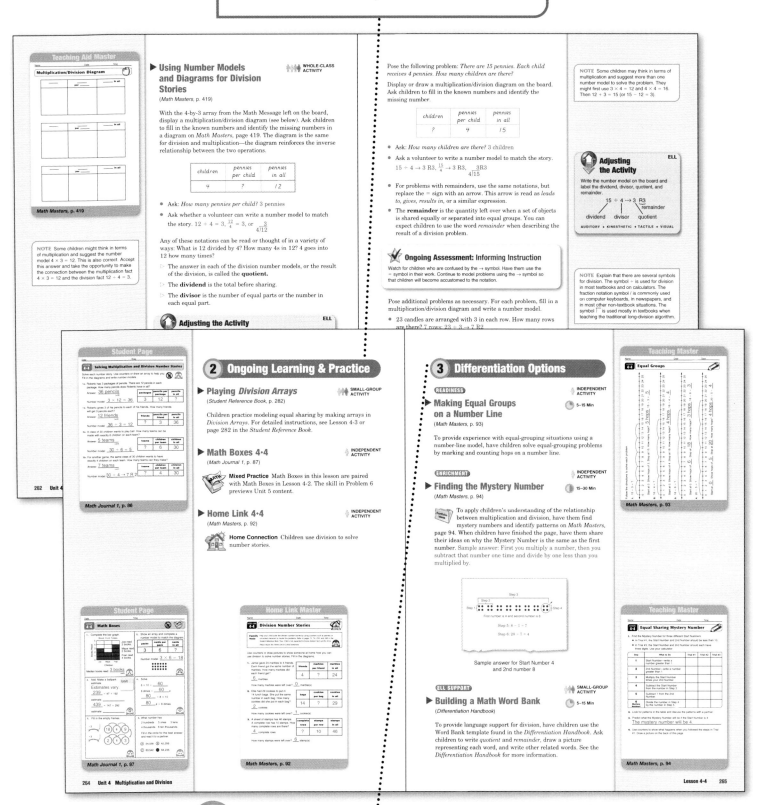

2 Ongoing Learning & Practice

Activities provide essential review and practice for maintaining skills. Includes *Everyday Mathematics* games appropriate for revisiting mathematics skills, as well as Math Boxes and Home/Study Links.

3 Differentiation Options

Includes Readiness activities which cover mathematical content necessary for student success in the lesson. English Language Learner support, Enrichment, and Extra Practice are also key features of the Differentiation Options.

Assessment

In *Everyday Mathematics,* assessment is like a motion picture revealing the development of each student's mathematical understanding over time, while giving the teacher useful feedback about the instructional needs of both individual students and the class as a whole.

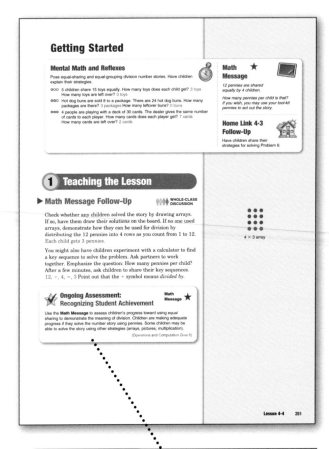

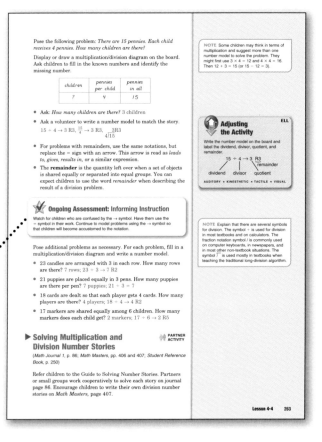

Types of Assessment

Ongoing Assessment Lessons feature Ongoing Assessment: Recognizing Student Achievement and Ongoing Assessment: Informing Instruction.

Periodic Assessment Formal assessments, such as the Progress Check, are built into the *Everyday Mathematics* curriculum.

Purposes of Assessment

Formative Assessment Formative assessments provide information about students' current knowledge and abilities and are used for effectively planning future instruction. In *Everyday Mathematics,* this is called Informing Instruction.

Summative Assessment Summative assessments measure student growth and achievement. Summative assessments are included in each lesson as Recognizing Student Achievement.

Recognizing Student Achievement

Each lesson contains a Recognizing Student Achievement note. The notes highlight tasks that can be used to monitor students' progress.

Informing Instruction

Suggests how to use observation of students' work to effectively adapt instruction.

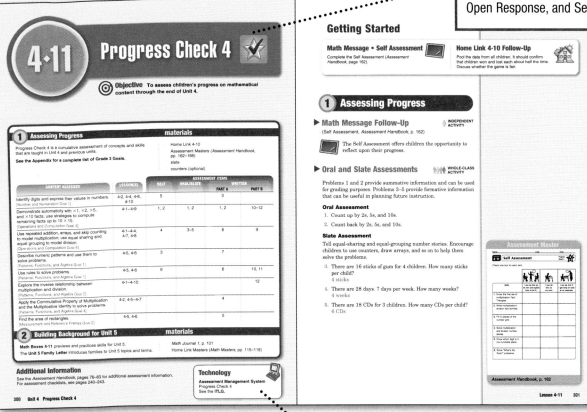

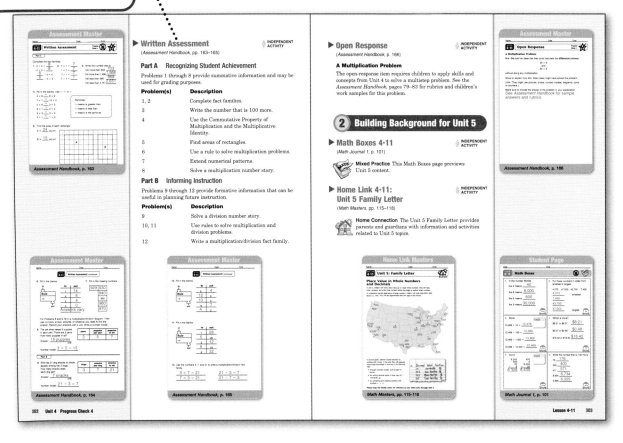

Technology Support

Technology Options

Everyday Mathematics offers teachers and students many technology options to make teaching easier and learning more fun! These options are available through the internet or on CD-ROM.

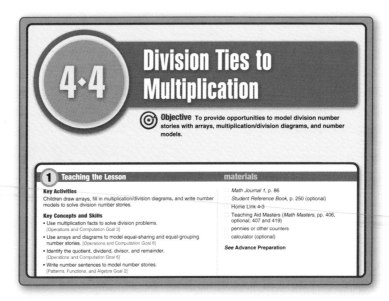

Interactive Teacher's Lesson Guide This grade-level specific software provides access to student and teacher materials. Content is searchable.

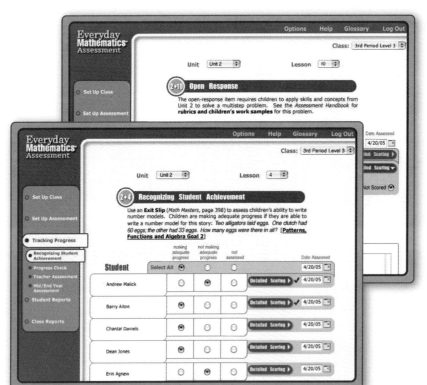

Assessment Management System Web-based software that provides teachers with the opportunity to track progress toward Grade-Level Goals.

Supporting Students and Home

Family Involvement

Within *Everyday Mathematics* there are several opportunities for supporting the home-school connection.

Family Letters Provide families with information on the *Everyday Mathematics* structure and curriculum. Each unit's Family Letter explains key content and vocabulary for the unit, directions for appropriate games, Do Anytime Activities, and answers to most Home/Study Links for the unit.

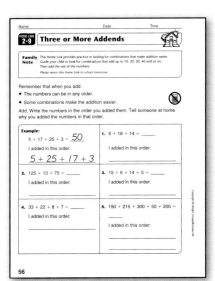

Home Links/Study Links Each lesson has a Home/Study Link. Home/Study Links include extensions of lessons and ongoing review problems. They show families what students are doing in mathematics.

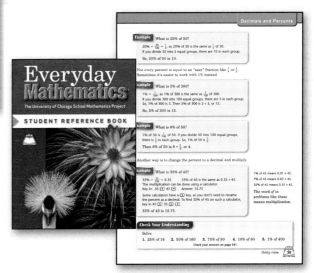

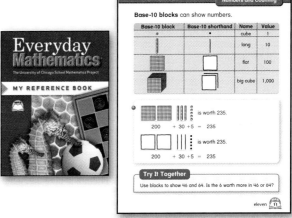

Home Connection Handbook This teacher- and administrator-focused handbook provides support for communicating with families. Includes blackline masters for easier communication.

Student Reference Book and My Reference Book These books are resources that can be sent home to provide parents with support on lesson content. The reference books include explanations and examples of mathematical topics, as well as directions for *Everyday Mathematics* games.

Contents

Volume 1

Volume 2

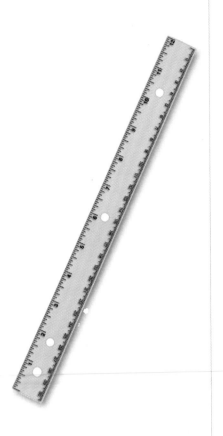

**W**elcome to *Everyday Mathematics,* the elementary school mathematics curriculum developed by the University of Chicago School Mathematics Project (UCSMP). *Everyday Mathematics* offers you and your children a broad, rich, and balanced experience in mathematics.

Second Grade Everyday Mathematics emphasizes the following content strands, skills, and concepts:

◆ **Number and Numeration** Counting; reading, writing, and modeling whole numbers; identifying place-value; comparing numbers; working with fractions; using money to develop place-value and decimal concepts.

◆ **Operations and Computation** Recalling addition and subtraction facts; working with fact families; adding and subtracting with tens and hundreds; making reasonable estimates; beginning multiplication and division; calculating values of coin and bill combinations.

◆ **Data and Chance** Collecting, organizing, and interpreting data using tables, charts, line plots, and graphs; exploring concepts of chance.

◆ **Measurement and Reference Frames** Using tools to measure length, weight, and temperature; using U.S. customary and metric measurement units; using clocks and calendars.

◆ **Geometry** Exploring 2- and 3-dimensional shapes; classifying polygons.

◆ **Patterns, Functions, and Algebra** Exploring number patterns, rules for number sequences, relations between numbers, and attributes.

Throughout *Everyday Mathematics,* emphasis is placed on:

◆ A realistic approach to problem solving in everyday situations, applications, and purely mathematical contexts.

◆ Frequent and distributed practice of basic skills through ongoing program routines and mathematical games.

◆ An instructional approach that revisits topics regularly to ensure full concept development and long-term retention of learning.

◆ Activities that explore a wide variety of mathematical content and offer opportunities for students to apply their skills and understandings to geometry, measurement, and algebra.

Everyday Mathematics is a comprehensive program for children and teachers. During your first months with the program, focus on Parts 1 and 2 of the lessons; these parts are the core of the program. As the year progresses, incorporate activities from Part 3 of the lesson as appropriate for your children. During your first year, you will become increasingly comfortable with the content, components, and strategies of *Second Grade Everyday Mathematics.* You and your children will experience mathematical processes as a part of everyday work and play. These processes will gradually shape children's ways of thinking about mathematics and will foster the development of their mathematical intuitions and understandings. By the end of the year, we think you will agree that the rewards are worth the effort.

Have an exciting year!

Professional Preparation

Components for *Second Grade Everyday Mathematics*

Go to...	When you need...	
Teacher's Lesson Guide	• daily lessons • unit support information • daily assessment suggestions • English language learners support	• readiness, enrichment and extra practice suggestions • Key Vocabulary • scope and sequence • Grade-Level Goals
Teacher's Reference Manual	• background on mathematical content	• ideas for curriculum and classroom management • a comprehensive glossary
Assessment Handbook	• Suggestions for ongoing and periodic assessment • Program Goals and Grade-Level Goals for all grades	• assessment masters • sample rubrics for open-response tasks
Differentiation Handbook	• suggestions for meeting diverse needs	• unit specific ideas
Minute Math®+	• brief activities for transition time and extra practice	
Content-by-Strand Poster	• Key Concepts and Skills organized by content strand and paced by month	• Program Goals and Grade-Level Goals
Home Connection Handbook	• suggestions for home-school communication	
My Reference Book	• concise explanations of mathematical concepts • worked examples	• game directions • a reference for children to read with teachers and/or parents and others
Student Math Journal	• lesson support material for children to analyze and complete • paired Math Boxes for mixed practice	• a yearlong record of each child's mathematical development • activity sheets
Math Masters	• blackline masters for lessons, Home Links, projects, teaching aids, and games	

Suggested Reading & Lesson Preparation

In order to prepare for effective classroom and curriculum management, we suggest the following before you teach *Everyday Mathematics* for the first time.

Reading and Planning

☐ Review each component in your Classroom Resource Package (CRP). Determine where information and materials are located so that you can find them as needed throughout the school year. See the chart on page xxv.

☐ Read the Management Guide in the *Teacher's Reference Manual,* which has many useful tips and explanations.

☐ Read the Unit 1 Organizer and the first three to four lessons in this *Teacher's Lesson Guide,* noting the Advance Preparation sections in each lesson.

☐ Make a list of coins for each student to bring from home (10 pennies, 5 nickels, 10 dimes, 2 quarters). Suggest that students bring the coins in a small plastic bag. An additional class collection of pennies is also useful.

☐ Create tool kits. See *Teacher's Lesson Guide,* Unit 1 Lesson 2, page 25.

☐ Prepare slates for children's use. See *Teacher's Lesson Guide,* Unit1 Lesson 2, page 24.

☐ Prepare a general daily math schedule. This schedule should include time for morning routines (calendar, weather, attendance, etc.), Teaching the Lesson, and Ongoing Learning and Practice activities such as games and Math Boxes.

☐ Prepare a supply of paper:
   Blank $8\frac{1}{2}$" by 11" (full-, half-, and quarter-size sheets)
   Handwriting paper
   Colored construction paper
   Graph paper (1-inch)

Before you teach subsequent units, you should read the Unit Organizer in the *Teacher's Lesson Guide* and the relevant sections of the *Teacher's Reference Manual,* the *Assessment Handbook,* and the *Differentiation Handbook.*

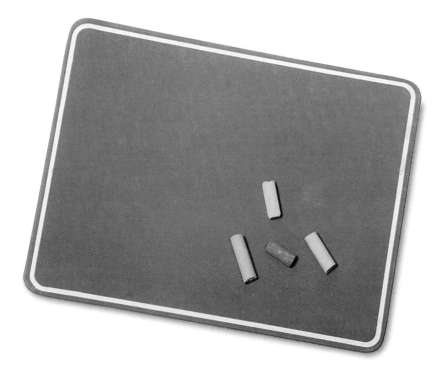

Organizing Your Classroom

Items for Display

Before the school year begins, we suggest that you prepare the following items for classroom display. By taking time to prepare these items your first year and laminating them if possible, you will be able to reuse them year after year. See the given sections in the Management Guide of your *Teacher's Reference Manual* for more information and suggestions.

- [ ] Number Line (−35 to 180) (Section 5.4)
- [ ] Class Data Pad (Section 5.3)
- [ ] Number Grid Poster (In your CRP)
- [ ] Thermometer Poster (In your CRP)
- [ ] Monthly Calendar (Section 5.2)
- [ ] Weather/Temperature Recording Chart (Section 5.8)
- [ ] Attendance Chart (Section 5.1)
- [ ] Daily Class Schedule (Section 5.6)
- [ ] Job Chart (Section 5.5)
- [ ] N, S, E, W directional indicators

Classroom Setup

The following items should be considered as you set up your classroom for *Everyday Mathematics*. Try several arrangements until you find one that is comfortable and effective for you and your children. Visit other classrooms in your building to observe and discuss what works for your colleagues.

- [ ] Prepare and label a location in the classroom where children can deposit their written work such as Math Messages, Home Links, Exit Slips, and so on.
- [ ] Arrange classroom desks/tables to allow for easy access to manipulatives and to facilitate efficient transitions for individual, partner, and small-group activities.

- [ ] Organize class and individual manipulatives for easy access and efficient use of storage space.
- [ ] Allow (table) space for math center(s). Selected games and activities can then be left in this space for ongoing practice or free exploration.
- [ ] One or more computers with Internet access can let children use software and Web sites that are recommended in *Second Grade Everyday Mathematics*.

Manipulatives

The table below lists the materials that are used throughout *Second Grade Everyday Mathematics.* Some lessons call for minor additional materials, which you or your students can bring in at the appropriate time.

Quantity	Item
1 set	Attribute Blocks
1 set	Base-10 Blocks
1 per student	Calculators (Texas Instruments TI-108 or Casio SL-450 recommended)*
1 per student	Clock Face
1 set	Clock Face Stamp
1 set	Coin Stamp Set, Heads
1 pkg. (2,000)	Connectors
1 pkg. (450)	Counters
1 pkg. (1,000)	Counting (Craft) Sticks
1 pkg. (16)	Dice, Blank
1 per student	Dice, Dot
3 pkgs. (18 total)	Dice, Polyhedral
5 sets	Dominoes, Double-9
15 decks	Everything Math Decks
8	Geoboards, Two-Sided, 7" × 7"
10	Metersticks, Dual Scale
1	Number Line, −35 to 180
2 sets	Pattern Blocks
1 per student	Pattern Block Template (in student material set)
10 sets	Play Money Bill Set
2 sets	Play Money Coin Set
1	Rocker Balance
1 pkg. (400)	Rubber Bands (for geoboards)
1 per student	Rulers, 6 in./15 cm
1 per student	Slates (chalk or marker boards)
1	Spring Scale
1	Stamp Pad
1 pkg. (500)	Straws
15	Tape Measures, Retractable
1	Thermometer, Classroom
1 per student	Tool-Kit Bags*
10	Yardsticks

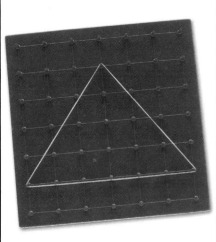

All of the items above are available from Wright Group/McGraw-Hill. They may be purchased either as a comprehensive classroom manipulatives kit or by individual components. The manipulatives kit provides multiple classroom quantities and comes packaged in durable plastic tubs with labels.

* *Calculators and tool-kit bags are available from Wright Group/McGraw-Hill for individual purchase only.*

Instruction

The following sections introduce instructional procedures and suggestions for implementing *Everyday Mathematics*. Teachers are encouraged to read these pages and refer to them as needed throughout the school year.

Daily Routines

In *Everyday Mathematics,* children learn a great deal of mathematics through daily individual and class routines. These daily activities may include tracking attendance, calendar, weather, temperature, and choral counting. Numerous mathematical concepts are reinforced on a daily basis so that children become aware of how mathematics pervades our everyday lives.

Most of the daily routines in *Second Grade Everyday Mathematics* are introduced in Unit 1 and should be maintained throughout the school year. Refer to Unit 1 lessons and the Management Guide of the *Teacher's Reference Manual* for more information.

Program Routines

Everyday Mathematics uses a number of program routines that are incorporated throughout all grade levels. These allow for ongoing developmental practice in a number of skill and content areas. Below is a list of the routines you will encounter in *Second Grade Everyday Mathematics.* The lesson in which each routine is first used has been noted. Refer to the Management Guide in the *Teacher's Reference Manual* for more information.

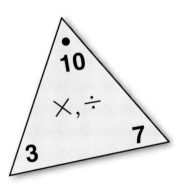

Mental Math and Reflexes (Lesson 1-1)
Math Message (Lesson 1-1)
Games (Lesson 1-4)
Math Boxes (Lesson 1-6)
Home Links (Lesson 1-11)
Fact Triangles/Fact Families (Lesson 2-7)
Name Collection Boxes (Lesson 2-9)
Frames and Arrows (Lesson 2-10)
"What's My Rule?"/Function Machines (Lesson 2-11)

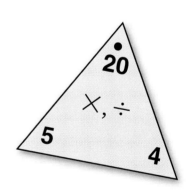

All of the above are used in *First Grade Everyday Mathematics.*

Games

Games are an integral component of *Everyday Mathematics*. They help children develop the ability to think critically and solve problems, and provide an enjoyable way for them to practice basic skills. Establish a games routine during the first unit and maintain it throughout the year. Make sure that all children are afforded time to play the games, especially those children who require the most practice.

Suggestions for building games into your instructional program:

◆ Include games as part of your daily morning routine.

◆ Devote the first or last 10 minutes of each math class to playing games from the current unit.

◆ Designate one math class per week as "Games Day." Set up stations that feature the unit games. Ask parent volunteers to assist in the rotation of students though these stations.

◆ Set up a Games Corner that features some of the children's favorite games. Encourage children to visit this corner during free choice time. Change the games frequently to maintain student interest.

Explorations

You will find an Explorations lesson in every unit in *Second Grade Everyday Mathematics*. These lessons include several independent, small-group activities that are informal and open-ended. The Explorations lessons have been designed so that you can place the activities at stations around the room and have small groups rotate among them.

Each Explorations lesson suggests up to three exploratory activities, with the option of adding other familiar activities as desired. In each lesson, Exploration A contains the main content and requires the most teacher facilitation, especially at the outset.

Explorations are not intended as optional activities for students to do when they have finished their other work, so be sure to set aside enough class time so that all students can experience them. Explorations provide critical initial exposure to content that is developed later in *Everyday Mathematics*.

Refer to the Management Guide in the *Teacher's Reference Manual* for more information.

Museums

Everyday Mathematics encourages the development of classroom museums using a bulletin board or table where related items can be collected, categorized, and labeled. For example, beginning in Lesson 5-6, second graders assemble a Shape Museum using models of 3-dimensional shapes.

Refer to the Management Guide in the *Teacher's Reference Manual* for more information.

Projects

Second Grade Everyday Mathematics provides eight projects, each of which includes an array of mathematics activities that focus on a theme that interests children. Projects are suggested in the Unit Organizers in the *Teacher's Lesson Guide* at appropriate times throughout the year. They typically take one to two days to complete, depending upon how many of the suggested activities are used. Projects involve a range of concepts and skills; integrate mathematics with science, social studies, art, and language arts; and allow the teacher to assess children's abilities to apply the mathematics they have learned in cross-curricular contexts. Projects are also often memorable events for children.

Refer to the Management Guide in the *Teacher's Reference Manual* and Unit Organizers in the *Teacher's Lesson Guide* for more information.

Assessment

Everyday Mathematics supports a balanced approach to assessment, one that provides information both for guiding instruction and for evaluating student performance. Assessment takes place on an ongoing basis as children complete their everyday work and in special periodic assessments, such as the assessment lesson at the end of each unit. Information for assessment is gathered both through teacher observations while children are working and through children's written products.

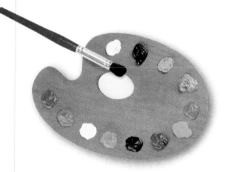

Refer to the *Assessment Handbook* and the Unit Organizers in the *Teacher's Lesson Guide* for detailed information regarding student assessment.

Differentiation

Everyday Mathematics has been designed from the ground up to accommodate a wide range of student backgrounds and abilities, including English language learners. The program also includes many tools and suggestions to help teachers differentiate instruction to meet children's diverse needs, including Enrichment, Readiness, ELL Support, Extra Practice activities in Part 3 of the lessons, and Adjusting the Activity suggestions in Parts 1 and 2.

Refer to the *Differentiation Handbook* and the Unit Organizers in the *Teacher's Lesson Guide* for detailed information about differentiation in *Everyday Mathematics*.

Providing for Home-School Connections

Comprehensive and consistent home-school communication is essential for successful implementation of *Everyday Mathematics*. The *Home Connection Handbook* has many suggestions and tools that can help you introduce parents and primary caregivers to the *Everyday Mathematics* curriculum. Grade-specific Family Letters and Home Links facilitate ongoing communication and engage parents as partners in the learning process.

Refer to the *Home Connection Handbook* for more information.

K–3 Games Correlation Chart

Game	K Activity	Grade 1 Lesson	Grade 2 Lesson	Grade 3 Lesson	Numeration	Mental Math	Basic Facts	Operations	Patterns	Geometry	Money	Time	Probability	Calculator
Addition Card Draw			12•5			●	●	●						
Addition Spin			4•2			●	●	●						
Addition Top-It	4•2	6•1	1•4	1•4	●	●	●	●						
Angle Race				6•9						●				
Animal Weight Top-It		5•5			●	●	●	●						
Array Bingo			6•9	9•6	●		●	●						
Attribute Train Game		7•2							●	●				
Base-10 Exchange		5•3	3•4	2•9	●									
Base-10 Trading Game			6•5		●		●	●						
Baseball Multiplication				4•7	●		●	●						
Basketball Addition			7•3			●	●	●						
Beat the Calculator		5•11	2•2	1•9		●	●	●						●
Beat the Calculator (Multiplication Version)			11•9	7•6		●	●	●						●
Before and After		3•1	*		●			●						
The Block-Drawing Game				8•2					●				●	
Bunny Hop Game		1•5			●		●							
Coin-Dice		3•12			●						●			
Coin Exchange		6•10	*		●						●			
Coin Top-It		2•13	1•4	1•10	●						●			
Decimal Solitaire				5•10	●				●					
Difference Game		5•7	2•12		●	●	●	●			●			
Digit Game		5•1	3•1		●	●		●						
Dime-Nickel-Penny Grab		3•13			●						●			
Division Arrays				4•3	●		●	●						
Dollar Rummy			3•5		●	●	●	●			●			
Domino Top-It		3•14	2•2		●	●	●	●						
Doubles or Nothing			2•3		●	●	●	●						
Equivalent Fractions Game			8•5	8•5	●									
Equivalent Fractions Game (Advanced Version)				8•5	●									
Fact Extension Game			4•8			●	●	●	●					
Fact Power Game		6•4				●	●	●						
Factor Bingo				9•6	●	●	●	●						
Finding Factors				9•6		●	●	●						
Fingers				11•3									●	
Fraction Top-It			8•7	8•6	●									
Fraction Top-It (Advanced)				8•6	●									
High Roller	8•4	2•12	3•7		●	●		●						
Hit the Target			7•2			●		●						●
Less Than You!				1•3	●	●		●						
Make My Design		7•1								●				
Memory Addition/Subtraction				10•8	●			●						●
Missing Terms			*											●
Money Exchange Game			1•5		●						●			
Monster Squeeze	3•6	1•2			●									

Number indicates first exposure at grade level. *Available in the Games section of *My Reference Book* or the *Student Reference Book*.

Games Correlation Chart *continued*

Game	K Activity	Grade 1 Lesson	Grade 2 Lesson	Grade 3 Lesson	Numeration	Mental Math	Basic Facts	Operations	Patterns	Geometry	Money	Time	Probability	Calculator
Multiplication Bingo				7◆3		●	●	●						
Multiplication Draw				11◆6		●	●	●						
Multiplication Top-It				10◆7	●	●	●	●						
Name That Number			2◆9	1◆6	●	●	●							
Nickel-Penny Grab		2◆11			●						●			
Number-Line Squeeze		1◆2	1◆1	1◆1	●									
Number-Grid Difference Game			6◆5	1◆8	●	●	●		●					
Number-Grid Game	5◆16	9◆2	1◆8						●					
Number Top-It			1◆11	5◆2	●									
Number Top-It (5-Digit Numbers)				5◆4	●									
Number Top-It (7-Digit Numbers)				5◆5	●									
Number Top-It (Decimals)				5◆10	●				●					
One-Dollar Exchange		8◆2	★		●						●			
$1, $10, $100 Exchange Game		10◆4			●	●	●	●			●			
Penny-Dice Game		1◆3			●						●			
Penny-Dime-Dollar Exchange			3◆2		●						●			
Penny-Drop Addition		2◆11			●		●	●			●			
Penny Grab		2◆8			●		●	●			●			
Penny Guessing		2◆9			●						●			
Penny-Nickel Exchange	5◆10	2◆10	1◆5		●						●			
Penny-Nickel-Dime Exchange		5◆13			●						●			
Penny Plate		2◆9	1◆6		●	●					●			
Pick-a-Coin			10◆3								●			●
Quarter-Dime-Nickel-Penny Grab		6◆9			●						●			
Robot Game				6◆3						●				
Rock, Paper, Scissors		1◆8											●	
Roll to 100				2◆1		●	●							
Rolling for 50		2◆1			●	●	●	●						
Shading Shapes				6◆5					●	●				
Shaker Addition Top-It		4◆12			●		●	●						
Simon Says			6◆8					●						
Soccer Spin			7◆8	11◆13		●			●				●	
Spinning for Money			3◆2	1◆11	●						●			
Spinning to Win				11◆5									●	
Subtraction Top-It			★	3◆7	●	●	●	●						
Target: 50				2◆7	●									
Three Addends			6◆1			●	●	●						
3, 2, 1 Game		8◆5	★		●	●	●	●	●					
Time Match	8◆12	4◆4	★									●		
Top-It	4◆2	1◆6	★		●									
Touch and Match Quadrangles				6◆5						●				
Tric-Trac		6◆8	★		●	●	●	●						
Two-Fisted Penny Addition			1◆6		●	●	●	●						
"What's My Attribute Rule?"				2◆3					●	●				

Number indicates first exposure at grade level. *Available in the Games section of *My Reference Book* or the *Student Reference Book.*

Unit

1

Organizer

Numbers and Routines

Overview

The organization of Everyday Mathematics is based on the observation that children learn best when they build on prior knowledge. Unit 1 suggests a number of review activities for mathematics that children have encountered in first grade. These will provide you with a snapshot of their mathematics background and capabilities as they begin a new school year. In addition, Unit 1 also establishes routines meant to be used all year to promote an active and cooperative learning environment. Unit 1 has five main areas of focus:

◆ To review number patterns, number sequences, number grids, and number lines,

◆ To review months, weeks, and days, and telling time,

◆ To practice addition facts,

◆ To give equivalent names for numbers, and

◆ To compare numbers using the symbols <, >, and =.

Contents

Learning In Perspective

	Lesson Objectives	Links to the Past	Links to the Future
1·1	To introduce the Math Message routine; and to review number sequences and number lines.	In first grade, children work with patterns, including skip counting. Children use calculators, number lines, and number grids to explore patterns.	In Unit 2, children use patterns to develop strategies for learning addition facts. They identify patterns to solve "What's My Rule?" and Frames-and-Arrows problems.
1·2	To introduce the tool kits; and to guide children as they find the values of coin combinations.	Children are introduced to coins and bills in Kindergarten. They count combinations of coins in first grade.	Children continue to develop money-counting and change-making skills and strategies throughout second grade. (Units 3–5, 10, and 11)
1·3	To review months, weeks, and days; and to review telling time.	In first grade children discuss months, weeks, and days. They practice telling time to the nearest half-hour and quarter-hour.	In second grade, children practice calendar skills and telling time. Fractions of an hour is introduced in third grade.
1·4	To provide practice with addition facts; and to establish partnership principles.	Children practice +1, +0, doubles, and sums of 10 addition facts in first grade.	Children construct and solve fact families in Unit 2. Basic facts are practiced through games and in a variety of problem-solving situations throughout the year.
1·5	To provide review for grouping by tens; and to provide practice for exchanging $1, $10, and $100 bills.	In first grade, children are introduced to place value for 100s, 10s, and 1s, using base-10 blocks (flats, longs, and cubes).	Place-value concepts are revisited in Unit 3 and used later to develop mental arithmetic strategies for adding and subtracting two- and three-digit numbers.
1·6	To introduce *My Reference Book;* and to introduce the Math Boxes routine.	In first grade, children are introduced to the Math Boxes routine and begin using *My Reference Book* in Unit 6.	Children continue to use the Math Boxes routine and a *Student Reference Book* throughout the grades.
1·7	To establish rules for working in small groups; and to review number patterns and sequences.	In first grade, children work with patterns, including skip counting. Children use calculators, number lines, and number grids to explore patterns.	In Unit 2, children use patterns to help develop strategies for learning addition facts. Identifying patterns will also be key to determining solutions for "What's My Rule?" and Frames-and-Arrows problems.
1·8	To guide children as they explore place-value patterns on number grids.	In first grade, children are introduced to place value for 100s, 10s, and 1s, using base-10 blocks (flats, longs, and cubes).	Place-value concepts will be revisited in Unit 3 and used later to develop mental arithmetic strategies for adding and subtracting two- and three-digit numbers.
1·9	To provide experiences with giving equivalent names for numbers; and to review calculator use.	First graders use name-collection boxes and play *Broken Calculator.* Children begin using different names for the same number in Kindergarten.	In second grade, children find different combinations of coins, construct fact families, and play *Broken Calculator.* They review name-collection boxes in Unit 2.
1·10	To guide children as they count and look for patterns on the calculator.	In Kindergarten and first grade, children begin skip counting by 2s, 5s, and 10s.	Skip counting will help children to count money, tell time, find number patterns, and learn multiplication facts throughout *Everyday Mathematics.*
1·11	To provide experiences with comparing numbers using the relation symbols <, >, and =; and to introduce Home Links.	In Kindergarten, children compare number size and order numbers. The symbols > and < are introduced in first grade.	Children make comparisons of many types throughout the grades.
1·12	To guide children as they read and display temperatures; combine values of ones, tens, and hundreds using base-10 blocks; and explore addition facts on dominoes.	In first grade, children record daily temperatures and become familiar with the Celsius and Fahrenheit scales. They are introduced to place value for 100s, 10s, and 1s, using base-10 blocks. They practice +1, +0, doubles, and sums of 10 addition facts	Beyond second grade, children use temperature as a context for exploring negative numbers. Place-value concepts are used later to develop mental arithmetic strategies for adding and subtracting two- and three-digit numbers.

Key Concepts and Skills

Key Concepts and Skills	Grade 2 Goals*
1·1 Count on by ones. Read and write numbers to 10s, 100s, and 1,000s. Compare and order numbers on a number line.	Number and Numeration Goal 1 Number and Numeration Goal 2 Number and Numeration Goal 7
1·2 Count by 1s, 5s, and 10s using coins. Use a counting-up strategy to calculate the total value of coin combinations. Calculate the values of coin combinations.	Number and Numeration Goal 1 Operations and Computation Goal 2 Operations and Computation Goal 2
1·3 Use probability terms to describe events. Name days in a week Tell and show time to the nearest half-hour. Describe calendar patterns and use them to solve problems.	Data and Chance Goal 3 Measurement and Reference Frames Goal 3 Measurement and Reference Frames Goal 6 Patterns, Functions, and Algebra Goal 1
1·4 Compare numbers in *Addition Top-It* Use *Addition Top-It* to practice addition facts. Write number sentences.	Number and Numeration Goal 7 Operations and Computation Goal 1 Patterns, Functions, and Algebra Goal 2
1·5 Count on by 1s, 10s, and 100s. Use counting up to calculate the value of bill combinations. Make exchanges among bills.	Number and Numeration Goal 1 Operations and Computation Goal 2 Measurement and Reference Frames Goal 4
1·6 Count objects. Explore money equivalencies. Explore analog and digital time pieces.	Number and Numeration Goal 1 Measurement and Reference Frames Goal 4 Measurement and Reference Frames Goal 6
1·7 Count by 2s, 5s, and 10s on the number grid. Write numbers to 1,000s. Identify odd and even numbers on the number grid. Use the number grid to find 1 more, 1 less, 10 more, or 10 less.	Number and Numeration Goal 1 Number and Numeration Goal 2 Number and Numeration Goal 4 Patterns, Functions, and Algebra Goal 1
1·8 Count on the number grid. Use place-value skills to complete number-grid puzzles. Use patterns to complete number-grid puzzles. Identify patterns on the number grid.	Number and Numeration Goal 1 Number and Numeration Goal 2 Patterns, Functions, and Algebra Goal 1 Patterns, Functions, and Algebra Goal 1
1·9 Count on by 2s and 10s on the calculator. Write equivalent names for numbers. Write equivalent names for numbers using facts; use facts to solve Broken Calculator problems.	Number and Numeration Goal 1 Number and Numeration Goal 5 Operations and Computation Goal 1
1·10 Count by 6s, 7s, and 4s on the calculator. Identify the ones digit in numbers. Identify patterns in counts and use the patterns to answer questions.	Number and Numeration Goal 1 Number and Numeration Goal 2 Patterns, Functions, and Algebra Goal 1
1·11 Compare numbers. Calculate and compare the values of combinations of coins. Read, write, and explain the <, >, and = symbols.	Number and Numeration Goal 7 Operations and Computation Goal 2 Patterns, Functions, and Algebra Goal 2
1·12 Count by 1s, 10s, and 100s with base-10 blocks. Use dominoes to identify equivalent names for numbers. Practice addition facts with dominoes. Read a thermometer and record the temperature.	Number and Numeration Goal 1 Number and Numeration Goal 5 Operations and Computation Goal 1 Measurement and Reference Frames Goal 5

* See the Appendix for a complete list of Grade 2 Goals.

Ongoing Learning and Practice

Math Boxes

Math Boxes are paired across lessons as shown in the brackets below. This makes them useful as assessment tools. Math Boxes also preview content of the next unit.

Mixed practice	[1◆7, 1◆9, 1◆11], [1◆8, 1◆10, 1◆12]

Mixed practice with multiple choice	1◆6, 1◆9, 1◆11, 1◆12

Mixed practice with writing/reasoning opportunity	1◆7, 1◆10

Practice through Games

Games are an essential component of practice in the *Everyday Mathematics* program. Games offer skills practice and promote strategic thinking.

Lesson	Game	Skill Practiced
1◆1	Number-Line Squeeze	**Sequencing numbers** Number and Numeration Goal 7
1◆4, 1◆5, 1◆7, 1◆11, 1◆12	Addition Top-It	**Addition** Number and Numeration Goal 1 Number and Numeration Goal 7 Operations and Computation Goal 1
1◆4	Coin Top-It	**Counting** Operations and Computation Goal 2
1◆5	Money Exchange Game	**Make exchanges between coins and bills** Measurement and Reference Frames Goal 4
1◆5	Penny-Nickel Exchange	**Trading pennies and nickels** Measurement and Reference Frames Goal 4
1◆6	Penny Plate	**Counting pennies; addition; subtraction** Number and Numeration Goal 1 Operations and Computation Goal 1
1◆6	Two-Fisted Penny Addition	**Counting pennies; naming parts of a whole** Number and Numeration Goals 1 and 3
1◆8	Number-Grid Game	**Exploring patterns on a number grid** Patterns, Functions, and Algebra Goal 1
1◆11	Number Top-It	**Comparing numbers** Number and Numeration Goal 7

See the *Differentiation Handbook* for ways to adapt games to meet children's needs.

Home Communication

Home Links provide homework and home communication.

◀ *Home Connection Handbook* provides more ideas to communicate effectively with parents.

Unit 1 Family Letter provides families with an overview, Do-Anytime Activities, Building Skills Through Games, and a list of vocabulary.

Problem Solving

Encourage children to use a variety of strategies to solve problems and to explain those strategies. Strategies that children might use in this unit:

- ◆ Modeling with manipulatives
- ◆ Using a number line
- ◆ Using a table
- ◆ Finding a pattern
- ◆ Listing possibilities
- ◆ Acting out the problem
- ◆ Using computation

Lessons that teach **through** *problem solving, not just* **about** *problem solving*

Lesson	Activity
1◆1	Find missing numbers on number lines.
1◆2	Find values of coin combinations.
1◆3	Build a monthly calendar.
1◆3	Display time using the tool-kit clock.
1◆4	Explore number-grid patterns.
1◆6	Name parts of a total in *Penny Plate*.
1◆7	Make a class number scroll.
1◆9	Solve Broken Calculator problems.
1◆11	Act as a pan balance for comparing numbers.
1◆12	Read and display temperature on a thermometer.

See Chapter 18 in the *Teacher's Reference Manual* for more information about problem solving.

Planning Tips

Pacing

Pacing depends on a number of factors, such as children's individual needs and how long your school has been using *Everyday Mathematics*. At the beginning of Unit 1, review your *Content by Strand* Poster to help you set a monthly pace.

← MOST CLASSROOMS →		
AUGUST	SEPTEMBER	OCTOBER

NCTM Standards

Unit 1 Lessons	1◆1	1◆2	1◆3	1◆4	1◆5	1◆6	1◆7	1◆8	1◆9	1◆10	1◆11	1◆12
NCTM Standards	1–2, 6–8	1, 3–4, 6–10	1, 4, 5, 6–10	1, 6–8	1, 4, 6, 8–10	1, 6–10	1–2, 6–10	1–2, 6, 7, 10	1–2, 6–10	1–2, 6–8	1–2, 6–10	1, 4, 6–10

Content Standards: **1** Number and Operations, **2** Algebra, **3** Geometry, **4** Measurement, **5** Data Analysis and Probability

Process Standards: **6** Problem Solving, **7** Reasoning and Proof, **8** Communication, **9** Connections, **10** Representation

Balanced Assessment

Ongoing Assessment

 Recognizing Student Achievement

Opportunities to assess children's progress toward Grade 2 Goals:

Lesson	Content Assessed
1◆1	Write and order numbers. [Number and Numeration Goal 7]
1◆2	Count coin combinations. [Operations and Computation Goal 2]
1◆3	Tell time to the nearest half-hour. [Measurement and Reference Frames Goal 6]
1◆4	Recall basic addition facts. [Operations and Computation Goal 1]
1◆5	Count bill combinations. [Operations and Computation Goal 2]
1◆6	Find missing addends. [Operations and Computation Goal 1]
1◆7	Complete and describe a number pattern. [Patterns, Functions, and Algebra Goal 1]
1◆8	Identify number-grid patterns. [Patterns, Functions, and Algebra Goal 1]
1◆9	Find equivalent names for numbers. [Number and Numeration Goal 5]
1◆10	Calculate the value of coin combinations. [Operations and Computation Goal 2]
1◆11	Compare numbers in the tens and hundreds. [Number and Numeration Goal 7]
1◆12	Identify odd and even numbers. [Number and Numeration Goal 4]

Use the **Assessment Management System** to collect and analyze data about children's progress throughout the year.

 Informing Instruction

To anticipate common child errors and to highlight problem-solving strategies:

Lesson 1◆1   Order numbers greater than 100

Lesson 1◆3   Differentiate between hours and minutes

Lesson 1◆5   Exchange dollar bills

Lesson 1◆6   Count pennies

Lesson 1◆7   Write numbers with the correct number of digits

Lesson 1◆11 Count coin combinations

Periodic Assessment

 1✦13 Progress Check 1

CONTENT ASSESSED	ASSESSMENT ITEMS			
	Self	Oral/Slate	Written	Open Response
Count up by 1s, 2s, 5s, 10s, 25s, and 100s to 1,000; count on and back using a number grid. [Number and Numeration Goal 1]	✔	✔	✔	✔
Use tally marks and numerical expressions to find equivalent names for numbers. [Number and Numeration Goal 5]	✔	✔	✔	
Practice and apply addition and subtraction facts through 10 + 10. [Operations and Computation Goal 1]	✔		✔	
Calculate and compare values of coins and bill combinations. [Operations and Computation Goal 2]	✔		✔	
Show and tell time on an analog clock to the nearest half-hour; write time in digital notation. [Measurement and Reference Frames Goal 6]	✔		✔	
Continue and describe simple numerical and nonnumerical patterns; find rules for patterns and use them to solve problems. [Patterns, Functions, and Algebra, Goal 1]	✔	✔	✔	✔

Portfolio Opportunities

Opportunities to gather samples of children's mathematical writings, drawings, and creations to add balance to the assessment process:

◆ Writing strategy used to solve number-grid problem, **Lesson 1✦7**

◆ Writing strategy used to solve coin-combination problem, **Lesson 1✦10**

Assessment Handbook ▶

Unit 1 Assessment Support

◆ Grade 2 Goals, pp. 37–50

◆ Unit 1 Assessment Overview, pp. 52–59

Unit 1 Assessment Masters

◆ Unit 1 Self Assessment, p. 154

◆ Unit 1 Written Assessment, pp. 155 and 156

◆ Unit 1 Open Response, p. 157

◆ Unit 1 Class Checklist, pp. 238, 239, and 293

◆ Unit 1 Open Response
  • Detailed rubric, p. 56
  • Sample student responses, pp. 57–59

◆ Unit 1 Individual Profile of Progress, pp. 236, 237, and 292

◆ Exit Slip, p. 295

◆ Math Logs, pp. 298–300

◆ Other Student Assessment Forms, pp. 296, 297 and 301–303

Differentiated Instruction

Daily Lesson Support

ENGLISH LANGUAGE LEARNERS

1•1 Discussing the Mathematics All Around bulletin board
1•3 Using the language of time and events
1•7 Building a Math Word Bank
1•12 Using temperature words

EXTRA PRACTICE

1•2 Counting on and back by 5s

Minute Math®+ **1•6** Practicing complements of 10; **1•7** Practicing number patterns; **1•12** Practicing arithmetic facts; solving problems involving temperature

READINESS

1•1 Sequencing numbers
1•2 Counting coin collections
1•3 Using ordinal numbers
1•4 Reviewing addition facts
1•5 Trading pennies and nickels
1•6 Naming parts of a whole
1•7 Counting on the number grid
1•8 Completing number-grid puzzles
1•9 Using a balance to explore equivalency
1•10 Counting by 2s, 5s, and 10s
1•11 Using a balance to compare quantities
1•12 Making a thermometer

ENRICHMENT

1•1 Using Roman numerals
1•2 Finding equivalent coin combinations
1•3 Calculating time spent on activities
1•4 Comparing values of coin combinations
1•5 Using a number grid to find number combinations
1•7 Making number scrolls in the thousands
1•8 Creating number-grid puzzle pieces
1•9 Solving place-value puzzles
1•10 Solving calculator-counting problems
1•11 Comparing numbers in *Number Top-It*

Adjusting the Activity

1•1 Numbering the days of school
1•1 Naming ways in which numbers are used
1•1 Individualizing number lines
1•2 Making tally marks
1•2 Identifying coin values **ELL**
1•3 Using ordinal numbers with a calendar **ELL**
1•3 Marking special events on a calendar **ELL**
1•4 Practicing with specific addition facts
1•5 Modeling problems with dollar bills **ELL**
1•7 Counting by 2s on a number grid **ELL**

1•7 Filling in numbers on a number grid
1•8 Completing number-grid puzzles
1•9 Collecting names for numbers
1•10 Counting by 2s to find a pattern **ELL**
1•11 Using a pan balance to compare numbers **ELL**
1•11 Using the symbols <, >, and =
1•12 Reading negative numbers on thermometers **ELL**
1•12 Using a thermometer
1•12 Modeling 2-dimensional structures **ELL**
1•12 Recording addition facts

A U D I T O R Y ◆ K I N E S T H E T I C ◆ T A C T I L E ◆ V I S U A L

Cross-Curricular Links

Literature
Lesson 1•2 Children will read *Arctic Fives Arrive* and practice counting by 5s.

Science
Lesson 1•12 Children will learn about the Fahrenheit scale.

Using the Projects

Use Project 2, Weather Station, on page 444 to reinforce reading a thermometer and collecting weather observations. See the *Differentiation Handbook* for modifications to Project 2.

Differentiation Handbook

See the *Differentiation Handbook* for materials on Unit 1.

Language Support

Everyday Mathematics provides lesson-specific suggestions to help all children, including non-native English speakers, to acquire, process, and express mathematical ideas.

Connecting Math and Literacy

Lesson 1•1 *A Day with No Math,* by Marilyn Kaye, Harcourt, Brace, Jovanovich, 1992

Lesson 1•2 *Arctic Fives Arrive,* by Elinor J. Pinczes, Scholastic Inc., 1996

Lesson 1•7 *Even Steven and Odd Todd,* by Kathryn Cristaldi, Scholastic Inc., 1996

Lesson 1•8 *One Hundred Hungry Ants,* by Elinor J. Pinczes, Scholastic Inc., 1993

Lesson 1•10 *12 Ways to Get to 11,* by Eve Merriam, Aladdin Paperbacks, 1996

Lesson 1•11 *Math Counts Pattern,* by Henry Pluckrose, Children's Press, 1995

 My Reference Book
pp. 122, 123, 142, 143, 146, and 147

Multiage Classroom ◆ Companion Lessons

Companion Lessons from Grades 1 and 3 can help you meet instructional needs of a multiage classroom. The full Scope and Sequence can be found in the Appendix.

Grade 1	1•2 3•5 4•1	1•3 1•11	1•9 2•5 6•10	1•10 4•11	5•1 8•2		1•10	2•1 3•3 9•1	6•2	3•2–3•4 9•1	1•6 5•3 5•6	1•12 2•7 4•1
Grade 2	1•1	1•2	1•3	1•4	1•5	1•6	1•7	1•8	1•9	1•10	1•11	1•12
Grade 3	1•1 1•12	1•10	1•13	2•1 2•2	5•1 5•5 9•1	5•1	1•12	1•2	1•6	1•12	1•10	5•6 5•7

Professional Development

Teacher's Reference Manual Links

Lesson	Topic	Section
1•1	Plain and Fancy Counting	9.2.2
	Number Grids, Scrolls, and Lines	9.7.2
	Math Messages	1.2.5
1•2	Money	14.9
	Tool Kits	3.3
	Slates	1.2.10
1•3	Clocks	15.2.1
	Calendars	15.2.2
	Class Calendar	5.2
1•4	Reading and Writing Number Sentences	10.1.2
	Cooperative Groupings	4.1
1•5	Money	14.9
1•6	Math Boxes	1.2.4
	My Reference Book/Student Reference Book	1.2.11

Lesson	Topic	Section
1•7	Plain and Fancy Counting	9.2.2
	Number Grids, Scrolls, and Lines	9.7.2
	Cooperative Groupings	4.1
1•9	Equality	9.6.1
	Games for Fact Practice	16.3.4
	Calculators	3.1.1
1•11	Numeric Relations	9.6
	Arithmetic Symbols	10.1.1
	Home Links and Family Letters	8.1
1•12	Thermometers	15.1.2
	Base-10 Blocks	9.7.1
	Explorations	1.2.1

Materials

Lesson	Masters	Manipulative Kit Items	Other Items
1•1	Teaching Master, p. 2* Home Link Masters, pp. 3–6 Game Master, p. 446	Class Number Line	Class Data Pad*; counters; stick-on notes
1•2	Teaching Master, p. 7	Pattern-Block Template tool-kit coins slate	tool kit; 20 pennies, 5 nickels, 10 dimes, and 4 quarters; overhead coins*; Lost-and-Found Box; *Arctic Fives Arrive;* Class Data Pad; crayons
1•3	Teaching Master, p. 8 transparency of *Math Masters,* p. 414*	tool-kit clock	large wall calendar; demonstration clock*
1•4	Teaching Aid Masters, p. 415 and 416* Game Masters, pp. 449* and 452 or 453	per group: 4 of each number cards 0–10 ; Class Number Grid Poster; slate; tool-kit coins*	Working with a Partner Poster*; per group: 40 pennies; scissors
1•5	Game Masters, pp. 449* and 458–461 transparency of *Math Masters,* p. 448 Teaching Aid Master, p. 417	per group: 4 of each number cards 0–10, dominoes, and 1 die	envelope or other device for storing money; scissors; per group: 20 pennies and 10 nickels; per group: 40 nickels and 20 dimes; crayons or markers; Class Data Pad
1•6	Game Master, p. 468	slate per group: 20 tool-kit pennies	per group: plate, cup, or other container
1•7	Teaching Masters, pp. 9–11 Teaching Aid Master, p. 415 Game Master, p. 449*	Number-Grid Poster; per group: number cards 4 of each 0–10, dominoes, or dice*; slate; calculator*	demonstration clock; Rules for Working in Small Groups Poster*; red and green cups*; paste or tape; empty paper-towel roll*; crayons
1•8	Teaching Aid Masters, pp. 416*, 417, and 418 Teaching Masters, pp. 12 and 13	Number-Grid Poster per group: 1 die	game marker; dry-erase marker or grease pencil; scissors; tape or paste*; half-sheets of paper*
1•9		tool-kit bills calculator	overhead calculator*; pan balance; 18 pencils, dominoes, pennies, or other small identical objects
1•10	Teaching Master, p. 14 Teaching Aid Master, p. 416*	slate calculator	
1•11	Teaching Aid Master, p. 415 Home Link Masters, pp. 15 and 16 Game Masters, pp. 449*, 465, and 466	tool-kit coins; slate per group: number cards 4 of each 0–10, dominoes, or dice*	pan balance; 20 pennies or other identical objects; glue or tape
1•12	Home Link 1•11 Teaching Masters, pp. 17–19 Home Link Master, p. 20 Game Master, p. 449*	per group: outdoor thermometer, base-10 blocks, number cards 0–18, double-9 dominoes meterstick; 4 of each number number cards 0–10	Class Thermometer Poster; Rules for Explorations Poster*; quarter-sheets of paper; chart paper; stick-on notes; marker
1•13	Home Link 1•12 Assessment Masters, pp. 154–157 Home Link Masters, pp. 21–24	slate	

Technology
Assessment Management System, Unit 1
iTLG, Unit 1

* Denotes optional materials

Mathematical Background

The discussion below highlights the major content ideas presented in Unit 1 and helps establish instructional priorities.

Routines and Devices

Most of the routines and devices initiated in Unit 1 and in later units have been introduced in prior grades. If you have not used *Everyday Mathematics* before, you are urged to read the Organizing Routines and Displays section of the Management Guide, which is found in the *Teacher's Reference Manual*.

The following tables list routines and devices that initially appear in Unit 1.

A Mathematics All Around bulletin board

Routines	Lesson
Family Letters	1♦1
Math Message	1♦1
Mental Math and Reflexes	1♦1
Oral counting	1♦1
School days on the Class Number Line	1♦1
Mathematics All Around bulletin board	1♦1
Monthly calendar	1♦3
Partner activities	1♦4
Math Boxes	1♦6
Home Links	1♦11

Devices	Lesson
Class Number Line	1♦1
Class Data Pad	1♦1
Tool kits, coins, Pattern-Block Template	1♦2
Clocks (demonstration and tool-kit)	1♦3
Everything Math Deck	1♦4
Class Number Grid Poster	1♦4
Money (bills)	1♦5
Number scrolls	1♦7
Calculators	1♦9

Reminders and Review Activities

When assessing children's level of understanding of previously taught concepts and skills, briefly review the topics before conducting the actual assessment. Without such review, children may not be able to demonstrate the full extent of their knowledge.

The following table lists the topics reviewed in Unit 1.

Reminders and Review	Lesson
Number sequences	1◆1
Number line	1◆1
Counts by 2s, 5s, 10s	1◆1
Coin values	1◆2
Tallies	1◆2
Months, weeks, days	1◆3
Time of day	1◆3
Addition facts	1◆4, 1◆6
Number-grid patterns	1◆4, 1◆7, 1◆8
Money values	1◆5
Place values	1◆5, 1◆8
Equivalent names for numbers	1◆9
Skip counting	1◆9, 1◆10
Numbers (<, >, =)	1◆11

In Lesson 1-3, Mental Math and Reflexes, children find ways to represent 35¢.

Math Message and Number Sequences (Lesson 1◆1)

Most Math Messages are designed to start children thinking about the main topic of the day. Some Math Messages may also review ideas covered in prior lessons.

The Mental Math and Reflexes routine mostly focuses on quick mental mathematics activities. In this unit, the routine involves whole-class oral responses. Starting in Lesson 1-2, children will often display their individual responses on slates.

The first lesson of the year emphasizes counting and number sequences, especially sequences on a number line. Children look for examples of number lines in everyday life (such as rulers) and begin keeping track of the number of school days on the Class Number Line. Children also share ideas about mathematics. The first Family Letter should be sent home to inform families about *Everyday Mathematics* in general and Unit 1 in particular.

PROFESSIONAL DEVELOPMENT

Before beginning Unit 1, read about the following routines and devices in the Management Guide, which is located in the *Teacher's Reference Manual:* Daily Routines, Math Messages, Mental Math and Reflexes, Class Data Pad, Home Links, and Family Letters.

Also decide on the following:

- *where you will post the Math Message*
- *how children will respond to the Math Message*
- *where you will post the current date*
- *how to keep track of the number of school days on the Class Number Line. Marking days can be a daily job for one of the children.*

Tools and Coins (Lesson 1♦2)

Doing mathematics involves using mathematical tools, such as rulers to measure length, straightedges and templates to draw shapes, and counters to model problem situations. Slates provide a quick way to check children's work as they respond to questions. In this lesson, procedures for storing and retrieving slates are determined, and slates are used for recording tallies.

Children also receive tool kits, which are convenient devices designed to store their individual materials. Children use coins in their tool kits to find the value of coin collections and explore making shape designs using the Pattern-Block Template.

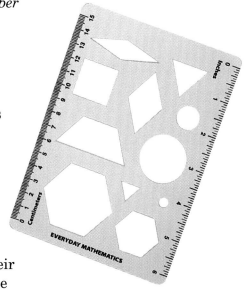

Pattern-Block Template

 You may want to read more about slates and tool kits in the Management Guide, which is located in the *Teacher's Reference Manual.*

Calendars and Clocks (Lesson 1♦3)

Children practice telling time. Most children should be able to tell time to 30-minute intervals; a few children may even be able to tell time to 5-minute intervals. Adjust examples to suit the level of your class. Telling time will be covered again in later units. Children fill in a calendar for the current month—a routine that can be done each month. The calendar is used to review ordinal numbers.

 You can read more about calendars and clocks in Section 15, Reference Frames, which is located in the *Teacher's Reference Manual.*

Partner Study Routines (Lesson 1♦4)

Because children will often work with partners, it is important to agree on guidelines for working together early in the year. You will want to establish a supportive classroom environment in which conversation and movement are welcome but wasting time and bothering others are not. In this lesson, children pair up to play a game that gives them practice with basic addition facts. Children also explore patterns on the Class Number-Grid Poster, which displays the numbers 0 through 110.

 Before beginning this lesson, read about Games and Cooperative Groupings in the Management Guide in the *Teacher's Reference Manual.*

Working with a Partner

- *Be polite.*
- *Help each other.*
- *Share.*
- *Listen to your partner.*
- *Praise your partner.*
- *Take turns.*
- *Talk about problems.*
- *Speak quietly.*

You may want to display a poster like this one in your classroom.

Grouping by Tens—$1, $10, $100
(Lesson 1♦5)

Children cut out the $1, $10, and $100 bills provided in their journals (or you can supply play money from another source). After counting the total amount of money, children strengthen their place-value skills by playing various versions of the *Money Exchange Game*. In this game, groups of ten bills are exchanged for one bill of the next-higher denomination.

 For information about money, see Section 14.9 in the *Teacher's Reference Manual.*

Math Boxes (Lesson 1♦6)

In this lesson, children are introduced to *My Reference Book*. Children will use this book to revisit topics that were introduced before and to look up information, such as a definition.

Math Boxes have proved to be a popular and effective routine for review and practice. Starting with this lesson, each lesson will have one page of Math Boxes problems. Usually, Math Boxes problems will be based on skills developed earlier, not on the content of the current lesson.

 Before beginning this lesson, read about Math Boxes in Section 1.2.4 of the Management Guide in the *Teacher's Reference Manual.*

Working in Small Groups (Lesson 1♦7)

In this lesson, the rules for working with partners established in Lesson 1-4 are extended to working in small groups. Children work in small groups to make a scroll of the numbers to 1,000. There is an opportunity to discuss even and odd numbers, as well as other patterns found in number grids.

 See the *Teacher's Reference Manual,* Section 4.1 for additional information about cooperative grouping.

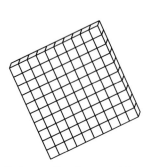

The Class Number Grid Poster helps children visualize numbers as they count by 2s, 5s, and 10s.

Number Grids (Lesson 1♦8)

Children find patterns on number grids and use place-value skills to fill in missing numbers. It is helpful for children to have their own laminated number grids, which can be used several times. *Math Masters* page 417 is available for this purpose.

 Before beginning this lesson, read about semipermanent chalk in the Organizing Routines and Displays section of the Management Guide, which is located in the *Teacher's Reference Manual.*

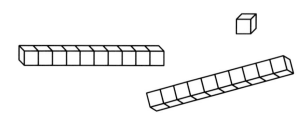
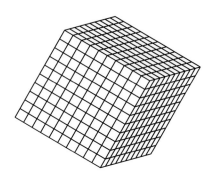

Equivalent Names for Numbers
(Lesson 1♦9); Counting Patterns (Lesson 1♦10)

One of the basic ideas of mathematics is that any number can be named in a variety of ways. For example, 4 + 6; 20 − 10; and 2 × 5 are all names for the number 10. This idea is reinforced in Lesson 1-9 in several ways—one of which is by solving *Broken Calculator* problems, in which one or more calculator keys are "broken" and numbers must be obtained without using the numbers on those keys.

In Lessons 1-9 and 1-10, children use calculators to skip count and explore patterns.

 Before beginning Lesson 1-9, you may want to read about calculators in Section 3.1.1 of the *Teacher's Reference Manual.*

Note

Children should not use calculators to solve basic facts or while practicing algorithms for adding, subtracting, or multiplying numbers. To remind children of this, journal pages, Home Links, and masters are marked with a "no calculator" icon.

Relations (<, >, =) and Home Links
(Lesson 1♦11)

Children compare numbers by first writing the phrases *is less than, is greater than*, or *is equal to* between pairs of numbers and then by writing the symbols <, >, or =. Mnemonic devices are reviewed to help children remember the meanings of < and >.

Home Links are described in detail in the Management Guide. The Home Links routine is begun in this lesson. Home Links, which include activities and problems for children to complete outside of school, are provided in each lesson.

Exploring Temperatures, Base-10 Structures, and Dominoes (Lesson 1♦12)

You will need to decide how you will organize the Explorations. Remember that Explorations are designed to be small-group activities. If you are going to run them simultaneously, you will need a plan for managing several different activities at the same time. Parent volunteers can be helpful.

In the first Exploration, children read and mark temperatures on the Class Thermometer Poster. In the second Exploration, children review the values that base-10 blocks represent. Then children build structures with the blocks and calculate the values of the structures. In this unit's final Exploration, children develop addition facts by sorting dominoes according to the sums of the dots.

Children build structures with cubes, longs, and flats. Then they find the numerical value of these structures based on the following system:

1 cube = 1

1 long = 10

1 flat = 100

 Explorations are discussed in the Managing the Curriculum section of the Management Guide, which is located in the *Teacher's Reference Manual* Section 1.2.1.

Math Message and Number Sequences

 Objectives To introduce the Math Message routine; and to review number sequences and number lines.

1 Teaching the Lesson — materials

Key Activities
Children are introduced to the Math Message routine and share ideas about mathematics. They complete and extend number sequences and number lines.

Key Concepts and Skills
- Count on by ones.
  [Number and Numeration Goal 1]
- Read and write numbers to 10s, 100s, and 1,000s.
  [Number and Numeration Goal 2]
- Compare and order numbers on a number line.
  [Number and Numeration Goal 7]

Key Vocabulary
Math Message • number line

Ongoing Assessment: Informing Instruction See page 20.

Ongoing Assessment: Recognizing Student Achievement Use journal page 1.
[Number and Numeration Goal 7]

materials
- ☐ *Math Journal 1*, p. 1
- ☐ Teaching Master (*Math Masters*, p. 2; optional)
- ☐ Class Data Pad (optional)
- ☐ Class Number Line

***See* Advance Preparation**

2 Ongoing Learning & Practice — materials

Children take home the Home Link Family Letter.

materials
- ☐ Home Link Masters (*Math Masters*, pp. 3–6)

3 Differentiation Options — materials

READINESS
Children play *Number-Line Squeeze* to explore comparing and ordering numbers.

ENRICHMENT
Children use Roman numerals to further explore ordering numbers.

ELL SUPPORT
Children discuss the Mathematics All Around bulletin board.

materials
- ☐ Game Master (*Math Masters*, p. 464)
- ☐ 2 counters
- ☐ Class Data Pad (optional)
- ☐ Class Number Line
- ☐ stick-on notes

Additional Information

Advance Preparation Start a Mathematics All Around bulletin board. Post items that show a variety of numbers and shapes—for example, advertisements with quantities and prices, schedules that list times, and pictures of designs and structures.

Technology
Assessment Management System
Journal page 1, Problems 1 and 2
See the **iTLG.**

Getting Started

Mental Math and Reflexes

- ○○○ Count on by 2s, 5s, and 10s.
- ○○○ Count back by 2s, 5s, and 10s.
- ○○○ Do stop-and-start counting. Have a group of children begin counting at a number you name; stop them; point at another group to continue where the count left off. If appropriate, try 3-digit counting, such as counting on by 2s starting at 150.

Math Message

With a partner, talk about what mathematics is. Look for items in the classroom that have to do with mathematics. Be prepared to share what you find.

---

1 Teaching the Lesson

▶ Math Message Follow-Up
 WHOLE-CLASS DISCUSSION

Point out the **Math Message.** Tell children that every day they will complete a Math Message before the math lesson begins.

Ask children to share their ideas about mathematics and what items they see in the classroom that have to do with mathematics. In addition to numbers, encourage children to look for other mathematical items, such as shapes, patterns, and mathematical tools. You may want to record the children's ideas on the Class Data Pad. (*See margin.*) Call children's attention to the Mathematics All Around bulletin board for other things to add to the data pad. As the year progresses, add ideas they suggest. Refer to the pad whenever a link can be made to a topic under discussion.

> **Adjusting the Activity**
>
> Ask children: *How old are you? What is your address? What do you do when you use the telephone? What number is on our classroom door? Why is this particular number on our door?*
>
> AUDITORY ♦ KINESTHETIC ♦ TACTILE ♦ VISUAL

> **NOTE Readiness** activities help children gain prerequisite skills so that they can be successful in the lesson. Some children may benefit from doing the Readiness activity before you begin Part 1 of the lesson. See the Readiness activity in Part 3 for details.

Counting
Measuring Distances and Lengths
Measuring Amounts
Buying Things
Knowing Shapes and Patterns
Solving Problems
Number Grid
Number Line

The Class Data Pad can be used to list children's ideas about mathematics.

▶ Number of School Days Routine
WHOLE-CLASS ACTIVITY

Tell children that the class is going to mark school days on the Class Number Line. Discuss and decide where to mark today on the **number line.** If today is the first day of school, the number 1 would be marked.

Have children describe other ways in which number lines can be used. Number lines are often used as scales for measuring things. The axes on a graph resemble number lines. Ask children to think of objects that remind them of number lines. Ruler, thermometer, measuring cup, weighing scale, radio dial

>  **Adjusting the Activity**
>
> Ask: *What number names the day before the first day of school?* 0 *What number names the day before the day before the first day of school?* −1 *What are numbers less than 0 called?* Negative numbers
>
> AUDITORY ♦ KINESTHETIC ♦ TACTILE ♦ VISUAL

▶ Writing Numbers in Sequence 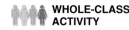 WHOLE-CLASS ACTIVITY

To support English language learners, write the word *sequence* on the board and discuss the meaning.

Write a partial sequence of numbers on the board. *For example:*

63, ――, ――, ――, 67, ――, ...

Ask children to copy the sequence and fill in the blanks.

1. Have a volunteer name the missing numbers. 64, 65, 66, 68

2. Ask whether anyone can explain the meaning of the ellipsis— the three dots—at the end. The dots show that the sequence goes on.

3. Ask children to write the next few numbers in the sequence.

Pose problems like the following:

▷ 42, 43, ――, ――, ―― , ... 44, 45, 46

▷ 310, 311, ――, ――, ―― , ... 312, 313, 314

▷ 727, 728, ――, ――, ―― , ... 729, 730, 731

 Ongoing Assessment: Informing Instruction

Watch for children who have difficulty ordering numbers greater than 100. Suggest that if the beginning digits of the numbers are the same, they can order the numbers based on the last two digits. For example, with 310, 311, 312, children cover the digit 3 in the hundreds place and look at 10, 11, 12.

▶ Reviewing Number Sequences Starting with 1,000  WHOLE-CLASS ACTIVITY

Write 1,000 on the board. Ask a volunteer to write the number that comes next while the class says the number in unison.

Remind children not to say *and* when reading large whole numbers. The number 1,001 is read *one thousand one*, not *one thousand and one*. The word *and* is used to indicate the decimal point when reading numbers.

▶ Introducing the Journal  WHOLE-CLASS DISCUSSION
(*Math Journal 1*)

Distribute *Math Journal 1* and have children write their names on the back cover. Briefly discuss how the journals will be used and stored.

Take a tour of the journal. Ask questions, such as the following:

● What information is in the table of contents?

● What information is inside the front cover?

● What should be recorded at the top of every journal page?

Writing Numbers on Number Lines

(Math Journal 1, p. 1; Math Masters, p. 2)

INDEPENDENT ACTIVITY

Have children turn to journal page 1. Remind them to write the date and time at the top of the page. Show them where the current date will be displayed in the classroom.

Have children fill in the missing numbers for the number lines. Review answers by counting in unison.

Ongoing Assessment: Recognizing Student Achievement

Journal page 1 Problems 1 and 2

Use **journal page 1, Problems 1 and 2** to assess children's abilities to write and order numbers. Children are making adequate progress if they successfully complete Problems 1 and 2. Some children may be able to complete the number line sequences in the hundreds and thousands.

[Number and Numeration Goal 7]

2 Ongoing Learning & Practice

Home Link Family Letter

INDEPENDENT ACTIVITY

(Math Masters, pp. 3–6)

Home Connection Distribute copies of the beginning-of-the-year Family Letter for children to take home.

Student Page

Math Journal 1, p. 1

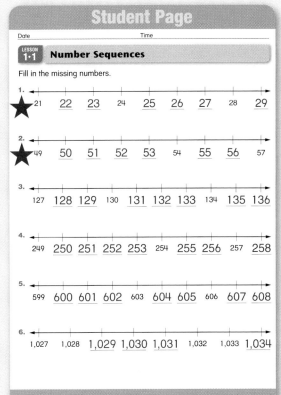

Date _____ Time _____

LESSON 1·1 Number Sequences

Fill in the missing numbers.

1. ★ 21 22 23 24 25 26 27 28 29

2. ★ 49 50 51 52 53 54 55 56 57

3. 127 128 129 130 131 132 133 134 135 136

4. 249 250 251 252 253 254 255 256 257 258

5. 599 600 601 602 603 604 605 606 607 608

6. 1,027 1,028 1,029 1,030 1,031 1,032 1,033 1,034

Adjusting the Activity

Use *Math Masters*, page 2 to create number lines that meet the needs of individual children.

AUDITORY ♦ KINESTHETIC ♦ TACTILE ♦ VISUAL

Teaching Master

Name _____ Date _____ Time _____

LESSON 1·1 Number Lines

1.
2.
3.
4.
5.
6.

Home Link Masters

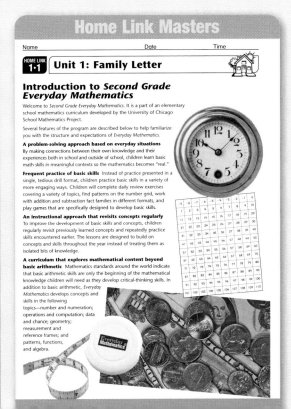

Name _____ Date _____ Time _____

HOME LINK 1·1 Unit 1: Family Letter

Introduction to *Second Grade Everyday Mathematics*

Welcome to *Second Grade Everyday Mathematics*. It is a part of an elementary school mathematics curriculum developed by the University of Chicago School Mathematics Project.

Several features of the program are described below to help familiarize you with the structure and expectations of *Everyday Mathematics*.

A problem-solving approach based on everyday situations By making connections between their own knowledge and their experiences both in school and outside of school, children learn basic math skills in meaningful contexts so the mathematics becomes "real."

Frequent practice of basic skills Instead of practice presented in a single, tedious drill format, children practice basic skills in a variety of more engaging ways. Children will complete daily review exercises covering a variety of topics, find patterns on the number grid, work with addition and subtraction fact families in different formats, and play games that are specifically designed to develop basic skills.

An instructional approach that revisits concepts regularly To improve the development of basic skills and concepts, children regularly revisit previously learned concepts and repeatedly practice skills encountered earlier. The lessons are designed to build on concepts and skills throughout the year instead of treating them as isolated bits of knowledge.

A curriculum that explores mathematical content beyond basic arithmetic Mathematics standards around the world indicate that basic arithmetic skills are only the beginning of the mathematical knowledge children will need as they develop critical-thinking skills. In addition to basic arithmetic, *Everyday Mathematics* develops concepts and skills in the following topics—number and numeration; operations and computation; data and chance; geometry; measurement and reference frames; and patterns, functions, and algebra.

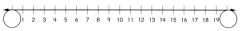

Roman Numerals

$I = 1$	$XX = 20$ (2 tens)
$II = 2$	
$III = 3$	$XL = 40$ (50 less 10)
$IV = 4$	$L = 50$
$V = 5$	$LX = 60$ (50 plus 10)
$VI = 6$	
$VII = 7$	$XC = 90$ (100 less 10)
$VIII = 8$	$C = 100$
$IX = 9$	$CX = 110$ (100 plus 10)
$X = 10$	
	$D = 500$
	$M = 1,000$

③ Differentiation Options

 READINESS   **SMALL-GROUP ACTIVITY** **5–15 Min**

▶ Playing *Number-Line Squeeze*

(*Math Masters*, p. 464)

To explore comparing and ordering numbers using a visual model, have children play *Number-Line Squeeze*. See *Math Masters*, page 464 for directions.

ENRICHMENT   **INDEPENDENT ACTIVITY** **5–15 Min**

▶ Counting with Roman Numerals

To further explore comparing and ordering numbers, introduce children to Roman numerals. Display a table of Roman numerals on the board or Class Data Pad. (*See margin.*) Discuss the patterns in the Roman numeral system.

Use Roman numerals along with the routine of counting the number of school days. Roman numerals can be written on large stick-on notes and attached to the Class Number Line.

 **ELL SUPPORT**   **SMALL-GROUP ACTIVITY** **5–15 Min**

▶ Discussing the Mathematics All Around Bulletin Board

To provide language support for understanding uses of numbers, have children look at the Mathematics All Around bulletin board. Ask them to describe some of the ways the numbers on the bulletin board are being used. Sample answers: An address on a door, a list of telephone numbers, how much something costs If several English language learners speak the same language, have them take a minute to discuss the bulletin board in their own language first and then share what they are able to in English.

Planning Ahead

▷ Beginning in Lesson 1-2, children will need 20 pennies, 5 nickels, 10 dimes, and 4 quarters. Be prepared to distribute either real or play coins for children to add to their tool kits in Lesson 1-2. Consider sending a note to parents requesting real coins for their children to use in class.

▷ You may also wish to send home a note asking that children bring clean, old socks to school to use as slate erasers. Alternatively, have children use tissues or paper towels for this purpose.

Tools and Coins

 Objectives To introduce the tool kits; and to guide children as they find the values of coin combinations.

1　Teaching the Lesson

materials

Key Activities
The teacher distributes and discusses mathematical tools and tool kits. Children find the values of coin combinations.

Key Concepts and Skills
• Count by 1s, 5s, and 10s using coins.
[Number and Numeration Goal 1]

• Use a counting-up strategy to calculate the total value of coin combinations.
[Operations and Computation Goal 2]

• Calculate the values of coin combinations.
[Operations and Computation Goal 2]

Key Vocabulary
slate • tool kit • Lost-and-Found Box • Pattern-Block Template

☑ **Ongoing Assessment: Recognizing Student Achievement** Use journal page 2.
[Operations and Computation Goal 2]

☐ *Math Journal 1*, p. 2
☐ slate
☐ tool kit
☐ Lost-and-Found Box
☐ 20 pennies, 5 nickels, 10 dimes, and 4 quarters
☐ overhead coins (optional)

See **Advance Preparation**

2　Ongoing Learning & Practice

materials

Children explore with Pattern-Block Templates.

☐ Pattern-Block Template
☐ Class Data Pad
☐ crayons

3　Differentiation Options

materials

READINESS
Children sort and count collections of coins.

ENRICHMENT
Children find equivalent coin combinations.

EXTRA PRACTICE
Children count on and back by 5s.

☐ *Math Journal 1*, p. 2
☐ Teaching Master (*Math Masters*, p. 7)
☐ tool-kit coins
☐ *Arctic Fives Arrive* by Elinor J. Pinczes

Additional Information

Advance Preparation Put a Lost-and-Found Box in a prominent place in the room. Before distributing the tool kits in Part 1, assign a number to each child. Some teachers assign numbers in the thousands. Label the tool kits and their contents with corresponding numbers. Be prepared to distribute real or play coins in case children did not bring enough from home.

For the optional Extra Practice activity in Part 3, obtain a copy of *Arctic Fives Arrive* by Elinor J. Pinczes (Houghton Mifflin, 1996).

Technology
Assessment Management System
Journal page 2, Problems 1–3
See the **iTLG**.

Getting Started

Mental Math and Reflexes

◉○○ Count on by 10s from a multiple of 10.

◉○○ Count on by 10s from 10; stop; continue to count on by 5s.

◉◉◉ Count on by 10s starting at 40; stop; continue to count on by 5s; stop; continue to count on by 1s.

Math Message

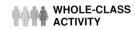

Take a slate, a piece of chalk, and an eraser. Make tally marks to show how many children are here today.

NOTE Some children may benefit from doing the **Readiness** activity before you begin Part 1 of the lesson. See the Readiness activity in Part 3 for details.

① Teaching the Lesson

▶ Math Message Follow-Up

👪👪 **WHOLE-CLASS ACTIVITY**

Have children share responses to the Math Message. Record the correct number of tallies on the board and have the class count them together. Be sure to count the groups of 5s first; for example, 5, 10, 15, 20, 25, 26, 27.

⬆ Adjusting the Activity

If children are not familiar with how to make tally marks, begin by making a separate mark for each child in attendance. Count the total by 1s. Then, show children how to make four marks with a fifth mark placed across the others ("four standing tall; then one takes a fall"). Make a tally count for the class total. Count by 5s for each group of tallies.

AUDITORY ◆ KINESTHETIC ◆ TACTILE ◆ VISUAL

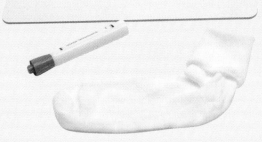

Children may use a sock for an eraser.

▶ Introducing the Slate Routine

👪👪 **WHOLE-CLASS ACTIVITY**

Discuss the care and use of **slates.** Explain where slates will be kept and how they will be distributed. Explain that during whole-class activities, the slates will provide everyone with a chance to answer quietly and at the same time.

Practice a routine, such as "Listen, Think, Write, Show, Erase." You may want to use some of the suggestions below to practice this routine. Encourage children to erase their slates completely between problems.

● Write the number that comes before 200. 199

● Write the number that comes before 1,001. 1,000

● Write the number that comes after 509. 510

▶ Distributing Tool Kits

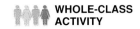 **WHOLE-CLASS ACTIVITY**

Ask questions such as the following:

- Who uses tools? Doctors? Plumbers? Who else?

- What tools do they use?

- What do they use their tools for?

- What tools belong in a toolbox for mathematics?

Tell children that they will each have a **tool kit** to help in their work with mathematics.

Distribute the tool kits. Point out that each tool kit has a number written on the outside of it. Explain that the numbers will help identify the owners of misplaced items. Show the **Lost-and-Found Box** and explain its purpose. Talk about the items that are now in the tool kits, identifying each item.

Call out the names of the children and have them say their tool-kit numbers. Be sure to keep a master list of children's names with their tool-kit numbers. Other small items, such as a ruler, tape measure, dice, play bills, clock face, and calculator, will be added to the tool kit as they are introduced.

NOTE It is important that the tool kits are available to children for use at any time during math lessons.

> **NOTE** You might want to distribute tool kits at random, or you might want to assign children their numbers (for example, in alphabetical order according to first names) ahead of time and then match children with tool-kit numbers. Children can then compare the order of letters in the alphabet with the order of numbers.

▶ Finding the Values of Coin Combinations

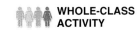 **WHOLE-CLASS ACTIVITY**

Have children show 2 quarters. Ask: *How much money do you have?* 50 cents Then have each child show 2 dimes and 2 nickels. Ask: *How much money do you have now?* 30 cents Continue with simple combinations. You might model these combinations on the overhead projector with overhead coins.

Ask children to show more complex coin combinations in random order of value, such as 2 dimes, 1 quarter, 2 pennies. Ask: *How much money do you have?* 47 cents Have children share strategies for solving this problem. If no one mentions it, have children line up their coins in order of value from greatest to least and count as a class: 25, 35, 45, 46, 47 cents.

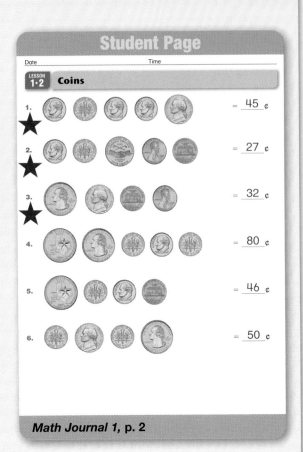

Date _____ Time _____

LESSON 1·2   **Coins**

1. = 45 ¢ ★

2. = 27 ¢ ★

3. = 32 ¢ ★

4. = 80 ¢

5. = 46 ¢

6. = 50 ¢

Math Journal 1, p. 2

NOTE Throughout *Everyday Mathematics,* various versions of nickels are pictured on children's pages. Point out to children the nickel backs shown on Math Journal, page 2. Explain that, in addition to the Monticello tails that they are familiar with, there are a few other nickel backs. Point out the Louisiana Purchase nickel. They will see different nickel backs throughout the year. Help children understand that all nickels, regardless of the images on them, are worth 5 cents. Draw their attention to the words *five cents* on the coin.

▶ **Counting Coins**

INDEPENDENT ACTIVITY

(*Math Journal 1,* p. 2)

Have children turn to journal page 2. They may use their coins to help them complete the page. Draw

 Ⓟ Ⓝ Ⓓ Ⓠ

on the board and remind children that these symbols stand for penny, nickel, dime, and quarter.

✔ **Ongoing Assessment:**
Recognizing Student Achievement

Journal page 2 Problems 1–3 ★

Use **journal page 2, Problems 1–3** to assess children's ability to count coin combinations. Children are making adequate progress if they successfully complete Problems 1–3 using real coins. Some children may successfully calculate all the coin combinations with or without using real coins.

[Operations and Computation Goal 2]

⬆⬇ **Adjusting the Activity**

ELL

Have children record the coin value above each coin:

   25¢   10¢   10¢   1¢

When the coins are displayed in random order, have children model the problem by placing real coins in order of value.

A U D I T O R Y ◆ K I N E S T H E T I C ◆ T A C T I L E ◆ V I S U A L

---

2 **Ongoing Learning & Practice**

▶ **Exploring the Pattern-Block Template**

INDEPENDENT ACTIVITY

Have children point to and name the shapes on the **Pattern-Block Template.** To support English language learners, write the name of each shape next to its picture on the Class Data Pad.

Review how to use the Pattern-Block Template to draw shapes. Then let children play freely with their Pattern-Block Templates, creating and coloring their designs.

③ Differentiation Options

READINESS

SMALL-GROUP ACTIVITY

▶ Sorting and Counting Coins

5–15 Min

(*Math Masters,* p. 7)

To provide experience with sorting and counting coins, have children sort collections of coins into piles of pennies, nickels, dimes, and quarters. They count the number of coins and calculate the total value of the coins in each pile.

ENRICHMENT

SMALL-GROUP ACTIVITY

▶ Finding Equivalent Coins

5–15 Min

(*Math Journal 1,* p. 2)

To apply what children know about coin combinations, have them find an equivalent coin combination using the least number of coins for each problem on journal page 2.

EXTRA PRACTICE

SMALL-GROUP ACTIVITY

▶ Counting by Fives in Literature

5–15 Min

Literature Link Read the following book to groups of children, or have children read the book themselves. Have children count on and back in unison by 5s to 100.

Arctic Fives Arrive by Elinor J. Pinczes (Houghton Mifflin, 1996) *Summary:* Arctic animals arrive in groups of five to view the Northern Lights. Then "their order reversed, the watchers dispersed."

Teaching Master

Name   Date   Time

LESSON 1·2 Sorting and Counting Coins

Sort your coins into piles of pennies, nickels, dimes, and quarters.

Count the number of coins you have in each pile. Record your total number of coins for each pile.

Calculate the total value for each pile of coins. Record your total value for each pile of coins.

Coin	Number of Coins	Value of Coins
Pennies		
	Answers vary.	
Nickels		
Dimes		
Quarters		

Try This

Calculate the total value of all of your coins.

***Math Masters,* p. 7**

1·3 Calendars and Clocks

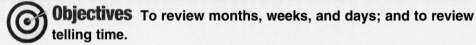

Objectives To review months, weeks, and days; and to review telling time.

---

1 Teaching the Lesson

materials

Key Activities

Children number and name months in a year, begin to build a calendar for the current month, and say and write ordinal numbers. They tell time using clocks in their tool kits and on their journal pages.

Key Concepts and Skills

- Use probability terms to describe events.
  [Data and Chance Goal 3]
- Name days in a week.
  [Measurement and Reference Frames Goal 3]
- Tell and show time to the nearest half-hour.
  [Measurement and Reference Frames Goal 6]
- Describe calendar patterns and use them to solve problems.
  [Patterns, Functions, and Algebra Goal 1]

Key Vocabulary

calendar • ordinal numbers

✔ **Ongoing Assessment: Informing Instruction** See page 31.

- ☐ *Math Journal 1*, pp. 3 and 159
- ☐ Transparency (*Math Masters*, p. 414; optional)
- ☐ large wall calendar
- ☐ tool-kit clock
- ☐ demonstration clock (optional)

***See* Advance Preparation**

---

2 Ongoing Learning & Practice

materials

Children tell time on an analog clock.

✔ **Ongoing Assessment: Recognizing Student Achievement** Use journal page 4.
  [Measurement and Reference Frames Goal 6]

- ☐ *Math Journal 1*, p. 4

---

3 Differentiation Options

materials

READINESS

Children listen for and say ordinal numbers while playing ordinal number games.

ENRICHMENT

Children make schedules of their daily activities and calculate the amount of time they spend on each activity.

ELL SUPPORT

Children answer questions using the language of time and events.

- ☐ Teaching Master (*Math Masters*, p. 8)

Additional Information

Advance Preparation Consider writing the names of the months on the board if they are not posted in the classroom.

Technology

Assessment Management System
Journal page 4, Problems 1, 2, 4, and 5
See the **iTLG.**

Getting Started

Mental Math and Reflexes

⊙○○ Count up and back by 2s, 5s, and 10s.

⊙⊙○ Do stop-and-start counting by 2s, 5s, and 10s. Have a group of children begin counting at a number you name; stop; point at another group to continue where the count left off.

⊙⊙⊙ Do stop-and-start counting by 2s, 5s, and 10s starting with 3-digit numbers.

Math Message

How many months are in a year? 12 *Can you name the months?* January, February, March, April, May, June, July, August, September, October, November, December

---

① Teaching the Lesson

> **NOTE** Some children may benefit from doing the **Readiness** activity before you begin Part 1 of the lesson. See the Readiness activity in Part 3 for details.

▶ Math Message Follow-Up

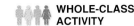 **WHOLE-CLASS ACTIVITY**

(*Math Journal 1*, p. 159)

Have children turn to journal page 159 and find the number of months in a year.

Have children name as many of the months as they can. Prompt them by asking questions like the following: *In what month were you born? What month is it now? In what month do we celebrate Valentine's Day?*

Say the months of the year in order together. If the months are displayed in the classroom, point to each name as you say it. If they are not displayed, write the names on the board as you say them.

▶ Building a Calendar for the Month

 **WHOLE-CLASS DISCUSSION**

(*Math Journal 1*, p. 3; *Math Masters*, p. 414)

Show children a large wall calendar, preferably one with more than one month. Remind them that we use a **calendar** to keep track of days, weeks, and months in a year.

Ask questions such as the following about the calendar:

● How many days are in a week? 7 days

● How many days are in a month? 28, 29, 30, or 31 days

● How many days does this month have? 30 or 31 days

● On what day of the week did this month begin? Do all months begin on the same day?

● What year, month, and day is today?

NOTE As children give answers, have them attach a unit to the number. One of the ongoing ideas in *Everyday Mathematics* is that numbers almost always occur in context.

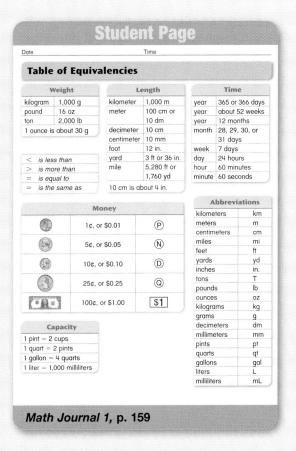

Student Page

Date _____ Time _____

Table of Equivalencies

Weight	
kilogram	1,000 g
pound	16 oz
ton	2,000 lb
1 ounce is about 30 g	

Length	
kilometer	1,000 m
meter	100 cm or
	10 dm
decimeter	10 cm
centimeter	10 mm
foot	12 in.
yard	3 ft or 36 in.
mile	5,280 ft or
	1,760 yd
10 cm is about 4 in.	

Time	
year	365 or 366 days
year	about 52 weeks
year	12 months
month	28, 29, 30, or 31 days
week	7 days
day	24 hours
hour	60 minutes
minute	60 seconds

<	is less than
>	is more than
=	is equal to
=	is the same as

Money		
	1¢, or $0.01	Ⓟ
	5¢, or $0.05	Ⓝ
	10¢, or $0.10	Ⓓ
	25¢, or $0.25	Ⓠ
	100¢, or $1.00	$1

Abbreviations	
kilometers	km
meters	m
centimeters	cm
miles	mi
feet	ft
yards	yd
inches	in.
tons	T
pounds	lb
ounces	oz
kilograms	kg
grams	g
decimeters	dm
millimeters	mm
pints	pt
quarts	qt
gallons	gal
liters	L
milliliters	mL

Capacity
1 pint = 2 cups
1 quart = 2 pints
1 gallon = 4 quarts
1 liter = 1,000 milliliters

Math Journal 1, p. 159

Date _____ Time _____

LESSON
1·3 **Calendar for the Month**

	Sunday	Monday	Tuesday	Wednesday	Thursday	Friday	Saturday
Month

Math Journal 1, p. 3

Month _September_

Sunday	Monday	Tuesday	Wednesday	Thursday	Friday	Saturday
			1 School starts	2	3	4
5	6 Labor Day holiday	7	8	9	10	11
12	13	14	15	16 Ann's birthday	17	18
19	20	21	22	23	24 Field trip to the zoo	25
26	27	28	29 storyteller assembly	30		

Children fill in dates and special days on
the calendar.

NOTE Use the blank calendar on *Math
Masters,* page 414 on a monthly basis to
provide continued calendar practice for
children.

You may also want to ask questions about the likelihood of certain
events related to the calendar:

● How certain are you that we will have five days of school
this week?

● Is it likely that our class will go on a field trip today?

Mention that people usually use **ordinal numbers** to say a date.
For example, people say *September fifth,* not *September five.*

Show children how to write today's date. You may wish to use a
transparency of *Math Masters,* page 414. Have them write the date
at the top of journal page 3. Then have them rotate the page and
write the month at the top of the calendar. Next, children write the
first seven numbers on the calendar.

Adjusting the Activity   ELL

For number-line and calendar activities, emphasize ordinal-number
words. For example, use expressions such as, "Today is September 12th. This is
the 4th day of school, the 3rd day of the week, the 1st hour of the school day, the
21st minute of the hour," and so on.

AUDITORY ◆ KINESTHETIC ◆ TACTILE ◆ VISUAL

▶ **Completing a Calendar Page**   INDEPENDENT ACTIVITY

(*Math Journal 1,* p. 3)

Children finish filling in the dates on the calendar page. They
should mark any special events, holidays, or days to remember.
For example, they might circle the first day of school, write in the
names of classmates or others who have birthdays this month, and
note any special events that will take place at school.

Adjusting the Activity   ELL

Children can record special events or activities by drawing small
pictures instead of writing words.

AUDITORY ◆ KINESTHETIC ◆ TACTILE ◆ VISUAL

▶ **Telling Time**   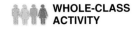 WHOLE-CLASS ACTIVITY

Distribute tool-kit clocks. Have children check that the number on
their clocks is the same as the number on their tool kits.

Ask a volunteer to tell what time it is now and to explain how he or
she knows what time it is. Sample answers: By using the hour and
minute hands on the classroom clock or by reading a digital watch
or clock Review the functions of the hour hand and minute hand.
Remind children that when people tell time it is always an estimate
because as soon as they say or write the time, the time in seconds
has changed, and the time in minutes may have also changed.

Have children show times such as the following on their clocks: 4:00, 3:30, 8:15, 7:45, 1:00, ten minutes to twelve, half-past six, quarter to five, and so on. For English language learners, it may be curious that the number 305 is read *three hundred five* and not read *three-oh-five*, but the time 3:05 is read *three-oh-five*. Three-oh-five doesn't make sense because it uses the letter *O* instead of the number zero. Explaining this difference may be important. Emphasize other ways to read 3:05 such as *5 past three*.

 Ongoing Assessment: Informing Instruction

Watch for children who confuse hours and minutes. Help them by saying an hour and have them set the hour hand for that time. Tell them to set the minute hand at 12, and then count off the minutes past the hour as they move the minute hand. Have children adjust the hour hand accordingly.

After children show each time on their clocks, you may want to display the correct time on your demonstration clock so children can check their own clocks.

2 Ongoing Learning & Practice

▶ Telling Time on Clocks

INDEPENDENT ACTIVITY

(*Math Journal 1*, p. 4)

Have children write the date and current time at the top of journal page 4. Tell them that from now on, they should always record the date and time when they begin a journal page. Children complete journal page 4. Briefly go over the answers.

 Ongoing Assessment: **Recognizing Student Achievement**

Journal page 4 Problems 1, 2, 4, and 5 ★

Use **journal page 4, Problems 1, 2, 4, and 5** to assess children's ability to tell time to the nearest half-hour. Children are making adequate progress if they can successfully complete Problems 1, 2, 4, and 5. Some children may be able to tell and write time to the nearest quarter-hour.

[Measurement and Reference Frames Goal 6]

NOTE Children will practice telling time on a daily basis by writing the start time on the top of each journal page. If children need more practice with specific intervals, consider setting a demonstration clock for the start time you want them to record. For more practice, consider having children record their start time on all class papers.

Math Journal 1, p. 4

Time	Picture of Clock	Class
9:00		Reading
10:00		Math
11:00		Science
12:00		Gym

3 Differentiation Options

READINESS **SMALL-GROUP ACTIVITY**

▶ Listening for Your Number

⏱ 5–15 Min

To further explore comparing and ordering numbers, arrange children in a line and assign each child an ordinal number. As you point to a child, they say their ordinal numbers. Rapidly repeat several times using the ordinal number words.

Then have children listen for their ordinal number and directions. For example, give the following instructions:

- First child, clap your hands once.
- Tenth child, find the sixth child; shake his or her hand and then return to your place in line.

To finish the activity and get children seated, give instructions such as the following:

- First child and (ordinal for last) child, take your seats.
- If your number ends in *-th,* take your seats (4th, 5th, 6th, and so on).

ENRICHMENT **INDEPENDENT ACTIVITY**

▶ Listing My Activities

⏱ 5–15 Min

(*Math Masters,* p. 8)

To apply children's understanding of telling time, have them list some of the activities they do on a school day. They record the start and stop times for each activity. They estimate which activity takes the most amount of time and which one takes the least amount of time.

ELL SUPPORT  **SMALL-GROUP ACTIVITY**

▶ Using the Language of Time and Events

⏱ 5–15 Min

To provide practice with the language of time and events, take a few extra minutes at different times of each day asking questions such as:

- What time is it now?
- What do we do at 12 o'clock?
- At what time does our school day end?
- How many minutes until lunch?

To support English language learners, attach a class schedule as shown in the margin to children's desks.

Partner Study Routines

 Objectives To provide practice with addition facts; and to establish partnership principles.

1 Teaching the Lesson

materials

Key Activities
Children review addition facts and then practice by playing *Addition Top-It*. Children discuss and practice working with a partner and explore the Everything Math Deck.

Key Concepts and Skills
- Compare numbers in *Addition Top-It*.
  [Number and Numeration Goal 7]
- Use *Addition Top-It* to practice addition facts.
  [Operations and Computation Goal 1]
- Write number sentences.
  [Patterns, Functions, and Algebra Goal 2]
- ✔ **Ongoing Assessment: Recognizing Student Achievement** Use an Exit Slip.
  [Operations and Computation Goal 1]

- ☐ *Math Journal 1*, p. 5
- ☐ Teaching Aid Master (*Math Masters*, p. 415)
- ☐ Game Master (Math Masters, p. 449; optional)
- ☐ Working with a Partner Poster (optional)
- ☐ per partnership: 4 each of number cards 0–10 (from the Everything Math Deck, if available)
- ☐ slate
- ☐ coin (optional)

See Advance Preparation

2 Ongoing Learning & Practice

materials

Children explore number-grid patterns.

- ☐ Teaching Aid Master (*Math Masters*, p. 416; optional)
- ☐ Number-Grid Poster

3 Differentiation Options

materials

READINESS

Children play a variation of *Addition Top-It* with pennies to review addition facts and compare numbers.

ENRICHMENT

Children play *Coin Top-It* to practice finding and comparing the values of coin combinations.

- ☐ Game Master (*Math Masters*, p. 452 or 453)
- ☐ per partnership: 4 each of number cards 0–10 (from the Everything Math Deck, if available)
- ☐ 40 pennies per partnership
- ☐ scissors
- ☐ tool-kit coins (optional)

Additional Information

Advance Preparation You may want to prepare a Working with a Partner poster to display in

Technology

Getting Started

Mental Math and Reflexes

Dictate numbers and ask children to write the next larger number on their slates.

○○○ 15, 20, 29

○○○ 135, 99, 104

●●● 109; 789; 1,000

Math Message

Write the date and time on the top of journal page 5. Then do Problems 1 through 7.

NOTE Some children may benefit from doing the **Readiness** activity before you begin Part 1 of the lesson. See the Readiness activity in Part 3 for details.

---

① Teaching the Lesson

▶ **Math Message Follow-Up**

 WHOLE-CLASS DISCUSSION

(*Math Journal 1*, p. 5)

Briefly review answers. Discuss the different formats of the addition-fact problems.

▶ **Discussing Partnership Principles**

 WHOLE-CLASS DISCUSSION

Review the partnership principles: Guide, Check, and Praise.

Ask children for suggestions to help make the classroom more pleasant while working as partners in a room full of people.

Show children the list of rules for working with a partner as shown below and discuss why each rule will help them work effectively.

Reinforce the partnership principles frequently. This will ensure that important partnership and small-group work can be carried on in the best possible environment.

Student Page

Date _____ Time _____

LESSON 1·4 Addition Facts

1. [dice: 2 dots] [dice: 4 dots]
2. [dice: 5 dots] [dice: 5 dots]

2 + 4 = _6_   5 + 5 = _10_

3. [domino]   3
            + 4
            ⬚7⬚

4. [domino]   7
            + 9
            ⬚16⬚

5. 6 + 8 = _14_   6. 8 + _3_ = 11   7. _6_ + 4 = 10

Addition Top-It

Write a number model for each player's cards.
Then write <, >, or = in the box.

___ ___ = ___   ⬚   ___ ___ = ___
___ ___ = ___   ⬚   ___ ___ = ___
___ ___ = ___   ⬚   ___ ___ = ___

Math Journal 1, p. 5

> ## Working with a Partner
>
> - Be polite.
> - Help each other.
> - Share.
> - Listen to your partner.
> - Praise your partner.
> - Take turns.
> - Talk about problems.
> - Speak quietly.

▶ Exploring the Everything Math Deck

PARTNER ACTIVITY

Form partnerships and distribute one Everything Math Deck to each pair. Allow time for children to explore the organization of the cards. Then bring the class together to discuss what has been found. Expect observations like the following:

▷ There are four cards for each of the numbers 0 through 10 and one card for each of the numbers 11 through 20.

▷ There are geometric figures with the appropriate number of sides on cards 0 through 10.

▷ A fraction is on one side of the cards 0 through 10. The fraction is pictured with blue shading.

▶ Demonstrating and Playing *Addition Top-It*

PARTNER ACTIVITY

(*Math Journal 1*, p. 5; *Math Masters*, pp. 415 and 449)

Have partners remove all the cards with numbers greater than 10 from the Everything Math Deck and put them aside. Explain the following rules of *Addition Top-It:*

Rules

1. Mix or shuffle the cards and place them in a pile facedown between the two players.

2. One player turns over two cards and says the sum of the numbers.

3. The other player turns over the next two cards and says the sum of the numbers.

4. The player with the higher sum takes all four cards.

5. In case of a tie, each player draws one more card to add to the sum. The higher sum wins all the cards.

6. Play ends when not enough cards remain for both players to have another turn. The winner is the player with more cards.

Variation: Children flip a coin to determine whether the player with more or fewer cards is the winner.

Have children record number models on the bottom half of journal page 5 for three rounds of the game. Children may use *Math Masters*, page 449 to record additional number models.

Circulate and observe how well children are following the partnership principles. Interrupt from time to time to comment on positive things you are seeing.

Game Master

Name _____ Date _____ Time _____

Addition Top-It Record Sheet

Write a number model for each player's cards.

Then write <, >, or = in the box.

Math Masters, p. 449

Teaching Aid Master

| Name | Date | Time |

My Exit Slip

415

✂ -

| Name | Date | Time |

My Exit Slip

Math Masters, p. 415

Adjusting the Activity

To practice with specific addition facts, you may have children keep one of the two numbers the same for each round so that it is always an addend. For example, one card is always a 5; draw another card each turn so the child is always adding $5 + n$.

To practice facts with numbers greater than 10, have children play with all cards, using the numbers 0 through 20.

AUDITORY ◆ KINESTHETIC ◆ TACTILE ◆ VISUAL

Ongoing Assessment:
Recognizing Student Achievement

Exit Slip

Use an **Exit Slip** (*Math Masters,* page 415) to assess children's knowledge of basic addition facts. Have children record three addition facts they know. Children are making adequate progress if they have written three correct addition facts. Some children may write facts with larger addends.

[Operations and Computation Goal 1]

② Ongoing Learning & Practice

▶ Exploring Number-Grid Patterns 👫👫 WHOLE-CLASS ACTIVITY

(*Math Masters,* p. 416)

Have children describe patterns they see or things they notice about the Number-Grid Poster. You may also wish to have them refer to a small number grid from *Math Masters,* page 416. Expect observations like the following:

▷ Every other number across is odd.

▷ Every number in the far-right column is a multiple of 10.

▷ The grid starts at 0 and ends at 110.

▷ The grid is like a chopped-up number line.

▷ Each number down a specific column has the same digit in the 1s place.

▷ Each number across a specific row has the same digit in the 10s place (except for the last number in the row).

Do counting-up and counting-back exercises, such as the following, on the Number-Grid Poster:

● If I start at 1 and count up 6, where do I stop? 7

● If I start at 8 and count back 2, where do I stop? 6

● If I start at 7 and count up 10, where do I stop? 17

● If I start at 15 and count back 5, where do I stop? 10

● If I start at 20 and count up 3, where do I stop? 23

Have children describe how they solved each problem.

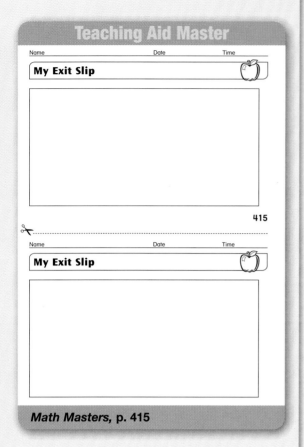

Teaching Aid Master

| Name | Date | Time |

Number Grid

−9	−8	−7	−6	−5	−4	−3	−2	−1	0
1	2	3	4	5	6	7	8	9	10
11	12	13	14	15	16	17	18	19	20
21	22	23	24	25	26	27	28	29	30
31	32	33	34	35	36	37	38	39	40
41	42	43	44	45	46	47	48	49	50
51	52	53	54	55	56	57	58	59	60
61	62	63	64	65	66	67	68	69	70
71	72	73	74	75	76	77	78	79	80
81	82	83	84	85	86	87	88	89	90
91	92	93	94	95	96	97	98	99	100
101	102	103	104	105	106	107	108	109	110

−9	−8	−7	−6	−5	−4	−3	−2	−1	0
1	2	3	4	5	6	7	8	9	10
11	12	13	14	15	16	17	18	19	20
21	22	23	24	25	26	27	28	29	30
31	32	33	34	35	36	37	38	39	40
41	42	43	44	45	46	47	48	49	50
51	52	53	54	55	56	57	58	59	60
61	62	63	64	65	66	67	68	69	70
71	72	73	74	75	76	77	78	79	80
81	82	83	84	85	86	87	88	89	90
91	92	93	94	95	96	97	98	99	100
101	102	103	104	105	106	107	108	109	110

Math Masters, p. 416

③ Differentiation Options

READINESS

PARTNER ACTIVITY

5–15 Min

▶ Playing *Addition Top-It* with Pennies

To provide experience with addition facts and comparing numbers using a concrete model, have children play *Addition Top-It* using pennies as counters.

Rules

1. Children put 40 pennies in a "bank" between them.

2. Mix or shuffle the cards and place them in a pile facedown between the two players.

3. During each turn, a player turns over two cards and counts out pennies for each of the numbers and then counts the total number of pennies. Encourage children to count on from the larger number.

4. The player with the higher sum takes all the cards and each player returns the pennies to the bank.

5. Play ends when not enough cards remain for another turn. The winner is the player with more cards.

ENRICHMENT

PARTNER ACTIVITY

5–15 Min

▶ Playing *Coin Top-It*

(*Math Masters,* p. 452 or 453)

To apply children's knowledge of addition facts, have them play *Coin Top-It* by adding and comparing coin combinations. Each player cuts apart a copy of *Math Masters,* page 452 or 453. Partners combine their cards.

Rules

1. Players mix the 32 cards and place the deck facedown.

2. Each player draws a card and says the total amount of the coins shown on his or her card. The player with the greater amount collects and keeps both cards. (Players draw again if the amounts are equal.)

3. The game ends when there are no cards left to draw. The winner is the player who collected more cards.

Variation: Children use their tool-kit coins to model the combinations pictured on the cards.

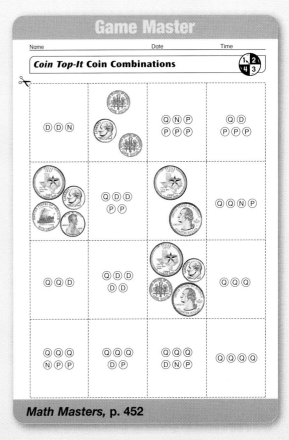

Game Master

| Name | | Date | Time |

Coin Top-It **Coin Combinations**

Math Masters, p. 452

1·5 Grouping by Tens—$1, $10, $100

 Objectives To provide review for grouping by tens; and to provide practice exchanging $1, $10, and $100 bills.

1 Teaching the Lesson

materials

Key Activities
Children find the total values of combinations of $1, $10, and $100 bills. They play the *Money Exchange Game* with $1, $10, and $100 bills.

Key Concepts and Skills
• Count on by 1s, 10s, and 100s.
[Number and Numeration Goal 1]

• Use counting up to calculate the value of bill combinations.
[Operations and Computation Goal 2]

• Make exchanges among bills.
[Measurement and Reference Frames Goal 4]

✔ **Ongoing Assessment:** Recognizing Student Achievement Use journal page 6.
[Operations and Computation Goal 2]

✔ **Ongoing Assessment:** Informing Instruction See page 40.

☐ *Math Journal 1,* p. 6
☐ Game Masters (*Math Masters,* pp. 458–461)
☐ Transparency (*Math Masters,* p. 458; optional)
☐ envelope or other device for storing play money
☐ scissors
☐ Class Data Pad
☐ 1 die per partnership

See **Advance Preparation**

2 Ongoing Learning & Practice

materials

Children continue playing the *Money Exchange Game* or play *Addition Top-It.*

☐ Game Masters (*Math Masters,* pp. 449, 458–461; optional)
☐ 1 die per partnership
☐ per partnership: 4 each of number cards 0–10 (from the Everything Math Deck, if available); 1 set of double-9 dominoes, or 1 die or 3 dice (optional)

3 Differentiation Options

materials

READINESS
Children play *Penny-Nickel Exchange* to explore trading pennies and nickels.

ENRICHMENT
Children use a number grid to find various combinations of numbers that add to 100.

☐ Teaching Aid Master (*Math Masters,* p. 417)
☐ 1 die per partnership
☐ per partnership: 20 pennies and 10 nickels; 40 nickels and 20 dimes (optional)
☐ crayons or markers

Additional Information

Advance Preparation Before the Math Message, you may want each child to cut out the paper money from *Math Masters,* pages 459–461. For the *Money Exchange Game* activity in Part 1, you might want to make an overhead transparency of *Math Masters,* page 458. Decide how children will store their paper money, such as in small envelopes, or bundled with paper clips or rubber bands. Label the envelopes with children's tool-kit numbers.

Technology
Assessment Management System
Journal page 6, Problems 1 and 2
See the **iTLG.**

Getting Started

Mental Math and Reflexes

- ○○○ Count up by 10s from a multiple of 10.
- ○○○ Count up by 10s from 50; stop; continue to count on by 5s.
- ○○○ Count up by 10s starting at 100; stop; continue to count on by 5s.

Math Message

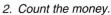

1. Cut out the play money from Math Masters, pages 459–461.
2. Count the money.
3. How much do you have?
4. Take an envelope. Write your tool-kit number on the front of it. Put the money inside.

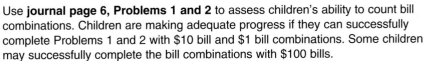
1 Teaching the Lesson

> **NOTE** Some children may benefit from doing the **Readiness** activity before you begin Part 1 of the lesson. See the Readiness activity in Part 3 for details.

 ## Math Message Follow-Up

WHOLE-CLASS ACTIVITY

Have children put their money into three piles—$100s, $10s, and $1s—and count all the money beginning with the $100s. $576

Add money to the list of ideas about mathematics on the Class Data Pad if it is not there from previous discussions.

Counting Money

INDEPENDENT ACTIVITY

(*Math Journal 1, p. 6*)

Make sure children write the date and time at the top of journal page 6. To support children new to the United States who are unfamilar with the different bills, discuss the similarities and differences of the bills pictured on journal page 6.

**✓ Ongoing Assessment:
Recognizing Student Achievement**

**Journal page 6
Problems
1 and 2** ★

Use **journal page 6, Problems 1 and 2** to assess children's ability to count bill combinations. Children are making adequate progress if they can successfully complete Problems 1 and 2 with $10 bill and $1 bill combinations. Some children may successfully complete the bill combinations with $100 bills.

[Operations and Computation Goal 2]

Briefly go over the answers. For Problem 5, discuss how to rearrange the bills to make the problem easier to solve. Sample answer: Group the bills by value and then count, beginning with bills of the greatest value.

 ## Adjusting the Activity

ELL

Have children use their tool-kit bills to model the problems.

AUDITORY ♦ KINESTHETIC ♦ TACTILE ♦ VISUAL

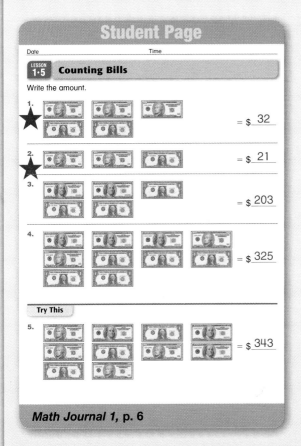

Student Page

Date _____ Time _____

LESSON 1·5 Counting Bills

Write the amount.

1. ★ = $ 32
2. ★ = $ 21
3. = $ 203
4. = $ 325

Try This

5. = $ 343

Math Journal 1, p. 6

Game Master

Money Exchange Game Mat

	One Hundred Dollars $100
	Ten Dollars $10
	One Dollar $1

Math Masters, p. 458

⭐ Ongoing Assessment: Informing Instruction

While the children play the *Money Exchange Game,* circulate and observe them making the bill exchanges. Watch for children who have more than ten $1 bills in the One Dollar column and are not making the exchanges. Remind the children to put the $1 bills into groups of tens and then to exchange each group for a $10 bill.

▶ **Playing the *Money Exchange Game* with $100 Bills**

PARTNER ACTIVITY

(*Math Masters,* pp. 458–461)

Provide each player with *Math Masters,* page 458 and the bills used in the Math Message Follow-Up. Show the class how to play the *Money Exchange Game* with $1, $10, and $100 bills.

Rules

1. Partners put all their bills together to form a "bank."

2. Player 1 rolls one die and takes from the bank the number of $1 bills shown on the die.

3. Player 1 places the $1 bills in the right-hand column (the $1 column) on his or her mat.

4. Player 2 repeats Steps 2 and 3.

5. Players continue in this way, taking turns.

6. Whenever possible, players trade ten $1 bills for one $10 bill and ten $10 bills for one $100 bill. They put the new bills in the correct column on their mats.

7. The first player to trade for a $100 bill wins.

Show the class how to collect and exchange bills. Have a volunteer roll a die to tell how much money to take. You might record the totals with tally marks on an overhead transparency of *Math Masters,* page 458. Act out the exchanges with bills when the total is $10 or more.

② Ongoing Learning & Practice

▶ **Playing the *Money Exchange Game* or *Addition Top-It***

PARTNER ACTIVITY

(*Math Masters,* pp. 449, 458–461)

Children continue playing the *Money Exchange Game* or play *Addition Top-It* as it was introduced in Lesson 1-4. They may want to play one of the following variations of *Addition Top-It:*

▷ Use double-9 dominoes instead of number cards.

▷ Draw three cards on each turn instead of two.

▷ Roll one die three times, or roll three separate dice together, to generate three addends.

③ Differentiation Options

READINESS

 PARTNER ACTIVITY

▶ Playing *Penny-Nickel Exchange*

🕐 5–15 Min

To explore trading pennies and nickels, have children play *Penny-Nickel Exchange.*

Rules

1. Partners put 20 pennies and 10 nickels in a pile. This is the "bank."

2. Players take turns. At each turn, a player rolls a die and collects the number of pennies shown on the die from the bank. Whenever a player has at least 5 pennies, he or she says "Exchange!" and trades 5 pennies for a nickel in the bank.

3. The game ends when there are no more nickels in the bank. The player who has more nickels wins. If players have the same number of nickels, the player with more pennies wins.

Variation: Increase the bank to 40 nickels and 20 dimes and trade for dimes.

ENRICHMENT

 PARTNER ACTIVITY

▶ Finding Number Grid Number Combinations to 100

🕐 5–15 Min

(Math Masters, p. 417)

To apply children's ability to find coin combinations for $1.00, have them find combinations of numbers that equal 100 on the number grid. They use crayons or markers to color each of their combinations a different color. For example, 49 and 51 may be yellow; 1, 30, and 69 may be blue. Encourage children to use three or more numbers in their combinations. Consider having children write a number sentence for each combination they find. Have children read their number sentences.

Teaching Aid Master

Name					Date				Time	

Number Grid 🍎

0	10	20	30	40	50	60	70	80	90	100	110
-1	9	19	29	39	49	59	69	79	89	99	109
-2	8	18	28	38	48	58	68	78	88	98	108
-3	7	17	27	37	47	57	67	77	87	97	107
-4	6	16	26	36	46	56	66	76	86	96	106
-5	5	15	25	35	45	55	65	75	85	95	105
-6	4	14	24	34	44	54	64	74	84	94	104
-7	3	13	23	33	43	53	63	73	83	93	103
-8	2	12	22	32	42	52	62	72	82	92	102
-9	1	11	21	31	41	51	61	71	81	91	101

Math Masters, p. 417

1·6 Math Boxes

 Objectives To introduce *My Reference Book;* and to introduce the Math Boxes routine.

1 Teaching the Lesson

materials

Key Activities
Children are introduced to *My Reference Book.* They are introduced to the Math Boxes routine and complete the first Math Boxes page.

Key Concepts and Skills
• Explore money equivalencies.
  [Measurement and Reference Frames Goal 4]
• Explore analog and digital time pieces.
  [Measurement and Reference Frames Goal 6]

Key Vocabulary
My Reference Book • Table of Contents • Math Boxes

☐ *Math Journal 1,* p. 7
☐ *My Reference Book*
☐ slate

2 Ongoing Learning & Practice

materials

Children play *Penny Plate* to practice naming parts of a whole.

✦ **Ongoing Assessment: Informing Instruction** See page 44.

✦ **Ongoing Assessment: Recognizing Student Achievement** Use *Math Masters,* page 468.
  [Operations and Computation Goal 1]

Per partnership:
☐ *My Reference Book,* pp. 146 and 147
☐ Game Master (*Math Masters,* p. 468)
☐ plate, cup, or other container
☐ 20 tool-kit pennies

***See* Advance Preparation**

3 Differentiation Options

materials

READINESS
Children play *Two-Fisted Penny Addition* to practice naming parts of a whole using concrete models.

EXTRA PRACTICE
Children solve problems with complements of 10 and 2-, 3-, and 4-digit numbers.

☐ *Minute Math®+,* pp. 9, 23, 32, and 33
☐ 10 or more pennies

Additional Information

Advance Preparation For *Penny Plate* in Part 2, obtain paper plates or other open-top, opaque containers. During the game, children will turn the containers upside down and arrange as many as 20 pennies on the containers' bottoms. Make sure the bottom of each container is wide and sturdy enough to hold the pennies.

Technology
Assessment Management System
Math Masters, page 468
See the **iTLG.**

Getting Started

Mental Math and Reflexes

On slates,

- ○○○ Write all the 1-digit numbers. How many are there? 10
- ○○○ Write two 2-digit numbers. Circle the larger one.
- ○○● Write two 3-digit numbers. Circle the digit in the ones place and put an X on the digit in the hundreds place.

Math Message

Spend a few minutes looking through your My Reference Book. *Be ready to share something you found interesting. Think about how this book can be helpful to you.*

---

1 Teaching the Lesson

▶ Math Message Follow-Up
WHOLE-CLASS ACTIVITY

(*My Reference Book*)

Have children briefly share some interesting things that they found. Discuss ways in which ***My Reference Book*** can be helpful.

With the class, look up the Table of Money Equivalencies in *My Reference Book*. Ask children simple questions regarding money equivalences. For example, ask: *How many pennies in a dime?* 10 *How many nickels in a dime?* 2 *How many nickels in a quarter?* 5

Discuss the sections of *My Reference Book*.

The **Table of Contents** may be used to find information about a particular topic. The Table of Contents also gives the page number of the first page of a topic.

Use the Table of Contents to look up information on clocks on pages 78 and 79. Discuss the information in *My Reference Book* regarding clocks. Be sure to allow the children enough time to explore the clock section.

Explain to the children that in today's lesson they will see how *My Reference Book* can be helpful to them as they work in their *Math Journals*.

▶ Introducing Math Boxes
WHOLE-CLASS DISCUSSION

(*Math Journal 1*, p. 7)

Ask children to name activities that people practice. Sample answers: Dancing, singing, playing a musical instrument, speaking a foreign language, playing basketball and other sports, and so on

NOTE Some children may benefit from doing the **Readiness** activity before you begin Part 1 of the lesson. See the Readiness activity in Part 3 for details.

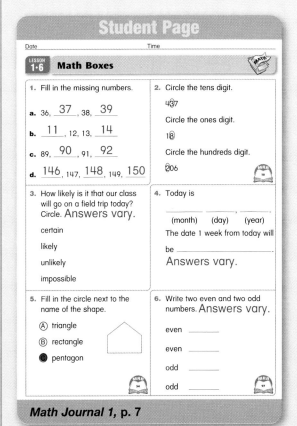

Student Page

Date _____ Time _____

LESSON 1·6 Math Boxes

1. Fill in the missing numbers.
   a. 36, __37__, 38, __39__
   b. __11__, 12, 13, __14__
   c. 89, __90__, 91, __92__
   d. __146__, 147, __148__, 149, __150__

2. Circle the tens digit.
   4(3)7
   Circle the ones digit.
   1(8)
   Circle the hundreds digit.
   (2)06

3. How likely is it that our class will go on a field trip today? Circle. **Answers vary.**
   certain
   likely
   unlikely
   impossible

4. Today is
   _____, _____, _____
   (month)   (day)   (year)
   The date 1 week from today will be _____.
   Answers vary.

5. Fill in the circle next to the name of the shape.
   Ⓐ triangle
   Ⓑ rectangle
   ● pentagon

6. Write two even and two odd numbers. **Answers vary.**
   even _____
   even _____
   odd _____
   odd _____

Math Journal 1, p. 7

Penny Plate

Materials ❑ 10 pennies
❑ 1 small plastic plate

Players 2

Skill Sum-equals-ten facts

Object of the game To get 5 points.

Directions

1. Player 1:
   • Turns the plate upside-down.
   • Hides some of the pennies under the plate.
   • Puts the remaining pennies on top of the plate.

My Reference Book, p. 146

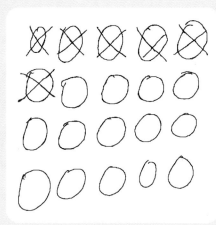

Children name the two parts of 20 shown here: 6 and 14.

Ask children: *What would happen if people never practiced? Is anyone familiar with the expression, "Practice makes perfect?" What does this mean?*

Explain that practice is necessary in mathematics, too. In *Everyday Mathematics,* one of the ways to practice is by doing a page of problems called **Math Boxes.**

Have children turn to journal page 7. Call children's attention to the *My Reference Book* icon in the Math Boxes. Discuss how this icon tells them which page to go to in *My Reference Book* if they need more information to complete the Math Boxes.

▶ **Completing a Math Boxes Page**   INDEPENDENT ACTIVITY

(*Math Journal 1,* p. 7)

 Mixed Practice Go over each problem so children understand what to do. Children complete the journal page independently or with a partner. When children have finished, briefly discuss the answers.

(2) Ongoing Learning & Practice

▶ **Playing** *Penny Plate*   PARTNER ACTIVITY

(*Math Masters,* p. 468; *My Reference Book,* pp. 146 and 147)

Have children read the rules for *Penny Plate* on pages 146 and 147 in *My Reference Book* and play the game in partnerships.

✓ Ongoing Assessment: Informing Instruction

Watch for children who are having difficulty determining the number of pennies. Suggest that they draw circles to represent all of the pennies. Then suggest that the children use one of the strategies below to figure out how many pennies are under the plate:

▷ Cross off one circle for each penny on top of the plate. Count the uncrossed circles to find the number of pennies under the plate.

▷ Use a second set of pennies as markers. Cover one circle for each penny on top of the plate. Count the uncovered circles to find the number of pennies under the plate.

---

③ Differentiation Options

READINESS

👥 PARTNER
ACTIVITY

🕐 5–15 Min

▶ Playing *Two-Fisted Penny Addition*

To explore finding sums to ten using a concrete model, have
children play *Two-Fisted Penny Addition.* Children count out 10
pennies and split them between their two hands. Help children
identify their left and right hands.

Call on several children to share amounts. *For example:*

▷ My left hand has 1 penny and my right hand has 9 pennies.

▷ My left hand has 3 pennies and my right hand has 7 pennies.

The various splits can be recorded on the board.

Repeat with other numbers of pennies. Partners can continue to
practice using different total numbers of pennies: 9, 12, 20, and
so on.

EXTRA PRACTICE

👥👤 SMALL-GROUP
ACTIVITY

🕐 5–15 Min

▶ *Minute Math+*

To offer children more experience with complements of 10, as well
as with 2-, 3-, and 4-digit numbers, see the following pages in
Minute Math+: pp. 9, 23, 32, and 33.

Student Page

Games

2. Player 2:
   • Counts the pennies on top of the plate.
   • Figures out how many pennies are hidden
     under the plate.

I see 6 pennies.
There are 10 pennies in all.
So there are 4 pennies
under the plate.

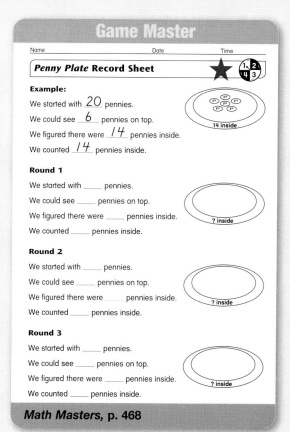

3. If the number is correct, Player 2 gets a point.

4. Players trade roles and repeat Steps 1 and 2.

5. Each player keeps a tally of their points.
   The first player to get 5 points is the winner.

Another Way to Play

Use a different number of pennies.

My Reference Book, p. 147

Game Master

Name _____ Date _____ Time _____

Penny Plate Record Sheet ★ (1,2,3,4)

Example:

We started with _20_ pennies.

We could see _6_ pennies on top.

We figured there were _14_ pennies inside.

We counted _14_ pennies inside.

14 inside

Round 1

We started with ____ pennies.

We could see ____ pennies on top.

We figured there were ____ pennies inside.

We counted ____ pennies inside.

? inside

Round 2

We started with ____ pennies.

We could see ____ pennies on top.

We figured there were ____ pennies inside.

We counted ____ pennies inside.

? inside

Round 3

We started with ____ pennies.

We could see ____ pennies on top.

We figured there were ____ pennies inside.

We counted ____ pennies inside.

? inside

Math Masters, p. 468

Working in Small Groups

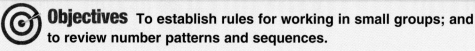

Objectives To establish rules for working in small groups; and to review number patterns and sequences.

1 Teaching the Lesson

materials

Key Activities

Children continue number sequences and explore patterns on the Number-Grid Poster. They learn rules for working in small groups. They make a class number scroll from 0 to 1,000.

Key Concepts and Skills

• Count by 2s, 5s, and 10s on the number grid. [Number and Numeration Goal 1]

• Write numbers to 1,000s. [Number and Numeration Goal 2]

• Identify odd and even numbers on the number grid. [Number and Numeration Goal 4]

• Use the number grid to find 1 more, 1 less, 10 more, or 10 less. [Patterns, Functions, and Algebra Goal 1]

Key Vocabulary number scroll • even number • odd number

☑ **Ongoing Assessment: Recognizing Student Achievement** Use the Math Message. [Patterns, Functions and Algebra Goal 1]

☑ **Ongoing Assessment: Informing Instruction** See page 49.

☐ Teaching Masters (*Math Masters,* pp. 9 and 10)
☐ Teaching Aid Master (*Math Masters,* p. 415)
☐ Number-Grid Poster
☐ demonstration clock; slate
☐ Rules for Working in Small Groups Poster (optional)
☐ red and green cups (optional)
☐ paste or tape
☐ empty paper-towel roll (optional)
☐ calculator (optional)

See **Advance Preparation**

2 Ongoing Learning & Practice

materials

Children review addition facts by playing *Addition Top-It.*

Children practice and maintain skills through Math Boxes.

☐ *Math Journal 1,* p. 8
☐ *My Reference Book,* pp. 122 and 123
☐ Game Master (*Math Masters,* p. 449; optional)
☐ per partnership: 4 each of number cards 0–10; double-9 dominoes or dice (optional)

3 Differentiation Options

materials

READINESS	**ENRICHMENT**	**EXTRA PRACTICE**	**ELL SUPPORT**
Children use patterns to count up and back on the number grid.	Children make number scrolls using greater numbers.	Children solve problems with number patterns.	Children add *odd* and *even* to their Math Word Banks.

☐ Teaching Masters (*Math Masters,* pp. 10 and 11)
☐ *Minute Math®+,* pp. 3, 5, 7, 27, 29, and 31
☐ *Differentiation Handbook*
☐ crayons
☐ tape; empty paper-towel roll (optional)

See **Advance Preparation**

Additional Information

Advance Preparation For Part 1, make a poster like the one shown on page 48. Also, in Part 1, the class will need 1 copy of *Math Masters,* page 9 to begin the scroll and at least 9 copies of *Math Masters,* page 10 to continue it. Make extra copies of *Math Masters,* page 10 for children who wish to continue scrolling and for the optional Enrichment activity in Part 3.

Technology

Assessment Management System
Math Message
See the **iTLG.**

Getting Started

Mental Math and Reflexes

Set the hands on your demonstration clock to various times. Children write these times on their slates.

●○○	12:00	●●○	4:15	●●●	3:40
	2:30		5:45		5:10
	9:00		9:45		10:25

Math Message ★

Write the next 3 numbers on an Exit Slip (Math Masters, page 415).

Suggestions: *12, 14, 16,* 18, 20, 22

36, 38, 40, 42, 44, 46

234, 236, 238, 240, 242, 244

---

1 Teaching the Lesson

NOTE Some children may benefit from doing the **Readiness** activity before you begin Part 1 of the lesson. See the Readiness activity in Part 3 for details.

▶ Math Message Follow-Up

WHOLE-CLASS ACTIVITY

> ✔ **Ongoing Assessment:** **Recognizing Student Achievement**
>
> Math Message ★
>
> Use the **Math Message** to assess the children's ability to complete and describe a number pattern. Children are making adequate progress if they can complete the first problem and describe it as counting by 2s. Some children may successfully complete problems starting with larger numbers.
>
> [Patterns, Functions and Algebra Goal 1]

Go over the answers. Ask someone to describe the pattern. Counting by 2s

▶ Exploring Counting Patterns on the Number-Grid Poster

WHOLE-CLASS ACTIVITY

Count by 2s in unison, starting at 0. Point to the numbers on the number-grid poster as you count. *What patterns do the count-by-2 numbers make on the grid?* Sample answers: They are every other number; the even numbers; the numbers in every other column.

Next, count by 5s and review the patterns. All the numbers fall in the middle column and end in 5 or in the last column and end in 0. Finally, count by 10s and review the patterns. All the numbers fall in the last column, with numbers ending in 0.

Class Number Grid

−9	−8	−7	−6	−5	−4	−3	−2	−1	0
1	2	3	4	5	6	7	8	9	10
11	12	13	14	15	16	17	18	19	20
21	22	23	24	25	26	27	28	29	30
31	32	33	34	35	36	37	38	39	40
41	42	43	44	45	46	47	48	49	50
51	52	53	54	55	56	57	58	59	60
61	62	63	64	65	66	67	68	69	70
71	72	73	74	75	76	77	78	79	80
81	82	83	84	85	86	87	88	89	90
91	92	93	94	95	96	97	98	99	100
101	102	103	104	105	106	107	108	109	110

Class Number Grid

> ⬆⬇ **Adjusting the Activity**
>
> **ELL**
>
> Ask a volunteer to color or cross out the multiples of 2 while the class counts by 2s. When the pattern begins to emerge, ask if there is an easier way to mark the 2s. Mark or color every other column. Use different colors or different marks for the 5s and 10s patterns.
>
> AUDITORY ◆ KINESTHETIC ◆ TACTILE ◆ VISUAL

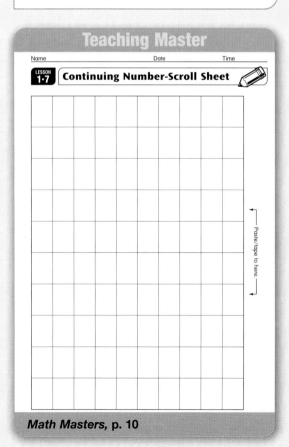

Math Masters, p. 9

NOTE Some teachers use green and red plastic cups for small-group management. Each group has one red and one green cup. The cups are stacked and displayed to indicate the following:

● Green cups: Everything is running smoothly.

● Red cups: We need help.

No group should display a red cup until every group member has tried to solve the problem or answer the question.

Teaching Master

Name   Date   Time

1·7 **Continuing Number-Scroll Sheet**

Paste/tape to here

Math Masters, p. 10

▶ # Establishing Rules for Small-Group Work

 **WHOLE-CLASS DISCUSSION**

Teaching and reinforcing orderly small-group interactions is well worth the time and effort. Effective small groups encourage cooperative learning and reduce children's reliance on you for answers.

Review the partnership principles: Guide, Check, and Praise. Have the class suggest additional rules that might help when doing activities in small groups.

Emphasize that children should ask you for help only when no one in the group can solve the problem or answer the question. This is very important for developing good group interaction.

> ## Rules for Working in Small Groups
>
> • Use quiet voices.
> • Be polite.
> • Share materials.
> • Take turns.
> • Help each other.

▶ # Making a Class Number Scroll from 1 to 1,000

 **SMALL-GROUP ACTIVITY**

(*Math Masters*, pp. 9 and 10)

Children work in small groups to create a **number scroll** for the numbers up to 1,000. The scroll will be made from separate number grids.

Have children count off into ten small groups with 2 to 4 children per group. Give one group a copy of *Math Masters*, page 9 to begin the scroll. Give each of the other groups a copy of *Math Masters*, page 10. Assign each group a different 3-digit number ending in 1 (101, 201, 301, and so on, up to 901).

Each group begins filling in the scroll by using its special 3-digit number.

As children work, circulate and ask questions about patterns on the grid. *For example:*

● Who can show me some **even numbers?**

● Some **odd numbers?**

● What is the pattern for counting by 10s?

Adjusting the Activity

Write several numbers on each grid before distributing the grids. Children can check their work as they fill in the remaining numbers. To find the number that comes next in the sequence, some children may find it helpful to ignore the hundreds place. For example, to find the number that comes after 839, ask what number comes after 39. Write 40 in the space. Now look at the hundreds place and write an 8 in front of the 40. 840 comes after 839.

AUDITORY ♦ KINESTHETIC ♦ TACTILE ♦ VISUAL

After all groups have completed their grids, bring the class together to review the completed grids. Tape or paste them together to make the number scroll. The first page of the class number scroll can be taped to an empty paper-towel roll for storage.

Ongoing Assessment: Informing Instruction

Watch for children who write 139 as 10039. They need to be reminded that a hundreds number has three digits. It may be helpful to enter each digit in a place-value chart on the board.

Also watch for children who have difficulty making the transition to the next decade. It may be helpful to provide children with a calculator so they can visualize the change from 9 to 0 in the ones place. Children may also use a number line.

2 Ongoing Learning & Practice

▶ Playing *Addition Top-It*

PARTNER ACTIVITY

(*Math Masters*, p. 449; *My Reference Book*, pp. 122 and 123)

Partners continue to play the game as it was introduced in Lesson 1-4, or they play one of the following variations:

▷ Use double-9 dominoes instead of number cards.

▷ Draw three cards on each turn instead of two.

▷ Roll three dice, or one die three times, to generate three addends.

▶ Math Boxes 1·7

INDEPENDENT ACTIVITY

(*Math Journal 1*, p. 8)

 Mixed Practice Math Boxes in this lesson are linked with Math Boxes in Lessons 1-9 and 1-11. The skills in Problems 5 and 6 preview Unit 2 content.

Writing/Reasoning Have children draw, write, or verbalize their answers to the following: *Explain your strategies for finding the missing numbers on the number grid in Problem 2.* Sample answer: I counted up by 1s, starting at 13.

Student Page

Games

Addition Top-It

Materials ❑ number cards 0–10 (4 of each)

Players 2 to 4

Skill Addition facts 0 to 10

Object of the game To collect the most cards.

Directions

1. Shuffle the cards. Place the deck number-side down on the table.

2. Each player turns over 2 cards and calls out the sum of the numbers.

3. The player with the largest sum wins the round and takes all the cards.

4. In case of a tie for the largest sum, each tied player turns over 2 more cards and calls out the sum of the numbers. The player with the largest sum then takes all the cards from both plays.

5. The game ends when not enough cards are left for each player to have another turn.

6. The player with the most cards wins.

My Reference Book, p. 122

NOTE Some children may have completed individual number scrolls in *First Grade Everyday Mathematics* using rather large numbers.

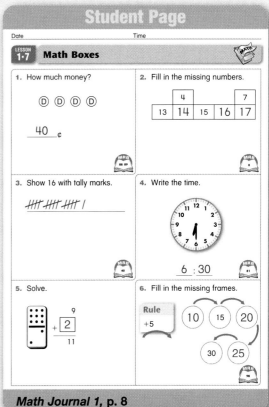

Math Journal 1, p. 8

3 Differentiation Options

READINESS

  INDEPENDENT ACTIVITY

▶ **Counting on the Number Grid**

⏱ **5–15 Min**

(*Math Masters,* p. 11)

To explore patterns on a number grid, have children count up and back on the number grid.

ENRICHMENT

  INDEPENDENT ACTIVITY

▶ **Making Individual Number Scrolls in the Thousands**

◑ **15–30 Min**

(*Math Masters,* p. 10)

To further explore patterns with larger numbers, have children create individual scrolls using numbers larger than 1,000. Let children select their starting numbers. Everyone who participates will need multiple copies of *Math Masters,* page 10. The first page of individual scrolls can be taped to empty paper-towel rolls for storage.

EXTRA PRACTICE

 **SMALL-GROUP ACTIVITY**

▶ *Minute Math+*

⏱ **5–15 Min**

To offer children more experience with number patterns, see the following pages in *Minute Math+*: pp. 3, 5, 7, 27, 29, and 31.

ELL SUPPORT

  SMALL-GROUP ACTIVITY

▶ **Building a Math Word Bank**

⏱ **5–15 Min**

(*Differentiation Handbook*)

To provide language support for the words *odd* and *even,* have children use the Word Bank template found in the *Differentiation Handbook.* Ask children to write the word *odd,* list examples of numbers that are odd, and draw an odd number of dots to represent the word. Ask children to do the same with *even.* See the *Differentiation Handbook* for more information.

1·8 Number Grids

 Objective To guide children as they explore place-value patterns on number grids.

1 Teaching the Lesson · materials

Key Activities
Children identify various number-grid patterns, such as 1 more, 10 more, 1 less, and 10 less. Children practice place-value skills by completing number-grid puzzles.

Key Concepts and Skills
- Count on the number grid. [Number and Numeration Goal 1]
- Use place-value skills to complete number-grid puzzles. [Number and Numeration Goal 2]
- Use patterns to complete number-grid puzzles. [Patterns, Functions, and Algebra Goal 1]
- Identify patterns on the number grid. [Patterns, Functions, and Algebra Goal 1]

Ongoing Assessment: Recognizing Student Achievement Use journal page 9.
[Patterns, Functions, and Algebra Goal 1]

☐ *Math Journal 1,* p. 9
☐ Teaching Aid Master (*Math Masters,* p. 416; optional)
☐ Number-Grid Poster

***See* Advance Preparation**

2 Ongoing Learning & Practice · materials

Children play the *Number-Grid Game.*

Children practice and maintain skills through Math Boxes.

☐ *Math Journal 1,* p. 10
☐ *My Reference Book,* pp. 142 and 143
☐ Teaching Aid Master (*Math Masters,* p. 418)
☐ one die per partnership
☐ one game marker for each player

3 Differentiation Options · materials

READINESS
Children use place-value patterns to create number-grid puzzles.

ENRICHMENT
Children create number-grid puzzle pieces.

☐ Teaching Masters (*Math Masters,* pp. 12 and 13)
☐ Teaching Aid Master (*Math Masters,* p. 417)
☐ dry-erase marker or grease pencil
☐ scissors
☐ tape or paste (optional)
☐ half-sheets of paper (optional)

***See* Advance Preparation**

Additional Information

Advance Preparation Before beginning the activities in Part 1, you may wish to draw a semipermanent 3-by-3 blank number grid on the board. You may find it helpful to provide small laminated grids for children to keep in their desks. *Math Masters,* page 416 can be used for this purpose. Also, display the Number-Grid Poster at all times. For the optional Readiness activity in Part 3, cut out and laminate the number-grid pieces from *Math Masters,* page 12.

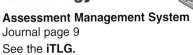

Technology
Assessment Management System
Journal page 9
See the **iTLG.**

Getting Started

Use the Number-Grid Poster and ask questions like the following:

○○○ I am counting by 2s. What number comes after 4? 6

I am counting by 5s. What number comes after 10? 15

I am counting by 10s. What number comes after 20? 30

●○○ I am counting by 4s. What number comes after 16? 20

I am counting by 3s. What number comes after 12? 15

I am counting by 6s. What number comes after 12? 18

●●○ I am counting by 10s. What number comes after 23? 33

I am counting by 20s. What number comes after 15? 35

I am counting by 10s. What number comes before 83? 73

Math Message

What number is 1 more than 46? 47

What number is 10 more than 46? 56

What number is 1 less than 46? 45

What number is 10 less than 46? 36

NOTE Some children may benefit from doing the **Readiness** activity before you begin Part 1 of the lesson. See the Readiness activity in Part 3 for details.

	45	
54	55	56
	65	

---

① Teaching the Lesson

▶ Math Message Follow-Up

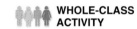
WHOLE-CLASS ACTIVITY

Ask a volunteer to point to a number that is 1 more than 46 on the Number-Grid Poster. 47 Ask other volunteers to point to the other answers for the Math Message. 56; 45; 36

Have children choose other numbers on the Number-Grid Poster and repeat this routine.

▶ Finding Patterns on a Number Grid

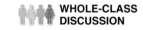
WHOLE-CLASS DISCUSSION

Tell children that today they will find patterns on a number grid and use the number grid to create number-grid puzzles.

Write 55 in the center of the 3-by-3 grid on the board. (*See margin.*) Ask for volunteers to write in the grid the number that is 1 more than 55 56; 1 less than 55 54; 10 more than 55 65; 10 less than 55 45. *What numbers go in the other squares on the grid?* 44; 46; 64; 66

Let the children choose other beginning numbers and repeat this procedure.

Tell the children to think of any number on the grid. Ask:

● Where is the number that is 1 more? To the right, or at the left end of the row below Where is the number that is 1 less? To the left, or at the right end of the row above

● Where is the number that is 10 more? One row down, directly below Where is the number that is 10 less? One row up, directly above

Completing Number-Grid Puzzles 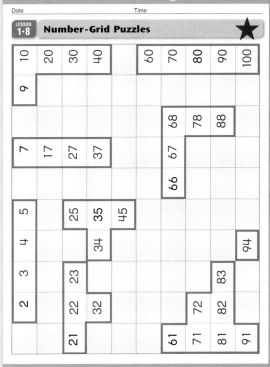 INDEPENDENT ACTIVITY

(*Math Journal 1*, p. 9)

Check to be sure children have recorded the date and time at the top of journal page 9. Children work alone or with a partner to complete the number-grid puzzles.

 Adjusting the Activity

Provide hints by filling in several of the surrounding blue boxes.

21			24	
		33		35

65	66	
	76	

Number-grid puzzles

A U D I T O R Y ◆ K I N E S T H E T I C ◆ T A C T I L E ◆ V I S U A L

Ongoing Assessment:
Recognizing Student Achievement

Journal page 9 ★

Use **journal page 9** to assess children's understanding of number-grid patterns. Children are making adequate progress if they are able to complete the journal page with the assistance of the Number-Grid Poster. Some children may use mental math to complete the journal page.

[Patterns, Functions, and Algebra Goal 1]

 (2) Ongoing Learning & Practice

▶ **Playing the *Number-Grid Game*** PARTNER ACTIVITY

(*Math Masters*, p. 418; *My Reference Book*, pp. 142 and 143)

Children will find directions for the *Number-Grid Game* on pages 142 and 143 of *My Reference Book*. They use the number grid from *Math Masters*, page 418 to play the game.

▶ **Math Boxes 1·8** INDEPENDENT ACTIVITY

(*Math Journal 1*, p. 10)

Mixed Practice Math Boxes in this lesson are linked with Math Boxes in Lessons 1-10 and 1-12. The skills in Problems 5 and 6 preview Unit 2 content.

Student Page

Date_____ Time_____

LESSON 1·8 **Number-Grid Puzzles** ★

Math Journal 1, p. 9

Student Page

Games

Number-Grid Game

Materials	❑ 1 number grid
	❑ 1 six-sided die
	❑ 1 game marker for each player
Players	2 or more
Skill	Counting on the number grid

Object of the game To land on 110 with an exact roll.

Roll	Spaces
•	1 or 10
••	2 or 20
•• •	3
•• ••	4
•• • ••	5
••• •••	6

Directions

1. Players put their markers at 0 on the number grid.

2. Take turns. When it is your turn:
   • Roll the die.
   • Use the table to see how many spaces to move your marker.
   • Move your marker that many spaces.

3. Continue playing. The winner is the first player to land on 110 with an exact roll.

My Reference Book, p. 142

Student Page

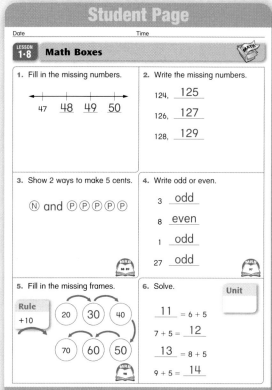

Math Journal 1, p. 10

Teaching Master

Name   Date   Time

LESSON 1·8 Number-Grid Cutouts

Math Masters, p. 13

3 Differentiation Options

READINESS

INDEPENDENT ACTIVITY

5–15 Min

► Filling In Pieces of a Number Grid

(*Math Masters*, pp. 12 and 417)

To explore patterns on a number grid, have children use patterns to complete number-grid puzzles. Cut out and laminate the number-grid shapes from *Math Masters*, page 12. The shapes will fit over the number grid on *Math Masters*, page 417.

Tell children to place the T on the number grid so it covers whole boxes. They can use a grease pencil or dry-erase marker to fill in the covered numbers. Then they lift the T to check their responses.

Discuss the numbers and their placement, especially counts by 10s. This procedure can be repeated many times, using different shapes and placements on the number grid.

11	12	13	14	15	16	17	18	
21	**22**	**23**	24	25	26	27	28	2
31	**32**	33	34	35	36	37	38	39
41	**42**	**43**	44	45	46	47	48	4
51	52	53	54	55	56	57	58	5
61	62	63	64	65	66	67	68	69
71	72	73	74	75	76	77	78	79
81	82	83	84	85	86	87	88	89
91	92	93	94	95	96	97	98	99
101	102	103	104	105	106	107	108	109

A cutout from *Math Masters*, page 12 is placed over the number grid found on *Math Masters*, page 417.

ENRICHMENT

INDEPENDENT ACTIVITY

5–15 Min

► Making Number-Grid Puzzle Pieces

(*Math Masters*, p. 13)

To apply children's understanding of patterns on the number grid, have them design their own number-grid puzzle pieces. This activity promotes number sequencing and patterns. Encourage children to use 3- and 4-digit numbers.

Children make number-grid puzzle pieces by cutting out grid pieces from *Math Masters*, page 13 and entering one or two numbers on each piece. You might want to suggest to children that their grid pieces have a minimum of five squares and can be in any shape.

These pieces can be taped or glued on half-sheets of paper and assembled into a class book. If the pages are laminated, the puzzles can be solved and erased many times.

Equivalent Names for Numbers

 Objectives To provide experiences with giving equivalent names for numbers; and to review calculator use.

---

1 Teaching the Lesson

materials

Key Activities
Children give equivalent names for people and numbers, review basic calculator functions, and skip count using their calculators. They find equivalent names for numbers by solving Broken Calculator problems.

Key Concepts and Skills
- Count on by 2s and 10s on the calculator.
  [Number and Numeration Goal 1]
- Write equivalent names for numbers.
  [Number and Numeration Goal 5]
- Write equivalent names for numbers using facts; use facts to solve Broken Calculator problems.
  [Operations and Computation Goal 1]

Key Vocabulary
equivalent names • program

☑ **Ongoing Assessment: Recognizing Student Achievement** Use journal page 11.
  [Number and Numeration Goal 5]

☐ *Math Journal 1,* p. 11
☐ calculator
☐ overhead calculator (optional)

***See* Advance Preparation**

---

2 Ongoing Learning & Practice

materials

Children review place value and money.

Children practice and maintain skills through Math Boxes.

☐ *Math Journal 1,* pp. 12 and 13
☐ tool-kit bills

---

3 Differentiation Options

materials

READINESS
Children use a pan balance for additional exposure to equivalency.

ENRICHMENT
Children solve place-value puzzles using a calculator.

☐ pan balance
☐ 18 pencils, dominoes, pennies, or other small identical objects
☐ calculator

***See* Advance Preparation**

Additional Information

Advance Preparation Before beginning the lesson, familiarize yourself with your class's calculators. Every calculator has a "repeat" key. On most basic calculators, this is the ⊜ key. Some calculators have an "operations" key that remembers and repeats operations.

For the optional Readiness activity in Part 3, set up a pan balance with a collection of identical objects.

Technology
Assessment Management System
Journal page 11, Problems 1 and 5
See the **iTLG.**

Getting Started

Math Message

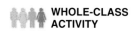

Write the name of someone at home. What other names does this person have?

NOTE Some children may benefit from doing the **Readiness** activity before you begin Part 1 of the lesson. See the Readiness activity in Part 3 for details.

---

1 Teaching the Lesson

▶ Math Message Follow-Up

 **WHOLE-CLASS ACTIVITY**

Ask a few volunteers to give several names for someone at home. For example, to most of her patients, Miguel's mother is known as Dr. Medina. Her friends call her Roberta. People in her family call her Mom, Grandma, and Aunt Roberta. All are names for the same person.

▶ Reviewing Equivalent Names for Numbers

WHOLE-CLASS DISCUSSION

Point out that numbers can also be called by many different names. Direct children's attention to the addition problems from Mental Math and Reflexes that you recorded on the board.

Ask children to suggest subtraction names for the number 10, such as $12 - 2 = 10$. Record these names on the board. Ask if anyone can think of ways to use words to name 10; for example, "ten" or "two less than a dozen."

Explain that names for the same number are called **equivalent names.** Write the word *equivalent* on the board to support English language learners.

Adjusting the Activity

Have children collect names for numbers greater than 10—for example, collect names for 40.

AUDITORY ◆ KINESTHETIC ◆ TACTILE ◆ VISUAL

▶ Reviewing Calculator Use

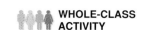 **WHOLE-CLASS ACTIVITY**

Many children will be familiar with calculators and can help those children who are not familiar with this tool. At this point, children should know how to do the following:

1. Turn on the calculator.

2. Enter numbers.

3. Key in addition and subtraction expressions.

4. Use the ⊜ key to display an answer.

5. Clear the calculator.

► Counting on a Calculator

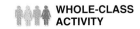 **WHOLE-CLASS ACTIVITY**

Use an overhead calculator, if possible, to guide the children through the steps for counting up and down by any number.

You can teach a calculator to count using a **program.** The program needs five steps: To *clear* the calculator memory, set a number to *count by,* set to *count up* or *count down,* and set a *starting number.* Finally, it needs to be instructed to *count.*

The order of these five steps in the program depends on your calculator. The following program will work on any calculator:

Clear the calculator. Press *s* (the starting number) ⊞ *n* (the number by which you want to count) ⊜ ⊞ *n* ⊜ ⊞ *n* ⊜ .... Two additional programs for counting by 2s starting at 4 are given below for demonstration purposes. Have children perform each step on their own calculators.

NOTE You can use any calculator to complete activities in *Second Grade Everyday Mathematics.* For demonstration purposes, key sequences for TI-108 and Casio SL-450 calculators are provided. Check your calculator users' manual and adjust the instructions accordingly.

For the Texas Instruments® TI-108:

1. Press the ⌷ON/C⌷ key to *clear.*

2. Enter a *starting number.* Enter ⌷4⌷ on your calculator.

3. Set to *count up* or *count down* by pressing ⌷+⌷ for up or ⌷−⌷ for down. Press ⌷+⌷ to count up.

4. Enter the number that you want to *count by.* Enter ⌷2⌷ on your calculator.

5. *Count* by pressing ⌷=⌷. Everyone count aloud while we press ⌷=⌷ repeatedly: 4, 6, 8, ...

For the Casio® SL-450:

1. Press the ⒶⒸ key to *clear.*

2. Enter the number that you want to *count by.* Enter ②　on your calculator.

3. Set to *count up* or *count down* by pressing ⊕ ⊕ for up or ⊝ ⊝ for down. Press ⊕ ⊕ to count up. (You will see a little K on the left of the display to show that the counter has been set, and a little + on the right to show it is counting up.)

4. Enter a *starting number.* Enter ④ on your calculator.

5. *Count* by pressing ⊜. Everyone count aloud while we press ⊜ repeatedly: 4, 6, 8, ...

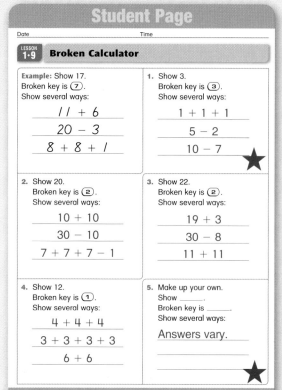

Math Journal 1, p. 11

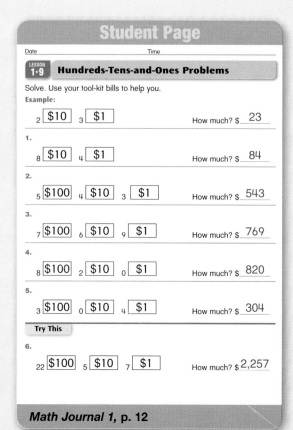

Math Journal 1, p. 12

Clear calculators and repeat the process, counting by a different number. Be sure to count both up and down by different numbers. For example, count up by 10s beginning with 40 and count down by 10s beginning with 100. Continue until children are comfortable with the procedure.

 Links to the Future

Have children count down below zero so negative numbers appear in the display. Do not expect children to understand or remember negative numbers at this time. Consider this activity as an exposure to the concept that there are numbers below zero. Comparing integers is a Grade 3 Goal.

▶ Solving Broken Calculator Problems

INDEPENDENT ACTIVITY

(*Math Journal 1*, p. 11)

Ask children to pretend that the 9 key on their calculator is broken. How can they display the number 9 without using the broken key? Share and note on the board several ways of doing this. Encourage children to try using three or more numbers.

Try other Broken Calculator problems like the following:

● Show 2. Pretend the 2 key is broken.

● Show 18. Pretend the 1 and 0 keys are broken.

● Show 21. Pretend the 2 key is broken.

Repeat the activity with other broken keys. If the children do well, make the problems more difficult.

Have children work alone or with partners to complete the problems on journal page 11. Point out that they are pretending different keys are broken for each problem.

 Ongoing Assessment: Recognizing Student Achievement

Journal page 11 Problems 1 and 5 ★

Use **journal page 11, Problems 1 and 5** to assess the children's understanding of equivalent names for numbers. Children are making adequate progress if they can write at least one equivalent number model for 1-digit numbers. Some children may be able to successfully complete equivalent names for 2- and 3-digit numbers and use more than one operation.

[Number and Numeration Goal 5]

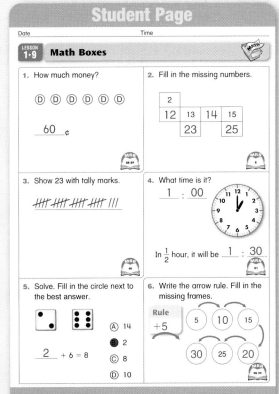

Math Journal 1, p. 13

2 Ongoing Learning & Practice

▶ Solving Hundreds-Tens-and-Ones Problems

INDEPENDENT ACTIVITY

(*Math Journal 1*, p. 12)

Children use their tool-kit bills to solve the place-value and money problems on journal page 12.

▶ Math Boxes 1•9

INDEPENDENT ACTIVITY

(*Math Journal 1*, p. 13)

Mixed Practice Math Boxes in this lesson are linked with Math Boxes in Lessons 1-7 and 1-11. The skills in Problems 5 and 6 preview Unit 2 content.

3 Differentiation Options

▶ Illustrating Equivalencies Using Pan Balance and Identical Objects

PARTNER ACTIVITY

5–15 Min

To explore the concept of equivalency using a concrete model, have children solve pan-balance problems.

Set up a pan balance. Mark or tape an = sign on the fulcrum. Show a few ways of arranging 7 or any other number of identical objects on each of the two pans. (*See margin.*) Ask children to suggest additional arrangements. For each arrangement, write number models. Vary the ways in which you express the situations, as shown below.

Repeat the process for other numbers.

You may want to use straws, blocks, or pencils to demonstrate different ways to say the same number. For example, $4 + 3 = 5 + 2$.

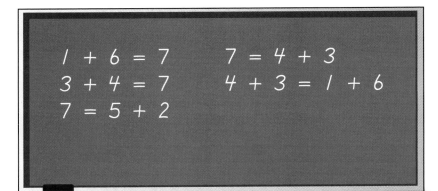

$$1 + 6 = 7 \qquad 7 = 4 + 3$$
$$3 + 4 = 7 \qquad 4 + 3 = 1 + 6$$
$$7 = 5 + 2$$

Enter	Change To	How?
35	85	+50

► Solving Calculator Place-Value Puzzles

To further explore equivalent names for numbers, have children solve calculator place-value puzzles. Pose the following problem: *Enter 35 into your calculator. Try to change the display to 85 by adding or subtracting a number.* Have children share solution strategies. Possible strategies might include:

▷ "The digits in the ones place are the same, so I know that I don't have to change them. I have to change the digit in the tens place from a 3 to an 8. That means the number has to increase by 5 tens, or 50, so I add 50 to get to 85."

▷ "I put my finger on 35 on my number grid and counted the number of rows to 85. It's 5 rows, and I know that means counting up 5 tens, or 50. So I added 50 to the 35 to get 85."

Record the answers in a table on the board. (*See margin.*)

Pose several other problems that involve adding and subtracting multiples of 10.

Try a couple of problems that involve adding and subtracting multiples of 100. *For example:*

● Enter 246 into your calculator. Try to change the display to 446. 200

● Enter 368 into your calculator. Try to change the display to 168. ☐ 200

Encourage children to make up problems for the group to solve.

1·10 Counting Patterns

 Objective To guide children as they count and look for patterns on the calculator.

---

1 Teaching the Lesson — materials

Key Activities
Children count by 10s. They count using a calculator and explore number patterns that result from counts.

Key Concepts and Skills
- Count by 6s, 7s, and 4s on the calculator.
  [Number and Numeration Goal 1]
- Identify the ones digit in numbers.
  [Number and Numeration Goal 2]
- Identify patterns in counts and use the patterns to answer questions.
  [Patterns, Functions, and Algebra Goal 1]

☐ *Math Journal 1*, p. 14
☐ calculator
☐ slate

---

2 Ongoing Learning & Practice — materials

Children find equivalent names for numbers by solving Broken Calculator problems.

Children practice and maintain skills through Math Boxes.

✔ **Ongoing Assessment: Recognizing Student Achievement** Use journal page 16.
  [Operations and Computation Goal 2]

☐ *Math Journal 1*, pp. 15 and 16
☐ calculator

---

3 Differentiation Options — materials

READINESS
Children practice counting by 2s, 5s, and 10s.

ENRICHMENT
Children solve calculator counting problems.

☐ Teaching Master (*Math Masters*, p. 14)
☐ Teaching Aid Master (*Math Masters*, p. 416; optional)
☐ calculator

Technology

Assessment Management System
Math Boxes, Problem 3
See the **iTLG**.

Getting Started

Mental Math and Reflexes

Children do problems like the following on their slates:

◉○○ Write 52. Circle the digit in the 10s place.
Write 83. Circle the digit in the 1s place.
Write 50. Circle the digit in the 1s place.

◉◉○ Write 120. Circle the digit in the 10s place. Put an X on the digit in the 1s place.
Write 143. Circle the digit in the 10s place. Put an X on the digit in the 1s place.
Write 209. Circle the digit in the 10s place. Put an X on the digit in the 1s place.

◉◉◉ Write 1,002. Circle the digit in the 10s place. Put an X on the digit in the 1s place.
Write 2,341. Circle the digit in the 100s place. Put an X on the digit in the 1s place.
Write 5,720. Circle the digit in the 10s place. Put an X on the digit in the 100s place.

Math Message

Count by 10s. Count as high as you can in 1 minute. Write the number you reach.

NOTE Some children may benefit from doing the **Readiness** activity before you begin Part 1 of the lesson. See the Readiness activity in Part 3 for details.

① Teaching the Lesson

▶ ## Math Message Follow-Up

WHOLE-CLASS ACTIVITY

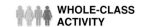

Count together by 10s up to 200.

▶ ## Counting with a Calculator

WHOLE-CLASS ACTIVITY

(Math Journal 1, p. 14)

Remind children that when they want to count using a calculator, they need to program it. The program needs five steps: To *clear* the calculator memory, set a number to *count by,* set to *count up* or *count down,* and set a *starting number.* Finally, it needs to be instructed to *count.*

Have children practice counting by 1s on their calculators.

Tell children that they are going to count by some uncommon skips in their counting today. Have them turn to journal page 14. Give children a few minutes to do the first problem. Check to see that everyone understands what to do. Children then complete the page.

When most of the children have finished, briefly discuss the answers and any patterns they found.

Ask why you might choose not to use the calculator to count by 2s, 5s, or 10s. It's faster to do those counts without the calculator.

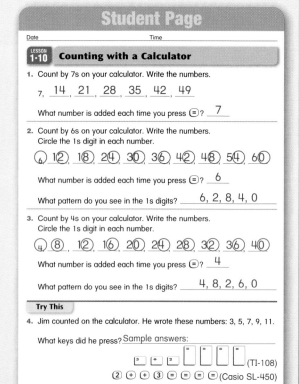

Adjusting the Activity

ELL

Count by 2s to 24. Write the counts on the board and circle the 1s digits. The circled digits are 2, 4, 6, 8, 0, 2, 4, 6, 8, 0, 2, 4.

Now write the digits 0, 2, 4, 6, and 8 evenly spaced around a pentagon. The circled digits repeat the same pattern as the digits around the pentagon.

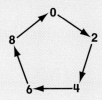

A U D I T O R Y ◆ K I N E S T H E T I C ◆ T A C T I L E ◆ V I S U A L

2 Ongoing Learning & Practice

▶ ## Solving Broken Calculator Problems

INDEPENDENT ACTIVITY

(*Math Journal 1*, p. 15)

Children have an opportunity to solve and pose equivalent name problems using their calculators. See Solving Broken Calculator Problems in Lesson 1-9.

▶ ## Math Boxes 1•10

INDEPENDENT ACTIVITY

(*Math Journal 1*, p. 16)

 Mixed Practice Math Boxes in this lesson are linked with Math Boxes in Lessons 1-8 and 1-12. The skills in Problems 5 and 6 preview Unit 2 content.

 Writing/Reasoning Have children draw, write, or verbalize their answers to the following: *For Problem 3, show 35¢ with the fewest number of coins. Explain how you know that you found the fewest number of coins.* Sample answer: ⓆⒹ I used the coins that are worth the most.

Ongoing Assessment: Recognizing Student Achievement

Math Boxes Problem 3 ★

Use **Math Boxes, Problem 3** to assess children's progress toward calculating coin values. Children are making adequate progress if they can correctly complete the problem. Some children may be able to add coin symbols to this amount to make a dollar.

[Operations and Computation Goal 2]

Student Page

Date _____ Time _____

LESSON 1•10 Broken Calculator

1. Show 8.
   Broken key is ⑧.
   Show several ways:
   2 + 6
   9 − 1
   4 + 4

2. Show 30.
   Broken key is ③.
   Show several ways:
   20 + 10
   15 + 15
   40 − 10

3. Show 15.
   Broken key is ⑤.
   Show several ways:
   11 + 4
   16 − 1
   7 + 7 + 1

4. Show 26.
   Broken key is ⑥.
   Show several ways:
   11 + 11 + 4
   30 − 4
   20 + 5 + 1

5. Make up your own.
   Show _____.
   Broken key is _____.
   Show several ways:
   Answers vary.

6. Make up your own.
   Show _____.
   Broken key is _____.
   Show several ways:
   Answers vary.

Math Journal 1, p. 15

Student Page

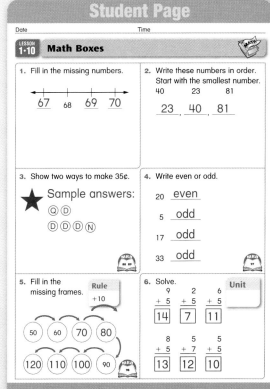

Date _____ Time _____

LESSON 1•10 Math Boxes

1. Fill in the missing numbers.

   67 68 69 70

2. Write these numbers in order.
   Start with the smallest number.
   40   23   81
   23 , 40 , 81

3. Show two ways to make 35¢.
   ★ Sample answers:
   ⓆⒹ
   ⒹⒹⒹⓃ

4. Write even or odd.
   20 even
   5 odd
   17 odd
   33 odd

5. Fill in the missing frames.
   Rule +10
   50 60 70 80
   120 110 100 90

6. Solve.
   Unit
   9   2   6
   + 5 + 5 + 5
   14   7   11

   8   5   5
   + 5 + 7 + 5
   13   12   10

Math Journal 1, p. 16

Lesson 1•10   **63**

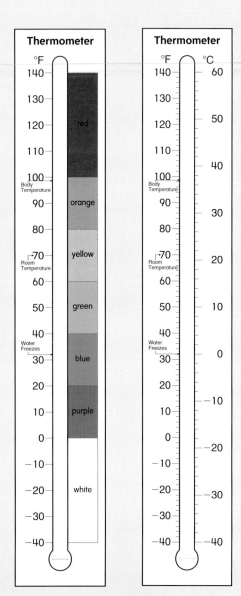

Teaching Master

Name _____ Date _____ Time _____

LESSON 1·10 | **Calculator Counting**

1. Use your calculator.

2. Choose a "count by" number.

3. Enter the key sequence to start your count and press the ⊟ key three times.

4. Show your partner the calculator.

5. Slowly press the ⊟ key four times while your partner writes the display numbers on the lines.

6. Your partner then guesses your "count by" number.

7. Switch turns.

1. _____ _____ _____ _____

   Guess _____

2. _____ _____ _____ _____

   Guess _____

3. _____ _____ _____ _____

   Guess _____

4. _____ _____ _____ _____

   Guess _____

Math Masters, p. 14

Class Thermometers

3 Differentiation Options

READINESS **SMALL-GROUP ACTIVITY**

🕐 5–15 Min

▶ Counting by 2s, 5s, and 10s

To provide experience with counting, have children do rhythmic counts. Try to correlate rhythmic counting with movement when chanting 2s, 5s, and 10s. *For example:*

● 1, 2 (clap), 3, 4 (clap), ...

● 1, 2, 3, 4, 5 (touch toes), 6, 7, 8, 9, 10 (touch toes), ...

● 1, 2, 3, 4, 5, 6, 7, 8, 9, 10 (jumping jack), ...

ENRICHMENT **PARTNER ACTIVITY**

🕐 5–15 Min

▶ Solving Calculator-Count Problems

(*Math Masters,* pp. 14 and 416)

To apply children's understanding of calculator counts, have children start counts on the calculator for their partners to guess. Partners record numbers and guess the "count by" number. Children may use the number grid, such as on *Math Masters,* page 416, to help solve the problem.

Planning Ahead

Before beginning Lesson 1-12, assemble the Class Thermometer Poster °F so the thermometer is full length.

Cut a long strip of red ribbon or crepe paper to represent the "mercury" in the thermometer tube. (The liquid is often called mercury, but may be something else.) Cut a slit in the thermometer bulb and pull the ribbon or crepe paper through the slit. Tape it at the top to hold it in place. Place a container beneath the poster to hold the excess ribbon or crepe paper. (Celsius temperatures will be introduced in Unit 4 using the Class Thermometer Poster (°F/°C).)

Note When you use the *Everyday Mathematics* posters with English language learners, you should display either the English version only or both the English and Spanish versions simultaneously.

1·11 Relations (<, >, =) and Home Links

 Objectives To provide experiences with comparing numbers using the relation symbols <, >, and =; and to introduce Home Links.

---

1 Teaching the Lesson

materials

Key Activities
Children compare numbers by using words, acting out pan-balance problems, and reading and writing number sentences with the relations symbols <, >, and =.

Key Concepts and Skills
- Compare numbers. [Number and Numeration Goal 7]
- Calculate and compare the values of combinations of coins. [Operations and Computation Goal 2]
- Read, write, and explain the <, >, and = symbols. [Patterns, Functions, and Algebra Goal 2]

Key Vocabulary
is equal to • is less than • is greater than

☑ **Ongoing Assessment: Recognizing Student Achievement** Use Mental Math and Reflexes. [Number and Numeration Goal 7]

☑ **Ongoing Assessment: Informing Instruction** See page 68.

- ☐ *Math Journal 1*, p. 17
- ☐ Teaching Aid Master (*Math Masters*, p. 415)
- ☐ slate
- ☐ tool-kit coins
- ☐ pan balance and pennies (optional)

---

2 Ongoing Learning & Practice

materials

Children review addition facts by playing *Addition Top-It*.

Children practice and maintain skills through Math Boxes and Home Link activities.

- ☐ *Math Journal 1*, p. 18
- ☐ *My Reference Book*, pp. 122 and 123
- ☐ Home Link Masters (*Math Masters*, pp. 15 and 16)
- ☐ Game Master (*Math Masters*, p. 449; optional)
- ☐ per partnership: 4 each of number cards 0–10; double-9 dominoes or dice (optional)

---

3 Differentiation Options

materials

READINESS

Children describe inequalities and equalities by using a pan balance to compare quantities.

ENRICHMENT

Children play *Number Top-It* with 5-digit numbers.

- ☐ Game Masters (*Math Masters*, pp. 465 and 466)
- ☐ pan balance; pennies or other identical objects
- ☐ per partnership: 4 each of number cards 0–9
- ☐ glue or tape

Technology

Assessment Management System
Mental Math and Reflexes
See the **iTLG**.

Getting Started

Mental Math and Reflexes

Name pairs of numbers. Children write them on an Exit Slip (*Math Masters,* page 415) and circle the larger or smaller number. Give problems like the following:

○○○ Write 15 and 18.
Circle the larger number.

Write 25 and 15.
Circle the larger number.

Write 68 and 86.
Circle the smaller number.

○○○ Write 115 and 107.
Circle the larger number.

Write 200 and 189.
Circle the larger number.

Write 250 and 205.
Circle the smaller number.

○○○ Write 1,245 and 1,189.
Circle the larger number.

Write 3,002 and 1,299.
Circle the larger number.

Write 4,132 and 4,122.
Circle the smaller number.

Math Message

Write "is less than" or "is greater than" between each pair of numbers.

20 is greater than 12

40 is greater than 38

30 is less than 35

70 is greater than 59

NOTE Some children may benefit from doing the **Readiness** activity before you begin Part 1 of the lesson. See the Readiness activity in Part 3 for details.

 Ongoing Assessment:
Recognizing Student Achievement

Mental Math and Reflexes

Use the **Mental Math and Reflexes** to assess the children's ability to compare numbers. Children are making adequate progress if they can successfully compare numbers in the tens and hundreds. Some children may be able to successfully compare numbers in the thousands.

[Number and Numeration Goal 7]

---

1 Teaching the Lesson

▶ Math Message Follow-Up

WHOLE-CLASS ACTIVITY

Have children stand. Tell them to pretend they are holding 25 pennies in their left hand. Have everyone hold up his or her left hand. Tell the children to pretend they are holding 12 pennies in their right hand. Have everyone hold up his or her right hand.

Which hand would be heavier? The hand with the 25 pennies Have children pretend they are pan balances and hold out their hands to show which hand would be lower. Ask why. The hand with 25 pennies would be lower, because 25 pennies are more than 12 pennies and the side with 25 pennies would be heavier.

Repeat the activity with 30 and 35 pennies. Encourage use of the language *30 is less than 35* and *35 is greater than 30.*

Adjusting the Activity

ELL

Use an actual pan balance to demonstrate that 25 pennies are heavier than 12 pennies. Once children have seen several examples with the pan balance, pose similar problems for which they pretend to be a pan balance.

A U D I T O R Y ◆ K I N E S T H E T I C ◆ T A C T I L E ◆ V I S U A L

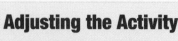

► Reviewing Relations: Less Than ($<$), Greater Than ($>$), Equal To ($=$)

Write the following sentences on the board: "1 and 1 is the same as 2" and "1 plus 1 **is equal to** 2." Ask children which symbol can replace the words *is the same as* or *is equal to*. $=$ Erase these words and write $=$ in their place. Ask which symbol can replace *and* or *plus* in these sentences. $+$ Erase these words and put $+$ in their place. Read the resulting sentences as "1 and 1 is the same as 2" and "1 plus 1 is equal to 2," pointing to the number sentences on the board. Remind children that they made equivalent names for numbers. (Point to one if they are still displayed.) Explain that sometimes numbers are written as words or in other languages. Some mathematical words are also written using symbols, such as writing $=$ for *equal* and $+$ for *plus*.

Write the following sentence on the board: "30 **is less than** 35." Remind children that symbols often replace words in mathematics. Ask if anyone knows which symbol can replace *is less than*. If no one suggests it, show children the symbol $<$. Erase *is less than* and replace the words with $<$.

Write "14 $<$ 16" on the board. Ask a volunteer to read the number sentence. 14 is less than 16. Do several similar examples.

Write "21 $>$ 15" on the board. Ask a volunteer to tell what the symbol $>$ means. **Is greater than,** *is more than, is larger than, or is bigger than*

Explain that the open side of the symbols $>$ and $<$ is always next to the larger number. The vertex or point always points to the smaller number. There are a number of strategies for remembering which is which.

▷ The "mouth" must be bigger to swallow the bigger number. (*See margin.*)

▷ The "less" looks like the left-hand finger and thumb. (*Less* and *left* start with the same letter.) (*See margin.*)

▷ The meeting point of the two lines always points to the smaller number.

▷ Draw dots on each open end of $>$ or $<$, and draw one dot on the vertex or point. The number that is larger is on the side with two dots. The number that is smaller is on the side with one dot. (*See margin.*)

▷ Draw two dots (:) next to the larger number and one dot next to the smaller number. Connect each of the two dots to the single dot, and the symbol will be correct. (*See margin.*)

$$5 > 2$$

$$2 < 5$$

$$3 < 5$$

$$5 > 3$$

Student Page

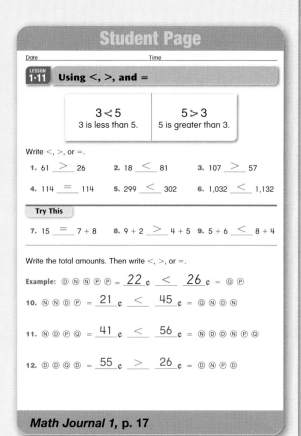

Date _____ Time _____

LESSON 1·11   **Using <, >, and =**

3 < 5	5 > 3
3 is less than 5.	5 is greater than 3.

Write <, >, or =.

1. 61 $>$ 26   2. 18 $<$ 81   3. 107 $>$ 57

4. 114 $=$ 114   5. 299 $<$ 302   6. 1,032 $<$ 1,132

Try This

7. 15 $=$ 7 + 8   8. 9 + 2 $>$ 4 + 5   9. 5 + 6 $<$ 8 + 4

Write the total amounts. Then write <, >, or =.

Example: Ⓓ Ⓝ Ⓝ Ⓟ Ⓟ = _22_ ¢ $<$ _26_ ¢ = Ⓠ Ⓟ

10. Ⓝ Ⓝ Ⓓ Ⓟ = _21_ ¢ $<$ _45_ ¢ = Ⓠ Ⓓ Ⓝ

11. Ⓝ Ⓓ Ⓟ Ⓠ = _41_ ¢ $<$ _56_ ¢ = Ⓝ Ⓓ Ⓓ Ⓝ Ⓟ Ⓠ

12. Ⓓ Ⓓ Ⓠ Ⓓ = _55_ ¢ $>$ _26_ ¢ = Ⓓ Ⓝ Ⓟ Ⓓ

Math Journal 1, p. 17

Write pairs of numbers on the board. *For example:*

15 < 25   40 > 34   20 = 20   102 > 27

Have volunteers come up and write the correct symbol between each pair of numbers.

▶ Practicing the Use of the Symbols <, >, and =

WHOLE-CLASS ACTIVITY

(*Math Journal 1*, p. 17)

Tell children pairs of numbers to write on their slates. Have them choose the symbol that goes between the numbers. Pose problems similar to those in the previous activity.

Adjusting the Activity

Try problems like the following: 7 > 3 + 2; 4 + 1 = 5; 9 + 4 > 14 − 3

AUDITORY ♦ KINESTHETIC ♦ TACTILE ♦ VISUAL

When children are ready, have them work alone or with a partner to complete journal page 17. Suggest that children use their tool-kit coins.

✓ Ongoing Assessment: Informing Instruction

Watch for children who have difficulty counting the coin combinations. Suggest that children write the values for the coin or place the actual coin above the symbol.

Student Page

Games

Addition Top-It

Materials ❑ number cards 0–10 (4 of each)

Players 2 to 4

Skill Addition facts 0 to 10

Object of the game To collect the most cards.

Directions

1. Shuffle the cards. Place the deck number-side down on the table.

2. Each player turns over 2 cards and calls out the sum of the numbers.

3. The player with the largest sum wins the round and takes all the cards.

4. In case of a tie for the largest sum, each tied player turns over 2 more cards and calls out the sum of the numbers. The player with the largest sum then takes all the cards from both plays.

5. The game ends when not enough cards are left for each player to have another turn.

6. The player with the most cards wins.

My Reference Book, p. 122

---

2   Ongoing Learning & Practice

▶ Playing *Addition Top-It*

 PARTNER ACTIVITY

(*Math Masters*, p. 449; *My Reference Book*, pp. 122 and 123)

Partners continue to play the game as it was introduced in Lesson 1-4, or they play one of the following variations:

▷ Use double-9 dominoes instead of number cards.

▷ Draw 3 cards on each turn instead of 2.

▷ Roll a single die three times, or roll three separate dice, to generate three addends.

▶ Math Boxes 1·11

(*Math Journal 1*, p. 18)

INDEPENDENT
ACTIVITY

Mixed Practice Math Boxes in this lesson are linked with Math Boxes in Lessons 1-7 and 1-9. The skills in Problems 5 and 6 preview Unit 2 content.

▶ Home Link 1·11

(*Math Masters*, pp. 15 and 16; *My Reference Book*)

INDEPENDENT
ACTIVITY

Home Connection Children explore *My Reference Book* with someone at home and record three interesting things. Children compare numbers and write the symbols <, >, and =.

Distribute Home Link 1-11. Discuss the purpose of Home Links and children's responsibilities:

● Put your name, the date, and the time on your Home Link.

● Take home the correct Home Link.

● Discuss and complete the Home Link with someone at home—a parent, guardian, older brother or sister, other relative, caretaker, and so on. Use *My Reference Book* to find <, >, and = symbols and their uses.

● Return the completed Home Link to school the next school day. (Occasionally, Home Links take several days to complete.)

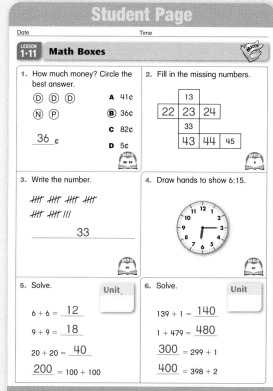

Math Journal 1, p. 18

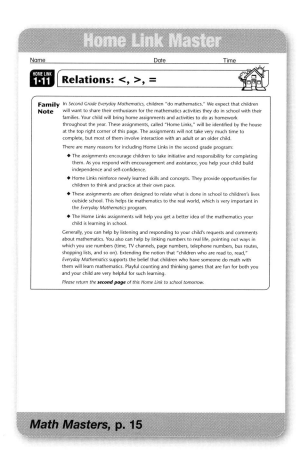

Math Masters, p. 15

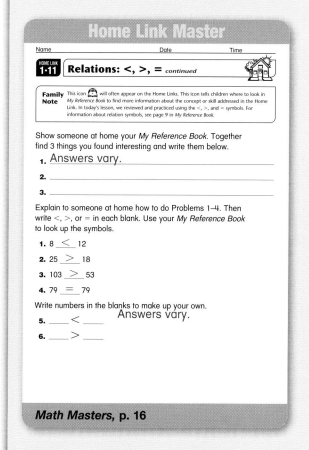

Math Masters, p. 16

READINESS

SMALL-GROUP ACTIVITY

▶ **Showing Equalities and Inequalities with a Pan Balance**

5–15 Min

To explore comparing the relative weight of objects, use a pan balance and objects to demonstrate and help children verbalize greater, less, and equal relationships. *For example:*

▷ "The things on this side weigh more than the things on that side."

▷ "These objects weigh less than those objects."

▷ "These things weigh about the same."

Repeat with various quantities of identical objects.

ENRICHMENT

PARTNER ACTIVITY

▶ **Playing *Number Top-It* (5-Digit Numbers)**

5–15 Min

(*Math Masters,* pp. 465 and 466)

To apply children's ability to compare numbers, have them play *Number Top-It.* Players make place-value mats by gluing or taping together *Math Masters,* pages 465 and 466. In the two-player version, players share a game mat. In the more-than-two-players version, players need additional game mats. Model by playing several rounds against the class before children play on their own.

Millions	Hundred-Thousands	Ten-Thousands	Thousands	Hundreds	Tens	Ones

Place-Value Mat from *Math Masters,* pages 465 and 466

Rules

1. Shuffle the cards. Place the deck number-side down.

2. Each player uses one row of boxes on the Place-Value Mat. Do not use the Millions box or the Hundred-Thousands box.

3. During each round, players take turns turning over the top card from the deck and placing it on any one of the empty boxes. Each player takes 5 turns and places 5 cards on his or her row of the Place-Value Mat.

4. At the end of each round, players read their numbers aloud and compare them. The player with the largest number for the round scores 1 point, the player with the next-largest number scores 2 points, and so on.

5. Players play five rounds per game. When all the cards in the deck are used, a player shuffles the discarded cards to make a new deck. The player with the smallest total number of points at the end of five rounds wins the game.

Variations: Children may play with less than 5 digits. If more than 2 players play, they could order all their numbers.

1·12 Exploring Temperatures, Base-10 Structures, and Dominoes

 Objective To guide children as they read and display temperatures, combine values of ones, tens, and hundreds using base-10 blocks, and explore addition facts on dominoes.

---

1 Teaching the Lesson

materials

Key Activities
Children are introduced to procedures and expectations for Explorations.

Exploration A: Children read and display temperatures on the Class Thermometer Poster.

Exploration B: Children build structures from base-10 blocks and calculate the values represented by the structures.

Exploration C: Children sort dominoes according to the sums of the domino dots.

Key Concepts and Skills
• Count by 1s, 10s, and 100s with base-10 blocks. [Number and Numeration Goal 1]
• Use dominoes to identify equivalent names for numbers.
  [Number and Numeration Goal 5]
• Practice addition facts with dominoes. [Operations and Computation Goal 1]
• Read a thermometer and record the temperature.
  [Measurement and Reference Frames Goal 5]

Key Vocabulary
temperature • thermometer • Fahrenheit • Explorations • base-10 blocks • cube • long • flat

☐ Home Link 1·11
☐ Rules for Explorations Poster (optional)
Exploration A: Per group:
☐ Teaching Master (*Math Masters*, p. 17)
☐ Class Thermometer Poster (°F)
☐ quarter-sheets of paper
☐ outdoor thermometer
Exploration B: Per group:
☐ Teaching Master (*Math Masters*, p. 18)
☐ base-10 blocks (cubes, longs, flats)
☐ quarter-sheets of paper
Exploration C: Per group:
☐ Teaching Master (*Math Masters*, p. 19)
☐ number cards 0–18
☐ 1 or 2 sets of double-9 dominoes

***See* Advance Preparation**

---

2 Ongoing Learning & Practice

materials

Children play *Addition Top-It*.
Children practice and maintain skills through Math Boxes and Home Link activities.

⭐ **Ongoing Assessment: Recognizing Student Achievement** Use journal page 19.
[Number and Numeration Goal 4]

☐ *Math Journal 1*, p. 19
☐ *My Reference Book*, pp. 122 and 123
☐ Home Link Master (*Math Masters*, p. 20)
☐ Game Master (*Math Masters*, p. 449; optional)
☐ per partnership: 4 each of number cards 0–10

---

3 Differentiation Options

materials

READINESS
Children use base-10 blocks to make and read a thermometer.

EXTRA PRACTICE
Children solve problems with arithmetic facts and temperature.

ELL SUPPORT
Children use temperature words to label the Class Thermometer Poster.

☐ *Minute Math*®+, pp. 10, 41, 97 and 136
☐ chart paper; marker; meterstick; base-10 longs
☐ stick-on notes; Class Thermometer Poster (°F)

Additional Information

Advance Preparation You may want to create a poster of Rules for Explorations like the one shown on page 73. Decide how many stations you will need to have children in groups of 3, 4, or 5. You will need an outdoor thermometer large enough so children can easily see the level of the liquid. Cover the Celsius scale with masking tape.

Technology
Assessment Management System
Math Boxes, Problem 4
See the **iTLG**.

Getting Started

Mental Math and Reflexes

Do stop-and-start counting. Have a group of children begin counting toward a number you name; stop; point at another group to continue where the count left off. Repeat.

- ●○○ Count on by 10s. Start at 10; 100
- ●●○ Count on by 2s. Start at 10; 38
- ●●● Count on by 10s. Start at 250; 500
- ●●● Count on by 2s. Start at 120; 200

Math Message

Make a list of words to describe the weather.

Home Link 1·11 Follow-Up

Briefly go over the answers.

Ask volunteers to share some of the problems they created.

NOTE Some children may benefit from doing the **Readiness** activity before you begin Part 1 of the lesson. See the Readiness activity in Part 3 for details.

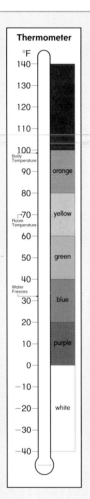

Thermometer

Class Thermometer Poster (°F)

Science Link Point out that the letter F stands for **Fahrenheit,** which is the name of the physicist, Gabriel Daniel Fahrenheit, who developed this thermometer scale. A Fahrenheit thermometer measures temperature in degrees Fahrenheit. The symbol for degrees appears before the letter F and is read *degrees Fahrenheit.* Write 60°F on the board. Say: *This is read "60 degrees Fahrenheit."*

---

1 Teaching the Lesson

▶ Math Message Follow-Up

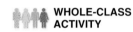 WHOLE-CLASS ACTIVITY

Record children's responses on the board. Ask children which words describe **temperature.** Possible answers: hot, cold, warm, cool, freezing, boiling Circle the temperature words on the board.

Display an outdoor **thermometer.** Explain that an outdoor thermometer makes it possible to not only say that it's cold or hot outside, but also to say how cold or hot it is. For example, 6°F might be the temperature on a colder day and 89°F might be the temperature on a hotter day.

Have children look at the Class Thermometer Poster (°F). Ask them to describe what they see. Sample answers: Numbers every 10 degrees; marks for degrees; the letter F at the top of the thermometer with the symbol ° in front of it; arrows indicating body temperature, room temperature, and the temperature at which water freezes; a red ribbon or strip of red crepe paper running next to the numbers of degrees

NOTE You may want to explain that there is a second scale on many thermometers. It is called the Celsius temperature scale. The Celsius scale will be introduced in Unit 4.

Put your finger on the scale at 0. Move it up the scale while children count in unison the numbers of degrees by 10s: *0 degrees, 10 degrees, 20 degrees,* and so on.

Repeat the activity with children counting the number of degrees by 2s. Point out the numbers below 0 with the negative signs in front of them: −10, −20. These temperatures are read *10 degrees below zero, 20 degrees below zero,* and so on.

Adjusting the Activity

ELL

Tell children that these temperatures can also be read *negative 10 degrees, negative 20 degrees,* and so on. Point out that, on a number line, negative numbers are displayed to the left of 0.

AUDITORY ◆ KINESTHETIC ◆ TACTILE ◆ VISUAL

▶ Discussing Procedures and Expectations for Explorations

 **WHOLE-CLASS DISCUSSION**

Review the expectations for small-group work from previous lessons. Talk about the purposes of and the management routines for **Explorations.** Model and explain the specific Explorations.

▶ Exploration A: Measuring Temperature

SMALL-GROUP ACTIVITY

(*Math Masters*, p. 17)

Have someone place the outdoor thermometer outside for a few minutes while you discuss the daily temperature routine.

Assign a child to be in charge of setting the temperature on the Class Thermometer Poster (°F) to show the outside temperature. On the Class Thermometer Poster, the red ribbon or crepe paper represents the mercury in a regular thermometer. At about the same time each day, a child should move the red ribbon on the Class Thermometer Poster to approximately match the temperature on the outdoor thermometer. Model how to do this and ask children to describe today's temperature reading. Encourage the use of such phrases as *between _____ and _____ degrees Fahrenheit, almost _____ degrees Fahrenheit,* and *about halfway between _____ and _____ degrees Fahrenheit.*

Once children are comfortable setting a temperature on the Class Thermometer Poster, have them work as a group to complete *Math Masters,* page 17.

 Adjusting the Activity

The Class Thermometer Poster (°F) was used at the beginning of *First Grade Everyday Mathematics*. By Unit 4 of Grade 1, children began to set daily temperatures the °F/°C poster. If the children in your class have had limited exposure to thermometers, you may wish to use the °F thermometer poster to begin the daily temperature routine. Once children are accustomed to reading the thermometer and setting the temperature, switch over to the °F/°C thermometer poster.

AUDITORY ◆ KINESTHETIC ◆ TACTILE ◆ VISUAL

▶ Exploration B: Calculating the Values of Base-10 Structures

SMALL-GROUP ACTIVITY

(*Math Masters*, p. 18)

Introduce this Exploration to the whole class before children form small groups. Show children a set of **base-10 blocks.** Hold up a **cube** and call it a *cube.* Explain that it represents one unit, or one. Hold up a **long** and call it a *long.* Ask: *What numerical value might a long represent?* 10 units, or 10 *How do you know?* Sample answers: There are 10 units marked on it. It is 10 times as long as a cube.

Repeat with a hundreds **flat.**

Rules for Explorations

1. Cooperate with others.
2. Move about quietly.
3. Keep voices low.
4. Treat materials as tools, not as toys.
5. Straighten up when finished. Put materials back where they belong.

NOTE You may want to add the daily temperature routine to your job chart. Frequently rotate the job among the children in your class. You will need to supervise this routine in the beginning, but with experience, children will be able to complete the job independently.

Teaching Master

Name _____ Date _____ Time _____

LESSON 1·12 **Temperature**

Work in a group of 3 or 4 children.

Materials ☐ Class Thermometer Poster
☐ quarter-sheets of paper

Directions

Activity 1

1. Take turns. One person names a temperature. Another person shows that temperature on the Class Thermometer Poster.
2. Everyone in the group checks to see that the temperature is shown correctly.
3. Keep taking turns until each person has named a temperature and has shown a temperature on the Class Thermometer Poster.

Activity 2

1. Take turns showing a temperature on the Class Thermometer Poster. Everyone reads the thermometer and writes that temperature.
2. Everyone in the group compares the temperatures they wrote. Did everyone write the same temperature? Discuss any differences.

[Follow-Up]

Look at all the temperatures that you recorded on your quarter-sheets of paper.

◆ Were some temperatures easier to read than others? Explain.

◆ Order the temperatures from coldest to hottest.

Math Masters, p. 17

Teaching Master

Name Date Time

LESSON 1·12 | **Base-10 Structures**

Work in a group of 3 or 4 children.

Materials ☐ base-10 blocks (cubes, longs, and flats)

☐ quarter-sheets of paper

Directions

1. Each person uses base-10 blocks to make a "building." The picture shows an example. 60

2. Each block has a value.

■	= 1
		= 10
☐	= 100

The value of the cube is 1.
The value of the long is 10.
The value of the flat is 100.

What number does your building show? Use the symbols in the box above to help you.

3. Draw your building on a quarter-sheet of paper. Write the number with your drawing.

4. Have a friend help you check the number.

5. If there is time, make more buildings. Draw each building and record the number of each building.

Follow-Up

◆ Look at the numbers shown by your group's buildings.

◆ Order the numbers from smallest to largest.

Math Masters, p. 18

Tell children that they will build structures with the base-10 blocks. Once children have built the structures, they can figure out how much each structure is worth by counting the number of cubes (1s), longs (10s), and flats (100s) that they used.

Explain to children that they will draw these structures and write their values on quarter-sheets of paper.

Children form small groups and proceed with the activity. If time permits, groups should arrange their written records in order from least to greatest value.

 Adjusting the Activity ELL

Model some simple 2-dimensional structures on the overhead so that children can practice evaluating them.

AUDITORY ◆ KINESTHETIC ◆ TACTILE ◆ VISUAL

▶ **Exploration C: Sorting Dominoes** **SMALL-GROUP ACTIVITY**

(*Math Masters, p. 19*)

Children work together in small groups to sort one or more sets of double-9 dominoes. Children first lay out the number cards from 0 through 18. They place each domino above the number card that shows the sum of the domino's dots. Each group makes a list of all the addition facts shown by the dominoes.

 Adjusting the Activity

Have children record the addition facts for only one number card.

AUDITORY ◆ KINESTHETIC ◆ TACTILE ◆ VISUAL

Teaching Master

Name Date Time

LESSON 1·12 | **Sorting Dominoes**

Work in a group of 3 or 4 children.

Materials ☐ 1 or 2 sets of double-9 dominoes

☐ number cards 0–18 (from the Everything Math Deck, if available)

Directions

1. Lay down the number cards in order from 0 through 18.

2. Place each domino above the number card that shows the sum of the domino dots.

5

3. List the addition facts shown by the dominoes on a sheet of paper. Before you begin, decide how your group will record the facts.

Follow-Up

◆ Look at the list of addition facts your group made.

◆ Try to think of a better way to record the facts.

◆ Talk about why you think the new way is better.

Math Masters, p. 19

② Ongoing Learning & Practice

▶ **Playing *Addition Top-It***  **PARTNER ACTIVITY**

(*Math Masters, p. 449; My Reference Book, pp. 122 and 123*)

Children practice addition skills for numbers from 0 through 10 by playing *Addition Top-It*. For instructions, see *My Reference Book*, pages 122 and 123.

▶ **Math Boxes 1·12** **INDEPENDENT ACTIVITY**

(*Math Journal 1, p. 19*)

Mixed Practice Math Boxes in this lesson are linked with Math Boxes in Lessons 1-8 and 1-10. The skills in Problems 5 and 6 preview Unit 2 content.

▶ **Home Link 1·12**

INDEPENDENT
ACTIVITY

(*Math Masters*, p. 20)

 Home Connection Children read Fahrenheit thermometers marked in 1-degree intervals.

(3) Differentiation Options

READINESS

SMALL-GROUP
ACTIVITY

5–15 Min

▶ **Making a Base-10 Blocks Thermometer**

To provide experience with reading the thermometer, have children make a thermometer from base-10 blocks. On a piece of chart paper, use a marker to draw a thick, straight line that is one meter long. Children line up base-10 longs on the line. They draw a tick mark at the end of each long and mark it with the number of cubes cumulatively. For example, mark 10 after the first long, mark 20 after the second long, and so on. They then locate room temperature, body temperature, and the temperature at which water freezes and mark these on the line. The base-10 blocks can help them identify these points.

EXTRA PRACTICE

SMALL-GROUP
ACTIVITY

5–15 Min

▶ *Minute Math+*

To offer children more experience with arithmetic facts and temperature, see the following pages in *Minute Math+*: pp. 10, 41, 97, and 136 (but work with Fahrenheit temperatures only).

ELL SUPPORT

SMALL-GROUP
ACTIVITY

5–15 Min

▶ **Labeling the Thermometer**

To provide language support for temperature words, place stick-on notes with temperature words from the Math Message, such as *hot, cold, warm, cool, freezing,* and *boiling,* next to the appropriate temperatures on the Class Thermometer Poster (°F). Have children write, say, and place the labels on the poster. Children may also draw pictures to represent events at certain temperatures.

Date   Time

LESSON 1·12 Math Boxes

1. Fill in the missing numbers.

135 136 137 138

2. Fill in the oval next to the numbers that are in order from the smallest to the largest.

○ 103, 29, 86
● 29, 86, 103
○ 29, 103, 86
○ 86, 29, 103

3. Write the amount.

Ⓠ Ⓓ Ⓝ Ⓝ Ⓝ Ⓟ

51 ¢

4. Write even or odd.

4 even
7 odd
10 even
46 even

5. Write the arrow rule. Fill in the missing frames.

Rule
+5   55   60   65
      85   80   75   70

6. Fill in the blanks.

25, 35, 45, 55, 65

Math Journal 1, p. 19

Name   Date   Time

HOME LINK 1·12 Temperatures

Family Note In today's lesson, the class examined thermometers and practiced reading Fahrenheit temperatures. We began a daily routine of recording the outside temperature. If you have a nondigital thermometer at home (inside or outside), encourage your child to read the Fahrenheit temperatures to you. We will introduce Celsius temperatures in a later unit.
Please return this Home Link to school tomorrow.

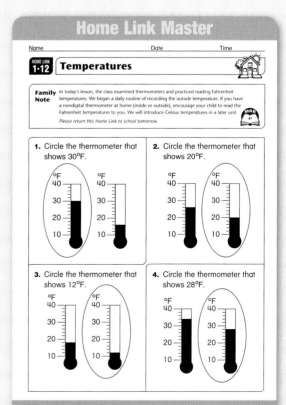

1. Circle the thermometer that shows 30°F.

2. Circle the thermometer that shows 20°F.

3. Circle the thermometer that shows 12°F.

4. Circle the thermometer that shows 28°F.

Math Masters, p. 20

Lesson 1·12 75

 **Progress Check 1**

 Objective To assess children's progress on mathematical content through the end of Unit 1.

---

1 Assessing Progress

Progress Check 1 is a cumulative assessment of concepts and skills taught in Unit 1.

See the Appendix for a complete list of Grade 2 Goals.

materials

☐ Home Link 1·12

☐ Assessment Masters (*Assessment Handbook,* pp. 154–157)

☐ slate

CONTENT ASSESSED	LESSON(S)	SELF	ORAL/SLATE	WRITTEN	
				PART A	PART B
Count up by 1s, 2s, 5s, 10s, 25s, and 100s to 1,000. [Number and Numeration Goal 1]	1·1–1·12	6	1–3	3	
Use tally marks and numerical expressions to find equivalent names for numbers. [Number and Numeration Goal 5]	1·7, 1·9, 1·11, 1·12	1	5	1, 4	
Practice and apply addition and subtraction facts through 10 + 10. [Operations and Computation Goal 1]	1·4–1·12	5			7–9
Calculate and compare values of coins and bill combinations. [Operations and Computation Goal 2]	1·2, 1·5–1·12	2		2	10
Show and tell time on an analog clock to the nearest half-hour; write time in digital notation. [Measurement and Reference Frames Goal 6]	1·3, 1·4, 1·6, 1·7, 1·9, 1·11	4		5	
Continue and describe simple numerical and nonnumerical patterns; find rules for patterns and use them to solve problems. [Patterns, Functions, and Algebra Goal 1]	1·3, 1·4, 1·7–1·10, 1·12	3	4	6	11

---

2 Building Background for Unit 2

materials

Math Boxes 1·13 previews and practices skills for Unit 2.

The **Unit 2 Family Letter** introduces families to Unit 2 topics and terms.

☐ *Math Journal 1,* p. 20

☐ Home Link Masters (*Math Masters,* pp. 21–24)

Additional Information

See *Assessment Handbook,* pages 52–59 for additional assessment information. For assessment checklists, see pages 236–239.

Technology

Assessment Management System
Progress Check 1
See the iTLG.

Getting Started

1 Assessing Progress

▶ Math Message Follow-Up

INDEPENDENT ACTIVITY

(Self Assessment, *Assessment Handbook,* p. 154)

 The Self Assessment offers children the opportunity to reflect upon their progress.

▶ Oral and Slate Assessments

SMALL-GROUP ACTIVITY

Problems 1–3 provide summative information and can be used for grading purposes. Problems 4 and 5 provide formative information that can be useful in planning future instruction.

Oral Assessment

1. Count up by 2s beginning with 0, 10, 26, and 50.

2. Count up by 5s beginning with 0, 15, 45, and 70.

3. Count up by 10s beginning with 0, 40, and 60.

Slate Assessment

4. Write the number that is ten more than (or ten less than) 15; 29; 72; 100.

5. Write another name for the number 20; 25; 50.

Assessment Master

| Name | | Date | | Time |

LESSON 1·13 | **Self Assessment** | Progress Check 1

Check one box for each skill.

Skills	I can do this by myself. I can explain how to do this.	I can do this by myself.	I can do this with help.
1. Draw tally marks.			
2. Count money.			
3. Solve number-grid puzzles.			
4. Tell and write time.			
5. Add numbers to 10.			
6. Find missing numbers on a number line.			

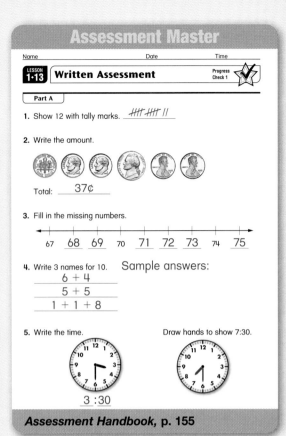

Assessment Handbook, p. 155

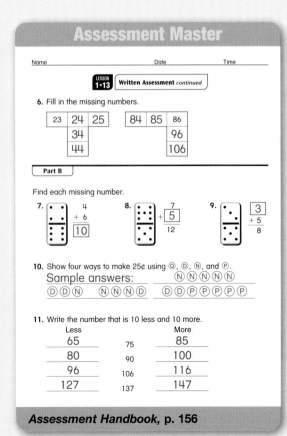

Assessment Handbook, p. 156

▶ **Written Assessment**

(*Assessment Handbook,* pp. 155 and 156)

Everyday Mathematics children are expected to master a variety of mathematical concepts and skills over time. The curriculum frequently revisits topics, concepts, and skills. For this reason, the written assessment includes items recently introduced as well as items that assess long-term retention and mastery.

The written assessment is only one part of a balanced assessment plan. Use it along with other assessment tools in the program. See the *Assessment Handbook* for additional information.

Part A   Recognizing Student Achievement

The Recognizing Student Achievement, or *summative,* part of the written assessment is designed to help teachers assess children's progress toward Grade 2 Goals. The items in this section can be used for grading purposes since the curriculum to this point has provided multiple exposures to the content of the problems that appear in this part.

Problem(s)	Description
1	Show 12 with tally marks.
2	Write the amount for a collection of coins.
3	Fill in missing numbers on a number line.
4	Write three names for 10.
5	Write the time. Draw hands to show 7:30.
6	Solve number-grid puzzles.

Part B   Informing Instruction

The Informing Instruction, or *formative,* part of the written assessment can help teachers make decisions about how best to approach concepts and skills the next time they appear. The items in this part of the written assessment are intended to inform future instruction.

Problem(s)	Description
7–9	Solve problems with addition facts.
10	Show four ways to make 25¢.
11	Write the number that is 10 less and 10 more.

▶ Open Response

(Assessment Handbook, pp. 55–59 and 157)

INDEPENDENT ACTIVITY

The Missing Locker Numbers

The open response item requires children to apply skills and concepts from Unit 1 to solve a multistep problem. See *Assessment Handbook*, pages 55–59 for rubrics and children's work samples for this problem.

---

② Building Background for Unit 2

▶ Math Boxes 1·13

(Math Journal 1, p. 20)

INDEPENDENT ACTIVITY

Mixed Practice This Math Boxes page previews Unit 2 content.

▶ Home Link 1·13: Unit 2 Family Letter

(Math Masters, pp. 21–24)

INDEPENDENT ACTIVITY

Home Connection The Unit 2 Family Letter provides parents and guardians with information and activities related to Unit 2 topics.

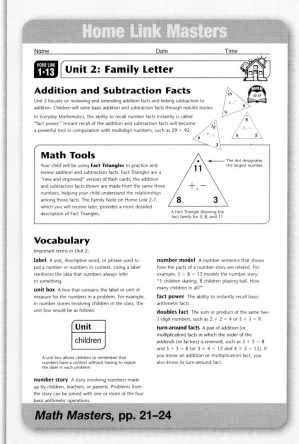

Student Page

Date _____ Time _____

LESSON 1·13 Math Boxes

1. Write 6 names for 9.

9 Sample answers:

nine	4 + 5
10 − 1	‖‖‖ ////
3 + 3 + 3	8 + 1

2. Solve.   Unit

$4 + 5 = \underline{9}$

$5 + 3 = \underline{8}$

$\begin{array}{r} 8 \\ + 5 \\ \hline 13 \end{array}$ $\begin{array}{r} 11 \\ + 5 \\ \hline 16 \end{array}$

3. Use a number grid. How many spaces from:

17 to 26? $\underline{9}$

49 to 65? $\underline{16}$

4. Solve.   Unit

$14 + 1 = \underline{15}$

$136 + 1 = \underline{137}$

$291 + 1 = \underline{292}$

$279 + 1 = \underline{280}$

5. Fill in the missing frames.

Rule +10

40 50 60

80 70

6. Solve.

$2 + \boxed{4} = 6$

Math Journal 1, p. 20

Home Link Masters

Name _____ Date _____ Time _____

HOME LINK 1·13 Unit 2: Family Letter

Addition and Subtraction Facts

Unit 2 focuses on reviewing and extending addition facts and linking subtraction to addition. Children will solve basic addition and subtraction facts through real-life stories.

In *Everyday Mathematics*, the ability to recall number facts instantly is called "fact power." Instant recall of the addition and subtraction facts will become a powerful tool in computation with multidigit numbers, such as 29 + 92.

Math Tools

Your child will be using **Fact Triangles** to practice and review addition and subtraction facts. Fact Triangles are a "new and improved" version of flash cards; the addition and subtraction facts shown are made from the same three numbers, helping your child understand the relationships among those facts. The Family Note on Home Link 2-7, which you will receive later, provides a more detailed description of Fact Triangles.

The dot designates the largest number.

11

+, −

8   3

A Fact Triangle showing the fact family for 3, 8, and 11.

Vocabulary

Important terms in Unit 2:

label A unit, descriptive word, or phrase used to put a number or numbers in context. Using a label reinforces the idea that numbers always refer to something.

unit box A box that contains the label or unit of measure for the numbers in a problem. For example, in number stories involving children in the class, the unit box would be as follows:

Unit
children

A unit box allows children to remember that numbers have a context without having to repeat the label in each problem.

number story A story involving numbers made up by children, teachers, or parents. Problems from the story can be solved with one or more of the four basic arithmetic operations.

number model A number sentence that shows how the parts of a number story are related. For example, 5 + 8 = 13 models the number story: "5 children skating. 8 children playing ball. How many children in all?"

fact power The ability to instantly recall basic arithmetic facts.

doubles fact The sum or product of the same two 1-digit numbers, such as 2 + 2 = 4 or 3 × 3 = 9.

turn-around facts A pair of addition (or multiplication) facts in which the order of the addends (or factors) is reversed, such as 3 + 5 = 8 and 5 + 3 = 8 (or 3 × 4 = 12 and 4 × 3 = 12). If you know an addition or multiplication fact, you also know its turn-around fact.

Math Masters, pp. 21–24

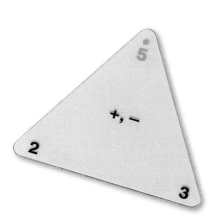

Addition and Subtraction Facts

Overview

Much of the material in this unit serves to remind children of content covered in *First Grade Everyday Mathematics*. Routines are reviewed and extended. Frequent experiences with these routines should enable children to demonstrate proficiency with addition and subtraction through 10 + 10 by the end of second grade. Subtraction is linked to addition to help children develop facility with subtraction facts. Unit 2 has three main areas of focus:

◆ To make up, represent, and solve addition and subtraction number stories,

◆ To review and apply alternative strategies for addition and subtraction, and

◆ To practice addition and subtraction facts for sums and differences up to and including 10.

Contents

Learning In Perspective

	Lesson Objectives	Links to the Past	Links to the Future
2·1	To guide children as they make up, represent, and solve addition number stories.	Children begin telling and solving number stories in Kindergarten and continue throughout first grade.	Throughout the grades, children continue to create and solve number stories.
2·2	To review +0 and +1 addition facts; and to provide practice with addition facts in which one of the addends is 0, 1, 2, or 3.	Children practice +0 and +1 facts during first grade and review addition facts in Unit 1.	Addition continues to be practiced through games and in a variety of problem-solving situations throughout second grade.
2·3	To review and provide practice for doubles facts.	Children are introduced to doubles facts during first grade and review addition facts in Unit 1.	Addition continues to be practiced through games and in a variety of problem-solving situations throughout second grade.
2·4	To review the turn-around shortcut for addition; and to discover and provide practice for a shortcut for addition facts that have 9 as an addend.	Children are introduced to the turn-around shortcut in first grade.	Throughout second grade, children practice addition facts through games and in a variety of problem-solving situations. Children continue to practice shortcuts for facts in the beginning of third grade.
2·5	To provide opportunities for children to explore and practice doubles-plus-1 and doubles-plus-2 facts.	Children practice basic addition facts in first grade and in Unit 1.	Children continue to practice shortcuts for facts and fact extensions in third grade.
2·6	To review the −0 and −1 shortcuts; and to guide children to identify the subtraction facts related to given addition facts.	Fact families are introduced in first grade using Fact Triangles. Children practice basic subtraction facts in first grade.	Fact Triangles are used for review of basic facts throughout second and third grades.
2·7	To demonstrate the inverse relationship between addition and subtraction; and to provide practice for addition and subtraction facts for sums up to and including 10.	Fact families are introduced in first grade using Fact Triangles.	Fact Triangles are used for basic fact review throughout second and third grades.
2·8	To guide children as they use a pan balance and spring scale, experience the ounce/pound relationship, and find the total number of objects in equal groups.	In first grade, children weigh objects using a pan balance and spring scale. They solve problems using the unit of pounds. Children investigate equal shares.	Children continue to investigate the concept of multiplication in third grade. In third grade, children review metric and U.S. customary units of weight.
2·9	To review the concept that a number can be named in many ways.	Children begin finding equivalent names for numbers in Kindergarten and make name-collection boxes in first grade.	Finding equivalent names for numbers is emphasized throughout the grades.
2·10	To guide children as they use a given addition or subtraction rule to generate a number sequence, and as they identify the rule for a given number sequence.	The Frames-and-Arrows routine is introduced in first grade using one rule.	Frames-and-Arrows is extended in second and third grades to incorporate more than one rule.
2·11	To provide experiences with identifying missing numbers in number pairs that are generated by a rule, and determining the rule used to generate number pairs.	Children are introduced to "What's My Rule?" problems in Kindergarten and begin using the function machine diagram in first grade.	In third grade, "What's My Rule?" problems are extended to include multiplication and division.
2·12	To review, develop, and provide practice for subtraction strategies.	Children begin learning basic subtraction facts in first grade. They also use Fact Triangles to practice subtraction facts.	Practice with subtraction facts is provided in relation to addition and through games and problem solving throughout the grades.
2·13	To guide children as they discover and practice shortcuts for subtracting 9 or 8 from any number.	Children are introduced to −9 and −8 subtraction facts in first grade.	Unit 11 provides focused practice with subtraction algorithms. A variety of subtraction algorithms are reviewed in third and fourth grades.

Key Concepts and Skills

	Key Concepts and Skills	Grade 2 Goals*
2·1	Solve number stories involving addition.	Operations and Computation Goal 1
	Write number stories that involve parts-and-total and change situations.	Operations and Computation Goal 4
	Write number models to summarize number stories.	Patterns, Functions, and Algebra Goal 2
2·2	Discuss +0 and +1 facts shortcuts.	Operations and Computation Goal 1
	Use *Beat the Calculator* to practice facts.	Operations and Computation Goal 1
	Identify patterns in addition facts.	Patterns, Functions, and Algebra Goal 1
	Identify patterns for +0 and +1 facts.	Patterns, Functions, and Algebra Goal 1
2·3	Use the Addition/Subtraction Fact Table to practice facts.	Operations and Computation Goal 1
	Solve facts involving doubles.	Operations and Computation Goal 1
	Identify patterns in the Addition/Subtraction Facts Table.	Patterns, Functions, and Algebra Goal 1
2·4	Identify and use patterns to solve +9 facts.	Patterns, Functions, and Algebra Goal 1
	Identify and use patterns on a number grid.	Patterns, Functions, and Algebra Goal 1
	Explore the turn-around rule for facts.	Patterns, Functions, and Algebra Goal 3
2·5	Practice doubles facts.	Operations and Computation Goal 1
	Develop and practice strategies for addition that use doubles facts.	Operations and Computation Goal 1
	Use doubles patterns to practice facts.	Patterns, Functions, and Algebra Goal 1
2·6	Practice subtraction facts.	Operations and Computation Goal 1
	Use dominoes to model related addition and subtraction facts.	Operations and Computation Goal 1
	Identify and use patterns to solve subtraction facts.	Patterns, Functions, and Algebra Goal 1
	Use symbols to write number sentences for fact families.	Patterns, Functions, and Algebra Goal 2
2·7	Practice basic facts in the context of Fact Triangles.	Operations and Computation Goal 1
	Use symbols to write number sentences for fact families.	Patterns, Functions, and Algebra Goal 2
	Construct fact families (using the turn-around rule for addition).	Patterns, Functions, and Algebra Goal 3
2·8	Use repeated addition to solve equal groups problems.	Operations and Computation Goal 4
	Use a spring scale to weigh objects that are about 1 pound.	Measurement and Reference Frames Goal 1
	Model the relationship between two objects.	Patterns, Functions, and Algebra Goal 2
2·9	Generate equivalent names for numbers in a name-collection box.	Number and Numeration Goal 5
	Use addition and subtraction facts in the *Name That Number* game.	Operations and Computation Goal 1
	Use symbols to write number sentences for *Name That Number.*	Patterns, Functions, and Algebra Goal 2
2·10	Practice facts in Frames-and-Arrows problems.	Operations and Computation Goal 1
	Use patterns to find rules for Frames-and-Arrows problems.	Patterns, Functions, and Algebra Goal 1
	Find missing numbers and rules for Frames-and-Arrows problems.	Patterns, Functions, and Algebra Goal 1
	Count on and back by 1s, 2s, 3s, 5s, and 10s.	Number and Numeration Goal 1
2·11	Practice facts in "What's My Rule?" problems.	Operations and Computation Goal 1
	Use patterns to find rules for "What's My Rule?" problems.	Patterns, Functions, and Algebra Goal 1
	Find missing numbers and rules for "What's My Rule?" problems.	Patterns, Functions, and Algebra Goal 1
2·12	Count up and back by 1s.	Number and Numeration Goal 1
	Use addition and subtraction facts to solve subtraction problems.	Operations and Computation Goal 1
	Use Fact Triangles to practice facts.	Operations and Computation Goal 1
	Use counting-up and counting-back strategies for subtraction.	Operations and Computation Goal 2
2·13	Solve −8 and −9 subtraction facts.	Operations and Computation Goal 1
	Use −8 and −9 facts to solve 2-digit by 1-digit subtraction problems.	Operations and Computation Goal 2
	Use patterns in subtraction facts to solve −8 and −9 facts.	Patterns, Functions, and Algebra Goal 1

* For a detailed listing of all Grade 2 Goals, see the Appendix.

Ongoing Learning and Practice

Math Boxes

Math Boxes are paired across lessons as shown in the brackets below. This makes them useful as assessment tools. Math Boxes also preview content of the next unit.

Mixed practice	[2•1, 2•3], [2•2, 2•4], [2•5, 2•7], [2•6, 2•8], [2•9, 2•11, 2•13], [2•10, 2•12]
Mixed practice with multiple choice	2•1, 2•2, 2•5, 2•6, 2•8, 2•9, 2•10, 2•13
Mixed practice with writing/reasoning opportunity	2•3, 2•4, 2•7, 2•8, 2•11, 2•12

Practice through Games

Games are an essential component of practice in the *Everyday Mathematics* program. Games offer skills practice and promote strategic thinking.

Lesson	Game	Skill Practiced
2•2, 2•4, 2•6, 2•8, 2•12	*Beat the Calculator*	**Addition facts** Operations and Computation Goal 1 Number and Numeration Goal 1
2•2, 2•5, 2•6	*Domino Top-It*	**Addition facts and comparing sums** Operations and Computation Goal 1 Number and Numeration Goal 1
2•3	*Doubles or Nothing*	**Addition facts with emphasis on doubles** Operations and Computation Goal 1
2•9, 2•10	*Name That Number*	**Addition and subtraction facts** Number and Numeration Goal 5; Operations and Computation Goal 1; Patterns, Functions, and Algebra Goal 2
2•9	*Two-Fisted Penny Addition*	**Addition; counting** Operations and Computation Goal 1 Number and Numeration Goal 1
2•12	*Difference Game*	**Subtraction facts; counting** Operations and Computation Goal 1
2•12	*Number-Grid Difference Game*	**Subtraction facts** Operations and Computation Goal 1

See the *Differentiation Handbook* for ways to adapt games to meet children's needs.

Home Communication

Home Links provide homework and home communication.

◄ *Home Connection Handbook* provides more ideas to communicate effectively with parents.

Unit 2 Family Letter provides families with an overview, Do-Anytime Activities, Building Skills Through Games, and a list of vocabulary.

Problem Solving

Encourage children to use a variety of strategies to solve problems and to explain those strategies. Strategies that children might use in this unit:

- ◆ Identifying and using patterns
- ◆ Working backward
- ◆ Using pictures and models
- ◆ Using manipulatives
- ◆ Using number models

Lessons that teach through *problem solving, not just* about *problem solving*

Lesson	Activity
2◆1	Write addition number stories.
2◆1	Solve number-grid puzzles.
2◆3	Explore Addition/Subtraction Facts Table.
2◆6	Use dominoes to generate related addition and subtraction facts.
2◆7	Identify fact families on Fact Triangles.
2◆10	Determine a pattern in a number sequence and state the rule.
2◆11	Solve "What's My Rule?" problems.
2◆12	Count back and count up for subtraction.

See Chapter 18 in the *Teacher's Reference Manual* for more information about problem solving.

Planning Tips

Pacing

Pacing depends on a number of factors, such as children's individual needs and how long your school has been using *Everyday Mathematics*. At the beginning of Unit 2, review your *Content by Strand* Poster to help you set a monthly pace.

←— MOST CLASSROOMS —→

SEPTEMBER	OCTOBER	NOVEMBER

NCTM Standards

Unit 2 Lessons	2◆1	2◆2	2◆3	2◆4	2◆5	2◆6	2◆7	2◆8	2◆9	2◆10	2◆11	2◆12	2◆13
NCTM Standards	1, 2, 6–8	1, 2, 6–8	1–3, 6, 7	1, 2, 6–8	1–3, 6–8	1, 2, 6–9	1, 2, 4–10	1, 2, 4, 6–9	1, 2, 6–10	1–3, 6–8, 10	1, 2, 4, 6–8, 10	1–3, 5–10	1–3, 6–8

Content Standards: **1** Number and Operations, **2** Algebra, **3** Geometry, **4** Measurement, **5** Data Analysis and Probability
Process Standards: **6** Problem Solving, **7** Reasoning and Proof, **8** Communication, **9** Connections, **10** Representation

Balanced Assessment

Ongoing Assessment

Recognizing Student Achievement

Opportunities to assess children's progress toward Grade 2 Goals:

Lesson	Content Assessed
2•1	Represent an "easy facts" number story using words, drawings, or tallies. [Operations and Computation Goal 1]
2•2	Record addition facts. [Operations and Computation Goal 1]
2•3	Count back by 5s. [Number and Numeration Goal 1]
2•4	Solve +0 and +1 facts. [Operations and Computation Goal 1]
2•5	Record doubles facts. [Operations and Computation Goal 1]
2•6	Recall and understand turn-around facts. [Patterns, Functions, and Algebra Goal 3]
2•7	Write a number story to explain a number sentence. [Patterns, Functions, and Algebra Goal 2]
2•8	Count by 1s on a number grid. [Patterns, Functions, and Algebra Goal 1]
2•9	Write addition and subtraction number sentences; generate equivalent names for a given number. [Number and Numeration Goal 5]
2•10	Extend a numeric pattern using addition and subtraction. [Patterns, Functions, and Algebra Goal 1]
2•11	Find missing numbers for "What's My Rule?" problems. [Patterns, Functions, and Algebra Goal 1]
2•12	Write a fact family from a Fact Triangle. [Operations and Computation Goal 1]
2•13	Demonstrate understanding of the − and = symbols in solving subtraction problems. [Patterns, Functions, and Algebra Goal 2]

Use the **Assessment Management System** to collect and analyze data about children's progress throughout the year.

Informing Instruction

To anticipate common child errors and to highlight problem-solving strategies:

Lesson 2•1   Work with unit boxes

Lesson 2•2   Find distances on a number grid

Lesson 2•3   Locate a cell on the Facts Table

Lesson 2•8   Make equal groups of objects

Periodic Assessment

2♦14 Progress Check 2

CONTENT ASSESSED	ASSESSMENT ITEMS			
	Self	Oral/Slate	Written	Open Response
Skip count forward by twos [Number and Numeration Goal 1]				✔
Read, write, and model with manipulatives whole numbers up to 10,000; identify the value of digits in numbers. [Number and Numeration Goal 2]		✔	✔	
Use tally marks and numerical expressions involving addition and subtraction to give equivalent names for whole numbers. [Number and Numeration Goal 5]	✔		✔	
Demonstrate automaticity with +/−0, +/−1, doubles, and sum-equals-ten facts, and proficiency with all addition and subtraction facts through 10 + 10. [Operations and Computation Goal 1]	✔	✔	✔	
Calculate and compare values of coins and bills. [Operations and Computation Goal 2]			✔	
Use graphs to ask and answer simple questions and draw conclusions. [Data and Chance Goal 2]			✔	
Extend numeric patterns; describe rules for patterns and use them to solve problems; describe, write and use rules for functions involving addition and subtraction. [Patterns, Functions, and Algebra Goal 1]	✔		✔	✔
Describe the Commutative Property of Addition and apply it to mental arithmetic problems. [Patterns, Functions, and Algebra Goal 3]			✔	

Portfolio Opportunities

Some opportunities to gather samples of children's mathematical writings, drawings, and creations to add balance to the assessment process:

- Writing number stories, **Lesson 2♦1**
- Determining the greater number, **Lesson 2♦3**
- Describing skip counts, **Lesson 2♦4**
- Recording doubles facts, **Lesson 2♦5**
- Designing a Doubles Facts Book, **Lesson 2♦5**

- Using addition facts, **Lesson 2♦7**
- Describing patterns, **Lesson 2♦8**
- Paying with the least amount of coins, **Lesson 2♦11**
- Using double facts, **Lesson 2♦12**

Assessment Handbook

Unit 2 Assessment Support

- Grade 2 Goals, pp. 37–50
- Unit 2 Assessment Overview, pp. 60–67

- Unit 2 Open Response
  - Detailed rubric, p. 64
  - Sample student responses, pp. 65–67

Unit 2 Assessment Masters

- Unit 2 Self Assessment, p. 158
- Unit 2 Written Assessment, pp. 159–161
- Unit 2 Open Response, p. 162
- Unit 2 Class Checklist, pp. 242, 243, and 293
- Unit 2 Individual Profile of Progress, pp. 240, 241, and 292

- Exit Slip, p. 295
- Math Logs, pp. 298–300
- Other Student Assessment Forms, pp. 296, 297, 301, 302, and 303

Differentiated Instruction

Daily Lesson Support

ENGLISH LANGUAGE LEARNERS

- **2•3** Building a Math Word Bank
- **2•4** Building a Math Word Bank
- **2•7** Making a fact family chain
- **2•12** Building a Math Word Bank

EXTRA PRACTICE

- **2•3** Writing doubles facts

Minute Math®+ **2•4** Using shortcuts for subtraction facts; **2•8** Exploring time, weight, volume, length, and area; **2•12** Solving addition and subtraction problems; **2•13** Using shortcuts for subtraction facts

READINESS

- **2•1** Solving addition number stories
- **2•2** Practicing addition facts
- **2•3** Practicing doubles addition facts
- **2•4** Solving +9 addition facts
- **2•5** Creating a Doubles Facts Book
- **2•6** Exploring addition and subtraction facts
- **2•7** Representing subtraction with counters
- **2•8** Comparing weights of two objects
- **2•9** Finding equivalent names for numbers
- **2•10** Exploring counting patterns
- **2•11** Identifying rules by sorting attributes
- **2•12** Practicing finding differences
- **2•13** Using a ten-frame card

ENRICHMENT

- **2•1** Creating a number-story bulletin board
- **2•2** Creating +0 and +1 number stories
- **2•3** Explaining patterns in the Facts Table
- **2•5** Exploring doubles facts
- **2•6** Exploring subtraction
- **2•7** Finding mystery numbers
- **2•8** Estimating and measuring weight
- **2•9** Finding names for facts
- **2•10** Solving Frames-and-Arrows problems
- **2•11** Creating "What's My Rule?" tables
- **2•12** Using a number grid to find differences

Adjusting the Activity

- **2•1** Representing number stories
- **2•1** Completing number-grid puzzles
- **2•2** Playing *Beat the Calculator*
- **2•3** Using a visual reminder **ELL**
- **2•4** Finding turn-around facts
- **2•4** Using a hand gesture **ELL**
- **2•4** Demonstrating the +9 shortcut **ELL**
- **2•6** Modeling change-to-less stories **ELL**
- **2•6** Recognizing subtraction facts
- **2•7** Practicing with Fact Triangles

- **2•8** Using a pan balance
- **2•9** Playing *Name That Number*
- **2•9** Solving pan-balance problems
- **2•10** Using a visual model **ELL**
- **2•10** Solving Frames-and-Arrows problems
- **2•11** Solving "What's My Rule?" problems
- **2•12** Counting up and back to solve problems **ELL**
- **2•13** Demonstrating the −9 shortcut **ELL**
- **2•13** Practicing −9 and −8 shortcuts

AUDITORY ♦ KINESTHETIC ♦ TACTILE ♦ VISUAL

⟳ Cross-Curricular Links

Literature

Lesson 2•3 Children read *Two of Everything: A Chinese Folktale* and write doubles facts.

Language

Lesson 2•9 Children learn how to say *eight* in different languages.

Using the Projects

Choose any of Projects 1 through 3 to introduce your class to the Projects during Unit 2. In Project 1, your class will name fractional parts, practice following directions, and use paper-folding techniques to make paper boxes. Project 2 provides an opportunity for children to read thermometers and to observe and collect data on weather conditions. Project 3 is an introduction to the 12-year cycle of the Chinese calendar.

Differentiation Handbook

See the *Differentiation Handbook* for materials on Unit 2.

Language Support

Everyday Mathematics provides lesson-specific suggestions to help all children, including non-native English speakers, to acquire, process, and express mathematical ideas.

Connecting Math and Literacy

Lesson 2✦1 *Math For All Seasons,* by Gregory Tang, Scholastic Press, 2002

Lesson 2✦1 *Mission: Addition,* by Loreen Leedy, Holiday House, 1999

Lesson 2✦3 *Two of Everything: A Chinese Folktale,* by Lily Toy Hong, Albert Whitman and Company, 1993

Lesson 2✦9 *12 Ways to Get to 11,* by Eve Merriam, Aladdin Paperbacks, 1996

Lesson 2✦12 *The Hershey's Kisses Subtraction Book,* by Jerry Pallotta, Cartwheel, 2002

 My Reference Book
   pp. 16, 27, 100, 101, 122–125, 130, 131, and 138–141

Multiage Classroom ✦ Companion Lessons

Companion Lessons from Grades 1 and 3 can help you meet instructional needs of a multiage classroom. The full Scope and Sequence can be found in the Appendix.

Grade 1	1✦13, 5✦6– 5✦8	4✦11, 6✦3, 6✦4	4✦11, 5✦10, 6✦1	4✦11, 6✦1	4✦12, 5✦10, 6✦1	3✦6, 5✦6, 6✦1	6✦3, 6✦4	5✦4, 5✦5	6✦2, 9✦8	3✦8, 3✦9	5✦11, 5✦12 6✦8	3✦6, 6✦5, 9✦2	3✦6, 6✦5, 9✦2
Grade 2	2✦1	2✦2	2✦3	2✦4	2✦5	2✦6	2✦7	2✦8	2✦9	2✦10	2✦11	2✦12	2✦13
Grade 3	2✦4, 2✦6	2✦1, 2✦2	2✦1, 2✦2	2✦1, 2✦2	2✦1, 2✦2	1✦8	2✦1	4✦1, 4✦3, 10✦3	1✦6, 8✦5		2✦3	1✦8, 2✦2, 2✦8	1✦8, 2✦2, 2✦8

Professional Development

Teacher's Reference Manual Links

Lesson	Topic	Section		Lesson	Topic	Section
2✦1	Addition and Subtraction use classes	10.2.1		**2✦8**	Weight and Mass	14.6
					Visual Patterns	17.1.1
	Number stroies	18.4.1		**2✦9**	Name-Collection Boxes	9.7.3
2✦2	Basic facts and Fact Power	16.3.2		**2✦10**	Functions	17.1.4
	Number and Counting Tools	3.2.1			Frames and Arrows Deagrams	1.3.2
2✦3	Fact Practice	16.3.3		**2✦11**	"What's My Rule?"/Function Machines	1.3.7
	Operations and Number Models Tools	10.3			Functions	17.1.4
2✦4	Games for Fact Practice	16.3.4		**2✦12**	Subtraction Algorithms	11.2.2
2✦5	Fact Practice	16.3.3				

Materials

Lesson	Masters	Manipulative Kit Items	Other Items
2•1	Home Link Master, p. 25 Teaching Aid Master, p. 419	slate	stick or strip of paper; 10 pennies or collection of small objects
2•2	Home Link 2•1; Teaching Aid Masters, pp. 415 and 419; Home Link Master, p. 26	dominoes; slate; calculator	large paper triangles*
2•3	Home Link 2•2; Teaching Aid Masters, pp. 420* and 421; transparency of *Math Masters*, p. 421*; Home Link Master, p. 27; Game Master, p. 456	per group: 4 each of number cards 1–10; penny stamp; slate calculator	pennies and/or cubes; colored pencils; Class Facts Table; *Two of Everything: A Chinese Folktale*
2•4	Home Link 2•3; Home Link Master, p. 28; Teaching Aid Master, p. 422		Class Number Grid Poster; 19 counters; Class Facts Table
2•5	Home Link 2•4; Home Link Master, p. 29 Teaching Master, p. 30	per group: 1 set of dominoes; pattern blocks; Pattern-Block Template; slate; calculator	envelope; paper and pencil; scissors
2•6	Home Link 2•5; Teaching Aid Master, p. 415; Home Link Master, p. 31; Teaching Masters, pp. 32 and 33	dominoes; dice; number line; slate; calculator	10 counters and 10 cubes*
2•7	Home Link 2•6 Home Link Masters, pp. 34 and 35 Teaching Master, p. 36 transparency of *Math Master*, p. 423* Teaching Aid Master, p. 415	number line dominoes* slate calculator	Fact Triangles cut from *Math Journal 1*, Activity Sheets 1 and 2 (see Lesson 2•5); 18 pennies or other counters per group; 8 1/2 x 11 paper
2•8	Home Link 2•7 Teaching Master, p. 37 Home Link Masters, pp. 38 and 39 *Math Master*, p. 416	tape measure six-sided dice spring scale	pennies; objects weighing between $\frac{1}{2}$ oz and 8 oz; pan balance; plastic bag; 6 quarter-sheets of paper; 1 sheet of plain paper; 36 counters; class number grid
2•9	Home Link 2•8; Game Master, p. 462; Home Link Masters, pp. 40 and 41; Teaching Master, p. 42; Teaching Aid Master, p. 422*	per group: 4 each of number; cards 1–10, 1 each of number cards 11–20; slate	10 pennies; half-sheet of paper; pan balance*
2•10	Home Link 2•9; transparency of *Math Masters*, p. 43*; Home Link Masters, pp. 44 and 45; Game Master, p. 462*; Teaching Master, p. 46; Teaching Aid Master, p. 424	number cards 0–9	counters, number line, or number grid*
2•11	Home Link 2•10; transparencies of *Math Masters*, pp. 425 and 426*; Home Link Masters, pp. 47 and 48; Teaching Aid Master, p. 426		envelope with Fact Triangles (from Lesson 2•5); number grid
2•12	Home Link 2•11 Home Link Master, p. 49 Game Master, p. 463	number cards 0–10; slate; calculator	envelope with Fact Triangles (from Lesson 2•5); per group: 40 pennies or markers; scissors; number grid; counters*
2•13	Home Link 2•12 Teaching Aid Masters, pp. 415 and 422 Home Link Masters, pp. 50 and 51	slate	18 counters per child; envelopes with Fact; Triangles (from Lessons 2•5 and 2•12); Number Grid Poster*; half-sheets of paper
2•14	Home Link 2•13 Assessment Masters, pp. 158–162 Home Link Masters, pp. 52–55	slate	

* Denotes optional materials

Technology
Assessment Management System, Unit 2
iTLG, Unit 2

Mathematical Background

The discussion below highlights the major content ideas presented in Unit 2 and helps establish instructional priorities.

Addition Number Stories

(Lesson 2◆1 and following)

Throughout *Everyday Mathematics,* children are encouraged to make up and solve number stories. In Unit 2, these stories are used to show that numbers are usually used in context, which we indicate by using a label or a unit. Labels are recorded in a unit box—a device used to give context to number models and to sets of practice problems.

You should write number models on the board as your class solves number stories, but do not require children to write number models at this stage. Be aware of the types of addition and subtraction number stories, but do not teach children to categorize problems at this time. In Unit 2, our goal is to show children these different types of problems. More formal discussions through diagrams will take place in later units.

Most addition number stories that children make up will be of two types:

◆ *Parts-and-total,* in which two or more separate parts are known, and the total is to be found. *For example:* "Beth has 7 dollars. Joe has 6 dollars. How many dollars in all?"

◆ *Change-to-more,* in which there is a starting quantity. The starting quantity is increased, and the new quantity is to be found. *For example:* "Beth has 7 dollars. Joe gives her 6 dollars. How many dollars does Beth have now?"

$$4 \text{ cups} + 3 \text{ cups} = 7 \text{ cups}$$

or

$$4 + 3 = 7$$

Unit
cups

Children use numbers in context. The unit box is a shortcut to assigning each number a label.

 PROFESSIONAL DEVELOPMENT You can read more about unit boxes in the Management Guide, which is located in the *Teacher's Reference Manual,* Section 1.3.6.

Addition and Subtraction Facts

(Lesson 2◆2 and following)

In *Everyday Mathematics,* the ability to recall number facts instantly is called *fact power.* Instant recall is indeed a powerful tool, for it facilitates computation with multidigit numbers. Fact power is also essential in solving multistep problems.

Lessons 2-2 and 2-3 quickly review "easy" addition facts: 0-facts, 1-facts, and doubles—44 facts in all. This leaves 56 remaining facts. Because these 56 facts include all of the turn-around facts, such as $2 + 3 = 5$ and $3 + 2 = 5$, there are really only 28 other facts that children need to learn.

Lessons 2-4 and 2-5 develop strategies for remembering most of these facts, such as the +9 shortcut and the doubles-plus-1 and doubles-plus-2 strategies.

The inverse relationship of subtraction to addition forms the basis for the study of the subtraction facts. This relationship is first established by observing patterns on dominoes (Lesson 2-6) and then on Fact Triangle flashcards (Lesson 2-7). Children then use Fact Triangles to generate fact families, which are sets of related addition and subtraction facts, for example, $4 + 5 = 9$, $5 + 4 = 9$, $9 - 5 = 4$, and $9 - 4 = 5$.

Subtraction strategies for harder subtraction facts (subtracting 8 and 9 from a number, known algebraically as $n - 8$ and $n - 9$) are discussed in Lesson 2-13.

Since addition and subtraction facts are the main focus of this unit, it is suggested that you hold frequent oral drills. This gives children a chance to practice with the facts and provides you with one way to assess their progress.

 PROFESSIONAL DEVELOPMENT Section 16.3.2 in the *Teacher's Reference Manual* can provide you with more information about basic facts and fact power.

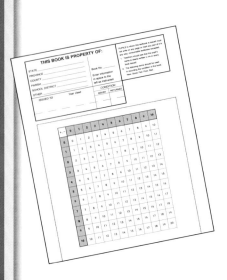

Zero-facts and doubles facts are two of the shortcuts children learn to help them recall "easy" addition facts.

Subtraction Number Stories

(Lesson 2◆6 and following)

Most subtraction number stories that children make up will be of two types:

◆ *Change-to-less,* in which there is a starting quantity. The quantity is decreased, and the new quantity is to be found. *For example:* "Bob has 10 model cars. He lost 3 of them. How many model cars does Bob have now?"

◆ *Comparison,* in which two separate quantities are compared by finding the difference (distance) between them. *For example:* "Bob has 10 model cars. Amit has 3 model cars. How many more model cars does Bob have?"

Again, you will want to expose children to these types of number stories, but do not ask children to categorize the stories by type at this time.

 PROFESSIONAL DEVELOPMENT Section 18.4.1 in the *Teacher's Reference Manual* provides more information about solving number stories.

Exploring Weights, Scales, Equal Groups (Lesson 2•8)

Another essential part of the program, Explorations, is continued in Lesson 2-8. Explorations provide children with access to limited manipulative materials and, along with projects, provide group problem-solving activities.

Two Explorations in Lesson 2-8 offer experiences with a pan balance and a spring scale. By using the scale, children develop an awareness of the relationship between a pound and an ounce. Children use counters during the partner activity "Egg Nests" to develop the basic idea of multiplication.

 See Chapter 14 in the *Teacher's Reference Manual* for more information about measurement concepts.

Frames-and-Arrows, "What's My Rule?", and Name-Collection Boxes (Lessons 2•9, 2•10, and 2•11)

Unit 2 extends other ideas introduced in *First Grade Everyday Mathematics:*

◆ *Frames-and-Arrows problems* provide experience with number sequences and their rules.

Frames and Arrows

◆ *"What's My Rule?" problems* develop the concept of a function—a rule relating the numbers in a number pair.

◆ *Name-collection boxes* stress that one number has many equivalent names. The fact that there are many ways to say the same number is a fundamental concept in mathematics.

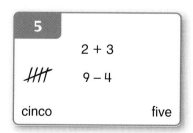

Name-collection box

 See Sections 9.7.3, 17.1.4, 1.3.2, and 1.3.7, located in the *Teacher's Reference Manual,* for additional information about these topics.

Children use a spring scale to find a set of objects whose combined weight is about 1 pound.

in	out
12	17
4	9
0	5
10	15
7	12
3	8

"What's My Rule?" table

2·1

Addition Number Stories

 Objective To guide children as they make up, represent, and solve addition number stories.

---

1 Teaching the Lesson — materials

Key Activities

Children review the need for labels to put numbers in context. They make up and solve addition number stories.

Key Concepts and Skills

• Solve number stories involving addition.
  [Operations and Computation Goal 1]

• Write number stories that involve parts-and-total and change situations.
  [Operations and Computation Goal 4]

• Write number models to summarize number stories.
  [Patterns, Functions, and Algebra Goal 2]

Key Vocabulary

addition number story • label • unit box • number model

✔ **Ongoing Assessment: Informing Instruction** See page 96.

✔ **Ongoing Assessment: Recognizing Student Achievement** Use journal page 21.
  [Operations and Computation Goal 1]

☐ *Math Journal 1,* p. 21

---

2 Ongoing Learning & Practice — materials

Children complete number-grid puzzles.

Children practice and maintain skills through Math Boxes and Home Link activities.

☐ *Math Journal 1,* pp. 22 and 23
☐ Home Link Master (*Math Masters,* p. 25)

---

3 Differentiation Options — materials

READINESS

Children solve addition number stories using a concrete model.

ENRICHMENT

Children create a bulletin board or book to display addition number stories.

☐ Teaching Aid Master (*Math Masters,* p. 419)
☐ slate
☐ stick or a strip of paper
☐ 10 pennies or a collection of small objects

Technology

Assessment Management System
Journal page 21
See the **iTLG.**

Getting Started

Mental Math and Reflexes

Pose simple distances on the number grid problems. *Suggestions:* How many spaces from:

◉○○ 21 to 31? 10   ◉◉○ 37 to 42? 5   ◉◉◉ 53 to 41? 12

      17 to 27? 10   35 to 64? 29   134 to 146? 12

Math Message

5 children are skating.

8 children are playing ball.

How many children in all? 13

---

1. Teaching the Lesson

▶ Math Message Follow-Up

WHOLE-CLASS ACTIVITY

Ask children to share their strategies for answering the question. Children may count on their fingers, make tallies for 5 and 8 and count them, or add 5 and 8 mentally and announce the total.

Write "5 children + 8 children = 13 children" under the Math Message and say that this is one way to show an **addition number story.** Discuss the idea that numbers almost always occur in context and have a **label.** Labels can be the name of a thing (for example, books) or a measurement unit (for example, hours). The word *label* can be used as a verb when we ask children to "label their answers" and as a noun when we refer to the "label on a can." To support English language learners, discuss these subtle differences.

Talk about writing a label for the numbers in the story in a **unit box** so you won't have to repeat the label. Using a unit box, the Math Message story can be shown this way: 5 + 8 = 13. Mention that 5 + 8 = 13 is called a **number model** for the story.

▶ Making Up and Solving Addition Number Stories

WHOLE-CLASS ACTIVITY

Ask children to make up addition number stories. Do the following for several stories:

1. Write the story on the board, or draw a picture to represent the story.

2. Draw an empty unit box under the story.

3. Have children write a label in the unit box and share how they would answer the question in the story.

4. Ask a volunteer to write a number model for the story.

NOTE Children are not expected to categorize addition number stories as parts-and-total or change-to-more at this time. Later lessons will include practice with both types of addition number stories.

2 ways to show a number story.

One way:

     5 children + 8 children = 13 children

Another way:

Unit

children

5 + 8 = 13

Most of the stories children make up will probably belong in one of these two categories:

Parts-and-Total

Two or more separate parts are known. Find the total.

For example: Beth has 7 dollars. Joe has 6 dollars. How many dollars do they have in all?

Change-to-More

Start with a number of things. Increase the number of things. Find how many things there are now.

For example: Beth has 7 dollars. Joe gives her 6 dollars. How many dollars does she have now?

 Adjusting the Activity

Have children represent their story using pictures or tallies, for example, ⧄⧄⧄⧄ / sitting. /// standing. How many in all? 9

A U D I T O R Y ◆ K I N E S T H E T I C ◆ T A C T I L E ◆ V I S U A L

▶ **Writing Number Stories**

(*Math Journal 1*, p. 21)

INDEPENDENT ACTIVITY

Children continue to make up and solve an addition number story by completing the journal page.

Examples:

Parts-and-Total Stories

● 7 ducks are swimming. 5 ducks are on the grass. How many ducks are there in all? 12 ducks; 7 + 5 = 12

● 6 children are sitting. 3 children are walking. How many children are there in all? 9 children; 6 + 3 = 9

Change-to-More Stories

● 7 ducks are swimming. 5 ducks enter the pond. How many ducks are swimming now? 12 ducks; 7 + 5 = 12

● 6 children are sitting. 3 children who were walking sit down. How many children are sitting now? 9 children; 6 + 3 = 9

NOTE While the focus of this lesson is on addition number stories, some children may write number stories for the picture that involve subtraction.

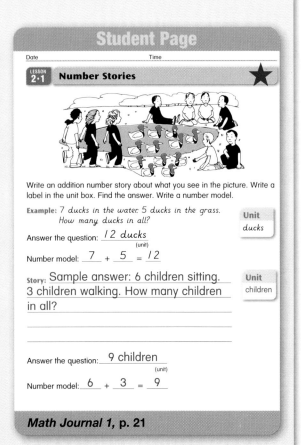

Student Page

Date _____ Time _____

LESSON 2·1 **Number Stories** ★

Write an addition number story about what you see in the picture. Write a label in the unit box. Find the answer. Write a number model.

Example: *7 ducks in the water. 5 ducks in the grass. How many ducks in all?*

Answer the question: _12 ducks_
                        (unit)

Number model: _7_ + _5_ = _12_

Story: Sample answer: 6 children sitting. 3 children walking. How many children in all?

Answer the question: _9 children_
                        (unit)

Number model: _6_ + _3_ = _9_

Unit
ducks

Unit
children

Math Journal 1, p. 21

Ongoing Assessment: Informing Instruction

Watch for children who put a number in the unit box. Daily use of a unit box during math time will give children practice with this skill. Assign a child each day to decide what the unit for the day will be. Children can choose to use the classroom unit or pick their own.

Student Page

Date _____ Time _____

Lorem

Ongoing Assessment:
Recognizing Student Achievement

Journal
page 21 ★

Use **journal page 21** to assess children's ability to write number stories using "easy" facts. Children are making adequate progress if they are able to represent an "easy" facts number story using words, drawings, or tallies; write a number model to represent their story; answer the question correctly; and complete the unit box. Some children will be able to complete all the number story components using larger numbers.

[Operations and Computation Goal 1]

2 Ongoing Learning & Practice

▶ ## Completing Number-Grid Puzzles
INDEPENDENT ACTIVITY

(*Math Journal,* p. 22)

Number-grid puzzles were introduced in Lesson 1-9.

If children are able to complete the first grid but not the second, tell them to ignore the digits in the hundreds place for the numbers in the second grid. Guide children by saying the following:

● What number comes after 332?

● Ignore the hundreds. Which number comes after 32? (Write 33 in the next space on the grid.)

● Now remember the hundreds place and write 3 in front of the 33.

● The number that comes after 332 is 333.

Adjusting the Activity

Provide additional clues for filling in the number-grid puzzles by filling in several of the blue cells. Children can also use their calculators to find 1 more, 1 less, 10 more, and 10 less.

AUDITORY ◆ KINESTHETIC ◆ TACTILE ◆ VISUAL

▶ ## Math Boxes 2•1
INDEPENDENT ACTIVITY

(*Math Journal 1,* p. 23)

Mixed Practice Math Boxes in this lesson are paired with Math Boxes in Lesson 2-3. The skill in Problem 6 previews Unit 3 content.

Student Page

Date _____ Time _____

LESSON
2•1 **Number-Grid Puzzles**

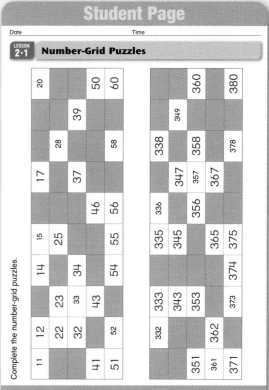

Math Journal 1, p. 22

Student Page

Date _____ Time _____

LESSON
2•1 **Math Boxes**

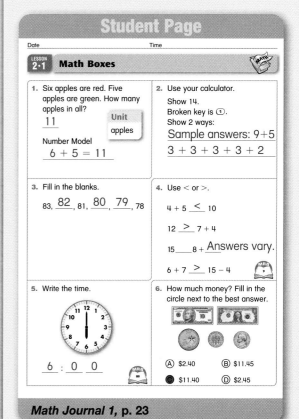

Math Journal 1, p. 23

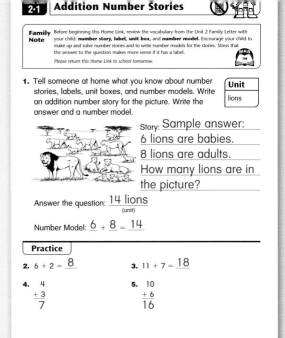

2-1 Addition Number Stories

Family Note Before beginning this Home Link, review the vocabulary from the Unit 2 Family Letter with your child: **number story, label, unit box,** and **number model.** Encourage your child to make up and solve number stories and to write number models for the stories. Stress that the answer to the question makes more sense if it has a label.

Please return this Home Link to school tomorrow.

1. Tell someone at home what you know about number stories, labels, unit boxes, and number models. Write an addition number story for the picture. Write the answer and a number model.

Unit
lions

Story: Sample answer:
6 lions are babies.
8 lions are adults.
How many lions are in the picture?

Answer the question: 14 lions
(unit)

Number Model: 6 + 8 = 14

Practice

2. 6 + 2 = 8

3. 11 + 7 = 18

4. 4
   + 3

   7

5. 10
   + 6

   16

Math Masters, p. 25

Teaching Aid Master

Name	Date	Time

A Number Story

Unit

Math Masters, p. 419

(Math Masters, p. 25)

Home Connection Since the vocabulary in today's lesson consists of terms that will be used throughout the year, it is important to share their meanings with children's families. Home Link 2-1 suggests that children explain these terms to someone at home. The Unit 2 Family Letter explains the terms.

3 Differentiation Options

READINESS

SMALL-GROUP ACTIVITY

▶ **Joining Objects**

5–15 Min

To provide experience with solving number stories using a concrete model, have children model addition number stories with counters on their slates. Children place dividers in the middle of their slates. Tell a number story. For example, say, "I had 5 shells. Then my mom gave me 3 more." Children place 5 objects on one side of the divider and 3 objects on the other. Have children remove the divider, combine the two parts and count the number of objects. Ask: *How many shells do I now have all together?* 8 Repeat with different number stories as needed.

ENRICHMENT

PARTNER ACTIVITY

▶ **Making a Number Stories Bulletin Board or Book**

15–30 Min

(Math Masters, p. 419)

To apply children's understanding of addition number stories, have them make up their own number stories. One partner tells the story and the other partner records the story by drawing pictures, writing words, or both. Partners then reverse roles and repeat the activity. Collect the stories for a bulletin board display or a classroom book. During the next few days, use some of these number stories during Mental Math and Reflexes.

As an alternative, children can make their own number stories book. Stories can be laminated and placed in the class library for silent reading time.

2·2 Review "Easy" Addition Facts

 Objectives To review +0 and +1 addition facts; and to provide practice with addition facts in which one of the addends is 0, 1, 2, or 3.

---

1 Teaching the Lesson

materials

Key Activities
Children make up addition stories, review the meaning of addition facts and the +0 and the +1 shortcuts, and review "easy" addition facts by playing *Beat the Calculator*.

Key Concepts and Skills
- Discuss +0 and +1 facts shortcuts.
  [Operations and Computation Goal 1]
- Use *Beat the Calculator* to practice facts.
  [Operations and Computation Goal 1]
- Identify patterns in addition facts.
  [Patterns, Functions, and Algebra Goal 1]
- Identify patterns for +0 and +1 facts.
  [Patterns, Functions, and Algebra Goal 1]

Key Vocabulary
addition fact • +0 facts • +1 facts • +0 shortcut • +1 shortcut • fact power

✔ **Ongoing Assessment: Recognizing Student Achievement** Use an Exit Slip.
  [Operations and Computation Goal 1]

- ☐ *Math Journal 1*, p. 24
- ☐ *My Reference Book*, pp. 124 and 125
- ☐ Home Link 2·1
- ☐ Teaching Aid Master (*Math Masters*, p. 415)
- ☐ slate
- ☐ 1 calculator per child
- ☐ large paper triangles (optional)

See Advance Preparation

---

2 Ongoing Learning & Practice

materials

Children find distances on a number grid.
Children practice and maintain skills through Math Boxes and Home Link activities.
✔ **Ongoing Assessment: Informing Instruction** See page 103.

- ☐ *Math Journal 1*, pp. 25 and 26
- ☐ Home Link Master (*Math Masters*, p. 26)

---

3 Differentiation Options

materials

READINESS

Children play *Domino Top-It* to practice addition facts.

ENRICHMENT

Children create +0 and +1 number stories.

- ☐ *My Reference Book*, pp. 122 and 123
- ☐ Teaching Aid Master (*Math Masters*, p. 419)
- ☐ dominoes

Additional Information

Advance Preparation For Part 1, mark the calculators with children's tool-kit numbers. You may provide children with a large paper triangle with corners labeled "Calculator," "Caller," and "Brain" for *Beat the Calculator*. See margin on page 101.

Technology
Assessment Management System
Exit Slip
See the **iTLG.**

Getting Started

Pose simple addition number stories. *Suggestions:*

●○○ Jackson has 8 books. His grandmother gives him 3 more books. How many books does Jackson have now? 11 books

●●○ Sally has 16 fish in her fish tank. Sam has 14 fish. How many fish in all? 30 fish

●●● Tonisha had 36 pennies. Her mother gave her 42 more. How many pennies does Tonisha have now? 78 pennies

Math Message

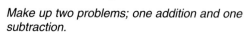

Make up two problems; one addition and one subtraction.

Tell what calculator keys to use to solve them.

Home Link 2·1 Follow-Up

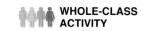

Have several children share their number stories with the class. Ask volunteers to solve the problems. During the next few days, you can use remaining number stories as Mental Math and Reflexes problems.

---

① Teaching the Lesson

▶ Math Message Follow-Up

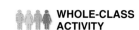 **WHOLE-CLASS ACTIVITY**

Ask a few children to share their addition and subtraction problems and to explain what keys they pressed on the calculator to solve them. Have the other children press the keys for each problem on their calculators.

Write 11 = 8 + 3 on the board. Review the key sequence to use for this number model. To support English language learners, explain the meaning of the phrase *key sequence* in this context.

Ask children to make up a number story for this number model. Sample answer: I had $8. I earned $3 more. Now I have $11. After a few minutes, ask children to share their stories and to suggest labels to write in the unit box. Write one of these labels, such as "dollars," in the box. Say that it will be the label for all numbers in this lesson that are not otherwise labeled.

Review the meaning of **addition fact.** Remind children that 11 = 8 + 3 is an example of an addition fact—the sum of two 1-digit numbers. Write this fact on the board horizontally and vertically.

$$8 + 3 = 11$$
$$11 = 8 + 3$$

$$\begin{array}{r} 8 \\ + 3 \\ \hline 11 \end{array}$$

Use all three forms, one as often as another.

▶ Reviewing +0 and +1 Shortcuts

WHOLE-CLASS ACTIVITY

Write some **+0 facts** and **+1 facts** on the board, without the sums. Use both horizontal and vertical forms, as shown in the margin.

Ask children to copy and complete the facts on their slates. See if they can find patterns for +0 facts and +1 facts. Discuss the **+0 shortcut** and the **+1 shortcut.** If 0 is added to any number,

or any number is added to 0, there is no change in the number. If 1 is added to any number, or any number is added to 1, the result is the next larger number. To support English language learners, clarify the meaning of *shortcut*.

Write the following problem on the board: 87 + 0 = _____.

After a volunteer has given the answer, ask someone else to check the answer on a calculator. Try several other +0 examples with 2-digit and 3-digit numbers—and with some very large numbers just for fun!

Follow the same routine with several +1 facts using 2-digit, 3-digit, and larger numbers.

> **Examples:**
>
> 5 + 0 = _____
>
> 0 + 8 = _____
>
> _____ = 1 + 9
>
> $\begin{array}{r} 3 \\ +1 \\ \hline \end{array}$ $\begin{array}{r} 0 \\ +6 \\ \hline \end{array}$

▶ # Demonstrating *Beat the Calculator*

👥👥 **WHOLE-CLASS ACTIVITY**

(*Math Journal 1*, p. 24)

Tell children that they are now going to use their calculators to practice some addition facts. Select three children to demonstrate the game and to record their results.

1. Designate one child as the "Caller," a second child as the "Calculator," and the third as the "Brain."

2. The Caller selects a problem at random from the unshaded area of the Fact Power Table on journal page 24. In this lesson, all fact problems should be selected from the unshaded area of the table.

3. The Calculator solves the problem with a calculator while the Brain solves it without a calculator. The Caller decides who gets the answer first.

If the Brain correctly beats the Calculator on a fact, the Caller makes a check mark in the box for the fact on the Brain's Fact Power Table.

Children trade roles every 10 turns or so.

NOTE You may assess children's mastery of addition facts by playing *Beat the Calculator* frequently. Use journal page 24 as a record sheet. Children receive a check mark each time they beat the calculator. When they receive three check marks next to a particular fact, they can write the sum in that box to indicate that the fact has been mastered.

NOTE Some teachers provide children with a large paper triangle with corners labeled "Calculator," "Caller," and "Brain." The children rotate the triangle to assist with the role assignments.

Student Page

Games

Beat the Calculator

Materials ❑ number cards 0–9
(4 of each)
❑ 1 calculator

Players 3

Skill Mental addition

Object of the game To add numbers faster than
a player using a calculator.

Directions

1. One player is the "Caller." A
   second player is the "Calculator."
   The third player is the "Brain."

2. Shuffle the cards. Place the deck
   number-side down on the table.

3. The Caller draws 2 cards from
   the number deck and asks for the
   sum of the numbers.

4. The Calculator solves the problem *with* a calculator.
   The Brain solves it *without* a calculator. The Caller
   decides who got the answer first.

My Reference Book, p. 124

Student Page

Games

5. The caller continues to draw 2 cards at a time
   from the number deck and to ask for the sum of
   the numbers.

6. Players trade roles every 10 turns or so.

● The Caller draws a 2 and a 9. The Caller says,
  "2 plus 9."

  The Brain and the Calculator each solve the problem.

  The Caller decides who got the answer first.

Caller — 2 plus 9

Calculator   Brain

Another Way to Play

The Caller can choose problems from
the Facts Table.

My Reference Book, p. 125

▶ Playing *Beat the Calculator*

**SMALL-GROUP
ACTIVITY**

(*Math Journal 1,* p. 24; *My Reference Book,* pp. 124 and 125)

Divide the class into groups of three. Children can read the
directions on pages 124 and 125 in *My Reference Book.*

Circulate as children play; offer guidance when needed. It is
important for children to understand the purpose of the game and
to help one another develop fact power. Praise those who display
a spirit of cooperation.

Adjusting the Activity

If children can beat the calculator for many unshaded facts, have the
Caller select fact problems from any part of the Fact Power Table.

Have children count up mentally or by using their fingers. Start with the
larger digit.

Examples:

9 + 2 = ? Think 9. Say "10, 11." The sum is 11.
3 + 7 = ? Think 7. Say "8, 9, 10." The sum is 10.

AUDITORY ◆ KINESTHETIC ◆ TACTILE ◆ VISUAL

▶ Stressing the Importance of "Fact Power"

WHOLE-CLASS
ACTIVITY

(*Math Masters,* p. 415)

Point out that the children who did not use calculators sometimes
beat those who did use them. They were able to do so because they
know those facts without having to take time to figure out the
answers. Tell children that they will be reviewing shortcuts to
help them beat the calculator, even on "harder" facts.

Explain that having **fact power** makes it much easier to solve
problems in mathematics because one knows the facts without
having to figure them out.

✓ Ongoing Assessment: Exit Slip
Recognizing Student Achievement

Use an **Exit Slip** (*Math Masters,* page 415) to have children record the facts for
which they beat the calculator. Children are making adequate progress if they
successfully record three facts. Some children may be able to beat the calculator
on more than three facts.

[Operations and Computation Goal 1]

2 Ongoing Learning & Practice

▶ Finding Distances on a Number Grid

INDEPENDENT ACTIVITY

(*Math Journal*, p. 25)

Use the example to demonstrate how to count moves ("spaces") when traveling from one number to another.

NOTE When finding the distance on a number grid, count the number of spaces from left to right until you reach the end of a line and continue counting at the beginning of the next line. See *My Reference Book,* pages 7 and 8.

▶ Math Boxes 2·2

INDEPENDENT ACTIVITY

(*Math Journal 1*, p. 26)

Mixed Practice Math Boxes in this lesson are paired with Math Boxes in Lesson 2-4. The skills in Problems 5 and 6 preview Unit 3 content.

▶ Home Link 2·2

INDEPENDENT ACTIVITY

(*Math Masters*, p. 26)

Home Connection Home Link 2-2 begins a maze practice routine that will be used several times. However, do not tell children that this is a maze problem. Simply tell them to answer all the problems on the page. (See Home Link 2-2 Follow-Up in Lesson 2-3.)

Student Page

Date   Time

LESSON 2·2   Distances on a Number Grid

Example: *How many spaces do you move to go from 17 to 23 on the number grid?*

Solution: *Place a marker on 17. You move the marker 6 spaces before landing on 23.*

11	12	13	14	15	16	(17)	(18)	(19)	(20)
(21)	(22)	(23)	24	25	26	27	28	29	30

How many spaces from:

23 to 28? __5__   15 to 55? __40__   39 to 59? __20__

27 to 42? __15__   34 to 26? __8__   54 to 42? __12__

15 to 25? __10__   26 to 34? __8__

1	2	3	4	5	6	7	8	9	10
11	12	13	14	15	16	17	18	19	20
21	22	23	24	25	26	27	28	29	30
31	32	33	34	35	36	37	38	39	40
41	42	43	44	45	46	47	48	49	50
51	52	53	54	55	56	57	58	59	60

***Math Journal 1*, p. 25**

★ Ongoing Assessment: Informing Instruction

Watch for children who include the starting space in their count when finding distances on a number grid. Many children will find that it is easier to count spaces if they use a penny to act out the moves from the starting to the ending number.

Student Page

Date   Time

LESSON 2·2   Math Boxes

1. Count by 3s. Use your calculator.

3, 6, 9, 12, 15, 18

2. Fill in the missing numbers.

455, __456__, __457__, 458

3. Solve.

4 + 3 = __7__ | Unit |

10 − 7 = __3__

5   8
+4   −3
‾‾   ‾‾
9   5

4. Show $1.00 three ways. Use Ⓠ, Ⓓ, and Ⓝ.

Sample answer:

Ⓠ Ⓠ Ⓠ Ⓠ

Ⓠ Ⓠ Ⓠ Ⓓ Ⓓ Ⓝ

Ⓠ Ⓠ Ⓓ Ⓓ Ⓓ Ⓓ Ⓝ Ⓝ

5. Mrs. Satz's Class's Favorite Colors

Colors	Tallies
Red	⁄⁄⁄⁄ ⁄⁄⁄⁄
Blue	⁄⁄⁄⁄ ⁄⁄⁄
Green	⁄⁄⁄⁄
Yellow	⁄⁄

Which color is the most popular? __Red__

6. Fill in the circle that names the number.

5 ones   Ⓐ 564

6 hundreds   Ⓑ 356

3 tens   ● 635

   Ⓓ 536

***Math Journal 1*, p. 26**

Home Link Master

Name   Date   Time

HOME LINK 2·2   Addition Facts

Family Note In class today, we continued working with addition stories. We reviewed shortcuts when adding 0 or 1 to a number. We also stressed the importance of memorizing the sum of two 1-digit numbers. Then we reinforced addition facts by playing a game called *Beat the Calculator.*

Please return this Home Link to school tomorrow.

Solve these addition fact problems.

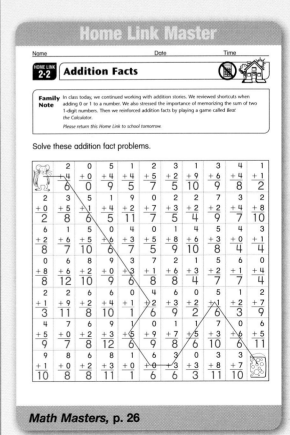

***Math Masters*, p. 26**

Student Page

Games

Addition Top-It

Materials ☐ number cards 0–10 (4 of each)

Players 2 to 4

Skill Addition facts 0 to 10

Object of the game To collect the most cards.

Directions

1. Shuffle the cards. Place the deck number-side down on the table.

2. Each player turns over 2 cards and calls out the sum of the numbers.

3. The player with the largest sum wins the round and takes all the cards.

4. In case of a tie for the largest sum, each tied player turns over 2 more cards and calls out the sum of the numbers. The player with the largest sum then takes all the cards from both plays.

5. The game ends when not enough cards are left for each player to have another turn.

6. The player with the most cards wins.

My Reference Book, p. 122

Teaching Aid Master

Name _____ Date _____ Time _____

A Number Story

	Unit

_____

_____

_____

_____

_____

_____

_____

_____

Math Masters, p. 419

③ Differentiation Options

READINESS

PARTNER ACTIVITY

▶ *Domino Top-It*

5–15 Min

(*My Reference Book,* pp. 122 and 123)

To provide addition fact practice using a concrete model, have children play *Domino Top-It*. Go over the game directions with children and have them play with a partner. See *My Reference Book,* pages 122 and 123.

Directions

1. Place all the dominoes facedown on the table.

2. Each player turns over a domino and finds the total number of dots.

3. The player with the larger total takes both dominoes. In case of a tie, each player turns over another facedown domino and the player with the larger total then takes all the faceup dominoes.

4. Play continues until all the dominoes have been played. The player who has more dominoes wins.

ENRICHMENT

INDEPENDENT ACTIVITY

▶ **Writing +0 and +1 Number Stories**

5–15 Min

(*Math Masters,* p. 419)

To further explore the +0 and +1 patterns in addition number stories, have children write +0 or +1 number stories. Encourage them to use large numbers. Remind them to fill in the unit box and write a number model to represent their story.

For example:

▷ Raimon was born in 1999 and his cousin Jorge was born 1 year later. In what year was Jorge born? $1999 + 1 = 2000$

Unit

year

$$1999 + 1 = 2000$$

▷ It was 65 degrees outside during recess. When Debby looked at the thermometer after school the temperature had risen 0 degrees. What was the temperature after school? $65 + 0 = 65$ degrees

Unit

degrees

$$65 + 0 = 65$$

2·3 Doubles Facts

 Objective To review and provide practice for doubles facts.

---

1 Teaching the Lesson

materials

Key Activities

Children write and practice doubles facts and "almost doubles" facts, and review using the Addition/Subtraction Facts Table to identify +0 and doubles patterns.

Key Concepts and Skills

- Use the Addition/Subtraction Fact Table to practice facts. [Operations and Computation Goal 1]
- Solve facts involving doubles. [Operations and Computation Goal 1]
- Identify patterns in Addition/Subtraction Facts Table. [Patterns, Functions, and Algebra Goal 1]

Key Vocabulary doubles facts • sum • Facts Table • row • column • diagonal

☑ **Ongoing Assessment: Informing Instruction** See page 107.

- ☐ *Math Journal 1*, pp. 27–29
- ☐ Home Link 2·2
- ☐ Teaching Aid Master (*Math Masters*, p. 420; optional)
- ☐ Transparency (*Math Masters*, p. 421; optional)
- ☐ per partnership: 4 each of number cards 1–10
- ☐ calculator; slate
- ☐ Class Facts Table

See Advance Preparation

---

2 Ongoing Learning & Practice

materials

Children practice doubles addition facts by playing *Doubles or Nothing*.

Children practice and maintain skills through Math Boxes and Home Link activities.

☑ **Ongoing Assessment: Recognizing Student Achievement** Use journal page 30. [Number and Numeration Goal 1]

- ☐ *Math Journal 1*, p. 30
- ☐ Home Link Master (*Math Masters*, p. 27)
- ☐ Game Master (*Math Masters*, p. 456)
- ☐ per partnership: 4 each of number cards 1–10
- ☐ calculator

---

3 Differentiation Options

materials

READINESS

Children practice doubles addition facts by using pennies and/or cubes.

ENRICHMENT

Children work in small groups to identify and explain patterns in the Facts Table.

EXTRA PRACTICE

Children write doubles facts.

ELL SUPPORT

Children add *sum* to their Math Word Banks.

- ☐ Teaching Aid Master (*Math Masters*, p. 421)
- ☐ *Differentiation Handbook*
- ☐ pennies and/or cubes; penny stamp
- ☐ colored pencil
- ☐ *Two of Everything: A Chinese Folktale*, by Lily Toy Hong

---

Additional Information

Advance Preparation Prepare a large class Facts Table like the one on journal page 27, using one of the following options: draw the table on the Class Data Pad or chart paper; tape together 4 copies of *Math Masters*, page 420 and fill in the facts; make an overhead transparency of *Math Masters*, page 421.

Before the lesson, draw a unit box on the board and fill it in with a label of your choice. Use the unit box and label for all the numbers that are not labeled in this lesson. See the Unit Organizer for Literature Links for this lesson.

Technology

Assessment Management System
Math Boxes, Problem 3
See the **iTLG**.

Getting Started

Mental Math and Reflexes

Pose easy addition facts. Have children answer orally.
Suggestions:

●○○ 4 + 2 = ? 6   ●●○ ? + 8 = 13 5
      3 + 6 = ? 9   6 + ? = 14 8
      7 + 1 = ? 8   50 + 40 = ? 90
●●○ ? = 5 + 4 9   60 + 60 = ? 120
      6 + 8 = ? 14
      7 + 5 = ? 12

Math Message

Write 2 + 2 = 4 and 5 + 5 = 10 on your slate. Write any other doubles facts that you know.

Home Link 2·2 Follow-Up

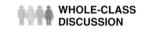

Briefly review the answers. Tell children that the mouse can only go through boxes with a sum of 6 to find the cheese. Ask children to draw the mouse's path. The mouse can move up, down, left, right, or diagonally. Ask a volunteer to display the page.

Children can find the path more easily if they first color in each box that has the sum of 6.

---

1 Teaching the Lesson

▶ **Math Message Follow-Up**   WHOLE-CLASS ACTIVITY

Ask children to share their **doubles facts** as you write them on the board. Skip duplicates. Do not erase the board after finishing the follow-up. You will use these doubles facts for the "Reviewing the Doubles Facts" activity on page 107.

▶ **Reviewing the Meaning of Sum**   WHOLE-CLASS DISCUSSION

Remind children that the number obtained by adding two or more numbers is called the **sum.** Encourage children to use the word *sum.* For example, if a child says, "The answer to 8 + 8 is 16," you might say, "Yes. You are adding numbers, so the answer is called the sum." Another way to say it is, "The sum of 8 and 8 is 16."

▶ **Reviewing the Facts Table**   WHOLE-CLASS ACTIVITY

(*Math Journal 1,* p. 27; *Math Masters,* p. 420 or 421)

Use the class **Facts Table** to review the meanings of **row, column,** and **diagonal.** As you explain these terms, have children follow along on the table on journal page 27. Then have children use the table to find the sums for several addition facts.

Student Page

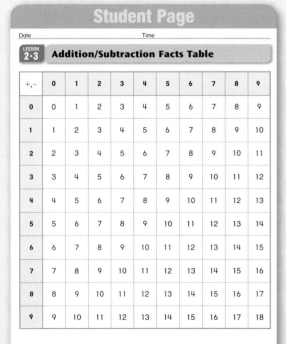

Date _____ Time _____

LESSON 2·3 **Addition/Subtraction Facts Table**

+,−	0	1	2	3	4	5	6	7	8	9
0	0	1	2	3	4	5	6	7	8	9
1	1	2	3	4	5	6	7	8	9	10
2	2	3	4	5	6	7	8	9	10	11
3	3	4	5	6	7	8	9	10	11	12
4	4	5	6	7	8	9	10	11	12	13
5	5	6	7	8	9	10	11	12	13	14
6	6	7	8	9	10	11	12	13	14	15
7	7	8	9	10	11	12	13	14	15	16
8	8	9	10	11	12	13	14	15	16	17
9	9	10	11	12	13	14	15	16	17	18

Math Journal 1, p. 27

Have children make a visual vocabulary reminder at the bottom of the journal page. Consider putting the example below on the board for children to copy:

```
ROW        C      D
           O       I
           L          A
           U            G
           M              O
           N                N
                            A
                          L
```

A U D I T O R Y ◆ K I N E S T H E T I C ◆ T A C T I L E ◆ V I S U A L

 Ongoing Assessment: Informing Instruction

Some children may have difficulty locating the cell where a row and column intersect. Suggest that they use a blank sheet of paper with an arrow drawn in the lower right hand corner as pictured to highlight the row and column of interest.

To find 9 + 7, say:

- Find the 9 row. Go across the 9 row to the 7 column. The number where the 9 row and the 7 column meet is 16. This tells you that 9 + 7 = 16. The sum is 16.

By exploring patterns in the Facts Table, children will accelerate their mastery of facts. Ask children to find the +0 facts in the Facts Table. The +0 facts appear in the top uncolored row and in the left uncolored column of the table. Have children use their pencils to lightly shade the +0 facts. See whether they can identify the pattern for +0 facts in the table. Sample answer: The sums increase by 1 as you move across the row from left to right. The sums increase by 1 as you move down the column.

Links to the Future

Notice that finding the sum of two numbers on the Facts Table is similar to locating a point on a coordinate grid using ordered pairs. This skill helps prepare children for using ordered pairs to find points on a coordinate grid, a Grade 4 Goal.

▶ **Reviewing the Doubles Facts**   **WHOLE-CLASS ACTIVITY**

(Math Journal 1, p. 27)

Use the Facts Table to verify the doubles facts that you wrote on the board during the Math Message Follow-Up. Ask children to examine the table to find any doubles facts that they may have overlooked. Have them lightly shade all of the doubles facts on the Facts Table with a pencil. Ask them to identify the pattern for doubles on the table. Doubles facts form a diagonal pattern from top left to bottom right. The sums increase by 2 as you move down diagonally.

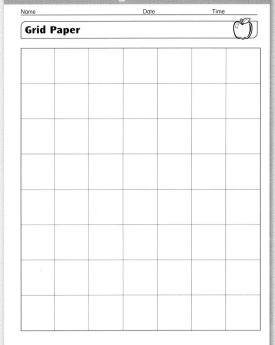

Teaching Aid Master

Name _____ Date _____ Time _____

Grid Paper

Math Masters, p. 420

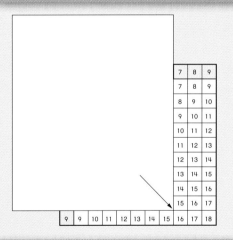

Teaching Aid Master

Name _____ Date _____ Time _____

Facts Table

+,−	0	1	2	3	4	5	6	7	8	9
0	0	1	2	3	4	5	6	7	8	9
1	1	2	3	4	5	6	7	8	9	10
2	2	3	4	5	6	7	8	9	10	11
3	3	4	5	6	7	8	9	10	11	12
4	4	5	6	7	8	9	10	11	12	13
5	5	6	7	8	9	10	11	12	13	14
6	6	7	8	9	10	11	12	13	14	15
7	7	8	9	10	11	12	13	14	15	16
8	8	9	10	11	12	13	14	15	16	17
9	9	10	11	12	13	14	15	16	17	18

Math Masters, p. 421

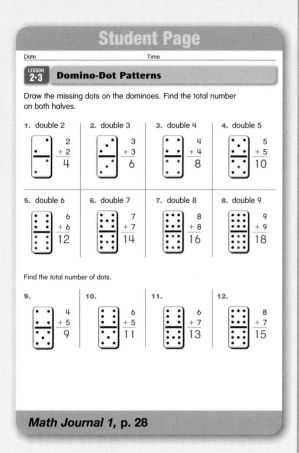

Math Journal 1, p. 28

▶ Practicing Doubles Facts and "Almost-Doubles" Facts

(*Math Journal 1,* p. 28)

Children practice doubles facts by exploring domino patterns. Problems 9 through 12 illustrate how knowing doubles facts can help with "almost-doubles" facts. This is revisited in Lesson 2-5.

Example: For $4 + 5 = ?$: Think $4 + 4$, and 1 more. 8; 9

▶ Demonstrating *Doubles or Nothing*

(*Math Journal 1,* p. 29)

Children have an opportunity to develop their recall of addition facts with emphasis on adding doubles. Each child uses journal page 29 as his or her record sheet. Each partnership uses number cards 0–9.

Directions

1. Shuffle the cards. Place the deck number-side down on the playing surface.

2. Take the top card from the pile and write the number in any square on your record sheet.

3. Take turns and continue until all squares are filled.

4. Add the scores across each row, down each column, and along each diagonal.

5. Circle any pairs of identical sums. Find the sum of the identical sums and record that number for each round total.

6. If there are no pairs, the total score is zero.

7. Use a calculator to find the total of all the rounds.

8. Flip a coin to see who wins. If it is heads, the higher total wins. If it is tails, the lower score wins.

---

② Ongoing Learning & Practice

▶ Playing *Doubles or Nothing*

(*Math Masters,* p. 456)

Children continue playing *Doubles or Nothing* to develop their recall of addition facts with emphasis on doubles facts. Children can use a copy of *Math Masters,* page 456 as a record sheet. This page is the same as journal page 29.

▶ Math Boxes 2·3

(*Math Journal 1*, p. 30)

Mixed Practice Math Boxes in this lesson are paired with Math Boxes in Lesson 2-1. The skill in Problem 6 previews Unit 3 content.

Writing/Reasoning Have children draw, write, or verbalize their answers to the following: *How did you know what symbol to put in each in Problem 4?* I added the numbers on each side, then I looked for the bigger number. I put the open side by the bigger number. If they were the same I put =.

Ongoing Assessment:
Recognizing Student Achievement

Math Boxes
Problem 3 ★

Use **Math Boxes, Problem 3** to assess children's understanding of counting back by 5s. Children are making adequate progress if they successfully count back to 5. Some children may be able to continue past 0.

[Number and Numeration Goal 1]

▶ Home Link 2·3

(*Math Masters*, p. 27)

Home Connection Children practice the doubles facts and use doubles facts to find the answers to "almost-doubles" facts.

---

③ Differentiation Options

▶ Representing Doubles

To explore doubles using a concrete model, have children use pennies and/or cubes to model doubles facts. Children select a particular number of pennies and then make another group of the same number of pennies. Write the number model to represent these groups on a sheet of paper. Have children use a penny stamp to design a picture to go with a doubles number model.

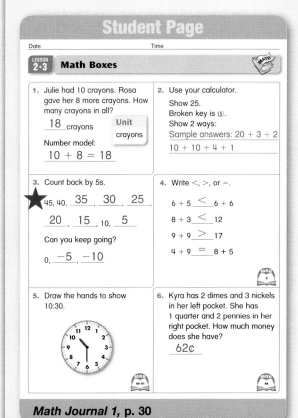

Math Journal 1, p. 30

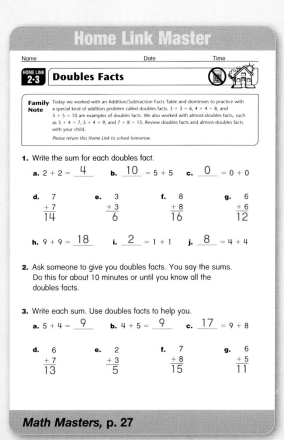

Math Masters, p. 27

▶ Finding Patterns in the Facts Table

(Math Masters, p. 421)

To further explore patterns in the Facts Table, have children identify and color patterns they see. Children work in small groups on *Math Masters,* page 421. When they think they have found an interesting pattern, they should color the grid to show the pattern they have found. At the bottom of *Math Masters,* page 421, consider having children describe in numbers or words the pattern they have colored. When groups are finished, have children share their results. Encourage the use of words like "row," "column," "diagonal," and "add."

Possible patterns:

▷ Each number is 1 less than the number to its right and 1 more than the number to its left.

▷ Each number is 1 less than the number below it. After the first row, each number is 1 more than the number above it.

▷ On the diagonal from top left to bottom right, the numbers increase by 2 as you move down the diagonal.

▷ On the diagonal from top right to bottom left, the numbers are the same.

 SMALL-GROUP ACTIVITY

5–15 Min

▶ Finding Doubles In Literature

 Literature Link Read the following book to groups of children, or have the children read the book themselves.

Two of Everything: A Chinese Folktale

Summary: Doubles facts are illustrated in the story of a brass pot that doubles whatever is put into it. Children can write a doubles fact for every item put into the pot.

 SMALL-GROUP ACTIVITY

5–15 Min

▶ Building a Math Word Bank

(Differentiation Handbook)

To provide language support for addition, have children use the Word Bank template found in the *Differentiation Handbook.* Ask the children to write the term *sum,* draw a picture representing the term, and write other related words. See the *Differentiation Handbook* for more information.

2·4 Turn-Around Facts and the +9 Shortcut

 Objectives To review the turn-around shortcut for addition; and to discover and provide practice for a shortcut for addition facts that have 9 as an addend.

1 Teaching the Lesson

materials

Key Activities
Children use the Facts Table and the Number-Grid Poster to discuss turn-around facts and to discover the +9 shortcut.

Key Concepts and Skills
• Identify and use patterns to solve +9 facts.
[Patterns, Functions, and Algebra Goal 1]

• Identify and use patterns on a number grid.
[Patterns, Functions, and Algebra Goal 1]

• Explore the turn-around rule for facts.
[Patterns, Functions, and Algebra Goal 3]

Key Vocabulary
turn-around facts • +9 facts • +9 shortcut

☐ *Math Journal 1*, pp. 27 and 31
☐ Home Link 2·3
☐ Facts Table
☐ Number-Grid Poster

***See* Advance Preparation**

2 Ongoing Learning & Practice

materials

Children practice basic facts through the *Beat the Calculator* game.

Children practice and maintain skills through Math Boxes and Home Link activities.

☑ **Ongoing Assessment: Recognizing Student Achievement** Use journal page 32.
[Operations and Computation Goal 1]

☐ *Math Journal 1*, pp. 24 and 32
☐ Home Link Master (*Math Masters*, p. 28)

3 Differentiation Options

materials

READINESS
Children solve +9 addition facts by using a ten-frame card and counters.

EXTRA PRACTICE
Children solve problems using shortcuts for subtraction facts.

ELL SUPPORT
Children add *turn-around facts* to their Math Word Banks.

☐ Teaching Aid Master (*Math Masters*, p. 422)
☐ *Differentiation Handbook*
☐ *Minute Math®+*, pp. 24 and 80
☐ 19 counters

Additional Information

Advance Preparation Before the lesson, draw a unit box on the board and fill it in with a label of your choice. Use the unit box and label for all the numbers that are not labeled in this lesson.

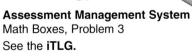

Technology
Assessment Management System
Math Boxes, Problem 3
See the **iTLG**.

Getting Started

Mental Math and Reflexes

Use the number grid to find the distance from one number to another. *Suggestions:*

◉○○ 24 to 44 20   ◉◉○ 26 to 47 21   ◉◉◉ 85 to 56 29

     13 to 53 40   15 to 59 44   103 to 49 54

Math Message

Find the sums. Look for patterns.

$1 + 6 = ?$ 7	$8 ? = 3 + 5$	$8 + 2 = ?$ 10
$6 + 1 = ?$ 7	$8 ? = 5 + 3$	$2 + 8 = ?$ 10

Home Link 2·3 Follow-Up

Briefly review the answers. Ask children how they solved the "almost doubles" facts in Problem 3.

---

1 Teaching the Lesson

▶ Math Message Follow-Up

WHOLE-CLASS ACTIVITY

Review the turn-around shortcut for addition facts illustrated in the Math Message. Ask children to share the patterns they saw. Select a pair of **turn-around facts,** such as $3 + 5 = 8$ and $5 + 3 = 8$. To support English language learners, discuss the everyday meaning of turnaround and its use in this context. Ask children to describe ways in which the facts are alike and different from each other. Sample answer: The facts are alike because the same numbers are added and they have the same sum. The facts are different because the numbers are not added in the same order.

Remind children that such facts are called turn-around facts. Ask: *Why is this a good name for such facts?* Sample answer: The numbers being added (the addends) are reversed or "turned around." Ask volunteers to give other examples of turn-around addition facts. Ask children to name a fact that does not have a different turn-around fact. A doubles fact and its turn-around fact are the same. Discuss why knowing the turn-around shortcut can help children gain fact power. If you know an addition fact, then you also know its turn-around fact.

Adjusting the Activity

Have children look at the Facts Table on journal page 27. The doubles facts form a diagonal. For each fact above the diagonal (such as $3 + 5 = 8$), the turn-around fact ($5 + 3 = 8$) is below the diagonal.

AUDITORY ◆ KINESTHETIC ◆ TACTILE ◆ VISUAL

Adjusting the Activity

ELL

Teach children a gesture to indicate "turn-around' facts. The gesture would demonstrate the idea of switching the numbers and could be used to remind children when the turn-around rule is being applied. See illustration.

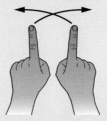 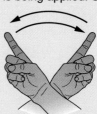

AUDITORY ◆ KINESTHETIC ◆ TACTILE ◆ VISUAL

NOTE Children who used *Everyday Mathematics* in first grade were introduced to the turn-around shortcut. The turn-around shortcut for addition is called the commutative property of addition. Do not require children to use this term.

► Introducing the +9 Shortcut

WHOLE-CLASS ACTIVITY

(Math Journal 1, p. 27)

Ask children to use the Facts Table on journal page 27 to name facts that include 9 as one of the addends. Write these **+9 facts** on the board.

Use the class Facts Table to help children notice that the +9 facts form patterns. If children have not already done so, point out the following:

▷ The +9 facts appear in the bottom row (the 9 row) and in the far right column (the 9 column) in the table.

▷ The digit in the ones place in the sum increases by 1 as you move across the 9 row from left to right and as you move down the 9 column.

▷ Beginning with the fact 1 + 9, the digit in the ones place in the sum is 1 less than the number added to 9. For example, 1 + 9 = 10. The digit 0 in the sum 10 is one less than the addend 1.

Have children shade all of the +9 facts on the Facts Table in the journal with their pencils. See whether children can discover the **+9 shortcut.** It may help if you write pairs of related +9 and +10 combinations on the board. *For example:*

9 + 1 = 10 → 10 + 1 = 11

9 + 2 = 11 → 10 + 2 = 12

9 + 3 = 12 → 10 + 3 = 13

9 + 6 = 15 → 10 + 6 = 16

9 + 9 = 18 → 10 + 9 = 19

Help children describe the +9 shortcut in their own words. *For example:*

▷ You add 10 instead of 9 and then count back 1.

▷ Add 10, but go back to 1 less.

Adjusting the Activity

ELL

Use the Number-Grid Poster to demonstrate the +9 shortcut. As you model the process on the class number grid, have the children model the process using the number grid in their journals.

To find the sum of 9 + 6, place your finger on number 6; add ten by moving your finger down one row; and subtract 1 by moving your finger one space left. The sum is 15.

AUDITORY ◆ KINESTHETIC ◆ TACTILE ◆ VISUAL

► Practicing +9 Facts

INDEPENDENT ACTIVITY

(Math Journal 1, p. 31)

Assign Problems 1 through 14 at the top of the page. Briefly review the answers. Then have children write a +9 number story.

Student Page

Date   Time

LESSON 2·3   Addition/Subtraction Facts Table

+,−	0	1	2	3	4	5	6	7	8	9
0	0	1	2	3	4	5	6	7	8	9
1	1	2	3	4	5	6	7	8	9	10
2	2	3	4	5	6	7	8	9	10	11
3	3	4	5	6	7	8	9	10	11	12
4	4	5	6	7	8	9	10	11	12	13
5	5	6	7	8	9	10	11	12	13	14
6	6	7	8	9	10	11	12	13	14	15
7	7	8	9	10	11	12	13	14	15	16
8	8	9	10	11	12	13	14	15	16	17
9	9	10	11	12	13	14	15	16	17	18

Math Journal 1, p. 27

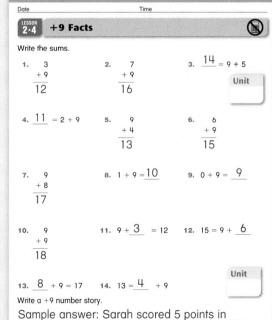

+9 shortcut on the number grid

Student Page

Date   Time

LESSON 2·4   +9 Facts

Write the sums.

1. 3
   + 9
   ‾‾‾
   12

2. 7
   + 9
   ‾‾‾
   16

3. _14_ = 9 + 5

   Unit

4. _11_ = 2 + 9

5. 9
   + 4
   ‾‾‾
   13

6. 6
   + 9
   ‾‾‾
   15

7. 9
   + 8
   ‾‾‾
   17

8. 1 + 9 = _10_

9. 0 + 9 = _9_

10. 9
    + 9
    ‾‾‾
    18

11. 9 + _3_ = 12

12. 15 = 9 + _6_

   Unit

13. _8_ + 9 = 17

14. 13 = _4_ + 9

Write a +9 number story.

Sample answer: Sarah scored 5 points in the game. Erin scored 9. How many points did they score all together? 14 points

Math Journal 1, p. 31

Date _____ Time _____

LESSON 2·2 Facts Power Table

0 + 0 0	0 + 1 1	0 + 2 2	0 + 3 3	0 + 4 4	0 + 5 5	0 + 6 6	0 + 7 7	0 + 8 8	0 + 9 9
1 + 0 1	1 + 1 2	1 + 2 3	1 + 3 4	1 + 4 5	1 + 5 6	1 + 6 7	1 + 7 8	1 + 8 9	1 + 9 10
2 + 0 2	2 + 1 3	2 + 2 4	2 + 3 5	2 + 4 6	2 + 5 7	2 + 6 8	2 + 7 9	2 + 8 10	2 + 9 11
3 + 0 3	3 + 1 4	3 + 2 5	3 + 3 6	3 + 4 7	3 + 5 8	3 + 6 9	3 + 7 10	3 + 8 11	3 + 9 12
4 + 0 4	4 + 1 5	4 + 2 6	4 + 3 7	4 + 4 8	4 + 5 9	4 + 6 10	4 + 7 11	4 + 8 12	4 + 9 13
5 + 0 5	5 + 1 6	5 + 2 7	5 + 3 8	5 + 4 9	5 + 5 10	5 + 6 11	5 + 7 12	5 + 8 13	5 + 9 14
6 + 0 6	6 + 1 7	6 + 2 8	6 + 3 9	6 + 4 10	6 + 5 11	6 + 6 12	6 + 7 13	6 + 8 14	6 + 9 15
7 + 0 7	7 + 1 8	7 + 2 9	7 + 3 10	7 + 4 11	7 + 5 12	7 + 6 13	7 + 7 14	7 + 8 15	7 + 9 16
8 + 0 8	8 + 1 9	8 + 2 10	8 + 3 11	8 + 4 12	8 + 5 13	8 + 6 14	8 + 7 15	8 + 8 16	8 + 9 17
9 + 0 9	9 + 1 10	9 + 2 11	9 + 3 12	9 + 4 13	9 + 5 14	9 + 6 15	9 + 7 16	9 + 8 17	9 + 9 18

Math Journal 1, p. 24

---

② Ongoing Learning & Practice

▶ Playing *Beat the Calculator*

 **SMALL-GROUP ACTIVITY**

(*Math Journal 1*, p. 24)

Children play *Beat the Calculator* to develop their recall of addition facts. They should record the facts for which they can beat the calculator by making a check mark in the box of that fact. When they receive three check marks next to a particular fact, they can write the sum in that box to indicate that the fact has been mastered. The Caller should select problems at random from the white area of the fact power table.

▶ Math Boxes 2·4

👤 **INDEPENDENT ACTIVITY**

(*Math Journal 1*, p. 32)

 Mixed Practice Math Boxes in this lesson are paired with Math Boxes in Lesson 2-2. The skills in Problems 5 and 6 preview Unit 3 content.

Writing/Reasoning Have children draw, write, or verbalize their answers to the following: *Describe how you used your calculator to find the answers for Problem 1.* I put in 6, then kept adding 6 more on the calculator to fill in the blanks.

✔️ **Ongoing Assessment: Recognizing Student Achievement**   **Math Boxes Problem 3** ★

Use **Math Boxes, Problem 3** to assess children's understanding of simple facts. Children are making adequate progress if they successfully complete the +0 and +1 facts. Some children may be able to complete the "harder fact."

[Operations and Computation Goal 1]

▶ Home Link 2·4

👤 **INDEPENDENT ACTIVITY**

(*Math Masters*, p. 28)

Home Connection Children practice facts by writing sums and finding missing addends.

Date _____ Time _____

LESSON 2·4 Math Boxes

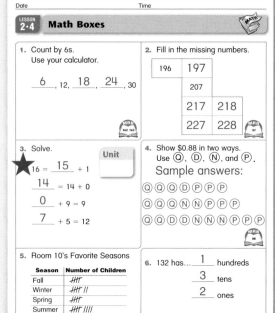

1. Count by 6s. Use your calculator.

   _6_, 12, _18_, _24_, 30

2. Fill in the missing numbers.

196	197
	207
217	218
227	228

3. Solve.

   ★ 16 = _15_ + 1

   _14_ = 14 + 0

   _0_ + 9 = 9

   _7_ + 5 = 12

   Unit

4. Show $0.88 in two ways. Use Ⓠ, Ⓓ, Ⓝ, and Ⓟ.
   Sample answers:

   ⓆⓆⓆⒹⓅⓅⓅ

   ⓆⓆⓃⓃⓅⓅⓅ

   ⓆⒹⒹⓃⓃⓃⓅⓅⓅ

5. Room 10's Favorite Seasons

Season	Number of Children
Fall	⁄⁄⁄⁄
Winter	⁄⁄⁄⁄ ⁄⁄
Spring	⁄⁄⁄⁄
Summer	⁄⁄⁄⁄ ⁄⁄⁄⁄

   Which seasons have the same number of votes?
   fall and spring

6. 132 has... _1_ hundreds

   _3_ tens

   _2_ ones

Math Journal 1, p. 32

READINESS

INDEPENDENT
ACTIVITY

5–15 Min

▶ Demonstrating the +9 Shortcut with Frames and Counters

(*Math Masters*, p. 422)

To explore the +9 shortcut using a concrete model, have children solve problems using the ten-frame card and counters. Each child needs a ten-frame card and 19 counters. To show $10 + 5$, the child fills the ten-frame card with 10 counters and places 5 counters outside the frame. The child writes "$10 + 5 = 15$." For $9 + 5$, the child takes one counter out of the frame and writes "$9 + 5 = 14$"; $9 + 5$ is 1 less than $10 + 5$. The activity can be repeated by placing a different number of counters (less than 10) outside of the frame each time.

EXTRA PRACTICE

SMALL-GROUP
ACTIVITY

5–15 Min

▶ Minute Math+

To offer children more experience with shortcuts for subtraction facts, see the following pages in *Minute Math+*: pp. 24 and 80.

ELL SUPPORT

SMALL-GROUP
ACTIVITY

5–15 Min

▶ Building a Math Word Bank

(*Differentiation Handbook*)

To provide language support for addition facts, have children use the Math Word Bank template found in the *Differentiation Handbook*. Ask the children to write the term *turn-around facts*, draw a picture representing the term, and write other related words. Encourage them to illustrate the action of switching of addends. See the *Differentiation Handbook* for more information.

Example:

$4 + 5 = 9 \longrightarrow 5 + 4 = 9$

Planning Ahead

For the Explorations in Lesson 2-8, each small group of children will need objects weighing between $\frac{1}{2}$ ounce and 8 ounces. Objects include student tape measures ($\frac{1}{2}$ oz each), full pads of stick-on notes ($\frac{1}{2}$ oz each), 2-inch binder clips (1 oz each), calculators (2–4 oz each), decks of cards (3 oz each), large scissors (5 oz each), mugs (6 oz each), full pads of lined paper (7 oz each), and small paperback books (4–8 oz each).

Name   Date   Time

HOME LINK 2·4   **Turn-Around, Doubles, and +9**

Family Note It is important for children to have instant recall of addition facts. They use shortcuts to help them learn the facts. For example, *turn-around facts* are facts that have the same sum, but the numbers being added are reversed or turned around. *Doubles facts* are facts in which the same number is added. When solving *+9 facts*, children are encouraged to think of the easier *+10* combinations and then subtract 1 from the sum.

Please return this Home Link to school tomorrow.

1. Write the sums. Tell someone at home what you know about turn-around facts.

  a. $6 + 1 = \underline{7}$ b. $\underline{11} = 3 + 8$ c. $5 + 2 = \underline{7}$

  d. $1 + 6 = \underline{7}$ e. $\underline{11} = 8 + 3$ f. $2 + 5 = \underline{7}$

2. Fill in the missing numbers. Tell someone at home what you know about doubles facts.

  a. $\underline{8} + 8 = 16$ b. $5 + \underline{5} = 10$ c. $12 = \underline{6} + 6$

  d. $6 = \underline{3} + 3$ e. $\underline{7} + 7 = 14$ f. $\underline{9} + 9 = 18$

3. Write the sums. Tell someone what you know about +9 facts.

  a. $10 + 1 = \underline{11}$ b. $\underline{15} = 5 + 10$ c. $6 + 10 = \underline{16}$

  d. $1 + 9 = \underline{10}$ e. $\underline{14} = 9 + 5$ f. $6 + 9 = \underline{15}$

  g. $10 + 7 = \underline{17}$ h. $\underline{14} = 4 + 10$ i. $8 + 10 = \underline{18}$

  j. $7 + 9 = \underline{16}$ k. $\underline{13} = 9 + 4$ l. $8 + 9 = \underline{17}$

Math Masters, p. 28

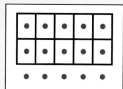

$$10 \atop \underline{+ 5} \atop 15$$

$$9 \atop \underline{+ 5} \atop 14$$

Name   Date   Time

Ten-Frame Card

Math Masters, p. 422

Addition Strategies That Use Doubles Facts

2·5

 Objective To provide opportunities for children to explore and practice doubles-plus-1 and doubles-plus-2 facts.

---

1 Teaching the Lesson

materials

Key Activities
Children identify and practice strategies for facts in which one addend is 1 or 2 more than the other addend.

Key Concepts and Skills
• Practice doubles facts.
[Operations and Computation Goal 1]

• Develop and practice strategies for addition that use doubles facts.
[Operations and Computation Goal 1]

• Use doubles patterns to practice facts.
[Patterns, Functions, and Algebra Goal 1]

Key Vocabulary
doubles-plus-1 facts • doubles-plus-2 facts

☑ **Ongoing Assessment:** Recognizing Student Achievement Use the Math Message.
[Operations and Computation Goal 1]

☐ *Math Journal 1*, pp. 27 and 33
☐ Home Link 2·4
☐ slate
☐ 1 sheet of paper per child

See Advance Preparation

---

2 Ongoing Learning & Practice

materials

Partners practice addition facts by playing *Domino Top-It*.

Children cut out the first set of 18 Fact Triangles.

Children practice and maintain skills through Math Boxes and Home Link activities.

☐ *Math Journal 1*, p. 34; Activity Sheets 1 and 2
☐ Home Link Master (*Math Masters*, p. 29)
☐ 1 set of dominoes per partnership
☐ scissors
☐ 1 envelope per child

---

3 Differentiation Options

materials

READINESS
Children create a Doubles Facts Book.

ENRICHMENT
Children use calculators to explore the concept of doubles addition facts.

☐ Teaching Master (*Math Masters*, p. 30)
☐ pattern blocks
☐ Pattern-Block Template
☐ paper and pencil
☐ calculator

Additional Information

Advance Preparation Before the lesson, draw a unit box on the board and fill it in with a label of your choice. Use the unit box and label for all the numbers that are not labeled in this lesson.

Technology
Assessment Management System
Math Message
See the **iTLG.**

Getting Started

Mental Math and Reflexes

Pose +9 facts. Encourage children to think +10, then count back 1.
Suggestions:

○○○ 1 + 9 = ? 10   ○○○ 9 + 5 = ? 14   ○○○ 9 + ? = 16 7
    2 + 9 = ? 11   ? = 9 + 6 15   4 + ? = 13 9
    3 + 9 = ? 12   ? = 7 + 9 16   ? + 9 = 17 8

Math Message ★

Write all the doubles addition facts on a sheet of paper.

Home Link 2·4 Follow-Up

Review answers as necessary.

1 Teaching the Lesson

▶ Math Message Follow-Up

WHOLE-CLASS ACTIVITY

(*Math Journal 1*, p. 27)

 Ongoing Assessment:
Recognizing Student Achievement

Math Message ★

Portfolio Ideas — Use the **Math Message** to assess children's knowledge of doubles facts. Children are making adequate progress if they can correctly record 5 of the 10 doubles facts. Some children may be able to record all the doubles.

[Operations and Computation Goal 1]

Ask children to turn to the Facts Table on journal page 27. Help them as needed while they check their list of doubles facts against the table.

▶ Discussing Doubles-Plus-1 Facts

WHOLE-CLASS ACTIVITY

Doubles-plus-1 facts include those addition facts in which one addend is 1 more than the other addend (for example, 3 + 2). Write some doubles-plus-1 facts on the board; leave out the sums. Use both horizontal and vertical forms. (See page 118.)

Ask children to copy and complete the facts on their slates. See whether any children mention a strategy that makes use of doubles. Discuss the doubles-plus-1 strategy. To add numbers where one addend is 1 more than the other, double the smaller number and then add 1.

NOTE Knowledge of doubles facts is important as this lesson focuses on strategies that assume quick recall of these facts. Daily chanting of the doubles will help reinforce this skill.

Student Page

Date _____ Time _____

LESSON 2·3 | Addition/Subtraction Facts Table

+,−	0	1	2	3	4	5	6	7	8	9
0	0	1	2	3	4	5	6	7	8	9
1	1	2	3	4	5	6	7	8	9	10
2	2	3	4	5	6	7	8	9	10	11
3	3	4	5	6	7	8	9	10	11	12
4	4	5	6	7	8	9	10	11	12	13
5	5	6	7	8	9	10	11	12	13	14
6	6	7	8	9	10	11	12	13	14	15
7	7	8	9	10	11	12	13	14	15	16
8	8	9	10	11	12	13	14	15	16	17
9	9	10	11	12	13	14	15	16	17	18

Math Journal 1, p. 27

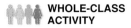

Discussing Doubles-Plus-2 Facts

Doubles-plus-2 facts are addition facts in which one addend is 2 more than the other addend (for example, 6 + 4). Write some doubles-plus-2 facts on the board; leave out the sums. Use both horizontal and vertical forms. (*See margin.*)

Ask children to copy and complete the facts on their slates. See whether any children mention a strategy that makes use of doubles. Discuss doubles-plus-2 strategies. To add numbers where one addend is 2 more than the other addend, double the smaller number and add 2.

Some children may discover that they can change a doubles-plus-2 fact into a doubles fact by subtracting 1 from the larger addend and adding 1 to the smaller addend, for example, they might change 4 + 6 into the doubles fact 5 + 5.

Practicing Addition Strategies That Use Doubles Facts

(*Math Journal 1*, p. 33)

Children practice and extend the doubles-plus-1 and doubles-plus-2 strategies and extend them to doubles-plus-3 facts.

(2) Ongoing Learning & Practice

Playing *Domino Top-It*

Have partners place dominoes facedown between them. Each player turns over a domino and calls out the sum of the dots on the two halves. The player with the higher sum wins and takes all the dominoes currently in play.

Domino Top-It is suggested in anticipation of Lesson 2-6, in which children use dominoes to construct subtraction facts.

Chalkboard 1:

$4 + 5 = \underline{}$ $\quad 7 \quad\quad 5$
$\underline{} = 9 + 8 \quad +6 \quad +6$

Chalkboard 2:

$4 + 6 = \underline{}$ $\quad 7 \quad\quad 6$
$\underline{} = 9 + 7 \quad +5 \quad +8$

Student Page

Date _____ Time _____

LESSON 2·5 Addition Facts

If you know a double, you know the 1-more and the 1-less sums.

Example:
If you know that 4 + 4 = 8,
You know 4 + 5 = 9,
And 4 + 3 = 7

1. 3 + 4 = $\underline{7}$ 2. 8 + 7 = $\underline{15}$

3. $\underline{13}$ = 6 + 7 4. $\begin{array}{r} 6 \\ + 5 \\ \hline 11 \end{array}$

5. $\begin{array}{r} 8 \\ + 9 \\ \hline 17 \end{array}$ 6. $\begin{array}{r} 7 \\ + 5 \\ \hline 12 \end{array}$ 7. $\begin{array}{r} 7 \\ + 9 \\ \hline 16 \end{array}$

8. 5 + 8 = $\underline{13}$ 9. $\underline{15}$ = 6 + 9 10. 8 + 6 = $\underline{14}$

Try This

11. 8 + 8 = $\underline{16}$ 12. 12 + 12 = $\underline{24}$
8 + 9 = $\underline{17}$ 12 + 13 = $\underline{25}$
8 + 7 = $\underline{15}$ 12 + 11 = $\underline{23}$

13. 15 + 15 = $\underline{30}$ 14. 14 + 12 = $\underline{26}$
16 + 15 = $\underline{31}$ 15 + 13 = $\underline{28}$
14 + 15 = $\underline{29}$

Math Journal 1, p. 33

▶ Cutting Out Fact Triangles

(*Math Journal 1,* Activity Sheets 1 and 2)

INDEPENDENT
ACTIVITY

Have children cut out the Fact Triangles from Activity Sheets 1 and 2. You might want to have them write their initials or draw a distinctive pattern on the back of each triangle. This will help children identify their individual sets.

Tell children to store the Fact Triangles in envelopes in their tool kits when they are not using them.

These Fact Triangles will be used in Lessons 2-7 and 2-11 through 2-13 as addition and subtraction flashcards. In Lesson 2-12, children will cut out a second set of Fact Triangles from Activity Sheets 3 and 4.

▶ Math Boxes 2·5

(*Math Journal 1,* p. 34)

INDEPENDENT
ACTIVITY

Mixed Practice Math Boxes in this lesson are paired with Math Boxes in Lesson 2-7. The skills in Problems 5 and 6 preview Unit 3 content.

▶ Home Link 2·5

(*Math Masters,* p. 29)

INDEPENDENT
ACTIVITY

Home Connection Children complete a page of addition facts and draw a path from the child to the ice-cream cone by connecting sums of 9, 10, or 11.

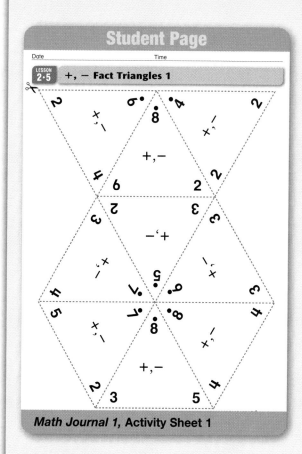

Math Journal 1, Activity Sheet 1

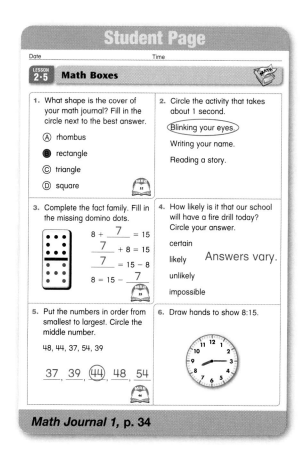

Math Journal 1, p. 34

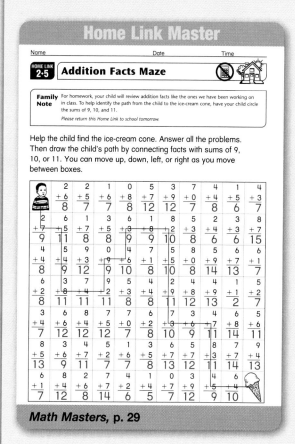

Math Masters, p. 29

③ Differentiation Options

▶ **Designing a Doubles Facts Book**

 INDEPENDENT ACTIVITY

🌓 **15–30 Min**

 To explore doubles facts using a concrete model, have children design a Doubles Facts Book using their Pattern-Block Template. First, have children create a doubles fact using pattern blocks of the same shape. Next, children copy the design onto a sheet of paper using their template. Each design shows a doubles fact accompanied by a number model. Staple the pages together to create a Doubles Facts Book. Have children describe their "double" designs using color and shape words. For example, "There are three sides on each green triangle. I have two green triangles. Three plus three equals six. There are six sides in my design." "There are two red trapezoids and two yellow hexagons. Two plus two equals four. There are four shapes in my design."

 PARTNER ACTIVITY

▶ **Exploring Calculator Doubles**

🕐 **5–15 Min**

(*Math Masters,* p. 30)

To further explore the concept of doubles addition facts, have children work with a partner to solve "doubles" problems on a calculator.

2·6 Subtraction from Addition

 Objectives To review the –0 and –1 shortcuts; and to guide children to identify the subtraction facts related to given addition facts.

---

1 Teaching the Lesson | materials

Key Activities
Children make up and share number stories that are solved by subtraction, discover and practice the –0 and –1 shortcuts, and use dominoes to generate related addition and subtraction facts.

Key Concepts and Skills
- Practice subtraction facts. [Operations and Computation Goal 1]
- Use dominoes to model related addition and subtraction facts.
  [Operations and Computation Goal 1]
- Identify and use patterns to solve subtraction facts. [Patterns, Functions, and Algebra Goal 1]
- Use symbols to write number sentences for fact families.
  [Patterns, Functions, and Algebra Goal 2]

Key Vocabulary
subtraction number story • –0 facts • –1 facts • –0 shortcut • –1 shortcut

⭐ **Ongoing Assessment: Recognizing Student Achievement** Use an Exit Slip.
[Patterns, Functions, and Algebra Goal 3]

☐ *Math Journal 1*, p. 35
☐ Home Link 2·5
☐ Teaching Aid Master
   (*Math Masters*, p. 415)
☐ 1 domino per child
☐ calculator; slate
☐ 10 counters and 10 cubes (optional)

---

2 Ongoing Learning & Practice | materials

Partners practice addition facts by playing *Beat the Calculator* or *Domino Top-It*.

Children practice and maintain skills through Math Boxes and Home Link activities.

☐ *Math Journal 1*, p. 24 (optional)
☐ *Math Journal 1*, p. 36
☐ Home Link Master (*Math Masters*, p. 31)
☐ 1 set of dominoes per partnership (optional)
☐ 1 calculator per group of 3 children (optional)

---

3 Differentiation Options | materials

READINESS
Children explore the relationship between addition and subtraction facts.

ENRICHMENT
Children use dice combinations to explore differences and patterns in subtraction.

☐ Teaching Masters (*Math Masters*, pp. 32 and 33)
☐ dominoes
☐ dice; number line

Technology
Assessment Management System
Exit Slip
See the **iTLG.**

Lesson 2·6 121

Getting Started

Mental Math and Reflexes

Pose doubles-plus-1 and doubles-plus-2 facts.
Suggestions:

⊚○○ 6 + 6 = ? 12	⊚⊚○ 6 + 7 = ? 13	⊚⊚⊚ 6 + 8 = ? 14
8 + 8 = ? 16	8 + 9 = ? 17	8 + 10 = ? 18
7 + 7 = ? 14	7 + 8 = ? 15	7 + 9 = ? 16

Math Message

Make up a story for the number model 10 − 3 = 7.

Home Link 2·5
Follow-Up

Check that children were able to find the correct path from the child to the ice-cream cone.

NOTE Change-to-less (also called take-away) is the meaning of subtraction most often encountered in schoolwork. The comparison meaning of subtraction does not involve take-away, because nothing is actually taken away; the two sets of cars are just being compared. Children are not expected to categorize subtraction stories as "change-to-less" or "comparison" at this time.

Adjusting the Activity   ELL

Children model change-to-less by representing the number of items in the story with counters. They remove the appropriate number of counters as described in the story. The number of counters remaining is the difference.

● ● ● ● ● ● ● ● ● ●

● ● ● ● ● ● ● ○ ○ ○

10 take away 3 is 7.

Children can also model comparison number stories by placing sets of connecting cubes side by side. The sets represent the numbers being compared. Children can determine the answer by visually comparing the two sets of cubes.

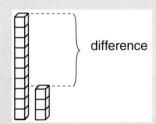

difference   The difference between 10 and 3 is 7.

AUDITORY ◆ KINESTHETIC ◆ TACTILE ◆ VISUAL

---

① Teaching the Lesson

▶ Math Message Follow-Up   WHOLE-CLASS ACTIVITY

Write 10 − 3 = 7 on the board. Ask children to share their **subtraction number stories.** Draw an empty unit box. Have children suggest a label for each number story and write it in the unit box. Expect most of the children's number stories to be one of two types:

Change-to-Less

Start with a number of items. Decrease the number of items. Find out the number of items after the number is decreased. *For example:* Tavon had 10 model cars. He lost 3 model cars. How many model cars does Tavon have now? 7 model cars

Comparison

Two separate quantities are known. Compare them by finding the difference between them. Tell how many more or less. *For example:* Supat has 10 model cars. Neal has 3 model cars. How many more model cars does Supat have? 7 more model cars

▶ Discussing the −0 and the −1 Shortcuts   WHOLE-CLASS ACTIVITY

Write some **−0 facts** and **−1 facts** on the board; do not include the differences. Use both horizontal and vertical forms.

Examples:

$$5 - 0 = \underline{\quad} \qquad \begin{array}{r} 3 \\ -1 \\ \hline \end{array} \qquad \begin{array}{r} 9 \\ -0 \\ \hline \end{array}$$

$$\underline{\quad} = 9 - 1$$

$$\underline{\quad} = 8 - 0$$

Ask children to copy and complete the facts on their slates. See whether they can describe the **−0 shortcut** and the **−1 shortcut.** If 0 is subtracted from any number, that number does not change. If 1 is subtracted from any number, the result is the next smaller number.

Write this problem on the board: $87 - 0 =$ ____. After a volunteer has given the answer, ask someone else to check the answer on a calculator. Try several other examples with 2- and 3-digit numbers, and with some large numbers, just for fun!

Follow the same procedure with several −1 examples. Use 2- and 3-digit numbers and a few large numbers.

▶ Using Dominoes to Generate Related Addition and Subtraction Facts

♦♦♦ WHOLE-CLASS ACTIVITY

Draw a domino on the board. Help children discover a set of related facts shown by the domino. For example, for a domino with 5 dots on one half and 4 dots on the other, ask:

● What is the total number of dots shown? 9

● Which addition facts describe this domino? $5 + 4 = 9$ and $4 + 5 = 9$

Remind children about turn-around facts.

Write the numbers 5, 4, and 9 on the board. Then write the two addition facts just named: $5 + 4 = 9$ and $4 + 5 = 9$.

● Which subtraction facts can you write using the three numbers 5, 4, and 9? $9 - 5 = 4$ and $9 - 4 = 5$ Write these two subtraction facts on the board.

Continue with other domino examples in the same way.

▶ Practicing Domino Facts

♦ INDEPENDENT ACTIVITY

(*Math Journal 1*, p. 35)

Children write the addition and subtraction facts generated by each domino pattern on the journal page. The final problems include special features that may cause some children difficulty. The double-9 domino has only two related facts, not four: $9 + 9 = 18$ and $18 - 9 = 9$. The domino with 9 dots on the top and zero dots on the bottom may confuse children. Make sure children realize that the blank half of the domino stands for zero. The four related facts for this domino are $9 + 0 = 9$, $0 + 9 = 9$, $9 - 0 = 9$, and $9 - 9 = 0$.

$$\begin{array}{cccc} 5 & 4 & 9 & 5 \\ +\ 4 & +\ 5 & -\ 5 & -\ 4 \\ \hline 9 & 9 & 4 & 5 \end{array}$$

⬆ Adjusting the Activity

So children can recognize the subtraction facts using dominoes, have them erase or cover up one side of the domino. *For example:* Nine dots in all. Take away the 5 dots on one side by erasing them. Four dots remain. So, $9 - 5 = 4$.

AUDITORY ♦ KINESTHETIC ♦ TACTILE ♦ VISUAL

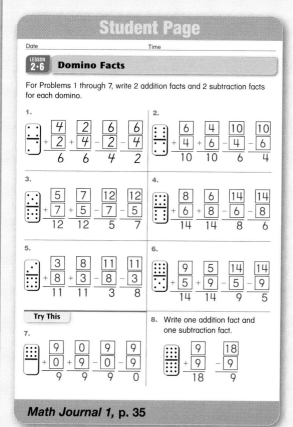

Student Page

Date _____ Time _____

LESSON 2·6 Domino Facts

For Problems 1 through 7, write 2 addition facts and 2 subtraction facts for each domino.

Math Journal 1, p. 35

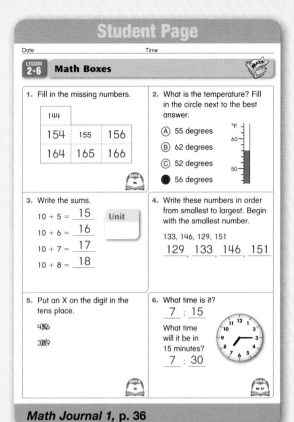

Date _____ Time _____

LESSON 2·6   **Math Boxes**

1. Fill in the missing numbers.

144		
154	155	156
164	165	166

2. What is the temperature? Fill in the circle next to the best answer.

Ⓐ 55 degrees
Ⓑ 62 degrees
Ⓒ 52 degrees
● 56 degrees

3. Write the sums.

$10 + 5 = \underline{15}$ Unit
$10 + 6 = \underline{16}$
$10 + 7 = \underline{17}$
$10 + 8 = \underline{18}$

4. Write these numbers in order from smallest to largest. Begin with the smallest number.

133, 146, 129, 151
$\underline{129}, \underline{133}, \underline{146}, \underline{151}$

5. Put an X on the digit in the tens place.

4⊗6

3⊗9

6. What time is it?

$\underline{7} : \underline{15}$

What time will it be in 15 minutes?

$\underline{7} : \underline{30}$

Math Journal 1, p. 36

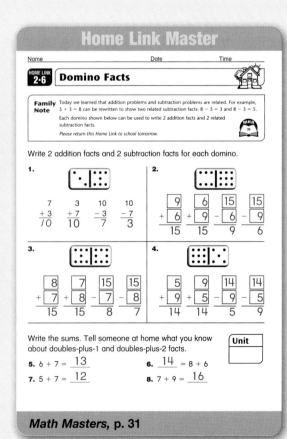

Name _____ Date _____ Time _____

HOME LINK 2·6   **Domino Facts**

Family Note   Today we learned that addition problems and subtraction problems are related. For example, $5 + 3 = 8$ can be rewritten to show two related subtraction facts: $8 - 5 = 3$ and $8 - 3 = 5$.

Each domino shown below can be used to write 2 addition facts and 2 related subtraction facts.

Please return this Home Link to school tomorrow.

Write 2 addition facts and 2 subtraction facts for each domino.

1.

7	3	10	10
+3	+7	-3	-7
10	10	7	3

2.

9	6	15	15
+6	+9	-6	-9
15	15	9	6

3.

8	7	15	15
+7	+8	-7	-8
15	15	8	7

4.

5	9	14	14
+9	+5	-9	-5
14	14	5	9

Write the sums. Tell someone at home what you know about doubles-plus-1 and doubles-plus-2 facts.   Unit

5. $6 + 7 = \underline{13}$ 6. $\underline{14} = 8 + 6$

7. $5 + 7 = \underline{12}$ 8. $7 + 9 = \underline{16}$

Math Masters, p. 31

Ongoing Assessment: **Exit Slip**
Recognizing Student Achievement

Use an **Exit Slip** (*Math Masters,* page 415) to assess children's understanding of the turn-around facts. Give each child a domino. Have them write two addition and two subtraction facts for that domino. Children are making adequate progress if they can write the corresponding addition problem and the turn-around fact. Some children may be able to successfully write two corresponding subtraction problems.

[Patterns, Functions, and Algebra Goal 3]

② Ongoing Learning & Practice

▶ Practicing Addition Facts   👥 PARTNER ACTIVITY

(*Math Journal 1,* p. 24)

Children may practice addition facts by playing *Beat the Calculator.* They may also practice with *Domino Top-It.*

▶ Math Boxes 2·6   👤 INDEPENDENT ACTIVITY

(*Math Journal 1,* p. 36)

Mixed Practice Math Boxes in this lesson are paired with Math Boxes in Lesson 2-8. The skills in Problems 5 and 6 preview Unit 3 content.

▶ Home Link 2·6   👤 INDEPENDENT ACTIVITY

(*Math Masters,* p. 31)

Home Connection Children use dominoes to generate and solve related addition and subtraction facts. Children also practice doubles-plus-1 and doubles-plus-2 facts.

③ Differentiation Options

READINESS   👤 INDEPENDENT ACTIVITY

▶ Exploring Domino Facts   🕐 5–15 Min

(*Math Masters,* p. 32)

To explore the relationship between addition and subtraction facts using a concrete model, have children use dominoes to model facts. Children complete *Math Masters,* page 32. When they have finished the page, discuss when they added and when they subtracted to find the missing numbers. (Note that some children may add up instead of subtracting when solving the domino problems.)

▶ **Exploring Dice Subtraction
with Negative Differences**

(*Math Masters*, p. 33)

👤 **INDEPENDENT
ACTIVITY**

🕐 **5–15 Min**

To apply children's understanding of subtraction, have them solve
randomly generated single-digit subtraction problems. They record
their work on *Math Masters,* page 33. Discuss the patterns they
see on the page. When the two numbers are switched in the
problem, the differences are the same distance from zero on the
number line. When you subtract the larger number from the
smaller number, the difference is a negative number.

Planning Ahead

If children have not cut out the Fact Triangles from Activity
Sheets 1 and 2, have them do that soon. They will be used in
Lesson 2-7.

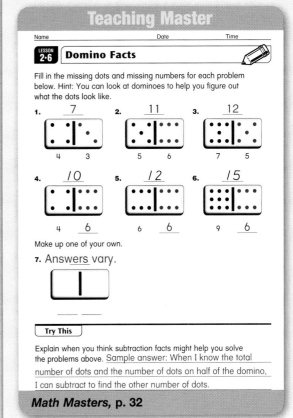

Teaching Master

Name   Date   Time

LESSON 2·6 Domino Facts

Fill in the missing dots and missing numbers for each problem
below. Hint: You can look at dominoes to help you figure out
what the dots look like.

1. 7   2. 11   3. 12
   4 3   5 6   7 5

4. 10   5. 12   6. 15
   4 6   6 6   9 6

Make up one of your own.

7. Answers vary.

Try This

Explain when you think subtraction facts might help you solve
the problems above. Sample answer: When I know the total
number of dots and the number of dots on half of the domino,
I can subtract to find the other number of dots.

***Math Masters*, p. 32**

Teaching Master

Name   Date   Time

LESSON 2·6 Dice Subtraction

For each problem below:

1. Roll two dice.

2. Record the numbers you rolled.

3. Write two subtraction number models for the numbers
   you rolled.

4. Use a number line to solve your problems. (Hint:
   Sometimes your answers will be negative numbers.)

Example:

I rolled 4 and 5.

5 − 4 = 1 and 4 − 5 = −1.

1. I rolled ____ and ____.

   ____ − ____ = ____   ____ − ____ = ____

2. I rolled ____ and ____.

   ____ − ____ = ____   ____ − ____ = ____

3. I rolled ____ and ____.

   ____ − ____ = ____   ____ − ____ = ____

Try This

Each time you roll the dice, how could you use one of your
subtraction problems to help you solve the other?

Sample answer: Each answer will be the same
distance from 0 on the number line.

***Math Masters*, p. 33**

2·7 Fact Families

 Objectives To demonstrate the inverse relationship between addition and subtraction; and to provide practice for addition and subtraction facts for sums up to and including 10.

1 Teaching the Lesson

materials

Key Activities
Children identify the fact families shown on Fact Triangles, and practice the "easier" addition and subtraction facts by using Fact Triangles as flashcards.

Key Concepts and Skills
• Practice basic facts in the context of Fact Triangles.
  [Operations and Computation Goal 1]
• Use symbols to write number sentences for fact families.
  [Patterns, Functions, and Algebra Goal 2]
• Construct fact families (using the turn-around rule for addition).
  [Patterns, Functions, and Algebra Goal 3]

Key Vocabulary
Fact Triangle • fact family

□ Fact Triangles cut from *Math Journal 1,* Activity Sheets 1 and 2 (see Lesson 2·5)
□ My Reference Book, p. 27
□ Home Link 2·6
□ Transparency (*Math Masters,* p. 423; optional)
□ slate

***See* Advance Preparation**

2 Ongoing Learning & Practice

materials

Children solve subtraction number stories.

Children practice and maintain skills through Math Boxes and Home Link activities.

✔️ **Ongoing Assessment: Recognizing Student Achievement** Use journal page 38.
  [Patterns, Functions, and Algebra Goal 2]

□ *Math Journal 1,* pp. 37 and 38
□ Home Link Masters (*Math Masters,* pp. 34 and 35)
□ Teaching Aid Master (*Math Masters,* p. 415)

3 Differentiation Options

materials

READINESS
Children use counters to represent subtraction.

ENRICHMENT
Children use subtraction to find mystery numbers.

ELL SUPPORT
Children make a fact family chain.

□ Teaching Master (*Math Masters,* p. 36)
□ 18 pennies or other counters per partnership
□ calculator
□ number line
□ dominoes (optional)
□ 1 8$\frac{1}{2}$ x 11 sheet of paper per child

Additional Information

Advance Preparation If children have not already cut out the Fact Triangles from Activity Sheets 1 and 2, they should do so before working on the Math Message.

For the Discussing Fact Families activity in Part 1, you may want to make an overhead transparency of *Math Masters,* p. 423.

Technology
Assessment Management System
Math Boxes, Problem 3
See the **iTLG.**

Getting Started

Mental Math and Reflexes

Pose simple **subtraction number story** problems. Have children share solution strategies. *Suggestions:*

○○○ Kevin had 9 pencils and he lost 3 pencils. How many pencils does Kevin have now? 6 pencils

June had 5 cookies and she shared 2 cookies with Juanita. How many cookies does June have left? 3 cookies

○○○ Denzel had $20 and spent $7. How much does Denzel have now? $13

Diego had $35 and he spent $15. How much does Diego have now? $20

There are 8 boys on Team A and 12 boys on Team B. How many more boys are on Team B? 4 boys

○○○ Barb scored 25 points. Dora scored 15 points. How many more points did Barb score? 10 points

Math Message

Take out your envelope of Fact Triangles. Write your name, and write "Fact Triangles" on the envelope.

Home Link 2·6 Follow-Up

Review answers as necessary.

---

1 Teaching the Lesson

▶ Math Message Follow-Up

WHOLE-CLASS DISCUSSION

Tell children to store the **Fact Triangles** in their tool kits when they are not using them. Explain that they will be using the Fact Triangles in this lesson to practice addition and subtraction facts.

▶ Discussing Fact Families

WHOLE-CLASS ACTIVITY

(*Math Masters,* p. 423)

Remind children that, in the previous lesson, the class discussed how to use addition number sentences to write related subtraction number sentences. Tell them that, in today's lesson, they will be using their knowledge of addition and subtraction number sentences to create fact families.

Draw a unit box on the board and ask a child to choose a label for the day. Then display an overhead transparency of *Math Masters,* page 423 or draw a large triangle on the board. Write 6, 3, and 9 (with a large dot above the 9) in the three corners. Ask children to describe ways in which the three numbers are related.

Show children that the three numbers can be used to make two addition facts ($6 + 3 = 9$ and $3 + 6 = 9$) and two subtraction facts ($9 - 6 = 3$ and $9 - 3 = 6$). This collection of facts is called a **fact family.** To support English language learners, discuss the everyday meaning of *family* and the meaning of *family* in this context. Point out that the large dot is used to identify the sum for addition facts and the first number (the minuend) for subtraction facts.

Teaching Aid Master

Name	Date	Time

Fact Triangle

Math Masters, p. 423

Student Page

Operations and Computation

Fact triangles show the 3 numbers in a fact family.

$3 + 5 = 8$ $8 - 5 = 3$
$5 + 3 = 8$ $8 - 3 = 5$

This is the fact family for 8, 5, and 3.

You can use fact triangles to practice facts.

To practice addition, cover the number by the dot.

Cover 8. Think:
$3 + 5 = ?$ $5 + 3 = ?$

To practice subtraction, cover one of the other numbers.

Cover 5. Think:
$8 - 3 = ?$ $3 + ? = 8$

Try It Together

Use your fact triangles to play *Beat the Calculator*.

My Reference Book, p. 27

NOTE Some teachers suggest having children write the fact families on the backs of the Fact Triangles. This could be an ongoing project, to be done a few at a time.

Student Page

Date _____   Time _____

LESSON 2·7   Subtraction Number Stories

Solve each problem.

1. Dajon has $11. He buys a book for $6. How much money does he have left?

$ __5__

2. Martin has 7 markers. Carlos has 4 markers. How many more markers does Martin have than Carlos?

__3__ markers

3. There are 11 girls on Tina's softball team. There are 13 girls on Lisa's team. How many more girls are on Lisa's team than on Tina's?

__2__ girls

4. Julia has 10 flowers. She gives 4 flowers to her sister. How many flowers does she have left?

__6__ flowers

5. Keisha has 8 chocolate cookies and 5 vanilla cookies. How many more chocolate cookies does she have than vanilla cookies?

__3__ chocolate cookies

6. Make up and solve your own subtraction story.

   Sample answer: Tyrell had $20. He spent $9.
   How much money does he have left? $11

Math Journal 1, p. 37

Ask someone to name three other numbers that are related by addition. Write these numbers in the corners of a triangle and have children write the fact family for the numbers on their slates. Repeat with other number sets as needed.

● How many different facts are there in the fact family for a doubles fact? 2; for example, $4 + 4 = 8$ and $8 - 4 = 4$

● Do subtraction facts have turn-around facts? No; for example, $9 - 3 = 6$ but $3 - 9 = -6$

▶ **Demonstrating the Use of +, − Fact Triangles**

 PARTNER ACTIVITY

(*My Reference Book,* p. 27)

For more information about Fact Triangles, read *My Reference Book* page 27 with your class. Demonstrate the flashcard procedure using an actual Fact Triangle, or the Fact Triangle on the transparency or board. Have partners practice it.

1. One partner covers one corner of a Fact Triangle with a finger or thumb.

2. The covered number is part of an addition or subtraction fact. The other partner says the complete fact.

Two journal pages with 9 Fact Triangles on each page are provided in this unit (*Math Journal 1,* Activity Sheets 1 and 2). The full set of 36 addition/subtraction Fact Triangles (Activity Sheets 1–4) includes all the facts except the 0 facts and the 1 facts. Encourage children to use the triangles at a pace that is comfortable for them. The first 18 triangles are used in this lesson and in Lessons 2-11 through 2-13; the remaining triangles are used in Lesson 2-13.

▶ **Practicing with Fact Triangles**

 PARTNER ACTIVITY

Children continue the flashcard procedure described above. You may wish to have children write facts on their slates rather than saying them aloud. Offer guidance to children as needed.

Adjusting the Activity

When a child misses a fact, the partner should flash the other fact problems on the triangle and then return to the fact that was missed. For example, Sue can't answer $10 - 6$. Alex flashes $6 + 4$, then $10 - 4$, and finally $10 - 6$ a second time.

AUDITORY ◆ KINESTHETIC ◆ TACTILE ◆ VISUAL

Use of the Fact Triangles will continually remind children that a good way to subtract is to ask, "How much do I add?" Each time a subtraction problem is posed, the child will receive two visual messages—a subtraction message and a related addition message.

$9 - 3 = ?$ and $3 + ? = 9$

2 Ongoing Learning & Practice

▶ Solving Subtraction Number Stories

INDEPENDENT ACTIVITY

(*Math Journal 1*, p. 37)

Change-to-less and comparison subtraction number stories were covered previously in Lesson 2-6 and practiced in the Mental Math and Reflexes problems in this lesson.

▶ Math Boxes 2·7

INDEPENDENT ACTIVITY

(*Math Journal 1*, p. 38)

Mixed Practice Math Boxes in this lesson are paired with Math Boxes in Lesson 2-5. The skills in Problems 5 and 6 preview Unit 3 content.

Writing/Reasoning Have children draw, write, or verbalize their answers to the following: *In Problem 3, how does writing two addition facts help you write two subtraction facts?* Sample answer: Since I know that a fact family has 3 numbers, I know to start with the largest number from my addition number sentence. I then subtract each of the other numbers from that number.

Ongoing Assessment:
Recognizing Student Achievement

Math Boxes Problem 3 ★

Use **Math Boxes, Problem 3** to assess children's progress toward writing a number story to explain a number sentence. Have children use an Exit Slip (*Math Masters,* p. 415) to write a number story that matches one of the four number sentences in Problem 3. Children are making adequate progress if they can successfully write a matching number story. Some children may write a number story for more than one number sentence.

[Patterns, Functions, and Algebra Goal 2]

▶ Home Link 2·7

INDEPENDENT ACTIVITY

(*Math Masters*, pp. 34 and 35)

Home Connection Children show someone at home how they practice with Fact Triangles. The family note explains Fact Triangles in more detail and suggests regular use at home to complement fact work in class.

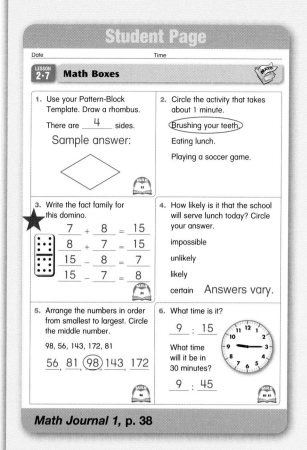
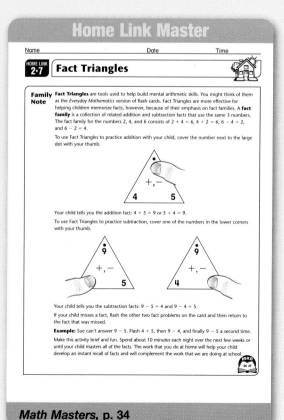

3 Differentiation Options

READINESS

PARTNER ACTIVITY

5–15 Min

▶ Solving Subtraction Facts with Counters

To explore subtraction facts using a concrete model, have children use counters to create subtraction number sentences.

1. Partners start with a known number of counters, such as 12.

2. Player 1 separates the counters into two groups; for example, one group of 7 and one group of 5.

● ● ● ● ● ● ●

● ● ● ● ●

3. The same child then covers one of the two groups with a piece of paper.

● ● ● ● ● ● ●

○ ○ ○ ○ ○

4. Player 2 writes the subtraction fact. *For example:* 12 *(whole)* – 7 *(known part)* = 5 *(unknown part)*. If necessary, the child may count the covered group to check the answer.

5. Player 2 now flips the paper over to cover the other group of counters.

6. Player 1 writes a different subtraction fact.

This activity can be repeated with any number of counters in different combinations.

ENRICHMENT

PARTNER ACTIVITY

5–15 Min

▶ Finding Subtraction Mystery Numbers

(*Math Masters*, p. 36)

To apply children's understanding of subtraction facts, have them find mystery numbers using the calculator as a subtraction-function machine. Make one copy of *Math Masters,* page 36 for each child. On the *Math Masters* page, directions for Calculator A will work on most calculators, including the TI-108, and Calculator B refers to the Casio SL-450.

NOTE You may want to suggest that children secretly write down their mystery number on their turn so that they do not forget it. This activity could involve exposure to negative numbers. Have a number line that extends from negative numbers to positive numbers available.

ELL SUPPORT

▶ Making a Fact Family Chain

To provide language support for fact families, have children create a fact family chain. To make the chain, take an $8\frac{1}{2}$ x 11 sheet of paper. Fold it in half so that the two $8\frac{1}{2}$ inch sides are touching. Fold again so that the two $8\frac{1}{2}$ inch sides are touching. (When you set the paper on the table with the middle fold pointing toward the ceiling, the paper should stand up like a tent.) Hold the folded paper and on one of the shorter sides cut off the two corners to form a triangular peak. Open the paper, and you have a chain of "Fact Family Houses." Write the three numbers of the fact family in the triangular "roof" of the house, and write the family of number sentences in the house explaining that only the numbers in the family can live in the house. Children can choose a domino to help them write a fact family or make up one of their own for each house.

3	8	14	18
2 1	5 3	7 7	10 8
$2 + 1 = 3$	$8 = 5 + 3$	$7 + 7 = 14$	$10 + 8 = 18$
$1 + 2 = 3$	$8 = 3 + 5$	$14 - 7 = 7$	$8 + 10 = 18$
$3 - 2 = 1$	$3 = 8 - 5$		$18 - 10 = 8$
$3 - 1 = 2$	$5 = 8 - 3$		$18 - 8 = 10$

Exploring Weights, Scales, Equal Groups

EXPLORATIONS

 Objective To guide children as they use a pan balance and spring scale, to experience the ounce/pound relationship, and find the total number of objects in equal groups.

---

1 Teaching the Lesson

Key Activities

Exploration A: Children use a pan balance to compare weights of different objects.

Exploration B: Children use a spring scale to find a set of objects whose combined weight is about 1 pound.

Exploration C: Children develop readiness for multiplication by making equal groups of objects and finding the total.

Key Concepts and Skills

• Use repeated addition to solve equal groups problems.
  [Operations and Computation Goal 4]

• Use a spring scale to weigh objects that are about 1 pound.
  [Measurement and Reference Frames Goal 1]

• Model the relationship between two objects.
  [Patterns, Functions, and Algebra Goal 2]

Key Vocabulary

ounce • pound • pan balance • heavier • lighter • in balance (balanced) • spring scale

Ongoing Assessment: Recognizing Student Achievement Use Mental Math and Reflexes. [Patterns, Functions, and Algebra Goal 1]

Ongoing Assessment: Informing Instruction See page 135.

materials

☐ Home Link 2·7

☐ number grid or *Math Masters*, p. 416; 1 half-sheet of paper per child

☐ tape measure; 10 pennies

Exploration A: Per small group:

☐ *Math Journal 1*, p. 39

☐ pan balance; objects weighing between $\frac{1}{2}$ oz and 8 oz

Exploration B: Per small group:

☐ *Math Journal 1*, p. 39

☐ spring scale; plastic bag; objects weighing between $\frac{1}{2}$ oz and 8 oz

Exploration C: Per partnership:

☐ Teaching Master (*Math Masters,* p. 37)

☐ 6 quarter sheets of paper; 1 six-sided die

☐ 36 counters, such as pennies, cubes, or beans; 1 sheet of plain paper

***See* Advance Preparation**

---

2 Ongoing Learning & Practice

Children practice basic addition facts by playing *Beat the Calculator.*

Children practice and maintain skills through Math Boxes and Home Link activities.

materials

☐ *Math Journal 1*, pp. 24 and 40

☐ *My Reference Book,* pp. 124 and 125

☐ Home Link Masters (*Math Masters,* pp. 38 and 39)

---

3 Differentiation Options

READINESS

Children compare the weights of two objects by hand and by pan balance.

ENRICHMENT

Children estimate and find the weights of objects.

EXTRA PRACTICE

Children solve problems with time, weight, length, volume, and area.

materials

☐ *Minute Math®+,* pp. 61 and 62

☐ pan balance; spring scale

☐ objects weighing between $\frac{1}{2}$ oz and 8 oz

Additional Information

Advance Preparation Collect objects found in the classroom that weigh between $\frac{1}{2}$ ounce and 8 ounces. Objects found in many rooms include a student tape measure ($\frac{1}{2}$ oz), a 2-inch binder clip (1 oz), a calculator (2 to 4 oz), a card deck (3 oz), a large pair of scissors (5 oz), a mug (6 oz), a full pad of lined paper (7 oz), and small paperback books (4 to 8 oz).

Technology

Assessment Management System
Mental Math and Reflexes
See the **iTLG.**

Getting Started

Mental Math and Reflexes

On a half-sheet of paper, ask children to use the number grid to find the number of spaces from one number to another. Have children demonstrate how they found their answers. *Suggestions:*

What is the number of spaces from:

⦿○○ 12 to 22? 10

⦿⦿○ 23 to 44? 21

⦿⦿⦿ 46 to 32? 14

Math Message

Which is heavier—1 ounce or 1 pound? 1 pound

Do you think your calculator weighs more than 1 pound or less than 1 pound? Less than 1 pound

Home Link 2·7 Follow-Up

Review answers as necessary.

 Ongoing Assessment: Recognizing Student Achievement   **Mental Math and Reflexes** ★

Use **Mental Math and Reflexes** to assess children's ability to use counting patterns on the number grid. Children are making adequate progress if they are able to find the answers using the number grid counting by ones. Some children may be able to count using tens and ones and still others may be able to find the answer using mental math.

[Patterns, Functions, and Algebra Goal 1]

---

1 Teaching the Lesson

▶ ## Math Message Follow-Up   WHOLE-CLASS DISCUSSION

Discuss children's answers. Say that **ounces** and **pounds** are different units of weight, just as inches and miles are different units of length. In the United States, short objects are measured in inches, and long distances are measured in miles. Light things are weighed in ounces, and heavy things are weighed in pounds. When discussing weight, children should have opportunities to hold different weights and compare them with one another. For example, each child should hold an object that weighs a pound and then one that weighs an ounce. Have children compare and discuss the weights of the two objects.

▶ ## Demonstrating the Pan Balance   WHOLE-CLASS ACTIVITY

Place two objects of different weights in the pans on the **pan balance.** The pan with the **heavier** object will go down. The pan with the **lighter** object will go up. Ask children when they have heard the words light and lighter before and discuss their meanings. Make sure to clarify the meaning of light and lighter in the context of this lesson. Point out that the balance does not have numbers on it like a bath scale.

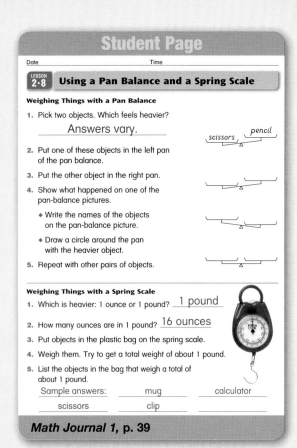

Date   Time

LESSON 2·8 Using a Pan Balance and a Spring Scale

Weighing Things with a Pan Balance

1. Pick two objects. Which feels heavier?

   _____Answers vary._____

   scissors   pencil

2. Put one of these objects in the left pan of the pan balance.

3. Put the other object in the right pan.

4. Show what happened on one of the pan-balance pictures.

   ◆ Write the names of the objects on the pan-balance picture.

   ◆ Draw a circle around the pan with the heavier object.

5. Repeat with other pairs of objects.

Weighing Things with a Spring Scale

1. Which is heavier: 1 ounce or 1 pound? 1 pound

2. How many ounces are in 1 pound? 16 ounces

3. Put objects in the plastic bag on the spring scale.

4. Weigh them. Try to get a total weight of about 1 pound.

5. List the objects in the bag that weigh a total of about 1 pound.

   Sample answers: mug   calculator

   scissors   clip   _____

Math Journal 1, p. 39

Place a student tape measure in one pan. Slowly add pennies to the other pan until the pans are **in balance.** (A student tape measure weighs about the same as 10 pennies.) Say that when the pans are equally balanced like this, the objects in the two pans are about the same weight.

▶ Demonstrating the Spring Scale 👨👧👩👦 WHOLE-CLASS ACTIVITY

Show children the marks and numbers on the **spring scale.** Say that they are like the marks and numbers on a bath scale that show weight in pounds. A spring scale, however, is usually used with objects that weigh less than a pound. Numbers on a spring scale represent ounces, not pounds.

Place an object that weighs more than 1 pound (for example, a book) in a plastic bag and hang the bag from the spring scale. The scale marker is pulled down to the bottom. The object is too heavy for this scale because it weighs more than 1 pound.

Pull the hook on the spring scale down until the marker is at 16 ounces. Say that this is what a 1-pound weight would do. Say that ounces are lighter than pounds, and there are 16 ounces in a pound.

Hang a pair of scissors on the scale. This time the scale marker moves down part of the way, but not all the way to the bottom. Read the number next to the marker and tell the class how many ounces the pair of scissors weighs. Point out that the plastic bag is necessary for weighing objects that cannot be hung easily on the scale (like books).

▶ Exploration A: Using a Pan Balance 👩👧 SMALL-GROUP ACTIVITY

(*Math Journal 1*, p. 39)

Help children understand the directions on the journal page. Two separate activities are recorded on this page: one using the pan balance and the other using the spring scale.

Children select two objects from the set of objects you have collected. They hold the objects and guess which is heavier. Then they use the pan balance to verify their guesses. For each pair of objects, they should write the names of the objects on one of the pan-balance pictures to show their results. For example, to show that a pair of student scissors weighs more than a calculator, children write "scissors" in the lower pan and "calculator" in the higher pan.

A pair of scissors weighs more than a calculator.

🔗 Links to the Future

In this lesson, children use a pan balance to compare weights of different objects. Some children may be able to transfer the work with the actual pan balances into pictorial representations in Lesson 2-9. These pan balance activities begin exposure to using a pan balance model to solve simple equations, which is a Grade 5 Goal.

Adjusting the Activity

Have children draw pictures of the objects on the pans rather than writing the names of the objects.

Have children place a light object in one pan and enough pennies in the other pan to put the pans in balance. Children can sketch this situation in the empty pans given on the journal page and record the object and number of pennies.

A U D I T O R Y ◆ K I N E S T H E T I C ◆ T A C T I L E ◆ V I S U A L

► ## Exploration B:
Using a Spring Scale

SMALL-GROUP ACTIVITY

(*Math Journal 1*, p. 39)

Have children hang a plastic bag from the hook on the spring scale. The challenge is to fill the bag with different objects so that it weighs about 1 pound. For example, a 6 oz mug, a 4 oz calculator, a 5 oz pair of scissors, and a 1 oz binder clip weigh about 16 oz, or 1 pound. Children record their work on the journal page.

► ## Exploration C:
Making Equal Groups of Objects

PARTNER ACTIVITY

(*Math Masters*, p. 37)

Partners follow instructions on *Math Masters*, page 37 to make "nests" that hold the same number of "eggs." This activity develops the basic concept of multiplication. This is the first exposure in second grade to the concept of multiplication.

✔ Ongoing Assessment: Informing Instruction

Watch how children answer the question "How many eggs are in all the nests?" Most will use repeated addition. For example, if there are 4 nests with 3 eggs in each nest, they will answer $3 + 3 + 3 + 3 = 12$. Make note of children who think in terms of multiplication and answer $4 \times 3 = 12$ or 4 [3s] equals 12.

---

2 Ongoing Learning & Practice

► ## Playing *Beat the Calculator*

SMALL-GROUP ACTIVITY

(*Math Journal 1*, p. 24; *My Reference Book*, pp. 124 and 125)

See *My Reference Book*, pages 124 and 125 for directions. Children play *Beat the Calculator* to develop their recall of addition facts. They should record the facts for which they can beat the calculator by making a check mark in the box of that fact.

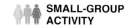

🔗 Links to the Future

Children will further explore the concept of multiplication in later units in Grade 2. Multiplication facts will be formally introduced in units 11 and 12.

Student Page

Date   Time

LESSON 2·2   **Facts Power Table**

0 + 0 0	0 + 1 1	0 + 2 2	0 + 3 3	0 + 4 4	0 + 5 5	0 + 6 6	0 + 7 7	0 + 8 8	0 + 9 9
1 + 0 1	1 + 1 2	1 + 2 3	1 + 3 4	1 + 4 5	1 + 5 6	1 + 6 7	1 + 7 8	1 + 8 9	1 + 9 10
2 + 0 2	2 + 1 3	2 + 2 4	2 + 3 5	2 + 4 6	2 + 5 7	2 + 6 8	2 + 7 9	2 + 8 10	2 + 9 11
3 + 0 3	3 + 1 4	3 + 2 5	3 + 3 6	3 + 4 7	3 + 5 8	3 + 6 9	3 + 7 10	3 + 8 11	3 + 9 12
4 + 0 4	4 + 1 5	4 + 2 6	4 + 3 7	4 + 4 8	4 + 5 9	4 + 6 10	4 + 7 11	4 + 8 12	4 + 9 13
5 + 0 5	5 + 1 6	5 + 2 7	5 + 3 8	5 + 4 9	5 + 5 10	5 + 6 11	5 + 7 12	5 + 8 13	5 + 9 14
6 + 0 6	6 + 1 7	6 + 2 8	6 + 3 9	6 + 4 10	6 + 5 11	6 + 6 12	6 + 7 13	6 + 8 14	6 + 9 15
7 + 0 7	7 + 1 8	7 + 2 9	7 + 3 10	7 + 4 11	7 + 5 12	7 + 6 13	7 + 7 14	7 + 8 15	7 + 9 16
8 + 0 8	8 + 1 9	8 + 2 10	8 + 3 11	8 + 4 12	8 + 5 13	8 + 6 14	8 + 7 15	8 + 8 16	8 + 9 17
9 + 0 9	9 + 1 10	9 + 2 11	9 + 3 12	9 + 4 13	9 + 5 14	9 + 6 15	9 + 7 16	9 + 8 17	9 + 9 18

Math Journal 1, p. 24

Student Page

Date   Time

LESSON 2·8 Math Boxes

1. Fill in the missing numbers.

12	13	14
	23	
	33	
	43	

2. What temperature is it? Fill in the circle next to the best answer.

°F 70

Ⓐ 61
● 62
Ⓒ 64
Ⓓ 78

60

50

3. Write the sums.

Unit

$10 + 7 = $ __17__

$10 + $ __2__ $= 12$

__30__ $= 10 + 20$

__51__ $= 10 + 41$

4. Write these numbers in order from smallest to largest. Circle the smallest number and draw a box around the largest number.

243, 156, 326, 256

(156), 243, 256, 326

5. Put an X on the digit in the tens place in each number.

3⊗2   1,0⊗3

1,2⊗9   5⊗6

6. What time is it?

9 : 15

What time will it be in 15 minutes?

9 : 30

Math Journal 1, p. 40

When they receive three check marks next to a particular fact, they can write the sum in that box to indicate that the fact has been mastered. The Caller should select problems at random from the white area of the fact power table.

▶ Math Boxes 2·8

(Math Journal 1, p. 40)

INDEPENDENT ACTIVITY

Mixed Practice Math Boxes in this lesson are paired with Math Boxes in Lesson 2-6. The skills in Problems 5 and 6 preview Unit 3 content.

Writing/Reasoning Have children draw, write, or verbalize their answers to the following: *Describe any patterns you see in the number grid piece in Problem 1.* Sample answer: Each time I go down the number in the ones place remains the same. The number in the tens place increases by one.

▶ Home Link 2·8

(Math Masters, pp. 38 and 39)

INDEPENDENT ACTIVITY

Home Connection Children tell someone at home how they used a pan balance and a spring scale. They compare the weights of objects and determine which objects in a group weigh less than 1 pound.

Home Link Master

Name   Date   Time

HOME LINK 2·8 Weighing Things

Family Note Today we worked with a pan balance to compare the weights of objects. We used a spring scale to weigh objects up to 1 pound. We introduced the word *ounce* as a unit of weight for light objects.

*Please return the **second page** of this Home Link to school tomorrow.*

1. Tell someone at home about how you used the pan balance to compare the weights of two objects.

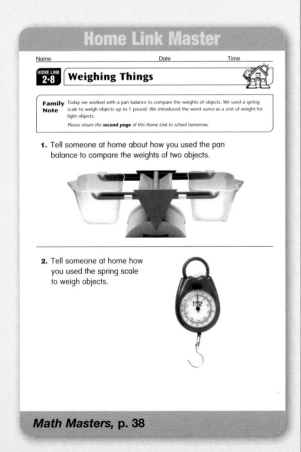

2. Tell someone at home how you used the spring scale to weigh objects.

Math Masters, p. 38

Home Link Master

Name   Date   Time

HOME LINK 2·8 Weighing Things *continued*

3. Look at the pairs of objects below. In each pair, circle the object that you think is heavier.

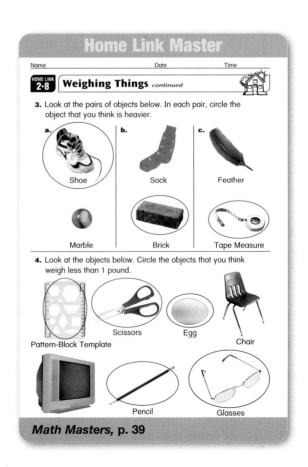

a. Shoe / Marble

b. Sock / Brick

c. Feather / Tape Measure

4. Look at the objects below. Circle the objects that you think weigh less than 1 pound.

Pattern-Block Template   Scissors   Egg   Chair

    Pencil   Glasses

Math Masters, p. 39

③ Differentiation Options

 PARTNER ACTIVITY

▶ Comparing Weight

🕐 5–15 Min

To explore the concept of weight, have children compare the weights of objects. Each partner may select two items to hold, one in each hand, and say which one feels lighter or heavier, and which are balanced. The items can be weighed in a pan balance to check their responses.

ENRICHMENT

 INDEPENDENT ACTIVITY

▶ Estimating Weight

🕐 5–15 Min

To apply children's understanding of concepts of weight, have children write an estimate of the weight of an object and then weigh it with a spring scale. As the activity proceeds, the estimates may get closer to the actual weight. This activity will help improve estimating skills.

EXTRA PRACTICE

  SMALL-GROUP ACTIVITY

▶ *Minute Math+*

🕐 5–15 Min

To offer children more experience with time, weight, length, volume, and area, see the following pages in *Minute Math+*: pp. 61 and 62.

2·9 Name Collections

 Objective To review the concept that a number can be named in many ways.

---

1 Teaching the Lesson

materials

Key Activities
Children use name-collection boxes to write equivalent names for numbers. They identify sums and differences that match a given number by playing *Name That Number*.

Key Concepts and Skills
• Generate equivalent names for numbers in a name-collection box.
[Number and Numeration Goal 5]
• Use addition and subtraction facts in the *Name That Number* game.
[Operations and Computation Goal 1]
• Use symbols to write number sentences for *Name That Number*.
[Patterns, Functions, and Algebra Goal 2]

Key Vocabulary
name-collection box

✓ **Ongoing Assessment: Recognizing Student Achievement** Use *Math Masters*, page 462.
[Number and Numeration Goal 5]

☐ *Math Journal 1*, p. 41
☐ *My Reference Book*, pp. 16, 138 and 139
☐ Home Link 2·8
☐ Game Master (*Math Masters*, p. 462)
☐ per partnership: 4 each of number cards 1–10 and 1 each of number cards 11–20 (from the Everything Math Deck, if available)
☐ slate

See Advance Preparation

---

2 Ongoing Learning & Practice

materials

Children represent weight comparisons by drawing pan-balance pictures.

Children practice and maintain skills through Math Boxes and Home Link activities.

☐ *Math Journal 1*, pp. 42–44
☐ Home Link Masters (*Math Masters*, pp. 40 and 41)
☐ pan balance (optional)

---

3 Differentiation Options

materials

READINESS
Children play *Two-Fisted Penny Addition* to practice finding equivalent names for numbers.

ENRICHMENT
Children find many names for facts.

☐ Teaching Master (*Math Masters*, p. 42)
☐ Teaching Aid Master (*Math Masters*, p. 422; optional)
☐ 10 pennies
☐ half-sheet of paper

Additional Information

Advance Preparation Before beginning the lesson, draw a unit box on the board. Fill in the unit box with a label of your choice (or the children's). Keep the unit box and label posted for all the numbers that are not labeled in this lesson.

Technology
Assessment Management System
Math Masters, page 462
See the **iTLG.**

Getting Started

Mental Math and Reflexes

Do place-value exercises on slates. *Suggestions:*

○○○ Write 56. Circle the digit in the 10s place. Put an X on the digit in the 1s place.

○○○ Write 506. Circle the digit in the 100s place. Put an X on the digit in the 1s place. Which digit is not marked? 0

○○○ Write 1,065. Circle the digit in the 1s place. What is the value of the digit in the 10s place? 60 What place is the 1 in? thousands

Math Message

Write as many different names for the number 8 as you can.

Sample answers: $5 + 3$, $9 - 1$, $2 + 2 + 2 + 2$

Home Link 2·8 Follow-Up

Ask children if they used the *Fact Triangles* to practice facts with someone at home. Remind children that the *Fact Triangles* can help them develop fact power, which makes it easier to solve problems.

---

1 Teaching the Lesson

▶ Math Message Follow-Up

 WHOLE-CLASS ACTIVITY

(*My Reference Book,* p. 16)

Draw a box on the board like the one in the margin. Tell children that this is called an 8 box. It is a **name-collection box** for the number 8. Ask several volunteers to write names for the number 8 in the box.

If children limit the names for 8 to addition and subtraction expressions, ask them to think of ways to write 8 without using numbers. If necessary, suggest a few other possibilities, such as the following:

Examples:

Tally marks: ///// ///

Pictures or diagrams:

octagon   4-by-2 array

Roman numeral: VIII

For more information about name-collection boxes, see additional names for the number 8 on *My Reference Book,* page 16. Read about name-collection boxes in *My Reference Book* with your class.

 Language Link Ask: "Does anyone know how to say *eight* in another language?" *acht* (axt) [*German*]; *ocho* (´oh cho) [*Spanish*]; *hachi* (hoch) [*Japanese*]; *huit* (weet) [*French*]; *bpatd* (bad) [*Thai*]; *nane* (´nah ney) [*Kiswahili*]

↙ Tag for the name-collection box

8

Name-collection box

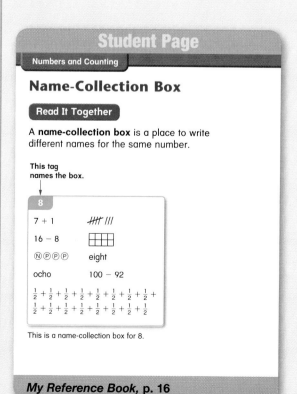

Student Page

Numbers and Counting

Name-Collection Box

Read It Together

A **name-collection box** is a place to write different names for the same number.

This tag names the box.

↓

8

7 + 1	///// ///
16 − 8	(grid)
Ⓝ Ⓟ Ⓟ Ⓟ	eight
ocho	100 − 92

$\frac{1}{2} + \frac{1}{2} + \frac{1}{2} + \frac{1}{2} + \frac{1}{2} + \frac{1}{2} + \frac{1}{2} + \frac{1}{2} +$
$\frac{1}{2} + \frac{1}{2} + \frac{1}{2} + \frac{1}{2} + \frac{1}{2} + \frac{1}{2} + \frac{1}{2} + \frac{1}{2}$

This is a name-collection box for 8.

My Reference Book, p. 16

Sample Round

Mae's turn:

The number to be named is 6.
The number 6 can be named
"4 + 2," "8 − 2," or "10 − 4."
Mae selects 4 + 2. She takes
the 4, 2, and 6 cards. She
replaces the 4 and 2 with
the top two cards from the
facedown deck and turns over
the next card to replace the 6,
as shown in Mike's turn below.

Mike's turn:

| 7 | 10 | 8 | 12 | 1 | | 16 |

The number to be named is 16.
Mike can't find two cards he
can use to name 16. He turns
over the next card from the
facedown deck and places it on
top of the 16. The next player
tries to name the new target
number.

A sample round for *Name That Number*

Name that Number

Materials ❑ number cards 0–20 (4 of each card
0–10, and 1 of each card 11–20)

Players 2 to 4 (the game is more fun when
played by 3 or 4 players)

Skill Using addition and subtraction to
name equivalent numbers

Object of the game To collect the most cards.

Directions

1. Shuffle the deck and place 5 cards number-side
up on the table. Leave the rest of the deck
number-side down. Then turn over the top card
of the deck and lay it down next to the deck.
The number on this card is the number to be
named. Call this number the *target number*.

2. Players take turns. When it is your turn:
   • Try to name the target number by adding or
   subtracting the numbers on 2 or more of the
   5 cards that are number-side up. A card may
   be used only once for each turn.

My Reference Book, p. 138

▶ Demonstrating *Name That Number* PARTNER ACTIVITY

(My Reference Book, pp. 138 and 139)

In *Name That Number,* children try to identify a sum or difference
that names a given target number. The target numbers play the
same role as numbers written on the tags of name-collection boxes.

Divide the class into groups of two, three, or four. Explain the
rules of *Name That Number.* Have children play a game while you
circulate and help groups that have questions. Praise good
group etiquette.

Go over the rules for *Name That Number* in the *My Reference
Book,* pages 138 and 139.

▶ Playing *Name That Number* PARTNER ACTIVITY

(Math Masters, p. 462)

Children continue playing the game.

Adjusting the Activity

Use any combination of two or more numbers and use both addition
and subtraction. For example, Mike could have named 16 as 10 + 7 = 17;
17 − 1 = 16, or 10 + 12 = 22; 22 − 7 = 15; 15 + 1 = 16, or 8 + 12 = 20;
20 − 10 = 10; 10 + 7 = 17; 17 − 1 = 16.

AUDITORY ◆ KINESTHETIC ◆ TACTILE ◆ VISUAL

✔ Ongoing Assessment: Recognizing Student Achievement
Math Masters Page 462 ★

Use *Math Masters,* **page 462** to assess children's ability to write number
sentences and generate equivalent names for a given number. Have children
record one of their best rounds of *Name That Number.*

Children are making adequate progress if they can correctly write an addition or
subtraction number sentence that uses at least two of the five faceup cards, and
the target card, as a sum or difference. Some children may be able to use more
than two cards and/or more than one operation.

[Number and Numeration Goal 5]

Practicing with Name-Collection Boxes

(Math Journal 1, p. 41)

INDEPENDENT ACTIVITY

Children solve problems that involve name-collection boxes.

---

2 Ongoing Learning & Practice

▶ Solving Pan-Balance Problems

INDEPENDENT ACTIVITY

(Math Journal, pp. 42 and 43)

Some food items and their weights are shown on journal page 42. Each problem on journal page 43 shows a pan balance tilted to the heavier side. Children imagine putting food items in the pans to make each balance tilt as shown. Work through a problem with children to be sure they understand what to do. The example from journal page 43 is shown in the margin.

Adjusting the Activity

Select an item for one of the pans and have the class record the item's name and weight on their journal page. The children must then, based on the position of the pans, decide whether to choose an item for the other pan that weighs more, less, or the same as the given item.

AUDITORY ◆ KINESTHETIC ◆ TACTILE ◆ VISUAL

▶ Math Boxes 2·9

INDEPENDENT ACTIVITY

(Math Journal 1, p. 44)

Mixed Practice Math Boxes in this lesson are linked with Math Boxes in Lessons 2-11 and 2-13. The skill in Problem 6 previews Unit 3 content.

▶ Home Link 2·9

INDEPENDENT ACTIVITY

(Math Masters, pp. 40 and 41)

Home Connection Children solve a name-collection box problem and then make up their own problem. The Family Note on the first page of Home Link 2-9 discusses name-collection boxes.

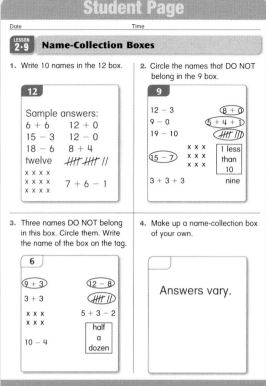

Date _____ Time _____

LESSON 2·9 Name-Collection Boxes

1. Write 10 names in the 12 box.

12

Sample answers:
6 + 6   12 + 0
15 − 3   12 − 0
18 − 6   8 + 4
twelve   //// //// //
x x x x
x x x x   7 + 6 − 1
x x x x

2. Circle the names that DO NOT belong in the 9 box.

9

12 − 3   ⟨8 + 0⟩
9 − 0   ⟨5 + 4 + 1⟩
19 − 10   ⟨//// ///⟩
           x x x   1 less
⟨15 − 7⟩   x x x   than
           x x x   10
3 + 3 + 3   nine

3. Three names DO NOT belong in this box. Circle them. Write the name of the box on the tag.

6

⟨9 + 3⟩   ⟨12 − 8⟩
3 + 3   ⟨//// //⟩
x x x   5 + 3 − 2
x x x
             half
10 − 4   a
             dozen

4. Make up a name-collection box of your own.

Answers vary.

Math Journal 1, p. 41

Links to the Future

Knowing and applying the order of operations is a Grade 6 Goal. Recognizing, understanding, and applying parentheses in number sentences are Grades 3, 4, and 5 Goals, respectively. Until children are able to insert parentheses into their recorded solutions, have them write each of their calculations separately. For example, the target number is 2. A child uses the following cards to name 2: 3, 4, and 5. The recorded steps could look like this: 4 + 3 = 7; 7 − 5 = 2. The solution could also be one step, as in 5 − 3 = 2.

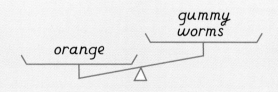

Example:

Weight: _8 ounces_   Weight: _4 ounces_

On journal page 43, children make up and solve pan-balance problems.

NOTE You may wish to provide time for children to further explore the pan balance with small objects such as pennies, craft sticks, or centimeter cubes.

Student Page

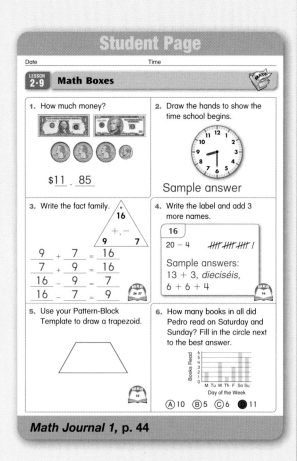

Math Journal 1, p. 44

Home Link Master

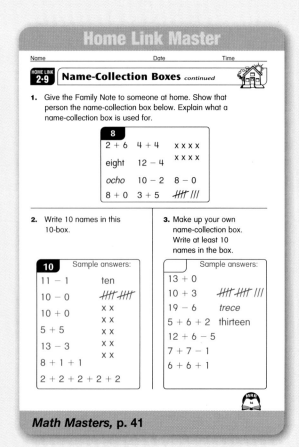

Math Masters, p. 41

3 Differentiation Options

PARTNER ACTIVITY

▶ **Playing** *Two-Fisted Penny Addition*

15–30 Min

To explore finding many ways to make ten, have children play *Two-Fisted Penny Addition*.

Have each child take out 10 pennies. Each child should grab some of their 10 pennies with one hand and the rest in the other hand. Children record each pair of numbers on a half-sheet of paper. Children continue to perform this activity with partners, recording the number of pennies in each hand on their half-sheets of paper. Children may begin to predict the number of pennies in the second hand before counting them. They can write their predictions and then count the pennies to check them. Ask children how many pennies there are in both hands. 10

PARTNER ACTIVITY

▶ **Exploring Name-Collection Boxes**

5–15 Min

(*Math Masters*, pp. 42 and 422)

To apply children's understanding of equivalent names for numbers, have them record number models to describe the way numbers are displayed in ten frames on *Math Masters*, page 42. When they have finished the page, consider having them share the ways they named eight, based on the ten-frame card illustrations. For example, "3 more than 5; 10 minus 2; 2 more than 3 doubled."

If children enjoy this activity, provide them with the blank ten-frame card from *Math Masters*, page 422 so they can create their own problems.

Planning Ahead

In preparation for tomorrow's class, make several copies of *Math Masters*, page 424 so that children can create more Frames-and-Arrows problems if they wish.

2·10 Frames-and-Arrows Routines

 Objective To guide children as they use a given addition or subtraction rule to generate a number sequence, and as they identify the rule for a given number sequence.

---

1 Teaching the Lesson

Key Activities
Children review the Frames-and-Arrows notation and routine that were introduced in first grade, and use addition or subtraction rules to fill in frames, arrow rules, or both.

Key Concepts and Skills
- Practice facts in Frames-and-Arrows problems.
  [Operations and Computation Goal 1]
- Use patterns to find rules for Frames-and-Arrows problems.
  [Patterns, Functions, and Algebra Goal 1]
- Find missing numbers and rules for Frames-and-Arrows problems.
  [Patterns, Functions, and Algebra Goal 1]
- Count on and back by 1s, 2s, 3s, 5s, and 10s.
  [Number and Numeration Goal 1]

Key Vocabulary
Frames-and-Arrows diagrams • frame • arrow • arrow rule

✔ **Ongoing Assessment:** Recognizing Student Achievement Use journal page 45.
  [Patterns, Functions, and Algebra Goal 1]

materials
- ☐ *Math Journal 1*, p. 45
- ☐ Home Link 2·9
- ☐ Transparency (*Math Masters*, p. 43; optional)
- ☐ counters, number line, or number grid (optional)

See Advance Preparation

---

2 Ongoing Learning & Practice

Children identify sums and differences that match a given number by playing *Name That Number*.

Children practice and maintain skills through Math Boxes and Home Link activities.

materials
- ☐ *Math Journal 1*, p. 46
- ☐ Home Link Masters (*Math Masters*, pp. 44 and 45)
- ☐ Game Master (*Math Masters*, p. 462)
- ☐ number cards 0–9 (see Lesson 2·9) (4 of each; from the Everything Math Deck, if available)

---

3 Differentiation Options

READINESS
Children count on a number line to explore counting patterns.

ENRICHMENT
Children make up and solve Frames-and-Arrows problems.

materials
- ☐ Teaching Master (*Math Masters*, p. 46)
- ☐ Teaching Aid Master (*Math Masters*, p. 424)

Additional Information

Advance Preparation Before beginning the lesson, draw a unit box on the board. Fill in the unit box with a label of your choice (or the children's). Keep the unit box and label posted for all the numbers that are not labeled in this lesson. You may also want to make an overhead transparency of *Math Masters*, page 43 for the first Frames-and-Arrows activity in Part 1.

Technology

Assessment Management System
Journal page 45, Problems 1 and 2
See the **iTLG.**

Getting Started

Mental Math and Reflexes

Count up and back on the number grid starting from different numbers. *Suggestions:*

◉○○ Count up by 10s starting at:
  10
  6
  12

◉◉○ Count backward by 10s starting at:
  54
  97
  109

◉◉◉ Count back by 5s starting at:
  108
  66
  89

Math Message

Which shape comes next? Draw it.

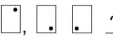

Home Link 2·9 Follow-Up

Ask volunteers to share the tag and one or two entries for the name-collection boxes they created. Can other children suggest additional entries?

---

1 Teaching the Lesson

▶ Math Message Follow-Up

WHOLE-CLASS ACTIVITY

Briefly go over children's responses and ask them to share how they found the answers. Help them state a rule for each pattern. *For example:*

▷ In the first pattern, the dot moves clockwise from corner to corner. The next shape is ⬚.

▷ The second pattern shows polygon shapes. Each shape has one more side than the preceding shape, so the shape following the pentagon has 6 sides (a hexagon). Ask children to name the shapes.

▶ Demonstrating Frames-and-Arrows Routines

WHOLE-CLASS ACTIVITY

(*Math Masters*, p. 43)

Frames-and-Arrows diagrams consist of **frames,** or shapes, which are connected by **arrows** that show the path from one frame to the next. Note that *frame* is an interesting word for children. It has social meanings, such as a picture frame or eyeglass frames, but also a mathematical meaning. Each frame contains a number, and the numbers form a sequence. Each arrow represents a rule—the **arrow rule**—that determines which number goes in the next frame. To support English language learners, you may want to explain that *rule* has an everyday usage, like the classroom rules that have been established, and *rule* also has a mathematical usage.

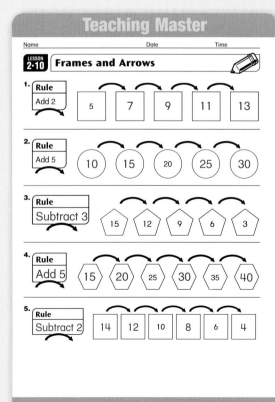

The Math Message problems and Frames-and-Arrows diagrams share a common feature. The problems and diagrams both use a rule to generate the pattern.

Use the Frames-and-Arrows diagram below as an example. Write the diagram on the board, or use an overhead transparency of *Math Masters,* page 43.

1.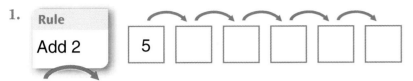

A possible Frames-and-Arrows diagram to put on the board.

Remind children that the squares are called frames and that the arrows stand for the rule that is written in the box. Ask children to use the rule "Add 2" to fill in the frames. Completed frames: 7, 9, 11, 13

Do a few more examples. Use different addition and subtraction rules, and fill in the first frame with a number.

Continue with other examples, but leave the first frames empty so that children will have to work both forward and backward to fill in the empty frames. *For example:*

2.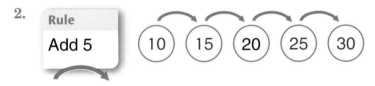

Next, try examples in which the frames are filled in, but the rule is missing. Ask children to identify the arrow rule. To support English language learners, write the list of children's rules on the board and discuss. For example, in the problem below, children may use terms such as "subtract," "get smaller," or "take away."

For example:

3.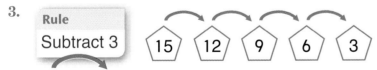

Write examples in which some of the frames are empty and the rule is missing. Ask children to find the rule and then fill in the missing frames. These problems are challenging; children must first discover the rule and then work both forward and backward to fill in the frames.

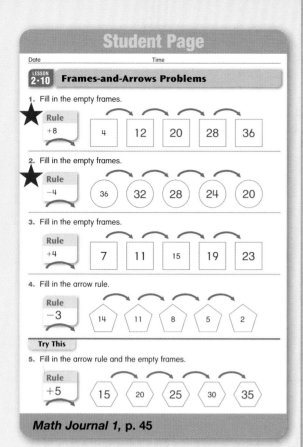

Date   Time

LESSON 2·10   **Frames-and-Arrows Problems**

1. Fill in the empty frames.

★ Rule
+8

| 4 | 12 | 20 | 28 | 36 |

2. Fill in the empty frames.

★ Rule
−4

36 32 28 24 20

3. Fill in the empty frames.

Rule
+4

| 7 | 11 | 15 | 19 | 23 |

4. Fill in the arrow rule.

Rule
−3

14 11 8 5 2

Try This

5. Fill in the arrow rule and the empty frames.

Rule
+5

15 20 25 30 35

Math Journal 1, p. 45

4.

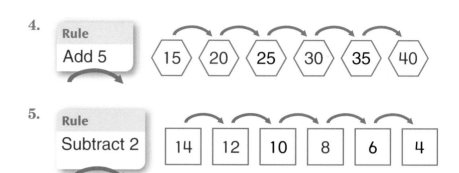

Rule
Add 5

15 20 25 30 35 40

5.

Rule
Subtract 2

| 14 | 12 | 10 | 8 | 6 | 4 |

▶ **Completing Frames-and-Arrows Diagrams**

INDEPENDENT ACTIVITY

(*Math Journal 1,* p. 45)

Have children fill in frames, arrow rules, or both. Circulate and offer help where needed.

 Adjusting the Activity

Fill in some of the empty frames to provide additional clues.

Also, when children are asked to find a rule, encourage them to think in two steps.

Step 1: Decide which operation is being used. Are the numbers in the pattern getting larger or smaller?

Step 2: Once the operation has been determined, children can figure out which number is being added or subtracted. Suggest counting up or counting back (with the use of fingers, counters, number line, or number grid to keep track, if necessary).

You might consider making a poster of these steps as a visual aid for your class.

A U D I T O R Y   ◆   K I N E S T H E T I C   ◆   T A C T I L E   ◆   V I S U A L

 Ongoing Assessment:
Recognizing Student Achievement

Journal page 45
Problems 1 and 2 ★

Use **journal page 45, Problems 1 and 2** to assess the children's progress toward extending a numeric pattern using addition and subtraction.

Children are making adequate progress if they correctly complete Problems 1 and 2 using a number grid, number line or counters. Some children may be able to complete a Frames-and-Arrows problem in which the first frame is empty. Others may be able to complete Frames-and-Arrows problems where they must fill in the arrow rule.

[Patterns, Functions, and Algebra Goal 1]

② Ongoing Learning & Practice

▶ Playing *Name That Number*

PARTNER ACTIVITY

(*Math Masters*, p. 462)

This game was introduced in Lesson 2-9. To make the game more challenging, have children play a variation in which players try to use two, three, four, or all five of the faceup cards to name the target number.

Example:

| 7 | 10 | 8 | 12 | 1 | | 16 |

Use 2 cards: no solution

Use 3 cards: $7 + 8 + 1 = 16$

Use 4 cards: $10 + 12 = 22; 22 + 1 = 23; 23 - 7 = 16$

Use 5 cards: $12 - 10 = 2; 2 + 8 = 10; 10 + 7 = 17; 17 - 1 = 16$

▶ Math Boxes 2·10

INDEPENDENT ACTIVITY

(*Math Journal 1*, p. 46)

 Mixed Practice Math Boxes in this lesson are paired with Math Boxes in Lesson 2-12. The skills in Problems 5 and 6 preview Unit 3 content.

▶ Home Link 2·10

INDEPENDENT ACTIVITY

(*Math Masters*, pp. 44 and 45)

 Home Connection Children complete Frames-and-Arrows problems. The Family Letter will help parents and guardians be more comfortable when assisting their children.

Date _____ Time _____

LESSON 2·10 Math Boxes

1. Write 4 doubles facts that you know.
   Sample answers:
   $4 + 4 = 8$
   $7 + 7 = 14$
   $5 + 5 = 10$
   $6 + 6 = 12$

2. Complete the Fact Triangle and the fact family.

   $12 = 9 + 3$
   $3 + 9 = 12$
   $12 - 3 = 9$
   $3 = 12 - 9$

3. Write the fact family for the domino.

   $11 = 6 + 5$
   $5 + 6 = 11$
   $11 - 6 = 5$
   $11 - 5 = 6$

4. Fill in the missing frames.

   Rule +2

   3 5 7 9
   15 13 11

5. The total cost is 16¢. I pay with 2 dimes. How much change do I get? Fill in the circle next to the best answer.

   Ⓐ 36¢   Ⓑ 6¢
   ● 4¢   Ⓓ 20¢

6. Draw a rectangle around the digit in the tens place.

   3 [4] 9
   4 [0] 6

Math Journal 1, p. 46

Name _____ Date _____ Time _____

HOME LINK 2·10 Frames-and-Arrows Problems

Family Note Today your child used **Frames-and-Arrows diagrams**. These diagrams show sequences of numbers—numbers that follow one after the other according to a rule. Frames-and-Arrows diagrams are made up of shapes called *frames* and arrows that connect the frames. Each frame contains one of the numbers in the sequence. Each *arrow* stands for a rule that tells which number goes in the next frame. Here is an example of a Frames-and-Arrows diagram. The arrow rule is "Add 2."

Rule | Add 2

2 4 6 8 10

In a Frames-and-Arrows problem, some of the information is left out. To solve the problem, you have to find the missing information.

Here are two examples of Frames-and-Arrows problems:

Example 1: Fill in the empty frames according to the rule.

Rule | Subtract 4

☐ 24 ☐ ☐ ☐

Solution: Write 28, 20, 16, and 12 in the empty frames.

Example 1: Write the arrow rule in the empty box.

Rule | ☐

10 15 20 25 30

Solution: The arrow rule is Add 5, or +5.

Ask your child to tell you about Frames-and-Arrows diagrams. Take turns making up and solving Frames-and-Arrows problems like the examples above with your child.

*Please return the **second page** of this Home Link to school tomorrow.*

Math Masters, p. 44

Home Link Master

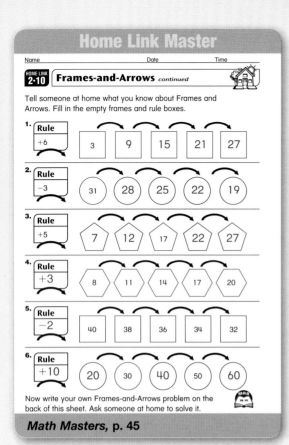

Math Masters, p. 45

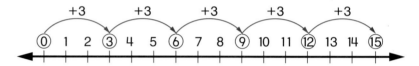

3 Differentiation Options

▶ **Counting on a Number Line**

(*Math Masters*, p. 46)

PARTNER ACTIVITY

5–15 Min

To explore counting patterns using a visual model, have children identify and record counting patterns on a number line on *Math Masters*, page 46. When children have finished the page, have them draw arrows to connect the circled numbers across the top of each number line with the "rule" (counting pattern) written above.

▶ **Making Up Frames-and-Arrows Problems**

(*Math Masters*, p. 424)

PARTNER ACTIVITY

5–15 Min

To apply children's understanding of using rules to generate and continue patterns in Frames-and-Arrows problems, have them create their own Frames-and-Arrows problems. They can exchange problems with a partner to solve. Encourage children to vary the types of problems they create

---

Teaching Master

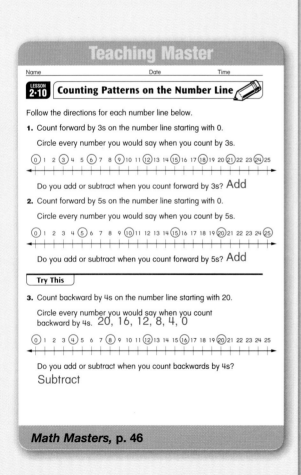

Math Masters, p. 46

Teaching Aid Master

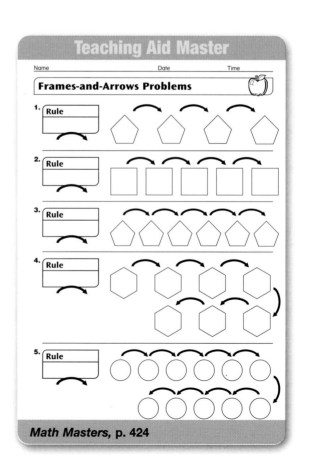

Math Masters, p. 424

2·11

"What's My Rule?" Routines

 Objective To provide experiences with identifying missing numbers in number pairs that are generated by a rule, and determining the rule used to generate number pairs.

---

1 Teaching the Lesson

materials

Key Activities

Children review the "What's My Rule?" routines and notation, use function machines to illustrate "What's My Rule?" tables, and solve "What's My Rule?" problems by determining missing numbers or rules.

Key Concepts and Skills

• Practice facts in "What's My Rule?" problems.
[Operations and Computation Goal 1]

• Use patterns to find rules for "What's My Rule?" problems.
[Patterns, Functions, and Algebra Goal 1]

• Find missing numbers and rules for "What's My Rule?" problems.
[Patterns, Functions, and Algebra Goal 1]

Key Vocabulary

"What's My Rule?" • function machine

✔ **Ongoing Assessment: Recognizing Student Achievement** Use journal page 47.
[Patterns, Functions, and Algebra Goal 1]

☐ *Math Journal 1,* p. 47
☐ *My Reference Book,* pp. 100 and 101
☐ Home Link 2·10
☐ Transparencies (*Math Masters,* pp. 425 and 426; optional)
☐ number grid

See Advance Preparation

---

2 Ongoing Learning & Practice

materials

Children practice addition and subtraction facts by using Fact Triangles as flashcards.

Children practice and maintain skills through Math Boxes and Home Link activities.

☐ *Math Journal 1,* p. 48
☐ Home Link Masters (*Math Masters,* pp. 47 and 48)
☐ envelope with Fact Triangles (from Lesson 2·5)

---

3 Differentiation Options

materials

READINESS
Children identify rules by sorting attributes.

ENRICHMENT
Children create "What's My Rule?" tables.

☐ Teaching Aid Master (*Math Masters,* p. 426)

Additional Information

Advance Preparation

For the "What's My Rule?" activities in Part 1, you may want to make overhead transparencies of *Math Masters,* pages 425 and 426.

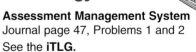

Technology

Assessment Management System
Journal page 47, Problems 1 and 2
See the **iTLG.**

Getting Started

Mental Math and Reflexes

Count up and back by 10s from different numbers on the number grid. *For example:*

- ●○○ Count up by 10s starting at 24. 34, 44, 54, and so on
- ●●○ Count back by 10s starting at 103. 93, 83, 73, and so on
- ●●● Count up by 10s starting at 224. 234, 244, 254, and so on

Math Message

June is 3 years older than Kevin. If Kevin is 7 years old, how old is June? 10 years old

Home Link 2·10 Follow-Up

Review the answers to the Frames-and-Arrows problems. If time allows, ask children to share the problems they created with the class. Ask other volunteers to solve the problems.

in	out
0	3
1	4
2	5
3	6

A table of values for +3

Unit

years

Kevin	June
7	10
8	
9	
10	
15	

Rule

+ 3

---

① Teaching the Lesson

▶ Math Message Follow-Up

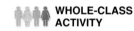 **WHOLE-CLASS ACTIVITY**

Ask children to share their strategies for solving the problem. They may draw pictures, use tallies, or count on their fingers. Help children summarize by writing a number model for the problem. $7 + 3 = 10$

▶ Establishing "What's My Rule?" Routines

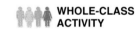 **WHOLE-CLASS ACTIVITY**

The first through third grade **"What's My Rule?"** routines include number pairs displayed in a table of values. The numbers in each pair are related, according to the same rule. The rule may be applied to any number in the left column (the *in* number) to generate the corresponding number in the right column (the *out* number). The table on the left shows a few pairs for the rule "add 3" or "+3."

Draw a unit box and table (as shown in the margin) on the board. Also, draw an empty rule box beneath the table. Leave out the numbers and the label in the unit box for the time being.

Remind children about the Math Message problem. Then write the entries 7 and 10 in the table, write +3 in the rule box, and write "years" in the unit box. Explain that this is one way to show the information in the problem.

Continue to fill in the table as you ask questions like the following. As children give each answer, help them to summarize by writing a number model on the board.

- What if Kevin is 8 years old? How old is June then? 11 years old; $8 + 3 = 11$

- What if Kevin is 9 years old? June is 12 years old. $9 + 3 = 12$

- What if Kevin is 10 years old? June is 13 years old.
  $10 + 3 = 13$

Now write 15 in the first column and ask questions like the following:

- Which number goes in the second column? 18 How do you know? Because the number in the second column is always 3 more than the number in the first column.

- Can anyone state a rule for finding June's age if you know Kevin's age? Add 3, or $+3$

Copy the table with an empty rule box (as shown in the margin) on the board. Ask questions like the following:

- Who is younger, Raissa or Joe? Joe How many years younger? 2 years

- What's the rule for finding Joe's age if you know Raissa's age? Subtract 2 from Raissa's age, or -2. Write -2 in the rule box for Table 2.

- What if Raissa is 10 years old? How old is Joe then? 8 years old; $10 - 2 = 8$

- What if Raissa is 15 years old? How old is Joe then? Joe is 13 years old. $15 - 2 = 13$

▶ **Using Function Machines to**
Illustrate "What's My Rule?" Tables

👥👥 **WHOLE-CLASS ACTIVITY**

(*Math Masters,* pp. 425 and 426; *My Reference Book,* pp. 100 and 101)

Draw the function machine and table shown in the margin on the board, or display an overhead transparency of *Math Masters,* page 425. Write "3," "+6," and "9," as shown in the margin.

Tell children that the diagram shows a **function machine.** The machine is set to follow a certain rule. Someone drops a number in the machine, the machine does something to the number according to the rule, and a new number comes out. You can read about function machines with your class on *My Reference Book,* pages 100 and 101.

Draw various "What's My Rule?" tables on the board, or use an overhead transparency of *Math Masters,* page 426. Complete the tables with children. Use a function machine to illustrate the process.

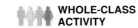

Raissa	Joe
7	5
8	6
9	7
10	
15	

Rule

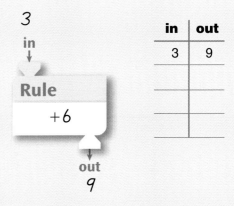

in	out
3	9

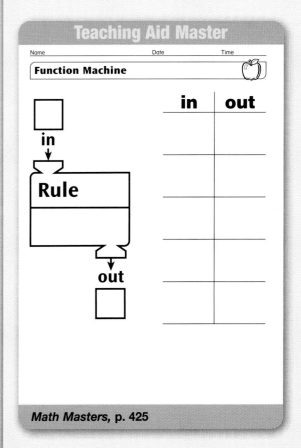

Math Masters, p. 425

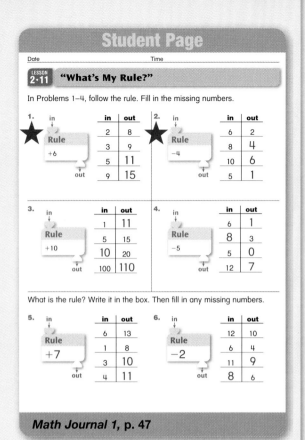

Try to include each type of table shown below.

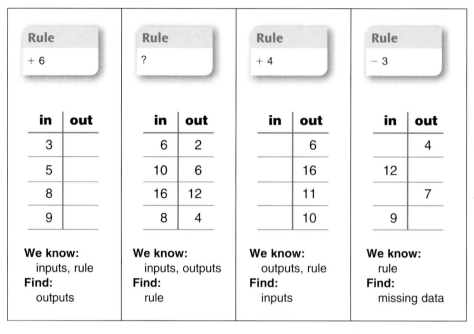

Rule	Rule	Rule	Rule
+ 6	?	+ 4	− 3

in	out		in	out		in	out		in	out
3			6	2		6				4
5			10	6		16			12	
8			16	12		11				7
9			8	4		10			9	

We know: inputs, rule **Find:** outputs	**We know:** inputs, outputs **Find:** rule	**We know:** outputs, rule **Find:** inputs	**We know:** rule **Find:** missing data

▶ ## Solving "What's My Rule?" Problems

PARTNER ACTIVITY

(*Math Journal 1*, p. 47; *Math Masters*, p. 426)

Partners practice solving problems in which the rule is given and numbers must be determined *and* in which numbers are given and the rule must be determined. An overhead transparency of *Math Masters*, page 426 may be used as an aid in discussing children's answers.

 Ongoing Assessment: Recognizing Student Achievement

Journal page 47 Problems 1 and 2

Use **journal page 47, Problems 1 and 2** to assess children's progress toward solving "What's My Rule?" problems using addition and subtraction with a known rule.

Children are making adequate progress if they successfully complete the problems with manipulatives. Some children may be able to complete "What's My Rule?" problems with unknown *ins* and unknown *Rules*.

[Patterns, Functions, and Algebra Goal 1]

Adjusting the Activity

You can use *Math Masters*, page 426 to create "What's My Rule?" problems tailored to your class.

AUDITORY ◆ KINESTHETIC ◆ TACTILE ◆ VISUAL

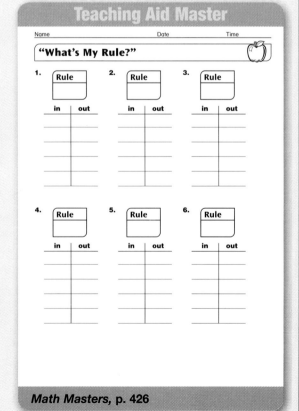

2 Ongoing Learning & Practice

▶ **Practicing with**
+, − Fact Triangles

PARTNER ACTIVITY

Partners practice addition and subtraction facts.

▶ **Math Boxes 2+11**

INDEPENDENT ACTIVITY

(*Math Journal 1*, p. 48)

Mixed Practice Math Boxes in this lesson are linked with Math Boxes in Lessons 2-9 and 2-13. The skill in Problem 6 previews Unit 3 content.

Writing/Reasoning Have children draw, write, or verbalize their answers to the following: *In Problem 1, if you want to pay with the least coins possible, what coins would you use to pay $1.50? Explain.* Sample answer: Six quarters, because quarters are worth the most and it takes fewer to make $1.50.

▶ **Home Link 2+11**

INDEPENDENT ACTIVITY

(*Math Masters*, pp. 47 and 48)

Home Connection Children solve "What's My Rule?" problems. The Family Note explains the "What's My Rule?" routine.

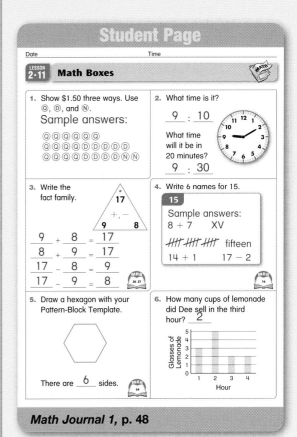

Math Journal 1, p. 48

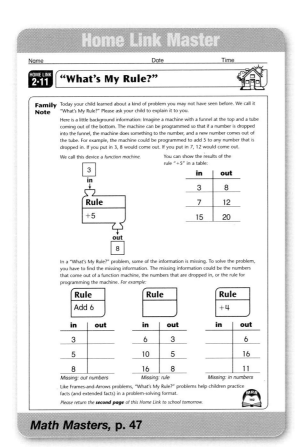

Math Masters, p. 47

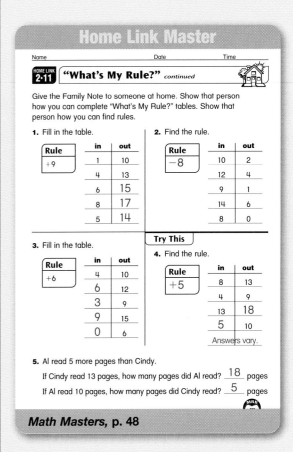

Math Masters, p. 48

▶ Fishing For The Rule

SMALL-GROUP ACTIVITY

 5–15 Min

To explore using patterns to determine rules, have children identify rules for selecting members of a group. "Fish" for children using some obvious attribute. For example, fish out a few people wearing brown, without explaining what you are fishing for. Ask: *What sort of fish am I going to catch next* (or "*What's My Rule?*")? Let children guess until someone says, "People wearing brown." Ask: *Who are the children not in my net?* All people not wearing brown. Use a different attribute and play again. Use obvious things at first (wearing red shirts or sneakers, for example). Once the children understand the game, let one of them do the fishing.

▶ Creating "What's My Rule?" Tables

PARTNER ACTIVITY

 5–15 Min

(*Math Masters*, p. 426)

To apply children's understanding of functions, have children create their own "What's My Rule?" tables. Encourage children to provide pairs of numbers without the rule along with tables that have various *in* and *out* numbers. They can exchange tables with a partner.

2·12 Counting Strategies for Subtraction

 Objective To review, develop, and provide practice for subtraction strategies.

---

1 Teaching the Lesson

materials

Key Activities

Children share and solve subtraction number stories. Children review and practice the counting-back and counting-up strategies for subtraction and use Fact Triangles to practice "easier" subtraction facts.

Key Concepts and Skills

- Count up and back by 1s. [Number and Numeration Goal 1]
- Use addition and subtraction facts to solve subtraction problems. [Operations and Computation Goal 1]
- Use Fact Triangles to practice facts. [Operations and Computation Goal 1]
- Use counting-up and counting-back strategies for subtraction. [Operations and Computation Goal 2]

Key Vocabulary difference

☐ Home Link 2·11
☐ counters (optional)
☐ envelope of Fact Triangles (from Lesson 2·5)
☐ slate
☐ number grid

---

2 Ongoing Learning & Practice

materials

Children practice "harder" addition facts by playing *Beat the Calculator.*

Children cut out a second set of 18 Fact Triangles.

Children practice and maintain skills through Math Boxes and Home Link activities.

✔ **Ongoing Assessment: Recognizing Student Achievement** Use journal page 49.
[Operations and Computation Goal 1]

☐ *Math Journal 1,* pp. 24 and 49; Activity Sheets 3 and 4
☐ Home Link Master (*Math Masters,* p. 49)
☐ calculator
☐ scissors

---

3 Differentiation Options

materials

READINESS

Children play the *Difference Game* to practice finding differences.

ENRICHMENT

Children use the number grid to find the difference between 2-digit numbers.

EXTRA PRACTICE

Children solve addition and subtraction problems.

ELL SUPPORT

Children add *difference* to their Math Word Banks.

☐ *My Reference Book,* pp. 130, 131, 140, and 141
☐ Game Master, (*Math Masters,* p. 463)
☐ *Differentiation Handbook*
☐ *Minute Math®+,* p. 39

☐ per partnership: 4 each of number cards 1–10; 40 pennies or markers
☐ per partnership: 4 each of number cards 0–9; number grid; calculator; 2 pennies or markers

---

Technology

Assessment Management System
Math Boxes, Problem 3
See the **iTLG.**

Getting Started

Adjusting the Activity

ELL

Have children use counters to solve subtraction problems by counting back. For 7 − 3, the child begins by placing seven counters on the table. The child removes three counters one by one while counting back. The child then writes the number model, 7 − 3 = 4. Repeat this activity for other facts in which 1, 2, or 3 is being subtracted.

AUDITORY ◆ KINESTHETIC ◆ TACTILE ◆ VISUAL

1 Teaching the Lesson

▶ ## Math Message Follow-Up

 **WHOLE-CLASS ACTIVITY**

Write "11 − 8 = 3" on the board and draw an empty unit box. Ask a few children to share their subtraction stories and to suggest labels to write in the unit box.

▶ ## Reviewing the Meaning of Difference

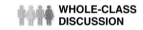 **WHOLE-CLASS DISCUSSION**

Remind children that the number obtained by subtracting one number from another is called the **difference.** Encourage them to use the word *difference.* For example, if a child says, "The answer to 11 − 8 is 3," you might say, "Yes. You are subtracting, so the answer is called the difference." Another way to say it is, "The difference between 11 and 8 is 3." To support English language learners, discuss the everyday as well as mathematical meaning of the word *difference.*

▶ ## Reviewing the Counting-Back Strategy for Subtraction

 **WHOLE-CLASS DISCUSSION**

There are 100 different subtraction facts that may be posed using the Facts Table. Thirty of these facts are the form $n - 1$, $n - 2$, or $n - 3$. Not all children will have achieved instant recall of these easier facts. The counting-back strategy shown in the following examples can enable these children to give answers quickly and achieve instant recall sooner.

Give several examples of counting back mentally. Use numbers in which the number being subtracted (subtrahend) is 1, 2, or 3. Count back, starting with the larger number (minuend).

Examples:

7 − 3 = ? Think 7. Say "6, 5, 4." The answer (difference) is 4.

37 − 2 = ? Think 37. Say "36, 35." The answer (difference) is 35.

Pose similar problems, and ask children to write the answers on their slates.

▶ Reviewing the Counting-Up Strategy for Subtraction

WHOLE-CLASS ACTIVITY

Forty of the subtraction facts on the Facts Table have differences of 0, 1, 2, or 3. Not all children will have instant recall of these easier facts. The counting-up strategy shown in the examples below can enable these children to give answers quickly and achieve instant recall sooner.

Give several examples of counting up mentally. Use subtraction problems that have a difference of 1, 2, or 3. Count up, starting with the smaller number (subtrahend).

Examples:

9 − 7 = ? Think 7. Say "8 is 1, 9 is 2." The answer (difference) is 2.

15 − 12 = ? Think 12. Say "13 is 1, 14 is 2, 15 is 3." The answer (difference) is 3.

Counting up using fingers can be efficient. Children raise a new finger for each number they count. The difference is the total number of fingers raised.

Examples:

9 − 7 = ? Think 7. Say "8 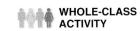, 9 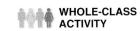."
The answer (difference) is 2.

36 − 33 = ? Think 33. Say "34 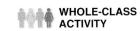, 35 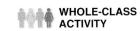, 36 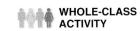."
The answer (difference) is 3.

Pose similar problems, and ask children to write the answers on their slates.

NOTE Use the number grid frequently to model the counting up and counting back strategy. The counting up method for multidigit subtraction is often the preferred subtraction algorithm for second graders.

Adjusting the Activity   ELL

Have children use counters to solve subtraction problems by counting up. For 9 − 7, a child begins by placing 9 counters on the table. The child touches 7 counters and counts up. "7, 8, 9; I counted up 2, so the difference is 2. 9 − 7 = 2." Repeat this activity for other facts for which the difference is 1, 2, or 3.

AUDITORY ◆ KINESTHETIC ◆ TACTILE ◆ VISUAL

▶ Practicing with +,− Fact Triangles

Children practice addition and subtraction facts.

The first set of Fact Triangles includes 18 individual Fact Triangles. All but four of these Fact Triangles include subtraction facts that may be answered by using the counting-up or counting-back strategies. With practice, children will rely less on strategies and more on memory as they begin to achieve instant recall of the facts.

② Ongoing Learning & Practice

▶ Playing *Beat the Calculator*

(*Math Journal 1*, p. 24)

The Caller should select problems at random from the gray area of the facts power table. Problems from the gray area include the "hardest" addition facts.

▶ Cutting Out +, − Fact Triangles

(*Math Journal 1*, Activity Sheets 3 and 4)

Have children cut out the Fact Triangles from Activity Sheets 3 and 4 and place them in an envelope. These Fact Triangles will be used in Lesson 2-13.

NOTE Children cut out the Fact Triangles from Activity Sheets 1 and 2 during Lesson 2-5.

▶ Math Boxes 2·12

(*Math Journal 1*, p. 49)

Mixed Practice Math Boxes in this lesson are paired with Math Boxes in Lesson 2-10. The skills in Problems 5 and 6 preview Unit 3 content.

Writing/Reasoning Have children draw, write, or verbalize their answers to the following: *How does a doubles fact like the one in Problem 1 help you solve other problems?* Sample answer: If I know 4 + 4 = 8, then I know that 4 + 5 = 9 because 5 is one more than 4. If I know 4 + 4 = 8, then I also know 4 + 3 = 7 because 3 is one less than 4.

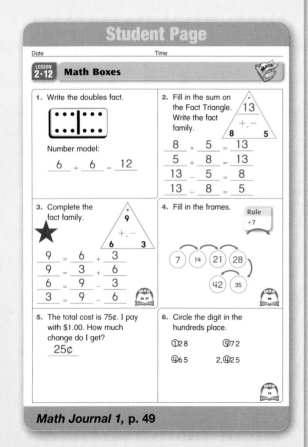

Student Page

Date   Time

LESSON 2·12   **Math Boxes**

1. Write the doubles fact.

Number model:

6 + 6 = 12

2. Fill in the sum on the Fact Triangle. Write the fact family.

13
+,−
8   5

8 + 5 = 13
5 + 8 = 13
13 − 5 = 8
13 − 8 = 5

3. Complete the fact family.

9
+,−
6   3

9 = 6 + 3
9 = 3 + 6
6 = 9 − 3
3 = 9 − 6

4. Fill in the frames.

Rule +7

7 14 21 28
42 35

5. The total cost is 75¢. I pay with $1.00. How much change do I get?

25¢

6. Circle the digit in the hundreds place.

①28   ⑨72
④65   2,④25

Math Journal 1, p. 49

Ongoing Assessment: Recognizing Student Achievement

Math Boxes Problem 3

Use **Math Boxes, Problem 3** to assess children's ability to write a fact family from a Fact Triangle. Children are making adequate progress if they can correctly write all four number sentences. Some children may be able to write a fact family with the extended facts.

[Operations and Computation Goal 1]

▶ Home Link 2·12

(*Math Masters*, p. 49)

INDEPENDENT ACTIVITY

 Home Connection Children solve subtraction facts and then trace a path through boxes with differences of 3, 4, or 5.

③ Differentiation Options

READINESS

PARTNER ACTIVITY

▶ Playing the *Difference Game*

(*My Reference Book*, pp. 130 and 131)

🌓 15–30 Min

To explore subtraction using a concrete model, have partners play the *Difference Game*. See *My Reference Book*, pages 130 and 131

Each child draws a card to determine how many pennies he or she will have for that turn. The pennies are then matched up in pairs. The player with more pennies gets to keep the extra pennies while the paired pennies go back into the bank. Play continues until there are not enough pennies in the bank to play another round. The player with more pennies wins the game.

ENRICHMENT

PARTNER ACTIVITY

▶ Playing the *Number-Grid Difference Game*

(*Math Masters*, p. 463; *My Reference Book*, pp. 140 and 141)

🌓 15–30 Min

To apply children's understanding of subtraction, have them find differences with 2-digit numbers in the *Number-Grid Difference Game*.

Name   Date   Time

HOME LINK 2·12 **Subtraction Maze**

Family Note For homework, your child will practice subtraction facts like the ones we have been working on in class. To help identify the path from the dog to the ball, have your child circle the differences of 3, 4, and 5.
Please return this Home Link to school tomorrow.

Help the dog find her ball. Solve all of the problems. Then draw the dog's path by connecting facts with answers of 3, 4, or 5. You can move up, down, left, right, or diagonally as you move between boxes.

Math Masters, p. 49

Student Page

Games

Difference Game

Materials ☐ number cards 1–10 (4 of each)
☐ 40 pennies
☐ 1 sheet of paper labeled "Bank"

Players 2

Skill Subtraction facts

Object of the game To take more pennies.

Directions

1. Shuffle the cards. Place the deck number-side down on the table.

2. Put 40 pennies in the bank.

3. To play a round, each player:
   • Takes 1 card from the top of the deck.
   • Takes the same number of pennies from the bank as the number shown on their card.

4. Find out how many more pennies one player has than the other. Pair as many pennies as you can.

5. The player with more pennies keeps the extra pennies. The rest of the pennies go back into the bank.

My Reference Book p. 130

Each player turns over 4 cards to make two 2-digit numbers. Players place their pennies on the number grid to mark their numbers. The difference between the numbers is their score for Round 1. Players record their scores. They play 5 rounds. After the fifth round, the players find the sum of their differences. Players may use the calculator to find the sum of their scores. The player with the highest sum wins the game.

EXTRA PRACTICE

SMALL-GROUP ACTIVITY

5–15 Min

▶ *Minute Math+*

To offer children more experience with addition and subtraction problems, see the following page in *Minute Math+*: page 39.

ELL SUPPORT

SMALL-GROUP ACTIVITY

5–15 Min

▶ **Building a Math Word Bank**
(Differentiation Handbook)

To provide language support for subtraction, have children use the Word Bank template found in the *Differentiation Handbook*. Ask children to write the term, *difference,* draw a picture representing the term, and write other related words. See the *Differentiation Handbook* for more information.

Student Page

Games

6. The game is over when there are not enough pennies in the bank to play another round.

7. The player with more pennies wins the game.

● Amy draws an 8. She takes 8 pennies from the bank.

John draws a 5. He takes 5 pennies from the bank.

Amy and John pair as many pennies as they can.

Amy has 3 more pennies than John. She keeps the 3 extra pennies and returns 5 of her pennies to the bank. John returns his 5 pennies to the bank.

Amy keeps the difference — 3 pennies.

Amy's Card **8**

John's Card **5**

My Reference Book, p. 131

2·13 Shortcuts for "Harder" Subtraction Facts

 Objective To guide children as they discover and practice shortcuts for subtracting 9 or 8 from any number.

---

1 Teaching the Lesson

materials

Key Activities
Children make up and share subtraction stories. They develop and practice the −9 and −8 shortcuts.

Key Concepts and Skills
• Solve −8 and −9 subtraction facts.
  [Operations and Computation Goal 1]

• Use −8 and −9 facts to solve 2-digit by 1-digit subtraction problems.
  [Operations and Computation Goal 2]

• Use patterns in subtraction facts to solve −8 and −9 facts.
  [Patterns, Functions, and Algebra Goal 1]

Key Vocabulary
−9 facts • −9 shortcut • −8 facts • −8 shortcut

Ongoing Assessment: Recognizing Student Achievement Use the Math Message.
  [Patterns, Functions, and Algebra Goal 2]

☐ *Math Journal 1,* p. 50
☐ Home Link 2·12
☐ Teaching Aid Master (*Math Masters,* p. 415)
☐ Number-Grid Poster (optional)
☐ slate
☐ half-sheets of paper

---

2 Ongoing Learning & Practice

materials

Children practice addition and subtraction facts by using Fact Triangles.

Children practice and maintain skills through Math Boxes and Home Link activities.

☐ *Math Journal 1,* p. 51
☐ Home Link Masters (*Math Masters,* pp. 50 and 51)
☐ envelopes with Fact Triangles (from Lessons 2·5 and 2·12)

***See* Advance Preparation**

---

3 Differentiation Options

materials

READINESS
Children use a ten-frame card to develop the −9 and −8 shortcuts.

EXTRA PRACTICE
Children solve problems with shortcuts for subtraction facts.

☐ Teaching Aid Master (*Math Masters,* p. 422)
☐ *Minute Math®+,* pp. 24, 41, and 42
☐ 18 counters per child

Additional Information

Advance Preparation Before beginning Part 2, children should cut out the Fact Triangles on Activity Sheets 3 and 4, if they have not already done so.

Technology
Assessment Management System
Math Message
See the **iTLG.**

Getting Started

Mental Math and Reflexes

Pose problems such as the following:

○○○ 14 − 10 = ? 4   ○○○ ? − 10 = 5 15
     18 − 10 = ? 8   ? − 10 = 16 26

○○○ 24 − 10 = ? 14
     32 − 10 = ? 22

Solving a set of −10 problems will aid in the discovery of the −9 and −8 shortcuts later in this lesson.

Math Message

On an Exit Slip (*Math Masters, p. 415*), *make up a story for the number model 16 − 9 = 7.*

Home Link 2·12
Follow-Up

Check that children were able to find the correct path through the maze.

14 − 9 = _____
_____ = 18 − 9   10   30
                 − 9   − 9

---

1 Teaching the Lesson

▶ Math Message Follow-Up

WHOLE-CLASS ACTIVITY

 Ongoing Assessment:
Recognizing Student Achievement

Math Message ★

Use the **Math Message** to assess children's understanding of the − and = symbols. Children are making adequate progress if their oral, pictorial, or written number story describes a change situation that matches the number sentence. Some children may create a parts-total or comparison number story.

[Patterns, Functions, and Algebra Goal 2]

Write 16 − 9 = 7 on the board and draw an empty unit box. Ask a few children to share their subtraction stories and to suggest labels to write in the unit box. Collect the number stories.

▶ Introducing the −9 Shortcut

WHOLE-CLASS ACTIVITY

Write some **−9 facts** and extended facts on the board but do not write the differences. Use both horizontal and vertical forms. (*See margin.*)

Ask children to copy and complete the facts on their slates. See if they can discover a **−9 shortcut** for subtracting 9 from any number.

It may help if you write pairs of related −9 facts and −10 facts on the board. (*See margin.*)

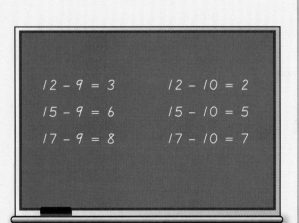

12 − 9 = 3   12 − 10 = 2
15 − 9 = 6   15 − 10 = 5
17 − 9 = 8   17 − 10 = 7

Ask children to describe the −9 shortcut in their own words. The following are good descriptions:

▷ Subtract 10 instead of 9, and then add 1.

▷ Subtract 10, but make your answer 1 bigger.

Adjusting the Activity   ELL

Use the Number-Grid Poster to demonstrate the −9 shortcut. As you model the process on the class number grid, have children model the process at their desks using the number grid in their journals. To find the difference of 17 − 9, place your finger on number 17; subtract 10 by moving your finger straight up to the row above; add one by moving right one space. The difference is 8.

1	2	3	4	5	6	7 →	8	9	10
11	12	13	14	15	16	(17)	18	19	20

A U D I T O R Y   ◆   K I N E S T H E T I C   ◆   T A C T I L E   ◆   V I S U A L

▶ Introducing the −8 Shortcut   WHOLE-CLASS ACTIVITY

Write some −**8 facts** and extended facts on the board, but do not write the differences. Use both horizontal and vertical forms. (*See margin.*)

Use the same approach as you did with the −9 shortcut to help children discover a −**8 shortcut** for subtracting 8 from any number. Demonstrate the −8 shortcut on the number grid. Children might describe the shortcut in the following ways:

▷ Subtract 10 instead of 8, and then add 2.

▷ Subtract 10, but make your answer 2 bigger.

Demonstrate the −8 shortcut on the number grid.

▶ Practicing −9 and −8 Shortcuts   INDEPENDENT ACTIVITY

(*Math Journal 1*, p. 50)

Children practice shortcuts for subtracting 9 or 8 from any number.

Adjusting the Activity

Have children write the −10 fact next to all the problems. For example, next to 17 − 9, write 17 − 10. Children find the answer to 17 − 10 and decide how that answer can be used to solve 17 − 9.

A U D I T O R Y   ◆   K I N E S T H E T I C   ◆   T A C T I L E   ◆   V I S U A L

Date   ·   Time

LESSON 2·13   Subtract 9 or 8

Reminder: To find 18 − 9, think 18 − 10 + 1.
          To find 18 − 8, think 18 − 10 + 2.

1. Subtract. Use the −9 and −8 shortcuts.

   a. 13 − 9 = __4__   b. 16 − 9 = __7__   c. 14 − 8 = __6__

   d. __4__ = 12 − 8   e. __8__ = 17 − 9   f. 12 − 9 = __3__

   g. __5__ = 13 − 8   h. 11 − 9 = __2__   i. __7__ = 15 − 8

   j.   15   k.   17   l.   11
      − 9   − 8   − 8
      ‾‾‾   ‾‾‾   ‾‾‾
       6   9   3

Try This

2. Find the differences.

   a. 43 − 9 = __34__   b. 56 − 8 = __48__   c. 65 − 9 = __56__

   d. 37 − 8 = __29__   e. 45 − 9 = __36__   f. 53 − 8 = __45__

3. Solve.

   a. 7 = __16__ − 9   b. 6 = __14__ − 8

Math Journal 1, p. 50

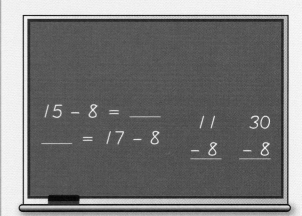

$15 - 8 = $ _____

_____ $= 17 - 8$

11	30
− 8	− 8

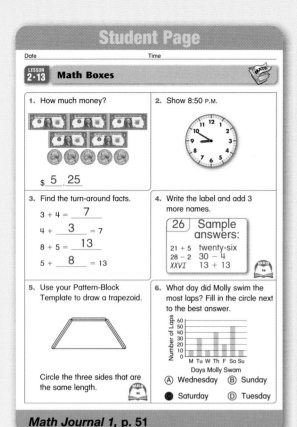

Student Page

Date   Time

LESSON
2·13 Math Boxes

1. How much money?

$ __5__ . __25__

2. Show 8:50 P.M.

3. Find the turn-around facts.

3 + 4 = __7__

4 + __3__ = 7

8 + 5 = __13__

5 + __8__ = 13

4. Write the label and add 3 more names.

26	Sample answers:
21 + 5	twenty-six
28 − 2	30 − 4
XXVI	13 + 13

5. Use your Pattern-Block Template to draw a trapezoid.

Circle the three sides that are the same length.

6. What day did Molly swim the most laps? Fill in the circle next to the best answer.

Number of Laps: 60 50 40 30 20 10
M Tu W Th F Sa Su
Days Molly Swam

Ⓐ Wednesday   Ⓑ Sunday
● Saturday   Ⓓ Tuesday

Math Journal 1, p. 51

NOTE The second Home Link page contains Fact Triangles that have been used in this lesson. With this page, children have separate sets of Fact Triangles for their use at school and at home.

---

② Ongoing Learning & Practice

▶ Practicing with +,− Fact Triangles

Have children practice addition and subtraction facts by using Fact Triangles as flashcards. This procedure was first described in Lesson 2-7. If children have instant recall for most of the easier facts, ask them to remove the Fact Triangles that have sums less than 10. Then, children will focus on practicing the harder facts.

▶ Math Boxes 2·13

(*Math Journal 1*, p. 51)

Mixed Practice Math Boxes in this lesson are linked with Math Boxes in Lessons 2-9 and 2-11. The skill in Problem 6 previews Unit 3 content.

▶ Home Link 2·13

(*Math Masters*, pp. 50 and 51)

Home Connection Children solve addition and subtraction facts, and then trace a path through boxes in which the answer is 6. The focus is on −9 and −8. Children practice with copies of the second set of fact triangles on *Math Masters*, page 51 at home.

Home Link Master

Name   Date   Time

HOME LINK
2·13 Addition/Subtraction Facts

Family Note For homework, your child will practice addition and subtraction facts like the ones we have been working on in class. Help your child solve the problems and identify the path from the bird to the seeds by circling all the cells with the answer 6.
Please return this Home Link to school tomorrow.

The bird wants to eat the seeds. Solve all of the problems below. Then draw the bird's path by connecting facts with an answer of 6. There are addition and subtraction facts. Watch for + or −.

Math Masters, p. 50

Home Link Master

Name   Date   Time

HOME LINK
2·13 Addition/Subtraction Facts *continued*

Cut out the Fact Triangles. Show someone at home how you use them to practice adding and subtracting.

Math Masters, p. 51

---

③ Differentiation Options

Ten-Frame Card

READINESS

INDEPENDENT ACTIVITY

5–15 Min

▶ ## Using a Ten-Frame Card to Demonstrate the −9 and −8 Shortcuts

(*Math Masters*, p. 422)

To explore subtraction using a visual model, have children use counters and a ten-frame card to model subtraction. Begin with a problem such as 15 − 9, and have a child place 9 counters on the ten-frame card. Ask the child how many more counters are needed to show 15. Focus on the idea of *one more to get 10* and then the rest of the number.

The child may think:

▷ I'm starting with 9.

▷ How much to 10? 1

▷ How much more to 15? 5

▷ 1 + 5 = 6, so 15 − 9 = 6.

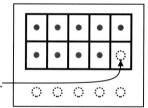

One more to get to 10.
Then 5 more.

Math Masters, p. 422

Repeat for other differences, such as 12 − 9 and 18 − 9.

Use the same procedure for the −8 facts by showing 8 counters in the ten-frame card. Focus on the idea of *two more to get 10* and then how many more to get to the starting number. Have children describe the steps they take to solve the problems.

EXTRA PRACTICE

SMALL-GROUP ACTIVITY

5–15 Min

▶ ## *Minute Math+*

To offer children more experience with shortcuts for subtraction facts, see the following pages in *Minute Math+*: pp. 24, 41, and 42.

Planning Ahead

To prepare for the activities in Lesson 3-1, organize a set of base-10 blocks for each partnership. Include 3 or 4 flats, 10 longs, and 10 cubes. Put the blocks into bags labeled with the children's tool-kit numbers. You will need a similar set for yourself. You may want to use base-10 blocks for the overhead projector.

 Objective To assess children's progress on mathematical content through the end of Unit 2.

---

1 Assessing Progress

Progress Check 2 is a cumulative assessment of concepts and skills taught in Unit 2 and in previous units.

See the Appendix for a complete list of Grade 2 Goals.

materials

☐ Home Link 2·13

☐ Assessment Masters, (*Assessment Handbook*, pp. 158–162)

☐ slate

CONTENT ASSESSED	LESSON(S)	SELF	ORAL/SLATE	WRITTEN PART A	WRITTEN PART B
Read, write, and model with manipulatives whole numbers up to 10,000; identify the value of digits in numbers. [Number and Numeration Goal 2]	2·7–2·10, 2·12		1, 2		10
Use tally marks and numerical expressions involving addition and subtraction to give equivalent names for whole numbers. [Number and Numeration Goal 5]	2·9, 2·11, 2·13	2			6
Demonstrate automaticity with +/-0, +/-1, doubles, and sum-equals-ten facts, and proficiency with all addition and subtraction facts through 10 + 10. [Operations and Computation Goal 1]	2·1–2·13	1, 5, 6	3, 4	2, 3, 4	8, 9
Calculate and compare values of coins and bills. [Operations and Computation Goal 2]	2·1–2·4, 2·9–2·13				11
Use graphs to ask and answer simple questions and draw conclusions. [Data and Chance Goal 2]	2·2, 2·4, 2·9, 2·11, 2·13				12
Extend numeric patterns; describe rules for patterns and use them to solve problems; describe, write, and use rules for functions involving addition and subtraction. [Patterns, Functions, and Algebra Goal 1]	2·2–2·6 2·10, 2·11, 2·13	3, 4		5	7
Describe the Commutative Property of Addition and apply it to mental arithmetic problems. [Patterns, Functions, and Algebra Goal 3]	2·4, 2·6, 2·7			1	

---

2 Building Background for Unit 3

Math Boxes 2·14 previews and practices skills for Unit 3.

The **Unit 3 Family Letter** introduces families to Unit 3 topics and terms.

materials

☐ *Math Journal 1*, p. 52

☐ Home Link Masters (*Math Masters*, pp. 52–55)

Additional Information

See *Assessment Handbook*, pages 60–67 for additional assessment information. For assessment checklists, see pages 240–243.

Technology

Assessment Management System
Progress Check 2
See the **iTLG.**

Getting Started

Math Message • Self Assessment | **Home Link 2·13 Follow-Up**

Complete the Self Assessment (Assessment Handbook, page 158). | Review answers as necessary.

---

1 Assessing Progress

▶ **Math Message Follow-Up**
INDEPENDENT ACTIVITY

(Self Assessment, *Assessment Handbook*, p. 158)

The Self Assessment page offers children the opportunity to reflect upon their progress.

▶ **Oral and Slate Assessments**
SMALL-GROUP ACTIVITY

Problems 1 and 2 provide summative information and can be used for grading purposes. Problems 3 and 4 provide formative information that can be useful in planning future instruction.

Oral Assessment

Write the following on the board. Have children read the numbers orally.

1. 34, 82, 96

2. 340, 995, 109

Slate Assessment Suggestions

3. Six dogs are in the park. Eight dogs enter the park. How many dogs are in the park now? 14 dogs

4. Marta has 4 stickers in her collection. Michelle has 7 stickers in her collection. How many stickers do the two girls have in all? 11 stickers

Assessment Master

Name _____ Date _____ Time _____

LESSON 2·14 Self Assessment Progress Check 2

Check one box for each skill.

Skills	I can do this by myself. I can explain how to do this.	I can do this by myself.	I can do this with help.
1. Write fact families.			
2. Fill in name-collection boxes.			
3. Solve Frames-and-Arrows problems.			
4. Solve "What's My Rule?" problems.			
5. Know addition facts.			
6. Know subtraction facts.			

Assessment Handbook, p. 158

Assessment Master

Name _____ Date _____ Time _____

LESSON 2·14 | **Written Assessment** | Progress Check 2 ✓

Part A

1. Add and write the turnaround.

   5 + 3 = ___8___   Turnaround 3 + 5 = 8

2. Write the fact family for 2, 11, and 9.

   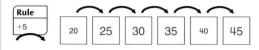

   2 + 9 = 11   9 + 2 = 11
   11 − 2 = 9   11 − 9 = 2

3. Add.

   a. 6 + 1 = ___7___
   b. 4 + 4 = ___8___
   c. 0 + 9 = ___9___

4. Subtract.

   a. 7 − 0 = ___7___
   b. ___10___ = 11 − 1
   c. 7 − 4 = ___3___

5. Fill in the empty frames.

   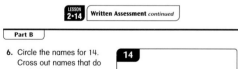

   | Rule +5 | | 20 | 25 | 30 | 35 | 40 | 45 |

Assessment Handbook, p. 159

▶ **Written Assessment**   INDEPENDENT ACTIVITY

(*Assessment Masters*, pp. 159–161)

Part A   Recognizing Student Achievement

Problems 1–5 provide summative information and may be used for grading purposes.

Problem(s)	Description
1	Add and write the turnaround.
2	Write the fact family for 2, 11, and 9.
3	Add.
4	Subtract.
5	Fill in the empty frames.

Part B   Informing Instruction

Problems 6–10 provide formative information that can be useful in planning future instruction.

Problem(s)	Description
6	Circle the names for 14.
7	Find the rule and complete the table.
8	Add.
9	Subtract.
10	Put an X on the number in the tens place.
11	Show $1.00 two ways using Q, D, and N.
12	Use the graph to answer the questions.

Assessment Master

Name _____ Date _____ Time _____

LESSON 2·14 | **Written Assessment** *continued*

Part B

6. Circle the names for 14. Cross out names that do not belong.

   14

   (9 + 5) (34 − 20) (8 + 6)
   ~~14~~ ⟨11⟩ (12 + 2) ~~5 × 6~~
   ~~7 × 3~~ 3 × 9
   (7 + 7) (18 − 4)

7. Find the rule and complete the table.

Rule +6	in	out
	9	15
	4	10
	6	12
	7	13
	8	14
	10	16

8. Add.

   a.   9
      + 6
      ‾15‾

   b.   5
      + 6
      ‾11‾

9. Subtract.

   a.   9
      − 5
      ‾4‾

   b.   13
      − 8
      ‾5‾

Assessment Handbook, p. 160

Assessment Master

Name _____ Date _____ Time _____

LESSON 2·14 | **Written Assessment** *continued*

10. Put an X on the number in the tens place.

    1X4   7X6

11. Show $1.00 two ways using ⓆⒹⓃ.

    Sample answers:

    Ⓠ Ⓠ Ⓠ Ⓠ
    Ⓠ Ⓠ Ⓓ Ⓓ Ⓓ Ⓓ

12.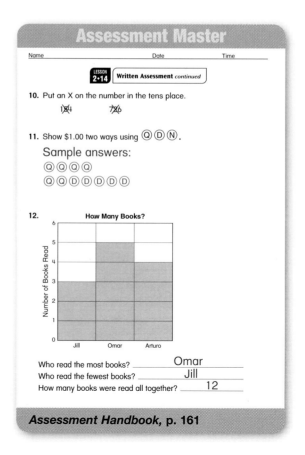

    How Many Books?

    Who read the most books? ___Omar___
    Who read the fewest books? ___Jill___
    How many books were read all together? ___12___

Assessment Handbook, p. 161

168   **Unit 2   Progress Check 2**

▶ Open Response

(*Assessment Handbook,* pp. 63–67, 162)

INDEPENDENT ACTIVITY

Train Boxes

The open response item requires children to apply skills and concepts from Unit 2 to solve a multistep problem. See *Assessment Handbook,* pages 63–67 for rubrics and children's work samples for this problem.

---

② Building Background for Unit 3

▶ Math Boxes 2•14

INDEPENDENT ACTIVITY

(*Math Journal 1,* p. 52)

Mixed Practice This Math Boxes page previews Unit 3 content.

▶ Home Link 2•14: Unit 3 Family Letter

INDEPENDENT ACTIVITY

(*Math Masters,* pp. 52–55)

Home Connection The Unit 3 Family Letter provides parents and guardians with information and activities related to Unit 3 topics.

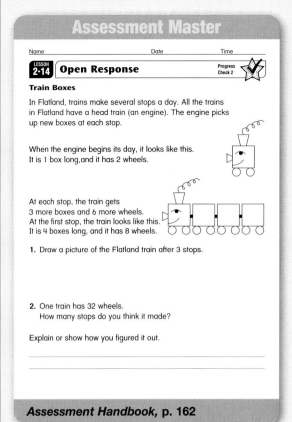

Assessment Master

Name _____ Date _____ Time _____

LESSON 2•14 Open Response — Progress Check 2

Train Boxes

In Flatland, trains make several stops a day. All the trains in Flatland have a head train (an engine). The engine picks up new boxes at each stop.

When the engine begins its day, it looks like this. It is 1 box long, and it has 2 wheels.

At each stop, the train gets 3 more boxes and 6 more wheels. At the first stop, the train looks like this. It is 4 boxes long, and it has 8 wheels.

1. Draw a picture of the Flatland train after 3 stops.

2. One train has 32 wheels. How many stops do you think it made?

Explain or show how you figured it out.

_____

Assessment Handbook, p. 162

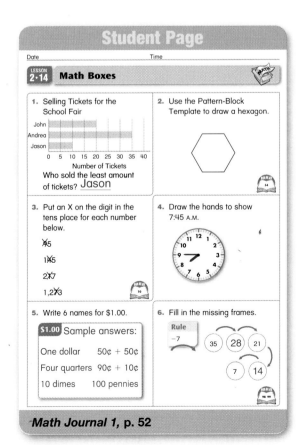

Student Page

Date _____ Time _____

LESSON 2•14 Math Boxes

1. Selling Tickets for the School Fair

   John
   Andrea
   Jason

   0 5 10 15 20 25 30 35 40
   Number of Tickets
   Who sold the least amount of tickets? **Jason**

2. Use the Pattern-Block Template to draw a hexagon.

3. Put an X on the digit in the tens place for each number below.

   X̶45
   1X̶5
   2X̶7
   1,2X̶3

4. Draw the hands to show 7:45 A.M.

5. Write 6 names for $1.00.

   $1.00 Sample answers:
   One dollar   50¢ + 50¢
   Four quarters   90¢ + 10¢
   10 dimes   100 pennies

6. Fill in the missing frames.

   Rule −7
   35 28 21
   7 14

Math Journal 1, p. 52

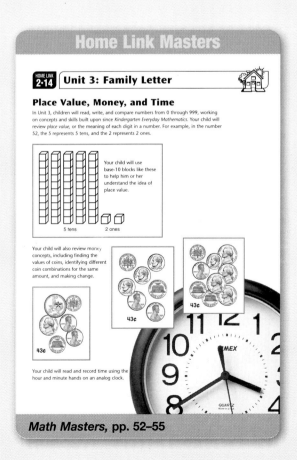

Home Link Masters

HOME LINK 2•14 Unit 3: Family Letter

Place Value, Money, and Time

In Unit 3, children will read, write, and compare numbers from 0 through 999, working on concepts and skills built upon since *Kindergarten Everyday Mathematics*. Your child will review *place value,* or the meaning of each digit in a number. For example, in the number 52, the 5 represents 5 tens, and the 2 represents 2 ones.

Your child will use base-10 blocks like these to help him or her understand the idea of place value.

5 tens   2 ones

Your child will also review money concepts, including finding the values of coins, identifying different coin combinations for the same amount, and making change.

43¢   43¢   43¢

Your child will read and record time using the hour and minute hands on an analog clock.

Math Masters, pp. 52–55

Unit 3 Organizer

Place Value, Money, and Time

Overview

Unit 3 continues the review and extension of topics introduced in First Grade Everyday Mathematics®: numeration and place value, money, time, and data collection and analysis. Few children will have mastered these concepts as a result of their first-grade experiences. As usual, keep the activities lively and set a brisk pace. These topics will be brought up repeatedly in review exercises, in Mental Math and Reflexes, and in other opportunities throughout the school day. Unit 3 has four main areas of focus:

◆ To review place value in 2-digit and 3-digit numbers,

◆ To review coin values and exchanges among coins,

◆ To tell time and to write time in digital-clock notation, and

◆ To gather data by counting and to analyze data.

Contents

Unit

3
Organizer

Learning In Perspective

	Lesson Objectives	Links to the Past	Links to the Future
3·1	To review place value in 2-digit and 3-digit numbers.	In first grade, children are introduced to place value for 100s, 10s, and 1s using base-10 blocks.	Place-value concepts are used later to develop mental arithmetic strategies for adding and subtracting 2- and 3-digit numbers. Children learn place value to the millions in third grade.
3·2	To review coin values and exchanges among coins; and to provide experiences with finding coin combinations needed to pay for items.	Children are introduced to coins and bills in Kindergarten and count combinations of coins in first grade.	Children continue to develop money-counting and change-counting skills and strategies throughout second grade and third grade.
3·3	To review telling time; and to provide experiences with writing time in digital-clock notation.	In first grade, children practice telling time to the nearest quarter hour and learn to use the minute hand.	Time telling practice continues throughout Grade 3. Children begin to learn how to calculate elapsed time in third grade.
3·4	To provide experiences with representing and renaming numbers with base-10 blocks; reviewing time; and making, describing, and comparing geoboard shapes.	In first grade, children are introduced to place value for 100s, 10s, and 1s using base-10 blocks. They practice telling time to the nearest half- and quarter-hour. Children begin to examine the properties of 2-dimensional shapes in Kindergarten.	Place-value concepts are used later to develop mental arithmetic strategies for adding and subtracting 2- and 3-digit numbers. Time telling practice continues through Grade 3. Children further explore and classify 2-dimensional and 3-dimensional shapes in third grade.
3·5	To provide experiences with gathering data, entering data in a table, and drawing a bar graph; and to demonstrate a strategy for finding the middle value in a data set.	In first grade, children are introduced to the statistical landmarks of maximum and minimum, and practice collecting data and making bar graphs.	In second grade, children continue to find the median and mode when analyzing data. In third grade, they are introduced to the mean.
3·6	To guide children as they solve Frames-and-Arrows problems having two rules.	The Frames-and-Arrows routine is introduced in first grade, using one rule.	Two-rule Frames-and-Arrows continue to be used throughout second and third grades. In third grade, children use Frames-and-Arrows with 3-digit numbers, multiplication, and division.
3·7	To guide children as they make change by counting up from the cost of an item to the amount tendered.	Children are introduced to coins and bills in Kindergarten and count combinations of coins in first grade.	Children continue to develop money-counting and change-making skills and strategies throughout second grade and third grade.
3·8	To guide children as they solve multistep problems for amounts under $1.00; and as they practice making change using nickels, dimes, and quarters.	Children are introduced to coins and bills in Kindergarten and count combinations of coins in first grade.	Children continue to develop money-counting and change-making skills and strategies throughout second grade.

Key Concepts and Skills

	Key Concepts and Skills	Grade 2 Goals*
3·1	Count by 1s, 10s, and 100s with base-10 blocks.	Number and Numeration Goal 1
	Explore place-value concepts with base-10 blocks; read and write 2- and 3-digit numbers.	Number and Numeration Goal 2
	Build numbers with base-10 blocks in preparation for modeling addition strategies.	Number and Numeration Goal 2
3·2	Count by 5s, 10s, and 25s.	Number and Numeration Goal 1
	Use dollars-and-cents notation.	Number and Numeration Goal 2
	Calculate coin combinations.	Operations and Computation Goal 2
	Exchange coins and dollar bills.	Measurement and Reference Frames Goal 4
3·3	Count by 5s.	Number and Numeration Goal 1
	Distinguish between analog and digital clocks.	Measurement and Reference Frames Goal 6
	Tell and write times.	Measurement and Reference Frames Goal 6
3·4	Model 2-digit numbers with base-10 blocks.	Number and Numeration Goal 2
	Write and tell time to the nearest hour, half-hour, and quarter-hour.	Measurement and Reference Frames Goal 6
	Model, describe, and compare shapes on a geoboard.	Geometry Goal 2
3·5	Compare and order numbers.	Number and Numeration Goal 7
	Use parts-and-total diagrams to find totals.	Operations and Computation Goal 4
	Make a tally chart and bar graph to represent data.	Data and Chance Goal 1
	Discuss data in a tally chart and bar graph.	Data and Chance Goal 2
3·6	Use dollars-and-cents notation.	Number and Numeration Goal 2
	Calculate values of coin and bill combinations.	Operations and Computation Goal 2
	Identify and use rules for a function involving addition and subtraction of coins.	Patterns, Functions, and Algebra Goal 1
3·7	Count by 1s, 5s, 10s, and 25s.	Number and Numeration Goal 1
	Write money amounts using cents notation.	Number and Numeration Goal 2
	Make change by counting up.	Operations and Computation Goal 2
	Show coin combinations for an amount.	Operations and Computation Goal 2
3·8	Count by 5s, 10s, and 25s.	Number and Numeration Goal 1
	Write amounts in dollars-and-cents notation.	Number and Numeration Goal 2
	Use strategies to make change.	Operations and Computation Goal 2
	Calculate coin amounts.	Operations and Computation Goal 2

* See the Appendix for a complete list of Grade 2 Goals.

Ongoing Learning and Practice

Math Boxes

Math Boxes are paired across lessons as shown in the brackets below. This makes them useful as assessment tools. Math Boxes also preview content of the next unit.

Mixed practice   [3◆1, 3◆3], [3◆2, 3◆4], [3◆5, 3◆7], [3◆6, 3◆8]
Mixed practice with multiple choice   3◆1, 3◆5, 3◆6
Mixed practice with writing/reasoning opportunity   3◆3, 3◆4, 3◆7, 3◆8

Practice through Games

Games are an essential component of practice in the *Everyday Mathematics* program. Games offer skills practice and promote strategic thinking.

Lesson	Game	Skill Practiced
3◆1, 3◆7	*Digit Game*	**Place value** Number and Numeration Goal 2
3◆2	*Spinning for Money*	**Coin and bill exchanges** Measurement and Reference Frames Goal 4
3◆2	*Penny-Nickel Exchange*	**Exchanging pennies and nickels** Measurement and Reference Frames Goal 4
3◆2	*Penny-Dime-Dollar Exchange*	**Coin and bill exchanges** Measurement and Reference Frames Goal 4
3◆4	*Base-10 Exchange*	**Place value** Number and Numeration Goal 2
3◆5	*Dollar Rummy*	**Finding value of coin combinations** Measurement and Reference Frames Goal 4 Operations and Computation Goal 2
3◆7	*High Roller*	**Counting up** Number and Numeration Goal 1

See the *Differentiation Handbook* for ways to adapt games to meet children's needs.

Home Communication

Home Links provide homework and home communication.

◀ *Home Connection Handbook* provides more ideas to communicate effectively with parents.

Unit 3 Family Letter provides families with an overview, Do-Anytime Activities, Building Skills Through Games and a list of vocabulary.

Problem Solving

Encourage children to use a variety of strategies to solve problems and to explain those strategies. Strategies that children might use in this unit:

◆ Acting out the problem   ◆ Using information to write a number story
◆ Working backward   ◆ Making and using a graph
◆ Using manipulatives as models   ◆ Using information from a picture

Lessons that teach **through** *problem solving, not just* **about** *problem solving*

Lesson	Activity
3◆2	Buy and sell things with coins.
3◆4	Solve magic squares problems.
3◆4	Create a clock booklet.
3◆4	Give directions for duplicating shapes.
3◆5	Make a bar graph of pockets data.
3◆6	Solve Frames-and-Arrows problems involving money.
3◆6	Read a bar graph.
3◆8	Make purchases and make change using Fruit and Vegetables Stand and Vending Machine Posters.

See Chapter 18 in the *Teacher's Reference Manual* for more information about problem solving.

Planning Tips

Pacing

Pacing depends on a number of factors, such as children's individual needs and how long your school has been using *Everyday Mathematics*. At the beginning of Unit 3, review your *Content by Strand* Poster to help you set a monthly pace.

← **MOST CLASSROOMS** →

SEPTEMBER	OCTOBER	NOVEMBER

NCTM Standards

Unit 3 Lessons	3◆1	3◆2	3◆3	3◆4	3◆5	3◆6	3◆7	3◆8
NCTM Standards	1–2, 6–8	1–2, 4, 6–10	4, 6, 8–10	1–4, 6–10	1–2, 5–10	1–2, 5–8, 10	1–2, 4, 6–10	1, 4, 6–10

Content Standards: 1 Number and Operations, **2** Algebra, **3** Geometry, **4** Measurement, **5** Data Analysis and Probability
Process Standards: 6 Problem Solving, **7** Reasoning and Proof, **8** Communication, **9** Connections, **10** Representation

Balanced Assessment

Ongoing Assessment

 Recognizing Student Achievement

Opportunities to assess children's progress toward Grade 2 Goals:

Lesson	Content Assessed
3•1	Understand place value. [Number and Numeration Goal 2]
3•2	Find values of coin combinations. [Operations and Computation Goal 2]
3•3	Record tally marks and correctly group tallies by 5s. [Number and Numeration Goal 5]
3•4	Show time to the nearest half-hour. [Measurement and Reference Frames Goal 6]
3•5	Show equivalent names for 20. [Number and Numeration Goal 5]
3•6	Create number patterns and rules in Frames-and-Arrows problems. [Patterns, Functions, and Algebra Goal 1]
3•7	Understand place value. [Number and Numeration Goal 2]
3•8	Find values of coin combinations. [Operations and Computation Goal 2]

Use the **Assessment Management System** to collect and analyze data about children's progress throughout the year.

 Informing Instruction

To anticipate common child errors and to highlight problem-solving strategies:

Lesson 3•1   Represent three-digit numbers with 0s

Lesson 3•3   Draw the hands of a clock correctly

Lesson 3•5   Count up on a number line

Lesson 3•6   Solve Frames-and-Arrows problems when the first frame is blank

Periodic Assessment

 3◆9 Progress Check 3

CONTENT ASSESSED	Self	ASSESSMENT ITEMS Oral/Slate	Written	Open Response
Count on by 1s, 2s, 5s, 10s, 25s, and 100s. [Number and Numeration Goal 1]	✔	✔	✔	
Read and write whole numbers to 1,000; identify place values in such numbers. [Number and Numeration Goal 2]		✔		
Know and apply addition facts through 10 + 10. [Operations and Computation Goal 1]	✔		✔	
Use and explain strategies to add and subtract 2-digit numbers. Calculate and compare values of coin and bill combinations [Operations and Computation Goal 2]	✔		✔	✔
Demonstrate, describe, and apply change, comparison, and parts-and-total situations. [Operations and Computation Goal 4]			✔	
Use graphs to ask and answer questions and draw conclusions. [Data and Chance Goal 2]	✔		✔	
Make exchanges between coins. [Measurement and Reference Frames Goal 4]				✔
Read temperature to the nearest degree on both the Fahrenheit and Celsius scales. [Measurement and Reference Frames Goal 5]	✔		✔	
Continue simple numerical patterns; find rules for patterns and use them to solve problems. [Patterns, Functions, and Algebra Goal 1]	✔		✔	

Portfolio Opportunities

Some opportunities to gather samples of children's mathematical writings, drawings, and creations to add balance to the assessment process:

◆ Explaining strategy used to solve addition problem, **Lesson 3◆3**
◆ Making a clock booklet to practice telling time, **Lesson 3◆4**
◆ Creating number patterns and rules in Frames-and-Arrows problems, **Lesson 3◆6**
◆ Explaining a strategy used to solve a problem with multiple addends, **Lesson 3◆8**

Assessment Handbook

Unit 3 Assessment Support

◆ Grade 2 Goals, pp. 37–50
◆ Unit 3 Assessment Overview, pp. 68–75

◆ Unit 3 Open Response
  • Detailed rubric, p.72
  • Sample student responses, pp. 73–75

Unit 3 Assessment Masters

◆ Unit 3 Self Assessment, p. 163
◆ Unit 3 Written Assessment, pp. 164–166
◆ Unit 3 Open Response, p. 167
◆ Unit 3 Class Checklist, pp. 246, 247, and 293
◆ Quarterly Checklist: Quarter 1, pp. 284 and 285

◆ Unit 3 Individual Profile of Progress, pp. 244, 245, and 292
◆ Exit Slip, p. 295
◆ Math Logs, pp. 298–300
◆ Other Student Assessment Forms, pp. 296, 297, and 301–303

Differentiated Instruction

Daily Lesson Support

ENGLISH LANGUAGE LEARNERS

- **3•2** Building a Math Word Bank
- **3•3** Building a Math Word Bank
- **3•5** Building a Math Word Bank

EXTRA PRACTICE

Minute Math®+ **3•4** Practicing with digits, shapes, and time; **3•8** Practicing with money

READINESS

- **3•1** Investigating place value using calculators
- **3•2** Practicing coin exchanges
- **3•3** Showing times on a clock face
- **3•4** Practicing place-value skills
- **3•5** Practicing tallying
- **3•6** Counting up and back on a number line
- **3•7** Counting up using dice
- **3•8** Counting with coins on a number grid

ENRICHMENT

- **3•1** Creating three-digit numbers
- **3•2** Writing number stories
- **3•3** Calculating elapsed time
- **3•5** Creating and comparing data sets
- **3•6** Solving Frames-and-Arrows puzzles
- **3•7** Solving a coin puzzle
- **3•8** Adding coin combinations

Adjusting the Activity

- **3•1** Working with a Place-Value Mat **ELL**
- **3•2** Discussing the meaning of *cents* **ELL**
- **3•2** Setting parameters for coin combinations
- **3•4** Writing times to the nearest 5 minutes or minute
- **3•5** Using calculators to analyze data

- **3•5** Labeling a bar graph with *maximum, minimum,* and *middle number* **ELL**
- **3•6** Solving Frames-and-Arrows puzzles
- **3•6** Completing frames and finding the rule
- **3•7** Practicing making change
- **3•8** Using coins to model purchases

A U D I T O R Y   ◆   K I N E S T H E T I C   ◆   T A C T I L E   ◆   V I S U A L

○ Cross-Curricular Links

Language Arts

Lesson 3•3 Children learn the meaning of A.M. and P.M.

Lesson 3•4 Children make up a story about a time.

Using the Projects

Use Project 4, Dates on Pennies, during or after Unit 3. This project provides an opportunity for your children to gain experience with 4-digit numbers in the form of notation for years (1998, 1999, and so on) and to tally, graph, and compare data. See the *Differentiation Handbook* for modifications to project 4.

◄ *Differentiation Handbook*

See the *Differentiation Handbook* for materials on Unit 3.

Language Support

Everyday Mathematics provides lesson-specific suggestions to help all children, including non-native English speakers, to acquire, process, and express mathematical ideas.

Connecting Math and Literacy

Lesson 3•1 *A Place for Zero: A Math Adventure,* by Angeline Sparagna LoPresti, Charlesbridge Publishing, 2003

Lesson 3•2 *26 Letters and 99 Cents,* by Tara Hoban, Mulberry, 1987

Lesson 3•2 *The Big Buck Adventure,* by Shelley Gill and Deborah Tobola, Scholastic, Inc., 2000

Lesson 3•3 *Pigs on a Blanket,* by Amy Axelrod, Scholastic, Inc., 1996

Lesson 3•5 *Bart's Amazing Charts,* by Dianne Ochiltree, Scholastic, 1999

Lesson 3•8 *How Much Is That Guinea Pig in the Window?,* by Joanne Rocklin, Scholastic, Inc., 1995

 My Reference Book
pp. 11, 78-81, 88, 89, 132, and 133

Multiage Classroom ◆ Companion Lessons

Companion Lessons from Grades 1 and 3 can help you meet instructional needs of a multiage classroom. The full Scope and Sequence can be found in the Appendix.

Grade 1	4•7 5•1 8•3	3•12 8•1 8•4	2•5 3•7 6•10	4•7 10•2	3•13 6•12 10•1	3•8 3•9	3•12 8•1 8•5	3•12 8•4 8•5
Grade 2	**3•1**	**3•2**	**3•3**	**3•4**	**3•5**	**3•6**	**3•7**	**3•8**
Grade 3	5•1– 5•7	1•10 9•5 9•7	1•13 11•1	5•6 9•3	1•5 5•12 10•6		1•10 9•5 9•7	1•11 9•5 9•7

Professional Development

Teacher's Reference Manual Links

Lesson	Topic	Section	Lesson	Topic	Section
3•1	Numeration and Place Value	9.2.1	3•5	Data Collection, Organization, and Analysis	12.2
	Operations and Number Models Tools and Techniques	10.3		Collecting and recording data	12.2.2
	Number and Counting tools	3.2.1		Organizing and Displaying Data	12.2.3
3•3	Clocks	15.2.1	3•6	Functions	17.1.4
3•4	Base-10 blocks	9.7.1	3•7	Addition Algorithms	11.2.1
	Polygons	13.4.2	3•8	Subtraction Algorithms	11.2.2
	Clocks	15.2.1			

Unit 3 Organizer

Materials

Lesson	Masters	Manipulative Kit Items	Other Items
3•1	Teaching Aid Master, p. 427 transparency of *Math Masters*, p. 56* Home Link Master, p. 57	base-10 blocks 4 of each number cards 0–9 calculator	
3•2	Home Link 3•1 Teaching Aid Masters, pp. 417*, 419, and 428 transparency of *Math Masters*, p. 58 Home Link Master, p. 59 Game Master, p. 472	bills coin stamps* per group: 1 or 2 dice	coins; scissors; large paper clip
3•3	Home Link 3•2 Teaching Masters, pp. 60*, 61*, and 64 Teaching Aid Master, p. 415 Home Link Masters, pp. 62 and 63	slate, tool-kit clock	demonstration clock (hour hand only); demonstration clock (minute and hour hands); variety of analog and digital clocks *; scissors; red and green markers, brad *; +, − Fact Triangles (with sums greater than 10); paper fastener
3•4	Home Link 3•3 Teaching Masters, pp. 65–69 Teaching Aid Masters, pp. 427, 428, and 429 or 430* Home Link Master, p. 70	base-10 blocks number cards 0–9 clock-face rubber stamp and stamp pad geoboard and rubber bands per group: 2 dice slate	scissors; stapler; paper
3•5	Home Link 3•4 Teaching Master, p. 71 transparencies of *Math Masters*, pp. 72 and 73 Home Link Master, p. 74 Game Masters, pp. 454 and 455	per group: 1 die calculator*	scissors; half-sheet of paper; Class Data Pad*
3•6	Home Link 3•5 Teaching Masters, pp. 75–77, 79, and 80 Teaching Aid Master, p. 431 transparencies of *Math Masters*, pp. 75–77 and 431* Home Link Master, p. 78		coins; red and blue crayons
3•7	Home Link 3•6 Home Link Masters, pp. 81 and 82 Teaching Aid Master, p. 415 Teaching Master, p. 83	dice Per group: 4 each of number cards 0–9 bills slate	coins; overhead coins*
3•8	Home Link 3•7 transparency of *Math Masters*, p. 84* Home Link Master, p. 85 Teaching Aid Master, p. 418	Per group: 2 dice tool-kit coins bills slate calculator*	coins; item to use as a bank, such as a cup, small box, or piece of paper
3•9 ✓	Home Link 3•8 Assessment Masters, pp. 163–167 Home Link Masters, p. 86–89	base-10 blocks slate	

Technology
Assessment Management System, Unit 3
iTLG, Unit 3

* Denotes optional materials

Mathematical Background

The notes below highlight the major content ideas presented in Unit 3. These notes may help establish instructional priorities.

Numeration and Place Value

(Lesson 3•1)

In *Kindergarten* and *First Grade Everyday Mathematics,* children had a great deal of experience with place value through free play and exploration with base-10 blocks. Most children will also be familiar with recording whole numbers on paper and slates, entering numbers into a calculator, and representing numbers with number cards.

This lesson allows you to assess how children are able to translate among spoken numbers, written numbers, displays of base-10 blocks, and numbers displayed on a Place-Value Mat. This lesson also provides opportunities for you to assess whether children can tell how many ones, tens, and hundreds are in a given number, and whether they can write numbers if given the number of ones, tens, and hundreds.

Keep in mind the importance of identifying the unit for different contexts. For example, if "cent" is given as the unit, then "dime" represents 10 cents and "dollar" represents 100 cents. If children understand the concept of unit, they will have no trouble grasping the relationship between whole numbers and decimals that they will encounter later in *Everyday Mathematics:* If "dollar" is the unit, then

"dime" represents $\frac{1}{10}$, or 0.1, and "penny" represents $\frac{1}{100}$, or 0.01.

Continue to remind children that numbers are used to describe something that is identified by a label or a unit. In each of the place-value drills, have children choose a unit as a context for the numbers.

 **PROFESSIONAL DEVELOPMENT** To learn more about numeration and place value, refer to Section 9.2.1 of the *Teacher's Reference Manual.*

Children practice place value by naming the hundreds, tens, and ones for numbers in a calculator display.

Money (Lessons 3•2, 3•7, and 3•8)

The lessons on money serve as a vehicle for adding and subtracting 2-digit numbers using manipulatives (coins). These activities prepare children for the focus on mental arithmetic in Unit 4. Actual or play money (at least 10 pennies, 6 nickels, 6 dimes, 4 quarters, and two $1 bills per child) is used in several lessons. Therefore, you may want to have children keep a set of coins and bills in their tool kits or in a classroom bank for the duration of the unit. If children store the coins in their tool kits, be sure they use a container such as an empty film canister or a resealable plastic bag.

Two posters form the basis for number stories about money: a Fruit and Vegetables Stand Poster (Lesson 3-2) and a Milk and Juice Vending Machine Poster (Lesson 3-8). As usual, partners make up and solve many problems and record just a few of them in their journals.

I bought a melon slice, two apples and a pear with half a dollar. Is my number story true?

A child's number story based on the Fruit and Vegetables Stand poster.

Children practice money skills by playing the roles of a customer paying for an item and a clerk giving the customer the appropriate change. Children also do a Making Change activity beginning in Lesson 3-8.

Telling Time (Lesson 3•3)

Because it takes many experiences over an extended period to develop time-telling skills, it would be unrealistic to expect mastery at this point. The objective of the lessons in this unit is to give children experiences in reading and recording time on analog clocks and to assess how often children need to practice these skills over the next few weeks. Children will benefit greatly from brief but regular activities like the following:

7:15
15 minutes after 7
quarter after 7
a little past 7 o'clock
15 past 7

Different ways to describe
the same time

◆ Ask children to read the time on the classroom clock.

◆ Say an approximate time. Ask children to show the time on their tool-kit clocks.

◆ Once your classroom schedule has become familiar to children, ask them to say and write the times that they need to be at certain activities, such as recess or lunch. About where will the hour hand be at that time? About where will the minute hand be?

◆ Have children record the time daily at the top of each journal page.

Repeat such activities often during the school year.

Children may know several equivalent names for the same time—7:15, quarter after 7, 15 minutes after 7, and so on. Encourage children to use the different terms shown in the margin.

PROFESSIONAL DEVELOPMENT Refer to Section 15.2 of the *Teacher's Reference Manual* for more information about telling time.

Explorations: Numbers, Time, and Geoboards (Lesson 3•4)

This lesson contains three activities designed as Explorations. (See "Explorations" in the Managing the Curriculum section 1.2.1 of the Management Guide, which is located in the *Teacher's Reference Manual.*)

In the first Exploration, children develop place-value concepts by using base-10 blocks to show 2- and 3-digit numbers in different ways; for example, 26 as 2 tens and 6 ones, as 1 ten and 16 ones, or as 26 ones.

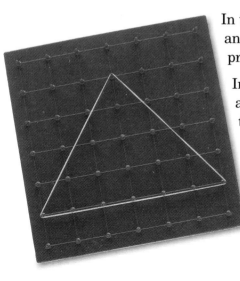

In the second Exploration, children make clock-face booklets showing analog and digital times. These booklets can be saved and used later to practice time-telling skills.

In the third Exploration, children make, describe, and compare shapes on a geoboard. Because one goal of this Exploration is to encourage children to communicate clearly about mathematics, children do these activities with a partner and in small groups.

The game *Dollar Rummy* is also introduced. This game strengthens counting and calculating skills as children find complements of 100.

Data Day: Pockets (Lesson 3•5)

Children count their pockets, tally their results, identify the middle value in their data, and represent their data by making a bar graph.

Name		Date		Time

LESSON 3•5 Pockets Data Table

Pockets	Children	
	Tallies	Number
0		
1		
2		
3		
4		
5		
6		
7		
8		
9		
10		
11		
12		
13 or more		

If there is an even number of values in a set of data, there is no single middle value; you and the children can decide how to handle this. The mathematical term for this middle value is *median*. In everyday life, people often refer to this as the "average." In mathematics and statistics, however, "average" usually refers to the "arithmetic average" (also called the "mean"), which is obtained by adding the numbers in the data set and dividing the sum by the number of data entries. The median usually gives an equally valid indication of what is "typical" and is usually much easier to obtain.

The data in this activity do not lend themselves to finding an arithmetic average. In other activities involving data, however, some second graders might enjoy using their calculators to find the arithmetic average and comparing it to the median.

Further information on Data Collection, Organization and Analysis can be found in Section 12.2 of the *Teacher's Reference Manual.*

Frames and Arrows with Two Rules (Lesson 3•6)

Frames-and-Arrows puzzles are extended to number sequences with two rules.

See "Frames-and-Arrows Diagrams" in the Managing the Curriculum section 1.3.2 of the Management Guide in the *Teacher's Reference Manual.*

Numeration and Place Value

 Objective To review place value in 2-digit and 3-digit numbers.

---

1 Teaching the Lesson

materials

Key Activities
Children are introduced to base-10 blocks and a simple way to draw them. They match numbers to base-10 blocks; model 2- and 3-digit numbers with one or two zeros; and translate among spoken and written numbers, displays of base-10 blocks, and number cards.

Key Concepts and Skills
• Count by 1s, 10s, and 100s with base-10 blocks.
 [Number and Numeration Goal 1]

• Explore place-value concepts with base-10 blocks; read and write 2-and 3-digit numbers.
 [Number and Numeration Goal 2]

• Build numbers with base-10 blocks in preparation for modeling addition strategies.
 [Number and Numeration Goal 2]

Key Vocabulary
base-10 system

☑ **Ongoing Assessment:** Informing Instruction See page 187.

☑ **Ongoing Assessment:** Recognizing Student Achievement Use journal page 53.
 [Number and Numeration Goal 2]

☐ *Math Journal 1,* p. 53
☐ *My Reference Book,* p. 11
☐ Teaching Aid Master (*Math Masters,* p. 427)
☐ Transparency (*Math Masters,* p. 56; optional)
☐ base-10 blocks
☐ number cards 0–9 (from the Everything Math Deck, if available)
☐ calculator

***See* Advance Preparation**

---

2 Ongoing Learning & Practice

materials

Children practice forming and comparing numbers by playing the *Digit Game.*

Children practice and maintain skills through Math Boxes and Home Link activities.

☐ *Math Journal 1,* p. 54
☐ *My Reference Book,* pp. 132 and 133
☐ Home Link Master (*Math Masters,* p. 57)
☐ per partnership: 4 each of number cards 0–9 (from the Everything Math Deck, if available)

---

3 Differentiation Options

materials

READINESS
Children use their calculators to investigate place value.

ENRICHMENT
Children create as many numbers as possible using three digits.

☐ calculator
☐ 10 flats, 10 longs, 10 cubes
☐ number cards 1–9 (from the Everything Math Deck, if available)

Additional Information

Advance Preparation You may want to spend two days on this lesson. For Part 1, you and each child or partnership will need a set of base-10 blocks (3 or 4 flats, 10 longs, and 10 cubes in bags labeled with children's tool-kit numbers). To display a Place-Value Mat, make an overhead transparency of *Math Masters,* page 56, or draw a Place-Value Mat on the board using semipermanent chalk.

Technology
Assessment Management System
Journal page 53, Problems 1 and 3
See the **iTLG.**

Getting Started

Mental Math and Reflexes

Pose number stories that involve addition and subtraction facts. *Suggestions:*

- ●○○ Keisha read 8 pages of her book last night and 6 pages this morning. How many pages did she read in all? 14 pages
- ●●○ Hana scored 7 points. Dakota scored 9. How many points did they score in all? 16 points
- ●●● Austin brought 17 cupcakes to school for his birthday. He gave 8 to his classmates. How many cupcakes does he have left? 9 cupcakes

Math Message

$52 = $ __5__ *tens and* __2__ *ones*

$25 = $ __2__ *tens and* __5__ *ones*

---

① Teaching the Lesson

▶ Math Message Follow-Up

👥 **WHOLE-CLASS DISCUSSION**

Briefly discuss children's responses. Ask children to explain how they decided which digit names the tens and which digit names the ones. These numbers will be revisited later in the lesson.

Explain to children that in today's lesson they will use base-10 blocks to create numbers.

▶ Exploring a Simple Way to Draw Base-10 Blocks

👥 **WHOLE-CLASS ACTIVITY**

(*My Reference Book,* p. 11)

Hold up a cube, a long, and a flat. Say: *These are called base-10 blocks.* Hold up a cube. Say: *This is a base-10 cube. It represents one.* Then hold up a long and say: *This is a long. It represents ten.* Ask children why they think a long represents ten. Because it is made up of 10 cubes Last, hold up a flat and say: *This is a flat. It represents one hundred.* Ask children why they think a flat represents one hundred. Because it is made up of 100 cubes Display the blocks on the overhead projector.

Remind children that our system for writing numbers is called the **base-10 system,** because it is based on grouping things by tens. Explain that base-10 blocks are useful for understanding numbers and solving problems.

Show children the pictures in the margin as a quick and easy way to draw base-10 blocks. Drawing pictures may be more convenient than using the actual blocks, and pictures are often useful for explaining and recording solutions.

Read about base-10 blocks with your class on page 11 of *My Reference Book.*

- On **Day 1** of this lesson, children should complete the Math Message Follow-Up, explore drawing base-10 blocks, and begin matching numbers and displays of base-10 blocks.

- On **Day 2** of this lesson, children should continue matching numbers and displays of base-10 blocks and do place-value exercises. Then have children complete Part 2 activities.

Base-10 blocks

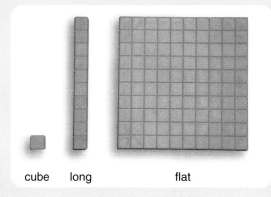

cube   long   flat

Base-10 drawings

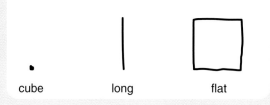

cube   long   flat

▶ Matching Numbers and Displays of Base-10 Blocks

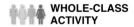

WHOLE-CLASS ACTIVITY

(*Math Masters,* pp. 56 and 427)

Give each child or partnership a set of number cards (0–9) and a Place-Value Mat. Display 3 flats, 5 longs, and 2 cubes on a Place-Value Mat. (*See Advance Preparation.*) Ask children to show the number 352 by putting cards on their Place-Value Mats. Children show 352 by putting the card for 3 in the hundreds place, the card for 5 in the tens place, and the card for 2 in the ones place. Ask:

● How many hundreds are in this number? 3

● How many tens? 5

● How many ones? 2

Then ask children to read the number in unison. Three hundred fifty-two

Repeat with other 2- and 3-digit numbers, including the numbers 52 and 25 from the Math Message. Ask children to explain what the digits 5 and 2 mean in each number. Display the place-value blocks at random without the mat. By doing this, children will have to sort the blocks mentally into ones, tens, and hundreds.

Then reverse the procedure. Write a 2- or 3-digit number on the board and ask children to show the number by placing base-10 blocks on their Place-Value Mats. Repeat with several other 2- or 3-digit numbers.

Adjusting the Activity

ELL

Write the numbers on a Place-Value Mat that you have drawn on the board or use the overhead transparency of *Math Masters,* page 56 to help children choose the correct base-10 blocks.

AUDITORY ◆ KINESTHETIC ◆ TACTILE ◆ VISUAL

Now, repeat the previous procedures using numbers with zero in the tens or ones place. For example, display 3 flats and 4 cubes and ask children to use number cards to show the number on their Place-Value Mats. Some children may put no digit card in the tens column; others will put a zero. Point out that not including the zero can cause problems when there is no Place-Value Mat.

Write 34 and 304 on the board and ask which number matches the base-10 blocks. 304 Ask which digit in 304 shows that there are no longs. The zero

Continue with a series of translations among spoken numbers, written numbers, base-10 blocks, number cards, and calculator displays. *For example:*

▷ Say: *Show the number 508 with base-10 blocks.* 5 flats, 8 cubes

▷ Say: *Use cards to show the number with 4 in the ones place, 0 in the tens place, and 8 in the hundreds place.* 804

Ask: *In 567, which number is in the ones place?* 7 *The tens place?* 6 *The hundreds place?* 5

▷ Write 749 on the board. Say: *Read the number on the board.* Seven hundred forty-nine.

▷ Say: *Use your calculator. Enter 708. Now use base-10 blocks to show 708.* 7 flats, 8 cubes

 Ongoing Assessment: Informing Instruction

Watch for children who enter 7008 on the calculator. When representing 708 with base-10 blocks, be sure to point out that there are three columns on the Place-Value Mat, therefore there should only be 3 digits.

▶ Doing Place-Value Exercises

INDEPENDENT ACTIVITY

(*Math Journal 1*, p. 53)

Children use base-10 blocks to complete journal page 53. Then review the answers with them. For Problem 3, make sure children have written 325 and not 532 or 235. Ask a volunteer to explain the answer to Problem 5. Have other children explain why they agree or disagree with the answer. Make sure children are able to identify each of the base-10 materials in the pictures.

 **Ongoing Assessment: Recognizing Student Achievement**

Journal page 53 Problems 1 and 3

Use **journal page 53, Problems 1 and 3** to assess children's understanding of place value. Children are making adequate progress if they can correctly answer the problems using base-10 blocks. Some children may be able to complete the problems that involve 0 as a placeholder.

[Number and Numeration Goal 2]

② Ongoing Learning & Practice

▶ Playing the *Digit Game*

PARTNER ACTIVITY

(*My Reference Book*, pp. 132 and 133)

Have children read the rules for the *Digit Game* on pages 132 and 133 of *My Reference Book*. Play several demonstration hands with the class.

Have partners play several rounds of the game.

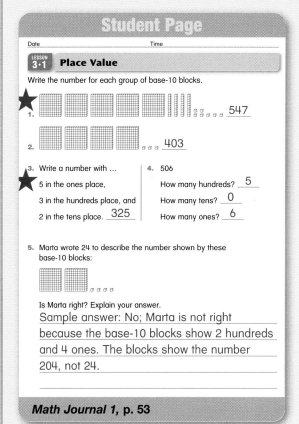

Student Page

Date _____ Time _____

LESSON 3·1 **Math Boxes**

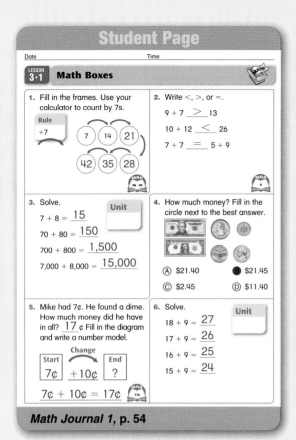

1. Fill in the frames. Use your calculator to count by 7s.

Rule +7

7 → 14 → 21 → 42 → 35 → 28

2. Write <, >, or =.

$9 + 7 \; > \; 13$

$10 + 12 \; < \; 26$

$7 + 7 \; = \; 5 + 9$

3. Solve.

Unit

$7 + 8 = 15$

$70 + 80 = 150$

$700 + 800 = 1,500$

$7,000 + 8,000 = 15,000$

4. How much money? Fill in the circle next to the best answer.

(A) $21.40   (B) $21.45

(C) $2.45   (D) $11.40

5. Mike had 7¢. He found a dime. How much money did he have in all? 17 ¢ Fill in the diagram and write a number model.

Start	Change	End
7¢	+10¢	?

$7¢ + 10¢ = 17¢$

6. Solve.

Unit

$18 + 9 = 27$

$17 + 9 = 26$

$16 + 9 = 25$

$15 + 9 = 24$

Math Journal 1, p. 54

▶ **Math Boxes 3·1**

👤 INDEPENDENT ACTIVITY

(*Math Journal 1*, p. 54)

 Mixed Practice Math Boxes in this lesson are paired with Math Boxes in Lesson 3-3. The skills in Problems 5 and 6 preview Unit 4 content.

▶ **Home Link 3·1**

👤 INDEPENDENT ACTIVITY

(*Math Masters*, p. 57)

Home Connection Children continue their work with base-10 blocks as they complete place-value exercises similar to those on journal page 53.

---

(3) Differentiation Options

(READINESS)

▶ **Counting Practice**

👥 SMALL-GROUP ACTIVITY

🕐 5–15 Min

To explore place value using a concrete model, have children use a calculator and base-10 blocks in a counting activity. Begin by reviewing how to count by 1s on the calculator. The following program will work on any calculator: Clear the calculator. Press 0 ⊞ 1 ⊜ ⊞ 1 ⊜ ⊞ 1 ⊜…. Two additional programs for counting by 1s are given below for demonstration purposes. Have children perform the steps on their own calculators.

For the Texas Instruments TI-108:

1. Press [ON/C] . This clears your calculator.
2. Press 0. This is the starting number.
3. Press ⊞ . This tells the calculator to count up.
4. Press 1. This tells the calculator to count by 1s.

For the Casio SL-450:

1. Press (AC) . This clears your calculator.
2. Press 1. This tells the calculator to count by 1s.
3. Press (+)(+) . This tells the calculator to count up.
4. Press 0. This is the starting number.

Home Link Master

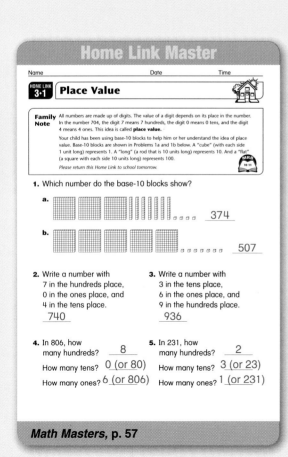

Name _____ Date _____ Time _____

HOME LINK 3·1 **Place Value**

Family Note All numbers are made up of digits. The value of a digit depends on its place in the number. In the number 704, the digit 7 means 7 hundreds, the digit 0 means 0 tens, and the digit 4 means 4 ones. This idea is called **place value**.

Your child has been using base-10 blocks to help him or her understand the idea of place value. Base-10 blocks are shown in Problems 1a and 1b below. A "cube" (with each side 1 unit long) represents 1. A "long" (a rod that is 10 units long) represents 10. And a "flat" (a square with each side 10 units long) represents 100.

Please return this Home Link to school tomorrow.

1. Which number do the base-10 blocks show?

   a. 374

   b. 507

2. Write a number with 7 in the hundreds place, 0 in the ones place, and 4 in the tens place. 740

3. Write a number with 3 in the tens place, 6 in the ones place, and 9 in the hundreds place. 936

4. In 806, how many hundreds? 8

   How many tens? 0 (or 80)

   How many ones? 6 (or 806)

5. In 231, how many hundreds? 2

   How many tens? 3 (or 23)

   How many ones? 1 (or 231)

Math Masters, p. 57

Now the calculator is ready to start counting by 1s. Without clearing their calculators, have children press the ⊜ key. Press the ⊜ key repeatedly together as the class counts together by 1s stopping at 9.

Ask children what comes next. Then have them press ⊜ once, observing the change from 9 to 0 in the ones place and the appearance of a 1 in the tens place. *What does the 1 stand for?* 1 ten

Clear the calculators and repeat the counting by 1s activity. This time, have the children work in partnerships. One partner does the calculator count while the other partner takes a cube each time one more is added. Compare what happens after 9 is displayed on the calculator (changing to 10) and the exchange of ten single cubes for one long.

Repeat the counting activity having all children count by 10s on the calculator from 0 to 100. Now have partnerships repeat the count switching roles so one partner counts on the calculator and the other partner takes longs. Repeat with 100s and flats.

If interest and time permit, change the start number and repeat counts by 10s and 100s using both the calculator and the blocks— for example, start at 14 (1 long, 4 cubes) and count by 10s (adding one long each time).

 **SMALL-GROUP ACTIVITY**

 5–15 Min

▶ Creating 3-Digit Numbers

To further explore 3-digit numbers, have children create as many 3-digit numbers as possible using the same three nonzero digits. Each child selects three cards from the Everything Math Deck (1–9). They create as many numbers as possible using the three cards and record their answers. Try three different cards. Ask: *How many combinations are possible using three cards?* 6 Have children try four cards. How many combinations are possible using four cards? 24

Planning Ahead

Before beginning Lesson 3-2, make an overhead transparency of *Math Masters,* page 58, the Fruit and Vegetables Stand Poster.

Using Coins to Buy Things

 Objectives To review coin values and exchanges among coins; and to provide experiences with finding coin combinations needed to pay for items.

1 Teaching the Lesson

materials

Key Activities
Children determine the total value of a set of coins and bills. Children review the values of coins and bills and the exchanges among them. Children name coin combinations to make purchases and make change while buying and selling items.

Key Concepts and Skills
• Count by 5s, 10s, and 25s. [Number and Numeration Goal 1]
• Use dollars-and-cents notation. [Number and Numeration Goal 2]
• Calculate coin combinations. [Operations and Computation Goal 2]
• Exchange coins and dollar bills. [Measurement and Reference Frames Goal 4]

Key Vocabulary
nickel • penny • dime • quarter • $1 bill

☑ **Ongoing Assessment: Recognizing Student Achievement** Use journal page 57. [Operations and Computation Goal 2]

☐ *Math Journal 1,* pp. 56 and 57
☐ *My Reference Book,* pp. 88 and 89
☐ Home Link 3·1
☐ Teaching Aid Master (*Math Masters,* p. 417; optional)
☐ Transparency (*Math Masters,* p. 58)
☐ coins and bills: 10 pennies, 6 nickels, 6 dimes, 4 quarters, and two $1 bills

***See* Advance Preparation**

2 Ongoing Learning & Practice

materials

Children practice coin and bill exchanges by playing *Spinning for Money.*

Children practice and maintain skills through Math Boxes and Home Link activities.

☐ *Math Journal 1,* pp. 55 and 58
☐ Home Link Master (*Math Masters,* p. 59)
☐ Game Master (*Math Masters,* p. 472)

☐ scissors; large paper clip
☐ coins and bills per player: 7 pennies, 5 nickels, 5 dimes, 4 quarters, and one $1 bill

3 Differentiation Options

materials

READINESS
Children play *Penny-Nickel Exchange* or *Penny-Dime-Dollar Exchange* to practice coin exchanges.

ENRICHMENT
Children write number stories using the Fruit and Vegetables Stand Poster.

ELL SUPPORT
Children add *penny, nickel, dime,* and *quarter* to their Math Word Banks.

☐ *Math Journal 1,* p. 56
☐ Teaching Aid Masters (*Math Masters,* pp. 419 and 428)
☐ *Differentiation Handbook*
☐ coin stamps (optional)

☐ per partnership: 20 pennies and 10 nickels; or 40 pennies, 40 dimes, and one $1 bill
☐ 1 or 2 dice per partnership

Additional Information

Advance Preparation For the Paying for Things with Coins activity in Part 1, create an overhead transparency of *Math Masters,* page 58.

Technology
Assessment Management System
Journal page 57
See the **iTLG.**

Getting Started

Mental Math and Reflexes

Count by 5s, 10s, and 25s.

○○○ Begin at 5. Count by 5s to 100.
  Begin at 30. Count by 10s to 150.
  Begin at 25. Count by 25s to 200.

●○○ Begin at 50. Count by 5s.
  Begin at 140. Count by 10s.
  Begin at 100. Count by 25s.

●●○ Begin at 115. Count by 5s.
  Begin at 153. Count by 10s.
  Begin at 175. Count by 25s.

Allow children to use coins or a number grid as they count.

Math Message

Take 10 Ⓟ, 6 Ⓝ, 6 Ⓓ, 4 Ⓠ, and 2 $1 from your tool-kit money. How much money is that? $4.00

Home Link 3·1 Follow-Up

Review answers as necessary.

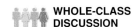

① Teaching the Lesson

▶ Math Message Follow-Up

⟪ WHOLE-CLASS DISCUSSION

Ask children to share the strategies they used to find the total amount ($4.00). You might model the strategies on an overhead projector.

One approach is to count the monetary units in order from greatest to least. The dollar bills are $2.00. Count on the four quarters to reach $3.00. Count by 10s from $3.00 for the six dimes to reach $3.60. Then count by 5s from $3.60 for the six nickels to reach $3.90. Finally, count by 1s from $3.90 for the ten pennies for a total of $4.00.

Another approach is to make exchanges: 10 pennies for a dime, 4 quarters for a $1 bill, and so on. In today's lesson children will exchange coins and $1 bills while buying and selling items from the Fruit and Vegetables Stand Poster.

▶ Reviewing the Exchanges for Coins and $1 Bills

⟪ WHOLE-CLASS DISCUSSION

(*My Reference Book,* pp. 88 and 89)

On the board, draw a unit box as shown in the margin. Read about money and equivalencies with your class on *My Reference Book,* pages 88 and 89. Have children respond in unison to questions about the coins and the $1 bill.

Hold up a **nickel.** Ask: *What is this called? How much is it worth?* 5 cents Write *nickel* and *5 cents* on the board. *How much are two nickels worth?* 10 cents Repeat with a **penny, dime, quarter,** and **$1 bill.**

> **NOTE** Although the focus of this lesson is not on money notation, such as 25¢ or $0.25; or $1, $1.00, or 100¢, be sure to use these different notations during this lesson.

> Unit
>
> *money*
> *$ and ¢*

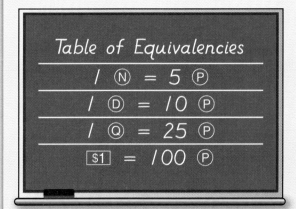

Table of Equivalencies
1 Ⓝ	=	5 Ⓟ
1 Ⓓ	=	10 Ⓟ
1 Ⓠ	=	25 Ⓟ
$1	=	100 Ⓟ

Children may find it helpful to refer to this Table of Equivalencies or *My Reference Book,* pages 88 and 89 during the remainder of the lesson.

Math Masters, p. 58

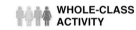

Cents is an interesting word because it has several homonyms. To support English language learners, clarify the meaning of *cents* in this context.

AUDITORY ◆ KINESTHETIC ◆ TACTILE ◆ VISUAL

Hold up a nickel. Ask: *How many pennies would you trade for a nickel?* 5 cents To support English language learners, draw a picture on the board illustrating that 1 nickel is equivalent to 5 pennies. Hold up the appropriate coins and draw corresponding pictures as you ask and discuss questions like the following:

● How many pennies would you trade for a dime? 10 pennies For a quarter? 25 pennies For one dollar? 100 pennies For two dollars? 200 pennies

● How many nickels would you trade for a dime? 2 nickels For a quarter? 5 nickels For a dollar? 20 nickels

● How many dimes would you trade for a dollar? 10 dimes

▶ Paying for Things with Coins

WHOLE-CLASS ACTIVITY

(*Math Masters,* p. 58)

Display an overhead transparency of the Fruit and Vegetables Stand Poster on *Math Masters,* page 58. (The poster is also found on journal page 56.) Ask children to count out the coins they would use to pay for one pear. Partners check each other's coin combinations.

Ask volunteers to share the coin combinations they used with the class. List their responses on the board.

Ⓟ Ⓟ Ⓟ Ⓟ Ⓟ	Ⓓ Ⓟ	Ⓝ Ⓟ	Ⓝ Ⓟ Ⓟ
Ⓟ Ⓟ Ⓟ Ⓟ Ⓟ	Ⓟ	Ⓝ Ⓟ	Ⓟ Ⓟ Ⓟ
Ⓟ Ⓟ Ⓟ	Ⓟ	Ⓟ	Ⓟ Ⓟ Ⓟ

Possible coin combinations for 13¢

Ask children if there are any other ways they could have paid for the pear. Sample answer: Pay for the pear with 1 dime and 1 nickel and receive 2 pennies as change.

Repeat the activity with other items until children are ready to work independently.

▶ Taking Turns Buying and Selling

PARTNER ACTIVITY

(*Math Journal 1,* pp. 56 and 57)

Partners take turns being customer and clerk at the Fruit and Vegetables Stand. The customer points to an item and pays the exact amount with coins. The clerk checks that the customer has

Date _____ Time _____

LESSON 3·2 **Buying Fruit and Vegetables** ★

Select the fruit and vegetables from journal page 56 that you would like to buy. Write the name of each item. Then draw the coins you could use to pay for each item. Write Ⓟ, Ⓝ, Ⓓ, or Ⓠ.

For Problems 3 and 4, write the total amount of money that you would spend. Sample answers:

I bought (Write the name.)	I paid (Draw coins.)	I paid (Draw coins another way.)
Example: one *orange*	Ⓓ Ⓝ Ⓟ Ⓟ Ⓟ	Ⓝ Ⓝ Ⓟ Ⓟ Ⓟ Ⓟ Ⓟ Ⓟ Ⓟ Ⓟ
1. one **melon slice**	Ⓠ Ⓝ	Ⓓ Ⓓ Ⓝ Ⓟ Ⓟ Ⓟ Ⓟ Ⓟ
2. one **head of lettuce**	Ⓠ Ⓝ Ⓝ Ⓝ Ⓝ	Ⓓ Ⓓ Ⓓ Ⓓ Ⓝ
3. one **apple** and one **plum**	Ⓝ Ⓝ Ⓟ Ⓟ Ⓝ Ⓟ	Ⓓ Ⓟ Ⓟ Ⓟ Ⓟ Ⓟ Ⓟ Ⓟ Ⓟ Total: 18¢
Try This		
4. one **ear of corn**, one **banana**, and one **green pepper**	Ⓠ Ⓓ Ⓓ Ⓟ Ⓟ Ⓟ	Ⓓ Ⓓ Ⓓ Ⓓ Ⓝ Ⓟ Ⓟ Ⓟ Total: 48¢

Math Journal 1, p. 57

paid the correct amount. Children record four of these transactions in their journals; they show two possible combinations for each transaction.

Ask children to share some of their answers from journal page 57. Have children divide the money and return it to their tool kits or to the classroom bank.

Adjusting the Activity

Set parameters for the coin combinations children make. For example, have them make and record coin combinations with the fewest possible coins or coin combinations without using nickels.

AUDITORY ◆ KINESTHETIC ◆ TACTILE ◆ VISUAL

✪ Ongoing Assessment: Recognizing Student Achievement

Journal Page 57 ★

Use **journal page 57** to assess children's ability to show coin combinations. Children are making adequate progress if they can show one coin combination for buying a pear, plum, onion, banana, apple, or ear of corn. Some children may be able to show coin combinations for the other fruits and vegetables. Others may be able to show two or more ways.

[Operations and Computation Goal 2]

---

2 Ongoing Learning & Practice

▶ Playing *Spinning for Money*   SMALL-GROUP ACTIVITY

(Math Journal 1, p. 55; Math Masters, p. 472)

Players put pennies, nickels, dimes, quarters, and $1 bills into a "bank." They then take turns spinning the *Spinning for Money* Spinner and taking the coins shown by the spinner from the bank. Whenever possible, players exchange coins for a single coin or bill of the same value. The first player to exchange for a $1 bill wins.

When introducing this game, use chance vocabulary. Discuss questions such as the following with the children:

- Which has a better chance, landing on 1 quarter or 1 dime? Equal chance

- Which has a better chance, landing on one of the penny spaces, or one of the dime spaces? Equal chance

- How likely is it that a spin will show more than 5 cents? Very likely
  More than 10 cents? Less likely than showing 10 cents or less
  More than 1 penny? certain
  More than 25 cents? impossible

Date   Time

LESSON 3·2   *Spinning for Money*

Materials ☐ *Spinning for Money* Spinner (*Math Masters*, p. 472)
  ☐ pencil   ☐ large paper clip
  ☐ 7 pennies, 5 nickels, 5 dimes, 4 quarters, and one $1 bill for each player
  ☐ sheet of paper labeled "Bank"

Players   2, 3, or 4
Skill   Exchange coins and dollar bills
Object of the Game To be first to exchange for a $1 bill
Directions

1. Each player puts 7 pennies, 5 nickels, 5 dimes, 4 quarters, and one $1 bill into the bank.

2. Players take turns spinning the *Spinning for Money* Spinner and taking the coins shown by the spinner from the bank.

3. Whenever possible, players exchange coins for a single coin or bill of the same value. For example, a player could exchange 5 pennies for a nickel, or 2 dimes and 1 nickel for a quarter.

4. The first player to exchange for a $1 bill wins.

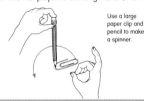

Use a large paper clip and pencil to make a spinner.

Math Journal 1, p. 55

NOTE Ask children to write their names on the backs of their *Spinning for Money* Spinners. Collect the spinners or have children store them in their tool kits for reuse.

Name   Date   Time

Spinning for Money Spinner

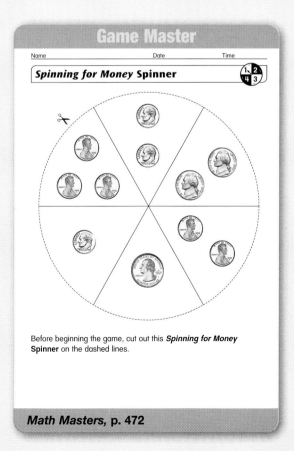

Before beginning the game, cut out this *Spinning for Money* Spinner on the dashed lines.

Math Masters, p. 472

Student Page

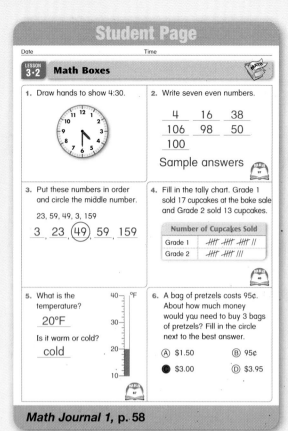

Date _____ Time _____

LESSON 3·2 Math Boxes

1. Draw hands to show 4:30.

2. Write seven even numbers.

4   16   38
106   98   50
100

Sample answers

3. Put these numbers in order and circle the middle number.

23, 59, 49, 3, 159

3 , 23 , (49) , 59 , 159

4. Fill in the tally chart. Grade 1 sold 17 cupcakes at the bake sale and Grade 2 sold 13 cupcakes.

Number of Cupcakes Sold	
Grade 1	~~HH~~ ~~HH~~ ~~HH~~ //
Grade 2	~~HH~~ ~~HH~~ ///

5. What is the temperature?

20°F

Is it warm or cold?

cold

6. A bag of pretzels costs 95¢. About how much money would you need to buy 3 bags of pretzels? Fill in the circle next to the best answer.

Ⓐ $1.50   Ⓑ 95¢
● $3.00   Ⓓ $3.95

Math Journal 1, p. 58

Home Link Master

Name _____ Date _____ Time _____

HOME LINK 3·2 How Much Does It Cost?

Family Note In this activity, your child looks through advertisements, selects items that cost less than $2.00, and shows how to pay for those items in more than one way. For example, your child could pay for an item that costs 79¢ by drawing 3 quarters and 4 pennies or by drawing 7 dimes and 9 pennies. If you do not have advertisements showing prices, make up some items and prices for your child.

Please return this Home Link to school tomorrow.

Look at newspaper or magazine advertisements. Find items that cost less than $2.00. Write the name and price of each item.

Show someone at home how you would pay for these items with coins and a $1 bill. Write Ⓟ, Ⓝ, Ⓓ, Ⓠ, and $1. Try to show amounts in more than one way. Answers vary.

1. I would buy _____. It costs _____.

This is one way I would pay: _____

This is another way: _____

2. I would buy _____. It costs _____.

This is one way I would pay: _____

This is another way: _____

3. I would buy _____. It costs _____.

This is one way I would pay: _____

This is another way: _____

Math Masters, p. 59

▶ Math Boxes 3·2

(*Math Journal 1*, p. 58)

Mixed Practice Math Boxes in this lesson are paired with Math Boxes in Lesson 3-4. The skills in Problems 5 and 6 preview Unit 4 content.

▶ Home Link 3·2

INDEPENDENT ACTIVITY

(*Math Masters*, p. 59)

Home Connection Children use store advertisements to find items that cost less than $2.00. They draw coins and bills to show two ways to pay for each item.

---

③ Differentiation Options

READINESS

▶ Playing *Penny-Nickel Exchange* or *Penny-Dime-Dollar Exchange*

PARTNER ACTIVITY

🕐 5–15 Min

(*Math Masters*, p. 428)

To provide concrete experience with coin exchanges, have children play *Penny-Nickel Exchange* or *Penny-Dime-Dollar Exchange*.

Penny-Nickel Exchange

Partners put 20 pennies and 10 nickels in a pile. This is the bank.

Players take turns. At each turn, a player rolls a die and collects the number of pennies shown on the die from the bank. Whenever players have at least 5 pennies, they say "Exchange!" and trade 5 of their pennies for a nickel in the bank. The game ends when there are no more nickels in the bank. The player who has more nickels wins. If players have the same number of nickels, the player with more pennies wins.

Penny-Dime-Dollar Exchange

Partners put 40 pennies, 40 dimes and 1 dollar in a pile. This is the bank. Each partnership shares one Place-Value Mat and a pair of dice.

Players take turns. They roll the dice, announce the total number of dots, take that number of cents from the bank, and place the coins on the mat. Whenever possible, they exchange 10 pennies for a dime. The partner who is not rolling the dice checks the accuracy of the transactions. The first player to make an exchange for a dollar wins the game.

▶ ENRICHMENT

▶ Writing Fruit and Vegetables Stand Number Stories

(*Math Journal 1,* p. 56; *Math Masters,* p. 419)

To further explore buying items with exact change, have children write number stories using items from the Fruit and Vegetables Stand Poster. Encourage children to buy multiple items at a time. Once the number stories are written they may exchange them with a classmate and solve them.

When children are finished, ask them to share their number stories and their strategies with the class.

▶ ELL SUPPORT

SMALL-GROUP ACTIVITY

5–15 Min

▶ Building a Math Word Bank

(*Differentiation Handbook*)

To provide language support for coins, have children use the Word Bank template found in the *Differentiation Handbook.* Ask children to write the terms *penny, nickel, dime,* and *quarter,* draw symbols and pictures representing each term, and write other related words. If available, have children stamp their page with the appropriate coin stamps. See the *Differentiation Handbook* for more information.

Planning Ahead

For the next lesson, you will need a demonstration clock with an hour hand only. Use *Math Masters,* page 60 and a paper fastener, or draw a clock face on the board with semipermanent chalk.

Each child will need a small tool-kit clock. If you prefer, clocks can be made from *Math Masters,* page 61, preferably copied onto stiff paper. See *Math Masters,* page 61 for instructions. Write each child's tool-kit number on his or her clock.

Name   Date   Time

Place-Value Mat

Math Masters, p. 428

Name   Date   Time

A Number Story

Unit

Math Masters, p. 419

3·3 Telling Time

 Objectives To review telling time; and to provide experiences with writing time in digital-clock notation.

---

① Teaching the Lesson

Key Activities
Children review the functions of the clock hands, use clocks to tell and show time, and practice writing and telling time.

Key Concepts and Skills
• Count by 5s.
  [Number and Numeration Goal 1]
• Distinguish between analog and digital clocks.
  [Measurement and Reference Frames Goal 6]
• Tell and write times.
  [Measurement and Reference Frames Goal 6]

Key Vocabulary
minute hand • hour hand • clock face • analog clock • digital clock

✔ **Ongoing Assessment: Recognizing Student Achievement**
Use Mental Math and Reflexes. [Number and Numeration Goal 5]

✔ **Ongoing Assessment: Informing Instruction** See page 199.

materials
☐ *Math Journal 1*, p. 59
☐ *My Reference Book*, pp. 78–81
☐ Home Link 3·2
☐ Teaching Master (*Math Masters*, p. 60; optional)
☐ Teaching Aid Master (*Math Masters*, p. 415)
☐ hour-hand-only demonstration clock
☐ a variety of analog and digital clocks (optional)
☐ tool-kit clock or clock made from *Math Masters*, p. 61
☐ red and green markers, scissors, brad (optional)
☐ demonstration clock with both minute and hour hands
☐ slate
☐ paper fastener

***See* Advance Preparation**

---

② Ongoing Learning & Practice

Children practice basic facts using Fact Triangles.

Children practice and maintain skills through Math Boxes and Home Link activities.

materials
☐ *Math Journal 1*, p. 60
☐ Home Link Masters (*Math Masters*, pp. 62 and 63)
☐ Teaching Master (*Math Masters*, p. 61; optional)

☐ +, − Fact Triangles per partnership (triangles with sums greater than 10)

***See* Advance Preparation**

---

③ Differentiation Options

READINESS
Children make drawings of daily activities and show the corresponding time on a clock face.

ENRICHMENT
Children calculate elapsed time.

ELL SUPPORT
Children add *almost* and *between* to their Math Word Banks.

materials
☐ *Math Journal 1*, p. 59
☐ Teaching Master (*Math Masters*, p. 64)
☐ *Differentiation Handbook*

☐ scissors
☐ demonstration clock
☐ tool-kit clock

Additional Information

Advance Preparation For the Math Message, each child will need a small tool-kit clock. See Planning Ahead at the end of Lesson 3·2. Children will need a clock for Home Link 3·3. They can take home the clock they made in this lesson, or make a clock at home using *Math Masters*, page 61.

Technology
Assessment Management System
Mental Math and Reflexes
See the **iTLG**.

Getting Started

Mental Math and Reflexes

Say a number and have children record tally marks for that number on an Exit Slip (*Math Masters*, page 415).
Suggestions:

○○○   3, 5, 10

○○○   8, 12, 14

○○●   16, 18, 23

Make tally marks for a number on the board. Have children count the marks and write the number on their slates.

Math Message

Find the clock with your tool-kit number on it. Set the hands to show the time when school starts.

or

Take a copy of Math Masters, *page 61.*

Home Link 3·2 Follow-Up

Ask several children to name the price of an item and the coin combination they chose to pay for it. Ask other children in the class to suggest other coin combinations for each item.

✔ Ongoing Assessment: Recognizing Student Achievement

Mental Math and Reflexes

Use **Mental Math and Reflexes** to assess children's ability to record tally marks for a given number. Children are making adequate progress if they can correctly group tallies by 5s. Some children may be able to count the tally marks by 5s and then 1s.

[Number and Numeration Goal 5]

---

1   Teaching the Lesson

▶ Math Message Follow-Up

 WHOLE-CLASS DISCUSSION

If you chose to have children make paper clocks from *Math Masters*, page 61, have them do so now. Children should fill in the 5-minute numbers around the clock face.

Ask children to set the hands to show the time when school starts. Ask children to display their clocks. Check several of them.

Explain to children that in today's lesson they will use clocks to tell and show time.

 Links to the Future

Children started telling time to the nearest hour in *First Grade Everyday Mathematics.* Children will continue telling time throughout second grade. This includes having children record the time on journal and masters pages as well as telling and writing times throughout the day. Telling time to the nearest five minutes is a Grade 2 Goal. Telling time to the nearest minute is a Grade 3 Goal.

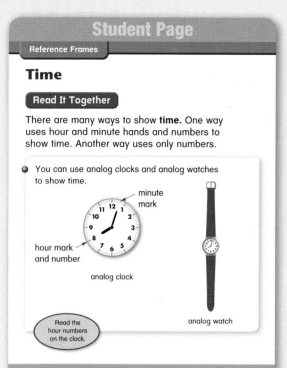
Language Arts Link Explain that A.M. means "before the middle of the day." It is an abbreviation for the Latin *ante meridiem*. Similarly, P.M. means "after the middle of the day." It is an abbreviation for *post meridiem*.

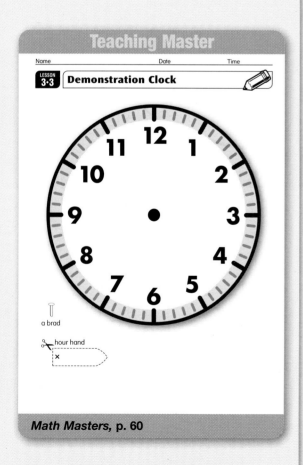
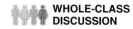

▶ Discussing the Functions of Clock Hands

WHOLE-CLASS DISCUSSION

(*My Reference Book*, pp. 78–81)

Use a demonstration clock to review the functions of the hands of a clock:

▷ The shorter (hour) hand shows the hour of the day. It takes 1 hour to move from 1 to 2, from 2 to 3, and so on. The hand moves completely around the clock face in 12 hours.

▷ The longer (minute) hand shows minutes after or before the hour. It takes 1 minute to move from one mark to the next on the clock face and 5 minutes to move from 1 to 2, from 2 to 3, and so on.

Set the hands on the demonstration clock so they show 9 o'clock. Slowly move the **minute hand** around the clock face, and ask children to observe the movement of the **hour hand** as you do so. To support English language learners, review the everyday meaning of *hand* as well as its specific meaning in this context. Ask questions like the following:

● Which hand do you think is more important—the hour hand or the minute hand?

● Could you estimate the time if your clock had only a minute hand? no What if it had only an hour hand? yes

Tell children that a clock with an hour hand, a minute hand, and numbers and marks around the **clock face** is called an **analog clock.** A clock that shows the hour and minutes with digits, separated by a colon, is called a **digital clock.** To support English language learners, write *analog clock* next to a sketch of one and write *digital clock* next to a sketch of one on the board. You can read about clocks and clock hands with your class in *My Reference Book,* pages 78–81.

NOTE You may want to display examples of analog and digital clocks for children to examine.

▶ Estimating Time with an Hour Hand Only

WHOLE-CLASS ACTIVITY

(*Math Masters*, p. 60 or 61)

Use the demonstration clock with an hour hand only, or draw a clock face on the board or on an overhead transparency. Move or draw the hour hand to various positions and ask children to tell the time shown. Remind them to use estimation language: *about _____ o'clock; just before (after) _____ o'clock; between _____ and _____ o'clock*. Remind children that telling time is always an estimate—by the time you say the time, it is a little later!

If clocks are made from *Math Masters,* page 61, have children put the two hands on their clocks together and pretend the clock has only an hour hand.

Partners take turns. One partner moves the two hands together to a certain position; the other estimates the time shown. Or partners ask each other to show the times when daily activities, such as going to lunch, take place.

▶ Estimating Time with the Hour Hand and the Minute Hand

WHOLE-CLASS DISCUSSION

(*Math Masters*, p. 61)

The minute hand makes it possible to tell time more precisely—to the nearest minute. In everyday situations, however, people are often less precise, giving the time to the nearest 5 minutes or quarter-hour: "about three-twenty," "almost quarter to six." With repeated experience over the next few weeks, children will develop the ability to estimate time to the nearest quarter-hour increment.

Start the discussion by reviewing the movement of the minute hand on the demonstration clock. Remind children that the distance between consecutive pairs of numbers on the clock face represents 5 minutes. Have them count by 5s in unison as you point to the numbers on the clock face.

Show several times on the demonstration clock, and have children estimate what time it is. Record the times on the board using digital notation (hour:minute)—about 9:00, about 3:30, and so on. Discuss the notation used to record the time: "It looks like the display of a digital clock; the hour of the day is first, then a colon, and then the number of minutes after the hour." Say an approximate time, such as "about 3:30," and write it on the board for children to show on their tool-kit clocks.

▶ Telling and Writing Time

PARTNER ACTIVITY

(*Math Journal 1*, p. 59; *My Reference Book*, pp. 80 and 81)

Partners take turns. One child sets the hands on a tool-kit clock; the other tells the time and records it on a piece of paper or a slate. Then they reverse the procedure. One child says a time and writes it on a piece of paper or a slate; the other sets the hands on the tool-kit clock.

Each child then completes the clock exercises on journal page 59. Remind children to write the time on the journal page. Children should be reminded to write the time at the top of their journal page each time they work in their journal.

⭐ Ongoing Assessment: Informing Instruction

Watch for children who are incorrectly drawing the hands of the clock. Note whether the difficulty involves drawing the hands the same length or in confusing which hand should be longer or shorter. Consider having a poster in the room with the parts of the clock labeled so children can refer to it. Also, you might direct children to *My Reference Book*, pages 80 and 81.

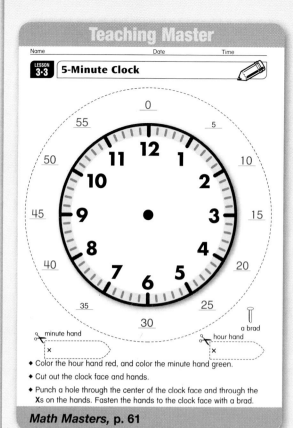

Math Masters, p. 61

NOTE Often during the next few weeks, ask children to tell about what time it is by looking at the classroom clock. Hold occasional practice sessions during which you say a time for children to show on their tool-kit clocks.

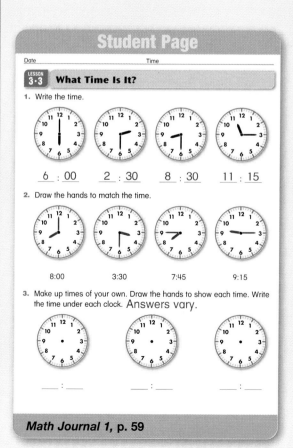

Math Journal 1, p. 59

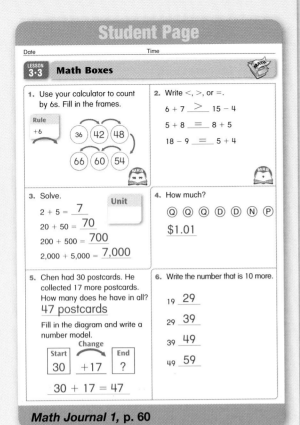

Math Journal 1, p. 60

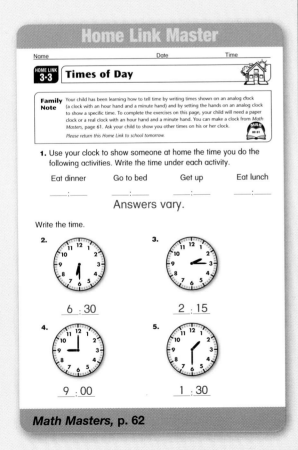

Math Masters, p. 62

2 Ongoing Learning & Practice

▶ Practicing with +, − Fact Triangles

Have children practice addition and subtraction facts using their Fact Triangles. Remove the Fact Triangles whose sums are less than 10.

As children practice, ask them to sort the Fact Triangles into two piles—facts they can recall quickly and facts that need more practice. Have them write those that need practice. Use these facts for later Mental Math and Reflexes exercises.

▶ Math Boxes 3·3

(Math Journal 1, p. 60)

 Mixed Practice Math Boxes in this lesson are paired with Math Boxes in Lesson 3-1. The skills in Problems 5 and 6 preview Unit 4 content.

Writing/Reasoning Have children draw, write, or verbalize their answers to the following: *Explain how you found the answers to Problem 3.* Sample answer: I know $2 + 5 = 7$. So 2 tens + 5 tens = 7 tens, 2 hundreds + 5 hundreds = 7 hundreds, and so on.

▶ Home Link 3·3

(Math Masters, pp. 62 and 63)

Home Connection Children use a clock to discuss time. They can take home the clock made in this lesson or a copy of *Math Masters*, page 61 to make a new clock.

3 Differentiation Options

▶ Illustrating Daily Activities

(Math Masters, p. 64)

To provide experience with telling time to the nearest hour, have children match activities with times of the day. Children cut apart *Math Masters*, page 64 and then draw pictures of things they do during the day on the blank sides of the cards. On the clock side, have them draw a minute hand and an hour hand to show the hour of the day when the activity occurs.

Partners mix up the completed cards clock-side up and put the clocks in order. They turn over the cards and use the pictures to check their answers. Partners trade cards and repeat the activity.

ENRICHMENT

▶ # Calculating Elapsed Time

(*Math Journal 1*, p. 59)

INDEPENDENT ACTIVITY

5–15 Min

To apply children's understanding of telling time, have them use tool-kit clocks to find elapsed time for pairs of clocks on journal page 59. Use the first two clocks (6:00 and 2:30) on the journal page to model the process. Begin with the hands set for 6:00. Remind children that you want to find how much time will pass between 6:00 and 2:30. (Consider attaching events to the time. For example, *I wake up at 6:00 in the morning and we finish school at 2:30. How long have I been awake when we finish school?*) Have the children follow along using their tool-kit clocks.

Model moving the minute hand around the tool-kit clock, stopping at each quarter hour to count 15-minute intervals. Each time the hour hand goes once around, the children make a tally to keep track of how many hours pass. When they get to 2:00, remind them that they will not be going all the way around again, so they may want to count by 15-minute intervals now.

Have children repeat the activity for other times on the journal page.

ELL SUPPORT

▶ # Building a Math Word Bank

(*Differentiation Handbook*)

SMALL-GROUP ACTIVITY

5–15 Min

To provide language support for time, have children use the Word Bank template found in the *Differentiation Handbook*. Ask children to write the words *almost* and *between*, draw a picture representing each term, and write other related words. See the *Differentiation Handbook* for more information.

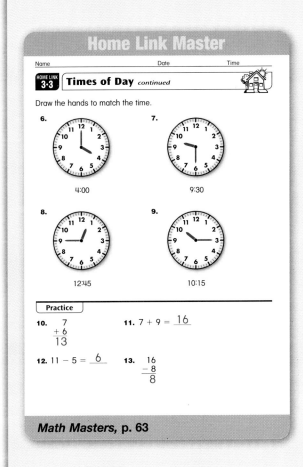

Math Masters, p. 63

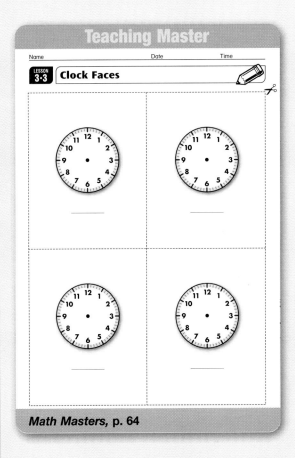

Math Masters, p. 64

3·4

EXPLORATIONS

Exploring Numbers, Time, and Geoboards

 Objective To provide experiences with representing and renaming numbers with base-10 blocks; reviewing time; and making, describing, and comparing geoboard shapes.

---

1 Teaching the Lesson

Key Activities

Exploration A: Children model place value for whole numbers using manipulatives.

Exploration B: Children practice writing and telling time by making clock-face booklets.

Exploration C: Children make, describe, and compare shapes on a geoboard.

Key Concepts and Skills

• Model 2-digit numbers with base-10 blocks.
[Number and Numeration Goal 2]

• Write and tell time to the nearest hour, half-hour, and quarter-hour.
[Measurement and Reference Frames Goal 6]

• Model, describe, and compare shapes on a geoboard.
[Geometry Goal 2]

materials

☐ Home Link 3·3
☐ slate

Exploration A:
Per partnership:
☐ *Math Journal 1,* p. 61
☐ Teaching Masters (*Math Masters,* pp. 65 and 66)
☐ Teaching Aid Master (*Math Masters,* p. 427)
☐ base-10 blocks: 9 longs and 30 cubes; 9 flats (optional)
☐ number cards 0–9 (from the Everything Math Deck, if available)

Exploration B:
Per partnership:
☐ Teaching Masters (*Math Masters,* pp. 67 and 68)
☐ scissors; stapler; paper
☐ clock-face rubber stamp and stamp pad

Exploration C:
☐ geoboard and several rubber bands
Per group:
☐ *Math Journal 1,* p. 62
☐ Teaching Master (*Math Masters,* p. 69)
☐ Teaching Aid Masters (*Math Masters,* pp. 429 or 430; optional)

---

2 Ongoing Learning & Practice

Children practice addition facts by completing magic squares.

Children practice and maintain skills through Math Boxes and Home Link activities.

⭐ **Ongoing Assessment:** Recognizing Student Achievement
Use journal page 64.
[Measurement and Reference Frames Goal 6]

materials

☐ *Math Journal 1,* pp. 63 and 64
☐ Home Link Master (*Math Masters,* p. 70)

---

3 Differentiation Options

READINESS

Children play *Base-10 Exchange* to practice place-value skills.

EXTRA PRACTICE

Children solve problems about digits, shapes, and time.

materials

☐ Teaching Aid Master (*Math Masters,* p. 428)
☐ *Minute Math®+,* pp. 33, 36, 53, 60, 71, and 73
☐ base-10 blocks: 20 longs and 20 cubes per partnership
☐ 2 dice per partnership

Technology

Assessment Management System
Math Boxes, Problem 1
See the **iTLG.**

Getting Started

Mental Math and Reflexes

Ask children to record on their slates the 100-complement of a number you say. If you say 90, children should write 10. Record the number model on the board: 90 + 10 = 100. *Suggestions:*

○●○   90   10

      50   50

      60   40

●●○   75   25

      70   30

      25   75

●●●   85   15

      65   35

      45   55

Math Message

The picture below shows one way to draw 36.

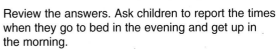

On your slates, draw at least two other ways to show 36.

Home Link 3·3 Follow-Up

Review the answers. Ask children to report the times when they go to bed in the evening and get up in the morning.

---

① Teaching the Lesson

▶ ## Math Message Follow-Up
    WHOLE-CLASS ACTIVITY

Ask children to share their solutions. For example, 36 can also be shown as follows:

▶ ## Exploration A: Building and Renaming Numbers
    PARTNER ACTIVITY

(*Math Journal 1*, p. 61; *Math Masters*, pp. 65, 66, and 427)

Partners follow instructions on *Math Masters,* pages 65 and 66 to build a 2-digit number by drawing cards from the deck of number cards. They build the numbers on the Place-Value Mat on *Math Masters,* page 427. As appropriate, children can draw three cards and build 3-digit numbers. Children record their work on journal page 61.

Links to the Future

This activity provides important practice for work with the partial-sums algorithm in Unit 4 and with trade-first subtraction in Unit 11.

Teaching Master

Name   Date   Time

LESSON 3·4 **Build a Number**

Do this activity with a partner.

Materials ☐ *Math Journal 1*, p. 61

☐ *Math Masters*, 427 (Place-Value Mat)

☐ base-10 blocks: 9 flats (optional), 9 longs, and 30 cubes

☐ number cards 0–9 (from the Everything Math Deck, if available)

1. Mix the cards and stack them facedown.

2. Take 2 cards.

3. Place the first card in the tens column of your Place-Value Mat. (If the card is a 0, put it back and take another.) Then put the second card in the ones column.

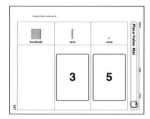

Math Masters, p. 65

Language Arts Link Children can work together to make up a story about a time shown in their booklets. They should write their stories on a separate piece of paper. You may wish to have children share their stories with the rest of the class or post the stories on a bulletin board.

Teaching Master

Name   Date   Time

LESSON 3·4 **Build a Number** *continued*

4. Build the number.

♦ Place longs in the tens column to show the tens digit.

♦ Place cubes in the ones column to show the ones digit.

5. Record your work in the table on journal page 61. Draw pictures of the longs and cubes you used.

6. Use the Place-Value Mat and blocks to build the same number in a different way. Draw the longs and cubes you used.

7. Build 3 or 4 more numbers in the same way. Record your numbers and draw pictures to show the two ways you built each number.

Try This

Take 3 cards instead of 2. Put 1 card in each column of the Place-Value Mat. Draw flats, longs, and cubes on journal page 61 to show your number.

Build the same number in a different way. Draw the blocks you used.

Math Masters, p. 66

▶ **Exploration B: Making a Clock Booklet**

PARTNER ACTIVITY

(*Math Masters,* pp. 67 and 68)

Partners follow instructions on *Math Masters,* pages 67 and 68 to make a booklet showing different times.

NOTE This activity provides a good opportunity to see how comfortable children are with telling time. You may wish to have children complete this several times a year as a portfolio item.

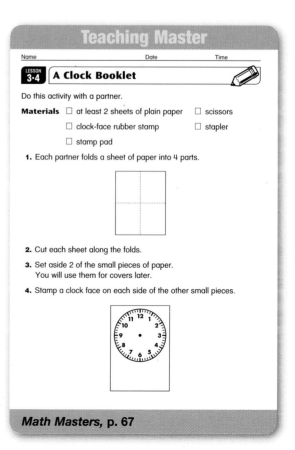

Children make clock booklets by following instructions on *Math Masters,* pages 67 and 68.

Adjusting the Activity

Encourage children to put times in their booklets to the nearest 5 minutes or even to the nearest minute.

AUDITORY ◆ KINESTHETIC ◆ TACTILE ◆ VISUAL

Teaching Master

Name   Date   Time

LESSON 3·4 **A Clock Booklet**

Do this activity with a partner.

Materials ☐ at least 2 sheets of plain paper   ☐ scissors

☐ clock-face rubber stamp   ☐ stapler

☐ stamp pad

1. Each partner folds a sheet of paper into 4 parts.

2. Cut each sheet along the folds.

3. Set aside 2 of the small pieces of paper. You will use them for covers later.

4. Stamp a clock face on each side of the other small pieces.

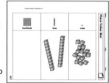

Math Masters, p. 67

▶ Exploration C: Making and Comparing Geoboard Shapes

 SMALL-GROUP ACTIVITY

(*Math Journal 1*, p. 62; *Math Masters*, pp. 69, 429, and 430)

Children record shapes, designs, or pictures on journal page 62, which is geoboard dot paper. *Math Masters,* pages 429 and 430 can be used to provide additional geoboard dot paper. Children will make a number of geoboard shapes. They will work independently, with partners, and in small groups. Guide children to give very clear directions so partners are able to duplicate the original shapes. You may wish to demonstrate this activity, modeling the vocabulary.

② Ongoing Learning & Practice

▶ Completing Magic Squares

PARTNER ACTIVITY

(*Math Journal 1*, p. 63)

Partners practice addition facts in a problem-solving format.

▶ Math Boxes 3•4

INDEPENDENT ACTIVITY

(*Math Journal 1*, p. 64)

Mixed Practice Math Boxes in this lesson are paired with Math Boxes in Lesson 3-2. The skills in Problems 5 and 6 preview Unit 4 content.

🔗 Links to the Future

Identifying likenesses and differences of shapes will prepare children for geometry in Unit 5. In that unit, children will compare 2-dimensional and 3-dimensional shapes.

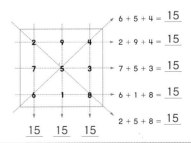

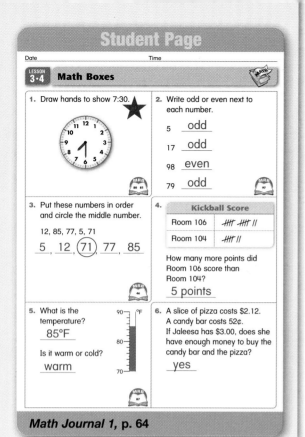

Student Page

Date _____ Time _____

LESSON 3·4 **Math Boxes**

1. Draw hands to show 7:30.

2. Write odd or even next to each number.

5 _odd_

17 _odd_

98 _even_

79 _odd_

3. Put these numbers in order and circle the middle number.

12, 85, 77, 5, 71

5 , 12 , (71) , 77 , 85

4.
Kickball Score	
Room 106	̶H̶H̶T̶ ̶H̶H̶T̶ //
Room 104	̶H̶H̶T̶ //

How many more points did Room 106 score than Room 104?

5 points

5. What is the temperature?

85°F

Is it warm or cold?

warm

6. A slice of pizza costs $2.12. A candy bar costs 52¢. If Jaleesa has $3.00, does she have enough money to buy the candy bar and the pizza?

yes

Math Journal 1, p. 64

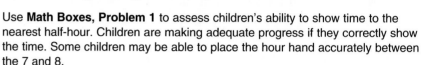

Writing/Reasoning Have children draw, write, or verbalize their answers to the following: *Explain how you found how many more points Room 106 scored than Room 104 in Problem 4.* Sample answer: I compared the tally marks in the table. Room 106 had 5 more tally marks.

✓ Ongoing Assessment: Recognizing Student Achievement

Math Boxes Problem 1 ★

Use **Math Boxes, Problem 1** to assess children's ability to show time to the nearest half-hour. Children are making adequate progress if they correctly show the time. Some children may be able to place the hour hand accurately between the 7 and 8.

[Measurement and Reference Frames Goal 6]

▶ **Home Link 3·4**   INDEPENDENT ACTIVITY

(*Math Masters*, p. 70)

Home Connection Children draw simple pictures of base-10 blocks to complete "What's My Rule?" tables.

---

3 Differentiation Options

READINESS   PARTNER ACTIVITY

▶ **Playing *Base-10 Exchange***   5–15 Min

(*Math Masters*, p. 428)

To provide experience with place-value using a concrete model, have children play *Base-10 Exchange*.

▷ The bank starts with 20 longs and 40 cubes. Each player has a Place-Value Mat. They share a pair of dice.

▷ Players take turns. They roll the dice, announce the total number of dots, take that number of cubes from the bank, and place the cubes on the mat. Whenever possible, they exchange 10 cubes for 1 long. The player who is not rolling the dice checks the accuracy of the exchanges.

▷ The game ends when there are no more longs. The player with the most longs wins. If there is a tie, the player with the most cubes wins.

EXTRA PRACTICE   SMALL-GROUP ACTIVITY

▶ *Minute Math+*   5–15 Min

To offer children more experience with digits, shapes, and time, see the following pages in *Minute Math+*: pp. 33, 36, 53, 60, 71, and 73.

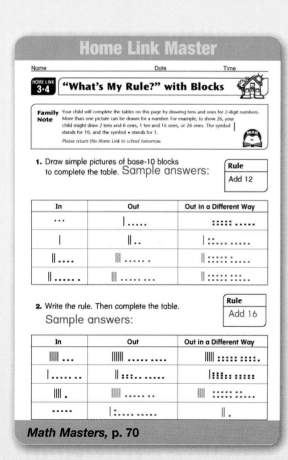

Home Link Master

Name _____ Date _____ Time _____

HOME LINK 3·4 **"What's My Rule?" with Blocks**

Family Note Your child will complete the tables on this page by drawing tens and ones for 2-digit numbers. More than one picture can be drawn for a number. For example, to show 26, your child might draw 2 tens and 6 ones, 1 ten and 16 ones, or 26 ones. The symbol | stands for 10, and the symbol • stands for 1.

Please return this Home Link to school tomorrow.

1. Draw simple pictures of base-10 blocks to complete the table. Sample answers:

Rule Add 12

In	Out	Out in a Different Way
•••		•••••	:::: •••••
		|| ••		:: ••••••
|| ••••	||| ••••••		:::: •••••
|| ••••••	||| ••••••		:::::: ••••

2. Write the rule. Then complete the table.

Sample answers:

Rule Add 16

In	Out	Out in a Different Way
||||| •••	||||| •••••••••	||||| :::::: :::••
	•••••••	|| ::::•• ••••••		::::•• ::::::
|||| •	|||| ••••••	|||| ••••• •• ••
••••••		|: ••••••••••	|| •

Math Masters, p. 70

3·5 Data Day: Pockets

 Objectives To provide experiences with gathering data, entering data in a table, and drawing a bar graph; and to demonstrate a strategy for finding the middle value in a data set.

1 Teaching the Lesson

materials

Key Activities
Children count the number of pockets on their clothes and compare the greatest and least number of pockets. Children tally the class pocket data and make a bar graph of the data. Children also identify the middle value (median) of the data by displaying the data in order.

Key Concepts and Skills
• Compare and order numbers. [Number and Numeration Goal 7]
• Use parts-and-total diagrams to find totals. [Operations and Computation Goal 4]
• Make a tally chart and bar graph to represent data. [Data and Chance Goal 1]
• Discuss data in a tally chart and bar graph. [Data and Chance Goal 2]

Key Vocabulary
predict • middle number • bar graph • range

☑ **Ongoing Assessment: Informing Instruction** See page 208.

☐ *Math Journal 1,* pp. 66 and 67
☐ Home Link 3·4
☐ Teaching Master (*Math Masters,* p. 71)
☐ Transparencies (*Math Masters,* pp. 72 and 73)
☐ calculator (optional)
☐ Class Data Pad (optional)

***See* Advance Preparation**

2 Ongoing Learning & Practice

materials

Children find complements of 100 by playing *Dollar Rummy.*

Children practice and maintain skills through Math Boxes and Home Link activities.

☑ **Ongoing Assessment: Recognizing Student Achievement** Use journal page 68.
[Number and Numeration Goal 5]

☐ *Math Journal 1,* pp. 65 and 68
☐ Home Link Master (*Math Masters,* p. 74)
☐ Game Masters (*Math Masters,* pp. 454 and 455)
☐ scissors

3 Differentiation Options

materials

READINESS
Children do a Dice-Roll and Tally activity to practice tallying.

ENRICHMENT
Children create and compare data sets.

ELL SUPPORT
Children add *middle number* to their Math Word Banks.

☐ *Differentiation Handbook*
☐ 1 die per partnership
☐ half-sheet of paper

Additional Information

Advance Preparation For the Math Message, make one copy of *Math Masters,* page 71 for every 2 children. Cut out the slips and place them near the Math Message. If your school requires a uniform, modify Part 1 activities to include the number of pencils, pens, or other objects children can tally. Make overhead transparencies of *Math Masters,* pages 72 and 73 for the last two pockets data activities.

Technology

Assessment Management System
Math Boxes, Problem 1
See the **iTLG.**

Getting Started

Mental Math and Reflexes

Pose -9 and -8 facts. *Suggestions:*

- ○○○ $13 - 9 = ?$ 4
-       $17 - 9 = ?$ 8
- ○○○ $? = 15 - 8$ 7
-       $? = 14 - 8$ 6
- ○○○ $? - 8 = 5$ 13
-       $? - 9 = 5$ 14

NOTE Remind children to think of "helper" 10-facts. For example, $13 - 10 = 3$, so $13 - 9 = 4$.

Math Message

Take one of the small pieces of paper labeled *Counting Pockets*. Follow the directions.

Home Link 3·4 Follow-Up

Have volunteers share the combinations of base-10 blocks that they used to represent numbers in the "What's My Rule?" table.

Links to the Future

The largest number in a data set is the maximum. The smallest number in a data set is the minimum. The children are not expected to use this vocabulary. Later lessons will include practice with both.

---

1   Teaching the Lesson

▶ Math Message Follow-Up

WHOLE-CLASS ACTIVITY

(*Math Masters*, p. 71)

Ask children to tell you how many pockets they have on their clothes. Have children with the greatest and least number of pockets stand. *Who has more? How many more?*

Ask children to explain their solution strategies. If no one mentions it, be sure to discuss and model the counting-up strategy for finding differences. For example, "The fewest number of pockets is 2. The greatest is 8. Count up from 2: 3 is 1 more, 4 is 2 more, ..., 8 is 6 more."

Ongoing Assessment: Informing Instruction

Watch for children who have difficulty understanding the counting-up strategy. Model the counting-up situation on the number line, as shown below.

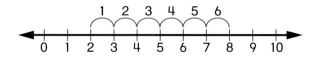

▶ Finding the Middle Number of Pockets

WHOLE-CLASS ACTIVITY

Ask children to pretend that a new child is joining the class. Ask them to **predict** how many pockets the new child will have. To support English language learners, discuss the meanings of the words *predict* and *prediction*.

Teaching Master

Name   Date   Time

LESSON 3·5   Counting Pockets

Name _____

Math Message: Counting Pockets

1. How many pockets are in the clothes you are wearing now?

2. Count the pockets on your shirt, on your pants or skirt, and on anything else that you are wearing.

3. Complete the diagram.

Total		
Shirt	Pants or Skirt	Other

4. Write your total number of pockets very large on the back of this sheet.

Name _____

Math Message: Counting Pockets

1. How many pockets are in the clothes you are wearing now?

2. Count the pockets on your shirt, on your pants or skirt, and on anything else that you are wearing.

3. Complete the diagram.

Total		
Shirt	Pants or Skirt	Other

4. Write your total number of pockets very large on the back of this sheet.

Math Masters, p. 71

Have children report their predictions and how they made them. Expect answers to be rather informal—"I think 5 pockets, because I have 5 pockets and I hope the new child will be like me." Some children may base their predictions on a middle number of pockets—"The fewest number of pockets is 2 and the greatest is 8. The new child might have 5, since 5 is in the middle."

Help children see that the **middle number** would be a good prediction for the new child. Then use the following procedure to find the middle, or median, number of pockets:

Step 1. Ask children with the greatest and least numbers of pockets to come to the front of the room and stand on opposite sides. They should face the class holding their Math Message slips so their total numbers of pockets can be easily seen.

Step 2. Ask the remaining children to come to the front, one by one, and to place themselves in order between the children already in line. Remind them to hold up their Math Message slips as they join the line. Children with the same number of pockets should stand next to one another, but their order doesn't matter.

Step 3. When all children are in line, check that they are in the correct order. While the children are lined up, emphasize which child has the *minimum* or *least* number of pockets and which child has the *maximum* or *greatest* number of pockets. This discussion will help English language learners build meanings for these concepts.

Step 4. Ask the two children on the ends of the line to take two big steps forward. Then ask the two children on the ends of the remaining line to step forward.

Step 5. Continue asking pairs of children on the ends to step forward until only one or two children are left. If one child is left, then the middle number of pockets is that child's number. If two children are left, the middle number of pockets is halfway between their numbers. Explain that the child (or pair of children) left represents the middle number of pockets today.

median

Children find the median number of pockets.

Discuss some of the following questions:

● Is the middle number a good prediction for the new child?

● Would you be surprised if the new child had more or fewer pockets than the middle number?

● Would it help if we knew whether the child was a boy or a girl?

● How do you think the greatest and fewest number of pockets would change if our school had uniforms? How do you think the middle number might change?

Date _____ Time _____

LESSON 3·5 Pockets Data Table

Count the pockets of children in your class. Sample answers:

Pockets	Children	
	Tallies	Number
0		0
1		0
2	//	2
3	//	2
4	///	3
5	////	4
6	///	3
7	////	4
8	//	2
9	/	1
10		0
11		0
12		0
13 or more		0

Math Journal 1, p. 66

 Links to the Future

The activities in this lesson include an early exposure to finding the median of a data set. This concept will be revisited throughout second grade. The most common number in a data set is called the mode. There may be more than one mode in a data set. Finding the mode will be discussed informally throughout second grade and in Unit 12.

Date _____ Time _____

LESSON 3·5 Graphing Pockets Data

Draw a bar graph of the pockets data. Sample answers:

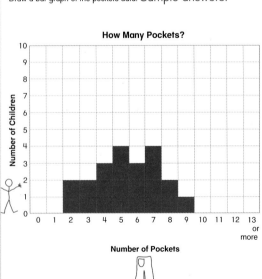

How Many Pockets?

Math Journal 1, p. 67

▶ **Tallying the Pockets Data**

 WHOLE-CLASS ACTIVITY

(*Math Journal 1*, p. 66; *Math Masters*, p. 72)

Ask each child to tell how many pockets they have. Tally these numbers on an overhead transparency of *Math Masters*, page 72. Have children tally them on journal page 66.

Count the tallies and have children complete the Number column. Then spend a few minutes talking about the table. Ask such questions as:

● How many children have 5 pockets? (Repeat for other numbers.)

● What is the most common number of pockets?

● What does this number mean? (Point to a number in the Number column.)

Adjusting the Activity

Using calculators, have children do one of the following:
▷ Determine the total number of pockets in the whole class.
▷ Find how many children have more than 3 pockets.

AUDITORY ◆ KINESTHETIC ◆ TACTILE ◆ VISUAL

▶ **Making a Bar Graph of the Pockets Data**

 INDEPENDENT ACTIVITY

(*Math Journal 1*, p. 67; *Math Masters*, p. 73)

After you have discussed the table, have children use journal page 67 to make a **bar graph** of the data. Use the Class Data Pad or an overhead transparency of *Math Masters*, page 73 to demonstrate.

Adjusting the Activity ELL

Label the sample bar graph with the words *maximum, minimum,* and *middle number* to help children make connections between the mathematical language and concepts.

AUDITORY ◆ KINESTHETIC ◆ TACTILE ◆ VISUAL

Display the graph for the entire lesson so it can be referred to easily later in the lesson. Because some children may confuse the numbers for pockets with the numbers for children, consider having them draw a stick figure under the Children label and draw pants with pockets under the Pockets label. (*See margin.*)

When children are finished, ask such questions as:

● Which bar is the tallest? What does that bar mean? What does the shortest bar tell you?

● Why are the bars taller near the middle of the graph and shorter near the ends?

- What number is the most common number in our data?

- The **range** of a set of data is the largest number minus the smallest number. What would our range for this set of data be?

To support English language learners, discuss the mathematical meaning of the word *range*.

2 Ongoing Learning & Practice

▶ Practicing Complements of 100 by Playing *Dollar Rummy*

 PARTNER ACTIVITY

(*Math Journal 1,* p. 65; *Math Masters,* pp. 454 and 455)

Explain the rules of *Dollar Rummy* on journal page 65. Using game cards cut from *Math Masters,* page 454, have children find as many different combinations of $1.00 as they can. For another version, use cards cut from *Math Masters,* page 455.

Prior to demonstrating the game, ask children which card would have a better chance of being picked:

- A 10¢ card or a 30¢ card? 10¢ card

- A 40¢ card or a 90¢ card? They have the same chance.

- A 50¢ card or a 10¢ card? 50¢ card

Play several demonstration rounds of the game before children begin to play with partners.

▶ Math Boxes 3·5

 INDEPENDENT ACTIVITY

(*Math Journal 1,* p. 68)

Mixed Practice Math Boxes in this lesson are paired with Math Boxes in Lesson 3-7. The skills in Problems 5 and 6 preview Unit 4 content.

Ongoing Assessment: **Recognizing Student Achievement**

Math Boxes **Problem 1** ★

Use **Math Boxes, Problem 1** to assess children's ability to show equivalent names for 20. Children are making adequate progress if they are able to find three names for 20. This may include +0 and +1. Some children may be able to find more than three names.

[Number and Numeration Goal 5]

▶ Home Link 3·5

 INDEPENDENT ACTIVITY

(*Math Masters,* p. 74)

 Home Connection Children count pockets of five people at home and make a bar graph using their data.

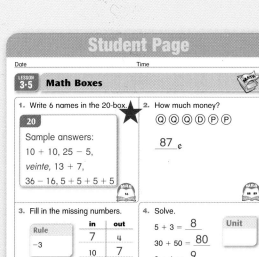

Name _____ Date _____ Time _____

HOME LINK
3·5

Pockets Bar Graph

Family Note Help your child fill in the table below. Then display the data by making a **bar graph.**
Please return this Home Link to school tomorrow.

1. Pick five people. Count the number of pockets that each person's clothing has. Complete the table.

2. Draw a bar graph for your data. First, write the name of each person on a line at the bottom of the graph. Then color the bar above each name to show how many pockets that person has.

Name	Number of Pockets
Jill	3
Lamar	5
Arturo	4

Sample answers

How Many Pockets?

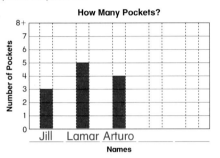

Math Masters, p. 74

Rolls of the Die

1	⊬⊬⊬ //
2	///
3	⊬⊬⊬ ///
4	⊬⊬⊬ ⊬⊬⊬
5	///
6	⊬⊬⊬ /

This child needs two rolls of 2 and two rolls of 5.

---

3 **Differentiation Options**

 PARTNER ACTIVITY

🕐 5–15 Min

▶ ## Recording Tally Marks

To provide experience with recording tally marks, have children do a Dice-Roll and Tally activity. Each partner sets up a table with the numbers 1 through 6 in the first column and blank spaces in the second column. Partners take turns rolling a die and putting a tally mark next to the appropriate number on their half-sheets of paper. (*See margin*). Partners continue until one child has at least five tally marks next to each number. After children finish the activity, have them discuss whether or not they have an equal chance of getting any number from 1 through 6.

 SMALL-GROUP ACTIVITY

🕐 5–15 Min

▶ ## Comparing Data

To apply children's understanding of bar graphs, have them collect data and compare data sets. Have children discuss, in small groups, whether they think all sets of people would have the same number of pockets. For example, if they surveyed the teachers in the school, would teachers have the same number of pockets as the children? Have each small group select a set of people to collect information about, such as teenagers, parents, men, and so on. Have children predict whether their selected set will have the same number, more, or fewer pockets than their class.

The next day, have the children in each small group combine their survey results into a bar graph that they can compare to their class graph. Discuss questions like the following: *Does one group have more pockets? Which data value should be used to answer that question? The middle value? The total? The maximum? Why might one group have more pockets?*

 **SMALL-GROUP ACTIVITY**

🕐 5–15 Min

▶ ## Building a Math Word Bank
(*Differentiation Handbook*)

To provide language support for data concepts, have children use the Word Bank template found in the *Differentiation Handbook*. Ask children to write the term *middle number,* draw a picture representing the term, and write other related words. See the *Differentiation Handbook* for more information.

Frames and Arrows Having Two Rules

 Objective To guide children as they solve Frames-and-Arrows problems having two rules.

---

1 Teaching the Lesson

Key Activities

Children make up and solve Frames-and-Arrows problems about coins and use coins to solve Frames-and-Arrows problems having two rules.

Key Concepts and Skills

• Use dollars-and-cents notation.
[Number and Numeration Goal 2]

• Calculate values of coin and bill combinations.
[Operations and Computation Goal 2]

• Identify and use rules for a function involving addition and subtraction of coins.
[Patterns, Functions, and Algebra Goal 1]

Ongoing Assessment: Informing Instruction See page 216.

Ongoing Assessment: Recognizing Student Achievement Use *Math Masters,* page 431. [Patterns, Functions, and Algebra Goal 1]

materials

☐ *Math Journal 1,* pp. 69 and 70
☐ Home Link 3·5
☐ Teaching Masters (*Math Masters,* pp. 75–77)
☐ Teaching Aid Master (*Math Masters,* p. 431)
☐ Transparencies (*Math Masters,* pp. 75–77 and 431; optional)
☐ coins per child: 5 quarters, 5 dimes, 5 nickels, and 5 pennies

***See* Advance Preparation**

---

2 Ongoing Learning & Practice

Children practice reading a bar graph.

Children practice and maintain skills through Math Boxes and Home Link activities.

materials

☐ *Math Journal 1,* pp. 71 and 72
☐ Home Link Master (*Math Masters,* p. 78)

---

3 Differentiation Options

READINESS

Children count up and back on a number line.

ENRICHMENT

Children solve Frames-and-Arrows puzzles.

materials

☐ Teaching Masters (*Math Masters,* pp. 79 and 80)
☐ red and blue crayons

Additional Information

Advance Preparation For the Math Message, make one copy of *Math Masters,* page 75 for every two children. Cut the copies apart and place them near the Math Message.

For Part 1, make overhead transparencies of *Math Masters,* pages 75–77 and 431, or draw a two-rule Frames-and-Arrows diagram on the board with semipermanent chalk.

Technology

Assessment Management System
Math Masters, page 431
See the **iTLG.**

Getting Started

Mental Math and Reflexes

Pose comparison number stories, which practice −9 and −8 subtraction facts or +9 and +8 addition facts, depending on which number model a child uses; for example, 4 + 8 = 12 or 12 − 4 = 8. Have children share strategies.
Suggestions:

- ○○○ Damian is 6 years old. Maya is 9 years older. How old is Maya? 15 years old

- ○○○ Jenna has $4. Martina has $12. How many more dollars does Jenna need in order to have the same amount of money as Martina? $8

- ○○○ Jackson has 14 sports magazines in his collection. Luis has 9. How many more magazines does Luis need in order to have the same number of magazines as Jackson? 5 magazines

Math Message

Here is a Frames-and-Arrows problem that uses nickels:

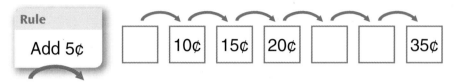

Rule
Add 5¢

| | 10¢ | 15¢ | 20¢ | | | 35¢ |

Take a blank Frames-and-Arrows diagram from Math Masters, *page 75. Make up a problem that uses nickels, dimes, or quarters. Hand in your problem.*

Home Link 3·5 Follow-Up

Have small groups of children compare their bar graphs by asking questions like the following:

- What is the greatest number of pockets shown by any graph? The least number?
- Use all of your group's graphs. What is the total number of people who had zero pockets? 1 pocket? (Continue with other numbers.)

---

(1) Teaching the Lesson

▶ Math Message Follow-Up

WHOLE-CLASS ACTIVITY

(*Math Masters,* p. 75)

Choose two of the children's Frames-and-Arrows problems. Review filling in frames and finding a missing rule. Share solution strategies with the class on an overhead transparency of *Math Masters,* page 75 or on the board. Make sure everyone understands these one-rule Frames-and-Arrows diagrams.

▶ Solving Frames-and-Arrows Diagrams Having Two Rules

WHOLE-CLASS ACTIVITY

(*Math Masters,* pp. 76, 77, and 431)

Display the example on *Math Masters,* page 76. Ask what is different about this Frames-and-Arrows diagram from Frames-and-Arrows diagrams that children have seen before. Sample answer: There are two kinds of arrows, one dashed and one solid. Explain that the two kinds of arrows stand for two different rules.

Have children act out the example with you. Start with a dime as indicated in the first frame, add a nickel (solid-arrow rule) to get the result shown in the second frame, add a dime (dashed-arrow rule) to get the result shown in the third frame, and so on.

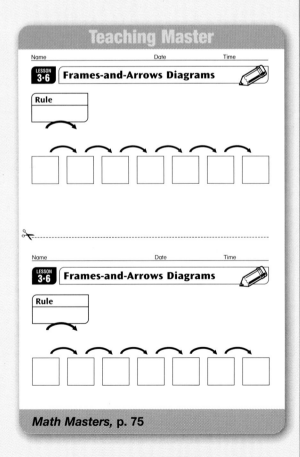

Teaching Master

Name _____ Date _____ Time _____

LESSON 3·6 Frames-and-Arrows Diagrams

Rule

Name _____ Date _____ Time _____

LESSON 3·6 Frames-and-Arrows Diagrams

Rule

Math Masters, p. 75

Adjusting the Activity

Have children write the appropriate rule above each arrow to help them navigate filling in the frames. For example, write +10¢ and −5¢ above the arrows in Problem 1 on *Math Masters*, page 76.

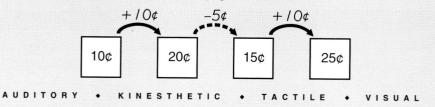

AUDITORY ◆ KINESTHETIC ◆ TACTILE ◆ VISUAL

Repeat the procedure with the other problems on *Math Masters*, pages 76 and 77. Use the Frames-and-Arrows blank diagrams on *Math Masters*, page 431 to make up more problems as necessary.

Adjusting the Activity

In Problems 4 and 5, children find one of the rules and complete the frames. To find the rule, children should use coins to act out the pattern. Children can then fill in the empty frames.

Focus on Problems 1–3. With additional practice on journal pages and in Math Boxes throughout the year, children will be better prepared for Problems like 4 and 5.

AUDITORY ◆ KINESTHETIC ◆ TACTILE ◆ VISUAL

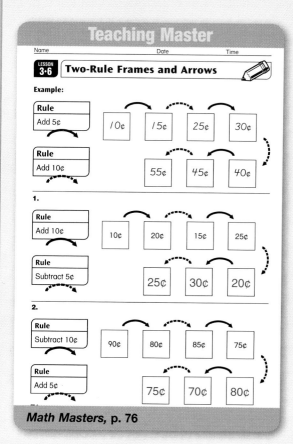

Math Masters, p. 76

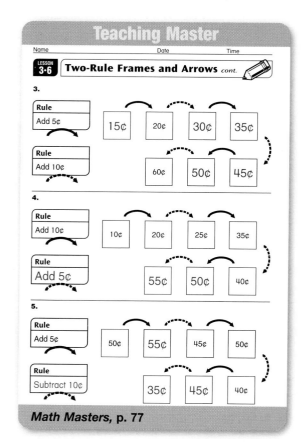

Math Masters, p. 77

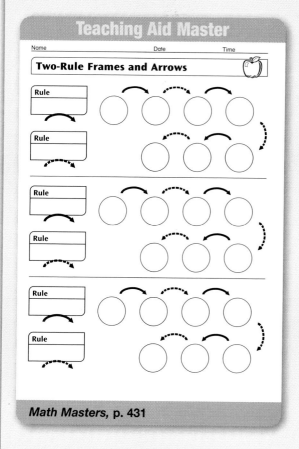

Math Masters, p. 431

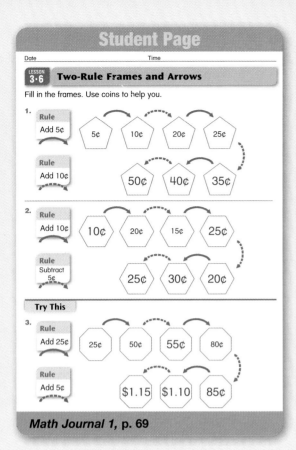

Student Page

Date _____ Time _____

LESSON 3·6   Two-Rule Frames and Arrows

Fill in the frames. Use coins to help you.

1.
Rule: Add 5¢

5¢   10¢   20¢   25¢

Rule: Add 10¢

50¢   40¢   35¢

2.
Rule: Add 10¢

10¢   20¢   15¢   25¢

Rule: Subtract 5¢

25¢   30¢   20¢

Try This

3.
Rule: Add 25¢

25¢   50¢   55¢   80¢

Rule: Add 5¢

$1.15 $1.10   85¢

Math Journal 1, p. 69

▶ **Solving Frames-and-Arrows Problems**

INDEPENDENT ACTIVITY

(*Math Journal 1*, pp. 69 and 70)

Children solve Frames-and-Arrows problems and use coins to help them. Encourage children to check each problem after they have completed it by applying the rules to the completed frames. For example, to check Problem 2, children begin with their answer of 10¢. The solid-arrow rule is Add 10¢. The second frame is 20¢. Does 10¢ + 10¢ = 20¢? Yes, so the answer is correct.

 Ongoing Assessment: Informing Instruction

Watch for children who do not have a strategy for completing Frames-and-Arrows problems where the first frame is blank. Suggest that the children write the rule above the arrows. Use either a number grid or a number line to demonstrate how to count up and back.

▶ **Creating Frames-and-Arrows Problems**

INDEPENDENT ACTIVITY

(*Math Masters*, p. 431)

Children create and solve their own two-rule Frames-and-Arrows problems. Encourage children to vary the operations and numbers they use for the rules.

You may want to have children trade papers with a partner to solve each other's problems. Children should check each other's work.

 Ongoing Assessment: Recognizing Student Achievement

Math Masters Page 431

Portfolio Ideas

Use *Math Masters*, page 431 to assess children's ability to create number patterns and rules in Frames-and-Arrows problems. Children are making adequate progress if they can make up a problem and complete it accurately. Some children may be able to include more difficult numbers for the rules.

[Patterns, Functions, and Algebra Goal 1]

Student Page

Date _____ Time _____

LESSON 3·6   Two-Rule Frames and Arrows *continued*

4. Fill in the frames. Use coins to help you.

Rule: Add 10¢

3¢   13¢   12¢   22¢

Rule: Subtract 1¢

30¢   31¢   21¢

Fill in the frames and find the missing rules. Use coins to help you.

5.
Rule: Add 2¢

1¢   3¢   4¢   6¢

Rule: Add 1¢

10¢   9¢   7¢

Try This

6.
Rule: Add 5¢

$1.00 $1.05 $1.15 $1.20

Rule: Add 10¢

$1.45 $1.35 $1.30

Math Journal 1, p. 70

② Ongoing Learning & Practice

▶ ## Reading a Bar Graph

INDEPENDENT ACTIVITY

(*Math Journal 1*, p. 71)

Children answer questions about a bar graph. Make sure they understand the difference between the two sets of numbers on the graph—one set names the number of brothers and sisters that children have, and the other set is used to tell how many children have a certain number of brothers and sisters.

▶ ## Math Boxes 3·6

INDEPENDENT ACTIVITY

(*Math Journal 1*, p. 72)

Mixed Practice Math Boxes in this lesson are paired with Math Boxes in Lesson 3-8. The skills in Problems 5 and 6 preview Unit 4 content.

▶ ## Home Link 3·6

INDEPENDENT ACTIVITY

(*Math Masters*, p. 78)

Home Connection Children use coins to solve Frames-and-Arrows problems that have two rules.

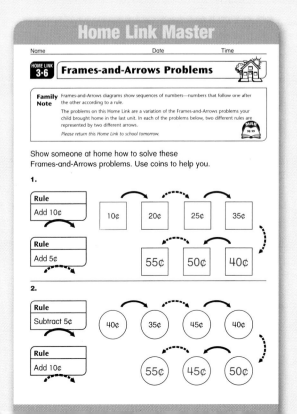

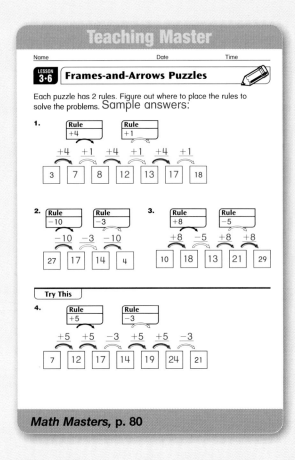

Math Masters, p. 79

Math Masters, p. 80

READINESS · SMALL-GROUP ACTIVITY · 5–15 Min

▶ Counting Up and Back on a Number Line

(Math Masters, p. 79)

To explore navigating on a number line, have children find the rules for skip counts on the number line. Introduce the activity by doing several counts with children on the first number line. They should follow along with their fingers and say each stopping point together. *Suggestions:*

▷ Start at 5 and count up by 2s on the number line. Say the stops together. 7, 9, 11, 13, 15, 17, 19 Ask them if they can think of a rule that would mean the same thing as "Count up by 2s." Add 2 Write the rule on the board.

▷ Start at 20 and count back by 3s on the number line. Say the stops together. 17, 14, 11, 8, 5, 2 Ask them if they can think of a rule that would mean the same thing as "Count up by 3s." Subtract 3 Write the rule on the board.

Now work on a couple of two-rule problems together, having children use their fingers to follow along on the number line. Tell children that they have been using only one rule, but that now they are going to do counts with two rules. *Suggestions:*

▷ Start at 1. Combine the "Add 3" rule and the "Add 2" rule. Say the stops together. 4, 6, 9, 11, 14, 16, 19

▷ Have children repeat this two-rule count. This time, have them draw the hops on the number line. Use the red crayon when they add 3 (3 hops) and use the blue crayon when they add 2 (2 hops).

Children work with a partner to complete the page.

ENRICHMENT · SMALL-GROUP ACTIVITY · 5–15 Min

▶ Solving Frames-and-Arrows Puzzles

(Math Masters, p. 80)

To further explore two-rule Frames-and-Arrows diagrams, have children solve frames-and-arrows puzzles on *Math Masters*, page 80. The arrows will not always alternate ABAB. Note that the order in which children place the rules will not matter as long as each rule is used the correct number of times. You may want to have children color-code their rules with crayons—underline the first rule in red and the second rule in blue for each problem; then draw the appropriate color arrow between the frames. Have children explain their solution strategies. Sample answer: I always take the biggest rule first until I am close to my number.

3·7 Making Change by Counting Up

Objective To guide children as they make change by counting up from the cost of an item to the amount tendered.

---

1 Teaching the Lesson

Key Activities
Children identify combinations of coins that can be used to make a purchase. They make change by counting up from the cost of an item to the amount tendered. They practice making change by acting out the roles of customer and clerk.

Key Concepts and Skills
- Count by 1s, 5s, 10s, and 25s.
  [Number and Numeration Goal 1]
- Write money amounts using cents notation.
  [Number and Numeration Goal 2]
- Make change by counting up.
  [Operations and Computation Goal 2]
- Show coin combinations for an amount.
  [Operations and Computation Goal 2]

Key Vocabulary
make change by counting up

materials
- ☐ *Math Journal 1*, p. 56 and 73
- ☐ Home Link 3·6
- ☐ coins per partnership: 10 pennies, 10 nickels, 5 dimes, 3 quarters, and one $1 bill
- ☐ overhead coins in the quantities given above (optional)
- ☐ slate

---

2 Ongoing Learning & Practice

Children practice forming and comparing numbers by playing the *Digit Game.*

Children practice and maintain skills through Math Boxes and Home Link activities.

✔️ **Ongoing Assessment: Recognizing Student Achievement** Use an Exit Slip.
  [Number and Numeration Goal 2]

materials
- ☐ *Math Journal 1*, p. 74
- ☐ *My Reference Book*, pp. 132 and 133
- ☐ Home Link Masters (*Math Masters*, pp. 81 and 82)
- ☐ Teaching Aid Master (*Math Masters*, p. 415)
- ☐ per partnership: 4 each of number cards 0–9 (from the Everything Math Deck, if available)

---

3 Differentiation Options

READINESS

Children play *High Roller* to practice addition skills by counting up using dice.

ENRICHMENT

Children solve a coin puzzle.

materials
- ☐ Teaching Master (*Math Masters*, p. 83)
- ☐ two dice

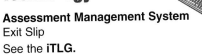

Technology
Assessment Management System
Exit Slip
See the **iTLG.**

Getting Started

Mental Math and Reflexes

Count by 5s, 10s, and 25s.

Suggestions:

○○○ Begin at 50. Count by 5s to 100.
  Begin at 25. Count by 10s to 105.
  Begin at 100. Count by 25s to 300.

●●○ Begin at 155. Count by 5s.
  Begin at 137. Count by 10s.
  Begin at 150. Count by 25s.

●●● Begin at 1,050. Count by 5s.
  Begin at 1,020. Count by 10s.
  Begin at 1,025. Count by 25s.

Math Message

You buy a toy that costs 48¢. Which coins would you use to pay for it? Draw the coins on your slate. Use *P, N, D, or Q.*

Home Link 3·6 Follow-Up

Ask volunteers to demonstrate how they found the numbers that belong in the empty frames for each problem. Show the children how to use coins to determine the missing numbers.

---

① Teaching the Lesson

▶ Math Message Follow-Up

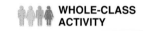 WHOLE-CLASS ACTIVITY

Ask several children to share their solutions. Explain that any group of coins that has a value of 48¢ is a correct solution. *How can you find the fewest number of coins that would be needed to buy the toy?* Sample answer: I start with the coin of the highest value, a quarter. I can use 1 quarter. Then I count on from 25¢ with the next-highest-value coin. I can use 2 dimes, so I count 25¢, 35¢, 45¢. I cannot use any nickels. So I count on from 45¢ with pennies: 45¢, 46¢, 47¢, 48¢. The fewest number of coins that I would need to buy the toy is 6: 1 quarter, 2 dimes, and 3 pennies.

▶ Demonstrating How to Make Change by Counting Up

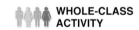 WHOLE-CLASS ACTIVITY

(*Math Journal 1*, p. 56)

Have children turn to the Fruits and Vegetables Stand Poster in their journals. Then pose this problem: *I buy an orange. I give the clerk 2 dimes. How much change will the clerk give me back?* To support English language learners, discuss the meaning of *make change.*

Date   Time

LESSON 3·2   Fruit and Vegetables Stand Poster

Math Journal 1, p. 56

Show how to **make change by counting up.**

1. Start with the cost of the item—18¢.

2. Count up to the amount of money used to pay for the item—20¢. Say "19, 20" while putting down 2 pennies.

3. Record the transaction on the board as follows:

I bought:	I paid:	My change was:
an orange for 18¢	Ⓓ Ⓓ	Ⓟ Ⓟ

4. Repeat this routine with several other examples.

Point out that the same transaction can involve different coin combinations. In the sample problem above, a child could have paid for the orange with a quarter. The change could have been 1 nickel and 2 pennies, or 7 pennies.

Partners take turns being the Customer and the Clerk. The Customer selects an item and gives the Clerk coins to pay for the item. The Clerk counts out the change. Encourage children to make change using the fewest possible number of coins. Have children share several transactions with the class and record them in the table on the board.

⬆⬇ Adjusting the Activity

Present examples where the Clerk uses no more than 4 pennies in change. Then move on to making change with nickels, dimes, and quarters.

Guide children to write number models for transactions: If you pay for a 13¢ pear with two dimes, you could use the number model 13¢ + 7¢ = 20¢ to show counting up to make the change. 13¢ is the cost, 20¢ is the amount used to pay, and 7¢ is the amount of change. If you pay for a 13¢ pear with two dimes, you could also use the number model 20¢ − 13¢ = 7¢.

A U D I T O R Y   ◆   K I N E S T H E T I C   ◆   T A C T I L E   ◆   V I S U A L

▶ ## Acting as Customer or Clerk

🧍🧍 **PARTNER ACTIVITY**

(*Math Journal 1*, p. 73)

Partners continue the shopping activity. They take turns being the Customer and the Clerk. Children record a few of their transactions in their journals, using the notation Ⓟ, Ⓝ, Ⓓ, Ⓠ, and 🔲$1🔲.

Date _____   Time _____

3·7 LESSON   **Shopping at the Fruit and Vegetables Stand**

Price per Item

pear	13¢	melon slice	30¢	lettuce	45¢
orange	18¢	apple	12¢	green pepper	24¢
banana	9¢	tomato	20¢	corn	15¢
plum	6¢	onion	7¢	cabbage	40¢

Complete the table. **Sample answer:**

I bought	I paid (Draw coins or $1 bill.)	I got in change
a pear	Ⓓ Ⓓ	7 ¢
		¢
		¢

Try This   Sample answer:

Buy 2 items. How much change from $1.00 will you get?

I bought	I paid	I got in change
lettuce		
and cabbage	$1	15 ¢

Math Journal 1, p. 73

Games

The Digit Game

Materials ☐ number cards 0–9 (4 of each)

Players 2

Skill Making and comparing numbers

Object of the game To collect more cards.

Directions

1. Shuffle the cards. Place the deck number-side down on the table.

2. Each player draws 2 cards from the deck and uses them to make the larger 2-digit number.

3. The player with the larger number takes all 4 cards.

4. The game is over when all of the cards have been used.

5. The player with more cards wins.

My Reference Book, p. 132

Student Page

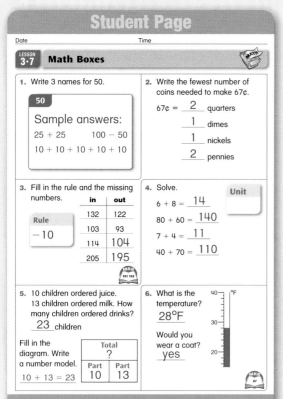

1. Write 3 names for 50.

   50

   Sample answers:
   25 + 25   100 − 50
   10 + 10 + 10 + 10 + 10

2. Write the fewest number of coins needed to make 67¢.

   67¢ = __2__ quarters
   __1__ dimes
   __1__ nickels
   __2__ pennies

3. Fill in the rule and the missing numbers.

   Rule **−10**

in	out
132	122
103	93
114	104
205	195

4. Solve.

   Unit

   6 + 8 = __14__
   80 + 60 = __140__
   7 + 4 = __11__
   40 + 70 = __110__

5. 10 children ordered juice. 13 children ordered milk. How many children ordered drinks?

   __23__ children

   Fill in the diagram. Write a number model.

Total	
?	
Part	**Part**
10	13

   10 + 13 = 23

6. What is the temperature?

   28°F

   Would you wear a coat?

   yes

2 Ongoing Learning & Practice

▶ Playing the *Digit Game*

PARTNER ACTIVITY

(*My Reference Book,* pp. 132 and 133)

The *Digit Game* was introduced in Lesson 3-1. Children will find game directions on pages 132 and 133 of *My Reference Book.* Play several demonstration hands with the class.

Have partners play several rounds of the game.

> ### ✓ Ongoing Assessment:
> **Recognizing Student Achievement**
>
> **Exit Slip**
>
> Use an **Exit Slip** (*Math Masters,* page 415) to assess the children's understanding of place value. Have children record two of their numbers from the *Digit Game.* Children are making adequate progress if they are able to make the largest number from the two digits. Some children may be able to use three or more cards successfully.
>
> [Number and Numeration Goal 2]

▶ Math Boxes 3·7

INDEPENDENT ACTIVITY

(*Math Journal 1,* p. 74)

Mixed Practice Math Boxes in this lesson are paired with Math Boxes in Lesson 3-5. The skills in Problems 5 and 6 preview Unit 4 content.

Writing/Reasoning Have children draw, write, or verbalize their answers to the following: *Explain how 6 + 8 helped you solve 80 + 60 in Problem 4. How will this strategy help you solve 600 + 800?* Sample answer: 6 + 8 is the same as 8 + 6. I used 8 + 6 = 14 to find 8 tens + 6 tens = 14 tens. I could use 6 + 8 = 14 to find 6 hundreds + 8 hundreds.

▶ Home Link 3·7

INDEPENDENT ACTIVITY

(*Math Masters,* pp. 81 and 82)

Home Connection With small items from home, children have a pretend garage sale. They "price" each item under $1; they "buy" each item with a $1 bill.

Home Link Master

Family Note Encourage your child to make change by counting up. Using real coins and dollar bills will make this activity easier. *For example:*
- Start with the cost of an item—65 cents.
- Count up to the money given—$1.00.

One way to make change: Put down a nickel and say "70." Then put down 3 dimes and say "80, 90, 1 dollar." *Another way:* Put down 3 dimes and say "75, 85, 95." Then put down 5 pennies and say "96, 97, 98, 99, 1 dollar."

The Practice section in the Home Link provides a review of previously learned skills.

Please return this Home Link to school tomorrow.

Pretend you are having a garage sale. Do the following:
- Find small items in your home to "sell."
- Give each item a price less than $1.00. Give each item a different price.
- Pretend that customers pay for each item with a $1 bill.
- Show someone at home how you would make change by counting up. Use Ⓟ, Ⓝ, Ⓓ, and Ⓠ.
- Show another way you can make change for the same item.

Example:

The customer buys _a pen_ for _65¢_.

One way I can make change: ___ Ⓝ Ⓓ Ⓓ Ⓓ

Another way I can make change: Ⓓ Ⓓ Ⓓ Ⓟ Ⓟ Ⓟ Ⓟ Ⓟ

3 Differentiation Options

READINESS

PARTNER ACTIVITY

▶ ## Playing *High Roller*

⏱ 5–15 Min

To provide concrete experience with counting on, have children play *High Roller*.

Rules

1. One player rolls two dice. The player keeps the die with the larger number (the High Roller) and throws the other die again.

2. The player counts up from the number rolled on the first die to get the sum of the two dice.

3. Each player repeats Steps 1 and 2. The winner is the player with the highest number after two rounds.

ENRICHMENT

INDEPENDENT ACTIVITY

▶ ## Solving a Coin Puzzle

⏱ 5–15 Min

(*Math Masters*, p. 83)

To apply children's understanding of coin values and coin combinations, have them solve coin puzzles. After completing the *Math Masters* page, have children write their own coin puzzles on the back of the page.

Name _____ Date _____ Time _____

HOME LINK 3·7 | **Change at a Garage Sale** *continued*

1. The customer buys _____ for _____.
   One way I can make change: _____
   Another way I can make change: _____

2. The customer buys _____ for _____.
   One way I can make change: _____
   Another way I can make change: _____

3. The customer buys _____ for _____.
   One way I can make change: _____
   Another way I can make change: _____

4. The customer buys _____ for _____.
   One way I can make change: _____
   Another way I can make change: _____

Practice

5. $7 + 5 = \underline{12}$

6. $8 + 6 = \underline{14}$

7. $\begin{array}{r} 4 \\ +9 \\ \hline 13 \end{array}$

8. $\begin{array}{r} 3 \\ +7 \\ \hline 10 \end{array}$

Math Masters, p. 82

Name _____ Date _____ Time _____

LESSON 3·7 | **Coin Puzzles**

Use the clues to solve the coin puzzles.

Example:

Clue 1: I have two coins.

Clue 2: Together they are worth 30¢.

Clue 3: One is not a nickel.

Coin Puzzle: What are the coins? *A quarter and a nickel*

1. Clue 1: I have 46¢.

   Clue 2: I have 7 coins.

   Coin Puzzle: Which coins do I have? Three dimes, three nickels, and one penny

2. Clue 1: I have 49¢ in one pocket.

   Clue 2: I have 16¢ in another pocket.

   Clue 3: When I put all my coins on the table, I count 10 pennies.

   Clue 4: None of the coins is a nickel.

   Coin Puzzle: What are the coins? One quarter, three dimes, and ten pennies

3. Clue 1: I have 5 coins.

   Clue 2: I have a total of 46¢.

   Clue 3: Three of the coins are not nickels.

   Coin Puzzle: Which coins do I have? One quarter, one dime, two nickels, and one penny

Math Masters, p. 83

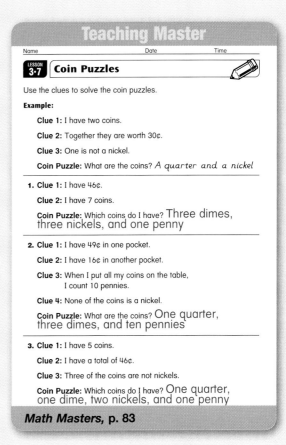

3·8 Coin Exchanges

 Objective To guide children as they solve multistep problems for amounts under $1.00 and as they practice making change using nickels, dimes, and quarters.

---

1 Teaching the Lesson

materials

Key Activities
Children identify the coins and bills that can be used to make a purchase under $1.00. They practice making change with nickels, dimes, and quarters by pretending to buy items from a milk and juice vending machine.

Key Concepts and Skills
• Count by 5s, 10s, and 25s. [Number and Numeration Goal 1]
• Write amounts in dollars-and-cents notation. [Number and Numeration Goal 2]
• Use strategies to make change. [Operations and Computation Goal 2]
• Calculate coin amounts. [Operations and Computation Goal 2]

Key Vocabulary
exact change light

✔ **Ongoing Assessment: Recognizing Student Achievement** Use journal page 76.
[Operations and Computation Goal 2]

□ *Math Journal 1*, pp. 76 and 77
□ Home Link 3·7
□ Transparency (*Math Masters*, p. 84; optional)
□ slate
□ coins per child (optional):
10 pennies, 10 nickels, 5 dimes, 3 quarters, and one $1 bill

See Advance Preparation

---

2 Ongoing Learning & Practice

materials

Children practice making coin combinations for a given amount.

Children practice and maintain skills through Math Boxes and Home Link activities.

□ *Math Journal 1*, pp. 75 and 78
□ Home Link Master (*Math Masters*, p. 85)
□ 2 dice per group

□ per child:
2 nickels, 2 dimes, 2 quarters, and one $1 bill
□ item to use as a bank, such as a cup, small box, or piece of paper

---

3 Differentiation Options

materials

READINESS
Children count by 5s, 10s, and 25s with coins on the number grid.

ENRICHMENT
Children add coin combinations.

EXTRA PRACTICE
Children solve problems about money.

□ Teaching Aid Master (*Math Masters*, p. 418)
□ *Minute Math®+*, pp. 22, 35, 67, 69, and 70
□ tool-kit coins
□ calculator (optional)

Additional Information

Advance Preparation For the Math Message Follow-Up in Part 1, you may want to create an overhead transparency of *Math Masters*, page 84.

Technology
Assessment Management System
Journal page 76, Problem 1
See the **iTLG.**

Getting Started

Mental Math and Reflexes

Show how you could pay for each item. Draw Ⓝ, Ⓓ, or Ⓠ on your slate.

○○○ A bottle of juice that costs 75¢

●○○ An apple that costs 55¢

○○○ A package of gum that costs 35¢

Math Message

Turn to page 76 in your journal. Do you know what this machine is called? Do you know how it works? Be ready to discuss this machine.

Home Link 3·7 Follow-Up

Ask volunteers to name an item they "sold," the price of the item, and how they made change. You may want to have children demonstrate their transactions using coins.

---

1 Teaching the Lesson

▶ Math Message Follow-Up

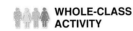 WHOLE-CLASS DISCUSSION

(*Math Journal 1*, p. 76; *Math Masters*, p. 84)

Display an overhead transparency of the Milk and Juice Vending Machine Poster (*Math Masters*, page 84), or have children turn to journal page 76. Ask:

● What is this machine? How does it work?

● Which coins or bills can you use in the machine? Nickels, dimes, quarters, and dollar bills

● Can you buy something if you don't have the exact amount? Yes, unless the "exact change" light is on. What does the **exact change light** mean? If it is on, the machine won't return change if the buyer puts in more money than an item costs.

Review the concept of making change: The buyer pays with coins or bills that add up to more than the cost of the item. The vending machine gives back the money owed (the difference).

▶ Buying Items with Exact Change Only

WHOLE-CLASS ACTIVITY

(*Math Journal 1*, p. 76)

Ask children to pretend that the exact change light is on and that they want to buy a can of grape juice. On their slates, have them draw the coins they would use. Sample answers: 1 quarter and 2 dimes, 4 dimes and 1 nickel, or 9 nickels. Have children share their coin combinations as you list them on the board. Repeat the question for other items from the vending machine.

Teaching Master

Name   Date   Time

LESSON 3·8 **Milk and Juice Vending Machine**

Math Masters, p. 84

Student Page

Date _____ Time _____

LESSON 3·8 **Buying from a Vending Machine**

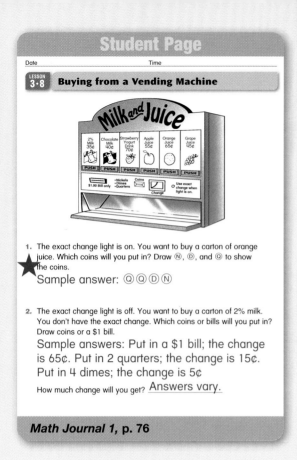

1. The exact change light is on. You want to buy a carton of orange juice. Which coins will you put in? Draw Ⓝ, Ⓓ, and Ⓠ to show the coins.

 Sample answer: Ⓠ Ⓠ Ⓓ Ⓝ

2. The exact change light is off. You want to buy a carton of 2% milk. You don't have the exact change. Which coins or bills will you put in? Draw coins or a $1 bill.

 Sample answers: Put in a $1 bill; the change is 65¢. Put in 2 quarters; the change is 15¢. Put in 4 dimes; the change is 5¢

 How much change will you get? **Answers vary.**

Math Journal 1, p. 76

▶ Buying Items without Exact Change

(*Math Journal 1*, p. 76)

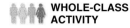

WHOLE-CLASS ACTIVITY

Ask children what happens when the exact change light is off. The buyer can put in more money than the cost of an item, and the machine will give change.

Ask children to pretend that they want to buy a carton of orange juice. Have them suggest various coin combinations they might use to pay with exact change.

Next, ask children to pretend that they don't have the exact change to buy the juice. Have them use their slates to draw the coins and bills they might put into the machine. Then they should draw the change that the machine would give back and write the amount. (*See below.*) Sample answers: Pay with $1 and receive 35¢ change; pay with 3 quarters and receive 1 dime change; or pay with 7 dimes and receive 1 nickel change. Have children share responses. Repeat the question for other items as necessary.

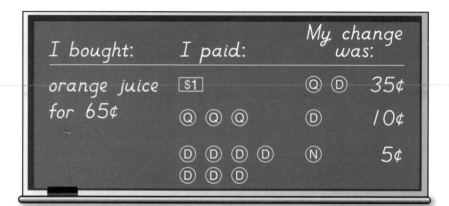

► Making Vending Machine Purchases

(Math Journal 1, p. 76 and 77)

PARTNER ACTIVITY

In Problems 1 and 3, the exact change light is on; in Problems 2 and 4, it is off.

In Problems 3 and 4, have children work with a partner. Partners take turns buying items from the vending machine and checking each other's work. The first two transactions in each problem are specified on the journal page; other transactions are of children's own choosing.

Adjusting the Activity

Encourage children to use coins to model the problems.

AUDITORY ◆ KINESTHETIC ◆ TACTILE ◆ VISUAL

Ongoing Assessment:
Recognizing Student Achievement

Journal Page 76 Problem 1

Use **journal page 76, Problem 1** to assess children's ability to combine coins to calculate an amount. Children are making adequate progress if they can use coins to solve the problem. Some children may be able to solve the problem without the use of coins.

[Operations and Computation Goal 2]

---

② Ongoing Learning & Practice

► Practice Making Change

(Math Journal 1, p. 75)

SMALL-GROUP ACTIVITY

Explain and demonstrate the directions on journal page 75. Then divide the class into groups of 2 or 3 children each and have them do the activity.

Student Page

Date   Time

LESSON 3·8 **Buying from a Vending Machine** *continued*

3. The exact change light is on.

You buy:	Draw the coins you put in.
chocolate milk	Sample answer: Ⓠ Ⓓ Ⓝ
strawberry yogurt drink	Sample answer: Ⓠ Ⓠ Ⓓ Ⓓ
Answers vary.	Coin combinations will vary but should equal the price of the chosen item.

4. The exact change light is off.

You buy:	Draw the coins or the $1 bill you put in.	What is your change?
orange juice	Ⓠ Ⓠ Ⓠ	10 ¢
chocolate milk	$1	60 ¢
Answers vary.		___ ¢
_____		___ ¢
_____		___ ¢

Math Journal 1, p. 77

Student Page

Date   Time

LESSON 3·8 **Making Change**

Materials ☐ 2 nickels, 2 dimes, 2 quarters, and one $1 bill for each child

☐ 2 six-sided dice

☐ a cup, a small box, or a piece of paper for a bank

Number of children 2 or 3

Directions

1. Each person starts with 2 nickels, 2 dimes, 2 quarters, and one $1 bill. Take turns rolling the dice and finding the total number of dots that are faceup.

2. Use the chart to find out how much money to put in the bank. (There is no money in the bank at the beginning of the activity.)

Making Change Chart

Total for Dice Roll	2	3	4	5	6	7	8	9	10	11	12
Amount to Pay the Bank	10¢	15¢	20¢	25¢	30¢	35¢	40¢	45¢	50¢	55¢	60¢

3. Use your coins to pay the amount to the bank. You can get change from the bank.

4. Continue until someone doesn't have enough money left to pay the bank.

Math Journal 1, p. 75

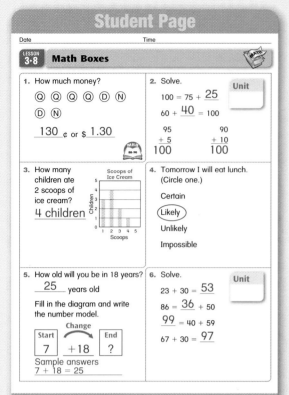

Date _____ Time _____

LESSON 3·8 Math Boxes

1. How much money?

Q Q Q Q D N
D N

___130___ ¢ or $ __1.30__

2. Solve.

$100 = 75 + \underline{25}$

$60 + \underline{40} = 100$

```
  95        90
+  5      + 10
 100       100
```
Unit

3. How many children ate 2 scoops of ice cream?

__4__ children

Scoops of Ice Cream

4. Tomorrow I will eat lunch. (Circle one.)

Certain

(Likely)

Unlikely

Impossible

5. How old will you be in 18 years?

__25__ years old

Fill in the diagram and write the number model.

Start	Change	End
7	+18	?

Sample answers
$7 + 18 = 25$

6. Solve.

$23 + 30 = \underline{53}$

$86 = \underline{36} + 50$

$\underline{99} = 40 + 59$

$67 + 30 = \underline{97}$

Unit

Math Journal 1, p. 78

Name _____ Date _____ Time _____

HOME LINK 3·8 Counting Up to Make Change

Family Note Help your child identify the amount of change that he or she would receive by "counting up" from the price of the item to the amount of money that was used to pay for the item. It may be helpful to act out the problems with your child using real coins and bills.

Please return this Home Link to school tomorrow.

Complete the table.

I buy:	It costs:	I pay with:	My change is:
a bag of potato chips	70¢	Q Q Q	__5__ ¢
a box of crayons	65¢	$1	__35__ ¢
a pen	59¢	Q Q Q	__16__ ¢
an apple	45¢	D D D D D	__5__ ¢
a notebook	73¢	Q Q D D N	__2__ ¢
a ruler	48¢	$1	__52__ ¢
Answers vary.	_____	_____	_____ ¢
Answers vary.	_____	_____	_____ ¢

Practice

1. $12 - 9 = \underline{3}$ 2. $15 - 7 = \underline{8}$ 3. $\begin{array}{r} 13 \\ -6 \\ \hline 7 \end{array}$ 4. $\begin{array}{r} 17 \\ -4 \\ \hline 13 \end{array}$

Math Masters, p. 85

▶ **Math Boxes 3·8**

INDEPENDENT ACTIVITY

(Math Journal 1, p. 78)

 Mixed Practice Math Boxes in this lesson are paired with Math Boxes in Lesson 3-6. The skills in Problems 5 and 6 preview Unit 4 content.

 Writing/Reasoning Have children draw, write, or verbalize their answers to the following: *Find how many children ate scoops of ice cream in Problem 3. Explain how you found the answer.* Sample answer: 10; I added the children for each number of scoops. $3 + 4 + 2 + 1 = 10$

▶ **Home Link 3·8**

INDEPENDENT ACTIVITY

(Math Masters, p. 85)

 Home Connection Children determine the amount of change they would receive when more than the required amount was paid.

---

3 Differentiation Options

 READINESS

SMALL-GROUP ACTIVITY

 5–15 Min

▶ **Counting on the Number Grid with Coins**

(Math Masters, p. 418)

To explore counting by 5s, 10s, and 25s using a visual model, have children count on the number grid. Place coins on the number grid as you count with a group of children. You may wish to start counting at zero and count up by nickels, then by dimes, then by quarters. As the children become more comfortable counting by 5s, 10s, and 25s, start at a number other than zero. As the children progress further, begin to count by quarters, then switch to nickels, then switch to dimes and continue to change the coin combinations.

▶ Calculating the Value of a Name

To apply children's understanding of coin values and coin combinations, have them calculate the value of their names. Begin by having children make a key for the value of each letter—that is, list the letters of the alphabet and record their values according to their order (A = 1¢, B = 2¢, C = 3¢, and so on). Children write their names (either first, or first and last). For each letter in their names, they assign the value according to the key. They find the total value of their names. (They can use a calculator.) They use their tool-kit coins to figure out how to represent the total value of their names with coins. If interest and time permits, they can try to find words worth exactly $1.

▶ Minute Math+

To offer children more experience with money, see the following pages in *Minute Math+*: pp. 22, 35, 67, 69, and 70.

Number Grid

−9	−8	−7	−6	−5	−4	−3	−2	−1	0
1	2	3	4	5	6	7	8	9	10
11	12	13	14	15	16	17	18	19	20
21	22	23	24	25	26	27	28	29	30
31	32	33	34	35	36	37	38	39	40
41	42	43	44	45	46	47	48	49	50
51	52	53	54	55	56	57	58	59	60
61	62	63	64	65	66	67	68	69	70
71	72	73	74	75	76	77	78	79	80
81	82	83	84	85	86	87	88	89	90
91	92	93	94	95	96	97	98	99	100
101	102	103	104	105	106	107	108	109	110

Math Masters, p. 418

3·9 Progress Check 3

Objective To assess children's progress on mathematical content through the end of Unit 3.

---

1 Assessing Progress

materials

Progress Check 3 is a cumulative assessment of concepts and skills taught in Unit 3 and in previous units.

See the Appendix for a complete list of Grade 2 Goals.

- ☐ Home Link 3·8
- ☐ Assessment Masters (*Assessment Handbook*, pp. 163–167)
- ☐ slate
- ☐ base-10 blocks

CONTENT ASSESSED	LESSON(S)	ASSESSMENT ITEMS			
		SELF	ORAL/SLATE	WRITTEN PART A	WRITTEN PART B
Count on by 1s, 2s, 5s, 10s, 25s, and 100s. [Number and Numeration Goal 1]	3·1–3·3, 3·6–3·8	3	2	3	10
Read and write whole numbers to 1,000; identify place values in such numbers. [Number and Numeration Goal 2]	3·1, 3·4, 3·7		1, 3, 4		
Know and apply addition facts through 10 + 10. [Operations and Computation Goal 1]	3·1, 3·3–3·5, 3·7	2		2	7
Use and explain strategies to add and subtract 2-digit numbers; calculate and compare values of coins and bills. [Operations and Computation Goal 2]	3·1–3·8	1		1	8, 9
Demonstrate, describe, and apply change, comparison, and parts-and-total situations. [Operations and Computation Goal 4]	3·1, 3·3, 3·5, 3·7, 3·8			5	
Use graphs to ask and answer questions and draw conclusions. [Data and Chance Goal 2]	3·4–3·6, 3·8	4		4	11
Read temperature to the nearest degree on both the Fahrenheit and Celsius scales. [Measurement and Reference Frames Goal 5]	3·2, 3·4, 3·5, 3·7	6			12
Continue simple numerical patterns; find rules for patterns and use them to solve problems. [Patterns, Functions, and Algebra Goal 1]	3·1, 3·3, 3·5–3·7	5			6

---

2 Building Background for Unit 4

materials

Math Boxes 3·9 previews and practices skills for Unit 4.

The **Unit 4 Family Letter** introduces families to Unit 4 topics and terms.

- ☐ *Math Journal 1,* p. 79
- ☐ Home Link Masters (*Math Masters,* pp. 86–89)

Additional Information

See *Assessment Handbook,* pages 68–75 for additional assessment information. For assessment checklists, see pages 244–247.

Technology

Assessment Management System
Progress Check 3
See the **iTLG.**

Getting Started

1 Assessing Progress

▶ Math Message Follow-Up

INDEPENDENT ACTIVITY

(Self Assessment, *Assessment Handbook*, p. 163)

 The Self Assessment offers children the opportunity to reflect upon their progress.

▶ Oral and Slate Assessments

SMALL-GROUP ACTIVITY

Problems 1 and 2 provide summative information and can be used for grading purposes. Problems 3 and 4 provide formative information that can be useful in planning future instruction.

Oral Assessment

1. Write the following numbers on the board. Have children read the numbers aloud.

   57

   101

   220

2. Count by 5s, 10s, and 25s.

Slate Assessment

3. Display sets of base-10 blocks—flats, longs, and cubes. Include some sets with no longs and/or no cubes. Children write the numbers shown.

4. Say 2- and 3-digit numbers. Children write the digits in the hundreds, tens, and ones places.

Assessment Master

Name ___ Date ___ Time ___

LESSON 3·9 | **Self Assessment** | Progress Check 3

Check one box for each skill.

Skills	I can do this by myself. I can explain how to do this.	I can do this by myself.	I can do this with help.
1. Add coins.			
2. Know addition facts.			
3. Count by 5s.			
4. Read a graph.			
5. Solve Frames and Arrows with 2 rules.			
6. Read the temperature.			

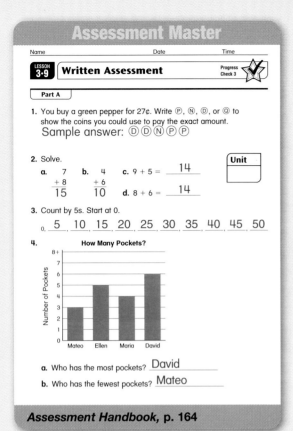

Assessment Master

Name _____ Date _____ Time _____

LESSON 3·9 | Written Assessment | Progress Check 3 ✓

Part A

1. You buy a green pepper for 27¢. Write Ⓟ, Ⓝ, Ⓓ, or Ⓠ to show the coins you could use to pay the exact amount.
   Sample answer: ⒹⒹⓃⓅⓅ

2. Solve.
   a. 7
      + 8
      ‾‾‾‾
      15
   b. 4
      + 6
      ‾‾‾‾
      10
   c. 9 + 5 = __14__
   d. 8 + 6 = __14__

   Unit ☐

3. Count by 5s. Start at 0.
   0, _5_, _10_, _15_, _20_, _25_, _30_, _35_, _40_, _45_, _50_

4. **How Many Pockets?**

   a. Who has the most pockets? __David__
   b. Who has the fewest pockets? __Mateo__

Assessment Handbook, p. 164

▶ **Written Assessment**

(*Assessment Handbook,* pp. 164–166)

INDEPENDENT ACTIVITY

Part A   Recognizing Student Achievement

Problems 1–5 provide summative information and may be used for grading purposes.

Problem(s)	Description
1	Show coins for 27¢.
2	Know addition facts.
3	Count by 5s.
4	Interpret a bar graph.
5	Solve an addition number-story problem.

Part B   Informing Instruction

Problems 6–12 provide formative information that can be useful in planning future instruction.

Problem(s)	Description
6	Solve a Frames-and-Arrows problem with 2 rules.
7	Solve extended addition facts.
8	Add or subtract 2-digit numbers.
9	Make change.
10	Count by 25s.
11	Interpret a bar graph.
12	Read a thermometer.

Assessment Master

Name _____ Date _____ Time _____

LESSON 3·9 | Written Assessment *continued*

5. Jamal has 30 toy cars. Eric has 8 toy cars.
   How many toy cars do Jamal and Eric have in all?

   Answer: __38 toy cars__
              (unit)

Part B

6. Fill in the frames.

   Rule: Subtract 10   65   55   59
   Rule: Add 4   43   53   49

7. Solve.
   a. __70__ = 20 + 50
   b. 30 + __40__ = 70
   c. 60
      + 20
      ‾‾‾‾
      80
   d. 70
      + 50
      ‾‾‾‾
      120

   Unit ☐

8. Solve.
   a. 35
      + 15
      ‾‾‾‾
      50
   b. 54
      − 12
      ‾‾‾‾
      42

   Unit ☐

Assessment Handbook, p. 165

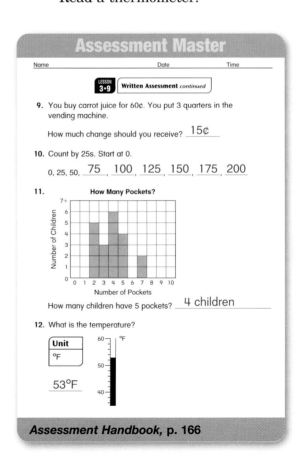

Assessment Master

Name _____ Date _____ Time _____

LESSON 3·9 | Written Assessment *continued*

9. You buy carrot juice for 60¢. You put 3 quarters in the vending machine.

   How much change should you receive? __15¢__

10. Count by 25s. Start at 0.
    0, 25, 50, _75_, _100_, _125_, _150_, _175_, _200_

11. **How Many Pockets?**

    How many children have 5 pockets? __4 children__

12. What is the temperature?

    Unit
    °F

    __53°F__

Assessment Handbook, p. 166

▶ Open Response

(*Assessment Handbook*, pp. 71–75 and 167)

INDEPENDENT ACTIVITY

Vending Machine Problem

The open response item requires children to apply skills and concepts from Unit 3 to solve a multistep problem. See *Assessment Handbook,* pages 71–75 for rubrics and children's work samples for this problem.

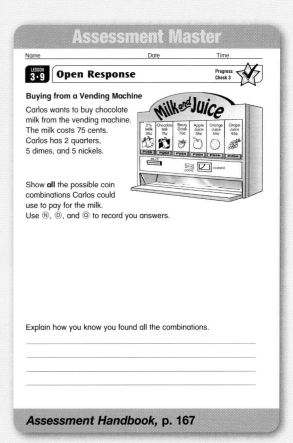

Name ___ Date ___ Time ___

LESSON 3·9 | **Open Response** | Progress Check 3

Buying from a Vending Machine

Carlos wants to buy chocolate milk from the vending machine. The milk costs 75 cents. Carlos has 2 quarters, 5 dimes, and 5 nickels.

Show **all** the possible coin combinations Carlos could use to pay for the milk.
Use Ⓝ, Ⓓ, and Ⓠ to record you answers.

Explain how you know you found all the combinations.

_____
_____
_____

Assessment Handbook, p. 167

---

② Building Background for Unit 4

▶ Math Boxes 3·9

INDEPENDENT ACTIVITY

(*Math Journal 1*, p. 79)

Mixed Practice This Math Boxes page previews Unit 4 content.

▶ Home Link 3·9: Unit 4 Family Letter

INDEPENDENT ACTIVITY

(*Math Masters*, pp. 86–89)

Home Connection The Unit 4 Family Letter provides parents and guardians with information and activities related to Unit 4 topics.

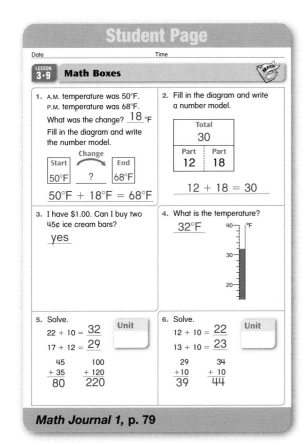

Date ___ Time ___

LESSON 3·9 **Math Boxes**

1. A.M. temperature was 50°F.
P.M. temperature was 68°F.
What was the change? __18__ °F
Fill in the diagram and write the number model.

Change
| Start | | End |
| 50°F | ? | 68°F |

50°F + 18°F = 68°F

2. Fill in the diagram and write a number model.

| Total |
| 30 |
| Part | Part |
| 12 | 18 |

12 + 18 = 30

3. I have $1.00. Can I buy two 45¢ ice cream bars?

yes

4. What is the temperature?

32°F

5. Solve.

22 + 10 = 32 | Unit |
17 + 12 = 29

45   100
+ 35   + 120
80   220

6. Solve.

12 + 10 = 22 | Unit |
13 + 10 = 23

29   34
+10   + 10
39   44

Math Journal 1, p. 79

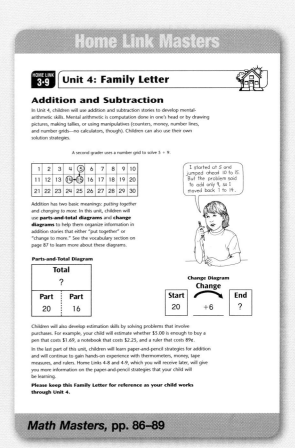

HOME LINK 3·9 **Unit 4: Family Letter**

Addition and Subtraction

In Unit 4, children will use addition and subtraction stories to develop mental-arithmetic skills. Mental arithmetic is computation done in one's head or by drawing pictures, making tallies, or using manipulatives (counters, money, number lines, and number grids—no calculators, though). Children can also use their own solution strategies.

A second grader uses a number grid to solve 5 + 9.

1	2	3	4	⑤	6	7	8	9	10
11	12	13	⑭-⑮	16	17	18	19	20
21	22	23	24	25	26	27	28	29	30

I started at 5 and jumped ahead 10 to 15. But the problem said to add only 9, so I moved back 1 to 14.

Addition has two basic meanings: *putting together* and *changing to more.* In this unit, children will use **parts-and-total diagrams** and **change diagrams** to help them organize information in addition stories that either "put together" or "change to more." See the vocabulary section on page 87 to learn more about these diagrams.

Parts-and-Total Diagram

| Total |
| ? |
| Part | Part |
| 20 | 16 |

Change Diagram
Change
| Start | | End |
| 20 | +6 | ? |

Children will also develop estimation skills by solving problems that involve purchases. For example, your child will estimate whether $5.00 is enough to buy a pen that costs $1.69, a notebook that costs $2.25, and a ruler that costs 89¢.

In the last part of this unit, children will learn paper-and-pencil strategies for addition and will continue to gain hands-on experience with thermometers, money, tape measures, and rulers. Home Links 4-8 and 4-9, which you will receive later, will give you more information on the paper-and-pencil strategies that your child will be learning.

Please keep this Family Letter for reference as your child works through Unit 4.

Math Masters, pp. 86–89

Addition and Subtraction

Overview

In Unit 4, addition and subtraction number stories are used as a vehicle for developing mental arithmetic skills. The unit ends with work on pencil-and-paper strategies. Unit 4 has three main areas of focus:

◆ To solve number stories,

◆ To read and show temperatures, and

◆ To develop different strategies for adding 2- and 3-digit numbers.

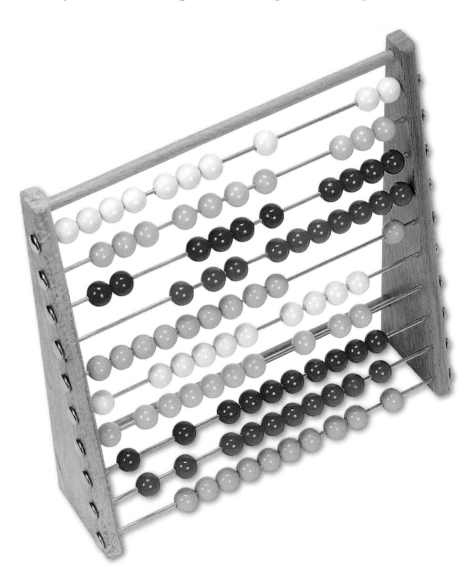

Contents

Unit 4 Organizer

	Lesson Objectives	Links to the Past	Links to the Future
4·1	To guide children as they solve change-to-more number stories.	Children tell and solve number stories in Kindergarten and first grade. In first grade, children are also introduced to change-to-more diagrams.	In Unit 6, children work with three or more addends. In Unit 7, children use counting patterns to help with mental arithmetic. In third grade, they add larger numbers.
4·2	To guide children as they solve parts-and-total number stories.	Children begin telling and solving number stories in Kindergarten. They are also introduced to parts-and-total diagrams in first grade.	In Unit 6, children work with three or more addends. In Unit 7, children use counting patterns to help with mental arithmetic. In third grade, they add larger numbers.
4·3	To guide children as they explore reading temperatures on a thermometer, practice finding the total value of a group of coins, and develop readiness for classifying geometric shapes.	In first grade, children record daily temperatures in both Celsius and Fahrenheit scales, count money, and sort attribute blocks.	Beyond second grade, children use temperature as a context for exploring negative numbers. They continue to develop money concepts and change-making skills.
4·4	To guide children as they read and show temperatures and solve number stories about temperature changes.	In first grade, children record daily temperatures in both Celsius and Fahrenheit scales. They learn ways to subtract smaller numbers.	In third grade, children use temperature as a context for exploring negative numbers. In Unit 6, children begin using strategies for solving 2-digit subtraction. In third grade, they subtract larger numbers using a variety of strategies.
4·5	To guide children as they use estimation to solve problems for which an exact answer is not necessary.	Children begin to work with estimates in first grade, when they estimate the lengths of objects and how many pattern blocks would fill an area.	Estimation and mental arithmetic are found throughout *Everyday Mathematics*. In Unit 10, children do further work with estimating costs.
4·6	To guide children as they develop strategies for adding 2-digit numbers mentally; to provide experiences with calculating the total cost of two items; and to demonstrate making change for whole-dollar amounts up to $100.	Children begin counting by 5s and 10s in Kindergarten. In first grade, children find ways to add smaller numbers.	In Unit 6, children work with three or more addends. In third grade, they add larger numbers. In Unit 7, children use counting patterns to help with mental arithmetic.
4·7	To guide children as they measure lengths and distances to the nearest inch and centimeter, explore area by tiling surfaces, and sort attribute blocks according to rules.	In first grade, children use rulers and tape measures with feet, inches, and centimeters. They are informally exposed to the idea of area. They also sort attribute blocks and play games such as the *Attribute Train Game*.	Throughout Grades 1–3, children measure lengths using standard units. They also collect, organize, and analyze data. They explore and construct 2-dimensional shapes.
4·8	To guide children as they develop paper-and-pencil strategies for adding 2- and 3-digit numbers; and to demonstrate using estimation to check If answers are reasonable.	Children work with estimates in first grade, by estimating the lengths of objects and how many pattern blocks would fill an area. They find ways to add smaller numbers.	Estimation and mental arithmetic are found throughout *Everyday Mathematics*. In Unit 10, they do further work with estimating costs. In third grade, children add larger numbers.
4·9	To introduce and practice the partial-sums addition algorithm.	Children begin counting by 10s in Kindergarten. In first grade, they are introduced to ways of adding smaller numbers. They work with single-digit addition and add multiples of 10s on the number grid.	In Unit 6, children work with three or more addends. In Unit 7, children use counting patterns to help with mental arithmetic. In third grade, they add larger numbers.

Key Concepts and Skills

Key Concepts and Skills	Grade 2 Goals*
4·1 Use basic addition and subtraction facts to compute extended facts.	Operations and Computation Goal 1
Use simple addition facts.	Operations and Computation Goal 1
Create and solve change-to-more number stories.	Operations and Computation Goal 4
Use a parts-and-total diagram.	Operations and Computation Goal 4
4·2 Count up by 5s and 10s to solve money number stories.	Number and Numeration Goal 1
Solve 2-digit by 2-digit addition number stories in the context of money.	Operations and Computation Goal 2
Solve parts-and-total number stories.	Operations and Computation Goal 4
4·3 Calculate and write the value of coin combinations.	Operations and Computation Goal 2
Explore equivalent temperatures between °F and °C.	Measurement and Reference Frames Goal 5
Read and record temperatures.	Measurement and Reference Frames Goal 5
Sort attribute blocks by three different attributes.	Patterns, Functions, and Algebra Goal 1
4·4 Count by 10s and 2s from a multiple of 10.	Number and Numeration Goal 1
Solve temperature-change problems.	Operations and Computation Goal 2
Demonstrate and explain temperature-change stories.	Operations and Computation Goal 4
Compare Fahrenheit and Celsius thermometers. Read and show temperatures on a Fahrenheit thermometer.	Measurement and Reference Frames Goal 5
4·5 Compare money amounts.	Operations and Computation Goal 2
Estimate money amounts to solve problems.	Operations and Computation Goal 3
Share strategies for estimating total money amounts.	Operations and Computation Goal 3
4·6 Identify the place value in two-digit numbers.	Number and Numeration Goal 2
Calculate money amounts.	Operations and Computation Goal 2
Use parts-and-total diagrams to solve multidigit addition problems.	Operations and Computation Goal 4
Write number models for parts-and-total problems.	Patterns, Functions, and Algebra Goal 2
4·7 Distinguish between centimeter and inch.	Measurement and Reference Frames Goal 1
Compare lengths in centimeters and inches.	Measurement and Reference Frames Goal 1
Measure to the nearest inch and centimeter.	Measurement and Reference Frames Goal 1
Find area by tiling with pattern blocks and counting shapes.	Measurement and Reference Frames Goal 2
Use rules to sort attribute blocks.	Patterns, Functions, and Algebra Goal 1
4·8 Share solution strategies for finding the sum of 2-digit numbers mentally.	Operations and Computation Goal 2
Use base-10 blocks to add two 2-digit numbers.	Operations and Computation Goal 2
Practice addition fact extensions.	Operations and Computation Goal 2
Estimate sums by changing the addends to "close but easier" numbers.	Operations and Computation Goal 3
4·9 Identify the value of digits in multidigit numbers.	Number and Numeration Goal 2
Use base-10 blocks and fact extensions to add two 2-digit whole numbers.	Operations and Computation Goal 2
Use ballpark estimates.	Operations and Computation Goal 3
Show understanding of addition and subtraction symbols.	Patterns, Functions, and Algebra Goal 2

* See the Appendix for a complete list of Grade 2 Goals.

Ongoing Learning and Practice

Math Boxes

Math Boxes are paired across lessons as shown in the brackets below. This makes them useful as assessment tools. Math Boxes also preview content of the next unit.

Mixed practice   [4♦1, 4♦3], [4♦2, 4♦4], [4♦5, 4♦7, 4♦9], [4♦6, 4♦8]

Mixed practice with multiple choice   4♦1, 4♦2, 4♦5, 4♦6, 4♦9, 4♦10

Mixed practice with writing/reasoning opportunity   4♦3, 4♦4, 4♦7, 4♦8, 4♦9

Practice through Games

Games are an essential component of practice in the *Everyday Mathematics* program. Games offer skills practice and promote strategic thinking.

Lesson	Game	Skill Practiced
4♦2, 4♦3, 4♦6	*Addition Spin*	Adding multiples of 5; adding 2-digit numbers Number and Numeration Goal 1 Operations and Computation Goal 2 Number and Numeration Goal 2
4♦5	*Name That Number*	Finding equivalent names for whole numbers Operations and Computation Goal 1 Number and Numeration Goal 5
4♦8, 4♦9	*Fact Extension Game*	Practicing fact extensions Operations and Computation Goal 2

See the *Differentiation Handbook* for ways to adapt games to meet children's needs.

Home Communication

Home Links provide homework and home communication.

◀ *Home Connection Handbook* provides more ideas to communicate effectively with parents.

Unit 4 Family Letter provides families with an overview, Do-Anytime Activities, Building Skills Through Games, and a list of vocabulary.

Problem Solving

Encourage children to use a variety of strategies to solve problems and to explain those strategies. Strategies that children might use in this unit:

- Using a diagram
- Using information from a table or picture
- Writing a number model
- Using estimation
- Acting out the problem

Lessons that teach through problem solving, not just about problem solving

Lesson	Activity
4◆1	Solve change-to-more problems involving fish weights.
4◆2	Solve parts-and-total problems about buying items at a snack bar.
4◆4	Solve problems involving temperature change.
4◆5	Estimate to solve money problems.
4◆6	Solve problems involving shopping and making change.
4◆7	Sort attribute blocks to fit a rule.

See Chapter 18 in the *Teacher's Reference Manual* for more information about problem solving.

Planning Tips

Pacing

Pacing depends on a number of factors, such as children's individual needs and how long your school has been using *Everyday Mathematics*. At the beginning of Unit 4, review your *Content by Strand* Poster to help you set a monthly pace.

	← MOST CLASSROOMS →	
OCTOBER	NOVEMBER	DECEMBER

NCTM Standards

Unit 4 Lessons	4◆1	4◆2	4◆3	4◆4	4◆5	4◆6	4◆7	4◆8	4◆9
NCTM Standards	1–2, 6–8	1–2, 4, 6–8	3, 4, 6–10	1–2, 4, 6–10	1, 4, 6–10	1, 4, 6–10	3–4, 6–10	1–2, 6–8	1, 6–8

Content Standards: 1 Number and Operations, **2** Algebra, **3** Geometry, **4** Measurement, **5** Data Analysis and Probability
Process Standards: 6 Problem Solving, **7** Reasoning and Proof, **8** Communication, **9** Connections, **10** Representation

Balanced Assessment

Ongoing Assessment

Recognizing Student Achievement

Opportunities to assess children's progress toward Grade 2 Goals:

Lesson	Content Assessed
4·1	Solve number stories using manipulatives. [Operations and Computation Goal 4]
4·2	Complete parts-and-total diagrams with or without the help of the number grid and/or manipulatives. [Operations and Computation Goal 4]
4·3	Write at least one equivalent name for $1.00. [Number and Numeration Goal 5]
4·4	Read and show temperatures; solve temperature-change problems. [Measurement and Reference Frames Goal 5]
4·5	Estimate. [Operations and Computation Goal 3]
4·6	Tell time to the nearest quarter hour. [Measurement and Reference Frames Goal 6]
4·7	Record at least ten known subtraction facts. [Operations and Computation Goal 1]
4·8	Make ballpark estimates. [Operations and Computation Goal 3]
4·9	Solve addition of multidigit multiples of ten. [Operations and Computation Goal 2]

Use the **Assessment Management System** to collect and analyze data about children's progress throughout the year.

Informing Instruction

To anticipate common child errors and to highlight problem-solving strategies:

Lesson 4·1   Complete change diagrams

Lesson 4·2   Complete parts-and-total diagrams

Lesson 4·3   Read thermometers

Lesson 4·5   Understand the importance of estimating

Lesson 4·6   Add multiples of 10

Periodic Assessment

4◆10 Progress Check 4

CONTENT ASSESSED	ASSESSMENT ITEMS			
	Self	Oral/Slate	Written	Open Response
Read and write whole numbers to 1,000 using standard base-ten place-value notation; identify digits and express their values in such numbers. [Number and Numeration Goal 2]			✔	✔
Recognize numbers as odd or even. [Number and Numeration Goal 6]	✔		✔	
Use and explain strategies for solving problems and number stories involving addition and subtraction of 2-digit whole numbers. Calculate and compare values of coin and bill combinations. [Operations and Computation Goal 2]	✔	✔	✔	✔
Use strategies to estimate solutions (ballpark estimates) for addition and subtraction problems. [Operations and Computation Goal 3]			✔	
Make exchanges between coins and bills. [Measurement and Reference Frames Goal 4]	✔		✔	
Read temperature to the nearest degree in both Fahrenheit and Celsius. [Measurement and Reference Frames Goal 5]	✔	✔	✔	
Continue simple numerical and non-numerical patterns; find rules for patterns and use them to solve problems. [Patterns, Functions, and Algebra Goal 1]	✔		✔	
Compare and order whole numbers. [Number and Numeration Goal 7]				✔

Portfolio Opportunities

Opportunities to gather samples of children's mathematical writings, drawings, and creations to add balance to the assessment process:

- Making coin-stamp booklets, **Lesson 4◆3**
- Counting by 100s, **Lesson 4◆3**
- Finding change, **Lesson 4◆4**
- Recording known subtraction facts, **Lesson 4◆7**
- Recognizing odd and even numbers, **Lesson 4◆7**
- Using a thermometer, **Lesson 4◆8**
- Telling time, **Lesson 4◆9**

Assessment Handbook

Unit 4 Assessment Support

- Grade 2 Goals, pp. 37–50
- Unit 4 Assessment Overview, pp. 76–83

- Unit 4 Open Response
  - Detailed rubric, p. 80
  - Sample student responses, pp. 81–83

Unit 4 Assessment Masters

- Unit 4 Self Assessment, p. 168
- Unit 4 Written Assessment, pp. 169–171
- Unit 4 Open Response, p. 172
- Unit 4 Class Checklist, pp. 250, 251, and 293
- Unit 4 Individual Profile of Progress, pp. 248, 249, and 292

- Exit Slip, p. 295
- Math Logs, pp. 298–300
- Other Student Assessment Forms, pp. 296, 297, and 301–303

Differentiated Instruction

Daily Lesson Support

ENGLISH LANGUAGE LEARNERS

- 4·3 Building a Math Word Bank
- 4·7 Building a Math Word Bank
- 4·8 Building a Math Word Bank

EXTRA PRACTICE

Minute Math®+ 4·6 Calculating costs of pairs of items 4·9 Adding multiples of 10

READINESS

- 4·1 Weighing objects on a scale
- 4·2 Solving parts-and-total problems
- 4·3 Making paper thermometers
- 4·4 Reading thermometers and comparing temperatures
- 4·5 Making coin combinations
- 4·6 Adding multiples of 10
- 4·8 Adding and subtracting 10s
- 4·9 Using base-10 blocks to review place-value concepts

ENRICHMENT

- 4·1 Writing change-to-more stories
- 4·2 Creating parts-and-total number stories
- 4·3 Comparing shapes
- 4·4 Experimenting with temperature changes
- 4·5 Estimating and comparing the sums of weights
- 4·7 Finding more than one way to measure
- 4·8 Solving 2- or 3-digit addition problems
- 4·9 Explaining addition strategies

Adjusting the Activity

- 4·2 Calculating money amounts
- 4·3 Adding the values of coins
- 4·3 Sorting attribute blocks **ELL**
- 4·4 Solving change-to-more/change-to-less problems
- 4·4 Reading a thermometer **ELL**
- 4·5 Estimating costs
- 4·5 Solving problems by estimation

- 4·6 Counting money to calculate cost **ELL**
- 4·6 Solving shopping problems
- 4·6 Using a parts-and-total diagram
- 4·7 Finding objects of given length
- 4·7 Sorting attribute blocks
- 4·8 Making ballpark estimates **ELL**
- 4·8 Solving addition problems **ELL**
- 4·8 Playing the *Fact Extension Game*

AUDITORY ◆ KINESTHETIC ◆ TACTILE ◆ VISUAL

◯ Cross-Curricular Links

Science

Lesson 4·3 Children compare Celsius and Fahrenheit temperatures.

Using the Projects

Use Project 5 to experiment with paper folding, creating snowflakes that represent real 6-sided water crystals. See the *Differentiation Handbook* for modifications to Project 5.

Differentiation
Handbook
cover

◄ *Differentiation Handbook*

See the *Differentiation Handbook* for materials on Unit 4.

Language Support

Everyday Mathematics provides lesson-specific suggestions to help all children, including non-native English speakers, to acquire, process, and express mathematical ideas.

Connecting Math and Literacy

Lesson 4◆3 *26 Letters and 99 Cents,* by Tana Hoban, Greenwillow Books, 1987
Lesson 4◆5 *Betcha!,* by Stuart J. Murphy, Scholastic Inc., 1997
Lesson 4◆6 *Math Man,* by Teri Daniels, Scholastic Inc., 2001
Lesson 4◆7 *A Cloak for the Dreamer,* by Aileen Friedman, Scholastic, 1995
Lesson 4◆7 *Inch by Inch,* by Leo Lionni, Harper Trophy, 1995

My Reference Book
p. 91–93, 116–118, 120, 121, 134, 135, 138, and 139

Multiage Classroom ◆ Companion Lessons

Companion Lessons from Grades 1 and 3 can help you meet instructional needs of a multiage classroom. The full Scope and Sequence can be found in the Appendix.

Unit 4 Vocabulary

algorithm
attribute blocks
ballpark estimate
centimeter (cm)
change diagram
change-to-more number story
degree marks
degrees Celsius (°C)
degrees Fahrenheit (°F)
estimate
inch (in.)
mental arithmetic
parts-and-total diagram
parts-and-total number story
thermometer
tiling

Grade 1	2◆11, 5◆6, 9◆4	1◆13,5◆9	1◆12,7◆2, 10◆6	1◆12,4◆1, 10◆6	8◆4,10◆3, 10◆4	8◆1–8◆5, 10◆3	4◆2–4◆7, 7◆1	2◆11,9◆2, 9◆4	5◆8,9◆2	
Grade 2	4◆1	4◆2	4◆3	4◆4	4◆5	4◆6	4◆7	4◆8	4◆9	4◆10
Grade 3	1◆11, 2◆5, 2◆9	1◆11, 2◆4, 2◆9	6◆4–6◆6, 11◆2		1◆11, 7◆7, 9◆5	1◆11, 7◆7, 9◆5	3◆1–3◆8	2◆7, 2◆9, 5◆5	2◆7, 2◆9, 5◆5	

Professional Development

Teacher's Reference Manual Links

Lesson	Topic	Section	Lesson	Topic	Section
4◆1	Number Stories	18.4.1	4◆7	Length	14.3
	Situation Diagrams	1.3.5		Area	14.4
4◆3	Temperature	15.1		Visual Patterns	17.1.1
	Geometry Tools and Techniques	13.10	4◆8	Addition Algorithms	11.2.1
4◆4	Temperature Scales	15.1.1		Estimates in Calculations	16.1.3
4◆5	Estimation	16.1	4◆9	Alternative and Focus Algorithms	11.1.3
4◆6	Addition and Subtraction Use Classes	10.2.1			
	Mental Calculation Strategies	16.3.1			

Materials

Lesson	Masters	Manipulative Kit Items	Other Items
4∙1	transparency of *Math Masters,* p. 432* Home Link Masters, pp. 90 and 91 Teaching Aid Master, p. 419		two paper towels; pan balance; water; semi-permanent chalk*; penny or other small object; bath scale; objects such as books
4∙2	Home Link 4∙1 transparency of *Math Masters,* p. 433* Home Link Masters, pp. 92 and 93 Game Masters, pp. 447 and 448 Teaching Master, p. 94 Teaching Aid Masters, pp. 419 and 433	per group: calculator	number grid or manipulatives*; semi-permanent chalk*; paper clip; scissors; paper plates; counters, coins
4∙3	Home Link 4∙2 Teaching Masters, pp. 95, 96, and 98 Teaching Aid Master, p. 415 Home Link Master, p. 97 Game Masters, pp. 447 and 448*	thermometer, preferably showing both °F and °C scales; rubber stamps of coins; stamp pad; slate; attribute blocks; calculator; pattern blocks	Class Thermometer Poster; per group: cups of hot tap water and ice water; scissors; stapler; sheets of paper; paper clip; Class Data Pad*
4∙4	Home Link 4∙3 transparency of *Math Masters,* p. 432* and 101 (1 per child) Home Link Masters, pp. 99 and 100 Teaching Masters, pp. 101–103 Teaching Aid Master, p. 419	slate	Class Thermometer Poster; index card or ruler*; glass of cold ice water; outdoor thermometer
4∙5	Home Link 4∙4 transparencies of *Math Masters,* pp. 99 and 100* Home Link Master, p. 104 Game Master, p. 462* Teaching Aid Master, p. 419	per group: 4 each of number cards 0–10 and 1 each of number cards 11–20; tool-kit coins	per group: 1 set of 3" by 5" cards labeled with the name and price of each object on journal page 93
4∙6	Home Link 4∙5 Teaching Aid Master, p. 433 *Math Masters,* p. 105 Home Link Master, p. 106 Game Master, pp. 447 and 448* Teaching Aid Master, p. 433	calculator; nine $1, eight $10 bills, and one $100 bill*; tool-kit money: ten $10 bills and eighteen $1 bills	paper clip
4∙7	Home Link 4∙6 Teaching Masters, pp. 107–109 Home Link Master, p. 110 Teaching Aid Master, p. 415	tape measure; yardstick; pattern blocks; Pattern-Block Template; playing cards or Everything Math Deck; slate; 1 set of attribute blocks; ruler	sheets of paper; scissors; red, yellow, and blue crayons; envelope with Fact Triangles (from Lesson 2∙5)
4∙8	Home Link 4∙7 Home Link Masters, pp. 111 and 112	per group: 1 die; number cards labeled 0–5; 0–9 number cards*; base-10 blocks*; number line	paper; Class Data Pad*; number grid; 1 penny or small object per child; large paper or posterboard
4∙9	Home Link 4∙8 Home Link Master, p. 113 Teaching Masters, pp. 114 and 115 Teaching Aid Master, p. 428	base-10 blocks; slate* number cards labeled 0–5; 0–9 number cards* per group: 1 die	overhead base-10 blocks*; number grid
4∙10 ✔	Home Link 4∙9 Assessment Masters, pp. 168–172 Home Link Masters, pp. 116–119	slate	Class Thermometer Poster

Technology
Assessment Management System, Unit 4
iTLG, Unit 4

* Denotes optional materials

Mathematical Background

The discussion below highlights the major content ideas presented in Unit 4 and helps establish instructional priorities.

Mental Arithmetic (Lesson 4♦1 and following)

The following routine for developing mental arithmetic skills is introduced in Lesson 4-1 with the help of a poster that displays the lengths and weights of fish (*Math Journal 1,* page 80).

Solving Number Stories

1. Children make up problems for the class to solve.

2. With a partner or individually, children devise solution strategies to solve the problems.

3. Children share their strategies. As children discuss these strategies, record them on the board by writing a label in the unit box, drawing the appropriate addition or subtraction diagram (see below), and writing a number model.

Addition has two basic meanings: putting together and changing to more. Change stories are discussed in Lessons 4-1 and 4-4. In Lessons 4-2 and 4-6, the focus is on parts-and-total stories, in which two or more parts are added (put together) to find a total.

Two diagrams are introduced for organizing the information in number stories—the **change diagram** and the **parts-and-total diagram.** Children are not expected to draw the diagrams themselves, but they should be able to fill in the diagrams that are provided in the journal.

In change number stories there is a starting quantity, and this quantity is increased (or decreased) so that the ending quantity is more (or less) than the starting quantity. Lesson 4-1 focuses on change-to-more number stories, and Lesson 4-4 focuses on change-to-less number stories.

Example	**Change-to-more number story**
	Amanda had $40. She earned $20 more mowing lawns. How much money did she have then?

Start	Change	End
40	+20	?

The starting quantity and the change are known, and we need to find the end quantity.

The change diagram in the margin displays the information in this story.

In parts-and-total number stories, two or more quantities (parts) are combined to form a total quantity.

Example	**Parts-and-total number story**
	There are 12 fourth graders and 23 third graders on a bus. How many children in all are on the bus?

The parts are known. The total is to be found.

The parts-and-total diagram in the margin displays the information in this story.

Once the known quantities (and a question mark for the unknown quantity) are put into a diagram, it becomes easy to write a number model and decide which operation is needed to solve the problem.

To practice the addition of multidigit numbers, children can play different versions of *Addition Spin*. These games may be played over and over and customized to your class's level of proficiency.

PROFESSIONAL DEVELOPMENT For additional information on mental arithmetic, see Section 16.3 of the *Teacher's Reference Manual*.

Unit

children

Total	
?	
Part	**Part**
12	23

Real-Life Themes (Lessons 4♦3 and following)

In addition to the work with fish weights, children solve many problems that involve purchases: food in a snack bar, school supplies, and so on.

Science Link Temperature is a major theme of this unit; in this unit the Fahrenheit scale is reviewed and the Celsius scale is introduced. Children read temperatures shown on a thermometer and solve a variety of problems involving temperature changes. You may want to give children some additional background information on thermometers:

- ♦ The invention of the thermometer is usually credited to Galileo Galilei (1564–1642).

- ♦ The German physicist Daniel Gabriel Fahrenheit (1686–1736) invented several accurate thermometers containing mercury and alcohol. He developed the Fahrenheit temperature scale sometime between 1700 and 1730.

- ♦ The Celsius scale was invented in 1742 by Swedish astronomer Anders Celsius (1701–1744). He originally designated the boiling point of water as 0 degrees and the freezing point of water as 100 degrees, but later the scale was reversed. The scale was called *centigrade* until it was officially renamed for Celsius in 1948.

Galileo Galilei

- ♦ Temperature scales are made by choosing a cold point and a hot point and then making an equal number of gradations between them.

- ♦ Pure water freezes at 32 degrees Fahrenheit.

- ♦ Fahrenheit made a mistake when he invented his temperature scale. He wanted 100° to signify the normal human body temperature, but he mistakenly used the body temperature of a cow. A cow's normal body temperature is about 100°F, but a human's normal body temperature is slightly less, about 98.6°F.

PROFESSIONAL DEVELOPMENT Refer to Sction 15.1 of the *Teacher's Reference Manual* for more information on temperature.

Pencil-and-Paper Addition
Strategies (Lessons 4♦8 and 4♦9)

Children are encouraged to develop their own strategies for addition. Their strategies usually are of three major types:

- ◆ counting up
- ◆ combining groups (ones, tens, etc.) separately
- ◆ adjusting and compensating

Examples of these three methods are illustrated in Lesson 4-8. The partial-sums addition algorithm is the topic of Lesson 4-9. The initial demonstration utilizes base-10 blocks, followed by the pencil-and-paper method.

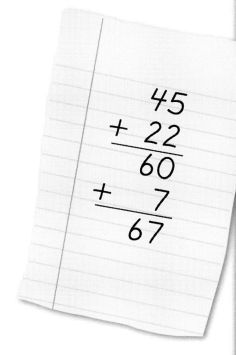

Example: 45 + 22

1. Add the tens. 4 tens + 2 tens = 6 tens, or 60. Write 60 below the line.

2. Add the ones. 5 ones + 2 ones = 7 ones, or 7. Write 7 below 60.

3. Add the partial sums. Draw a second line beneath the 60 and 7. Write 67 beneath this line.

 To find more information about pencil-and-paper addition algorithms, see Section 11.2 of the *Teacher's Refernece Manual.*

Explorations: Temperature, Money, and Shapes (Lesson 4♦3)

In Lesson 4-3, Exploration A provides hands-on experience with thermometers. In Exploration B, children reinforce their knowledge of money by making booklets that show sets of coins and their values. In Exploration C, children sort attribute blocks by shape, color, and size.

 See Sections 15.1 and 14.9 of the *Teacher's Reference Manual* for more information on temperature and money.

Explorations: Length, Area, and Attributes (Lesson 4♦7)

In Lesson 4-7, Explorations D and E provide hands-on measuring experiences using tape measures and different objects to tile. In Exploration F, children sort attribute blocks according to a rule.

 More information about length and area can be found in Sections 14.3 and 14.4 of the *Teacher's Reference Manual.*

4·1 Change-to-More Number Stories

 Objective To guide children as they solve change-to-more number stories.

---

1 Teaching the Lesson

Key Activities
Children are introduced to the change diagram for recording known and missing information in change-to-more number stories. They then solve change-to-more number stories, displaying the information in change diagrams.

Key Concepts and Skills
• Use basic addition and subtraction facts to compute extended facts.
[Operations and Computation Goal 1]
• Use simple addition facts.
[Operations and Computation Goal 1]
• Create and solve change-to-more number stories.
[Operations and Computation Goal 4]
• Use a parts-and-total diagram.
[Operations and Computation Goal 4]

Key Vocabulary
change-to-more number story • change diagram • mental arithmetic

✔ **Ongoing Assessment:** Informing Instruction See page 251.

✔ **Ongoing Assessment:** Recognizing Student Achievement Use journal page 81.
[Operations and Computation Goal 4]

materials
☐ *Math Journal 1*, pp. 80–82
☐ Transparency (*Math Masters,* p. 432; optional)
☐ two paper towels; pan balance; water
☐ semipermanent chalk (optional)

See Advance Preparation

---

2 Ongoing Learning & Practice

Children find distances (number of jumps) between numbers on a number grid.

Children practice and maintain skills through Math Boxes and Home Link activities.

materials
☐ *Math Journal 1*, pp. 83 and 84
☐ Home Link Masters (*Math Masters,* pp. 90 and 91)
☐ penny or other small object

---

3 Differentiation Options

READINESS
Children are introduced to the concept of change-to-more by weighing objects on a scale.

ENRICHMENT
Children write change-to-more stories.

materials
☐ *Math Journal 1*, p. 80
☐ Teaching Aid Master (*Math Masters,* p. 419)
☐ bath scale
☐ objects such as books

Additional Information

Advance Preparation Decide how you will display a change diagram:
▷ Make an overhead transparency of *Math Masters,* page 432.
▷ Draw one on the board with semipermanent chalk.
▷ Draw and erase them on the board as needed.

Technology
Assessment Management System
Journal page 81, Problems 1–3
See the **iTLG.**

Getting Started

Math Message

Which weighs more—a dry paper towel or a wet paper towel? Why? Wet; the water adds weight.

1 Teaching the Lesson

▶ Math Message Follow-Up

WHOLE-CLASS ACTIVITY

The weight of the paper towel increases, or changes to more, when it absorbs liquid. Do the following demonstration with the class. Fold or wad two paper towels of the same size, and place one on each side of a pan balance. The pans will be in balance. Then soak one of the towels in water, wring it out, and put it back in the empty pan. Ask children to explain how they know which towel is heavier. Sample answer: The wet towel is heavier because that pan is lower.

▶ Introducing the Change Diagram

WHOLE-CLASS DISCUSSION

(*Math Journal 1*, p. 80)

In a change number story, there is a starting quantity. This quantity is increased (or decreased) so the ending quantity is more (or less) than the starting quantity. The focus in this lesson is on change-to-more number stories, in which the starting quantity is increased. Change-to-less number stories will be discussed in Lesson 4-4.

Have children turn to the Fish Poster on journal page 80. Make up a **change-to-more number story** based on the Fish Poster. *For example:*

● Fish K weighs 35 pounds. It swallows Fish D, which weighs 5 pounds. How much does Fish K weigh now?

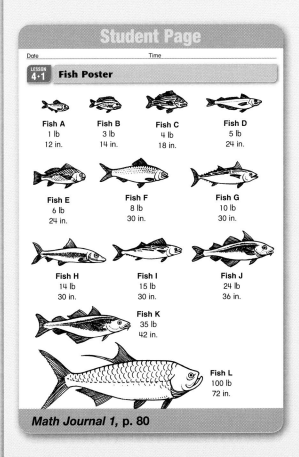

Student Page

Date   Time

LESSON 4·1 Fish Poster

Fish A — 1 lb, 12 in.
Fish B — 3 lb, 14 in.
Fish C — 4 lb, 18 in.
Fish D — 5 lb, 24 in.

Fish E — 6 lb, 24 in.
Fish F — 8 lb, 30 in.
Fish G — 10 lb, 30 in.

Fish H — 14 lb, 30 in.
Fish I — 15 lb, 30 in.
Fish J — 24 lb, 36 in.

Fish K — 35 lb, 42 in.

Fish L — 100 lb, 72 in.

Math Journal 1, p. 80

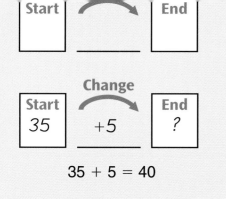

Start | End

Change

Start | End
35 | +5 | ?

$$35 + 5 = 40$$

> **NOTE** Children are not expected to draw change diagrams at this time. Situation diagrams are provided to help children organize information to solve number stories. Some children may find other strategies more helpful than situation diagrams.

> **NOTE** Encourage children to use the number line or number-grid to assist them in finding their solutions.

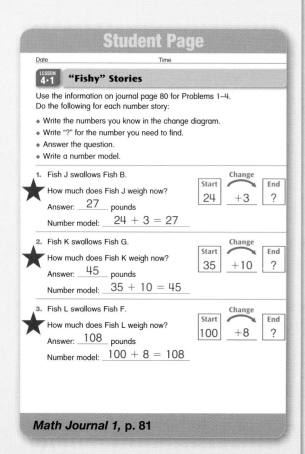

Student Page

Date _____ Time _____

LESSON 4·1 **"Fishy" Stories**

Use the information on journal page 80 for Problems 1–4.
Do the following for each number story:

♦ Write the numbers you know in the change diagram.
♦ Write "?" for the number you need to find.
♦ Answer the question.
♦ Write a number model.

1. Fish J swallows Fish B.
   How much does Fish J weigh now?
   Answer: __27__ pounds
   Number model: __24 + 3 = 27__

   Change
   Start | End
   24 | +3 | ?

2. Fish K swallows Fish G.
   How much does Fish K weigh now?
   Answer: __45__ pounds
   Number model: __35 + 10 = 45__

   Change
   Start | End
   35 | +10 | ?

3. Fish L swallows Fish F.
   How much does Fish L weigh now?
   Answer: __108__ pounds
   Number model: __100 + 8 = 108__

   Change
   Start | End
   100 | +8 | ?

Math Journal 1, p. 81

• Which label goes in the unit box? pounds

• Do we know Fish K's weight before it swallowed Fish D? Yes, 35 pounds

Write 35 in the Start box.

• What change occurred? Fish K gained 5 pounds. Is this a change to more or to less? To more

Write +5 in the Change box. Then write ? in the End box.

• How do we find Fish K's weight after it has swallowed Fish D? Add 35 + 5 What is Fish K's final weight? 40 pounds

• What number model can we write for this number story? 35 + 5 = 40

Together with the children, make up other change-to-more number stories using the Fish Poster. Emphasize stories for which Start and Change are known and End is to be found, but include some stories for which Start or Change is not known and must be found. *For example:*

▷ Fish J swallowed another fish. Fish J now weighs 29 pounds. How much does the fish weigh that Fish J swallowed? 24 + ? = 29; 5 pounds Which fish did Fish J swallow? Fish D

▷ A fish that swallowed Fish A now weighs 36 pounds. How much did the fish weigh before it swallowed Fish A? ? + 1 = 36; 35 pounds

Model children's solutions on the board by doing the following:

Step 1

Fill in a change diagram for each problem. Write in the numbers that are known, and write ? for the number that is to be found.

Step 2

Describe each solution using children's language and procedures as much as possible.

Step 3

Write a number model that summarizes the problem.

▶ Solving Change-to-More Number Stories

(Math Journal 1, pp. 81 and 82)

PARTNER ACTIVITY

Partners complete the problems on journal pages 81 and 82. Check that children are recording the known information in the correct boxes in the change diagram, writing "?" for the unknown number, and writing a number model. Encourage children to use **mental arithmetic** to obtain answers.

Ongoing Assessment: Recognizing Student Achievement

Journal Page 81 Problems 1–3

Use **journal page 81, Problems 1–3** to assess children's ability to solve a number story. Children are making adequate progress if they correctly solve the problems using manipulatives. Some children may be able to solve the problems using other strategies including the diagram.

[Operations and Computation Goal 4]

Ongoing Assessment: Informing Instruction

Watch for children who are having difficulty filling in the change diagram. They may find it helpful to record the weight of each object above its name in the problem. This may make it easier for children to fill in the change diagram.

Bring the class together and have partners share their solution strategies.

NOTE Lesson commentaries often suggest that children share solution strategies, and sometimes possible strategies are described. This does not mean, however, that children must be comfortable with every strategy. Have children share their strategies. Children will benefit from hearing strategies that others have used. Assist children in choosing a strategy that will work best for them. If none of the children mentions using the number grid to explain their strategy, model a problem using this helpful tool.

② Ongoing Learning & Practice

▶ Finding Distances on a Number Grid

INDEPENDENT ACTIVITY

(Math Journal 1, p. 83)

Use the first problem to demonstrate how children should count moves (jumps) in traveling from one number to another. Many children will find that it is easier to find the distance if they use a penny or another small object to act out the jumps from the starting number to the ending number. Encourage children to find the distance between numbers by moving vertically among the rows counting by 10s and moving horizontally counting by 1s.

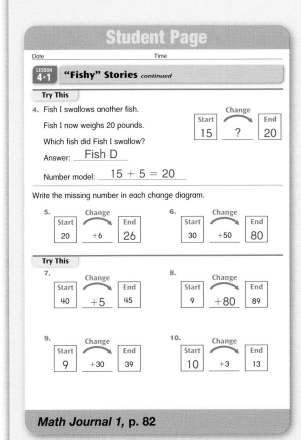

Math Journal 1, p. 82

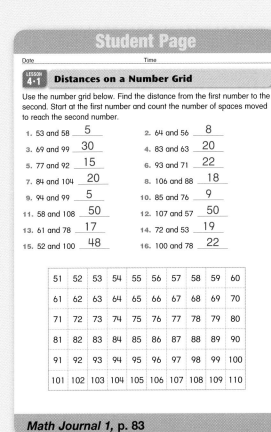

Math Journal 1, p. 83

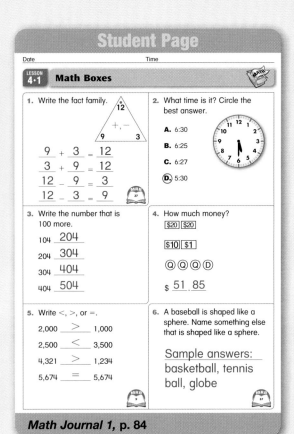

Math Journal 1, p. 84

Math Boxes 4·1

INDEPENDENT ACTIVITY

(*Math Journal 1*, p. 84)

Mixed Practice Math Boxes in this lesson are paired with Math Boxes in Lesson 4-3. The skill in Problem 6 previews Unit 5 content.

Home Link 4·1

INDEPENDENT ACTIVITY

(*Math Masters*, pp. 90 and 91)

Home Connection Children solve change-to-more number stories. They fill in a change diagram and write a number model for each problem. Children also solve problems in which they:

▷ add and subtract multiples of 10.

▷ add a 1-digit number to a multiple of 10.

▷ subtract a 1-digit number from a 2-digit number where the answer is a multiple of 10.

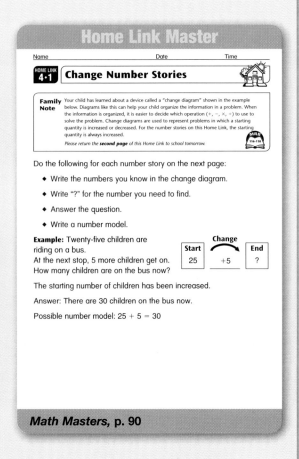

Math Masters, p. 90

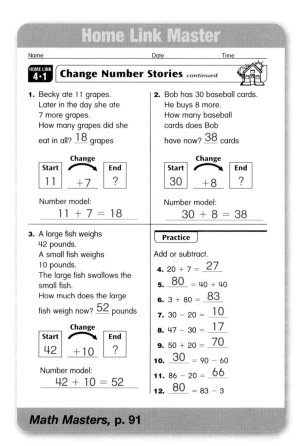

Math Masters, p. 91

③ Differentiation Options

READINESS

▶ Using a Scale to Show More (or Less)

SMALL-GROUP ACTIVITY

🕐 5–15 Min

To provide experience with the concept of change-to-more using a concrete model, have children weigh objects on a scale. Select a few objects (books, for example) and place them on the scale. Observe the weight. Add more objects to the scale. Ask: *What changed?* Sample answers: The number of books or the weight. *How did it change?* Sample answers: There are more books; the weight is greater; it changed to more. To support English language learners, emphasize and record measurement and comparison vocabulary. Select a number of objects to start with and take some away (change to less). Try several demonstrations with different objects. Remind children that as the number of objects increases, the weight changes to more. As the number of objects decreases, the weight changes to less.

ENRICHMENT

▶ Writing Change-to-More Stories

INDEPENDENT ACTIVITY

🕐 5–15 Min

(*Math Journal 1*, p. 80; *Math Masters*, p. 419)

To apply their knowledge of solving change-to-more stories, have children write change-to-more stories using the Fish Poster on journal page 80. Encourage children to write stories that involve a missing number in the Change or Start boxes. *For example:*

▷ Fish J swallows another fish. Fish J now weighs 27 pounds. Which fish did he swallow? Fish B

▷ A fish weighs 13 pounds after eating a fish that weighed 3 pounds. Which fish swallowed the 3-pound fish? Fish G

Children then exchange the problems with a partner and solve them. Finally, children choose one problem and explain how they solved the problem.

4·2 Parts-and-Total Number Stories

 Objective To guide children as they solve parts-and-total number stories.

---

1 Teaching the Lesson

materials

Key Activities
Children are introduced to the parts-and-total diagram for recording known and missing information in number stories that involve combining quantities (parts) to find a total. Children solve parts-and-total number stories, displaying information in parts-and-total diagrams.

Key Concepts and Skills
• Count up by 5s and 10s to solve money number stories. [Number and Numeration Goal 1]
• Solve 2-digit by 2-digit addition number stories in the context of money. [Operations and Computation Goal 2]
• Solve parts-and-total number stories. [Operations and Computation Goal 4]

Key Vocabulary parts-and-total diagram • parts-and-total number story

✔ **Ongoing Assessment: Informing Instruction** See page 256.

✔ **Ongoing Assessment: Recognizing Student Achievement** Use journal page 85. [Operations and Computation Goal 4]

☐ *Math Journal 1*, p. 85
☐ Home Link 4·1
☐ Transparency (*Math Masters,* p. 433; optional)
☐ number grid or manipulatives (optional)
☐ semipermanent chalk (optional)

See Advance Preparation

---

2 Ongoing Learning & Practice

materials

Children practice adding multiples of 5 by playing *Addition Spin.*

Children practice and maintain skills through Math Boxes and Home Link activities.

☐ *Math Journal 1*, p. 86
☐ *My Reference Book,* pp. 120 and 121
☐ Home Link Masters (*Math Masters,* pp. 92 and 93)
☐ Game Masters (*Math Masters,* pp. 447 and 448)
☐ per partnership: calculator and paper clip
☐ scissors

---

3 Differentiation Options

materials

READINESS

Children explore a physical model for solving parts-and-total problems.

ENRICHMENT

Children create parts-and-total number stories that involve a missing part.

☐ *Math Journal 1*, p. 85
☐ Teaching Master (*Math Masters,* p. 94)
☐ Teaching Aid Masters, (*Math Masters*, pp. 419 and 433)
☐ paper plates
☐ counters, coins

See Advance Preparation

Additional Information

Advance Preparation Decide which of the following you will use to display a parts-and-total diagram: Make an overhead transparency of *Math Masters,* page 433; Draw one on the board with semipermanent chalk; or Draw and erase parts-and-total diagrams on the board as needed. For the optional Readiness activity in Part 3 of this lesson, you will need a paper dinner plate divided into three sections labeled with a marker for each child. You may want to choose children's number stories from journal page 21.

Technology

Assessment Management System
Journal page 85, Problem 3
See the **iTLG.**

Getting Started

Mental Math and Reflexes

Children use nickels and dimes to show various amounts. They share their solutions with the class. Instead of actual coins, children can use the symbols Ⓓ and Ⓝ. *For example:*

○○○ 15¢ Ⓓ Ⓝ

　　20¢ Ⓓ Ⓓ, Ⓓ Ⓝ Ⓝ, or Ⓝ Ⓝ Ⓝ Ⓝ

○○○ 40¢ Sample answers: Ⓓ Ⓓ Ⓓ Ⓓ or Ⓓ Ⓓ Ⓓ Ⓝ Ⓝ

　　30¢ Sample answers: Ⓓ Ⓓ Ⓓ or Ⓓ Ⓓ Ⓝ Ⓝ

○○○ 60¢ Sample answers: Ⓓ Ⓓ Ⓓ Ⓓ Ⓓ Ⓓ or Ⓓ Ⓓ Ⓓ Ⓝ Ⓝ Ⓝ Ⓝ Ⓝ

　　65¢ Sample answers: Ⓓ Ⓓ Ⓓ Ⓓ Ⓓ Ⓓ Ⓝ or Ⓝ Ⓝ Ⓝ Ⓝ Ⓝ Ⓝ Ⓝ Ⓓ Ⓓ Ⓓ

Math Message

What is the total number of dots? 17

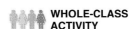

A hot dog costs 45¢. An orange costs 25¢. What is the total cost? 70¢

Home Link 4·1 Follow-Up

Review answers as necessary. Have children share solution strategies.

---

① Teaching the Lesson

▶ Math Message Follow-Up
WHOLE-CLASS ACTIVITY

Draw a unit box with the label dots. Display a **parts-and-total diagram.** (*See* Advance Preparation.) Write 8 and 9 in the two boxes labeled Part. Write 17 in the box labeled Total.

Tell children that the diagram is a convenient way to describe the domino in the Math Message. The boxes labeled Part show the number of dots on each part of the domino; the box labeled Total shows the total number of dots on the domino.

Erase the label in the unit box and the numbers in the parts-and-total diagram. Write the label ¢ in the unit box. Discuss why the diagram is a good one to use for the **parts-and-total number story** in the Math Message about the cost of a hot dog and an orange. The cost of a hot dog is one part of the total cost, and the cost of an orange is the other part. Write 45 and 25 in the two Part boxes. The total cost is unknown; write ? in the Total box.

Ask children to share solution strategies for finding the total cost.

For example:

▷ Count up from the larger addend by using the values of dimes and nickels. 45¢, 55¢, 65¢, 70¢

▷ Think of 45¢ as 4 dimes and 1 nickel. Think of 25¢ as 2 dimes and 1 nickel. Add the dimes, and then add the nickels. Then find the total cost. 4 dimes + 2 dimes = 6 dimes; 1 nickel + 1 nickel = 2 nickels; 6 dimes + 2 nickels = 70¢

▷ Use the number grid. Start at 45. Go down two tens (55, 65) then go to the right 5 to 70.

Unit
dots

Total
17

Part	Part
8	9

A parts-and-total diagram for the domino in the Math Message

Total
?

Part	Part
45	25

A parts-and-total diagram for the hot dog-and-orange problem in the Math Message

NOTE Since children have solved similar problems in Unit 3 by using coins, some may be ready to use more abstract techniques.

Date _____ Time _____

LESSON 4·2 Parts-and-Total Number Stories

Lucy's Snack Bar Menu

Sandwiches		Drinks		Desserts	
Hamburger	65¢	Juice	45¢	Apple	15¢
Hot dog	45¢	Milk	35¢	Orange	25¢
Cheese	40¢	Soft drink	40¢	Banana	10¢
Peanut butter and jelly	35¢	Water	25¢	Cherry pie	40¢

For Problems 1–4, you are buying two items. Use the diagrams to record both the cost of each item and the total cost.

1. a soft drink and a banana

Total
50¢

Part	Part
40¢	10¢

2. a hot dog and an apple

Total
60¢

Part	Part
45¢	15¢

3. a soft drink and a slice of pie

Total
80¢

Part	Part
40¢	40¢

4. a hamburger and juice

Total
$1.10

Part	Part
65¢	45¢

Try This

5. Jean buys milk and an orange. The cost is __60¢__.

Jean gives the cashier 3 quarters.

How much change does she get? __15¢__

Math Journal 1, p. 85

Name _____ Date _____ Time _____

***Addition Spin* Spinners**

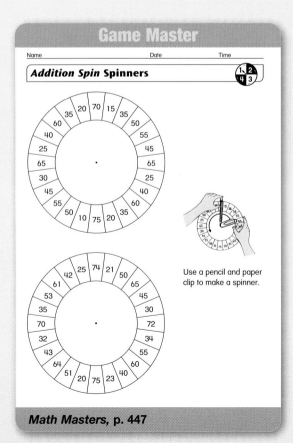

Use a pencil and paper clip to make a spinner.

***Math Masters*, p. 447**

► **Finding the Cost of Two or More Items**

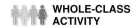 **WHOLE-CLASS ACTIVITY**

(*Math Journal 1*, p. 85)

Working together as a class, make up and solve several number stories like Problem 1 on the journal page. Display and use parts-and-total diagrams.

Working alone or with a partner, children find the costs of the items in Problem 1 on the journal page. Go over the answers and have children share solution strategies. Draw parts-and-total diagrams as children share their solutions. From the discussion, you should be able to determine how much help they will need to complete the rest of the journal page.

✔ Ongoing Assessment: Informing Instruction

Watch for children who are having difficulty finding the total. Use the number grid or base-10 blocks to model adding the two parts.

⬆⬇ Adjusting the Activity

Ask children the following questions:

- What is the total cost of all of the items on the snack bar menu? $4.20 Use a calculator to check the total.
- Josh has $1.00. He buys a hot dog and milk. What can he buy for dessert? An apple or a banana
- Choose a sandwich, a drink, and a dessert for yourself. How much will they cost? Write a number model. Answers vary.

A U D I T O R Y ◆ K I N E S T H E T I C ◆ T A C T I L E ◆ V I S U A L

✔ Ongoing Assessment: Recognizing Student Achievement

Journal Page 85 Problem 3 ★

Use **journal page 85, Problem 3** to assess children's progress toward solving parts-and-total situations. Children are making adequate progress if they correctly find the total using the number grid or manipulatives. Some children may be able to find the total without the use of manipulatives.

[Operations and Computation Goal 4]

NOTE Children are not expected to draw parts-and-total diagrams at this time. These diagrams help children organize the information to solve number stories. Some children may find other strategies more helpful.

---

2 Ongoing Learning & Practice

▶ Playing *Addition Spin*

 PARTNER ACTIVITY

(*Math Masters*, pp. 447 and 448; *My Reference Book*, pp. 120 and 121)

Explain the rules of *Addition Spin* on *My Reference Book*, page 120.

Play a demonstration game using the top spinner on *Math Masters*, page 447. Then divide the class into partners and have the children play.

To extend the game, players spin 3 times and add 3 numbers for each turn.

NOTE *Addition Spin* can be played throughout the year, using a variety of numbers and operations. The game, which is played by using the top spinner on *Math Masters*, page 447, focuses on addition of numbers that are multiples of 5. Blank *Addition Spin* mats have been provided on *Math Masters*, page 448 so you can customize the game for your class as the year progresses.

▶ Math Boxes 4·2

INDEPENDENT ACTIVITY

(*Math Journal 1*, p. 86)

 Mixed Practice Math Boxes in this lesson are paired with Math Boxes in Lesson 4-4. The skill in Problem 6 previews Unit 5 content.

Games

Addition Spin

Materials	❏ 1 *Addition Spin* spinner
	❏ 1 paper clip
	❏ 1 pencil
	❏ 1 calculator
	❏ 2 sheets of paper

Players 2

Skill Mental addition

Object of the game To have the larger total.

Directions

1. Players take turns being the "Spinner" and the "Checker."

2. The Spinner uses a pencil and a paper clip to make a spinner.

3. The Spinner spins the paper clip.

4. The Spinner writes the number that the paper clip points to. If the paper clip points to more than one number, the Spinner writes the smaller number.

My Reference Book, p. 120

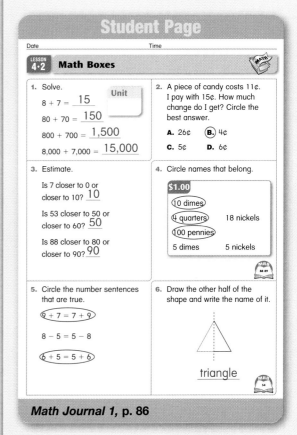

Student Page

Date _____ Time _____

LESSON 4·2 Math Boxes

1. Solve.

   8 + 7 = __15__ **Unit**

   80 + 70 = __150__

   800 + 700 = __1,500__

   8,000 + 7,000 = __15,000__

2. A piece of candy costs 11¢. I pay with 15¢. How much change do I get? Circle the best answer.

   A. 26¢ **B.** 4¢
   C. 5¢   D. 6¢

3. Estimate.

   Is 7 closer to 0 or closer to 10? __10__

   Is 53 closer to 50 or closer to 60? __50__

   Is 88 closer to 80 or closer to 90? __90__

4. Circle names that belong.

   $1.00

   (10 dimes)   18 nickels
   (4 quarters)
   (100 pennies)
   5 dimes   5 nickels

5. Circle the number sentences that are true.

   (9 + 7 = 7 + 9)

   8 − 5 = 5 − 8

   (6 + 5 = 5 + 6)

6. Draw the other half of the shape and write the name of it.

   triangle

Math Journal 1, p. 86

Name _____ Date _____ Time _____

HOME LINK 4·2 **Parts-and-Total Number Stories**

Family Note Today your child learned about another device to use when solving number stories. We call it a parts-and-total diagram. Parts-and-total diagrams are used to organize the information in problems in which two or more quantities (parts) are combined to form a total quantity.

*Please return the **second page** of this Home Link to school tomorrow.*

Large Suitcase	Small Suitcase	Backpack	Package
45 pounds	30 pounds	17 pounds	15 pounds

Use the weights shown in these pictures. Then do the following for each number story on the next page:

- ◆ Write the numbers you know in each parts-and-total diagram.
- ◆ Write "?" for the number you want to find.
- ◆ Answer the question.
- ◆ Write a number model.

Example: Twelve fourth graders and 23 third graders are on a bus. How many children in all are on the bus?

The parts are known. The total is to be found.

Answer: 35 children

Possible number model: 12 + 23 = 35

Total	
?	
Part	**Part**
12	23

Math Masters, p. 92

▶ **Home Link 4·2**

(*Math Masters*, pp. 92 and 93)

Home Connection Children solve parts-and-total number stories. They fill in a parts-and-total diagram and write a number model for each problem.

③ Differentiation Options

READINESS   **SMALL-GROUP ACTIVITY**

▶ **Solving Parts-and-Total Problems**   🕐 15–30 Min

(*Math Masters*, p. 94)

To explore solving parts-and-total problems using a physical model, have children act out number stories on a plate divided into three sections. For each number story, children put counters in each of the Part sections of the plate, then move the parts into the Total section to solve the problem. For example, say: *Mark had 3 new crayons and 4 old crayons. How many crayons did he have?* Children first put three counters in one of the Part sections and four counters in the other Part section. To solve the problem, they move all the counters to the Total section of the plate. Tell simple number stories for children to act out. Including stories with coin combinations will help prepare them for the content of this lesson. For example, say: *Luis had 24 cents and Javanda had 18 cents. How much money did they have when they put their money together?*

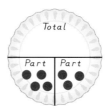   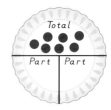

Name _____ Date _____ Time _____

HOME LINK 4·2 **Number Stories** *continued*

1. You wear the backpack and carry the small suitcase. How many pounds do you carry in all? **47** pounds

Total	
?	
Part	**Part**
17	30

Number model: 17 + 30 = 47

2. You carry the large suitcase and the small suitcase. How many pounds do you carry in all? **75** pounds

Total	
?	
Part	**Part**
45	30

Number model: 45 + 30 = 75

3. You carry the package and the large suitcase. How many pounds do you carry in all? **60** pounds

Total	
?	
Part	**Part**
15	45

Number model: 15 + 45 = 60

Try This

4. You wear the backpack and carry both of the suitcases. How many pounds do you carry in all? **92** pounds

Total		
?		
Part	**Part**	**Part**
17	45	30

Number model: 17 + 45 + 30 = 92

Math Masters, p. 93

▶ **Creating Missing-Part Number Stories**

PARTNER ACTIVITY

🕐 5–15 Min

(*Math Masters,* pp. 419 and 433; *Math Journal 1,* p. 85)

To apply children's understanding of parts-and-total number stories, have them create a problem that involves a missing part on a blank parts-and-total diagram.

Children use a blank parts-and-total diagram and Lucy's Snack Bar Menu (*Math Journal 1,* page 85) to create a number story that involves a missing part. *For example:*

▷ Yoshi spent $1.05 at the Snack Bar. He bought a hamburger. What else could he have bought? A soft drink, a cherry pie, or a cheese sandwich

Partners exchange number stories to find other possible menu selections.

Some children may be ready to work with three or more parts. *For example:*

▷ Kristen spent $1.00 at the Snack Bar. She bought a peanut butter and jelly sandwich. What two other items could Kristen have bought? Sample answers: Water and a cherry pie; a soft drink and an orange

---

Planning Ahead

At the end of the lesson, collect unused copies of:

▷ *Math Masters,* page 433 to use in Lesson 4-6.

▷ *Math Masters,* pages 447 and 448 to use in Lesson 4-3 and later lessons.

Before beginning Lesson 4-3, assemble the Class Thermometer Poster (°F/°C) so the thermometer is full length.

As you did for the Class Thermometer Poster (°F) used in Lesson 1-12, cut a long strip of red ribbon or crepe paper to represent the "mercury" in the thermometer tube. (The liquid is often called mercury, but may be something else.) Cut a slit in the thermometer bulb and pull the ribbon or crepe paper through the slit. Tape it at the top to hold it in place. Place a container beneath the poster to hold the excess ribbon or crepe paper.

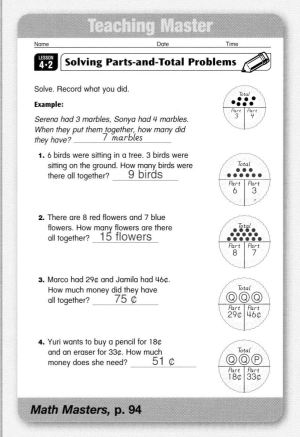

Math Masters, p. 94

Math Masters, p. 433

4·3 EXPLORATIONS

Exploring Temperature, Money, and Shapes

 Objective To guide children as they explore reading temperatures on a thermometer, practice finding the total value of a group of coins, and develop readiness for classifying geometric shapes.

1 Teaching the Lesson

materials

Key Activities

Children are introduced to the Celsius scale and learn how to find equivalent temperatures.

Exploration A: Children use a thermometer to measure temperatures and choose the more sensible temperature for a given situation.

Exploration B: Children make coin booklets showing groups of coins and the total value.

Exploration C: Children develop readiness for classifying geometric shapes by sorting attribute blocks.

Key Concepts and Skills

- Calculate and write the value of coin combinations. [Operations and Computation Goal 2]
- Explore equivalent temperatures between °F and °C. [Measurement and Reference Frames Goal 5]
- Read and record temperatures. [Measurement and Reference Frames Goal 5]
- Sort attribute blocks by three different attributes. [Patterns, Functions, and Algebra Goal 1]

Key Vocabulary

degrees Fahrenheit (°F) • degrees Celsius (°C) • thermometer • degree marks

✓ **Ongoing Assessment: Informing Instruction** See page 262.

✓ **Ongoing Assessment: Recognizing Student Achievement** Use an Exit Slip. [Number and Numeration Goal 5]

☐ Home Link 4·2

Exploration A:

☐ *Math Journal 1*, p. 87
☐ Class Thermometer Poster (°F/°C)
☐ per group of 3 or 4 children: cups of hot tap water and ice water
☐ thermometer, preferably showing both °F and °C scales

Exploration B: Per partnership:

☐ Teaching Master (*Math Masters*, p. 95)
☐ Teaching Aid Master (*Math Masters*, p. 415)
☐ rubber stamps of coins; stamp pad
☐ scissors; stapler; slate; paper

Exploration C: Per group:

☐ Teaching Master (*Math Masters*, p. 96)
☐ set of attribute blocks; sheets of paper

See **Advance Preparation**

2 Ongoing Learning & Practice

materials

Children practice adding 2-digit numbers by playing *Addition Spin*.

Children practice and maintain skills through Math Boxes and Home Link activities.

☐ *Math Journal 1*, p. 88
☐ Home Link Master (*Math Masters*, p. 97)

Per partnership:

☐ Game Masters (*Math Masters*,

pp. 447 and 448; optional)
☐ paper clip, calculator
☐ scissors (optional)

3 Differentiation Options

materials

READINESS

Children practice reading and setting temperatures.

ENRICHMENT

Children compare and contrast the attributes of two shapes.

ELL SUPPORT

Children enter *degree* in their Math Word Bank.

☐ Teaching Master (*Math Masters*, p. 98)
☐ *Differentiation Handbook*
☐ scissors, pattern blocks
☐ Class Data Pad (optional)

Additional Information

Advance Preparation Spend most of your time with children working on Exploration A.

Technology

Assessment Management System
Exit Slip
See the **iTLG**.

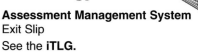

Getting Started

Math Message

Why are there two sets of marks and numbers on our Class Thermometer Poster? Two different temperature scales: one for Celsius, one for Fahrenheit

Home Link 4·2 Follow-Up

Review answers as necessary. Choose one problem and have children share their solution strategies.

---

1 Teaching the Lesson

► Math Message Follow-Up

WHOLE-CLASS DISCUSSION

Point out that there are two different scales that are most often used to measure temperature. To support English language learners, discuss the various meanings of *scale* and its meaning in this context. Temperatures in weather reports in the United States are usually given in **degrees Fahrenheit (°F).** Temperatures used in science are almost always given in **degrees Celsius (°C).** Celsius temperature readings are also becoming more common in everyday life in the United States.

► Translating between Fahrenheit and Celsius Temperatures

WHOLE-CLASS DISCUSSION

Science Link Begin with the benchmark temperatures indicated on the Class Thermometer Poster (°F/°C). For example, set the "mercury" in the **thermometer** at the room temperature line. What is room temperature on the Fahrenheit side of the thermometer? 70 degrees On the Celsius side? About 20 degrees Point out that there are **degree marks** on each scale at every degree. Extend questions to other temperatures.

For example:

▷ Set the mercury at 90°F. Ask what the equivalent temperature is on the Celsius scale. About 32°C

▷ Set the mercury at 10°C side. Ask what the equivalent temperature is on the Fahrenheit side. 50°F

Date _____ Time _____

LESSON 4·3   Temperatures

Fahrenheit Thermometer °F
Celsius Thermometer °C

Water boils. 212°F, 100°C

Normal body temperature 98.6°F, 37°C

Room temperature 70°F, 21°C

Water freezes. 32°F, 0°C

1. Use a thermometer to measure and record the temperatures of the following:

   a. your classroom   70 °F   21 °C

   b. hot water from a faucet   130 °F   55 °C

   c. ice water   43 °F   6 °C

   Sample answers

2. Which temperature makes more sense? Circle it.

   a. temperature in a classroom:

   40°F or (70°F)

   b. temperature of hot tea:

   100°F or (180°F)

   c. temperature of a person with a fever:

   (100°F) or 100°C

   d. temperature on a good day for ice-skating outside:

   (−10°C) or 10°C

Math Journal 1, p. 87

Links to the Future

Thermometer activities are a beginning exposure to signed numbers (negative numbers). Solving problems involving the addition and subtraction of signed numbers is a Grade 5 Goal.

▶ Exploration A: Measuring Temperatures

(*Math Journal 1*, p. 87)

If the thermometer you are using has only a single scale (°F or °C), tell children to find and record this reading. They can then use the Class Thermometer Poster (°F/°C) or the thermometer pictures on the journal page to translate any temperature to the other scale.

When children take temperature readings of hot water or ice water, they should leave the thermometer in the water for about 30 seconds, remove it, and read the temperature promptly.

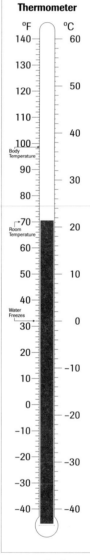

Thermometer

The Class Thermometer Poster (°F/°C) displaying room temperature

---

✓ Ongoing Assessment: Informing Instruction

Watch for children who have trouble reading the actual thermometer because it is much smaller than the thermometer pictured on the poster. Lesson 4-4 will focus on developing skills for reading a thermometer. For now, work closely with children to help them interpret their thermometer readings.

► Exploration B: Making Coin-Stamp Booklets

(*Math Masters,* p. 95)

Portfolio Ideas

Partners follow instructions on the master page to make a booklet showing different groups of coins and their values.

1. First, each partner folds a sheet of paper into fourths and cuts along the fold lines. They set aside two quarter sheets to use as covers.

2. Next, each partner uses the coin stamps to stamp a group of coins on one side of each quarter sheet.

3. Each partner writes the total value of the group of coins on the other side of the sheet using dollars-and-cents notation ($0.00).

4. Partners check each other's work.

5. When all the amounts are correct, partners stack the pages with the coins facing up, add the blank sheets as covers, and staple the pages together to make a booklet.

6. Partners write their names on the cover of their booklets.

Partners use the new booklets to practice determining the value of a group of coins. One partner counts the coin values and writes the total on a slate; the other partner checks the answer. Partners take turns with each role.

PARTNER ACTIVITY

⬆ Adjusting the Activity

Have children find the total value of all the coins stamped in a booklet. Have partners check each other's answers.

AUDITORY ◆ KINESTHETIC ◆ TACTILE ◆ VISUAL

✔ Ongoing Assessment: Recognizing Student Achievement

Exit Slip

Use an **Exit Slip** (*Math Masters,* page 415) to assess children's ability to write equivalent names for $1.00. Children are making adequate progress if they can successfully write one equivalent name for $1.00. Some children may be able to show $1.00 in multiple ways.

[Number and Numeration Goal 5]

Teaching Master

Name _____ Date _____ Time _____

LESSON 4·3 Coin-Stamp Booklets

Work with a partner.

Materials ☐ coin stamps ☐ stamp pad ☐ stapler
☐ scissors ☐ sheets of plain paper ☐ slates

1. Each partner folds a sheet of paper into 4 parts.

2. Cut the sheet along the folds.

3. Put aside 2 pieces of paper. Use them later for a book cover.

4. Stamp a group of coins on one side of each of the other six pieces of paper.

5. Write the total value of the coins on the other side of the paper. Use a dollar sign and a decimal point: $0.00. Check your partner's work.

6. Stack the pieces. Put the sides with the coins faceup.
   ◆ Put 1 blank piece of paper on top of the stack.
   ◆ Put the other blank piece at the bottom.
   ◆ Staple the pieces together to make a small book.
   ◆ Write your names on the cover of the book.

Follow-Up

◆ Take turns. One partner counts the value of the coins on a page and writes the total value on a slate. The other partner checks that the value is correct.

◆ Work together. Make up a story about the coins on a page and write it on a piece of paper.

Math Masters, **p. 95**

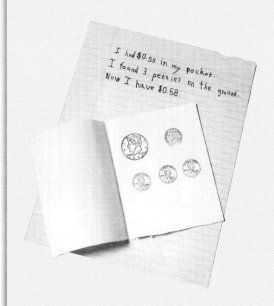

▶ **Exploration C: Sorting Attribute Blocks**

 **SMALL-GROUP ACTIVITY**

(*Math Masters,* p. 96)

Group members work together to sort the set of attribute blocks in three different ways: by color, by size, and by shape.

For each sort, they separate the blocks according to attributes, trace the blocks onto paper to make a record, and label the sort.

> **Adjusting the Activity**   **ELL**
>
> Prepare sorting sheets for children. For the color sort, for example, provide children with sheets of paper that have the color-coded labels Red, Blue, and Yellow. You can model the process by tracing and coloring one or two blocks that fit the rule on each sheet. For example, on the Red sheet, trace and color a small red triangle and a large red circle.
>
> **A U D I T O R Y   ♦   K I N E S T H E T I C   ♦   T A C T I L E   ♦   V I S U A L**

(2) Ongoing Learning & Practice

▶ **Playing *Addition Spin***

 PARTNER ACTIVITY

(*Math Masters,* pp. 447 and 448)

This game was introduced in Lesson 4-2. In that lesson, children used the top spinner on *Math Masters,* page 447, which is numbered with multiples of 5. Children could use the bottom spinner on this page to give them practice adding other 2-digit numbers. If you prefer, create your own spinner by using a blank spinner on *Math Masters,* page 448.

▶ **Math Boxes 4·3**

 INDEPENDENT ACTIVITY

(*Math Journal 1,* p. 88)

 Mixed Practice Math Boxes in this lesson are paired with Math Boxes in Lesson 4-1. The skill in Problem 6 previews Unit 5 content.

Writing/Reasoning Have children draw, write, or verbalize their answers to the following: *In Problem 3, continue counting by 100s for 5 more spaces. What pattern do you see?* Sample answer: 725, 825, 925, 1,025, 1,125; every number ends in 25; the numbers count up by ones in the 100s and 1,000s places.

▶ Home Link 4·3

(*Math Masters*, p. 97)

INDEPENDENT ACTIVITY

Home Connection Children practice reading thermometers to identify which of two thermometers shows a specific temperature.

③ Differentiation Options

▶ Reading and Setting Temperatures

(*Math Masters*, p. 98)

PARTNER ACTIVITY

15–30 Min

To provide experience with reading a thermometer using a concrete model, have children assemble their own paper thermometers and practice reading various temperatures.

Partners help each other set the indicator strips on their thermometers to temperatures you list on the board or Class Data Pad. Begin with multiples of 10. Have children fold their paper thermometers for storage in their tool kits.

ENRICHMENT

▶ Finding Pattern-Block Attributes

INDEPENDENT ACTIVITY

5–15 Min

To further explore sorting attribute blocks, have children identify and describe attributes of pattern blocks. Children select two pattern blocks. Make two columns on a piece of paper. Label one Same and one Different. Children can compare and contrast the attributes of the two shapes in writing. For example, children may talk about the color or the number of sides or angles. Children may select two other shapes and repeat the activity.

ELL SUPPORT

▶ Building a Math Word Bank

(*Differentiation Handbook*)

SMALL-GROUP ACTIVITY

5–15 Min

To provide language support for weather concepts, use the Word Bank Template in the *Differentiation Handbook*. Ask children to write the terms *temperature, thermometer,* and *degrees*. Children describe the term with words, pictures, and real-life examples. See the *Differentiation Handbook* for more information.

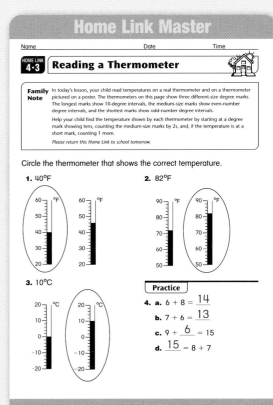

Reading a Thermometer

Family Note In today's lesson, your child read temperatures on a real thermometer and on a thermometer pictured on a poster. The thermometers on this page show three different-size degree marks. The longest marks show 10-degree intervals, the medium-size marks show even-number degree intervals, and the shortest marks show odd-number degree intervals.

Help your child find the temperature shown by each thermometer by starting at a degree mark showing tens, counting the medium-size marks by 2s, and, if the temperature is at a short mark, counting 1 more.

Please return this Home Link to school tomorrow.

Circle the thermometer that shows the correct temperature.

1. 40°F   2. 82°F

3. 10°C

Practice

4. a. $6 + 8 = \underline{14}$
   b. $7 + 6 = \underline{13}$
   c. $9 + \underline{6} = 15$
   d. $\underline{15} = 8 + 7$

***Math Masters*, p. 97**

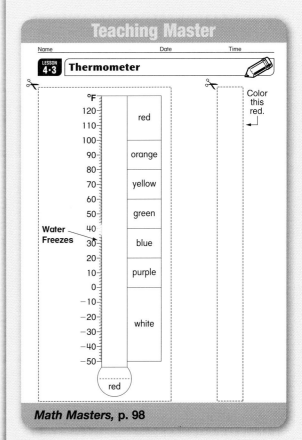

Thermometer

***Math Masters*, p. 98**

4·4 Temperature Changes

 Objective To guide children as they read and show temperatures and solve number stories about temperature changes.

---

1 Teaching the Lesson

materials

Key Activities
Children review thermometers and compare Fahrenheit and Celsius scales. Children solve temperature-change problems, including change-to-less, using change diagrams.

Key Concepts and Skills
- Count by 10s and 2s from a multiple of 10.
  [Number and Numeration Goal 1]
- Solve temperature-change problems.
  [Operations and Computation Goal 2]
- Demonstrate and explain temperature-change stories.
  [Operations and Computation Goal 4]
- Compare Fahrenheit and Celsius thermometers. Read and show temperatures on a Fahrenheit thermometer.
  [Measurement and Reference Frames Goal 5]

✔ **Ongoing Assessment: Recognizing Student Achievement** Use journal page 90.
  [Measurement and Reference Frames Goal 5]

□ *Math Journal 1*, pp. 87, 90, and 91
□ *My Reference Book,* pp. 116–118
□ Home Link 4·3
□ Transparency (*Math Masters,* p. 432; optional)
□ Class Thermometer Poster (°F/°C)
□ index card or ruler (optional)
□ slate

***See* Advance Preparation**

---

2 Ongoing Learning & Practice

materials

Children solve and make up parts-and-total number stories.

Children practice and maintain skills through Math Boxes and Home Link activities.

□ *Math Journal 1*, pp. 89 and 92
□ Home Link Masters (*Math Masters,* pp. 99 and 100)

---

3 Differentiation Options

materials

READINESS
Children compare temperatures visually using thermometers.

ENRICHMENT
Children experiment with temperature changes and write change number stories.

□ Teaching Masters (*Math Masters,* pp. 101 and 102) (1 per child)
□ Teaching Master (*Math Masters,* p. 103) (1 per 2 children)
□ Teaching Aid Master (*Math Masters,* p. 419)
□ Transparency (*Math Masters,* p. 101)
□ Class Thermometer Poster (°F/°C), ice water, outdoor thermometer

---

Additional Information

Advance Preparation Decide how you will display change diagrams. For the optional Readiness activity in Part 3 of this lesson, each child will need a transparency and a paper copy of *Math Masters,* page 101. Make several copies of *Math Masters,* page 102 and cut apart the different length bars. For the Enrichment, 1 glass of ice water is needed.

Technology
Assessment Management System
Journal page 90
See the **iTLG.**

Getting Started

Mental Math and Reflexes

Children practice counting by 10s and 2s from a multiple of 10. Counting by 2s is a useful skill for reading temperatures on a thermometer with a scale having 2-degree intervals.

The class counts orally in unison:

- ○○○ by 10s from 0 to 100.
- ○○○ by 2s from 60 to 70.
- ○○○ by 2s from 20 back to 10.
- ○○○ by 2s from 0 to 20.
- ○○○ by 10s from 100 back to 0.
- ○○○ by 2s from 60 back to 50.

Math Message

At what temperature does water freeze (turn to ice)? 32°F or 0°C

Home Link 4·3 Follow-Up

Ask volunteers to explain how they determined which thermometer showed the correct temperature. Children tell the temperature that is shown on the thermometer that was not circled.

1 Teaching the Lesson

▶ Math Message Follow-Up

WHOLE-CLASS DISCUSSION

(*Math Journal 1*, p. 87)

Ask the class to look at the Class Thermometer Poster (°F/°C) and the thermometers on journal page 87. Point out that a thermometer shows how hot or cold something is (relative to the number scale on that thermometer). Cover the following points:

▷ The narrow glass tube on a thermometer contains a liquid that expands when the temperature gets warmer. This causes the liquid to rise in the tube. The warmer the temperature is, the higher the liquid rises.

▷ In the United States, everyday temperatures, such as those in weather reports and recipes, are usually given in degrees Fahrenheit (°F). In science, temperatures are almost always given in degrees Celsius (°C). Celsius temperature readings are also becoming common in everyday life. Ask children to identify zones on the thermometer that might correspond to *hot, cold, warm,* and *cool*. You may want to place a picture next to each zone (for example, children building a snowman or swimming in a lake).

Compare the Fahrenheit and Celsius thermometers.

▷ Each multiple of 10 degrees is written as a number.

▷ Between the multiples of 10 degrees, the longer degree marks are spaced at 2-degree intervals; for example, at 72, 74, 76, and 78 degrees.

Ask:

- On which thermometer are the distances between degree marks greater? Celsius
- At what Fahrenheit temperature does water freeze? 32°F
- At what Celsius temperature does water freeze? 0°C

(Cooler)?" Problems

(*Math Masters,* p. 432; *My Reference Book,* pp. 116–118)

You may wish to review change diagrams by reading *My Reference Book,* pages 116–118 with your class. Page 118 provides an example using temperatures in which the change is unknown. Display a change diagram (*Math Masters,* p. 432) and draw a unit box labeled degrees Fahrenheit (°F).

Using temperatures that are multiples of 5 or 10, pose several temperature-change problems like those below. Have children write the answers on their slates.

Adjusting the Activity

Have children count by 5s or 10s with their fingers to keep track of the change to more or change to less. An alternate method is to have children use a number grid to find the distance between the two numbers or to count up or back.

AUDITORY ◆ KINESTHETIC ◆ TACTILE ◆ VISUAL

● It was 50°F at 9 o'clock in the morning and 70°F at noon. Did it get warmer or cooler? warmer

● By how many degrees? 20°F

Have children share their solution strategies while you write the information in the change diagram you displayed. Write:

1. 50 in the Start box.

2. 70 in the End box.

3. ? on the Change line.

Model the change on the number grid.

Most children should be able to identify the change as 20 degrees. Be sure that they also identify the change as change to more. For example, children might say "The temperature goes up" or "It gets warmer." Write +20 on the Change line.

● It was 40°F at 6 o'clock. By 10 o'clock, the temperature had gone down 30 degrees. What was the temperature at 10 o'clock? 10°F

Fill in the change diagram by writing:

1. 40 in the Start box.

2. −30 in the Change box.

3. ? in the End box.

Model the change on the number grid.

Remind children that the minus sign in −30 indicates a change to less: The temperature goes down, and it gets colder. When children conclude that the final temperature is 10 degrees, write 10 in the End box.

Expand the range of temperatures to include two 2-digit numbers whose difference is a multiple of 10. *For example:*

● If the temperature is 72°F and then goes down 20 degrees, what is the new temperature? 52°F

Student Page

Number Stories

Sometimes you need to find the change in a change story. You can use a change diagram to help you solve this kind of number story.

● The morning temperature was 50°F.
The afternoon temperature was 63°F.
What was the temperature change?

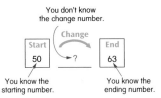

You don't know
the change number.

You know the   You know the
starting number.   ending number.

Number model: 50 + **13** = 63
The temperature change was +**13**°F.

Try It Together

Take turns with a partner making up and solving number stories.

***My Reference Book,* p. 118**

► Reading and Showing Temperatures and Solving Temperature-Change Problems

(*Math Journal 1*, pp. 90 and 91)

PARTNER ACTIVITY

Partners work through the journal pages and check each other's work. Problems include reading temperatures, marking a thermometer to show a temperature, and using change diagrams.

 Ongoing Assessment:
Recognizing Student Achievement

Journal Page 90 ★

Use **journal page 90** to assess children's ability to read, show temperatures, and solve temperature-change problems. Children are making adequate progress if they find the end number using the number grid and correctly fill in the end thermometer. Some children will be able to find the end number mentally.

[Measurement and Reference Frames Goal 5]

---

② Ongoing Learning & Practice

► Solving Parts-and-Total Number Stories

(*Math Journal 1*, p. 89)

INDEPENDENT ACTIVITY

Children solve parts-and-total number stories. They complete parts-and-total diagrams and write number models for these stories.

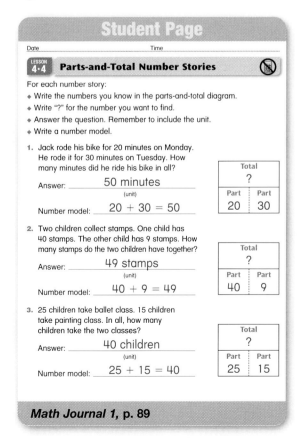

Math Journal 1, p. 89

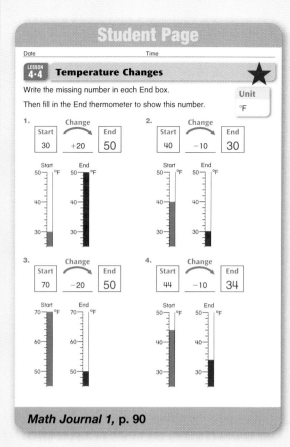

Math Journal 1, p. 90

⬆⬇ Adjusting the Activity

ELL

On journal pages 90 and 91, children can place the top of a card or ruler horizontally at the top of the "mercury" in one thermometer. They then slide the card up or down, counting by 2s until the card reaches the top of the other "mercury."

AUDITORY ◆ KINESTHETIC ◆ TACTILE ◆ VISUAL

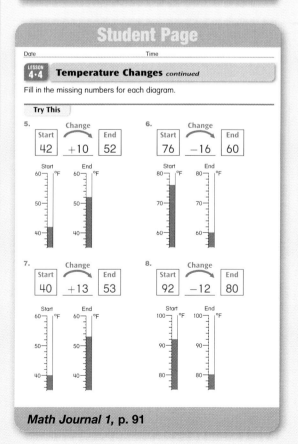

Math Journal 1, p. 91

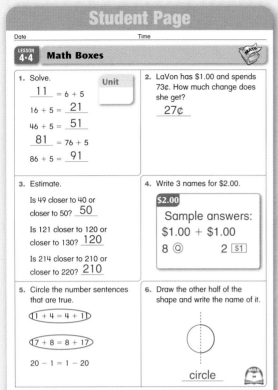

Math Journal 1, p. 92

Math Boxes 4·4

(*Math Journal 1*, p. 92)

INDEPENDENT ACTIVITY

Mixed Practice Math Boxes in this lesson are paired with Math Boxes in Lesson 4-2. The skill in Problem 6 previews Unit 5 content.

 Writing/Reasoning Have children draw, write, or verbalize their answers to the following: *Explain how you solved how much change LaVon will receive in Problem 2.*

Sample answers: I counted up 7 to 80 and added 20; I subtracted 73 from 100.

Home Link 4·4

(*Math Masters*, pp. 99 and 100)

INDEPENDENT ACTIVITY

Home Connection The Home Link provides children practice with two skills: reading the temperature shown on a thermometer and marking a thermometer to show a given temperature.

---

③ Differentiation Options

READINESS

SMALL-GROUP ACTIVITY

▶ Comparing Thermometers

15–30 Min

(*Math Masters*, pp. 101–103)

To provide experience with comparing temperatures using a visual model, have children solve problems using the thermometer on *Math Masters*, page 101. For each problem, children place one of the thermometer pieces from *Math Masters*, page 102 on the paper copy of the thermometer on *Math Masters*, page 101 (lining it up with 0). Ask children to tell what the temperature is if the liquid in the thermometer is as high as shown. On the overhead transparency of *Math Masters*, page 101, have children use an overhead marker and draw a line at the height of a second temperature you give them. They take the overhead transparency and line it up over the thermometer on the paper copy of *Math Masters*, page 101. They count the intervals between the two temperatures to find the difference (or change) between the two temperatures and record their answers on *Math Masters*, page 103.

Example:

▷ Place the 40-degree piece on the paper copy of *Math Masters*, page 101.

▷ Draw a line for 50 degrees on the transparency.

▷ Lay the transparency over the paper copy of *Math Masters*, page 101.

Home Link Master

Name　　　　　　Date　　　　Time

HOME LINK 4·4 **Temperature**

Family Note In today's lesson, your child solved problems involving temperatures. On the thermometers on this Home Link, the longer degree marks are spaced at 2-degree intervals. Point to these degree marks while your child counts by 2s; 40, 42, 44, 46, 48, 50 degrees.

Problems 6 and 12 involve temperatures that are an odd number of degrees. Help your child use the shorter degree marks to get the correct answers.

Please return this Home Link to school tomorrow.

Write the temperature shown on each thermometer.

1. 20°F　　2. 34°F　　3. 52°F

4. 96°F　　5. 48°F　　6. 73°F

Math Masters, p. 99

Say: *Imagine that the temperature this morning was 40 degrees, but now it is 50 degrees.*

Ask: *Did the temperature change? Did the temperature go up or down? Did the temperature increase or decrease? Is it warmer or colder now? By how many degrees did the temperature change?* To support English language learners, write the answers to the questions on the board as the children discuss them: *The temperature changed. The temperature went up. The temperature increased. The temperature is now warmer. The temperature increased by 10 degrees.*

ENRICHMENT

▶ # Writing Number Stories about Thermometer Experiments

 SMALL-GROUP ACTIVITY

◗ 15–30 Min

(*Math Masters*, p. 419)

To provide experience with temperature changes using a concrete model and to explore writing change number stories, have children participate in a temperature experiment.

Bring the outdoor thermometer inside and wait a few minutes until it shows the approximate room temperature.

1. Display the room temperature on the Class Thermometer Poster (°F). Ask: *In which color zone is the temperature now?*

Record and label the outside and room temperatures on the board. Give children some time to write a number story for what happened with the temperature. Have a couple of volunteers share their stories. If appropriate, have children write number models and complete change diagrams for their stories.

2. Ask a child to put his or her hand over the bulb at the bottom of the glass tube on the outdoor thermometer and hold it for about 30 seconds. While waiting, ask the children to predict what will happen. Then display the new temperature on the Class Thermometer Poster. Ask: *In which color zone is the temperature now?*

Record and label the temperature of a hand on the board.

3. Ask another child to place the bulb of the outdoor thermometer in a glass of ice cold water for about 30 seconds. Again ask the children to predict what will happen. Then display the new temperature on the Class Thermometer Poster. Ask: *In which color zone is the temperature now?*

Record and label the temperature of cold water on the board.

Have children write another number story using the information on the board. If appropriate, have children write number models and complete change diagrams for their stories.

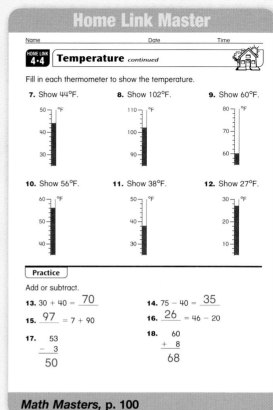

Math Masters, p. 100

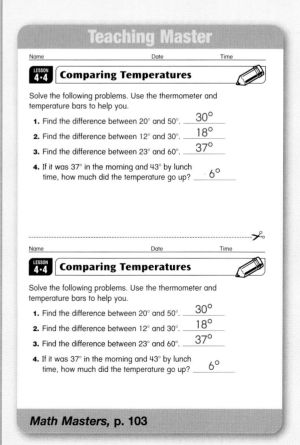

Math Masters, p. 103

4·5 Estimating Costs

 Objective To guide children as they use estimation to solve problems for which an exact answer is not necessary.

---

1 Teaching the Lesson

materials

Key Activities
Children are introduced to estimation. They use estimation to solve problems.

Key Concepts and Skills
• Compare money amounts. [Operations and Computation Goal 2]
• Estimate money amounts to solve problems. [Operations and Computation Goal 3]
• Share strategies for estimating total money amounts. [Operations and Computation Goal 3]

Key Vocabulary estimate

✔ **Ongoing Assessment: Informing Instruction** See page 274.

✔ **Ongoing Assessment: Recognizing Student Achievement** Use journal page 93.
[Operations and Computation Goal 3]

☐ *Math Journal 1*, p. 93
☐ Home Link 4·4
☐ Transparencies (*Math Masters,* pp. 99 and 100; optional)

***See* Advance Preparation**

---

2 Ongoing Learning & Practice

materials

Children identify sums and differences that match a given number by playing *Name That Number.*

Children practice and maintain skills through Math Boxes and Home Link activities.

☐ *Math Journal 1*, p. 94
☐ *My Reference Book,* pp. 138 and 139
☐ Home Link Master (*Math Masters,* p. 104)
☐ Game Master (*Math Masters,* p. 462; optional)
☐ per partnership: 4 each of number cards 0–10 and 1 each of number cards 11–20

---

3 Differentiation Options

materials

READINESS
Children make coin combinations.

ENRICHMENT
Children use estimation to compare sums of weights.

☐ *Math Journal 1*, p. 80
☐ Teaching Aid Master (*Math Masters,* p. 419)
☐ tool-kit coins; one set of 3-by-5 cards labeled with the name and price of each object on journal page 93 (per partnership)

Additional Information

Advance Preparation For the Home Link 4·4 Follow-Up, create overhead transparencies of *Math Masters,* pages 99 and 100. For the optional Readiness activity in Part 3 of this lesson, partnerships will need 3-by-5 cards labeled with the name and price of each object on journal page 93 and one 3-by-5 card labeled $1. To support English language learners, consider making an enlarged copy of the items pictured on the top of the page. Label each item with its name. Children cut apart the labeled images and use these instead of index cards.

Technology
Assessment Management System
Journal page 93, Problems 1–3
See the **iTLG.**

Getting Started

Math Message

Eraser: 28¢

Notebook: 69¢

You have $1.00. Do you have enough money to pay for both items? yes *Be prepared to explain your answer.*

Home Link 4·4 Follow-Up

Use an overhead transparency of Home Link Lesson 4-4 as you review the answers. Pay special attention to Problems 6 and 12, in which the temperature is an odd number of degrees. Children must read between the 2-degree intervals to get the correct answer.

① Teaching the Lesson

▶ Math Message Follow-Up

 **WHOLE-CLASS DISCUSSION**

Ask children to share their solution strategies. Some children may have tried to find the exact cost of the two items (28¢ + 69¢ = 97¢). Others may have found that they had enough money without actually finding the exact cost. *For example:*

▷ Some children might have reasoned that 69¢ + 20¢ is 89¢, and adding another 8¢ would not bring the cost to more than $1.00.

▷ Other children might have thought that 69¢ is just a little less than 70¢. Because 70¢ + 28¢ is 98¢, the actual cost must be slightly less than $1.00.

▶ Discussing Estimation

 **WHOLE-CLASS DISCUSSION**

There are many problems for which an exact answer is not required. The Math Message problem, for example, asks only whether the total cost is $1.00 or less; the exact total is not needed.

Ask children to think of other questions for which a close answer is good enough. *For example:*

▷ How old am I?

▷ What is the temperature today?

▷ What is the distance from my home to school?

Careful counting or measuring can furnish precise answers, but close answers are usually good enough for these situations. A close answer is called an **estimate.** Write *estimate* on the board. Explain that an estimate is like a guess except that you have some information to think about when you make an estimate.

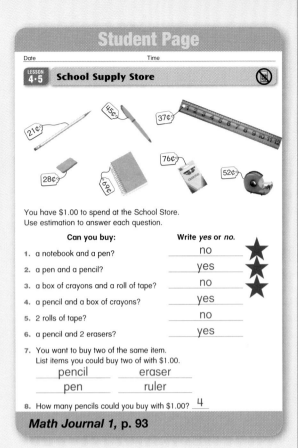

Date _____ Time _____

LESSON 4·5 **School Supply Store**

You have $1.00 to spend at the School Store.
Use estimation to answer each question.

Can you buy:	Write *yes* or *no.*
1. a notebook and a pen?	no
2. a pen and a pencil?	yes
3. a box of crayons and a roll of tape?	no
4. a pencil and a box of crayons?	yes
5. 2 rolls of tape?	no
6. a pencil and 2 erasers?	yes

7. You want to buy two of the same item.
   List items you could buy two of with $1.00.

   pencil   eraser
   pen   ruler

8. How many pencils could you buy with $1.00? __4__

Math Journal 1, p. 93

▶ **Estimating Costs**

(*Math Journal 1,* p. 93)

 WHOLE-CLASS DISCUSSION

Use the information at the top of journal page 93 to make up estimation problems for children to solve. Tell them that it is not necessary to calculate exact answers. Close answers, or estimates, will be good enough to answer the questions.

Examples:

● Is $1.00 enough to pay for a notebook and tape? No; each item costs more than 50¢, so the total must be more than $1.00.

● You have 80¢ to spend. You buy a pen. Do you have enough money left to buy a ruler? No; the pen costs 45¢ and the ruler costs 37¢. 40¢ + 30¢ = 70¢. Because 5¢ + 7¢ is greater than 10¢, the total is greater than 80¢.

● You buy an eraser and a ruler. The clerk says, "That will be 80 cents." Should you pay that amount? No; 28¢ + 37¢ is less than 30¢ + 40¢, which is 70¢. The clerk is wrong.

✔ **Ongoing Assessment:** Informing Instruction

Watch for children who think there is little reason to estimate when they know how to calculate an exact answer to a problem. Identify situations where an estimate is appropriate and those where an exact answer is necessary. Also point out that it is much faster to estimate money amounts.

At this time, it is best not to teach any formal estimation techniques, such as rounding, since children may then use such techniques by rote for all problems.

Have children share estimation strategies. Encourage them to devise several strategies of their own and then have them choose the strategy that best fits a particular situation.

⬆ **Adjusting the Activity**
⬇

Have children make estimates for problems containing more than two items. For example, ask: *Is $2.00 enough to buy a ruler, a box of crayons, and a notebook?* Yes. 37¢ + 76¢ + 69¢ is less than 40¢ + 80¢ + 70¢, which is $1.90. $1.90 is less than $2.00.

AUDITORY ◆ KINESTHETIC ◆ TACTILE ◆ VISUAL

NOTE To get an estimate, children should use numbers that are close to the numbers in the problems but easier to work with.

▶ **Solving Problems by Estimation**

(*Math Journal 1,* p. 93)

PARTNER ACTIVITY

When children feel comfortable dealing with estimation situations, have them complete journal page 93 with a partner. Do not permit the use of calculators. Circulate and help as needed.

Adjusting the Activity

Have children write the cost of each item directly above its name in the problem.

AUDITORY ◆ KINESTHETIC ◆ TACTILE ◆ VISUAL

Ongoing Assessment: Recognizing Student Achievement

Journal Page 93 Problems 1–3 ★

Use **journal page 93, Problems 1–3** to assess children's ability to make reasonable estimates. Children are making adequate progress if they can successfully answer Problems 1–3. Some children may be able to estimate the amount of change from $1.00 for Problem 2.

[Operations and Computation Goal 3]

2 Ongoing Learning & Practice

▶ Playing *Name That Number*

🧍🧍 **PARTNER ACTIVITY**

(*Math Masters*, p. 462; *My Reference Book*, pp. 138 and 139)

This game was introduced in Lesson 2-9. For another version, have children play a variation in which players try to use two, three, four, or all five of the faceup cards to name the target number. *Math Masters*, page 462 is an optional record sheet.

Use 2 cards: no solution

Use 3 cards: **7 + 8 + 1 = 16**

Use 4 cards: **10 + 12** = 22, 22 **+ 1** = 23, 23 **− 7** =16

Use 5 cards: **12 − 10** = 2, 2 **+ 8** = 10, 10 **+ 7** = 17, 17 **− 1** = 16

▶ Math Boxes 4·5

🧍 **INDEPENDENT ACTIVITY**

(*Math Journal 1*, p. 94)

 Mixed Practice Math Boxes in this lesson are linked with Math Boxes in Lessons 4-7 and 4-9. The skill in Problem 6 previews Unit 5 content.

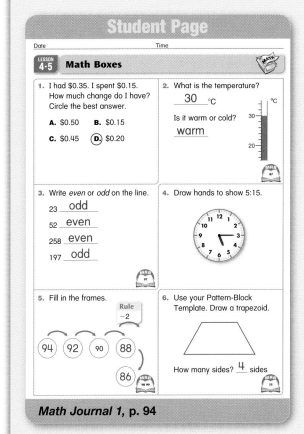

Math Journal 1, p. 94

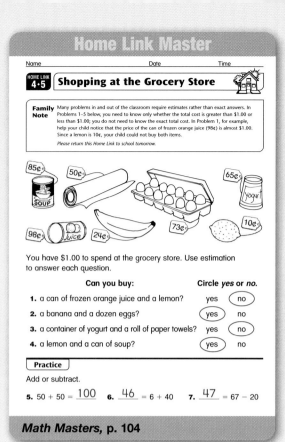
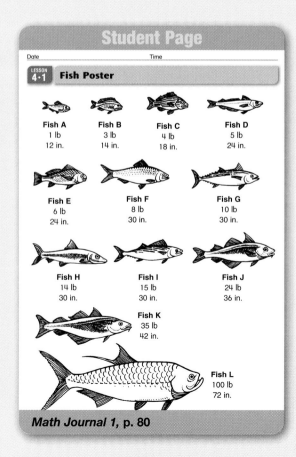

▶ **Home Link 4·5**

(Math Masters, p. 104)

INDEPENDENT ACTIVITY

 Home Connection Children use estimation to solve problems about buying items at the grocery store. They also determine whether they can buy two items with $1.00.

③ Differentiation Options

READINESS

SMALL-GROUP ACTIVITY

▶ **Making Coin Combinations**

🕐 15–30 Min

To provide experience with making coin combinations, have children use coins to show given amounts. Give children a set of labeled 3 by 5 cards or a set of images from journal page 93. For each image, have children make a coin combination using as few coins as possible. They can record these combinations and use them for reference during the lesson. As time permits, have children make as many coin combinations as they can for $1.

ENRICHMENT

INDEPENDENT ACTIVITY

▶ **Using Estimation to Compare Sums of Weights**

🕐 15–30 Min

(Math Journal 1, p. 80; Math Masters, p. 419)

To apply children's understanding of making ballpark estimates, have them solve comparison problems.

Give children the following problems about the Fish Poster on journal page 80 to practice using estimation skills.

▷ Choose a fish and ask children to name pairs of fish whose combined weights are less than, greater than, or equal to the weight of the chosen fish. For example, Fish A and Fish D together weigh less than Fish G. Children should explain why they think the weight of the pair is less than, greater than, or equal to that of the chosen fish.

▷ Name two pairs of fish. For example, Fish E and Fish C are one pair and Fish H and Fish J are the other pair. Ask: *Which pair weighs more?* or *Which pair weighs less?* Encourage children to explain their answers.

Finally, children create stories using the Fish Poster.

4·6 A Shopping Activity

 Objectives To guide children as they develop strategies for adding 2-digit numbers mentally; to provide experiences with calculating the total cost of two items; and to demonstrate making change for whole-dollar amounts up to $100.

1 Teaching the Lesson

materials

Key Activities
Children discuss strategies for adding 2-digit numbers. Then they add 2-digit numbers to solve problems about buying items.

Children calculate the total cost for a pair of items and use play money to pay and make change by doing a Shopping activity.

Key Concepts and Skills
• Identify the place value in two-digit numbers. [Number and Numeration Goal 2]
• Calculate money amounts. [Operations and Computation Goal 2]
• Use parts-and-total diagrams to solve multidigit addition problems. [Operations and Computation Goal 4]
• Write number models for parts-and-total problems. [Patterns, Functions, and Algebra Goal 2]

✔ **Ongoing Assessment: Informing Instruction** See page 279.

□ *Math Journal 1*, pp. 95–97
□ Home Link 4·5
Per partnership:
□ Teaching Aid Master (*Math Masters*, p. 433)
□ Shopping cards cut from *Math Masters*, p. 105
□ calculator; nine $1 bills, and eight $10 bills
□ one $100 bill (optional)

***See* Advance Preparation**

2 Ongoing Learning & Practice

materials

Children practice adding 2-digit numbers by playing *Addition Spin*.

Children practice and maintain skills through Math Boxes and Home Link activities.

✔ **Ongoing Assessment: Recognizing Student Achievement** Use journal page 98.
[Measurement and Reference Frames Goal 6]

□ *Math Journal 1*, p. 98
□ *My Reference Book*, pp. 120 and 121
□ Home Link Master (*Math Masters*, p. 106)
□ Game Masters (*Math Masters*, p. 447 and p. 448; optional)
Per partnership:
□ paper clip; calculator

3 Differentiation Options

materials

READINESS
Children add multiples of 10 using a concrete model.

EXTRA PRACTICE
Children solve number stories involving money.

□ Teaching Aid Master (*Math Masters*, p. 433)
□ *Minute Math®+*, pp. 141, 144, and 145
□ tool kit money; ten $10 bills eighteen $1 bills

Additional Information
Advance Preparation If you need more bills before doing the Shopping activity in Part 1, make copies of *Math Masters*, pages 459–461.

Technology
Assessment Management System
Math Boxes, Problem 4
See the **iTLG.**

Getting Started

Mental Math and Reflexes

Solve each problem.

- ●○○   70 + 30 = ?   100
-       30 + 40 = ?   70
-       50 + 20 = ?   70

- ●●○   36 + 40 = ?   76
-       50 + 24 = ?   74
-       ? = 58 + 20   78

- ●●●   87 + 30 = ?   117
-       ? = 60 + 69   129
-       ? = 70 + 33   103

Pose other addition problems with addends that are a multiple of 10 and any 2-digit number.

Math Message

You buy a clock that costs $78. You pay with a $100 bill. How much is your change? $22 *Be prepared to share your solution strategy.*

Home Link 4·5 Follow-Up

Ask volunteers to explain their answers.

---

1   Teaching the Lesson

▶ Math Message Follow-Up

 **WHOLE-CLASS DISCUSSION**

Ask children to share their solution strategies. In Unit 3, children practiced making change by counting up with coins. Invite a volunteer to make change for the clock purchase by counting up with play money. *For example:*

▷ Start with $78—the cost of the clock. Count up to $100—the money used to pay. Say 79, 80, 90, 100 while putting down two $1 bills and then two $10 bills. The change is $22.

To support English language learners, discuss the various meanings of the word *bill*.

Making change by counting up can be practiced as a variation of the Shopping activity.

▶ Discussing Strategies for Adding 2-Digit Numbers

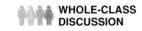 **WHOLE-CLASS DISCUSSION**

(*Math Journal 1*, p. 96)

Select a pair of items from journal page 96, such as the telephone ($46) and the toaster ($29). Ask children how they might find the total cost of these two items.

NOTE The items and prices shown on *Math Masters*, page 105 are the same as those shown on journal page 96.

Student Page

Date   Time

LESSON 4·6   Shopping Poster

Telephone $46	Camera $43	CD Player $25	Calculator $17
Toaster $29	Iron $32	CD $14	Radio $38

Math Journal 1, p. 96

You or the children might suggest the following strategies:

Strategy 1

Start with the larger addend, 46. To add 29, note that there are 2 tens in 29. Count up by 10s. 56, 66 Then add 9. $66 + 9 = 75$ The total cost is \$75.

Strategy 2

Think of \$10 bills and \$1 bills. Add the \$10 bills. 4 tens + 2 tens = 6 tens, or \$60. Add the \$1 bills. 6 ones + 9 ones = 15 ones, or \$15. Add the tens and the ones. $\$60 + \$15 = \$75$

Strategy 3

29 is 1 less than 30. Add 30 to 46. $30 + 46 = 76$ Then subtract 1 to make up for the extra 1. $76 - 1 = 75$

Strategy 4

29 is 1 less than 30, and 46 is 4 less than 50. Add 30 and 50. $30 + 50 = 80$ Then subtract the extra 1 and the extra 4. $1 + 4 = 5; 80 - 5 = 75$ or $80 - 1 = 79; 79 - 4 = 75.$

 Adjusting the Activity ELL

Have children model Strategy 2 with play money. Have them take \$10 bills and \$1 bills to represent the cost of each item. They combine the \$10 bills for both items and the \$1 bills for both items then count the money to calculate the total cost.

AUDITORY ♦ KINESTHETIC ♦ TACTILE ♦ VISUAL

Ongoing Assessment: Informing Instruction

Watch for children who still have difficulty adding multiples of 10. Use the number grid daily to count by 10 and to model adding 10s. Children need to practice this skill in anticipation of the partial-sums addition algorithm in Lesson 4-9.

▶ Using Shopping Strategies

 PARTNER ACTIVITY

(*Math Journal 1*, p. 95; *Math Masters*, p. 433 and Shopping cards cut from *Math Masters*, p. 105)

Divide the class into partnerships. Partners place the Shopping cards facedown. There should be 8 cards per partnership. Partners take turns being Customer and Clerk. Partners follow the steps given on journal page 95.

NOTE The main objective of this lesson is to develop and practice strategies for mental addition of 2-digit numbers. Making change by counting up is also practiced. The Shopping activity is done using *Math Masters*, page 433 to keep the parts-and-total diagram in children's minds.

Total

Part   Part

 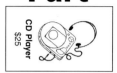

Children do the Shopping activity with the Shopping cards from *Math Masters*, page 105 and the parts-and total diagram from *Math Masters*, page 433.

NOTE At this point, do not take the time to teach children a traditional paper-and-pencil algorithm for addition. The purpose of this lesson is to allow children to experiment with their own mental addition methods. Formal addition methods are addressed in Lessons 4-8 and 4-9.

Total	
?	
Part	Part
43	32

Only essential information is recorded.

Total	
? cost of both	
Part	Part
$43 camera	$32 iron

Information with added descriptions

Adjusting the Activity

Have children count out the bills for each item separately. (If this is done, the Customer would need seventeen $1 bills.) For example, if the selected items are a camera ($43) and an iron ($32), the Customer can count out $43 and place these bills in one Part box, and then count out $32 and place these bills in the second Part box. The Customer then combines the bills, slides them to the Total box, and counts the bills to determine the total cost.

For another version, the Customer does not count out bills. Instead, the Customer says or writes the total cost of the selected items. The Customer pays with a $100 bill. The Clerk must return the correct change.

A U D I T O R Y ◆ K I N E S T H E T I C ◆ T A C T I L E ◆ V I S U A L

▶ **Solving Shopping Problems**   **PARTNER ACTIVITY**

(*Math Journal 1,* pp. 96 and 97)

Children solve the problems with their partners. Partners check each other's work. There is more than one possible correct answer for Problems 3–5. For Problems 1 and 2, children should indicate the known and missing information in the parts-and-total diagram.

Adjusting the Activity

Have children write words or short phrases in the parts-and-total diagram to remind them what the numbers mean. See examples in the margin.

A U D I T O R Y ◆ K I N E S T H E T I C ◆ T A C T I L E ◆ V I S U A L

2 Ongoing Learning & Practice

▶ **Playing *Addition Spin***  **PARTNER ACTIVITY**

(*Math Masters,* pp. 447 and 448; *My Reference Book,* pp. 120 and 121)

Children use a spinner from *Math Masters,* page 447 to construct 2-digit addition problems. The master includes two spinners. Children should now use the spinner at the bottom of the page.

The rules for *Addition Spin* are in *My Reference Book,* pages 120 and 121.

Math Masters, page 448 provides blank spinners for creating spinners with different numbers.

▶ **Math Boxes 4·6** **INDEPENDENT ACTIVITY**

(*Math Journal 1,* p. 98)

Mixed Practice Math Boxes in this lesson are paired with Math Boxes in Lesson 4-8. The skills in Problems 5 and 6 preview Unit 5 content.

Ongoing Assessment: Recognizing Student Achievement

Math Boxes Problem 4

Use **Math Boxes, Problem 4** to assess children's ability to tell time to the nearest quarter hour. Children are making adequate progress if they complete Problem 4 correctly. Some children may be able to tell time to the nearest 5 minutes.

[Measurement and Reference Frames Goal 6]

▶ **Home Link 4·6**   INDEPENDENT ACTIVITY

(*Math Masters*, p. 106)

Home Connection Children use change diagrams to solve problems mentally.

---

③ Differentiation Options

READINESS   INDEPENDENT ACTIVITY

▶ **Adding Multiples of 10**   5–15 Min

(*Math Masters*, p. 433)

To provide experience with adding 2-digit numbers using a concrete model, have children solve problems on a parts-and-total diagram using $10 bills and $1 bills. (*See margin.*)

Pose sets of problems like the following:

4 + 2 = ____ 6	9 + 3 = ____ 12
40 + 20 = ____ 60	90 + 30 = ____ 120
____ = 7 + 9 16	____ = 70 + 90 160

Remind children that another way to think of 40 is as 4 tens or 4 [10s]; another way to think of 20 is as 2 tens or 2 [10s]. So 40 + 20 = 4 [10s] + 2 [10s] = 6 [10s], or 60.

The sets of problems can then be rewritten as follows:

4 [1s] + 2 [1s] = ____ [1s] 6	4 [10s] + 2 [10s] = ____ [10s] 6
9 [1s] + 3 [1s] = ____ [1s] 12	9 [10s] + 3 [10s] = ____ [10s] 12
____ [1s] = 7 [1s] + 9 [1s] 16	____ [10s] = 7 [10s] + 9 [10s] 16

EXTRA PRACTICE   SMALL-GROUP ACTIVITY

Student Page

Date _____ Time _____

LESSON 4·6 **Math Boxes**

1. 45 cents = 1 quarter and __2__ dimes

   60 cents = 3 dimes and __6__ nickels

2. A.M. temperature was 50°F. P.M. temperature is 68°F. What was the change? __18__ °F Fill in the diagram and write the number model.

Start	Change	End
50	?	68

   $68 - 50 = 18.\ 50 + 18 = 68$

3. 20 airplanes. 8 take off. How many stay? __12__ airplanes stay. Fill in the diagram and write a number model.

Start	Change	End
20	−8	?

   $20 - 8 = 12$

4. Draw hands to show 8:15. ★

5. Measure the length of this line segment. Circle the best answer.

   _____

   A. about 7 cm
   B. about 6 cm
   C. about 8 cm
   D. about 10 cm

6. Draw a rectangle. Two sides are 4 cm long and two sides are 3 cm long.

Math Journal 1, p. 98

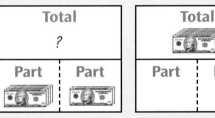

Total		Total	
?		🗎🗎	
Part	Part	Part	Part

$40 + 20 = ?$

Slide all bills to the Total box and count. $40 + 20 = 60$

Home Link Master

Name _____ Date _____ Time _____

HOME LINK 4·6 **Addition Number Stories**

Family Note In today's lesson, your child solved problems by adding 2-digit numbers mentally. For example, to find 34 + 23, you might first add the tens: 30 + 20 = 50. Then add the ones: 4 + 3 = 7. Finally, combine the tens and ones: 50 + 7 = 57.

Please return this Home Link to school tomorrow.

Try to solve Problems 1 and 2 mentally. Fill in the diagrams. Then write the answers and number models.

1. Ruth had 20 marbles in her collection. Her brother gave her 10 more. How many marbles does Ruth have now?

Start	Change	End
20	+10	30

   Answer: 30 marbles
   (unit)

   Number model:
   $20 + 10 = 30$

2. Tim baked 30 ginger snaps and 24 sugar cookies. How many cookies did he bake?

Total	
?	
Part	Part
30	24

   Answer: 54 cookies
   (unit)

   Number model:
   $30 + 24 = 54$

Exploring Length, Area, and Attributes

 Objective To guide children as they measure lengths and distances to the nearest inch and centimeter, explore area by tiling surfaces, and sort attribute blocks according to rules.

---

1 Teaching the Lesson

Key Activities
Children examine and discuss inch and centimeter scales.

Exploration D: Children use a tape measure to measure lengths and distances in the classroom.

Exploration E: Children use pattern blocks, playing cards, and quarter-sheets of paper to tile surfaces.

Exploration F: Children sort a set of attribute blocks by determining which blocks fit a given set of rules and which do not.

Key Concepts and Skills
• Distinguish between centimeter and inch.
  [Measurement and Reference Frames Goal 1]
• Compare lengths in centimeters and inches.
  [Measurement and Reference Frames Goal 1]
• Measure to the nearest in. and cm. [Measurement and Reference Frames Goal 1]
• Find area by tiling with pattern blocks and counting shapes.
  [Measurement and Reference Frames Goal 2]
• Use rules to sort attribute blocks. [Patterns, Functions, and Algebra Goal 1]

Key Vocabulary inch (in.) • centimeter (cm) • tiling • attribute blocks

materials
☐ Home Link 4•6
☐ tape measure and yardstick
Exploration D: Per small group:
☐ *Math Journal 1,* pp. 99 and 100
☐ tape measure
Exploration E: Per partnership:
☐ *Math Journal 1,* pp. 101 and 102
☐ pattern blocks; Pattern-Block Template
☐ playing cards or Everything Math Deck, if available
☐ slate; sheets of paper; scissors
Exploration F: Per group:
☐ *Math Journal 1,* p. 103
☐ Teaching Masters (*Math Masters,* pp. 107–109)
☐ 1 set of attribute blocks; scissors; envelope
☐ 2 sheets of paper
☐ red, yellow, and blue crayons

See **Advance Preparation**

---

2 Ongoing Learning & Practice

Children practice subtraction facts using fact triangles.

Children practice and maintain skills through Math Boxes and Home Link activities.

✓ **Ongoing Assessment: Recognizing Student Achievement** Use an Exit Slip.
  [Operations and Computation Goal 1]

materials
☐ *Math Journal 1,* p. 104
☐ Home Link Master (*Math Masters,* p. 110)
☐ Teaching Aid Master (*Math Masters,* p. 415)
☐ envelope with Fact Triangles (from Lesson 2•5)

---

3 Differentiation Options

ENRICHMENT
Children find different ways to measure the same length with a tape measure.

ELL SUPPORT
Children add *inch* and *centimeter* to their Math Word Banks.

materials
☐ *Math Journal 1,* pp. 99 and 100
☐ ruler
☐ *Differentiation Handbook*

Additional Information

Advance Preparation Spend the most time on Explorations D and E. Children should write tool-kit numbers on their tape measures. Have children use heavier stock paper for Exploration E. For Exploration F, place copies of *Math Masters,* pages 107 and 108 at workstations.

Technology
Assessment Management System
Exit Slip
See the **iTLG.**

Getting Started

Mental Math and Reflexes

Pose problems like these:

○○○ 95 − 5 = ? 90   74 − 4 = ? 70

○○○ ? = 39 − 30 9   ? = 27 − 10 17

○○○ 45 − 20 = ? 25   62 − 40 = ? 22

Math Message

Name two things you would measure with a ruler.

Name two things you would measure with a tape measure.

Home Link 4·6 Follow-Up

Ask volunteers to explain how they solved each problem. Assess whether most children were able to find the answers to the problems mentally.

---

1 Teaching the Lesson

▶ Math Message Follow-Up

 WHOLE-CLASS DISCUSSION

Discuss children's answers. Sample answers: ruler: the width of a hand, the length of a crayon; tape measure: the width of a desk, the distance around a person's waist It is important to select the correct measuring tool for the task at hand. Children's tool-kit rulers are best suited for measuring lengths and distances that are shorter than the ruler. Tape measures and yardsticks are longer. They are used to measure longer lengths. Tape measures are also useful for measuring things that are not flat, and for measuring around things.

Pull out a tool-kit tape measure to its full length (5 feet) and hold this alongside a yardstick. Ask why the tape measure would be a more convenient tool than the yardstick for measuring the heights of children in the class. Sample answer: Most of the children are taller than a yardstick, but shorter than the 5-foot tape.

▶ Examining Inch and Centimeter Scales

WHOLE-CLASS DISCUSSION

Discuss the **inch (in.)** and **centimeter (cm)** scales on rulers and tape measures. Ask children to examine their rulers and tape measures, and ensure that they can correctly identify the two scales on each. Explain the inch scale is more commonly used in the United States. In science, lengths are reported in centimeters or other metric units. Write the units and their abbreviations on the board.

Ask children which unit is longer—the inch or the centimeter. The inch Have children carefully pull their tape measures out to their full lengths. How long is your tape measure? 60 inches on the inch side; 150 cm on the centimeter side

> **NOTE** If children are using retractable tape measures, teach and enforce the "2-inch, no zap" rule: You may "zap" the tape measure only when no more than 2 inches are showing. Following this rule will extend the life of the tape measures.

Date _____ Time _____

LESSON 4·7 Measuring Lengths with a Tape Measure

1. Measure the height from the top of your desk or table to the floor. Measure to the nearest inch.

   The height from my desk or table to the floor is about _____ inches.
   Answers vary.

2. Measure the height from the top of your chair to the floor. Measure to the nearest inch.

   The height from the top of my chair to the floor is about _____ inches.
   Answers vary.

3. Measure the width of your classroom door.

   The classroom door is about _____ inches wide.
   Answers vary.

Math Journal 1, p. 99

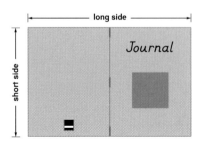

Adjusting the Activity

Have children find an object in your classroom that is about 50 inches long. Then have them find an object in your classroom that is about 50 centimeters long.

AUDITORY ◆ KINESTHETIC ◆ TACTILE ◆ VISUAL

Date _____ Time _____

LESSON 4·7 Measuring Lengths with a Tape Measure *cont.*

4. Open your journal so it looks like the drawing below.

   a. Measure the long side and the short side to the nearest inch.

   The long side is about __17__ inches.

   The short side is about __11__ inches.

   b. Now measure your journal to the nearest centimeter.

   The long side is about __44__ centimeters.

   The short side is about __28__ centimeters.

|←——————— long side ———————→|

Journal

short side

Math Journal 1, p. 100

Ask children to compare lengths on the two sides of their tape measures at different points along the tape. *For example:*

▷ It's 20 on the inch side and about 51 on the centimeter side.

▷ It's 30 on the inch side and about 76 on the centimeter side.

▷ It's 100 on the centimeter side and about 39 on the inch side.

Help children summarize the comparison. If you measure a length in centimeters, you will get a larger number than if you measure the same length in inches.

▶ Exploration D: Measuring Lengths with a Tape Measure

 **SMALL-GROUP ACTIVITY**

(*Math Journal 1,* pp. 99 and 100)

Children who used *Everyday Mathematics* in first grade have had considerable practice using rulers and tape measures to measure lengths to the nearest inch, but limited practice in measuring to the nearest centimeter. As you circulate, make sure children are lining up one end of the object or distance to be measured with the end (zero mark) of the tape measure. If a measured length falls between the inch (or centimeter) marks on their tapes, some children may need help deciding which is the nearest inch (or centimeter).

▶ Exploration E: Tiling Surfaces with Different Shapes

 PARTNER ACTIVITY

(*Math Journal 1,* pp. 101 and 102)

Children use multiples of the same pattern-block shape to cover a playing card as completely as possible. There should be no spaces between the blocks, nor should the blocks overlap or extend beyond the card. This activity is called **tiling.** To support English language learners, discuss the meaning of the words *tile* and *tiling.* Ask the children if they have tiles in their homes or if they see any in the classroom.

Children record the number of block shapes needed to tile the card. Any space around the edges of the card that cannot be covered by a whole block but that can be covered by more than half a block can be counted as 1 block. Any uncovered spaces less than half of a block should not be counted.

Next, children tile their slates and templates with playing cards and record the result. Then they fold an $8\frac{1}{2}$" by 11" sheet of paper into fourths, cut out the fourths, and use them to tile larger items, such as their desktops or a tabletop. Again, they record what they did. Ask children to find things in the room that are tiled or covered with a pattern.

► Exploration F: Sorting Attribute Blocks

(*Math Journal 1*, p. 103; *Math Masters*, pp. 107–109)

 **SMALL-GROUP ACTIVITY**

Children sort **attribute blocks** with these steps:

1. Cut apart the cards on *Math Masters,* page 109.

2. Shuffle the cards and put them in a pile facedown.

3. Label one sheet of paper These Fit the Rule. Label a second sheet These Do Not Fit the Rule.

4. Children take turns being the Rule Maker. The Rule Maker draws a card from the shuffled pile and puts it out for all to see.

5. The other children take turns putting blocks on the appropriate sheets labeled These Fit the Rule and These Do Not Fit the Rule.

Children record one of their rules on journal page 103 and describe those attribute blocks that fit the rule and those that don't.

⬆ Adjusting the Activity

Encourage children to work in partnerships when taking turns putting blocks on the appropriate sheet. In this way, children are able to discuss their choices. Alternately, the whole group can work together as a team to decide which blocks fit the rule and which do not.

Have children make up their own rules and write them on the two blank cards on *Math Masters,* page 109.

A U D I T O R Y ◆ K I N E S T H E T I C ◆ T A C T I L E ◆ V I S U A L

NOTE The Attribute Rule Cards from *Math Masters,* page 109 will be needed again in Lesson 5-1. Collect the cards and store them in envelopes.

Name   **Date**   **Time**

LESSON 4·7   Attribute Rule Cards ✏

small blue shapes	large red shapes	large shapes, but not triangles	circles, but not red
blue and yellow shapes, but not circles	red and yellow small shapes	not triangles or squares	large triangles, but not yellow

Math Masters, page 109

Date   Time

LESSON 4·7   Tiling Surfaces with Shapes

Materials ☐ pattern blocks
☐ slates
☐ sheets of paper
☐ Pattern-Block Template
☐ scissors
☐ Everything Math Deck cards, if available

1. Pick one pattern-block shape. **Tile** a card by covering it with blocks of this shape.
   - ◆ Lay the blocks flat on the card.
   - ◆ Don't leave any spaces between blocks.
   - ◆ Keep the blocks inside the edges of the card. There may be open spaces along the edges.

   Count the blocks on the card. If a space could be covered by more than half of a block, count the space as one block. Do not count spaces that could be covered by less than half of a block.

   Which pattern-block shape did you use?
   Answers vary.

   Number of blocks needed to tile the card:
   Answers vary.

   Trace the card. Use your Pattern-Block Template to draw the blocks you used to tile the card.

Math Journal 1, p. 101

Date   Time

LESSON 4·7   Tiling Surfaces with Shapes *continued*

2. Use Everything Math Deck cards to tile both a slate and a Pattern-Block Template. How many cards were needed to tile them?

   Slate: _____ cards **Answers vary.**

   Pattern-Block Template: _____ cards **Answers vary.**

3. Fold a sheet of paper into fourths. Cut the fourths apart. Use them to tile larger surfaces, such as a desktop.

Surface	Number of Fourths
Answers vary.	

Follow-Up

With a partner, find things in the classroom that are tiled or covered with patterns. Make a list. Be ready to share your findings.

Math Journal 1, p. 102

Student Page

Date _____ Time _____

LESSON 4·7 An Attribute Rule

Choose an Attribute Rule Card. Copy the rule below.

Rule: Rules, drawings, and descriptions vary.

Draw or describe all the attribute blocks that fit the rule.

Draw or describe all the attribute blocks that do *not* fit the rule.

These blocks fit the rule:

_____

_____

_____

_____

These blocks do *not* fit the rule:

_____

_____

_____

_____

_____

Math Journal 1, p. 103

2 Ongoing Learning & Practice

▶ Practicing with +, − Fact Triangles

PARTNER ACTIVITY

Partners practice subtraction facts and record the ones they know.

Ongoing Assessment:
Recognizing Student Achievement

Exit Slip

Use an **Exit Slip** (*Math Masters,* page 415) to have children record the subtraction facts they know. Children are making adequate progress if they demonstrate automaticity with −0, −1, and doubles (8−8=0). Some children may be able to demonstrate automaticity with the differences from 10 facts. For example, 10−7=3.

[Operations and Computation Goal 1]

▶ Math Boxes 4·7

INDEPENDENT ACTIVITY

(*Math Journal 1,* p. 104)

Mixed Practice Math Boxes in this lesson are linked with Math Boxes in Lesson 4-5 and Lesson 4-9. The skill in Problem 6 previews Unit 5 content.

Writing/Reasoning Have children draw, write, or verbalize their answers to the following: *For Problem 3, explain how you know a number is even or odd.* Sample answer: A number is even if it ends in 2, 4, 6, 8, or 0. A number is odd if it ends in 1, 3, 5, 7, or 9.

▶ Home Link 4·7

INDEPENDENT ACTIVITY

(*Math Masters,* p. 110)

Home Connection Children measure sections of a path to the nearest inch. Then they combine their measurements to find the total length of the path.

Teaching Master

Name _____ Date _____ Time _____

LESSON 4·7 What's My Attribute?

Work with a small group.

Materials
- ☐ *Math Journal 1,* p. 103
- ☐ Attribute Rule Cards (*Math Masters,* p. 109)
- ☐ scissors
- ☐ 2 sheets of paper
- ☐ 1 set of attribute blocks: triangles, circles, squares (large and small; red, yellow, and blue)
- ☐ red, yellow, and blue crayons

Directions

1. Cut apart the Attribute Rule Cards on *Math Masters,* page 109.
2. Mix the cards. Stack them facedown.
3. Label one sheet of paper "These Fit the Rule."
4. Label another sheet "These Do Not Fit the Rule."
5. Take turns being the Rule Maker.
6. The Rule Maker takes the top card from the stack.
7. The Rule Maker puts the card faceup for everyone to see.
8. Group members take turns choosing a block.

Math Masters, p. 107

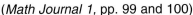

3 Differentiation Options

▶ ## Finding More Than One Way

(*Math Journal 1*, pp. 99 and 100)

PARTNER ACTIVITY

5–15 Min

To apply children's knowledge of linear measure, have them find different ways to measure the same length with a ruler. Children should measure the objects on journal pages 99 and 100 with a ruler using different strategies. Children could start from either end, start at a point not at the end, or measure different parts of the object and add the results. Watch for children whose answers differ from the measurements on the journal pages. Remind children that using the ruler a different way does not change the length of an object.

▶ ## Building a Math Word Bank

(*Differentiation Handbook*)

SMALL-GROUP ACTIVITY

5–15 Min

To provide language support for measurement concepts, use the Word Bank Template in the *Differentiation Handbook*. Ask children to write the terms *inch* and *centimeter*. Children describe the terms with words, pictures, and real-life examples. See the *Differentiation Handbook* for more information.

Teaching Master

Name   Date   Time

LESSON 4·7 | **What's My Attribute?** *continued*

9. If the block fits the rule on the card, place it on the paper that says "These Fit the Rule."

10. If the block does not fit the rule, place it on the paper that says "These Do Not Fit the Rule."

11. Repeat Steps 6–10 until everyone has been the Rule Maker.

Follow-Up

◆ Write one of the rules on journal page 103.

◆ Draw or describe all of the blocks that fit the rule.

◆ Draw or describe all of the blocks that do not fit the rule.

Try This

Make up two rules of your own. Write them on the two blank cards given on *Math Masters*, page 109.

Answers will vary. Sample answers: Not circles or triangles; small shapes, but not blue or red

Math Masters, p. 108

Student Page

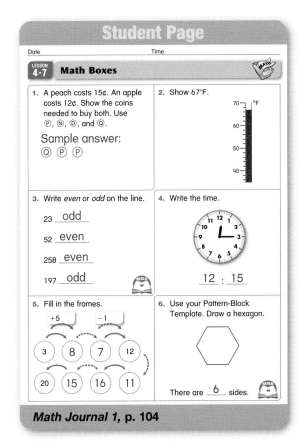

Math Journal 1, p. 104

Home Link Master

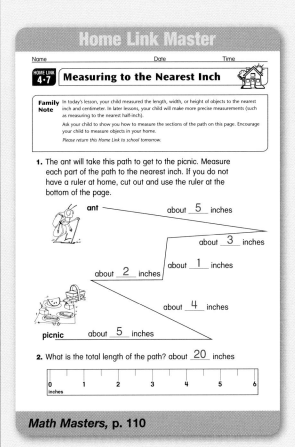

Math Masters, p. 110

4·8 Paper-and-Pencil Addition Strategies

 Objectives To guide children as they develop paper-and-pencil strategies for adding 2- and 3-digit numbers; and to demonstrate using estimation to check if answers are reasonable.

---

1 Teaching the Lesson

Key Activities
Children solve 2-digit addition problems, record their work with paper and pencil, share solution strategies, and use ballpark estimates to check whether their answers are reasonable. Children practice adding 2-, 3-, and 4-digit numbers.

Key Concepts and Skills
• Share solution strategies for finding the sum of 2-digit numbers mentally.
  [Operations and Computation Goal 2]
• Use base-10 blocks to add two 2-digit numbers. [Operations and Computation Goal 2]
• Practice addition fact extensions. [Operations and Computation Goal 2]
• Estimate sums by changing the addends to "close but easier" numbers.
  [Operations and Computation Goal 3]

Key Vocabulary
ballpark estimate

Ongoing Assessment: Recognizing Student Achievement
Use journal page 105. [Operations and Computation Goal 3]

materials
☐ *Math Journal 1*, p. 105
☐ *My Reference Book*, pp. 92–94
☐ Home Link 4·7
☐ base-10 blocks (optional): 18 cubes, 18 longs, and 6 flats
☐ paper
☐ Class Data Pad (optional)

See Advance Preparation

---

2 Ongoing Learning & Practice

Children practice fact extensions by playing the *Fact Extension Game*.

Children practice and maintain skills through Math Boxes and Home Link activities.

materials
☐ *Math Journal 1*, p. 106
☐ *My Reference Book*, pp. 134 and 135
☐ Home Link Masters (*Math Masters*, pp. 111 and 112)
☐ per partnership: number cards labeled 0–5 (from the Everything Math Deck, if available) (optional: 0–9 number cards)
☐ 1 die per partnership

---

3 Differentiation Options

READINESS
Children practice adding and subtracting 10s using a number grid and a penny.

ENRICHMENT
Children find new methods to solve 2- or 3-digit addition problems.

ELL SUPPORT
Children enter *ballpark estimate* in their Math Word Bank.

materials
☐ *Differentiation Handbook*
☐ number grid
☐ 1 penny or small object per child
☐ number line; base-10 blocks (optional)
☐ large paper or posterboard

Additional Information

Advance Preparation Plan to spend a total of two days on this lesson and three days on Lesson 4·9.

Technology
Assessment Management System
Journal page 105, Problems 1–3
See the **iTLG.**

Getting Started

Mental Math and Reflexes

Pose pairs of problems similar to the following:

◐○○   30 + 40 = ?   70
     ? = 50 + 20   70
     ? = 60 + 30   90
◐◐○   30 + 46 = ?   76
     ? = 58 + 20   78
     ? = 60 + 37   97
◐◐◐   124 + 30 = ?   154
     268 + 50 = ?   318
     1,210 + 40 = ?   1,250

Math Message

Make an estimate for the answer to each problem. Be prepared to tell how you found your answer.
75 + 8; 57 + 22

Home Link 4·7 Follow-Up

Review answers as necessary. Ask children to explain how they determined the nearest inch and their strategies for finding the total length of the path.

---

1   Teaching the Lesson

▶ Math Message Follow-Up

WHOLE-CLASS DISCUSSION

Have children share and explain their answers. Explain to the class that they will use estimating strategies to find **ballpark estimates**—an answer that may not be exact but that is close enough. To support English language learners, discuss the meaning of *ballpark*.

▶ Discussing the Use of Ballpark Estimates to Check Answers

WHOLE-CLASS DISCUSSION

(*My Reference Book,* pp. 92–94)

Remind the class that one way to decide whether an answer is reasonable is to make a ballpark estimate. One way to estimate a sum is to change the addends to close-but-easier numbers and then to add those numbers. To support English language learners, clarify the meaning of close-but-easier. You may want to demonstrate on a number line how some numbers are close to others but easier to work with than the others. To review estimation concepts, you may wish to read *My Reference Book,* pages 92–94 with your class.

⬆ Adjusting the Activity   ELL

Draw a "ballpark" on the board (a square oriented like a baseball field). Figure out the answer and write it where home plate would be. As children suggest possible ballpark estimates, the class should decide if the number is near enough to be in the ballpark, in which case, the number would go inside the diamond. If the number would not be in the ballpark, it would be written outside the ballpark and appropriately far away.

AUDITORY ◆ KINESTHETIC ◆ TACTILE ◆ VISUAL

- On **Day 1** of this lesson, children should complete the Math Message Follow-Up, discuss the use of ballpark estimates to check answers, and solve addition problems.

- On **Day 2** of this lesson, children should solve addition problems with two multidigit numbers. Then have children complete Part 2 activities.

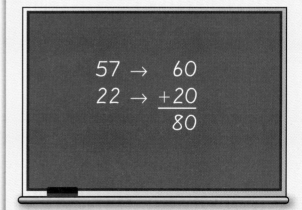

$$
\begin{array}{r}
57 \rightarrow 60 \\
22 \rightarrow +20 \\
\hline
80
\end{array}
$$

For the problem 57 + 22, suggest changing the first addend to 60 and the second addend to 20. Because 60 + 20 = 80, any answers that are not close to 80 are likely to be incorrect.

NOTE Although problems written in a horizontal format probably encourage more varied responses than problems written in a vertical format, the vertical format is often more efficient when children need to perform more complex computations.

▶ Solving Addition Problems; Keeping a Paper-and-Pencil Record

SMALL-GROUP ACTIVITY

Write problems like the following on the board, some in a horizontal format and some in a vertical format. Ask someone to suggest a unit and record it in a unit box. Be sure that the class number grid or individual number grids are available for the children to use.

29 + 37 66	76 + 23 99
52 + 29 81	163 + 56 219
26 + 74 100	219 + 352 571

Unit

Have children work on the problems together in small groups, recording their work with paper and pencil and checking whether each answer is reasonable by making a ballpark estimate.

After groups have done two or three problems, bring the class together to share solution strategies. Record successful strategies on the board or on the Class Data Pad. When most children seem to understand, let groups complete the rest of the problems. Then bring the class together for discussion.

Adjusting the Activity

ELL

Have children act out the problems with base-10 blocks, using longs and cubes to represent each addend separately. Then have children combine the longs and cubes into a single pile. If 10 or more cubes are in the pile, children replace 10 cubes with one long (regrouping). Then they simply count the number of longs (10s) and the number of cubes (1s) to find the sum.

If children are curious, show them how to reduce problems with 3-digit addends to 2-digit addition. For example, with $219 + 352$, add the hundreds first: $200 + 300 = 500$. Record or remember this. That leaves $19 + 52$. Find this sum. 71 Add 500 to get the final answer. 571

It is often convenient to think of 3- and 4-digit addition problems as dollars-and-cents problems. **Example:**

To add:	2,354	Think:	$23.54
	+ 4,667		+ 46.67

Add the dollars:	23	Add the cents:	54
	+ 46		+ 67
	60		110
	9		11
	69		121

Combine dollars and cents: $69 + $1.21 = $70.21.
So $2,354 + 4,667 = 7,021$.

AUDITORY ◆ KINESTHETIC ◆ TACTILE ◆ VISUAL

NOTE In Lesson 4-6, children discussed mental arithmetic strategies for adding 2-digit numbers. In this lesson, children continue to develop and share their solution strategies for solving addition problems and keep a paper-and-pencil record of their solutions.

The goal is to develop, over time, a number of systematic paper-and-pencil procedures—**algorithms**—that can be applied to any addition problem, including those with 3- and 4-digit addends.

Children usually use three major types of strategies:

Counting Up

My problem:	$47 + 33 = ?$
Start at 47. Count up 30 more: 47 57 67 77	
Add on 3 more:	+ 3
The answer is 80:	80

Combining Groups (1s, 10s ...) Separately

My problem:	$29 + 37 = ?$
Add the tens:	$20 + 30 = 50$
Add the ones:	$9 + 7 = 16$
Put these together. 50 + 16. The answer is 66:	66

Adjusting and Compensating

My problem:	$52 + 29 = ?$
30 is close to 29, just 1 more:	30
52 plus 30 is 82:	$52 + 30 = 82$
Take away 1, because I added 30 instead of 29:	-1
The answer is 81:	81

▶ Finding the Sum of Two Multidigit Numbers

PARTNER ACTIVITY

(*Math Journal 1*, p. 105)

Ask partners to solve problems like the following:

63 + 27 90   26 + 31 57   54 + 82 136

Share solution strategies as a class. Model counting up, combining groups, and adjusting and compensating, if no one mentions them.

Have partners work together to solve the addition problems on journal page 105. Tell children to show their computations in the workspaces on the journal page.

Children should record their answers and write a number model for their ballpark estimate to check their work. Remember that ballpark estimates can vary depending on which close, but easier to add, numbers are used. In Problems 7–10, children can use the first sum to find the second sum, the second sum to find the third sum, and the third sum to find the fourth sum.

Circulate and listen to the interactions as children work on the problems, but let them figure out the answers with as little help from you as possible. Suggest that children try one of the procedures that you recorded on the board earlier.

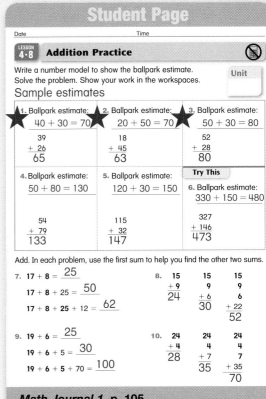

Student Page

Date _____ Time _____

LESSON 4·8 Addition Practice

Write a number model to show the ballpark estimate.
Solve the problem. Show your work in the workspaces.

Unit

Sample estimates

1. Ballpark estimate:
$40 + 30 = 70$
$\begin{array}{r} 39 \\ + 26 \\ \hline 65 \end{array}$

2. Ballpark estimate:
$20 + 50 = 70$
$\begin{array}{r} 18 \\ + 45 \\ \hline 63 \end{array}$

3. Ballpark estimate:
$50 + 30 = 80$
$\begin{array}{r} 52 \\ + 28 \\ \hline 80 \end{array}$

4. Ballpark estimate:
$50 + 80 = 130$
$\begin{array}{r} 54 \\ + 79 \\ \hline 133 \end{array}$

5. Ballpark estimate:
$120 + 30 = 150$
$\begin{array}{r} 115 \\ + 32 \\ \hline 147 \end{array}$

Try This

6. Ballpark estimate:
$330 + 150 = 480$
$\begin{array}{r} 327 \\ + 146 \\ \hline 473 \end{array}$

Add. In each problem, use the first sum to help you find the other two sums.

7. $17 + 8 =$ __25__
$17 + 8 + 25 =$ __50__
$17 + 8 + 25 + 12 =$ __62__

8. $\begin{array}{r} 15 \\ + 9 \\ \hline 24 \end{array}$ $\quad \begin{array}{r} 15 \\ 9 \\ + 6 \\ \hline 30 \end{array}$ $\quad \begin{array}{r} 15 \\ 9 \\ 6 \\ + 22 \\ \hline 52 \end{array}$

9. $19 + 6 =$ __25__
$19 + 6 + 5 =$ __30__
$19 + 6 + 5 + 70 =$ __100__

10. $\begin{array}{r} 24 \\ + 4 \\ \hline 28 \end{array}$ $\quad \begin{array}{r} 24 \\ 4 \\ + 7 \\ \hline 35 \end{array}$ $\quad \begin{array}{r} 24 \\ 4 \\ 7 \\ + 35 \\ \hline 70 \end{array}$

Math Journal 1, p. 105

Games

Fact Extension Game

Materials
- ❑ number cards 0–9 (4 of each)
- ❑ 1 six-sided die
- ❑ 1 calculator
- ❑ 1 sheet of paper for each player

Players 2

Skill Finding sums of 2-digit numbers and multiples of 10

Object of the game To have the higher total.

Directions

1. Shuffle the cards. Place the deck number-side down on the table.

2. Each player draws 2 cards from the deck and makes the larger 2-digit number.

3. Players take turns rolling the die and making another 2-digit number by using the number on the die in the tens place and a zero in the ones place.

4. Each player adds his or her 2 numbers and records the sum on a sheet of paper.

My Reference Book, p. 134

Adjusting the Activity

For the *Fact Extension Game*, suggest that children may add more than one zero.

AUDITORY ◆ KINESTHETIC ◆ TACTILE ◆ VISUAL

Date _____ Time _____

4·8 Math Boxes

1. How much?

   $10 $10 $5

   Q D D D D
   N N P P P

   $ 25.78

2. The temperature was 73°F. It got 13°F colder. What is the temperature now? __60__ °F
   Fill in the diagram and write a number model.

   Change

Start		End
73	−13	?

   73 − 13 = 60

3. 25 books. Bought 15 more. How many now? __40__ books

   Fill in the diagram and write a number model.

   Change

Start		End
25	+15	?

   25 + 15 = 40

4. What time is it?

   10 : 15

   What time will it be in a half hour?

   10 : 45

5. Draw a line segment 6 cm long. Underneath it, draw a line segment that is 2 cm longer.

6. Draw a rectangle. Two sides are 3 cm long and two sides are 5 cm long.

Math Journal 1, p. 106

2 Ongoing Learning & Practice

▶ Playing the *Fact Extension Game*

PARTNER ACTIVITY

(*My Reference Book*, pp. 134 and 135)

Children practice fact extension by playing the *Fact Extension Game*. See *My Reference Book* pages 134 and 135 for the rules of the game.

▶ Math Boxes 4·8

INDEPENDENT ACTIVITY

(*Math Journal 1*, p. 106)

Mixed Practice Math Boxes in this lesson are paired with Math Boxes in Lesson 4-6. The skills in Problems 5 and 6 preview Unit 5 content.

Writing/Reasoning Have children draw, write, or verbalize their answers to the following: *Explain how you know that your answer for Problem 2 is correct.* Sample answers: I know when the temperature gets colder the number goes lower. I used my number grid and put my finger on 73. I went back to 63 and jumped back 3 more. I stopped at 60; I counted back on the thermometer.

▶ Home Link 4·8

INDEPENDENT ACTIVITY

(*Math Masters*, pp. 111 and 112)

Home Connection Children add two multidigit numbers and record their strategies.

The Family Note on the Home Link explains paper-and-pencil strategies other than the traditional right-to-left method.

3 Differentiation Options

READINESS

▶ Modeling Addition and Subtraction Properties of 10s

SMALL-GROUP ACTIVITY

 15–30 Min

To provide experience with adding and subtracting 10s using a visual model, have children use the number grid to model the pattern. Begin by posing problems with numbers that are multiples of 5 or 10.

Example: $30 + 10 =$ ___ 40

Using the number grid, children place a penny on 30. Children use the penny to help them add 10 or jump 10 spaces forward. Ask: *What number are you on now?* 40 Have children move a finger down the column from 30 to 40, pointing out that when adding ten, you go down one space on the number grid.

Example: $25 - 10 =$ ___ 15

Again using the number grid, children lay a penny on 25. Children use the penny to help them subtract 10 or jump 10 spaces back. Ask: *What number are you on now?* 15

Have children move a finger up from 25 to 15 on the number grid. Point out that when subtracting 10 you go up one space on the number grid. Demonstrate that the digit in the tens place changes by 1 while the digit in the ones place stays the same when adding and subtracting 10.

Continue posing problems, working up to adding or subtracting 10 to or from any 2-digit number. For example, $17 + 10 =$ ___. 27 Then, add or subtract 100 or 1,000 to or from any number. For example, $23 + 100 =$ ___. 123

ENRICHMENT

▶ Finding New Methods to Solve Multidigit Addition Problems

SMALL-GROUP ACTIVITY

🕐 30+ Min

To further explore solving 2-digit addition problems, have children find different methods to solve 2- or 3-digit addition problems.

Small groups of children work together to pose a 2- or 3-digit addition problem. They find as many methods as they can to solve the problem. Possible manipulatives include the number grid, a number line, or base-10 blocks. They may also discover paper-and-pencil methods, such as counting up, combining groups, or adjusting and compensating. Invite children to create a poster of their methods to share with the class.

ELL SUPPORT

▶ Building a Math Word Bank

(*Differentiation Handbook*)

SMALL-GROUP ACTIVITY

🕐 5–15 Min

To provide language support for estimation, use the Word Bank Template in the *Differentiation Handbook*. Ask children to write the term *ballpark estimate*. Children describe the terms with words, pictures, and real-life examples. See the *Differentiation Handbook* for more information.

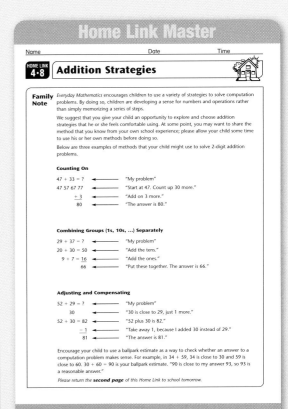

Math Masters, p. 111

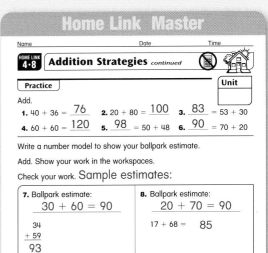

Math Masters, p. 112

The Partial-Sums Addition Algorithm

 Objective To introduce and practice the partial-sums addition algorithm.

1 Teaching the Lesson

materials

Key Activities
Children are introduced to the partial-sums algorithm using base-10 blocks and paper-and-pencil computation. Children practice adding 2- and 3-digit numbers using the partial-sums algorithm and make ballpark estimates to check their answers.

Key Concepts and Skills
- Identify the value of digits in multidigit numbers. [Number and Numeration Goal 2]
- Use base-10 blocks and fact extensions to add two 2-digit whole numbers. [Operations and Computation Goal 2]
- Use ballpark estimates. [Operations and Computation Goal 3]
- Show understanding of addition and subtraction symbols. [Patterns, Functions, and Algebra Goal 2]

Key Vocabulary algorithm

⭐ **Ongoing Assessment: Recognizing Student Achievement** Use Mental Math and Reflexes. [Operations and Computation Goal 2]

- ☐ *Math Journal 1*, pp. 107 and 108
- ☐ Home Link 4·8
- ☐ base-10 blocks: 2 flats, 18 longs, 18 cubes
- ☐ overhead base-10 blocks (optional): 8 longs, 13 cubes
- ☐ slate (optional)

See Advance Preparation

2 Ongoing Learning & Practice

materials

Children answer questions about the times before or after a given time of an event.

Children practice fact extensions by playing the *Fact Extension Game*.

Children practice and maintain skills through Math Boxes and Home Link activities.

- ☐ *Math Journal 1*, pp. 109 and 110
- ☐ *My Reference Book*, pp. 134 and 135
- ☐ Home Link Master (*Math Masters*, p. 113)
- ☐ per partnership: number cards labeled 0–5 (optional: 0–9 number cards)
- ☐ 1 die per partnership

3 Differentiation Options

materials

READINESS
Children use base-10 blocks to review place-value concepts.

ENRICHMENT
Children explain addition strategies.

EXTRA PRACTICE
Children solve problems using multiples of 10.

- ☐ Teaching Masters (*Math Masters*, pp. 114 and 115)
- ☐ Teaching Aid Master (*Math Masters*, p. 428)
- ☐ *Minute Math*®+, p. 42
- ☐ number cards
- ☐ base-10 blocks: 9 cubes, 9 longs, 9 flats
- ☐ number grid

Additional Information

Background Information The problems in Mental Math and Reflexes give children practice with quickly solving mental addition. This skill is needed for making ballpark estimates and carrying out the partial-sums algorithm.

Advance Preparation Plan to spend three days on this lesson. Decide how you will demonstrate the partial-sums algorithm using base-10 blocks—on a flat surface with children gathered around or with blocks on the overhead projector.

Technology
Assessment Management System
Mental Math and Reflexes
See the **iTLG.**

Getting Started

Mental Math and Reflexes ★

Pose pairs of problems, such as the following:

- ○○○ 30 + 40 = ? 70
  300 + 400 = ? 700
- ○○○ ? = 20 + 50 70
  ? = 200 + 500 700
- ○○○ 90 + 30 = ? 120
  900 + 300 = ? 1,200

Math Message

Make a ballpark estimate for each answer. Write a number model for each estimate.

37 + 58 = ?
40 + 60 = 100

473 + 234 = ?
500 + 200 = 700

Unit

people

Home Link 4·8 Follow-Up

Review answers and ask volunteers to explain the strategies they used to add and to make ballpark estimates. Problems 11 and 12 involve adding 3-digit numbers.

✓ Ongoing Assessment: Recognizing Student Achievement

Mental Math and Reflexes ★

Use **Mental Math and Reflexes** to assess children's progress toward solving problems involving addition of multidigit multiples of ten. Children are making adequate progress if they are able to successfully complete Level 1. Some children may be able to solve problems that have a 4-digit number as a sum.

[Operations and Computation Goal 2]

---

1 Teaching the Lesson

▶ Math Message Follow-Up

 WHOLE-CLASS DISCUSSION

Remind children that one way to make a ballpark estimate is to change the numbers in the problem to close but easier numbers that can be added mentally. *For example:*

- 37 + 58 is close to 40 + 60, or 100, or 30 + 50, or 80. The exact answer to 37 + 58 should be close to 100.

- 473 + 234 is close to 500 + 200, or 700, or 400 + 200, or 600. The exact answer should be near 700. Or notice that 400 + 200 is 600. That leaves 73 + 34, which is close to 70 + 30, or 100. Thus, 473 + 234 is close to 600 + 100, or 700.

▶ Introducing the Partial-Sums Addition Algorithm Using Base-10 Blocks

 WHOLE-CLASS DISCUSSION

Today children will learn and practice a single strategy for addition. (Encourage children to continue using other favorite strategies they may have for adding numbers.)

- On **Day 1** of this lesson, children should complete the Math Message Follow-Up and be introduced to and practice the partial-sums addition algorithm using base-10 blocks. Then children should play the *Fact Extension Game* in Part 2.

- On **Day 2** of this lesson, children should be introduced to and practice the partial-sums algorithm as a paper-and-pencil method. Then children should complete journal page 109 in Part 2.

- On **Day 3** of this lesson, children should continue to practice the partial-sums algorithm. Then have children complete the other Part 2 activities.

Example 1:

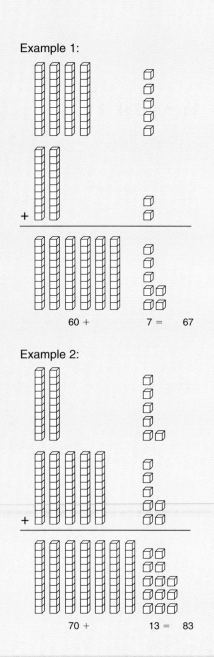

$$60 + \qquad 7 = \qquad 67$$

Example 2:

$$70 + \qquad 13 = \qquad 83$$

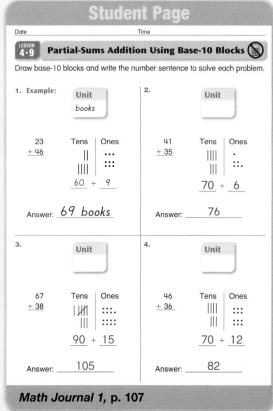
Write these two problems on the board, in vertical form:

$$\begin{array}{r} 45 \\ + 22 \end{array} \qquad\qquad \begin{array}{r} 26 \\ + 57 \end{array}$$

Ask children to gather around as you demonstrate how to use base-10 blocks. You may wish to use an overhead. Refer to the longs as tens and the cubes as ones. For each problem, model addition as a three-part operation: adding the 10s, adding the 1s, and then adding the partial sums.

Example 1: Model 45 + 22 with base-10 blocks.

1. Make a ballpark estimate before or after solving the problem. Sample answers: 50 + 20; 45 + 20; 40 + 20

2. Count out 4 tens and 5 ones to represent 45. Count out 2 tens and 2 ones to represent 22.

3. Arrange the blocks so that they resemble the vertical addition problem. (See the first model in the margin.)

4. Collect the tens into one pile. Collect the ones into a second pile.

5. Count the tens. 6 tens, or 60

6. Count the ones. 7 ones, or 7

7. Add the counts of tens and ones. 60 + 7 = 67 Record the answer on the board. The ballpark estimates are close to this answer, so the answer is reasonable.

Example 2: Model 26 + 57 with base-10 blocks.

For the second example, follow the same procedure. When you count the ones, some children may notice that 10 cubes in the ones pile can be replaced by 1 long; you can make this substitution. There are still two piles of blocks: the tens pile (with 8 tens), and the revised ones pile (with 3 ones).

Summary

These examples using base-10 blocks illustrate the steps of the partial-sums method for addition:

1. Add the tens.

2. Add the ones.

3. Add the partial sums of tens and ones to obtain the final answer.

Children do several problems at their desk. Have them describe exactly what they are doing at each step.

▶ **Practicing Addition Using Base-10 Blocks**

 PARTNER ACTIVITY

(*Math Journal 1*, p. 107)

Partners use base-10 blocks to practice the partial-sums algorithm.

Introducing the Partial-Sums Algorithm as a Paper-and-Pencil Method

WHOLE-CLASS DISCUSSION

Review the partial-sums addition with base-10 blocks using the same two problems: 45 + 22 and 26 + 57.

Next, on the board or overhead, demonstrate the paper-and-pencil method for solving these problems. As a reminder of place value, write "10s" and "1s" above the columns and use the same language to describe 10s and 1s.

Example: 45 + 22

1. Find a ballpark estimate. 50 + 20; 45 + 20; 40 + 20

2. Add the tens. 4 tens + 2 tens = 6 tens, or 60. Write 60 below the line.

3. Add the ones. 5 ones + 2 ones = 7 ones, or 7. Write 7 below 60.

4. Add the partial sums. Draw a second line beneath 60 and 7. Write 67 beneath this line.

In this example, the tens were added first. However, the partial sums may be calculated in either order—it does not matter whether the tens or the ones are added first.

For the second example, follow the same procedure again to find and add the partial sums 70 and 13, checking the answer against a ballpark estimate.

Tell children that the method illustrated by these examples is called an **algorithm.** An algorithm is a step-by-step set of instructions for doing something. Write *algorithm* on the board.

Practicing the Partial-Sums Algorithm

WHOLE-CLASS DISCUSSION

Write several multidigit addition problems on the board. Start by adding together a 2-digit and a 1-digit number. Most problems should have 2-digit addends. Using slates or paper, have children describe exactly what they are doing at each step. Correct errors in calculation and in method, making sure the numbers are aligned in columns.

Continuing Practice with the Partial-Sums Algorithm

WHOLE-CLASS DISCUSSION

(*Math Journal 1*, p. 108)

Review the partial-sums algorithm. Most problems should have 2-digit addends, but include at least one with 3-digit addends. When you discuss the problem with 3-digit addends, write "100s," "10s," and "1s" above the columns as a reminder of place value. Most children will realize that the partial-sums method works the same way for 3-digit numbers as for 2-digit numbers.

Date _____ Time _____

LESSON 4·9 Addition Practice

Write a number model to show your ballpark estimate. Solve the problem. Show your work. Use the ballpark estimate to check whether your exact answer makes sense. Sample estimates:

Unit

1. Ballpark estimate:	2. Ballpark estimate:	3. Ballpark estimate:
60 + 10 = 70	70 + 10 = 80	50 + 30 = 80
59 + 8 67	67 + 7 74	47 + 32 79
4. Ballpark estimate:	5. Ballpark estimate:	6. Ballpark estimate:
60 + 30 = 90	120 + 50 = 170	140 + 160 = 300
58 + 26 84	122 + 53 175	136 + 157 293

Math Journal 1, p. 108

	10s	1s			10s	1s
	4	5			2	6
+	2	2		+	5	7
	6	0			7	0
+		7		+	1	3
	6	7			8	3

Links to the Future

This is the first time that children have been exposed to a formal paper-and-pencil addition algorithm. They will have plenty of opportunities to practice the partial-sums algorithm throughout the year. Do not expect all children to be able to perform the algorithm at the conclusion of this lesson.

	100s	10s	1s
	4	7	3
+	2	3	4
	6	0	0
	1	0	0
+			7
	7	0	7

NOTE Provide base-10 blocks for children to use when working on journal page 108. This concrete experience is essential to prepare children for the transition from concrete to abstract thought.

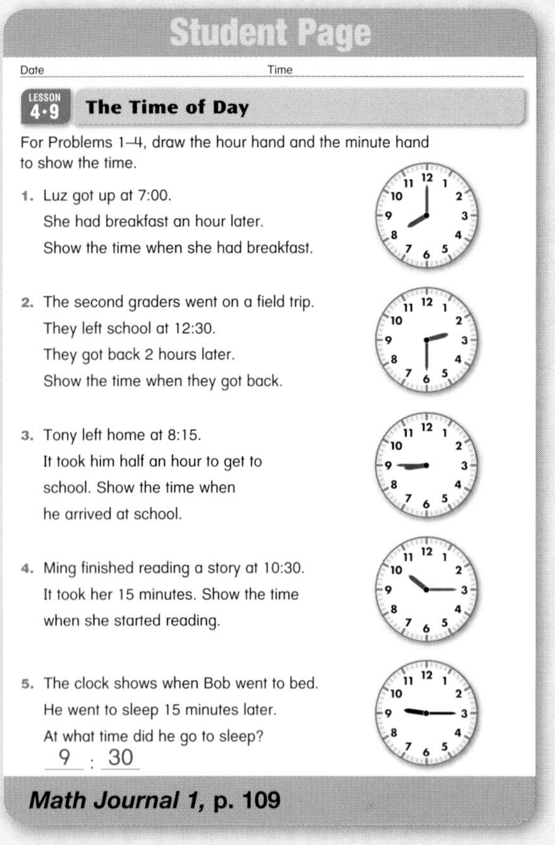

Student Page

Date Time

LESSON 4·9 **The Time of Day**

For Problems 1–4, draw the hour hand and the minute hand to show the time.

1. Luz got up at 7:00. She had breakfast an hour later. Show the time when she had breakfast.
2. The second graders went on a field trip. They left school at 12:30. They got back 2 hours later. Show the time when they got back.
3. Tony left home at 8:15. It took him half an hour to get to school. Show the time when he arrived at school.
4. Ming finished reading a story at 10:30. It took her 15 minutes. Show the time when she started reading.
5. The clock shows when Bob went to bed. He went to sleep 15 minutes later. At what time did he go to sleep? 9 : 30

Math Journal 1, p. 109

Student Page

Date Time

LESSON 4·9 **Math Boxes**

1. I bought a radio for $67.00. I paid with $100.00. How much change did I get? $33.00
2. What is the temperature? Circle the best answer. (A.) 34°F B. 36°F C. 32°F D. 4°F
3. Write three even and three odd 2-digit numbers. Circle the even numbers. Sample answers: (22) 31 (68) 39 (74) 23
4. What time is it? 6 : 15 What time will it be in 15 minutes? 6 : 30
5. Find the rules. +4 −6 11 15 9 13 11 7
6. Use your Pattern-Block Template. Draw the triangles. What is the difference between the triangles? One is larger.

Math Journal 1, p. 110

2 Ongoing Learning & Practice

▶ Reviewing Telling Time

INDEPENDENT ACTIVITY

(*Math Journal 1,* p. 109)

Children answer questions in which they determine the times before or after the given time of an event.

This activity is related to the partial-sums algorithm. In adding an initial time and an elapsed time, a common strategy is to add the hours and minutes separately and then trade 60 minutes for an hour if the total number of minutes is 60 or greater.

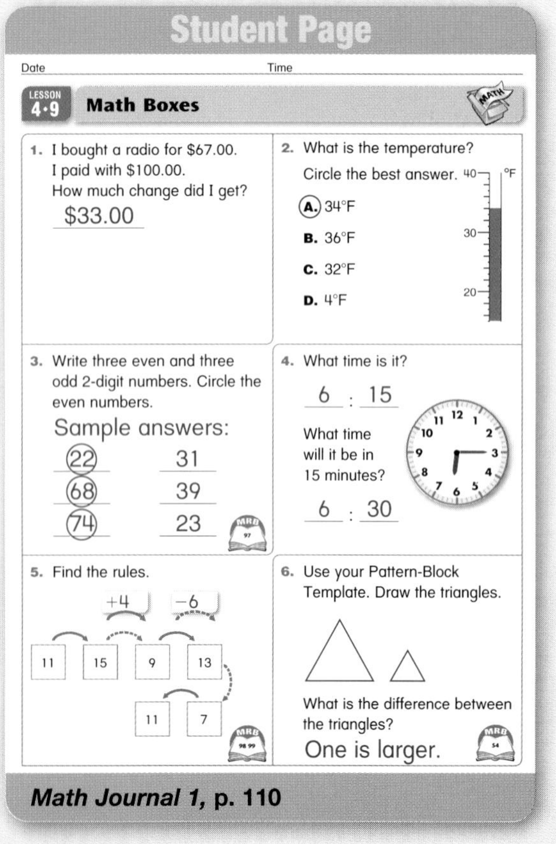

▶ Playing the *Fact Extension Game*

PARTNER ACTIVITY

(*My Reference Book*, pp. 134 and 135)

Children practice fact extensions through the *Fact Extension Game* first introduced on page 292 in Lesson 4-8.

▶ Math Boxes 4·9

INDEPENDENT ACTIVITY

(*Math Journal 1,* p. 110)

Mixed Practice Math Boxes in this lesson are linked with Math Boxes in Lessons 4-5 and 4-7. The skill in Problem 6 previews Unit 5 content.

Writing/Reasoning Have children draw, write, or verbalize their answers to the following: *In Problem 4, what time will it be in 12 hours? Explain how you solved this problem.* Sample answer: 6:15. I counted up 12 hours. 7:15, 8:15, 9:15, 10:15, and so on.

▶ Home Link 4·9

INDEPENDENT ACTIVITY

(*Math Masters,* p. 113)

Home Connection Children use the partial-sums algorithm to solve multidigit addition problems.

3 Differentiation Options

READINESS

PARTNER ACTIVITY

▶ Reviewing Place-Value Concepts

30+ Min

(*Math Masters,* pp. 114 and 428)

To provide experience with place value, have children use base-10 blocks to explore a strategy for using the fewest base-10 blocks.

Use base-10 blocks: Partners shuffle number cards, place the deck facedown between them, and draw two cards. They place the first card in the ones column on the Place-Value Mat (*Math Masters,* page 428) and the second card in the tens column. They use the *fewest* base-10 blocks possible to build the number. On a sheet of paper, they record the number shown, as well as the number of tens (longs) and the number of ones (cubes).

Then partners switch the two cards on the mat and repeat the procedure. Vary the activity by having children draw three cards to make 3-digit numbers.

Use *Math Masters,* page 114: For each group of base-10 blocks, children represent the same number using the fewest flats, longs, and cubes.

 ENRICHMENT

> ▶ **Using Addition Strategies**
(*Math Masters,* p. 115)

INDEPENDENT ACTIVITY

15–30 Min

To apply children's understanding of multidigit addition, have them determine the steps of an addition strategy on *Math Masters,* page 115. Have children explain how the strategies work. Briefly discuss which strategy they thought was easier and why.

 EXTRA PRACTICE

> ▶ *Minute Math+*

SMALL-GROUP ACTIVITY

5–15 Min

Children practice adding multiples of 10. Model this, using the number grid to find the answer. See the following page in *Minute Math+:* p. 42.

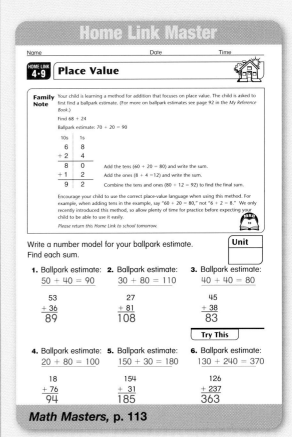

Home Link Master

HOME LINK 4·9 **Place Value**

Family Note Your child is learning a method for addition that focuses on place value. The child is asked to first find a ballpark estimate. (For more on ballpark estimates see page 92 in the *My Reference Book*.)

Find 68 + 24

Ballpark estimate: 70 + 20 = 90

10s	1s	
6	8	
+ 2	4	
8	0	Add the tens (60 + 20 = 80) and write the sum.
+ 1	2	Add the ones (8 + 4 =12) and write the sum.
9	2	Combine the tens and ones (80 + 12 = 92) to find the final sum.

Encourage your child to use the correct place-value language when using this method. For example, when adding tens in the example, say "60 + 20 = 80," not "6 + 2 = 8." We only recently introduced this method, so allow plenty of time for practice before expecting your child to be able to use it easily.

Please return this Home Link to school tomorrow.

Write a number model for your ballpark estimate. Find each sum.

Unit

1. Ballpark estimate:
50 + 40 = 90

53
+ 36
89

2. Ballpark estimate:
30 + 80 = 110

27
+ 81
108

3. Ballpark estimate:
40 + 40 = 80

45
+ 38
83

Try This

4. Ballpark estimate:
20 + 80 = 100

18
+ 76
94

5. Ballpark estimate:
150 + 30 = 180

154
+ 31
185

6. Ballpark estimate:
130 + 240 = 370

126
+ 237
363

Math Masters, p. 113

Teaching Master

LESSON 4·9 **Base-10 Blocks**

For each problem, draw a new set of base-10 blocks that uses the fewest possible number of flats, longs, and cubes.

1. ||| :::: :....	|||| ....
2. ||||| :....	|||||| .
3. || ▦ ::::	|||||	...
4. |||| :::: ::::	||||||	....
5. ☐ ||||| |||||	....	☐☐	....
6. ☐ ||||| ||||| ||| :::...	☐☐ |||| ..

Math Masters, p. 114

Teaching Master

LESSON 4·9 **Addition Strategies**

Addition Strategies

Look at the two addition strategies below. See if you can figure out how they work.

Louisa's Strategy	**Li's Strategy**
37 + 44 = ?	37 + 44 = ?
37 + 40 = 77	40 + 44 = 84
77 + 4 = 81	84 − 3 = 81
37 + 44 = 81	37 + 44 = 81

Now try to use either Louisa's Strategy or Li's Strategy to solve the problems below.

29 + 56 = ?   65 + 27 =

Sample answers:

Louisa's Strategy	Li's Strategy
29 + 50 = 79	65 + 30 = 95
79 + 6 = 85	95 − 3 = 92
29 + 56 = 85	65 + 27 = 92

Which strategy do you think is easier? Explain. ____

Sample answer: Louisa's strategy is easier because she is adding the tens and then adding the ones. She doesn't have to subtract anything.

Math Masters, p. 115

4·10 Progress Check 4

 Objective To assess children's progress on mathematical content through the end of Unit 4.

---

1 Assessing Progress

materials

Progress Check 4 is a cumulative assessment of concepts and skills taught in Unit 4 and in previous units.

See the Appendix for a complete list of Grade 2 Goals.

☐ Home Link 4·9   ☐ slate
☐ Assessment Masters (*Assessment Handbook,* pp. 168–172)
☐ Class Thermometer Poster (°F/°C)

CONTENT ASSESSED	LESSON(S)	SELF	ORAL/SLATE	WRITTEN PART A	WRITTEN PART B
Read and write whole numbers to 1,000 using standard base-ten place-value notation; identify digits and express their values in such numbers. [Number and Numeration Goal 2]	4·1, 4·3, 4·9			3a, 3b	13
Recognize numbers as odd or even. [Number and Numeration Goal 6]	4·5, 4·7	6		4a–4d	
Use and explain strategies for solving problems and number stories involving addition and subtraction of 2-digit whole numbers. Calculate and compare values of coin and bill combinations. [Operations and Computation Goal 2]	4·1–4·9	1–3	4–7	1	6, 7, 8b, 9b, 10b
Use strategies to estimate solutions (ballpark estimates) for addition and subtraction problems. [Operations and Computation Goal 3]	4·5, 4·8, 4·9				8a, 9a, 10a
Read temperature to the nearest degree in both Fahrenheit and Celsius. [Measurement and Reference Frames Goal 5]	4·3–4·9	4	1–3	2a, 2b	11, 12
Continue simple numerical and non-numerical patterns; find rules for patterns and use them to solve problems. [Patterns, Functions, and Algebra Goal 1]	4·1–4·5, 4·7, 4·9	5		5	

---

2 Building Background for Unit 4

materials

Math Boxes 4·10 previews and practices skills for Unit 5.
The Unit 5 Family Letter introduces families to Unit 5 topics and terms.

☐ *Math Journal 1,* p. 111
☐ Home Link Masters (*Math Masters,* pp. 116–119)

Additional Information

See *Assessment Handbook,* pages 76–83, for additional assessment information. For assessment checklists, see pages 248–251.

Technology

Assessment Management System
Progress Check 4
See the **iTLG.**

Getting Started

Math Message • Self Assessment

Complete the Self Assessment (Assessment Handbook, page 168).

Home Link 4·9 Follow-Up

Review answers as necessary.

① Assessing Progress

▶ ## Math Message Follow-Up

INDEPENDENT ACTIVITY

(Self Assessment, *Assessment Handbook,* p. 168)

The Self Assessment page offers children the opportunity to reflect upon their progress.

▶ ## Oral and Slate Assessments

WHOLE-CLASS ACTIVITY

Problems 1–3 provide summative information and can be used for grading purposes. Problems 4–7 provide formative information that can be useful in planning future instruction.

Oral Assessment

Using the Class Thermometer Poster (°F/°C), pose temperature situations and ask children to identify the more sensible measure.

Suggestions:

1. A good day for swimming outside: 28°C or 60°C? 28°C

2. A good day for ice fishing: 50°F or 20°F? 20°F

3. A good day to watch a baseball game outside: 20°C or 40°F? 20°C

Slate Assessment

Write the sums.

4. 20 + 9 29

5. 30 + 8 38

6. 2 + 30 32

7. 60 + 9 69

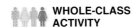

Name   Date   Time

LESSON 4·10   **Self Assessment**   Progress Check 4

Check one box for each skill.

Skills	I can do this by myself. I can explain how to do this.	I can do this by myself.	I can do this with help.
1. Add coins.			
2. Solve 2-digit addition.			
3. Find change.			
4. Read the temperature.			
5. Find patterns on the number grid.			
6. Recognize odd and even numbers.			

Assessment Handbook, p. 168

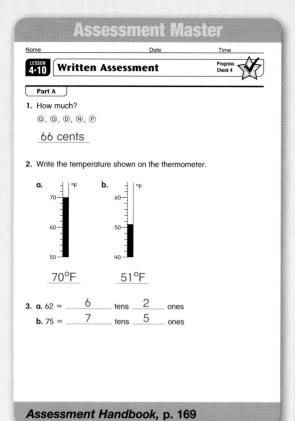

Assessment Handbook, p. 169

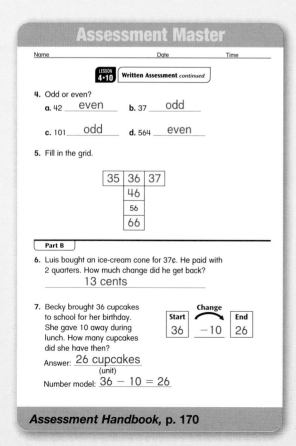

Assessment Handbook, p. 170

▶ Written Assessment

(*Assessment Handbook*, pp. 169–171)

👤 INDEPENDENT ACTIVITY

Part A   Recognizing Student Achievement

Problems 1–5 provide summative information and may be used for grading purposes.

Problem(s)	Description
1	Calculate the value of a coin combination.
2a, 2b	Write the temperature.
3a, 3b	Write whole numbers using base-ten notation.
4a–4d	Recognize numbers as odd or even.
5	Fill in the number grid puzzle.

Part B   Informing Instruction

Problems 6–13 provide formative information that can be useful in planning future instruction.

Problem(s)	Description
6	Calculate the amount of change.
7	Solve the change-to-less problem.
8a, 9a, 10a	Solve the problems using ballpark estimates.
8b, 9b, 10b	Solve problems involving multidigit addition.
11, 12	Mark each thermometer to show the temperature.
13	Circle the digit in the 100s place.

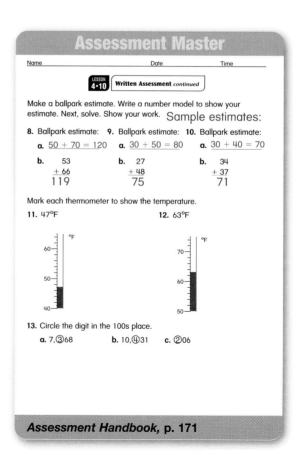

Assessment Handbook, p. 171

▶ Open Response

(*Assessment Handbook,* pp. 79–83 and 172)

Finding the Largest Sum

The open response problem requires children to apply skills and concepts from Unit 4 to solve a multistep problem. See *Assessment Handbook,* pages 79–83 for rubrics and children's work samples for this problem.

② Building Background for Unit 5

▶ Math Boxes 4·10

(*Math Journal 1,* p. 111)

Mixed Practice This Math Boxes page previews Unit 5 content.

▶ Home Link 4·10: Unit 5 Family Letter

(*Math Masters,* pp. 116–119)

Home Connection The Unit 5 Family Letter provides parents and guardians with information and activities related to Unit 5 topics.

Assessment Master

Name   Date   Time

LESSON 4·10 Open Response   Progress Check 4

Finding the Largest Sum
Cut out the 4 digits from the bottom of this page.

Make two 2-digit numbers in the boxes below so that when you add them you get the largest possible sum.

Use the digits you cut out to help you try different combinations. When you find the combination that makes the largest sum, write the numbers in the boxes.

```
  □   □
+ □   □
―――――――――
```

Show your work. Explain how you know you found the largest sum.

| 4 | 3 | 7 | 5 |

Assessment Handbook, p. 172

Home Link Masters

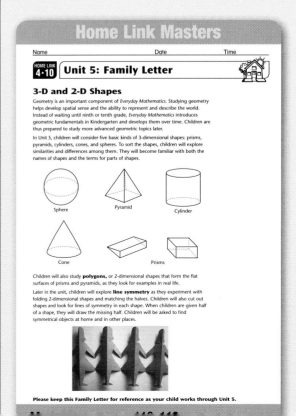

Name   Date   Time

HOME LINK 4·10 Unit 5: Family Letter

3-D and 2-D Shapes

Geometry is an important component of *Everyday Mathematics*. Studying geometry helps develop spatial sense and the ability to represent and describe the world. Instead of waiting until ninth or tenth grade, *Everyday Mathematics* introduces geometric fundamentals in Kindergarten and develops them over time. Children are thus prepared to study more advanced geometric topics later.

In Unit 5, children will consider five basic kinds of 3-dimensional shapes: prisms, pyramids, cylinders, cones, and spheres. To sort the shapes, children will explore similarities and differences among them. They will become familiar with both the names of shapes and the terms for parts of shapes.

Sphere   Pyramid   Cylinder

Cone   Prisms

Children will also study **polygons**, or 2-dimensional shapes that form the flat surfaces of prisms and pyramids, as they look for examples in real life.

Later in the unit, children will explore **line symmetry** as they experiment with folding 2-dimensional shapes and matching the halves. Children will also cut out shapes and look for lines of symmetry in each shape. When children are given half of a shape, they will draw the missing half. Children will be asked to find symmetrical objects at home and in other places.

Please keep this Family Letter for reference as your child works through Unit 5.

Unit 5
Organizer

3-D and 2-D Shapes

Overview

This unit contains mathematical terms that may be new to your students. The primary purpose of this unit, however, is to develop classification skills, not to teach vocabulary. This objective is accomplished through hands-on activities, in which children observe similarities and differences among various shapes and explore spatial relationships. Unit 5 has four main areas of focus:

- ◆ To develop the concepts of point and line segment,
- ◆ To identify, name, and classify polygons,
- ◆ To observe similarities and differences among 3-dimensional shapes, and
- ◆ To explore symmetry.

Contents

Learning In Perspective

	Lesson Objectives	Links to the Past	Links to the Future
5·1	To demonstrate rules used to classify shapes; to develop readiness for division; and to demonstrate telling time using digital and analog notation.	In first grade, children sort attribute blocks and play games such as the *Attribute Train Game*. They practice telling time to the nearest half-hour and quarter-hour. They begin exploring equal shares.	Fractions of an hour and minutes before and after the hour are introduced in third grade. Division models are introduced in Unit 11. In third grade, children continue to focus on number models and diagrams for division stories.
5·2	To guide children as they define, name, and draw line segments.	In earlier grades, children are introduced to rulers and straightedges. They measure and draw line segments to the nearest centimeter.	In third grade, children identify, draw, name, and model line segments, lines, and rays.
5·3	To introduce the concepts of parallel and parallel line segments.	In first grade, children explore drawing and measuring line segments.	In third grade, children construct 2- and 3-dimensional figures to model and explore the relationship among parallel and intersecting line segments, lines, and rays.
5·4	To review names and classify polygons; to develop readiness for multiplication; and to provide opportunities to explore similarities and differences of attribute blocks.	Children examine the properties of 2-dimensional shapes in Kindergarten. They create models of polygons in first grade. Beginning in Kindergarten, children informally explore multiplication through skip counting. Children in Kindergarten and first grade sort attribute blocks.	Exploration and construction of 2-dimensional shapes are continued in third grade, where, using their knowledge of shapes, children classify 3-dimensional shapes. Children model multiplication with arrays and diagrams.
5·5	To guide children as they identify the names and the characteristics of various quadrangles, and as they explore similarities and differences among quadrangles.	Children examine the properties of 2-dimensional shapes in Kindergarten. They create models of polygons in first grade.	In third grade, exploration and construction of 2-dimensional shapes continues. Children also classify 3-dimensional shapes using their general knowledge of shapes.
5·6	To guide children as they compare and contrast the characteristics of 3-dimensional shapes.	Beginning in Kindergarten, children work with 3-dimensional shapes. They create a Shapes Museum. First graders explore the cube as a special rectangular prism and construct paper tetrahedrons.	Beyond third grade, lessons highlight clear notation, definitions, comparisons, and statements of properties and relationships.
5·7	To guide children as they construct pyramids and explore the relationship among the number of faces, edges, and vertices in pyramids.	Since Kindergarten children work with 3-dimensional shapes. They create a Shapes Museum. First graders explore the cube as a special rectangular prism and construct 3-dimensional shapes.	Beyond third grade, lessons highlight clear notation, definitions, comparisons, and statements of properties and relationships.
5·8	To guide children as they find lines of symmetry in objects and complete drawings to create symmetrical shapes.	In Kindergarten, children begin exploring symmetry through art activities. In first grade, children use pattern blocks and drawings to explore symmetry.	In third grade, children explore the properties of symmetrical shapes.

Key Concepts and Skills

Key Concepts and Skills	Grade 2 Goals*
5·1 Count a collection of objects.	Number and Numeration Goal 1
Match the time on a clock face with the digital notation.	Measurement and Reference Frames Goal 6
Find the rules for a group of sorted attribute blocks.	Patterns, Functions, and Algebra Goal 1
5·2 Solve number stories using addition facts.	Operations and Computation Goal 1
Connect points in a sequence.	Geometry Goal 1
Use a straightedge to draw a line segment.	Geometry Goal 1
5·3 Use a straightedge to draw a line segment.	Geometry Goal 1
Identify parallel line segments.	Geometry Goal 1
Draw a quadrangle.	Geometry Goal 2
5·4 Count the total number of cubes.	Number and Numeration Goal 1
Create and record cube arrays.	Operations and Computation Goal 4
Name, compare, and construct polygons.	Geometry Goal 2
Sort attributes according to a rule.	Patterns, Functions, and Algebra Goal 1
5·5 Create shapes out of triangles and rectangles.	Geometry Goal 2
Identify characteristics of quadrangles.	Geometry Goal 2
Compare quadrangles.	Geometry Goal 2
5·6 Identify cones, pyramids, prisms, cubes, and cylinders.	Geometry Goal 2
Compare cones, pyramids, prisms, cubes, and cylinders.	Geometry Goal 2
Describe 3-dimensional shapes.	Geometry Goal 2
5·7 Construct 2-dimensional shapes using straws and twist-ties.	Geometry Goal 2
Construct pyramids using straws and twist-ties.	Geometry Goal 2
Describe different pyramids.	Geometry Goal 2
Identify patterns and relationships among pyramids.	Patterns, Functions, and Algebra Goal 1
5·8 Divide shapes into equal parts.	Number and Numeration Goal 3
Locate the line of symmetry in 2-dimensional shapes.	Geometry Goal 3
Create symmetric shapes.	Geometry Goal 3

* For a detailed listing of all Grade 2 Goals, see pages 491–502.

Ongoing Learning and Practice

Math Boxes

Math Boxes are paired across lessons as shown in the brackets below. This makes them useful as assessment tools. Math Boxes also preview content of the next unit.

Mixed practice   [5♦1, 5♦3], [5♦2, 5♦4], [5♦5, 5♦7], [5♦6, 5♦8]

Mixed practice with multiple choice   5♦1, 5♦2, 5♦7, 5♦8

Mixed practice with writing/reasoning opportunity   5♦3, 5♦4, 5♦5, 5♦6

Practice through Games

Games are an essential component of practice in the *Everyday Mathematics* program. Games offer skills practice and promote strategic thinking.

Lesson	Game	Skill Practiced
5♦1	*Addition Spin*	**Addition of 2-digit numbers** Operations and Computation Goal 1
5♦4	*Dollar Rummy*	**Creating coin combinations equal to $1.00** Operations and Computation Goal 2
5♦5	*Name That Number*	**Addition and subtraction facts** Operations and Computation Goal 1 Number and Numeration Goal 5
5♦7	*Beat the Calculator*	**Addition facts** Operations and Computation Goal 1
5♦8	*Fact Extension Game*	**Extensions of basic facts** Operations and Computation Goal 2

See the *Differentiation Handbook* for ways to adapt games to meet children's needs.

Home Communication

Home Links provide homework and home communication.

◀ *Home Connection Handbook* provides more ideas to communicate effectively with parents.

Unit 5 Family Letter provides families with an overview, Do-Anytime Activities, Building Skills Through Games, and a list of vocabulary.

Problem Solving

Encourage children to use a variety of strategies to solve problems and to explain those strategies. Strategies that children might use in this unit:

◆ Identifying a pattern
◆ Identifying important information
◆ Making an organized list
◆ Using logical reasoning
◆ Acting out the problem

Lesson	Activity
5◆1	Figure out attribute rules.
5◆1	Solve problems involving equal sharing.
5◆4	Follow directions to make figures on a geoboard.
5◆4	Find attribute blocks that differ by one or more attributes.
5◆5, 5◆6	Find similarities and differences among shapes.

Lessons that teach **through** *problem solving, not just* **about** *problem solving*

See Chapter 18 in the *Teacher's Reference Manual* for more information about problem solving.

Planning Tips

Pacing

Pacing depends on a number of factors, such as children's individual needs and how long your school has been using *Everyday Mathematics*. At the beginning of Unit 5, review your *Content by Strand* Poster to help you set a monthly pace.

← **MOST CLASSROOMS** →

DECEMBER	JANUARY	FEBRUARY

NCTM Standards

Unit 5 Lessons	5◆1	5◆2	5◆3	5◆4	5◆5	5◆6	5◆7	5◆8
NCTM Standards	2–10	3, 6–10	3, 6–10	1, 2, 3–4, 6–7, 10	3, 8–10	3, 7–10	2, 3, 7, 8, 10	3, 6–10

Content Standards: 1 Number and Operations, **2** Algebra, **3** Geometry, **4** Measurement, **5** Data Analysis and Probability
Process Standards: 6 Problem Solving, **7** Reasoning and Proof, **8** Communication, **9** Connections, **10** Representation

Balanced Assessment

Ongoing Assessment

 Recognizing Student Achievement

Opportunities to assess children's progress toward Grade 2 Goals:

Lesson	Content Assessed
5•1	Read the time and match it to digital notation. [Measurement and Reference Frames Goal 6]
5•2	Use a straightedge to draw a line segment. [Geometry Goal 1]
5•3	Identify parallel lines. [Geometry Goal 1]
5•4	Identify plane figures. [Geometry Goal 2]
5•5	Make reasonable estimates for addition problems. [Operations and Computation Goal 3]
5•6	Find the difference between two 2-digit numbers. [Operations and Computation Goal 2]
5•7	Complete patterns on a number grid. [Patterns, Functions, and Algebra Goal 1]
5•8	Complete symmetric shapes. [Geometry Goal 3]

Use the **Assessment Management System** to collect and analyze data about children's progress throughout the year.

 Informing Instruction

To anticipate common child errors and to highlight problem-solving strategies:

Lesson 5•3   Understand parallel line segments

Lesson 5•5   Recognize square corners

Lesson 5•6   Recognize differences between shapes

Lesson 5•6   Name shapes

Periodic Assessment

5✦9 Progress Check 5

CONTENT ASSESSED	ASSESSMENT ITEMS			
	Self	Oral/Slate	Written	Open Response
Count up by 1s, 2s, 5s, 10s, 25s, and 100s to 1,000. [Number and Numeration Goal 1]	✔		✔	✔
Order and compare whole numbers. [Number and Numeration Goal 7]			✔	
Know and apply addition facts. [Operations and Computation Goal 1]		✔	✔	
Use and explain strategies for solving problems involving the addition of 2-digit whole numbers. [Operations and Computation Goal 2]		✔		
Show and tell time on an analog and digital clock. [Measurement and Reference Frames Goal 6]		✔		
Draw line segments and identify parallel line segments. [Geometry Goal 1]	✔		✔	
Identify, describe, and model plane and solid figures. [Geometry Goal 2]	✔		✔	
Create and complete simple 2-dimensional symmetric shapes or designs. [Geometry Goal 3]	✔		✔	
Extend, describe, and use numeric patterns to solve problems. [Patterns, Functions, and Algebra Goal 1]				✔

Portfolio Opportunities

Opportunities to gather samples of children's mathematical writings, drawings, and creations to add balance to the assessment process:

◆ Exploring equal sharing, **Lesson 5✦1**

◆ Identifying plane figures, **Lesson 5✦4**

◆ Making centimeter-cube arrays, **Lesson 5✦4**

◆ Explaining how to identify odd and even numbers, **Lesson 5✦4**

◆ Making reasonable estimates for addition problems, **Lesson 5✦5**

◆ Solving an addition problem with four addends, **Lesson 5✦6**

Assessment Handbook

Unit 5 Assessment Support

◆ Grade 2 Goals, pp. 37–50

◆ Unit 5 Assessment Overview, pp. 84–91

◆ Unit 5 Open Response
  • Detailed rubric, p. 88
  • Sample student responses, pp. 89–91

Unit 5 Assessment Masters

◆ Unit 5 Self Assessment, p. 173

◆ Unit 5 Written Assessment, pp. 174–176

◆ Unit 5 Open Response, p. 177

◆ Unit 5 Class Checklist, pp. 254, 255, and 293

◆ Unit 5 Individual Profile of Progress, pp. 252, 253, and 292

◆ Exit Slip, p. 295

◆ Math Logs, pp. 298–300

◆ Other Student Assessment Forms, pp. 296, 297, 301, 302, and 303

Differentiated Instruction

Daily Lesson Support

ENGLISH LANGUAGE LEARNERS

5◆3 Building a Math Word Bank
5◆5 Using a Venn diagram
5◆7 Describing and comparing shapes

EXTRA PRACTICE

5◆4 Finding shapes around the room

Minute Math®+
5◆1 Gaining experience telling time
5◆6 Identifying shapes

READINESS

5◆1 Using the body as a clock
5◆2 Making designs from line segments
5◆3 Drawing line segments
5◆4 Identifying pattern-block shapes
5◆5 Sorting pattern-block shapes
5◆7 Reviewing and constructing polygons
5◆8 Exploring symmetry with pattern blocks

ENRICHMENT

5◆2 Drawing line segments in a sequence
5◆3 Solving pattern-block puzzles
5◆4 Investigating properties of polygons
5◆5 Exploring tangrams
5◆6 Solving and posing shape riddles
5◆7 Describing attributes of pyramids
5◆8 Making a symmetry booklet

Adjusting the Activity

5◆1 Figuring out attribute rules
5◆1 Writing the time in words
5◆2 Understanding lesson vocabulary **ELL**
5◆3 Understanding parallel lines and line segments **ELL**
5◆3 Adding to the Word Wall **ELL**
5◆4 Finding attribute blocks that are different

5◆5 Comparing shapes
5◆6 Adding to the Word Wall **ELL**
5◆6 Using a Venn diagram for understanding shapes **ELL**
5◆7 Constructing pyramids
5◆8 Adding to the Word Wall **ELL**

AUDITORY ◆ KINESTHETIC ◆ TACTILE ◆ VISUAL

⊙ Cross-Curricular Links

Language Arts
Lesson 5◆4 Children are taught the Greek roots of the word *polygon*.

Literature
Lesson 5◆4 Children read *The Greedy Triangle* and look for shapes around the classroom.

Differentiation Handbook
See the *Differentiation Handbook* for materials on Unit 5.

Language Support

Everyday Mathematics provides lesson-specific suggestions to help all children, including non-native English speakers, to acquire, process, and express mathematical ideas.

Connecting Math and Literacy

Lesson 5◆4 *The Greedy Triangle* by Marilyn Burns, Scholastic Press, 1995

Lesson 5◆4 *Shapes, Shapes, Shapes* by Tana Hoban, HarperTrophy, 1996

Lesson 5◆5 *Grandfather Tang's Story* by Ann Tompert, Dragonfly Books, 1997

Lesson 5◆5 *Three Pigs, One Wolf and Seven Magic Shapes* by Grace Maccarone, Cartwheel, 1998

Lesson 5◆6 *The Art of Shapes: For Children and Adults* by Margaret Steele and Cindy Estes, Moca Store, 1997

 My Reference Book
pp. 50, 55, 60, 120, 121, 124, 125, 134, 135, 138, and 139

<table>
<tr><td colspan="2">Unit 5 Vocabulary</td></tr>
<tr><td>angle</td><td>pentagon</td></tr>
<tr><td>apex</td><td>pentagonal pyramid</td></tr>
<tr><td>base</td><td>point</td></tr>
<tr><td>cone</td><td>polygon</td></tr>
<tr><td>congruent</td><td>pyramid</td></tr>
<tr><td>cube</td><td>quadrangle</td></tr>
<tr><td>curved surface</td><td>rectangle</td></tr>
<tr><td>cylinder</td><td>rectangular prism</td></tr>
<tr><td>edge</td><td>rectangular pyramid</td></tr>
<tr><td>endpoint</td><td>rhombus</td></tr>
<tr><td>face</td><td>side</td></tr>
<tr><td>flat surface</td><td>sphere</td></tr>
<tr><td>heptagon</td><td>square</td></tr>
<tr><td>hexagon</td><td>square corner</td></tr>
<tr><td>hexagonal pyramid</td><td>square pyramid</td></tr>
<tr><td>kite</td><td>straightedge</td></tr>
<tr><td>line of symmetry</td><td>symmetrical</td></tr>
<tr><td>line segment</td><td>trapezoid</td></tr>
<tr><td>line symmetry</td><td>triangle</td></tr>
<tr><td>octagon</td><td>triangular pyramid</td></tr>
<tr><td>parallel</td><td>vertex</td></tr>
<tr><td>parallelogram</td><td>vertices</td></tr>
</table>

Multiage Classroom ◆ Companion Lessons

Companion Lessons from Grades 1 and 3 can help you meet instructional needs of a multiage classroom. The full Scope and Sequence is on pages 503–524.

Grade 1	4◆7, 6◆10, 7◆1	1◆3, 2◆7, 4◆5	2◆7, 4◆5, 7◆4	7◆1–7◆4, 4◆5	7◆3, 7◆4	7◆5, 7◆6, 10◆5	7◆6	7◆7
Grade 2	**5◆1**	**5◆2**	**5◆3**	**5◆4**	**5◆5**	**5◆6**	**5◆7**	**5◆8**
Grade 3	1◆4	6◆1	6◆2	4◆8, 6◆6	3◆7, 6◆5, 9◆3	6◆11, 6◆12	6◆11	6◆9

Professional Development

Teacher's Reference Manual Links

Lesson	Topic	Section	Lesson	Topic	Section
5◆1	Multiplication and Division Use Classes	10.2.2	**5◆5**	Polygons	13.4.2
	Clocks	15.2.1	**5◆6**	Polyhedrons	13.5.2
5◆2	Points, Lines, Segments, and Rays	13.2; 13.3	**5◆7**	Polyhedrons	13.5.2
5◆3	Parallel and Perpendicular	13.6.1	**5◆8**	Line Symmetry	13.8.1
5◆4	Geometry Tools	3.2.4			

Materials

Lesson	Masters	Manipulative Kit Items	Other Items
5•1	Teaching Masters, pp. 120–124 Attribute Rule Cards (cut from *Math Masters*, p. 109) Teaching Aid Master, p. 415 10 index cards or 2 copies of *Math Masters*, p. 125 Home Link Master, p. 126 Game Masters, pp. 447 and 448	per group: set of attribute blocks, 1 six-sided die, clock-face stamp and stamp pad, calculator	per group: quarter-sheets of paper, about 35 centimeter cubes, pennies, dried beans, or other small counters, scissors, envelope, paper clip
5•2	Home Link 5•1 Teaching Aid Master, p. 415 Home Link Master, p. 127 Teaching Masters, pp. 123*, 124 128, and 129 Clock Concentration cards (made from index cards or from *Math Masters*, p. 125)	clock-face stamp and stamp pad* geoboards; rubber bands	straightedge; crayons
5•3	Home Link 5•2 Home Link Master, p. 130 Teaching Masters, pp. 131 and 132	Pattern-Block Template pattern blocks	straightedge; notebook paper and tape*
5•4	Home Link 5•3 Teaching Aid Masters, pp. 415, 429 or 430, and 434 Teaching Masters, pp. 133–135, 137, and 138 Home Link Master, p. 136 Dollar Rummy cards (cut from *Math Masters*, pp. 454 and 455)	Pattern-Block Template per group: two six-sided dice, attribute blocks slate geoboard; rubber bands	per group: straightedge, about 40 centimeter cubes, red, yellow, and blue crayons or pencils; *The Greedy Triangle*
5•5	Home Link 5•4 Teaching Masters, pp. 139 and 140 Teaching Aid Master, p. 415 Home Link Master, p. 141 Game Master, p. 462* tangram pieces and a square (cut from *Math Masters*, p. 142)	Pattern-Block Template pattern blocks per group: 4 each of number cards 0–10 and 1 each of number cards 11–20	index card*; scissors; glue or tape; envelope
5•6	Home Link 5•5 Home Link Master, p. 143	slate	3-D Shapes Poster*; 3-dimensional models: rectangular prism, cube, cylinder, cone, sphere, and pyramid; items from home for the Shapes Museum; labeled index cards for the Shapes Museum; straightedge
5•7	Home Link 5•6 Teaching Masters, pp. 144*, 146*, 147, and 148 Home Link Master, p. 145 Teaching Aid Master, p. 418*	slate calculator	models of a cone and a pyramid; per group: 15 four-inch straws, 15 six-inch; straws, and 20 twist-ties; table of pyramid edges, faces, and vertices; 3-D Shapes Poster*
5•8	Home Link 5•7 Teaching Masters, pp. 149 and 150 Home Link Master, p. 151	Pattern-Block Template pattern blocks per group: 4 of each number cards 0–9; 1 die slate; calculator	scissors; magazines; backing paper; glue
5•9	Home Link 5•8 Assessment Masters, pp. 173–177 Home Link Masters, pp. 152–155	pattern blocks Pattern-Block Template slate	straightedge; demonstration clock

Technology
Assessment Management System, Unit 5
iTLG, Unit 5

* Denotes optional materials

Mathematical Background

The discussion below highlights the major content ideas presented in Unit 5 and helps establish instructional priorities.

Explorations (Lessons 5♦1 and 5♦4)

Unit 5 has six Explorations. Three of the Explorations in this unit develop children's abilities to classify shapes, identify similarities and differences among shapes, and represent shapes on paper. The remaining three cover time and readiness for multiplication and division.

 PROFESSIONAL DEVELOPMENT Read Section 1.2.1 of the *Teacher's Reference Manual* for more about Explorations.

Points and Line Segments (Lessons 5♦2 and 5♦3)

Everyday Mathematics develops the fundamental concepts of points and line segments. Children learn how to name line segments, draw line segments that are parallel, and draw line segments that are not parallel.

Polygons (Lessons 5♦4, 5♦5, and following)

Children identify shapes that are polygons and non-polygons. They note that it is possible to trace the sides of a polygon and come back to the starting point without retracing or crossing any part. They classify and name polygons according to the number of sides and angles. These lessons include many hands-on activities. Children draw polygons by tracing pattern blocks; they draw polygons using a straightedge; they make polygons out of triangular and rectangular pieces; and they form them on a geoboard.

3-D Shapes (Lessons 5♦6 and 5♦7)

Before you begin Lesson 5-6, you and the children should bring enough 3-dimensional objects to school to create an extensive shapes museum. These objects are sorted into basic categories: prisms, pyramids, cylinders, cones, spheres, cubes, and others. Children observe the similarities and differences among 3-dimensional shapes, such as flat and curved surfaces. Children also identify the parts of shapes, such as faces, bases, edges, and vertices. In Lesson 5-7, they use straws and twist-ties to construct pyramids whose bases are squares, triangles, rectangles, pentagons, and hexagons. As you use the names of the shapes and their parts, children will be exposed to many words that are probably unfamiliar to them. Don't let this deter you from using the words, but do keep in mind that you should not expect children to memorize them at this time. With repeated exposure, these words will gradually become part of the children's vocabularies.

> **Note**
>
> Many vocabulary words are used in this unit. Children are not expected to memorize them, but they should be encouraged to use them. It may be helpful to write the words on a "Word Wall" so that children can refer to them as often as needed. Next to each word, include a picture as well as a written description. Numerous suggestions for the Word Wall are given throughout this unit.

Line Symmetry (Lesson 5♦8)

Children explore symmetry through folding and drawing activities. As with other topics, they look to the real world for examples of symmetry.

 PROFESSIONAL DEVELOPMENT For additional information about geometry concepts, including points, line segments, polygons, 3-dimensional shapes, and line symmetry, see Section 13 in the *Teacher's Reference Manual.*

Exploring Rules, Sharing, and Time

EXPLORATIONS

 Objectives To demonstrate rules used to classify shapes; to develop readiness for division; and to demonstrate telling time using digital and analog notation.

1 Teaching the Lesson

Key Activities

Exploration A: Children use the "What's My Attribute Rule?" activity to determine the rule (involving color, shape, and size) used to sort a set of attribute blocks.

Exploration B: Children act out an equal-sharing situation.

Exploration C: Children make activity cards and match clock faces with digital times.

Key Concepts and Skills

• Count a collection of objects.
[Number and Numeration Goal 1]

• Match the time on a clock face with the digital notation.
[Measurement and Reference Frames Goal 6]

• Find the rules for a group of sorted attribute blocks.
[Patterns, Functions, and Algebra Goal 1]

✓ **Ongoing Assessment: Recognizing Student Achievement**
Use an Exit Slip. [Measurement and Reference Frames Goal 6]

materials

Exploration A: Per group:
☐ Teaching Masters (*Math Masters*, pp. 120 and 121)
☐ Attribute Rule Cards (cut from *Math Masters*, p. 109)
☐ set of attribute blocks; 1 six-sided die

Exploration B: Per partnership:
☐ Teaching Masters (*Math Masters*, p. 122)
☐ quarter-sheets of paper
☐ about 35 centimeter cubes, pennies, dried beans, or other counters; 1 six-sided die or number cube

Exploration C: Per group:
☐ Teaching Masters (*Math Masters*, pp. 123 and 124)
☐ Teaching Aid Master (*Math Masters*, p. 415)
☐ 10 index cards or 2 copies of *Math Masters*, p. 125
☐ clock-face stamp and stamp pad (or *Math Masters*, p. 125)
☐ scissors; envelope

See **Advance Preparation**

2 Ongoing Learning & Practice

Children practice adding 2-digit numbers by playing *Addition Spin*.

Children practice and maintain skills through Math Boxes and Home Link activities.

materials

☐ *Math Journal 1*, p. 112
☐ *My Reference Book*, pp. 120 and 121
☐ Home Link Master (*Math Masters*, p. 126)
☐ Game Masters (*Math Masters*, pp. 447 and 448; per partnership)
☐ per partnership: paper clip; calculator

3 Differentiation Options

READINESS

Children use their arms and body as a clock to show a given time.

EXTRA PRACTICE

Children tell time to the nearest hour, half-hour, and 5 minutes.

materials

☐ *Minute Math®+*, p. 71

Additional Information

Advance Preparation For the Math Message, draw and color in three large circles—one yellow, one blue, and one red—on a piece of paper. Label the sheet, "These fit the rule." On another sheet, draw and color in a small yellow triangle, a small blue square, and a small red circle. Label this sheet, "These do NOT fit the rule." (Or, you could tape attribute blocks to labeled pieces of paper.) Post both sheets near the Math Message. (See the illustration on the next page.) Plan to spend most of your time working with children on Exploration A.

Technology

Assessment Management System
Exit Slip
See the **iTLG.**

Getting Started

Mental Math and Reflexes

Problems like the following give children practice in the quick mental-addition skills that are needed for making ballpark estimates and for carrying out the partial-sums algorithm:

○○○ 50 + 30 = ? 80
70 + 40 = ? 110
? = 40 + 60 100

○○○ 500 + 300 = ? 800
700 + 400 = ? 1,100
? = 400 + 600 1,000

○○○ 5,000 + 3,000 = ? 8,000
7,000 + 4,000 = ? 11,000
? = 4,000 + 6,000 10,000

Math Message

(See Advance Preparation.)

I am the Rule Maker. Look at the pictures of the attribute blocks labeled "These fit the rule." Look at the pictures labeled "These do NOT fit the rule." What is my rule?

① Teaching the Lesson

► Math Message Follow-Up

 WHOLE-CLASS DISCUSSION

The rule is "only large circles." Instead of explaining the rule, ask a child to bring you an attribute block that fits the rule. Say "yes" if the block fits the rule, and place it on the paper labeled "These fit the rule." If the block does not fit the rule, say "no" and place the block on the paper labeled "These do NOT fit the rule."

Continue until the majority of the class has figured out the rule.

These fit the rule.

These do NOT fit the rule.

NOTE At the beginning of this activity, children may logically think that the rule is "only circles." Point out to children, however, that a small red circle does not fit the rule.

Teaching Master

Name _____ Date _____ Time _____

LESSON 5·1 "What's My Attribute Rule?"

Work with a small group.

Materials ☐ set of attribute blocks

☐ Attribute Rule Cards (*Math Masters*, p. 109)

☐ 1 six-sided die

Directions

1. Label one sheet of paper: **These fit the rule.**

2. Label another sheet of paper: **These do NOT fit the rule.**

3. Take turns. Roll the die once. The person with the lowest number is the first "Rule Maker."

4. The Rule Maker mixes the Attribute Rule Cards and then stacks them facedown.

5. The Rule Maker picks up the top Attribute Rule Card but does not show it to the other group members or tell them what the rule is.

large shapes, but not triangles

Sample Attribute Rule Card

Math Masters, p. 120

6. The Rule Maker chooses 3 or 4 attribute blocks that fit the rule on the card. The Rule Maker puts them on the sheet labeled "These fit the rule."

These fit the rule.

7. The Rule Maker chooses 3 or 4 blocks that do NOT fit the rule. The Rule Maker puts them on the sheet labeled "These do NOT fit the rule."

These do NOT fit the rule.

8. The other group members are the "Guessers." The Guessers take turns. Each one chooses a block that he or she thinks might fit the rule.

9. The Rule Maker tells each Guesser "yes" or "no." The Guesser puts the block on the correct sheet. The Guesser suggests what the rule might be. The Rule Maker tells the Guesser if his or her rule is correct.

10. The Guessers continue until someone figures out the rule. Then that person becomes the Rule Maker for the next round.

Math Masters, p. 121

Attribute Rules

(Math Masters, pp. 109, 120, and 121)

Children find rules in the "What's My Attribute Rule?" activity which is similar to the Math Message activity. See *Math Masters,* pages 120 and 121 for instructions. In Lesson 4-7, children cut out the necessary Attribute Rule Cards from *Math Masters,* page 109.

Adjusting the Activity

Select two children to be Rule Makers. Together, they can choose the initial blocks that do and do not fit the rule and determine whether the blocks chosen by the Guessers fit the rule.

Ask the Rule Maker to make up his or her own rule rather than using an Attribute Rule Card. The Rule Maker can record the rule on a separate sheet of paper before laying out blocks that do and do not fit the rule.

AUDITORY ◆ KINESTHETIC ◆ TACTILE ◆ VISUAL

▶ Exploration B: Exploring Equal Sharing

PARTNER ACTIVITY

(Math Masters, p. 122)

Children choose numbers between 8 and 32 and take as many counters ("eggs") as the number they choose. Then they roll the die to determine how many quarter-sheets of paper ("nests") to take. They share (divide) the eggs among the nests. Children keep a record of what they did by showing the number of eggs with which they started, the number of nests, and the number of eggs in each nest. They also record how many eggs, if any, were left over (the remainder).

Links to the Future

This activity provides important practice for division. This skill will be explored further in Unit 6. Using equal sharing and equal grouping to demonstrate the meaning of division is a Grade 3 Goal.

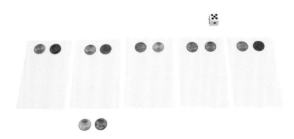

12 eggs are divided equally among 5 nests with 2 eggs left over.

Name _____ Date _____ Time _____

LESSON 5·1 **Sharing Equally**

Work with a partner.

Materials ☐ quarter-sheets of paper ☐ plain paper
☐ 1 six-sided die or number cube
☐ centimeter cubes, pennies, or dried beans

Directions

1. Think of the quarter-sheets of paper as "nests." Think of the cubes, pennies, or beans as "eggs."

2. Choose a number between 8 and 32. Then count out that many eggs.

3. Roll the die once. The number that lands faceup tells how many nests (quarter-sheets) to lay out.

4. Work together to share the eggs equally among all the nests. When you finish, count the eggs in each nest. Make sure each nest has the same number of eggs.

5. Make a record of your work on the sheet of plain paper.

   ◆ Show the number of eggs you started with.

   ◆ Show the nests and the eggs in each nest.

   ◆ Show any eggs that were left over.

6. Choose a different number of eggs. Then follow Steps 1–5 again.

Math Masters, p. 122

 **SMALL-GROUP ACTIVITY**

▶ Exploration C: Making Cards and Doing a Clock Concentration Activity

(*Math Masters,* pp. 123–125 and 415)

Each group makes a set of Clock Concentration cards using a clock-face stamp and index cards. Once the cards are made, children match times given on a clock face and in digital notation. Directions are on *Math Masters,* pages 123 and 124.

Children should be able to create cards that show times on the hour and the half-hour.

NOTE If clock stamps are not available, make copies of *Math Masters,* page 125, preferably on tagboard. If you use ordinary paper, tell children to write the times and draw the hands of the clocks lightly in pencil. By doing this, the times and clocks will not show through the paper when the cards are turned facedown. Have children cut the clock cards apart.

 ## Adjusting the Activity

Have children write the time in words rather than digital notation. Children should use expressions like *quarter past 6, ten till 7, half past 9,* and *noon.*

When doing the Clock Concentration activity, you may choose to limit the number of pairs in the array. For example, instead of 10 **C**s and 10 **T**s, use only 5 **C**s and 5 **T**s. Then, after each round, change the set of cards to provide practice using all 20 cards. Alternatively, do the activity with all the cards faceup so children can focus on matching the **C** and **T** cards.

A U D I T O R Y   ◆   K I N E S T H E T I C   ◆   T A C T I L E   ◆   V I S U A L

 ## Ongoing Assessment: Recognizing Student Achievement

Exit Slip

Use an **Exit Slip** (*Math Masters,* page 415) to assess children's ability to read the time and match it to its digital notation. Have children record three of their matches in the Clock Concentration activity. Children are making adequate progress if they matched times to the hour and half-hour. Some children may be able to match times to the quarter-hour and others may be able to match times to the 5-minute increment.

[Measurement and Reference Frames Goal 6]

Links to the Future

Showing and telling time to the nearest 5 minutes is a Grade 2 Goal. Showing and telling time to the nearest minute is a Grade 3 Goal.

Teaching Master

Name   Date   Time

LESSON 5·1 **Making Clock Concentration Cards**

Materials ☐ 10 index cards
              ☐ clock-face stamp
              ☐ stamp pad
              ☐ envelope
              ☐ scissors

Directions

Make a set of Clock Concentration cards.

1. Fold each index card in half. Then unfold it.

2. Stamp a clock face on one half of the card. Then draw an hour hand and a minute hand on the face to show a time.

3. Write the matching digital time on the other half. Check one another's work.

4. Cut the card in half.

5. Write **C** on the back of each card with a clock face.

6. Write **T** on the back of each card with a time.

7. Choose a mark your group will use to identify your cards. Make that mark in the same corner on the back of every card.

C **T**
XX   XX

Math Masters, **p. 123**

Math Masters, page 125 includes 5 sets of Clock Concentration cards.

Teaching Master

Name   Date   Time

LESSON 5·1 **Clock Concentration** *continued*

Materials ☐ 1 set of Clock Concentration Cards

Directions

1. Shuffle the cards and place them facedown in an array.

C	T	C	T	C
T	C	T	C	C
C	T	T	T	C
C	T	C	T	T

2. Take turns. For each turn, turn a **C** card and a **T** card faceup. If the cards match, pick up both cards and take another turn.

3. If the cards do not match, put them back in the array facedown. Then the next person takes a turn.

4. Continue until time is up or until all the cards have been matched.

5. Store your group's cards in an envelope.

Student Page

Games

Addition Spin

Materials ❑ 1 *Addition Spin* spinner
       ❑ 1 paper clip
       ❑ 1 pencil
       ❑ 1 calculator
       ❑ 2 sheets of paper

Players 2

Skill Mental addition

Object of the game To have the larger total.

Directions

1. Players take turns being the "Spinner" and the "Checker."

2. The Spinner uses a pencil and a paper clip to make a spinner.

3. The Spinner spins the paper clip.

4. The Spinner writes the number that the paper clip points to. If the paper clip points to more than one number, the Spinner writes the smaller number.

***My Reference Book*, p. 120**

② Ongoing Learning & Practice

▶ Playing *Addition Spin*

PARTNER ACTIVITY

(*Math Masters*, p. 447 or 448; *My Reference Book*, pp. 120 and 121)

This game was introduced in Lesson 4-2. The instructions are in *My Reference Book*. You can customize the game for your class in different ways. If children use the top spinner on *Math Masters*, page 447, they will practice adding 2-digit numbers that are multiples of 5. If they use the bottom spinner on *Math Masters*, page 447, they will practice adding other 2-digit numbers. *Math Masters*, page 448 provides blank *Addition Spin* spinners. You can write numbers on these spinners so your children can practice adding 2-digit numbers with regrouping or practice adding 3-digit numbers.

▶ Math Boxes 5·1

INDEPENDENT ACTIVITY

(*Math Journal 1*, p. 112)

Mixed Practice Math Boxes in this lesson are paired with Math Boxes in Lesson 5-3. The skill in Problem 6 previews Unit 6 content.

Student Page

Games

5. The Spinner spins a second time and writes the new number.

6. The Spinner adds the 2 numbers and writes the sum. The Checker checks the sum of the 2 numbers by using a calculator.

7. If the sum is correct, the Spinner circles it. If the sum is incorrect, the Spinner corrects it but does not circle it.

8. Players switch roles. They stop after they have each played 5 turns. Each player uses a calculator to find the total of his or her circled scores.

9. The player with the larger total wins.

● Sam spins 5 and 25. He writes 30.
   Mia spins 10 and 10. She writes 20.
   Sam has the larger sum.

***My Reference Book*, p. 121**

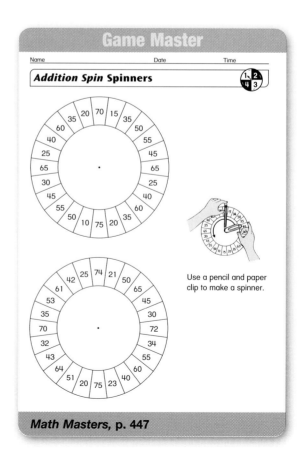

Game Master

Name   Date   Time

Addition Spin Spinners

Use a pencil and paper clip to make a spinner.

***Math Masters*, p. 447**

▶ Home Link 5·1

(Math Masters, p. 126)

INDEPENDENT ACTIVITY

Home Connection Children determine an unknown rule by looking at shapes that fit the rule and shapes that do not fit the rule. Children then write the rule and choose and draw shapes that fit it.

③ Differentiation Options

READINESS

SMALL-GROUP ACTIVITY

5–15 Min

▶ Showing the Time

To provide experience with telling time using a concrete model, have children use their arms and body as a clock to show different times. Ask children to stand and face you. If there is room, have them spread out a bit, each child extending one arm to the side to establish correct spacing. First, stand with your back to the class and model each of the following times.

Raise both of your arms straight up over your head to show 12:00. Keeping your left arm over your head, move your right arm to show 3:00, then straight down to show 6:00. Next, give several different times and have the children be the "body clocks."

EXTRA PRACTICE

SMALL-GROUP ACTIVITY

5–15 Min

▶ *Minute Math+*

To offer children more experience in telling time, see page 71 in *Minute Math+*.

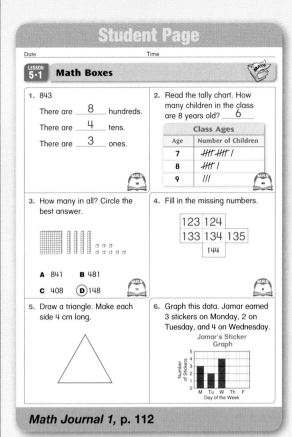

5·2 Points and Line Segments

 Objective To guide children as they define, name, and draw line segments.

---

1 Teaching the Lesson

materials

Key Activities
Children define and name points and line segments with letter labels. They also practice drawing line segments with a straightedge according to a code.

Key Concepts and Skills
- Solve number stories using addition facts. [Operations and Computation Goal 1]
- Connect points in a sequence. [Geometry Goal 1]
- Use a straightedge to draw a line segment. [Geometry Goal 1]

Key Vocabulary
point • straightedge • line segment • endpoint

✔ **Ongoing Assessment: Recognizing Student Achievement** Use an Exit Slip.
[Geometry Goal 1]

☐ *Math Journal 1*, p. 113
☐ *My Reference Book*, p. 50
☐ Home Link 5·1
☐ Teaching Aid Master (*Math Masters*, p. 415)
☐ straightedge

---

2 Ongoing Learning & Practice

materials

Children match clock faces with digital times by doing a Clock Concentration activity.

Children practice and maintain skills through Math Boxes and Home Link activities.

☐ *Math Journal 1*, p. 114
☐ Home Link Master (*Math Masters*, p. 127)
☐ Teaching Masters (*Math Masters*, p. 123, optional; and p. 124)
☐ Clock Concentration cards (made from index cards or from *Math Masters*, p. 125; per small group)
☐ clock-face stamp and stamp pad (optional)

---

3 Differentiation Options

materials

READINESS

Children explore making designs from line segments on a geoboard.

ENRICHMENT

Children explore drawing line segments in a sequence.

☐ Teaching Masters (*Math Masters*, pp. 128 and 129)
☐ geoboard; rubber bands
☐ straightedge
☐ crayons

Technology

Assessment Management System
Exit Slip
See the **iTLG**.

Getting Started

Mental Math and Reflexes

Pose number stories with "harder" addition and subtraction facts:

- ⊙○○ Alexi has 8 toy cars. Theo has 7 toy cars. How many do they have in all? 15 toy cars
- ⊙○○ Jillian had 9 crayons. She found 6 more. How many crayons in all? 15 crayons
- ⊙⊙○ Shantell brought 14 lollipops to school. She gave away 8 during lunch. How many does she have now? 6 lollipops
- ⊙○○ Maya went down the slide 17 times during recess. Jason went down 9 times. Maya went down the slide how many more times than Jason? 8 times

Math Message

Write a sentence that has the word point *or* points *in it.*

Home Link 5·1 Follow-Up

Review the rule and write it on the board. Ask volunteers to draw shapes that fit that rule.

---

1 Teaching the Lesson

▶ Math Message Follow-Up

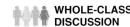 **WHOLE-CLASS DISCUSSION**

Write a few of the children's sentences on the board. If interest in this activity is high, add a few sentences of your own. *For example:*

▷ My pencil has a sharp *point*.

▷ The football team scored 21 *points*.

▷ This number has a decimal *point* in it.

▷ Can you *point* out the picture you like the best?

Discuss the meaning of the word **point** in geometry—an exact location in space, the tiniest part of a figure, an object without length, something represented by a dot, and so on.

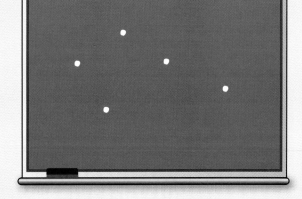

▶ Discussing How Points Are Named

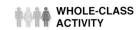 **WHOLE-CLASS ACTIVITY**

Draw five dots on the board. Ask someone to choose one of the dots and to tell you which one it is without pointing to it. He or she will probably have a hard time doing this.

Explain that an easy way to talk about points is to give them labels. Points are usually labeled with capital letters, such as *A*, *B*, and *C*. Label each of the dots on the board, calling them by name as you do so: "Point *A*," "Point *B*," and so on.

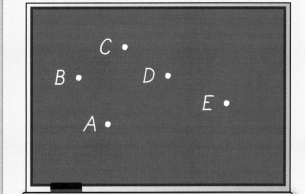

Links to the Future

This is a preliminary exposure to drawing and labeling points. Identifying and drawing points are Grade 3 Goals.

Adjusting the Activity

ELL

Consider posting *point, straightedge, line segment,* and *endpoint* on the Word Wall so children can refer to them as necessary. Include a picture and a written description from the glossary next to each word.

AUDITORY ✦ KINESTHETIC ✦ TACTILE ✦ VISUAL

Drawing a line segment labeled *AB*

Student Page

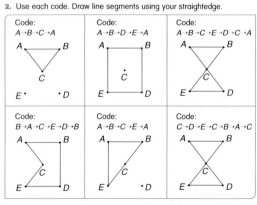

Math Journal 1, p. 113

▶ **Defining and Naming Line Segments**

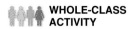

WHOLE-CLASS ACTIVITY

(*Math Masters,* p. 415; *My Reference Book,* p. 50)

Ask children what they think *straight* means. "Not curved" or "goes in one direction" are good responses. Point out that a **straightedge** is a tool used for drawing straight lines.

On blank sheets of paper, have children draw two dots as you do the same on the board. Label the dots *A* and *B*. Then demonstrate how to draw a "straight line" connecting them: Place the straightedge just under the dots and draw from point to point, not from letter to letter, and not past the points. Tell children that they just drew a **line segment** whose **endpoints** are points *A* and *B*. The segment can be called "line segment *AB*" or "line segment *BA*"—the names of the endpoints can be in either order. Write $\overline{AB}$ and $\overline{BA}$ on the board and say that sometimes the symbols are used for "line segment *AB*" or "line segment *BA*." For a summary of these concepts, read *My Reference Book,* page 50 with your class.

Ask children to draw three points (that are not in a straight line) on their papers and to label each point with a *different* letter. Explain that in any problem or example, all the points must have different names; two points may not have the same letter label. Have children use a straightedge to connect each of the three points to each of the other points. Ask children to name the shape they have formed. A triangle

✓ Ongoing Assessment: Recognizing Student Achievement

Exit Slip

Use an **Exit Slip** (*Math Masters,* page 415) to assess children's ability to use a straightedge to draw a line segment. Have children use a straightedge to draw line segment *EF*. Children are making adequate progress if they are able to use the straightedge to draw a line segment. Some children may indicate the endpoints and still others may label the endpoints.

[Geometry Goal 1]

▶ **Drawing Line Segments with a Straightedge**

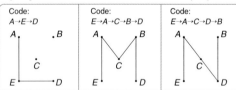

PARTNER ACTIVITY

(*Math Journal 1,* p. 113)

The first part of the journal page shows points connected by line segments, along with a code that specifies the sequence in which the points have been connected. For example, the code $A{\rightarrow}B{\rightarrow}C{\rightarrow}A$ means: "First draw a line segment from *A* to *B*, then a line segment from *B* to *C*, and finally one from *C* to *A*." Give partners 2 or 3 minutes to figure out the codes. Then go over the three codes with the class.

In the second part of the activity, children draw line segments according to given codes. Partners can work on these problems while you circulate and assist children who need help.

② Ongoing Learning & Practice

▶ Doing a Clock Concentration Activity

SMALL-GROUP ACTIVITY

(*Math Masters*, pp. 123–125)

The Clock Concentration activity was introduced in Lesson 5-1. If children have not done this activity, they will need to follow the directions to make a set of Clock Concentration cards. The activity can be modified by using fewer pairs of cards or by keeping the cards faceup.

▶ Math Boxes 5·2

INDEPENDENT ACTIVITY

(*Math Journal 1*, p. 114)

Mixed Practice Math Boxes in this lesson are paired with Math Boxes in Lesson 5-4. The skill in Problem 6 previews Unit 6 content.

▶ Home Link 5·2

INDEPENDENT ACTIVITY

(*Math Masters*, p. 127)

Home Connection Children connect 6 points with line segments in different ways to form a 6-pointed star and a hexagon. Children connect other line segments and answer a question about the shapes that are formed.

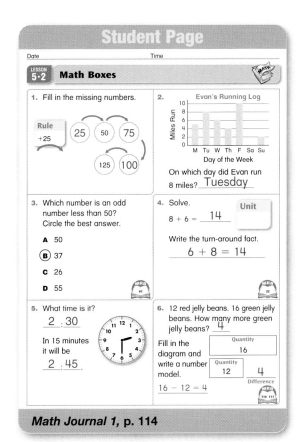

Math Journal 1, p. 114

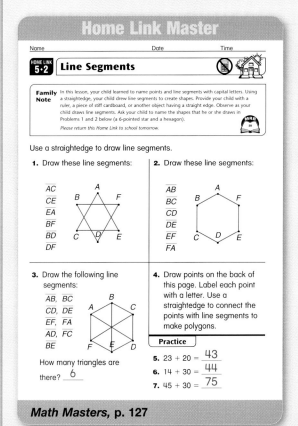

Math Masters, p. 127

Teaching Master

Name   Date   Time

LESSON 5·2   **Geoboard Designs**

1. Use 3 rubber bands to make a design. Record your design.

2. Use 6 rubber bands to make a design. Record your design.

3. Use 8 rubber bands to make a design. Record your design.

4. Make up your own. I used _____ rubber bands to make a design. Record your design.

Answers vary.

Math Masters, p. 128

Teaching Master

Name   Date   Time

LESSON 5·2   **A Line Segment Design**

Use a straightedge and a crayon.

Connect the dots below according to the following pattern:
$A \rightarrow B \rightarrow C \rightarrow D \rightarrow E \rightarrow F \rightarrow A$

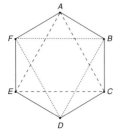

What shape did you make with line segments? __hexagon__

Use a different color. Connect the dots again in a different way. Follow this pattern:
$A \rightarrow C \rightarrow E \rightarrow A$

What shape did you make with line segments? __triangle__

Use a different color. Connect the dots one more time. Follow this pattern:
$B \rightarrow D \rightarrow F \rightarrow B$

What shapes do you see in your design?
Hexagons, triangles, star, rectangles

Color your design.

Math Masters, p. 129

---

③ Differentiation Options

READINESS   INDEPENDENT ACTIVITY

▶ Making Geoboard Designs

5–15 Min

(*Math Masters*, p. 128)

To explore drawing line segments, have children use rubber bands to make designs on a geoboard. The rubber bands can only be used with a row or column of pins enclosed, so that children are making designs from line segments. (*See margin.*) They can make shapes or simple designs with intersecting or parallel line segments. This should be an exploration with line segments—not an introduction to them. When children are satisfied which each design, they use a straightedge to record their designs on *Math Masters*, page 128.

ENRICHMENT   INDEPENDENT ACTIVITY

▶ Creating a Line Segment Design

5–15 Min

(*Math Masters*, p. 129)

To explore using line segments in a design, have children follow directions for drawing line segments in a sequence. As children complete *Math Masters*, page 129, they should recognize some of the shapes that they draw. Have children describe the process for drawing the shapes. Encourage the use of vocabulary such as *point, line segment, endpoint, connect,* and shape names.

Planning Ahead

In preparation for the Shapes Museum that will be introduced in Lesson 5-6, collect a few objects or pictures of objects having the following shapes:

Cylinders: coffee cans, rolls of paper towels, rolls of toilet paper, drinking straws, mugs, fluorescent lightbulbs

Spheres: tennis balls, oranges, globes

Rectangular prisms: books, cereal boxes, cartons, chalkboard erasers, pictures of a file cabinet, pictures of a bookcase

Cones: ice cream cones, party hats, conical paper cups, pictures of traffic cones

Pyramids: pictures of pyramids or pyramid-shaped roofs

Cubes: notepaper cubes, regular dice, centimeter cubes, a liter (cubic decimeter) box

5·3 Parallel Line Segments

 Objective To introduce the concepts of parallel and parallel line segments.

---

1 Teaching the Lesson

materials

Key Activities
Children are introduced to the meaning of the word *parallel,* and they identify examples of parallel line segments in the real world. They also examine diagrams of parallel and nonparallel line segments, draw parallel and nonparallel line segments, and identify parallel and nonparallel sides of quadrangles.

Key Concepts and Skills
• Use a straightedge to draw a line segment.
  [Geometry Goal 1]
• Identify parallel line segments.
  [Geometry Goal 1]
• Draw a quadrangle.
  [Geometry Goal 2]

Key Vocabulary
parallel

✔ **Ongoing Assessment:** Informing Instruction See page 329.

✔ **Ongoing Assessment:** Recognizing Student Achievement Use journal page 116.
  [Geometry Goal 1]

☐ *Math Journal 1,* pp. 115–117
☐ Home Link 5·2
☐ straightedge
☐ notebook paper and tape (optional)

---

2 Ongoing Learning & Practice

materials

Children solve "What's My Rule?" and Frames-and-Arrows problems.

Children practice and maintain skills through Math Boxes and Home Link activities.

☐ *Math Journal 1,* pp. 118 and 119
☐ Home Link Master (*Math Masters,* p. 130)

---

3 Differentiation Options

materials

READINESS

Children draw line segments using a straightedge.

ENRICHMENT

Children solve pattern-block puzzles.

ELL SUPPORT

Children add *parallel* to their Math Word Banks.

☐ Teaching Masters (*Math Masters,* pp. 131 and 132)
☐ *Differentiation Handbook*
☐ straightedge
☐ Pattern-Block Template
☐ pattern blocks

Technology
Assessment Management System
Journal page 116, Problems 1 and 2
See the **iTLG.**

Getting Started

Mental Math and Reflexes

Pose problems about making change. Have children share their solution strategies. *Suggestions:*

⊙○○ You buy a candy bar for 50 cents. You pay with a $1 bill. How much change should you receive? 50 cents

You buy a notebook for 70 cents. You pay with a $1 bill. How much change should you receive? 30 cents

⊙⊙○ You buy a pen for 68 cents. You pay with $1.00. How much change should you receive? 32 cents

You buy an eraser for 37 cents. You pay with $1.00. How much change should you receive? 63 cents

⊙⊙⊙ You buy an apple for 27 cents. You pay with 2 quarters. How much change should you receive? 23 cents

You buy a can of soup for 66 cents. You pay with 3 quarters. How much change should you receive? 9 cents

Math Message

Think of the lines printed on a sheet of notebook paper. Imagine that the lines could go on forever. Do you think the lines would ever meet?

Home Link 5·2 Follow-Up

Quickly check children's drawings to see if they drew the correct line segments. Ask volunteers to identify the shapes that were drawn in Problems 1 and 2. A 6-pointed star and a hexagon Ask several children to show the line segments and polygons they drew for Problem 4. If possible, have children name the specific polygons.

NOTE Theoretically, the lines on notebook paper would never meet, if extended infinitely. But in practice, no lines drawn on paper are perfectly parallel, so they would meet at some point. Not all lines that never meet are parallel. They must be in the same plane.

Student Page

Date   Time

LESSON 5·3 Parallel or Not Parallel?

These line segments are **parallel**.

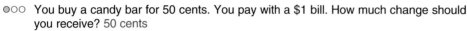

These line segments are **not parallel**.

Quadrangles (Quadrilaterals)
These polygons are quadrangles (quadrilaterals).

square   rectangle   parallelogram

rhombus   trapezoid   kite

Math Journal 1, p. 115

328   Unit 5   3-D and 2-D Shapes

---

1 Teaching the Lesson

▶ Math Message Follow-Up

WHOLE-CLASS DISCUSSION

Although we cannot see a line that goes on "forever" in the real world, it is possible to imagine it. Ask children to give reasons they think the lines printed on the notebook paper would or would not meet if extended forever in both directions. Some children may understand intuitively that the lines on notebook paper will always be the same distance apart.

Adjusting the Activity

ELL

Display a sheet of notebook paper rather than asking children to visualize the lines on the sheet. Tape the sheet to the board and use a straightedge and chalk to extend the lines in either or both directions.

AUDITORY ◆ KINESTHETIC ◆ TACTILE ◆ VISUAL

▶ Discussing the Meaning of Parallel Line Segments

WHOLE-CLASS DISCUSSION

(*Math Journal 1*, p. 115)

Mention that the "lines" on notebook paper are really line segments. To support English language learners, clarify the difference between *lines* and *line segments*. Continue to make this distinction and use the language correctly throughout the unit.

Discuss the idea of **parallel** in the real world. Give examples such as parallel railroad tracks, shelves on bookcases, and so on. The lines on notebook paper are parallel line segments.

Ask children to suggest other examples of parallel line segments in the classroom or hallway. *Sample answers: parallel edges of doors, opposite edges of books, opposite edges of chalkboards*

With the children, examine the parallel line segments at the top of the journal page. Mention that parallel line segments do not need to be the same length. Discuss why the line segments in the second row are not parallel. *Sample answers: Some of the line segments meet; others would meet if extended.*

 Ongoing Assessment: Informing Instruction

Watch for children who think parallel line segments only go in one direction. Have children draw parallel line segments on paper and then rotate the paper so they can see that the line segments remain parallel regardless of the direction.

Next, examine the quadrangles at the bottom of the page. Have children point to opposite sides that are parallel and to opposite sides that are not parallel.

 Adjusting the Activity **ELL**

Add the word *parallel* to the Word Wall along with a picture and a written description. Include a mnemonic device to help children remember the meaning: "The three *l*s in *parallel* are parallel!"
Introduce the mathematical symbol that is used to indicate parallel line segments. For example, "Line segment *AB* is parallel to line segment *CD*" can be written symbolically as $\overline{AB} \parallel \overline{CD}$.

AUDITORY ♦ KINESTHETIC ♦ TACTILE ♦ VISUAL

▶ ## Drawing Line Segments That Are or Are Not Parallel

INDEPENDENT ACTIVITY

(*Math Journal 1,* pp. 116 and 117)

In Problems 1–5, children draw line segments that are parallel, as well as those that are not parallel. In Problems 6–9, children apply their knowledge of parallel line segments to drawing quadrangles. Give children plenty of time to solve Problems 6–9. These problems prepare children for further work with quadrangles in Lesson 5-5, so they should complete the problems before going on to the next lesson.

 **Ongoing Assessment: Recognizing Student Achievement**

Journal page 116 Problems 1 and 2 ★

Use **journal page 116, Problems 1 and 2** to assess children's ability to identify parallel lines. Children are making adequate progress if they are able to use a straightedge to connect the points to make line segments and recognize that they are parallel. Some children may be able to successfully complete Problem 5 and draw a line segment that is not parallel to the others.

[Geometry Goal 1]

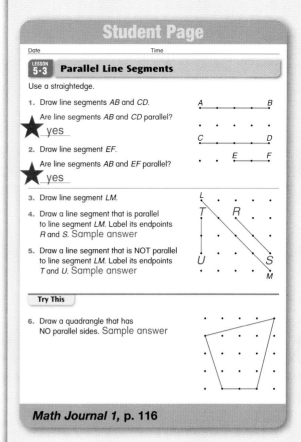

Math Journal 1, p. 116

NOTE Some children may ask about the symbol in the corner of the square and the rectangle. It is used to indicate a right angle. Tell children it simply means *square corner.* Square corners will be covered in Lesson 5-5.

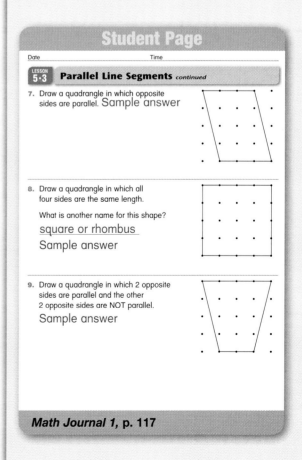

Math Journal 1, p. 117

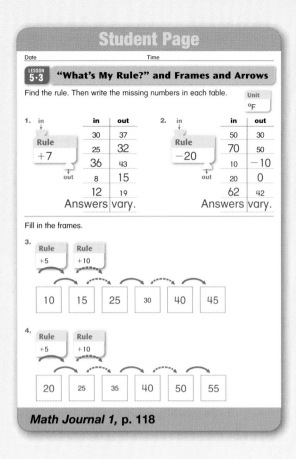

Student Page

Date _____ Time _____

LESSON 5·3 "What's My Rule?" and Frames and Arrows

Find the rule. Then write the missing numbers in each table.

Unit °F

1.
in → Rule +7 → out

in	out
30	37
25	32
36	43
8	15
12	19

Answers vary.

2.
in → Rule −20 → out

in	out
50	30
70	50
10	−10
20	0
62	42

Answers vary.

Fill in the frames.

3.
Rule +5   Rule +10

10   15   25   30   40   45

4.
Rule +5   Rule +10

20   25   35   40   50   55

Math Journal 1, p. 118

 Links to the Future

Expect that children will be able to describe parallel lines as lines that never meet, but do not expect that all children will be able to draw parallel lines at this time. Drawing parallel lines is a Grade 3 Goal.

2 Ongoing Learning & Practice

▶ **Solving "What's My Rule?" and Frames-and-Arrows Problems**

INDEPENDENT ACTIVITY

(*Math Journal 1*, p. 118)

In Problems 1 and 2, remind children to look at the completed rows in the tables to help them determine the rule.

▶ **Math Boxes 5·3**

INDEPENDENT ACTIVITY

(*Math Journal 1*, p. 119)

Mixed Practice Math Boxes in this lesson are paired with Math Boxes in Lesson 5-1. The skill in Problem 6 previews Unit 6 content.

Writing/Reasoning Have children draw, write, or verbalize their answers to the following: *Explain how you know that you made the largest number in Problem 1.* Sample answer: I picked the largest digit to be in the hundreds place, the second largest digit to be in the tens place, and the smallest digit to be in the ones place. Then I tested 531 against the other combinations and it was the largest number.

▶ **Home Link 5·3**

INDEPENDENT ACTIVITY

(*Math Masters*, p. 130)

Home Connection Children draw line segments and identify parallel line segments. They also begin collecting 3-dimensional objects for the Shapes Museum that will be introduced in Lesson 5-6.

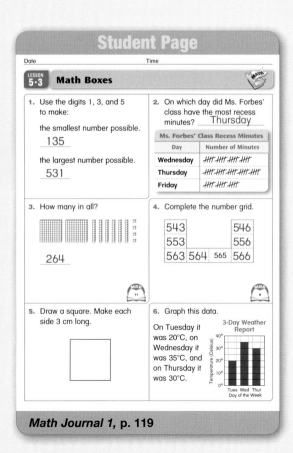

Student Page

Date _____ Time _____

LESSON 5·3 Math Boxes

1. Use the digits 1, 3, and 5 to make:

the smallest number possible.
135

the largest number possible.
531

2. On which day did Ms. Forbes' class have the most recess minutes? __Thursday__

Ms. Forbes' Class Recess Minutes	
Day	**Number of Minutes**
Wednesday	₴₴₴ ₴₴₴ ₴₴₴ ₴₴₴
Thursday	₴₴₴ ₴₴₴ ₴₴₴ ₴₴₴ ₴₴₴
Friday	₴₴₴ ₴₴₴ ₴₴₴

3. How many in all?

264

4. Complete the number grid.

543			546
553			556
563	564	565	566

5. Draw a square. Make each side 3 cm long.

6. Graph this data.

On Tuesday it was 20°C, on Wednesday it was 35°C, and on Thursday it was 30°C.

3-Day Weather Report

Math Journal 1, p. 119

3 Differentiation Options

INDEPENDENT
ACTIVITY

⏱ 5–15 Min

▶ Drawing Line Segments

(*Math Masters*, p. 131)

To explore relationships between line segments, have children use a straightedge to complete *Math Masters*, page 131. Ask children to describe the picture they have drawn. A house

---

ENRICHMENT

INDEPENDENT
ACTIVITY

⏱ 5–15 Min

▶ Solving Pattern-Block Puzzles

(*Math Masters*, p. 132)

To apply children's understanding of parallel line segments and 2-dimensional shapes, have them solve pattern-block puzzles. Have children share their solutions.

ELL SUPPORT

SMALL-GROUP
ACTIVITY

⏱ 5–15 Min

▶ Building a Math Word Bank

(*Differentiation Handbook*)

To provide language support for geometry, have children use the Word Bank template found in the *Differentiation Handbook*. Ask children to write the term *parallel,* draw a picture representing the term, and write other related words. See the *Differentiation Handbook* for more information.

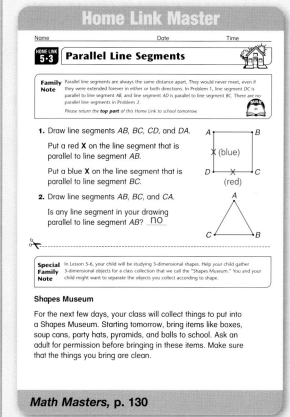

Home Link Master

Name   Date   Time

HOME LINK 5·3 Parallel Line Segments

Family Note Parallel line segments are always the same distance apart. They would never meet, even if they were extended forever in either or both directions. In Problem 1, line segment *DC* is parallel to line segment *AB*, and line segment *AD* is parallel to line segment *BC*. There are no parallel line segments in Problem 2.

*Please return the **top part** of this Home Link to school tomorrow.*

1. Draw line segments *AB*, *BC*, *CD*, and *DA*.

Put a red **X** on the line segment that is parallel to line segment *AB*.

Put a blue **X** on the line segment that is parallel to line segment *BC*.

2. Draw line segments *AB*, *BC*, and *CA*.

Is any line segment in your drawing parallel to line segment *AB*? __no__

✂- -

Special Family Note In Lesson 5-6, your child will be studying 3-dimensional shapes. Help your child gather 3-dimensional objects for a class collection that we call the "Shapes Museum." You and your child might want to separate the objects you collect according to shape.

Shapes Museum

For the next few days, your class will collect things to put into a Shapes Museum. Starting tomorrow, bring items like boxes, soup cans, party hats, pyramids, and balls to school. Ask an adult for permission before bringing in these items. Make sure that the things you bring are clean.

Math Masters, p. 130

Teaching Master

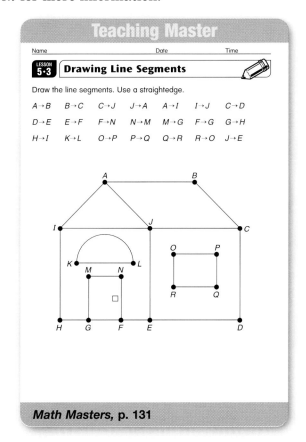

Name   Date   Time

LESSON 5·3 Drawing Line Segments

Draw the line segments. Use a straightedge.

A→B   B→C   C→J   J→A   A→I   I→J   C→D

D→E   E→F   F→N   N→M   M→G   F→G   G→H

H→I   K→L   O→P   P→Q   Q→R   R→O   J→E

Math Masters, p. 131

Teaching Master

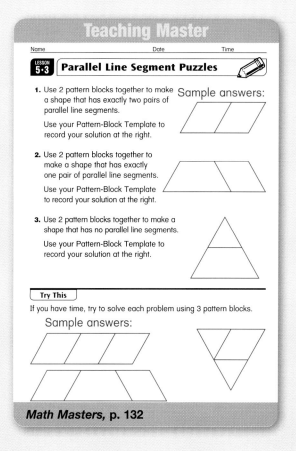

Name   Date   Time

LESSON 5·3 Parallel Line Segment Puzzles

1. Use 2 pattern blocks together to make a shape that has exactly two pairs of parallel line segments.

Use your Pattern-Block Template to record your solution at the right.

Sample answers:

2. Use 2 pattern blocks together to make a shape that has exactly one pair of parallel line segments.

Use your Pattern-Block Template to record your solution at the right.

3. Use 2 pattern blocks together to make a shape that has no parallel line segments.

Use your Pattern-Block Template to record your solution at the right.

Try This

If you have time, try to solve each problem using 3 pattern blocks.

Sample answers:

Math Masters, p. 132

Exploring Polygons, Arrays, and Attributes

EXPLORATIONS

 Objectives To review names and classify polygons; to develop readiness for multiplication; and to provide opportunities to explore similarities and differences of attribute blocks.

---

1 Teaching the Lesson

Key Activities

Children review the shapes on the Pattern-Block Template and the characteristics and names of polygons.

Exploration D: Children construct polygons on their geoboards, copy them onto dot paper, and compare them.

Exploration E: Children explore multiplication concepts by making rectangular arrays with centimeter cubes and recording them on grid paper.

Exploration F: Children find sets of attribute blocks that differ by at least one attribute: size, shape, or color.

Key Concepts and Skills
• Count the total number of cubes. [Number and Numeration Goal 1]
• Create and record cube arrays. [Operations and Computation Goal 4]
• Name, compare, and construct polygons. [Geometry Goal 2]
• Sort attributes according to a rule. [Patterns, Functions, and Algebra Goal 1]

Key Vocabulary trapezoid • rhombus • polygon • side • vertex • vertices • angle • triangle • quadrangle • pentagon • hexagon • heptagon • octagon

⭐ **Ongoing Assessment: Recognizing Student Achievement**
Use the Math Message. [Geometry Goal 2]

materials

☐ *Math Journal 1*, p. 120
☐ Home Link 5•3
☐ Teaching Aid Master (*Math Masters*, p. 415)
☐ Pattern-Block Template
☐ slate
Exploration D: Per group:
☐ Teaching Master (*Math Masters*, p. 133)
☐ geoboard; rubber bands; straightedge
Exploration E: Per partnership:
☐ Teaching Master (*Math Masters*, p. 134)
☐ Teaching Aid Master (*Math Masters*, p. 434)
☐ about 40 centimeter cubes; 2 six-sided dice
Exploration F: Per group:
☐ Teaching Master (*Math Masters*, p. 135)
☐ attribute blocks
☐ red, yellow, and blue crayons or pencils

***See* Advance Preparation**

---

2 Ongoing Learning & Practice

Children practice identifying complements of 100 by playing *Dollar Rummy*.

Children practice and maintain skills through Math Boxes and Home Link activities.

materials

☐ *Math Journal 1*, pp. 65 and 121
☐ Home Link Master (*Math Masters*, p. 136)
☐ *Dollar Rummy* cards (cut from *Math Masters*, pp. 454 and 455)

---

3 Differentiation Options

READINESS
Children identify pattern-block shapes.

ENRICHMENT
Children investigate relationships and properties of polygons with geoboards.

EXTRA PRACTICE
Children find shapes around the room and draw pictures of the items found.

materials

☐ Teaching Masters (*Math Masters*, pp. 137 and 138)
☐ Teaching Aid Master (*Math Masters*, p. 429 or 430)
☐ Pattern-Block Template; geoboard; rubber bands
☐ *The Greedy Triangle* by Marilyn Burns

***See* Advance Preparation**

Additional Information

Advance Preparation You may want to write the vocabulary words on the Word Wall. For the optional Extra Practice activity in Part 3, obtain the book *The Greedy Triangle* by Marilyn Burns (Scholastic, 1995).

Technology
Assessment Management System
Math Message
See page **iTLG.**

Getting Started

Mental Math and Reflexes

Say a number and ask children to record the 100-complement of that number on their slates.

For example, you say 90 and the class writes 10. Write the number model on the board: 90 + 10 = 100. *Suggestions:*

- ●○○ Multiples of 10: 90 10, 40 60, 70 30
- ●●○ Multiples of 25: 50 50, 25 75, 75 25
- ●●● Multiples of 5: 95 5, 45 55, 65 35

Math Message

Write the names of the Pattern-Block Template shapes on an Exit Slip (Math Masters, page 415).
Hexagon, circle, triangle, trapezoid, rhombus, square

Home Link 5·3 Follow-Up

Review answers. Discuss why there are no parallel line segments in Problem 2. Sample answer: Each line segment meets the other two line segments.

---

① Teaching the Lesson

▶ Math Message Follow-Up

WHOLE-CLASS DISCUSSION

 Ongoing Assessment:
Recognizing Student Achievement

Math Message

Use the **Math Message** to assess the children's ability to identify plane figures. Children are making adequate progress if they are able to name the triangle, circle, and square. Some children may be able to name the hexagon, trapezoid, and rhombus as well.

[Geometry Goal 2]

As children identify shapes on their Pattern-Block Templates, draw the shapes and write their names on the board. Remind children that the square, **trapezoid,** larger triangle, hexagon, and two **rhombuses** are the same size and shape as the pattern blocks. To distinguish between the two rhombuses, you might refer to them as the narrow rhombus and the wide rhombus.

> **NOTE** Although the word *diamond* is often used to describe a rhombus, and even though *rhombus* is defined in this way by some dictionaries, use the word *rhombus* since it is the formal term used in geometry.

▶ Reviewing Characteristics of Polygons

WHOLE-CLASS ACTIVITY

(*Math Journal 1*, p. 120)

Remind the class that the pattern-block shapes are examples of **polygons.** Draw a polygon on the board. Identify and discuss its parts.

▷ Polygons are made up of straight **sides** (line segments).

▷ Sides meet at their endpoints. A point at which two sides meet is a **vertex** of the polygon. The plural of *vertex* is **vertices.**

▷ Any two sides that meet form an **angle.**

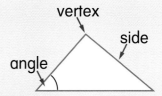

> **Links to the Future**
>
> Do not expect children to memorize the words *vertex, angle,* and *side.* Using this geometric language is a Grade 4 Goal.

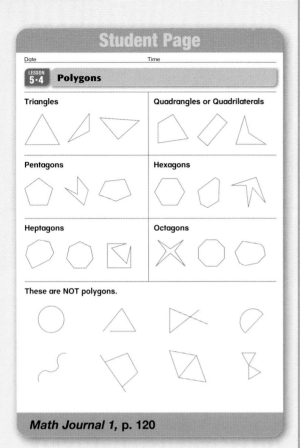

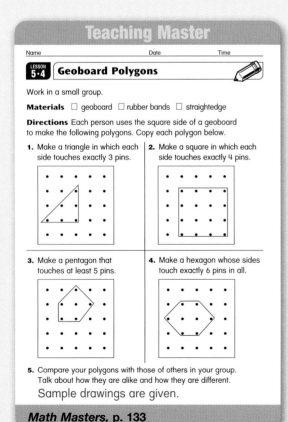
334 **Unit 5** **3-D and 2-D Shapes**

To support English language learners, ask children to identify polygons around the classroom.

With children, examine the shapes on journal page 120. Mention that polygons are "closed" figures—you can trace their sides and come back to where you started without retracing or crossing any part. Ask children to trace a couple of the polygons with their fingers.

Call children's attention to the last two rows of the journal page and discuss why these shapes are not polygons. Children should have no trouble with most of the shapes. Ask them to trace each of the three shapes located on the right of the final row. First, draw a dot anywhere on the shape to identify a starting point. Can they return to the starting point without retracing or crossing any part of the shape? no

▶ Naming Polygons by the Number of Their Sides or Angles

WHOLE-CLASS DISCUSSION

(*Math Journal 1,* p. 120)

Language Arts Link Explain that the word *polygon* comes from the Greek language: *poly-* means *many,* and *-gon* means *angle.* Point out that polygons are named according to the number of sides or angles they have.

3 Sides or Angles

Ask: *How many angles does a* **triangle** *have?* 3 *How many sides?* 3 Point out that *tri-* means *three.* Ask children to name other words that start with *tri-.* To support English language learners, show pictures as these words are introduced. Sample answers: tricycle, triple, triceratops (a dinosaur with three horns)

4 Sides or Angles

Ask: *How many angles does a* **quadrangle** *have?* 4 *How many sides?* 4 Point out that *quad-* means *four.* Other words that start with *quad-* include *quadruped* (a four-legged animal), *quadruple* (to multiply by four), and *quadrille* (a square dance for four couples; also a card game played by four people).

Quadrangles are often called *quadrilaterals.* The root *later* means *side.*

5 and More Sides or Angles

Discuss the other polygons on the page in a similar manner: **pentagon**—5 angles and 5 sides; **hexagon**—6 angles and 6 sides; **heptagon**—7 angles and 7 sides; and **octagon**—8 angles and 8 sides.

► Exploration D: Constructing Polygons on a Geoboard

(*Math Masters*, p. 133)

SMALL-GROUP ACTIVITY

Children make a triangle, a square, a pentagon, and a hexagon on a square geoboard. Children use their straightedges to copy each polygon onto dot paper. Note the restrictions: The rubber band may touch only a given number of pins. This is done in order to limit the size of the constructions.

When everyone in a group has copied all four shapes, ask group members to compare their shapes. Children should notice that polygons come in many sizes and shapes.

► Exploration E: Making Centimeter-Cube Arrays

PARTNER ACTIVITY

(*Math Masters*, pp. 134 and 434)

Portfolio Ideas

Partners complete the steps to make arrays with centimeter cubes. Children record at least 5 rectangular arrays by filling in the correct number and arrangement of centimeter-grid squares. For each array, children write how many rows, how many in each row, and how many in all.

► Exploration F: Finding Attribute Blocks That Differ by One Attribute or More

SMALL-GROUP ACTIVITY

(*Math Masters*, p. 135)

Children follow the directions on *Math Masters*, page 135 to find sets of attribute blocks that differ by at least one of the three attributes—size, shape, or color. To support English language learners, discuss the meaning of the word *attribute*. Children trace blocks and color the drawings on a sheet of paper to show their answers. Encourage children to find sets of blocks that are not the same as those of other children.

⬆️⬇️ Adjusting the Activity

Give children the first block and then guide them through a process of elimination to find the second block. For example, in Problem 1, say:

- Start with a small red triangle.
- The second block may not be small. Make a pile with only large blocks.
- The second block may not be a triangle. Remove all triangles from the pile of large blocks.
- The second block may not be red. Remove all red blocks from the pile of large circles, squares, rectangles, and hexagons.

All of the shapes that remain in the pile are not the same size, shape, or color as the original block, the small red triangle.

AUDITORY ◆ KINESTHETIC ◆ TACTILE ◆ VISUAL

Teaching Master

Name   Date   Time

LESSON 5·4 | **Cube Arrays**

Work with a partner or a small group.

Materials ☐ centimeter grid paper from *Math Masters*, p. 434
     ☐ 2 six-sided dice
     ☐ about 40 centimeter cubes

Directions

Follow these steps to build arrays with centimeter cubes:

1. Pick one member of your group to roll the dice.
2. Use the number that is faceup on one die for the number of rows in the array. Use the number that is faceup on the other die for the number of cubes in each row.

Example: If you roll this: You can make either array:

3. Work together. Use centimeter cubes to build the array.
4. On grid paper, fill in squares to show your array. Underneath the array, write
   - how many rows are in the array
   - how many cubes are in each row
   - how many cubes there are in all
5. Take turns rolling the dice. Together, make at least five different arrays. Record each array on grid paper.

Math Masters, p. 134

NOTE For Exploration E, you might want to provide children with additional copies of the centimeter grid paper on *Math Masters*, page 434.

Teaching Master

Name   Date   Time

LESSON 5·4 | **Attributes**

Work with a small group.

Materials ☐ attribute blocks
     ☐ sheet of paper
     ☐ red, yellow, and blue crayons or pencils

Directions

Solve each problem. On a separate sheet of paper, trace and color the blocks to show your answers.

1. Find 2 blocks that are NOT the same size, NOT the same shape, and NOT the same color.
2. Find 2 blocks that have the same shape, but are NOT the same size and NOT the same color.
3. Find 3 blocks that are the same size and the same color, but are NOT the same shape.
4. Find 4 small blocks that are the same color, but are NOT the same shape.

Sample answers:
1. Drawings of a small yellow triangle and a large red rectangle
2. Drawings of a small yellow triangle and a large blue triangle
3. Drawings of a large red triangle, a large red circle, and a large red square
4. Drawings of a small red triangle, a small red rectangle, a small red circle, and a small red square

Math Masters, p. 135

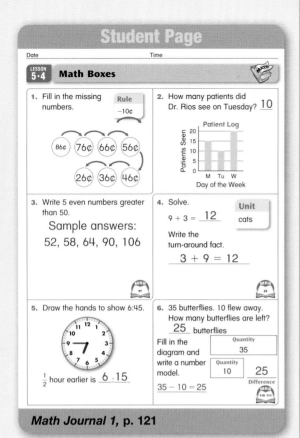

Date _____ Time _____

LESSON 5·4 **Math Boxes**

1. Fill in the missing numbers.

Rule −10¢

86¢ 76¢ 66¢ 56¢

26¢ 36¢ 46¢

2. How many patients did Dr. Rios see on Tuesday? 10

Patient Log

3. Write 5 even numbers greater than 50.
Sample answers:
52, 58, 64, 90, 106

4. Solve.

9 + 3 = 12

Unit cats

Write the turn-around fact.

3 + 9 = 12

5. Draw the hands to show 6:45.

½ hour earlier is 6 :15.

6. 35 butterflies. 10 flew away. How many butterflies are left?
25 butterflies

Fill in the diagram and write a number model.

| Quantity |
| 35 |

| Quantity |
| 10 |

| 25 |
| Difference |

35 − 10 = 25

Math Journal 1, p. 121

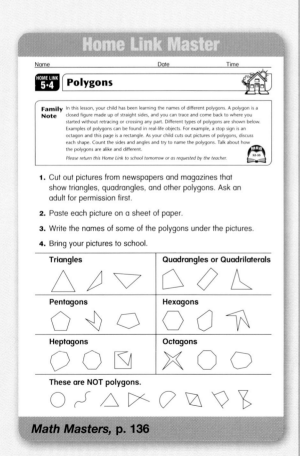

Name _____ Date _____ Time _____

HOME LINK 5·4 **Polygons**

Family Note In this lesson, your child has been learning the names of different polygons. A polygon is a closed figure made up of straight sides, and you can trace and come back to where you started without retracing or crossing any part. Different types of polygons are shown below. Examples of polygons can be found in real-life objects. For example, a stop sign is an octagon and this page is a rectangle. As your child cuts out pictures of polygons, discuss each shape. Count the sides and angles and try to name the polygons. Talk about how the polygons are alike and different.

Please return this Home Link to school tomorrow or as requested by the teacher.

1. Cut out pictures from newspapers and magazines that show triangles, quadrangles, and other polygons. Ask an adult for permission first.

2. Paste each picture on a sheet of paper.

3. Write the names of some of the polygons under the pictures.

4. Bring your pictures to school.

Triangles	Quadrangles or Quadrilaterals
Pentagons	**Hexagons**
Heptagons	**Octagons**

These are NOT polygons.

Math Masters, p. 136

---

2 **Ongoing Learning & Practice**

▶ **Playing** *Dollar Rummy*

PARTNER ACTIVITY

(*Math Journal 1,* p. 65; *Math Masters,* pp. 454 and 455)

Dollar Rummy was introduced in Lesson 3-5. The cards on *Math Masters,* page 454 have money amounts less than $1.00 in multiples of 10¢. You may wish to add the cards from *Math Masters,* page 455, which have amounts in multiples of 5¢.

▶ **Math Boxes 5·4**

INDEPENDENT ACTIVITY

(*Math Journal 1,* p. 121)

Mixed Practice Math Boxes in this lesson are paired with Math Boxes in Lesson 5-2. The skill in Problem 6 previews Unit 6 content.

Writing/Reasoning Have children draw, write, or verbalize their answers to the following: *Explain how you know your numbers are even numbers in Problem 3.* Sample answer: They all end in 2, 4, 6, 8, or 0.

▶ **Home Link 5·4**

INDEPENDENT ACTIVITY

(*Math Masters,* p. 136)

Home Connection Children cut out pictures of polygons from newspapers and magazines. They bring the pictures to school to use in a bulletin-board display or class polygon book. You may wish to allow children to have more than one day to complete this assignment. If so, be sure to tell the children.

---

3 **Differentiation Options**

READINESS

▶ **Identifying Pattern-Block Template Shapes**

SMALL-GROUP ACTIVITY

5–15 Min

(*Math Masters,* pp. 137 and 138)

To explore polygons using concrete models, have children use their Pattern-Block Templates to identify and draw shapes on *Math Masters,* pages 137 and 138. When they have completed the pages, encourage children to describe the shapes' similarities and differences.

▶ Investigating Polygons with Geoboards

(*Math Masters,* p. 429 or 430)

PARTNER ACTIVITY

15–30 Min

To explore naming and classifying polygons, have children transform one polygon into another using geoboards.

Children work in partnerships. One child begins by making a square on the geoboard. Partners record the square on *Math Masters,* page 429 (5-by-5 geoboards) or page 430 (7-by-7 geoboards). Partners take turns moving either one corner or one side of the rubber-band shape so that there are no loops, twists, or crossovers. With each move, partners try to create a new polygon, recording each new shape as they make it. They should try to create a different polygon with each move. For example, they change a square to an irregular quadrangle to a triangle, or change a square to a pentagon to a hexagon.

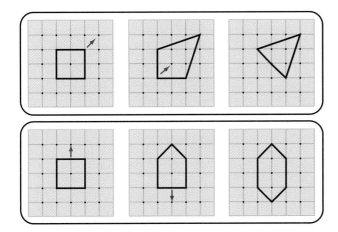

▶ Finding Shapes Around the Room

SMALL-GROUP ACTIVITY

5–15 Min

Literature Link Read the following book to groups of children, or have children read the book themselves. Children can look for shapes around the classroom and draw pictures of the items found.
The Greedy Triangle by Marilyn Burns (Scholastic, 1995)
Summary: This book focuses on the characteristics of different polygons. A triangle, dissatisfied with its life, asks for one more angle and one more side until it realizes staying its own shape is best.

Planning Ahead

In the Lesson 5-5 activity Making Shapes out of Triangles and Rectangles, children use shapes cut from *Math Masters,* pages 139 and 140 to form other shapes. This activity works best if the triangles and rectangles have been carefully cut out. You may wish to prepare the sets of triangles and rectangles ahead of time.

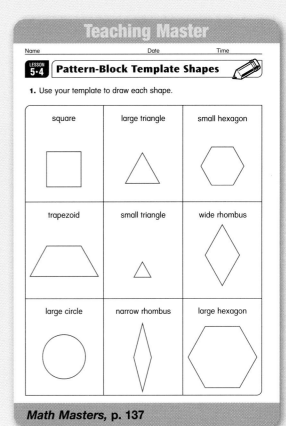

Teaching Master

Name _____ Date _____ Time _____

LESSON 5·4 | **Pattern-Block Template Shapes**

1. Use your template to draw each shape.

square	large triangle	small hexagon
trapezoid	small triangle	wide rhombus
large circle	narrow rhombus	large hexagon

Math Masters, p. 137

Teaching Master

Name _____ Date _____ Time _____

LESSON 5·4 | **Pattern-Block Template Shapes** *cont.*

2. Draw the shapes that have exactly 4 sides and 4 corners. Write their names.

square _____   trapezoid _____

narrow rhombus _____   wide rhombus _____

Math Masters, p. 138

5·5 Quadrangles

 Objectives To guide children as they identify the names and the characteristics of various quadrangles, and as they explore similarities and differences among quadrangles.

1 Teaching the Lesson

materials

Key Activities
Children discuss features and names of various quadrangles and identify the types of quadrangles they drew in Lesson 5·3. They also cut out triangles and rectangles, put them together to make other shapes, and write the names of the shapes.

Key Concepts and Skills
• Create shapes out of triangles and rectangles. [Geometry Goal 2]
• Identify characteristics of quadrangles. [Geometry Goal 2]
• Compare quadrangles. [Geometry Goal 2]

Key Vocabulary
square corner • square • rhombus • rectangle • trapezoid • parallelogram • kite

⭐ **Ongoing Assessment: Recognizing Student Achievement**
Use Mental Math and Reflexes. [Operations and Computation Goal 3]

⭐ **Ongoing Assessment: Informing Instruction** See page 339.

☐ *Math Journal 1,* pp. 115 and 117
☐ *My Reference Book,* p. 55
☐ Home Link 5·4
☐ Teaching Masters (*Math Masters,* pp. 139 and 140)
☐ Teaching Aid Master (*Math Masters,* p. 415)
☐ Pattern-Block Template
☐ index card (optional)
☐ scissors
☐ glue or tape

***See* Advance Preparation**

2 Ongoing Learning & Practice

materials

Children identify sums and differences that match a given number by playing *Name That Number.*

Children practice and maintain skills through Math Boxes and Home Link activities.

☐ *Math Journal 1,* p. 122
☐ *My Reference Book,* pp. 138 and 139
☐ Home Link Master (*Math Masters,* p. 141)
☐ Game Master (*Math Masters,* p. 462; optional)
☐ per partnership: 4 each of number cards 0–10 and 1 each of number cards 11–20

3 Differentiation Options

materials

READINESS
Children sort pattern-block shapes.

ENRICHMENT
Children explore tangrams.

ELL SUPPORT
Children use a Venn diagram to organize information about shapes.

☐ pattern blocks
☐ tangram pieces and a square (cut from *Math Masters,* p. 142)
☐ envelope

***See* Advance Preparation**

Additional Information

Advance Preparation You may want to spend two days on this lesson. For the optional Enrichment activity in Part 3, copy *Math Masters,* page 142 (tangram shapes) onto cardstock.

Technology
Assessment Management System
Mental Math and Reflexes
See the **iTLG.**
See Web site on page 342.

Getting Started

Mental Math and Reflexes ★

Children make ballpark estimates for sums. Have them record the number models on an Exit Slip (*Math Masters,* page 415). Pose problems like the following:

◐○○ 29 + 46 30 + 50 = 80
17 + 84 20 + 80 = 100; or 15 + 85 = 100

◐◐○ 67 + 98 70 + 100 = 170
76 + 123 80 + 120 = 200

◐◐◐ 153 + 239 150 + 240 = 390
198 + 256 200 + 250 = 450; or 200 + 256 = 456

Math Message

Trace each quadrangle that you find on your Pattern-Block Template.
Square, trapezoid, two rhombuses

Home Link 5·4 Follow-Up

Ask children how they identified shapes in pictures they brought to school.

Ongoing Assessment: Recognizing Student Achievement

Mental Math and Reflexes ★

Use **Mental Math and Reflexes** to assess children's ability to make reasonable estimates for addition problems. Children are making adequate progress if they make reasonable estimates using numbers that are close to the exact numbers in the problem. Some children may use numbers that are closer.

[Operations and Computation Goal 3]

- On **Day 1** of this lesson, children should complete the Math Message Follow-Up, explore similarities and differences among quadrangles, cut out the triangles and rectangles, and begin to form shapes.

- On **Day 2** of this lesson, children should finish forming shapes. Then have children complete Part 2 activities.

① Teaching the Lesson

▶ Math Message Follow-Up

👥👥 **WHOLE-CLASS DISCUSSION**

(*My Reference Book,* p. 55)

If children need help identifying which shapes are quadrangles, read *My Reference Book,* page 55 with your class. Briefly check children's drawings. Ask which shapes have **square corners.** *The square* You may wish to tell children that square corners are also called *right angles.*

Ongoing Assessment: Informing Instruction

If children are unable to determine which corners are square corners, they can check the shapes by using the corner of an index card.

  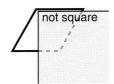

Student Page

Geometry

These 2-dimensional shapes are all **quadrangles.**
Quadrangles are also called **quadrilaterals.**

● A quadrangle has 4 sides, 4 angles, and 4 vertices.

square corner

| square | rectangle | parallelogram |

| rhombus | trapezoid | kite |

Try It Together

Choose one of the 2-dimensional shapes on pages 54–55.
Describe it to a partner without saying the shape's name.
Can your partner tell what shape you are describing?

My Reference Book, p. 55

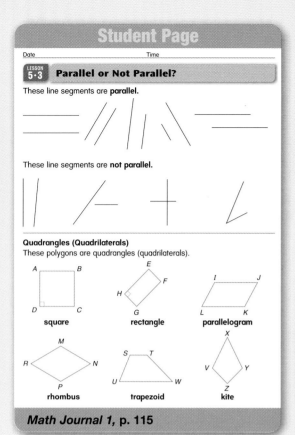
NOTE A square is a special kind of rhombus, one with all square corners. Similarly, a square is a special kind of rectangle, one with all sides the same length. Squares, rectangles, and rhombuses are special kinds of parallelograms, shapes with two pairs of parallel sides. This kind of classification of quadrangles will be discussed in *Third Grade Everyday Mathematics.*

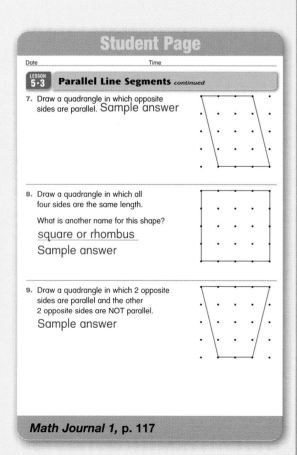
▶ # Exploring Similarities and Differences among Quadrangles

WHOLE-CLASS DISCUSSION

(*Math Journal 1,* pp. 115 and 117)

Ask children to examine the quadrangles on journal page 115. Call attention to the symbol ⌐ in the square and rectangle, indicating square corners. Discuss the features and names of the quadrangles. Ask questions like the following:

Adjusting the Activity

Draw the two shapes that are being compared on the board.

AUDITORY ◆ KINESTHETIC ◆ TACTILE ◆ VISUAL

- How are the **square** and the **rhombus** alike? All four sides are the same length. How are they different? A square has square corners; a rhombus may or may not have square corners.

- How are the square and the **rectangle** alike? Both have four square corners. How are they different? All four sides of a square are the same length; the adjacent sides of a rectangle do not need to be the same length.

- How are the **trapezoid** and **parallelogram** different? A parallelogram has two pairs of parallel sides. A trapezoid has only one pair of parallel sides.

- How are the parallelogram and the **kite** alike? Both have two pairs of sides that are the same length. How are they different? The opposite sides of a parallelogram are parallel; the opposite sides of a kite are not parallel. The sides of a kite that are the same length meet at a vertex; the sides of a parallelogram that are the same length may or may not meet at a vertex.

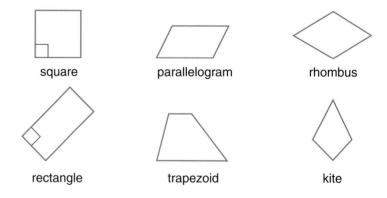

square   parallelogram   rhombus

rectangle   trapezoid   kite

Ask the class to turn to journal page 117. Volunteers show and name the shapes they drew in Problems 7–9. If the class did not come up with all possible shapes for Problem 7 or 8, ask: *What other shape could you have drawn?*

Links to the Future

Exploring similarities and differences among quadrangles is a beginning exposure to classifying plane figures. Children will continue to compare plane figures in third grade. Classifying plane figures is a Grade 4 Goal.

Making Shapes out of Triangles and Rectangles

INDEPENDENT ACTIVITY

(*Math Masters*, pp. 139 and 140)

Children cut out the triangles and rectangles on *Math Masters*, page 139. They put them together to form various shapes, which they paste or tape onto sheets of paper. If children need more triangles and rectangles, they can cut out additional shapes from *Math Masters*, page 140.

Below are some possible constructions. Encourage children who enjoy this activity to attempt more complex constructions.

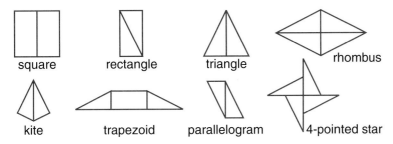

square   rectangle   triangle   rhombus

kite   trapezoid   parallelogram   4-pointed star

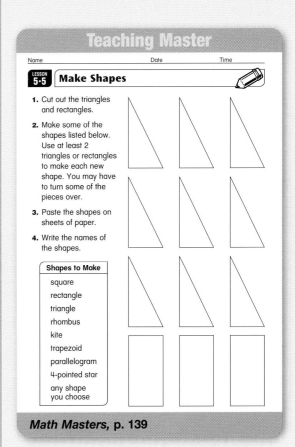

Math Masters, p. 139

(2) Ongoing Learning & Practice

Playing *Name That Number*

PARTNER ACTIVITY

(*Math Masters*, p. 462; *My Reference Book*, pp. 138 and 139)

This game was introduced in Lesson 2-9. To make the game more challenging, children may use two, three, four, or all five of the faceup cards to name the target number.

Math Boxes 5•5

INDEPENDENT ACTIVITY

(*Math Journal 1*, p. 122)

Mixed Practice Math Boxes in this lesson are paired with Math Boxes in Lesson 5-7. The skills in Problems 5 and 6 preview Unit 6 content.

Writing/Reasoning Have children draw, write, or verbalize their answers to the following: *Explain the strategy you used to fill in the number grid in Problem 2.* Sample answer: When I moved up, I subtracted 10. When I moved down, I added 10. Going left, I subtracted 1. Going right, I added 1.

Home Link 5•5

INDEPENDENT ACTIVITY

(*Math Masters*, p. 141)

Home Connection In each set of four quadrangles, three quadrangles have something in common that is not a feature of the fourth. Children decide which quadrangle is different.

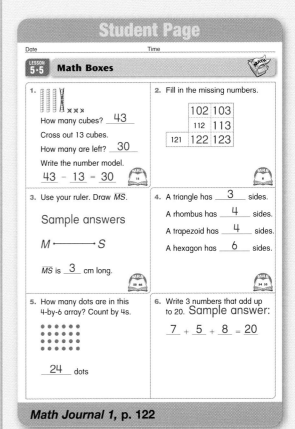

Math Journal 1, p. 122

5·5 Quadrangles

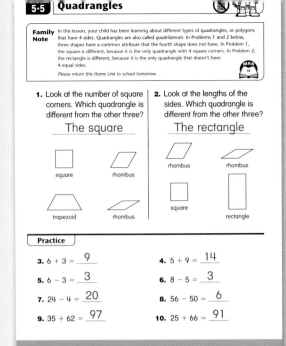

Family Note In this lesson, your child has been learning about different types of quadrangles, or polygons that have 4 sides. Quadrangles are also called *quadrilaterals*. In Problems 1 and 2 below, three shapes have a common attribute that the fourth shape does not have. In Problem 1, the square is different, because it is the only quadrangle with 4 square corners. In Problem 2, the rectangle is different, because it is the only quadrangle that doesn't have 4 equal sides.

Please return this Home Link to school tomorrow.

1. Look at the number of square corners. Which quadrangle is different from the other three?

The **square**

square   rhombus

trapezoid   rhombus

2. Look at the lengths of the sides. Which quadrangle is different from the other three?

The **rectangle**

rhombus   rhombus

square

rectangle

Practice

3. 6 + 3 = __9__

4. 5 + 9 = __14__

5. 6 − 3 = __3__

6. 8 − 5 = __3__

7. 24 − 4 = __20__

8. 56 − 50 = __6__

9. 35 + 62 = __97__

10. 25 + 66 = __91__

Math Masters, p. 141

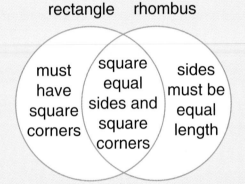

rectangle   rhombus

must have square corners | square equal sides and square corners | sides must be equal length

Teaching Master

Name _____ Date _____ Time _____

LESSON 5·5 Tangram Puzzle

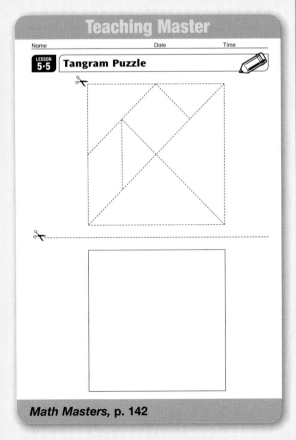

Math Masters, p. 142

③ Differentiation Options

READINESS

PARTNER ACTIVITY

▶ Sorting Pattern Blocks

🕐 5–15 Min

To explore 2-dimensional shapes, have children sort pattern-block shapes. Children need one of each pattern-block shape. With a partner, children decide how to sort the shapes into two groups, and then do the sorting. Have children describe how they sorted the shapes. *Sample answers: Shapes with four sides and shapes that do not have four sides; blocks you can make with other block shapes and blocks you cannot make with other block shapes*

Now have children only use blocks that have four sides—the trapezoid, square, and two rhombuses. Ask children to sort the shapes again and describe how they sorted them. *Sample answers: Shapes that have four equal sides and shapes that do not; shapes that have slanted sides and shapes that do not*

ENRICHMENT

PARTNER ACTIVITY

▶ Exploring Tangrams

🕐 5–15 Min

(*Math Masters,* p. 142)

To further explore the characteristics of 2-dimensional shapes, have children work with tangrams. Copy *Math Masters,* page 142 onto cardstock. Cut it in half along the dashed line, and cut apart the seven tangram shapes on the top half of the page. (Children can store the pieces in an envelope.) Provide the bottom half of the master as a template. Have children put the seven pieces together to form the square.

If interest in this activity is high, additional tangram puzzles can be found in many commercially available books.

NOTE Consider visiting the National Council of Teachers of Mathematics Web site where there is an interactive tangram set:
http://standards.nctm.org/document/eexamples/chap4/4.4/#applet

ELL SUPPORT

SMALL-GROUP ACTIVITY

▶ Using a Venn Diagram

🕐 5–15 Min

To provide language support for understanding similarities and differences between shapes, have children draw a Venn diagram to use as a tool for organizing the information. (*See margin.*) Encourage children to use the vocabulary they have been working on in this unit.

 **3-Dimensional Shapes**

Objective To guide children as they compare and contrast the characteristics of 3-dimensional shapes.

---

1 Teaching the Lesson

materials

Key Activities

Children review the names and parts of 3-dimensional objects by using the 3-D Shapes Poster and models. They also compare and contrast 3-dimensional shapes, collect objects for a Shapes Museum, and classify real objects by the names of their 3-dimensional shapes.

Key Concepts and Skills

- Identify cones, pyramids, prisms, cubes, and cylinders.
  [Geometry Goal 2]
- Compare cones, pyramids, prisms, cubes, and cylinders.
  [Geometry Goal 2]
- Describe 3-dimensional shapes.
  [Geometry Goal 2]

Key Vocabulary

cylinder • cone • sphere • curved surface • rectangular prism • cube • pyramid • flat surface • face • edge • vertex • vertices • congruent

⭐ **Ongoing Assessment: Informing Instruction** See pages 345 and 347.

- ☐ *Math Journal 1,* pp. 124 and 125
- ☐ Home Link 5·5
- ☐ 3-D Shapes Poster (optional)
- ☐ 3-dimensional models: rectangular prism, cube, cylinder, cone, sphere, and pyramid
- ☐ slate
- ☐ items from home for the Shapes Museum
- ☐ labeled index cards for the Shapes Museum

***See* Advance Preparation**

---

2 Ongoing Learning & Practice

materials

Children draw and count line segments and triangles.

Children practice and maintain skills through Math Boxes and Home Link activities.

⭐ **Ongoing Assessment: Recognizing Student Achievement** Use journal page 126.
  [Operations and Computation Goal 2]

- ☐ *Math Journal 1,* pp. 123 and 126
- ☐ Home Link Master (*Math Masters,* p. 143)
- ☐ straightedge

---

3 Differentiation Options

materials

ENRICHMENT
Children solve and pose shape riddles.

EXTRA PRACTICE
Children practice identifying shapes.

- ☐ *Minute Math®+,* pp. 18 and 56
- ☐ 3-dimensional models

Additional Information

Advance Preparation For Part 1, you might make a large poster with a labeled picture of each 3-dimensional shape to help children learn their names. For the Shapes Museum, write the words *rectangular prism, cube, cylinder, cone, sphere, pyramid,* and *other* on index cards. Gather models of 3-dimensional shapes and items for the museum. See the Planning Ahead section on page 326 for suggestions.

Technology

Assessment Management System
Math Boxes, Problem 5
See the **iTLG.**

Getting Started

Mental Math and Reflexes

Make a ballpark estimate for each sum. Record it as a number model on your slate.

○○○ 48 + 46 = ? 50 + 50 = 100; or 50 + 45 = 95

13 + 59 = ? 10 + 60 = 70; or 13 + 60 = 73

●○○ 76 + 188 = ? 80 + 190 = 270

85 + 165 = ? 80 + 160 = 240; or 90 + 170 = 260

●●○ 183 + 211 = ? 180 + 210 = 390; or 200 + 200 = 400

296 + 173 = ? 300 + 170 = 470; or 300 + 173 = 473

Math Message

Find two things in the room that have only flat sides. Find two things that have round sides. Sample answers: A book and a desk have flat sides. A roll of paper towels and a piece of chalk have round sides.

Home Link 5·5 Follow-Up

For each problem, have children name the quadrangle that doesn't belong and explain how they chose that quadrangle.

---

1 Teaching the Lesson

▶ Math Message Follow-Up

WHOLE-CLASS DISCUSSION

Children name the objects they found in the room. If children are having difficulty finding items, pose the question in the following way: *Find two things in the room that will not roll. Find two things that will roll.*

▶ Reviewing the Names of the Basic 3-Dimensional Shapes

WHOLE-CLASS DISCUSSION

(*Math Journal 1,* p. 124)

Ask children to examine the shapes on your class's 3-D Shapes Poster or on the journal page. (*See Advance Preparation.*) Have children say the names of the shapes. Then use your models of 3-dimensional shapes to name the parts of each shape. Introduce the following terms:

▷ **Cylinders, cones,** and **spheres** have **curved surfaces.**

▷ **Rectangular prisms, cubes, pyramids,** cylinders, and cones have **flat surfaces** called **faces.**

▷ An **edge** of a prism or pyramid is a line segment where two faces meet.

▷ A **vertex** (plural: **vertices**) of a prism or pyramid is a point at which at least three edges meet.

Adjusting the Activity

ELL

Add the shape words to the Word Wall so children can refer to them as often as necessary. Include a picture, as well as a written description from the glossary, for each word.

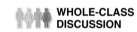

AUDITORY ◆ KINESTHETIC ◆ TACTILE ◆ VISUAL

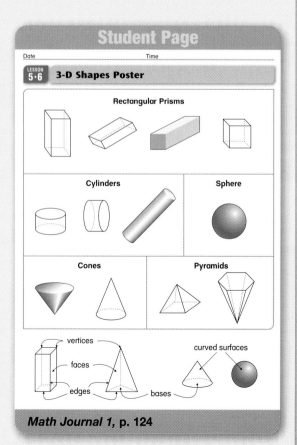

▶ Discussing Similarities and Differences among Shapes

 **WHOLE-CLASS DISCUSSION**

Compare and contrast shapes, two at a time.

Cylinder and Cone

Hold up the models of the cylinder and the cone. How are they alike? How are they different? Ask children to describe the shapes; accept unclear and informal descriptions. *Some possible responses:*

▷ Both the cylinder and the cone have a round side, but they don't look the same. The round side of the cylinder goes straight up and down. The round side of the cone comes to a point.

▷ Both the cylinder and the cone can roll.

▷ The cylinder has two (flat) faces; the cone has only one (flat) face.

▷ The (flat) faces in both shapes are circles.

Continue the discussion with other pairs of shapes. *For example:*

Pyramid and Cone

▷ The pyramid has no curved surfaces and can't be rolled.

▷ Both shapes come to a point.

▷ The faces of the pyramid that come to a point at the top are all triangles.

▷ The cone has a curved edge. The pyramid has only straight edges.

During the discussion of shapes, you may wish to present the term **congruent** to the class. Explain that congruent figures have the same size and shape. They can be 2-dimensional or 3-dimensional.

 Links to the Future

Children will be exposed to many geometric words that might be unfamiliar to them. Do not expect children to memorize them at this time. With repeated exposure, these words will gradually become part of the children's vocabularies. Identifying and describing these shapes is a Grade 2 Goal. Describing, comparing, and classifying solid figures using appropriate geometric terms— including *vertex, base, face, edge,* and *congruent*—are Grade 4 Goals.

Models of a cylinder and cone

Models of a pyramid and cone

Models of a pyramid and rectangular prism

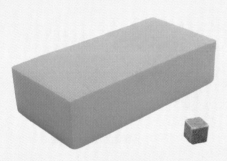

Models of a cylinder and rectangular prism

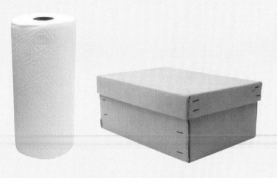

Models of a rectangular prism and cube

Pyramid and Rectangular Prism

▷ Both have vertices, faces, and edges.

▷ Neither has a curved surface.

▷ All but one (the bottom face) of the pyramid's faces come to a single point (vertex). Any three of the faces of the rectangular prism come together at a single point (vertex).

▷ At least two of the faces of the rectangular prism are rectangles. At least four of the faces of the pyramid are triangles.

▷ If you turn the prism upside down, it sits flat. If you turn the pyramid upside down, it tips over.

Cylinder and Rectangular Prism

▷ The cylinder has a curved surface; the prism does not.

▷ The cylinder has no vertices; the rectangular prism has eight vertices.

▷ The cylinder has two curved edges but no straight edges; the prism has 12 straight edges but no curved edges.

▷ If you closed your eyes and your partner turned a cylinder or prism upside down, you wouldn't be able to tell that the shape had been turned upside down by touching it.

Rectangular Prism and Cube

▷ They have the same number of faces, vertices, and edges.

▷ All the faces of a cube are squares.

▷ The faces of a rectangular prism can be squares or rectangles. Those that have all square faces are cubes. A cube is a special kind of rectangular prism.

Continue to compare and contrast pairs of shapes only as long as children remain interested. You can revisit other pairs of shapes in future lessons.

▶ Starting a Shapes Museum with a Display of 3-Dimensional Objects

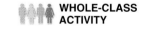 **WHOLE-CLASS ACTIVITY**

Tell children that they are going to make a Shapes Museum. Help them set up the museum by placing the items they brought from home near the correct name cards. Shapes that do not fit in any of the six categories are placed near the "other" card. Add some of your own items to the museum.

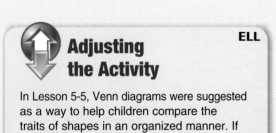

Adjusting the Activity ELL

In Lesson 5-5, Venn diagrams were suggested as a way to help children compare the traits of shapes in an organized manner. If the diagrams proved to be a useful tool, consider using them for this activity.

AUDITORY ◆ KINESTHETIC ◆ TACTILE ◆ VISUAL

▶ Identifying the Shapes of Real Objects

(*Math Journal 1*, p. 125)

Children complete the page on their own. Point out that real-life objects can resemble 3-dimensional shapes, but they often have other parts as well. For example, the wrapped package in Problem 3 is a rectangular prism, but it also has a bow attached to it.

✓ Ongoing Assessment: Informing Instruction

Watch for children who have difficulty naming the shapes. Have 3-dimensional shapes and real-life objects labeled and available for the children to compare.

② Ongoing Learning & Practice

▶ Drawing and Counting Line Segments

(*Math Journal 1*, p. 123)

For Problems 1 and 2, children draw line segments between pairs of points and count the total number of line segments they drew. In Problem 3, children draw line segments and then identify triangles and a four-sided figure.

▶ Math Boxes 5·6

(*Math Journal 1*, p. 126)

Mixed Practice Math Boxes in this lesson are paired with Math Boxes in Lesson 5-8. The skill in Problem 6 previews Unit 6 content.

Writing/Reasoning Have children draw, write, or verbalize their answers to the following: *How many children traveled to school in all in Problem 3? Explain how you found your answer.* Sample answer: 30 children; I added the number of children in each group together.
$4 + 6 + 8 + 12 = 30$

✓ Ongoing Assessment: Recognizing Student Achievement

Math Boxes Problem 5 ★

Use **Math Boxes, Problem 5** to assess children's ability to find the difference between two 2-digit numbers. Children are making adequate progress if they correctly complete the problem using manipulatives. Some children may be able to solve the problem without the use of manipulatives.

[Operations and Computation Goal 2]

Date _____ Time _____

LESSON 5·6 What's the Shape?

Write the name of each shape.

1. sphere
2. cylinder
3. rectangular prism
4. rectangular prism
5. pyramid
6. cylinder
7. cylinder
8. sphere
9. pyramid
10. cone

Math Journal 1, p. 125

Date _____ Time _____

LESSON 5·6 Connecting Points

Draw a line segment between each pair of points.
Record how many line segments you drew.

Example:

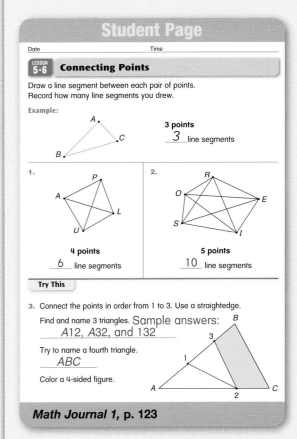

3 points
3 line segments

1. 4 points
6 line segments

2. 5 points
10 line segments

Try This

3. Connect the points in order from 1 to 3. Use a straightedge.
Find and name 3 triangles. Sample answers:
A12, A32, and *132*

Try to name a fourth triangle.
ABC

Color a 4-sided figure.

Math Journal 1, p. 123

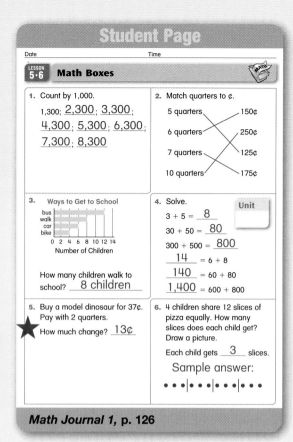

Date   Time

LESSON 5·6   Math Boxes

1. Count by 1,000.

1,300; **2,300**; **3,300**;
4,300; **5,300**; **6,300**;
7,300; **8,300**

2. Match quarters to ¢.

5 quarters → 150¢
6 quarters → 250¢
7 quarters → 125¢
10 quarters → 175¢

3. Ways to Get to School

bus
walk
car
bike

0 2 4 6 8 10 12 14
Number of Children

How many children walk to
school? **8 children**

4. Solve.   Unit

$3 + 5 = $ **8**
$30 + 50 = $ **80**
$300 + 500 = $ **800**
14 $ = 6 + 8$
140 $ = 60 + 80$
1,400 $ = 600 + 800$

5. Buy a model dinosaur for 37¢.
Pay with 2 quarters.

★ How much change? **13¢**

6. 4 children share 12 slices of
pizza equally. How many
slices does each child get?
Draw a picture.

Each child gets **3** slices.

Sample answer:

• • • | • • • | • • • | • • •

Math Journal 1, p. 126

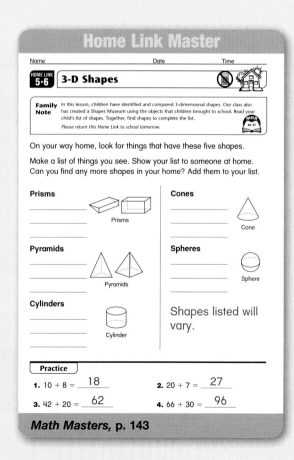

Name   Date   Time

HOME LINK 5·6   **3-D Shapes**

Family Note   In this lesson, children have identified and compared 3-dimensional shapes. Our class also has created a Shapes Museum using the objects that children brought to school. Read your child's list of shapes. Together, find shapes to complete the list.

Please return this Home Link to school tomorrow.

On your way home, look for things that have these five shapes.

Make a list of things you see. Show your list to someone at home.
Can you find any more shapes in your home? Add them to your list.

Prisms

Prisms

Cones

Cone

Pyramids

Pyramids

Spheres

Sphere

Cylinders

Cylinder

Shapes listed will
vary.

Practice

1. $10 + 8 = $ **18**   2. $20 + 7 = $ **27**

3. $42 + 20 = $ **62**   4. $66 + 30 = $ **96**

Math Masters, p. 143

Home Link 5·6

(*Math Masters*, p. 143)

Home Connection Children make a list of things seen on their way home and classify them by shape.

---

③ Differentiation Options

Solving Shape Riddles

INDEPENDENT ACTIVITY

15–30 Min

To apply children's understanding of the characteristics of 3-dimensional shapes, have them solve and pose Shape Riddles. Display a set of solids where children can see and handle them. Pose riddles like the following:

● I am thinking of a shape that has a face that is a circle and a point. cone

● I am thinking of a shape that has 5 faces. pyramid

Have children make up their own Shape Riddles. Consider making a class collection of Shape Riddles. These could be posted on a bulletin board, or laminated and left in a Shapes Station.

Minute Math+

SMALL-GROUP ACTIVITY

5–15 Min

To offer children more experience with identifying shapes, see the following pages in *Minute Math+*: pp. 18 and 56.

Planning Ahead

Before Lesson 5-7, you may wish to build your own square pyramid out of straws and twist-ties. See page 353 for directions. For the Lesson 5-7 Math Message, you will need 8 straws of equal length and 12 twist-ties per child. The pyramid constructions in Part 1 of Lesson 5-7 require 15 four-inch straws, 15 six-inch straws, and 20 twist-ties per partnership. You might want to place these items in three separate containers before beginning the lesson.

Pyramids

Objective To guide children as they construct pyramids and explore the relationship among the number of faces, edges, and vertices in pyramids.

Key Activities

Children construct pyramids whose bases are squares, triangles, rectangles, pentagons, and hexagons. Children count the numbers of edges, faces, and vertices in pyramids.

Key Concepts and Skills

- Construct 2-dimensional shapes using straws and twist-ties. [Geometry Goal 2]
- Construct pyramids using straws and twist-ties. [Geometry Goal 2]
- Describe different pyramids. [Geometry Goal 2]
- Identify patterns and relationships among pyramids.
  [Patterns, Functions, and Algebra Goal 1]

Key Vocabulary

base • apex • square pyramid • triangular pyramid • rectangular pyramid • pentagonal pyramid • hexagonal pyramid

□ Home Link 5·6
□ Teaching Master (*Math Masters,* p. 144; optional)
□ models of a cone and a pyramid
□ slate
□ 8 straws; 12 twist-ties
□ per partnership: 15 four-inch straws, 15 six-inch straws, and 20 twist-ties
□ 3-D Shapes Poster (optional)

***See* Advance Preparation**

---

2   Ongoing Learning & Practice

materials

Children practice addition facts by playing *Beat the Calculator.*

Children practice and maintain skills through Math Boxes and Home Link activities.

✔ **Ongoing Assessment: Recognizing Student Achievement** Use journal page 127.
[Patterns, Functions, and Algebra Goal 1]

□ *Math Journal 1,* pp. 24 and 127
□ *My Reference Book,* pp. 124 and 125
□ Home Link Master (*Math Masters,* p. 145)
□ Teaching Master (*Math Masters,* p. 146; optional)
□ Teaching Aid Master (*Math Masters,* p. 418; optional)
□ calculator

---

3   Differentiation Options

materials

READINESS

Children describe characteristics of polygons and construct polygons out of straws and twist-ties.

ENRICHMENT

Children describe the relationship between the numbers of edges, faces, and vertices of different kinds of pyramids.

ELL SUPPORT

Children describe, compare, and contrast shapes in the Shapes Museum.

□ Teaching Masters (*Math Masters,* pp. 147 and 148)
□ straws and twist-ties
□ table of pyramid edges, faces, and vertices

Additional Information

Advance Preparation You may want to spend two days on this lesson. Place 8 straws of equal length and 12 twist-ties per child (and a few extras) in separate boxes near the Math Message. If children need a visual aid to compare a pyramid and cone in the Math Message, display models or the 3-D Shapes Poster.

Technology

Assessment Management System
Math Boxes, Problem 2
See the **iTLG.**

Getting Started

Mental Math and Reflexes

Have children record addition problems and their sums on slates. *For example:*

◉○○ 63 + 24 = ? 87   ◉◉○ 36 + 48 = ? 84   ◉◉◉ ? = 257 + 136 393
      37 + 41 = ? 78   66 + 79 = ? 145   ? = 152 + 146 298

Math Message

Take 8 straws and 12 twist-ties.
How are pyramids and cones alike and different?

Home Link 5·6 Follow-Up

Ask volunteers to name some of the things on their lists and to describe how they determined where to list the items.

- On **Day 1** of this lesson, children should complete the Math Message Follow-Up and construct the pyramids.

- On **Day 2** of this lesson, children should discuss the constructions. Then have children complete Part 2 activities.

① Teaching the Lesson

▶ Math Message Follow-Up

ŧŧŧŧ WHOLE-CLASS DISCUSSION

Briefly discuss similarities and differences between cones and pyramids. List children's responses on the board.
Possible responses:

▷ Both shapes come to a point.

▷ The cone has one (flat) face; the pyramid has more than one (flat) face.

▷ The cone can be rolled; the pyramid cannot.

▷ The cone has a curved edge; the pyramid has only straight edges.

Place a model of a cone on its flat face. Say that this face is called the **base** of the cone. The "tip" of the cone—the vertex opposite the base—is called the **apex.**

Next, place a model of a pyramid in the same position as the cone. The face on which the pyramid "sits" is also called the base, and the tip of the pyramid is also called the apex. All of the faces of the pyramid, except the base, meet at the apex of the pyramid.

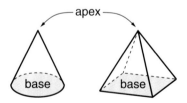

NOTE It is not important that children master this new vocabulary at this time. Through repeated exposure, these words will become part of the children's vocabularies. They should understand that pyramids are named after the shape of the base and that all pyramids with the same-shape base have the same number of faces, edges, and vertices.

▶ Constructing a Pyramid out of Straws

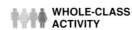 **WHOLE-CLASS ACTIVITY**

Demonstrate how to build a pyramid, one step at a time, as children follow your directions. As indicated in the Math Message, each child should have 8 straws of equal length and 12 twist-ties.

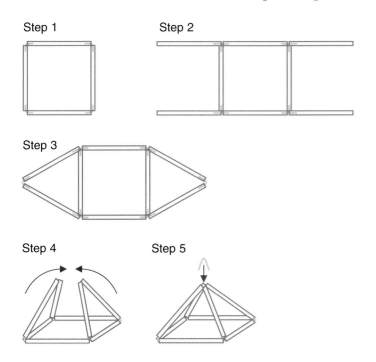

Step 1

Step 2

Step 3

Step 4

Step 5

When children have finished their constructions, ask them to name the shape of the base of their pyramids. A square Tell them that a pyramid is named after the shape of its base—a pyramid whose base is a square is called a **square pyramid.**

Ask: *Do you think you can build a cone out of straws? Why or why not?* Sample response: No. The base of a cone is a circle. You can't make a circle out of straight straws.

▶ Constructing Four Kinds of Pyramids out of Straws

 PARTNER ACTIVITY

(*Math Masters*, p. 144)

Children work in partnerships. Each partnership will make one pyramid.

Each partnership should have 15 four-inch straws, 15 six-inch straws, and about 20 twist-ties. Assign each of the following pyramids, one to each partnership: **triangular pyramid, rectangular pyramid, pentagonal pyramid,** or **hexagonal pyramid.** Children should use the shorter straws for the base. If they are building the rectangular pyramid, they will need to use 2 shorter straws and 2 longer straws. Children should use longer straws for the other edges.

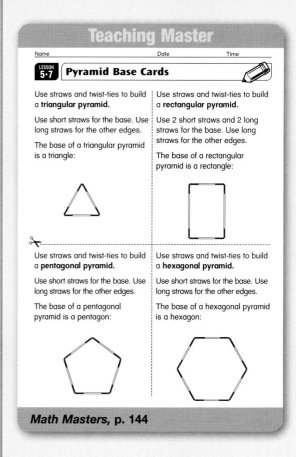

Math Masters, p. 144

NOTE Since a square is a special kind of rectangle, a square pyramid is a special kind of rectangular pyramid (a pyramid whose base is a rectangle).

Beat the Calculator

Materials ❑ number cards 0–9
(4 of each)
❑ 1 calculator

Players 3

Skill Mental addition

Object of the game To add numbers faster than a player using a calculator.

Directions

1. One player is the "Caller." A second player is the "Calculator." The third player is the "Brain."

2. Shuffle the cards. Place the deck number-side down on the table.

3. The Caller draws 2 cards from the number deck and asks for the sum of the numbers.

4. The Calculator solves the problem *with* a calculator. The Brain solves it *without* a calculator. The Caller decides who got the answer first.

My Reference Book, p. 124

NOTE Any face of a triangular pyramid can be chosen to be its base. Once a face is chosen as a base, the other three faces are not bases. You need not discuss this with children unless the question comes up.

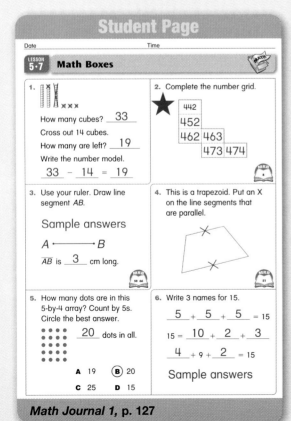

Date _____ Time _____

LESSON 5·7 **Math Boxes**

1. How many cubes? __33__
Cross out 14 cubes.
How many are left? __19__
Write the number model.
__33__ – __14__ = __19__

2. Complete the number grid.

	442	
	452	
	462	463
		473	474

3. Use your ruler. Draw line segment *AB*.

Sample answers

A •———→ B

$\overline{AB}$ is __3__ cm long.

4. This is a trapezoid. Put an X on the line segments that are parallel.

5. How many dots are in this 5-by-4 array? Count by 5s. Circle the best answer.

__20__ dots in all.

A 19 **(B)** 20
C 25 D 15

6. Write 3 names for 15.

__5__ + __5__ + __5__ = 15

15 = __10__ + __2__ + __3__

__4__ + 9 + __2__ = 15

Sample answers

Math Journal 1, p. 127

If you wish, provide each partnership with the appropriate Pyramid Base Card from *Math Masters,* page 144 to help them with their constructions.

Circulate and assist. Store children's constructions for use during the next math class.

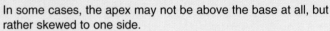

Adjusting the Activity

Have children use a mixture of short and long straws for the bases and edges of the pyramids. Be aware that these constructions are more difficult to make.

Encourage children to pay close attention to the resulting faces of the pyramids. The triangular faces will no longer be identical. Ask children to notice the position of the apex. Using both short and long straws will result in an apex that is not directly above the center of the base.

In some cases, the apex may not be above the base at all, but rather skewed to one side.

Assure children that these are all examples of pyramids

A U D I T O R Y ◆ K I N E S T H E T I C ◆ T A C T I L E ◆ V I S U A L

▶ # Discussing Pyramid Constructions

WHOLE-CLASS DISCUSSION

The purpose of this discussion is to observe patterns and relationships among various parts of pyramids.

A pyramid whose base is a triangle is called a triangular pyramid. Ask children who have constructed triangular pyramids to display them. Then ask:

● How many faces does your pyramid have? 4 Do these pyramids all have the same number of faces? yes

● How many edges does your pyramid have? 6 Do these pyramids all have the same number of edges? yes

● How many vertices does your pyramid have? 4 Do these pyramids all have the same number of vertices? yes

● Are all of the faces the same kind of polygon? Yes, triangles

Record the information in a table on the board. Repeat the procedure for the other three kinds of pyramids. The completed table should look like this:

Pyramid	Shape of Base	Number of Sides in Base	Number of Edges	Number of Faces	Number of Vertices
triangular	triangle	3	6	4	4
rectangular	rectangle	4	8	5	5
pentagonal	pentagon	5	10	6	6
hexagonal	hexagon	6	12	7	7

Ask: *What is the shape of the faces that meet at the apex of any pyramid?* triangle

② Ongoing Learning & Practice

▶ **Playing** *Beat the Calculator*   👥👥👥 **SMALL-GROUP ACTIVITY**

(*Math Journal 1*, p. 24; *My Reference Book*, pp. 124 and 125)

Children play *Beat the Calculator* to develop their recall of addition facts. They should record the facts for which they can beat the calculator by making a check mark in the box for that fact. The Caller should select problems at random.

▶ **Math Boxes 5·7**   👤 **INDEPENDENT ACTIVITY**

(*Math Journal 1*, p. 127)

 Mixed Practice Math Boxes in this lesson are paired with Math Boxes in Lesson 5-5. The skills in Problems 5 and 6 preview Unit 6 content.

✓ **Ongoing Assessment:**   **Math Boxes**
Recognizing Student Achievement   **Problem 2** ⭐

Use **Math Boxes, Problem 2** to assess children's ability to complete the patterns in the number grid. Children are making adequate progress if they can fill in the spaces using manipulatives (number grid, calculator, and so on). Some children may be able to complete the grid without using the number grid tool.

[Patterns, Functions, and Algebra Goal 1]

▶ **Home Link 5·7**   👤 **INDEPENDENT ACTIVITY**

(*Math Masters*, pp. 145 and 146)

 Home Connection Children construct a triangular pyramid out of a paper pattern. If you wish to have children construct a square pyramid as well, send home *Math Masters*, page 146.

③ Differentiation Options

READINESS   👥👥 **PARTNER ACTIVITY**

▶ **Constructing Polygons out of Straws and Twist-Ties**   ◐ 15–30 Min

(*Math Masters*, pp. 147 and 148)

To provide experience with the attributes of polygons using concrete models, have children construct polygons out of straws and twist-ties.

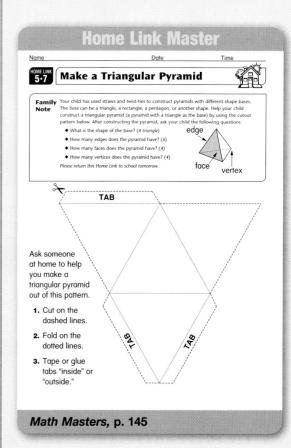

Name   Date   Time

HOME LINK 5·7 | **Make a Triangular Pyramid**

Family Note Your child has used straws and twist-ties to construct pyramids with different-shape bases. The *base* can be a triangle, a rectangle, a pentagon, or another shape. Help your child construct a triangular pyramid (a pyramid with a triangle as the base) by using the cutout pattern below. After constructing the pyramid, ask your child the following questions:

♦ What is the shape of the base? (*A triangle*)
♦ How many edges does the pyramid have? (6)
♦ How many faces does the pyramid have? (4)
♦ How many vertices does the pyramid have? (4)

Please return this Home Link to school tomorrow.

Ask someone at home to help you make a triangular pyramid out of this pattern.

1. Cut on the dashed lines.
2. Fold on the dotted lines.
3. Tape or glue tabs "inside" or "outside."

Math Masters, p. 145

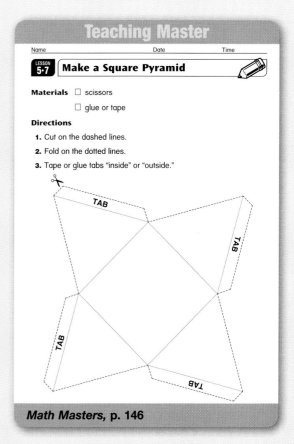

Name   Date   Time

LESSON 5·7 | **Make a Square Pyramid**

Materials ☐ scissors
             ☐ glue or tape

Directions

1. Cut on the dashed lines.
2. Fold on the dotted lines.
3. Tape or glue tabs "inside" or "outside."

Math Masters, p. 146

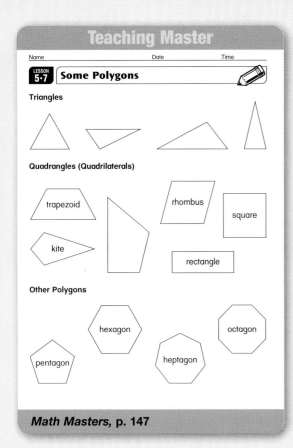
Review the characteristics of polygons:

▷ Polygons are made up of straight sides.

▷ The vertex of a polygon is the point where two sides meet.

Working with a partner, children construct various polygons and answer the questions on *Math Masters,* page 148. It is not necessary for each child to construct every polygon.

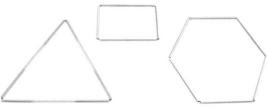

Examples of constructions from straws and twist-ties

ENRICHMENT

👥 SMALL-GROUP ACTIVITY

🕐 5–15 Min

▶ **Discussing Pyramid Construction**

To further explore pyramids, consider having children extend the table of pyramid edges, faces, and vertices created by the class.

Ask children to imagine a pyramid whose base has 10 sides. *How many edges would such a pyramid have?* 20; 10 edges around the base and 10 edges that meet at the apex of the pyramid. *How many faces?* 11; 1 base and 10 triangles *How many vertices?* 11; 10 vertices at the base and 1 apex

A ten-sided polygon is a decagon, so a pyramid whose base is a decagon is called a decagonal pyramid. Add this pyramid information to the table.

Have children use the table to describe the relationship among the numbers of edges, faces, and vertices in a pyramid. The relationship is:

$$\frac{\text{number}}{\text{of edges}} + 2 = \frac{\text{number}}{\text{of faces}} + \frac{\text{number}}{\text{of vertices}}$$

This relationship is true for these five kinds of pyramids and for other 3-dimensional shapes (polyhedra) as well. Challenge children to find other pyramids to add to the table.

ELL SUPPORT

👥 SMALL-GROUP ACTIVITY

🕐 5–15 Min

▶ **Discussing the Shapes Museum**

To provide language support for geometry, have children look at the Shapes Museum and describe the shapes. They may describe attributes of the shapes, or compare and contrast shapes.

5·8 Line Symmetry

 Objective To guide children as they find lines of symmetry in objects and complete drawings to create symmetrical shapes.

1 Teaching the Lesson

materials

Key Activities
Children name examples of symmetrical objects, fold pictures to find lines of symmetry, identify lines of symmetry in objects, and complete half-pictures to draw symmetrical template shapes.

Key Concepts and Skills
- Divide shapes into equal parts. [Number and Numeration Goal 3]
- Locate the line of symmetry in 2-dimensional shapes. [Geometry Goal 3]
- Create symmetric shapes. [Geometry Goal 3]

Key Vocabulary
line symmetry • line of symmetry • symmetrical

✓ **Ongoing Assessment: Recognizing Student Achievement** Use journal page 128.
[Geometry Goal 3]

☐ *Math Journal 1*, p. 128
☐ *My Reference Book*, p. 60
☐ Home Link 5·7
☐ Teaching Masters (*Math Masters*, p. 149; per partnership: *Math Masters*, p. 150)
☐ slate
☐ scissors
☐ Pattern-Block Template

***See* Advance Preparation**

2 Ongoing Learning & Practice

materials

Children practice fact extensions by playing the *Fact Extension Game*.

Children practice and maintain skills through Math Boxes and Home Link activities.

☐ *Math Journal 1*, p. 129
☐ *My Reference Book*, pp. 134 and 135
☐ Home Link Master (*Math Masters*, p. 151)
☐ per partnership: 4 each of number cards 0–9 (from the Everything Math Deck, if available)
☐ per partnership: die; calculator

3 Differentiation Options

materials

READINESS
Children explore symmetry with pattern blocks.

ENRICHMENT
Children cut symmetrical pictures from magazines and create a booklet.

☐ pattern blocks
☐ magazines; backing paper
☐ glue; scissors

Additional Information

Advance Preparation Before doing the Home Link 5·7 Follow-Up, use Home Link 5·7 to make a triangular pyramid.

Technology
Assessment Management System
Journal page 128
See the **iTLG**.

Getting Started

Mental Math and Reflexes

Children solve addition problems on slates.
Suggestions:

⦿○○ 32 + 61 = ? 93   ⦿⦿○ ? = 124 + 133 257
     78 + 22 = ? 100   ? = 236 + 148 384

⦿⦿○ 58 + 87 = ? 145
     27 + 46 = ? 73

Math Message

Take a copy of Math Masters, *page 149. It shows half of a picture. What do you think the whole picture looks like?*

Home Link 5·7 Follow-Up

Display a triangular pyramid made from the pattern. Review names of the parts of a pyramid.

---

1 Teaching the Lesson

▶ Math Message Follow-Up

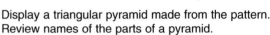 **WHOLE-CLASS ACTIVITY**

(*Math Masters*, p. 149; *My Reference Book*, p. 60)

Briefly go over the answer. A star *How many points does the star have?* 5

Ask children to do the following:

1. Fold the paper along the dashed fold line.

2. Carefully cut along the solid lines.

3. Unfold the cutout picture.

Point out that when the picture is folded, the two halves match. Such shapes are said to have **line symmetry.** The fold line is called the **line of symmetry.** Have children turn to *My Reference Book,* page 60 and read about line symmetry together.

> ### Adjusting the Activity ELL
>
> Add the terms *line symmetry* and *line of symmetry* to the Word Wall so children may refer to them as often as necessary. Include a picture, as well as a written description, next to each term. To support English language learners, clarify the difference between *line symmetry* and *line of symmetry.*
>
> A U D I T O R Y ◆ K I N E S T H E T I C ◆ T A C T I L E ◆ V I S U A L

Ask the class to give other examples of things that look **symmetrical.** If children have trouble getting started, suggest categories. *For example:*

▷ Things in nature: pumpkins, leaves, butterflies

▷ Things in school: tables, open books

▷ Things at home: spoons, chairs

▷ Tools: scissors, screwdrivers

▷ Things outside: buildings, fences

Teaching Master

Name _____ Date _____ Time _____

LESSON 5·8 What's Missing?

Math Masters, p. 149

► Finding Lines of Symmetry

(*Math Masters*, p. 150)

PARTNER ACTIVITY

Pass out a copy of *Math Masters,* page 150 to each partnership. Partners cut out each shape.

Start with the leaf. Ask children to fold it so the two halves match. Can they fold it another way so the two halves match? no The leaf has just one line of symmetry.

Repeat the process with the football. Can they fold it in more than one way? Yes, in 2 ways The football has two lines of symmetry.

Partners look for all lines of symmetry in the rectangle and the square. Ask for volunteers to demonstrate how they got their answers. Rectangle: 2 lines of symmetry; square: 4 lines of symmetry

► Completing Half-Pictures of Template Shapes

INDEPENDENT ACTIVITY

(*Math Journal 1*, p. 128)

Go over the example. Make sure children understand that the dashed line is a line of symmetry for the whole shape. Children use their Pattern-Block Templates to complete each shape. Circulate and assist as needed.

After children have completed the page, discuss how many lines of symmetry the circle has. An unlimited or infinite number (*See margin.*)

Ask volunteers to draw any additional lines of symmetry for some of the other shapes. *How many lines of symmetry does the rhombus have?* 2 *The trapezoid?* 1 *The square?* 4 *The hexagon?* 6 *The triangle?* 3

 Ongoing Assessment: Recognizing Student Achievement

Journal Page 128 ★

Use **journal page 128** to assess children's ability to complete 2-dimensional symmetric shapes. Children are making adequate progress if they successfully complete the shapes using a template. Some children may be able to create 2-dimensional symmetric shapes or designs.

[Geometry Goal 3]

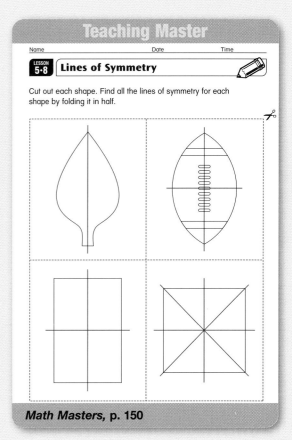
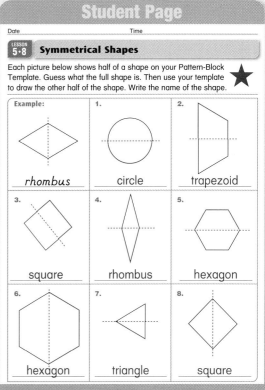

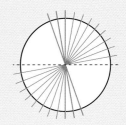

Student Page

Games

Fact Extension Game

Materials
- ❑ number cards 0–9 (4 of each)
- ❑ 1 six-sided die
- ❑ 1 calculator
- ❑ 1 sheet of paper for each player

Players 2

Skill Finding sums of 2-digit numbers and multiples of 10

Object of the game To have the higher total.

Directions

1. Shuffle the cards. Place the deck number-side down on the table.

2. Each player draws 2 cards from the deck and makes the larger 2-digit number.

3. Players take turns rolling the die and making another 2-digit number by using the number on the die in the tens place and a zero in the ones place.

4. Each player adds his or her 2 numbers and records the sum on a sheet of paper.

My Reference Book, p. 134

▶ **Playing the *Fact Extension Game***

 PARTNER ACTIVITY

(*My Reference Book*, pp. 134 and 135)

Children practice fact extension by playing the *Fact Extension Game*. Children will find directions on pages 134 and 135 of *My Reference Book*.

▶ **Math Boxes 5•8**

INDEPENDENT ACTIVITY

(*Math Journal 1*, p. 129)

 Mixed Practice Math Boxes in this lesson are paired with Math Boxes in Lesson 5-6. The skill in Problem 6 previews Unit 6 content.

▶ **Home Link 5•8**

INDEPENDENT ACTIVITY

(*Math Masters*, p. 151)

 Home Connection Children make a list of symmetrical objects found in their homes and draw a picture of one of those objects.

Student Page

Games

5. After 4 rounds, players use a calculator to find the total of their 4 sums.

6. The player with the higher total wins.

● Anna draws a 3 and a 5. She makes the number 53. Then Anna rolls a 6. She makes the number 60.

| 5 | 3 |

53   60

Anna finds the sum of her numbers.

53 + 60 = 113

My Reference Book, p. 135

Student Page

Date _____ Time _____

LESSON 5•8 Math Boxes

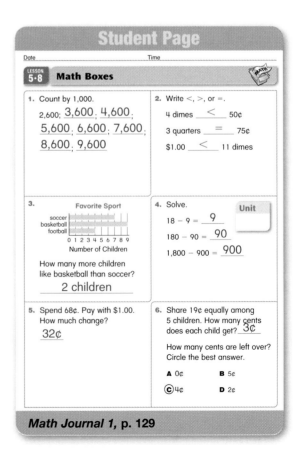

1. Count by 1,000.

2,600; 3,600; 4,600; 5,600; 6,600; 7,600; 8,600; 9,600

2. Write <, >, or =.

4 dimes ___<___ 50¢

3 quarters ___=___ 75¢

$1.00 ___<___ 11 dimes

3. **Favorite Sport**

How many more children like basketball than soccer?

2 children

4. Solve.

18 − 9 = __9__

180 − 90 = __90__

1,800 − 900 = __900__

Unit

5. Spend 68¢. Pay with $1.00. How much change?

32¢

6. Share 19¢ equally among 5 children. How many cents does each child get? _3¢_

How many cents are left over? Circle the best answer.

A 0¢   B 5¢

C 4¢   D 2¢

Math Journal 1, p. 129

③ Differentiation Options

READINESS

 PARTNER ACTIVITY

 5–15 Min

▶ Exploring Line Symmetry with Pattern Blocks

To provide experience with creating symmetrical designs using concrete models, have children use pattern blocks to create half of a shape on one side of a line of symmetry and their partners finish the shape by building on the other side.

First, children fold a blank sheet of paper in half widthwise to create a line of symmetry. Then they unfold the paper and lay it flat on the table.

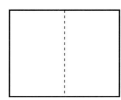

Paper provides the background for a symmetric design.

Next, children make a simple design with pattern blocks on the right side of the paper. Then a partner creates the other half of the design on the left side of the paper.

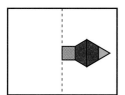 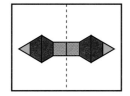

One-half of a design   A partner completes the design.

ENRICHMENT

INDEPENDENT ACTIVITY

 15–30 Min

▶ Making a Symmetry Booklet

To further explore symmetrical shapes and lines of symmetry, have children create a symmetry booklet. Provide a variety of magazines for children to look through and from which they can cut out pictures of symmetrical objects. After cutting out the picture, children should draw the lines of symmetry on the object. Encourage children to flip, slide, and rotate their shapes. Note that changing the position of the shape does not affect the number of lines of symmetry. Some children may notice that some shapes, such as squares or triangles, have rotational symmetry (that is, they can be rotated less than 360 degrees and appear identical). Children can then glue the picture onto a piece of paper. The pictures can be displayed in "symmetrical" booklets, either as individual booklets or as a class booklet.

Home Link Master

Name   Date   Time

HOME LINK 5·8   **Symmetry Hunt**

Family Note   In this lesson, your child has been determining whether shapes are symmetrical. A shape has *symmetry* if it has two halves that look alike but face in opposite directions. A *line of symmetry* divides the shape into two matching parts. Lines of symmetry are shown in the objects below. Help your child find other objects that are symmetrical. Remember that some shapes, such as the mirror below, may be symmetrical in more than one way.

Please return this Home Link to school tomorrow.

1. Ask someone to help you make a list of things at home that have symmetry. For example, you might list a window, a sofa, or a mirror.

My list: _____

_____

2. Draw a picture of one thing on your list. Draw as many lines of symmetry as you can.

3. If you find pictures in books or magazines that show symmetry, bring them to school.

Practice

4. $4 + 8 = \underline{12}$ 5. $6 + 9 = \underline{15}$ 6. $8 + 8 = \underline{16}$

7. $8 - 5 = \underline{3}$ 8. $9 - 4 = \underline{5}$ 9. $7 - 4 = \underline{3}$

Math Masters, p. 151

5·9 Progress Check 5

 Objective To assess children's progress on mathematical content through the end of Unit 5.

---

1 Assessing Progress — materials

Progress Check 5 is a cumulative assessment of concepts and skills taught in Unit 5 and in previous units.

See the Appendix for a complete list of Grade 2 Goals.

☐ Home Link 5·8
☐ Assessment Masters (*Assessment Handbook*, pp. 173–177)
☐ straightedge
☐ pattern blocks; Pattern-Block Template
☐ slate
☐ demonstration clock

CONTENT ASSESSED	LESSON(S)	ASSESSMENT ITEMS			
		SELF	ORAL/SLATE	WRITTEN PART A	PART B
Count up by 1s, 2s, 5s, 10s, 25s, and 100s to 1,000. [Number and Numeration Goal 1]	5·1–5·8	5		2	
Order and compare whole numbers. [Number and Numeration Goal 7]	5·1, 5·4, 5·8			3	
Know and apply addition facts. [Operations and Computation Goal 1]	5·1, 5·2, 5·4–5·8		4	1	
Use and explain strategies for solving problems involving the addition of 2-digit whole numbers. [Operations and Computation Goal 2]	5·1, 5·2, 5·4, 5·7, 5·8		1, 2		
Show and tell time on an analog and digital clock. [Measurement and Reference Frames Goal 6]	5·1, 5·2, 5·4		3		
Draw line segments and identify parallel line segments. [Geometry Goal 1]	5·2, 5·3, 5·5–5·7	4, 6		4	10–12
Identify, describe, and model plane and solid figures. [Geometry Goal 2]	5·3–5·7	1, 2		5, 6	7–9
Create and complete simple 2-dimensional symmetric shapes or designs. [Geometry Goal 3]	5·8	3			13

2 Building Background for Unit 6 — materials

Math Boxes 5·9 previews and practices skills for Unit 6.

The **Unit 6 Family Letter** introduces families to Unit 6 topics and terms.

☐ *Math Journal 1*, p. 130
☐ Home Link Masters (*Math Masters*, pp. 152–155)

Additional Information

See the *Assessment Handbook,* pages 84–91, for additional assessment information. For assessment checklists, see pages 252–255.

Technology

Assessment Management System
Progress Check 5
See the **iTLG.**

Getting Started

1 Assessing Progress

▶ Math Message Follow-Up

INDEPENDENT ACTIVITY

(Self Assessment, *Assessment Handbook*, p. 173)

 The Self Assessment offers children the opportunity to reflect upon their progress.

▶ Oral and Slate Assessments

WHOLE-CLASS ACTIVITY

Problems 3 and 4 provide summative information and can be used for grading purposes. Problems 1 and 2 provide formative information that can be useful in planning future instruction.

Oral Assessment

1. Say a number and have children respond with the 100-complement of that number. For example, say 80. 20 Begin with multiples of 10, then multiples of 25, and finally, multiples of 5.

2. Pose extended addition facts. Children state the sums.

   $30 + 40 = 70$

   $300 + 400 = 700$

   $120 = 50 + 70$

   $1,200 = 500 + 700$

   $20 + 90 = 110$

   $200 + 900 = 1,100$

   $120 = 60 + 60$

   $1,200 = 600 + 600$

Slate Assessment

3. Show the following times on a demonstration clock. Children record the times on their slates. 2:30, 12:00, 6:30, 8:00

4. Pose the following addition facts.

   $5 + 5 = ?$ 10 $6 + 6 = ?$ 12

   $7 + 2 = ?$ 9 $4 + 5 = ?$ 9

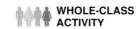

Assessment Master

Name _____ Date _____ Time _____

LESSON 5·9 | **Self Assessment** | Progress Check 5

Check one box for each skill.

Skills	I can do this by myself. I can explain how to do this.	I can do this by myself.	I can do this with help.
1. Name polygons.			
2. Identify 3-D shapes.			
3. Find the lines of symmetry.			
4. Draw line segments.			
5. Count numbers in the thousands.			
6. Identify parallel lines.			

Assessment Handbook, p. 173

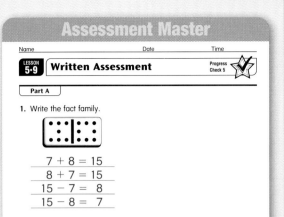

▶ Written Assessment

INDEPENDENT ACTIVITY

(*Assessment Handbook,* pp. 174–176)

Part A   Recognizing Student Achievement

Problems 1–6 provide summative information and may be used for grading purposes.

Problem(s)	Description
1	Write the fact family.
2	Count in the thousands.
3	Order whole numbers in the 100s and 1,000s.
4	Draw line segments.
5, 6	Identify 2-dimensional figures.

Part B   Informing Instruction

Problems 7–13 provide formative information that can be useful in planning future instruction.

Problem(s)	Description
7–9	Identify 3-dimensional figures.
10	Draw a line segment.
11, 12	Draw parallel and nonparallel line segments.
13	Draw lines of symmetry.

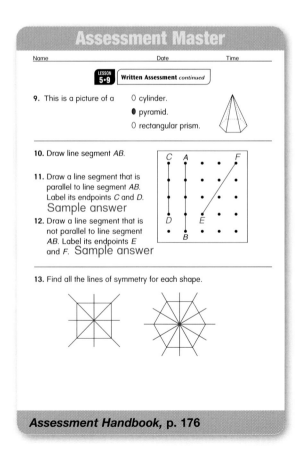

▶ Open Response

(*Assessment Handbook,* pp. 87–91, 177)

INDEPENDENT ACTIVITY

Making Polygons

The open response item requires children to apply skills and concepts from Unit 5 to solve a multistep problem. See *Assessment Handbook,* pages 87–91 for rubrics and children's work samples for this problem.

---

② Building Background for Unit 6

▶ Math Boxes 5·9

(*Math Journal 1,* p. 130)

INDEPENDENT ACTIVITY

Mixed Practice This Math Boxes page previews Unit 6 content.

▶ Home Link 5·9: Unit 6 Family Letter

(*Math Masters,* pp. 152–155)

INDEPENDENT ACTIVITY

Home Connection The Unit 6 Family Letter provides parents and guardians with information and activities related to Unit 6 topics.

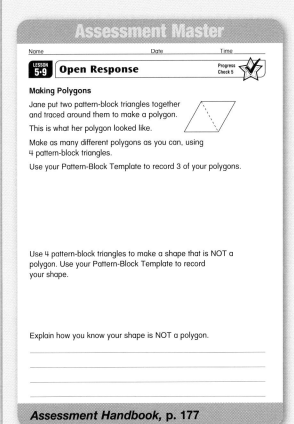

Assessment Master

Name	Date	Time

LESSON 5·9 Open Response — Progress Check 5

Making Polygons

Jane put two pattern-block triangles together and traced around them to make a polygon.

This is what her polygon looked like.

Make as many different polygons as you can, using 4 pattern-block triangles.

Use your Pattern-Block Template to record 3 of your polygons.

Use 4 pattern-block triangles to make a shape that is NOT a polygon. Use your Pattern-Block Template to record your shape.

Explain how you know your shape is NOT a polygon.

_____

_____

_____

Assessment Handbook, p. 177

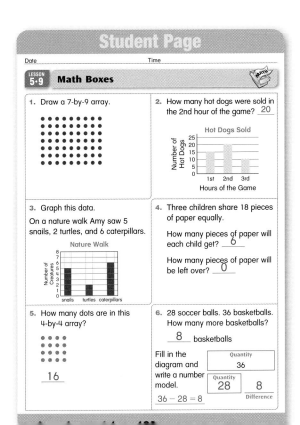

Student Page

Date	Time

LESSON 5·9 Math Boxes

1. Draw a 7-by-9 array.

2. How many hot dogs were sold in the 2nd hour of the game? __20__

Hot Dogs Sold

3. Graph this data.

On a nature walk Amy saw 5 snails, 2 turtles, and 6 caterpillars.

Nature Walk

4. Three children share 18 pieces of paper equally.

How many pieces of paper will each child get? __6__

How many pieces of paper will be left over? __0__

5. How many dots are in this 4-by-4 array?

__16__

6. 28 soccer balls. 36 basketballs. How many more basketballs?

__8__ basketballs

Fill in the diagram and write a number model.

Quantity
36

Quantity
28

8
Difference

$36 - 28 = 8$

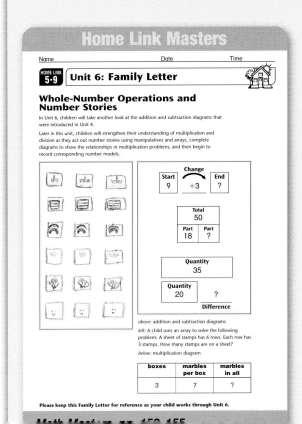

Home Link Masters

Name	Date	Time

HOME LINK 5·9 Unit 6: Family Letter

Whole-Number Operations and Number Stories

In Unit 6, children will take another look at the addition and subtraction diagrams that were introduced in Unit 4.

Later in this unit, children will strengthen their understanding of multiplication and division as they act out number stories using manipulatives and arrays, complete diagrams to show the relationships in multiplication problems, and then begin to record corresponding number models.

Change

Start	End
9	+3	?

Total
50

Part	Part
18	?

Quantity
35

Quantity
20	?

Difference

above: addition and subtraction diagrams

left: A child uses an array to solve the following problem: A sheet of stamps has 6 rows. Each row has 3 stamps. How many stamps are on a sheet?

below: multiplication diagram

boxes	marbles per box	marbles in all
3	7	?

Please keep this Family Letter for reference as your child works through Unit 6.

Math Masters, pp. 152–155

Unit 6
Organizer

Whole-Number Operations and Number Stories

Overview

In the context of number stories, children will review earlier work with addition and subtraction and begin formal work with multiplication and division in Unit 6. This unit has three main areas of focus:

◆ To introduce and practice array models,

◆ To review strategies for solving addition and subtraction problems, and

◆ To develop procedures for multiplication/division problems.

Contents

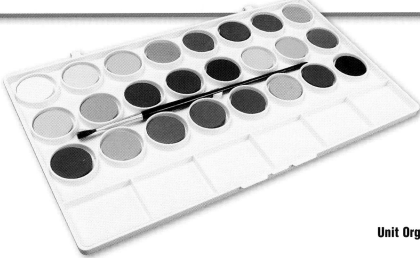

Unit 6 Organizer

Learning In Perspective

	Lesson Objectives	Links to the Past	Links to the Future
6·1	To review strategies for solving addition problems, with emphasis on problems having three addends.	Children solve addition number stories using a variety of strategies beginning in Kindergarten.	In Grade 2, with mental math and reflex problems children find easier combinations for adding three numbers. In Grade 3, children continue working with three addends in problem situations.
6·2	To introduce comparison number stories by using comparison diagrams.	Children begin telling and solving number stories in Kindergarten. This work continues throughout Grade 1.	Children continue to create and solve number stories throughout the grades.
6·3	To provide experiences with collecting, sorting, tallying, and graphing data.	Children begin collecting and organizing data in Kindergarten to create class-constructed graphs. Children continue to collect and organize data in Grade 1.	Children continue to collect and organize data throughout the grades.
6·4	To guide children in selecting and completing an appropriate diagram to help solve an addition or subtraction problem.	Children begin telling and solving number stories in Kindergarten. This work continues throughout Grade 1.	Children continue to create and solve number stories throughout the grades.
6·5	To review solution strategies for subtraction of 2-digit numbers.	In Unit 4, children use the number grid and/or mental arithmetic to find differences. Children begin counting up and back by 10s in Kindergarten.	In Unit 11, children are introduced to a formal algorithm for subtraction. Children continue to work with a variety of algorithms for subtraction in Grade 3.
6·6	To develop readiness for multiplication; to guide children in finding coin combinations equivalent to $1.00; and to explore one meaning of division.	In Grade 1, children have informal experiences with arrays. Children count combinations of coins in Grade 1. In Kindergarten, they explore equal sharing.	Children are introduced to multiplication facts in Unit 11, and continue in Grade 3. Division number models are introduced in Unit 11. Work with arrays continues in Grade 3.
6·7	To introduce multiplication as a way to find the total number of things in several equal groups.	In Kindergarten and first grade children explore multiples of equal groups informally and by skip counting.	*Third Grade Everyday Mathematics* focuses extensively on multiplication.
6·8	To introduce everyday examples of rectangular arrays; and to provide experiences with solving multiplication problems using multiplication diagrams and array models.	Children explore multiples of equal groups informally and by skip counting starting in Kindergarten. Children have informal experiences with arrays in Kindergarten and in Grade 1.	Work with arrays continues in *Third Grade Everyday Mathematics,* which focuses extensively on multiplication.
6·9	To introduce everyday examples of arrays; and to provide experiences with solving multiplication problems using multiplication diagrams and array models.	Children have informal experiences with arrays in Kindergarten and in Grade 1. Children skip count by 2s, 3s, 5s, and 10s in Kindergarten and in Grade 1.	Work with arrays continues in *Third Grade Everyday Mathematics,* which focuses extensively on multiplication.
6·10	To guide children as they explore situations that require equal sharing or making equal groups of things.	Children have many informal experiences with equal grouping and equal sharing in Kindergarten and in Grade 1.	Equal sharing is closely related to fractions, which is a focus of Unit 8. Division number models are introduced in Unit 11.

Key Concepts and Skills

Key Concepts and Skills	Grade 2 Goals*
6·1 Use and explain strategies for adding three or more numbers.	Operations and Computation Goal 2
Write number models with three or more numbers.	Patterns, Functions, and Algebra Goal 2
Describe and apply the Associative Property of Addition.	Patterns, Functions, and Algebra Goal 3
6·2 Share number story solution strategies.	Operations and Computation Goal 2
Describe and solve comparison number stories.	Operations and Computation Goal 4
Write number models to summarize addition and subtraction number stories.	Patterns, Functions, and Algebra Goal 2
6·3 Generate whole numbers from sets of tally marks.	Number and Numeration Goal 5
Collect data and tabulate it in a tally chart.	Data and Chance Goal 1
Use data in a tally chart to draw and interpret a bar graph.	Data and Chance Goal 1
Draw conclusions and answer questions from tally-chart and bar-graph data.	Data and Chance Goal 2
6·4 Explain solution strategies.	Operations and Computation Goal 2
Solve 2-digit addition and subtraction problems within number stories.	Operations and Computation Goal 2
Identify change, parts-and-total, and comparison number stories.	Operations and Computation Goal 4
6·5 Count up and back by 1s and 10s.	Number and Numeration Goal 1
Model 2-digit numbers using base-10 blocks.	Number and Numeration Goal 2
Develop counting up and back strategies for subtraction.	Operations and Computation Goal 2
Use and explain strategies for solving 2-digit by 2-digit subtraction problems.	Operations and Computation Goal 2
6·6 Count dots in an array.	Number and Numeration Goal 1
Create equal-size groupings.	Operations and Computation Goal 4
Use geoboards to create arrays.	Operations and Computation Goal 4
Create complements of $1.00 using nickels, dimes, and quarters.	Measurement and Reference Frames Goal 4
6·7 Count the total number of objects in several groups.	Number and Numeration Goal 1
Make arrays to represent equal groups.	Operations and Computation Goal 4
Use various strategies to solve equal-groups number stories.	Operations and Computation Goal 4
6·8 Solve multiplication number stories using rectangular arrays.	Operations and Computation Goal 4
Create multiplication number stories using rectangular arrays.	Operations and Computation Goal 4
Write a number model that represents a rectangular array.	Patterns, Functions, and Algebra Goal 2
6·9 Count objects in an array.	Number and Numeration Goal 1
Create rectangular arrays using concrete objects.	Operations and Computation Goal 4
6·10 Explore the concept of equal sharing and equal grouping.	Operations and Computation Goal 4
Create rectangular arrays.	Operations and Computation Goal 4
Solve division number stories using concrete objects.	Operations and Computation Goal 4

* See the Appendix for a complete list of Grade 2 Goals.

Ongoing Learning and Practice

Math Boxes

Math Boxes are paired across lessons as shown in the brackets below. This makes them useful as assessment tools. Math Boxes also preview content of the next unit.

Mixed practice   [6◆1, 6◆3, 6◆5], [6◆2, 6◆4], [6◆6, 6◆8, 6◆10], [6◆7, 6◆9]

Mixed practice with multiple choice   6◆1, 6◆4, 6◆5, 6◆8, 6◆9, 6◆10

Mixed practice with writing/reasoning opportunity   6◆2, 6◆3, 6◆6, 6◆7

Practice through Games

Games are an essential component of practice in the *Everyday Mathematics* program. Games offer skills practice and promote strategic thinking.

Lesson	Game	Skill Practiced
6◆1, 6◆6	*Three Addends*	**Addition with three addends** Operations and Computation Goal 2 Patterns, Functions and Algebra Goal 3
6◆2	*Addition Top-It*	**Addition with three or four addends; comparing sums** Number and Numeration Goal 7 Operations and Computation Goal 2 Patterns, Functions and Algebra Goal 3
6◆5, 6◆10	*Number-Grid Difference Game*	**Subtraction** Operations and Computation Goal 2
6◆5	*Base-10 Trading Game*	**Place-value exchanges** Operations and Computation Goal 1 Number and Numeration Goal 2 Operations and Computation Goal 2
6◆8	*Fact Extension Game*	**Fact extensions** Operations and Computation Goal 2
6◆8	*Simon Says*	**Making arrays** Operations and Computation Goal 4
6◆9	*Array Bingo*	**Recognizing arrays** Number and Numeration Goal 1 Operations and Computation Goal 4

See the *Differentiation Handbook* for ways to adapt games to meet children's needs.

Home Communication

Home Links provide homework and home communication.

◀ *Home Connection Handbook* provides more ideas to communicate effectively with parents.

Unit 6 Family Letter provides families with an overview, Do-Anytime Activities, Building Skills Through Games, and a list of vocabulary.

Problem Solving

Encourage children to use a variety of strategies to solve problems and to explain those strategies. Strategies that children might use in this unit:

- ◆ Using a situation diagram
- ◆ Writing a number model
- ◆ Using and making a graph
- ◆ Using information in a picture
- ◆ Trying and checking
- ◆ Modeling with manipulatives
- ◆ Drawing a picture

*Lessons that teach **through** problem solving, not just **about** problem solving*

Lesson	Activity
6◆1	Write number model with 3 addends.
6◆2	Solve comparison number stories.
6◆3	Make a bar graph of favorite foods.
6◆3	Solve comparison number stories.
6◆4	Solve addition and subtraction number stories.
6◆4	Use a situation diagram to solve addition and subtraction stories.
6◆5	Use manipulatives to model subtraction.
6◆9	Use arrays to model multiplication.
6◆7, 6◆8, 6◆10	Solve number stories involving equal groupings and equal sharing.

See Chapter 18 in the *Teacher's Reference Manual* for more information about problem solving.

Planning Tips

Pacing

Pacing depends on a number of factors, such as children's individual needs and how long your school has been using *Everyday Mathematics*. At the beginning of Unit 6, review your *Content by Strand* Poster to help you set a monthly pace.

← MOST CLASSROOMS →		
JANUARY	FEBRUARY	MARCH

NCTM Standards

Unit 6 Lessons	6◆1	6◆2	6◆3	6◆4	6◆5	6◆6	6◆7	6◆8	6◆9	6◆10
NCTM Standards	1, 2, 6–8	1, 2, 6–10	1, 2, 5, 6–10	1, 2, 6–8	1, 4, 6–8	1–3, 6–10	1, 2, 6–10	1–3, 6–10	1, 3, 4, 6–8, 10	1, 6–8

Content Standards: **1** Number and Operations, **2** Algebra, **3** Geometry, **4** Measurement, **5** Data Analysis and Probability
Process Standards: **6** Problem Solving, **7** Reasoning and Proof, **8** Communication, **9** Connections, **10** Representation

Balanced Assessment

Ongoing Assessment

 Recognizing Student Achievement

Opportunities to assess children's progress toward Grade 2 Goals:

Lesson	Content Assessed
6•1	Add three 1-digit numbers. [Operations and Computation Goal 2]
6•2	Solve comparison number stories. [Operations and Computation Goal 4]
6•3	Read graphs. [Data and Chance Goal 2]
6•4	Solve number stories. [Operations and Computation Goal 2]
6•5	Make a probability statement. [Data and Chance Goal 3]
6•6	Make bill and coin exchanges. [Measurement and Reference Frames Goal 4]
6•7	Combine equal groups to find totals. [Operations and Computation Goal 4]
6•8	Show arrays. [Operations and Computation Goal 4]
6•9	Draw and measure a 3-inch line segment. [Measurement and Reference Frames Goal 1]
6•10	Solve equal-sharing problems. [Operations and Computation Goal 4]

Use the **Assessment Management System** to collect and analyze data about children's progress throughout the year.

 Informing Instruction

To anticipate common child errors and to highlight problem-solving strategies:

Lesson 6•2   Write a number model

Lesson 6•3   Fill in a bar graph

Lesson 6•4   Choose a diagram to match a problem

Lesson 6•5   Use the counting up strategy

Periodic Assessment

6•11 Progress Check 6

CONTENT ASSESSED	ASSESSMENT ITEMS			
	Self	Oral/Slate	Written	Open Response
Use manipulatives, mental arithmetic paper and pencil algorithms, and calculators to solve 2-digit addition and subtraction problems. [Operations and Computation Goal 2]	✔	✔	✔	✔
Make reasonable estimates. [Operations and Computation Goal 3]	✔		✔	
Use arrays to model multiplication; identify and describe parts-and-total comparison situations. [Operations and Computation Goal 4]	✔	✔	✔	
Tell and show time. [Measurement and Reference Frames Goal 6]	✔		✔	
Extend, describe, and create numberic patterns; describe rules for patterns and use them to solve problems. Complete the "What's My Rule?" table. [Patterns, Functions, and Algebra Goal 1]	✔		✔	
Use the <, >, and = symbols. [Patterns, Functions, and Algebra Goal 2]	✔		✔	✔

Portfolio Opportunities

Opportunities to gather samples of children's mathematical writings, drawings, and creations to add balance to the assessment process:

- Finding all possible coin combinations, **Lesson 6•2**
- Explaining measurement segments, **Lesson 6•3**
- Finding many ways to make $1.00, **Lesson 6•6**
- Drawing shapes with a line of symmetry, **Lesson 6•6**
- Describing age differences, **Lesson 6•7**
- Solving an equal-sharing problem, **Lesson 6•10**

Assessment Handbook

Unit 6 Assessment Support

- Grade 2 Goals, pp. 37–50
- Unit 6 Assessment Overview, pp. 92–101

- Unit 6 Open Response
  - Detailed rubric, p. 96
  - Sample student responses, pp. 97–99

Unit 6 Assessment Masters

- Unit 6 Self Assessment, p. 178
- Unit 6 Written Assessment, pp. 179 and 180
- Unit 6 Open Response, p. 181
- Unit 6 Class Checklist, pp. 258, 259, and 293
- Quarterly Checklist: Quarter 2, pp. 286 and 287
- Mid-Year Assessment: pp. 223–227

- Unit 6 Individual Profile of Progress, pp. 256, 257, and 292
- Exit Slip, p. 295
- Math Logs, pp. 298–300
- Other Student Assessment Forms, pp. 296, 297, 301, 302, and 303

Differentiated Instruction

Daily Lesson Support

ENGLISH LANGUAGE LEARNERS

6◆7 Building a Math Word Bank
6◆8 Building a Math Word Bank
6◆10 Identifying phrases associated with multiplication and division

EXTRA PRACTICE

6◆3 Making and counting tally marks
6◆7 Solving multiplication problems

Minute Math®+

6◆4 Making up number stories
6◆6 Solving problems including money

READINESS

6◆1 Practicing with sums to ten
6◆2 Practicing comparing numbers
6◆4 Solving number stories with counters
6◆5 Practicing place-value exchanges
6◆7 Solving equal-groups problems
6◆8 Making equal rows
6◆9 Building arrays with pattern blocks
6◆10 Solving repeated subtraction problems

ENRICHMENT

6◆1 Adding four or more numbers
6◆2 Comparing number stories
6◆3 Making a bar graph and comparing data results
6◆4 Writing number stories
6◆5 Analyzing subtraction strategies
6◆6 Solving dollar riddles
6◆7 Solving equal-groups riddles
6◆8 Creating array number stories
6◆9 Building rectangular arrays
6◆10 Exploring the relationship between multiplication and division

Adjusting the Activity

6◆1 Varying the *Three Addends* game
6◆2 Filling in the comparison diagram
6◆3 Filling in a bar graph
6◆3 Make *difference* comparisons
6◆5 Using play money to model subtraction **ELL**
6◆6 Finding coin combinations with half-dollars

6◆7 Solving equal groups number stories using larger numbers
6◆8 Describing arrays in different ways **ELL**
6◆8 Solving multiplication number stories **ELL**
6◆8 Making and recording arrays with counters **ELL**
6◆9 Playing *Array Bingo*

AUDITORY ◆ KINESTHETIC ◆ TACTILE ◆ VISUAL

Cross-Curricular Links

Literature

Lesson 6◆7 Children read *Each Orange Had Eight Slices: A Counting Book* and discuss equal groups.

Using the Projects

Use Project 5 to experiment with paper folding, creating snowflakes that represent real 6-sided water crystals. See the *Differentiation Handbook* for modifications to Project 5.

Differentiation Handbook

See the *Differentiation Handbook* for materials on Unit 6.

Language Support

Everyday Mathematics provides lesson-specific suggestions to help all children, including non-native English speakers, to acquire, process, and express mathematical ideas.

Connecting Math and Literacy

Lesson 6·7 *Each Orange Had Eight Slices: A Counting Book,* by Paul Giganti, Greenwillow Books, 1992

Lesson 6·8 *Sea Squares,* by Joy N. Hulme, Hyperion Books for Children, 1991

Lesson 6·8 *Amanda Bean's Amazing Dream,* by Cindy Neuschwander, Scholastic Inc., 1998

Lesson 6·9 *The King's Commissioners,* by Aileen Friedman, Scholastic Inc., 1994

Lesson 6·9 *One Hundred Hungry Ants,* by Elinor J. Pinczes, Scholastic Inc., 1993

Lesson 6·11 *A Remainder of One,* by Elinor J. Pinczes, Houghton Mifflin, 1995

Lesson 6·11 *One Hungry Cat,* by Joanne Rocklin, Scholastic Inc., 1997

My Reference Book

pp. 110–113, 122, 123, 134, 135, 140 and 141

Unit 6 Vocabulary

bar graph
basic food groups
comparison diagram
comparison number story
data table
difference
division
equal grouping
equal groups
equal sharing
multiplication
multiplication diagram
multiplied by
remainder
times
trade (a base-10 long for 10 cubes)
x-by-*y* array

Multiage Classroom ◆ Companion Lessons

Companion Lessons from Grade 1 and Grade 3 can help you meet instructional needs of a multiage classroom. The full Scope and Sequence can be found in the Appendix.

Grade 1	5·9, 6·7, 6·8	1·13, 2·13, 5·7	3·13, 6·12, 10·1	3·6, 5·6–5·8	9·2–9·4	8·6, 9·5			8·6	
Grade 2	6·1	6·2	6·3	6·4	6·5	6·6	6·7	6·8	6·9	6·10
Grade 3	2·9	2·6	1·5, 11·1–11·5	1·11, 2·4–2·6	1·8, 2·2, 2·8	4·2–4·4	4·2–4·4, 4·8	4·2–4·4, 4·7	4·2–4·4, 4·8	4·4, 7·6, 9·1

Professional Development

Teacher's Reference Manual Links

Lesson	Topic	Section	Lesson	Topic	Section
6·1	Number Sentences and Number Models	10.1	6·4	Addition and Subtraction Use Classes	10.2.1
	Fact Practice	16.3.3	6·6	Multiplication and Division Use Classes	10.2.2
6·2	Number Stories	18.4.1		Equality	9.6.1
	Use classes and situation diagrams	10.2	6·8	Fact Practice	16.3.3
6·3	Collecting and Recording Data	12.2.2	6·9	Games for Fact Practice	16.3.4
	Organizing and Displaying Data	12.2.3			
	Data Analysis	12.2.4			

Materials

Lesson	Masters	Manipulative Kit Items	Other Items
6·1	Game Master, p. 473* Home Link Masters, pp. 156 and 157 Teaching Master, p. 158 Teaching Aid Master, 422	per group: set of number cards 0–20; calculator*	10 blue counters; 10 red counters; number grid; counters; per child: one half-sheet of paper; blue and red crayons
6·2	Home Link 6·1 transparency of *Math Masters,* p. 436* Home Link Masters, pp. 159 and 160 Game Masters, pp. 449* and 473* Teaching Master, p. 161	per group: set of number cards 0–20; number line	semi-permanent chalk*; 30 pennies or small counters; number grid*
6·3	Home Link 6·2 Teaching Masters, pp. 162 and 166 Teaching Aid Master, p. 415 transparencies of *Math Masters,* pp. 162*, 163*, and 164 Home Link Master, p. 165	slate	pennies; can or other container; Class Data Pad*; crayons or colored pencils
6·4	Home Link 6·3 Teaching Aid Masters, pp. 419 and 437 transparency of *Math Masters,* p. 437* Home Link Masters, pp. 167 and 168	tool-kit coins; slate; calculator; number line*	counters; number grid
6·5	Home Link 6·4 Home Link Masters, pp. 169 and 170 Teaching Aid Masters, pp. 418 and 427 Teaching Master, p. 171 Game Master, p. 463	per group: base-10 blocks: 6 longs and 30 cubes; 2 flats, 20 longs 40 cubes; play money*; 4 of each number cards 0–9; calculator; 2 dice	overhead base-10 blocks* pennies or other counters*; number grid
6·6	Home Link 6·5 Teaching Masters, pp. 172–176 Teaching Aid Master, p. 415 Game Master, p. 473 Home Link Master, p. 177 *Math Masters,* p. 178	per group: geoboard and rubber band; 1 regular die; per group: number cards 0–20; tool-kit coins; slate	overhead geoboard*; scissors; per group: large sheet of paper and glue or paste; per child: 20 nickels, 10 dimes, 4 quarters, 2 half-dollars; 50 pennies or other counters per group; paper
6·7	Home Link 6·6 Teaching Aid Master, p. 415 Home Link Master, p. 179 Teaching Masters, pp. 180 and 181	calculator	per group: 40 pennies or other counters; 6 boxes or bags to hold pennies and other counters; addition/subtraction Fact Triangles in an envelope; *Each Orange Had Eight Slices: A Counting Book*
6·8	Home Link 6·7 Teaching Master, pp. 182* and 183 Teaching Aid Masters, pp. 419 and 438 transparency of *Math Masters,* p. 438* Home Link Master, p. 183	calculator	50 pennies or other counters per group*; 24 counters
6·9	Home Link 6·8 Game Master, p. 450 Home Link Masters, pp. 184 and 185 Teaching Masters, pp. 186 and 187 Teaching Aid Master, p. 420	per group: 1 twenty-sided die or number cards 0–20*; pattern blocks; Pattern-Block Template; dice; centimeter cubes	per group: 2 six-sided dice, 1 twelve-sided die, or an egg-carton, number generator; per group: 40 counters; 40 overhead counters*; paper clip; envelope; scissors
6·10	Home Link 6·9 Teaching Aid Masters, pp. 415 and 418 Home Link Master, p. 188 Game Master, p. 463 Teaching Masters, pp. 189 and 190	number cards 0–9 (4 of each); slate; calculator	per group: 30 pennies or counters
6·11	Home Link 6·10 Assessment Masters, pp. 178–181 and 223–226 Home Link Masters, pp. 191–194	slate	counters

* Denotes optional materials

Technology
Assessment Management System, Unit 6
iTLG, Unit 6

Mathematical Background

The discussion below highlights the major context ideas presented in Unit 6 and helps establish instructional priorities.

Addition and Subtraction

(Lesson 6♦1 and following)

In *Everyday Mathematics,* the operations are developed gradually, in three stages:

1. Children explore an operation by using concrete objects (such as number grids, counters, pictures, doodles, or tallies) to solve real-life problems.

2. Children are exposed to more formal representations through diagrams and number models, but they are not yet expected to produce these representations by themselves.

3. Children choose and fill in appropriate diagrams; they also represent their solutions by writing number models.

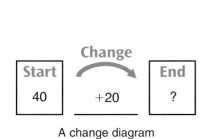
A change diagram

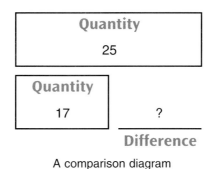
A comparison diagram

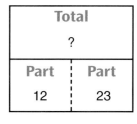
A parts-and-total diagram

Up to this point, the first two stages of the process have been used in developing addition and subtraction. Children solved simple problems with concrete objects in Kindergarten and in first grade. Then, in the first five units of second grade, they were exposed to addition and subtraction diagrams and number models. This was done informally: The teacher drew diagrams as part of the discussion, but children were not expected to do so themselves.

In Unit 6, the development of addition and subtraction is extended to the third stage. The following procedure for solving addition and subtraction problems is formally established:

1. Choose an appropriate addition/subtraction diagram: change, comparison, or parts-and-total.

2. Enter the known quantities and identify which quantity is unknown.

3. Choose the operation needed to find the missing information.

4. Solve the problem and write a number model.

 PROFESSIONAL DEVELOPMENT See Section 10.2 in the *Teacher's Reference Manual* for additional information about addition and subtraction.

Data Day (Lesson 6◆3)

The important topic of nutrition provides a context for the collection, analysis, and representation of data. The teacher discusses the basic food groups, referring to the Food Guide Pyramid. Food preferences of children are surveyed, tallied, and graphed.

 **PROFESSIONAL DEVELOPMENT** For more information about data concepts, see Sections 12.2.2, 12.2.3, and 12.2.4 in the *Teacher's Reference Manual.*

Note

Children are accustomed to seeing horizontal addition and subtraction problems with the answer (or answer spaces) written to the right of the equal sign. In *Everyday Mathematics,* children will also see problems with the answer (or answer spaces) written to the left of the equal sign. It is important that children regularly see both of these horizontal forms of addition and subtraction.

Multiplication and Division

(Lesson 6◆6 and following)

Children have been exposed to the underlying concepts of multiplication and division in a variety of contexts: addition involving equal groups of objects; oral counts by 1-digit numbers; counting by using a calculator; arrays; equal sharing; and finding fractional quantities (for example, give your friend half of your counters).

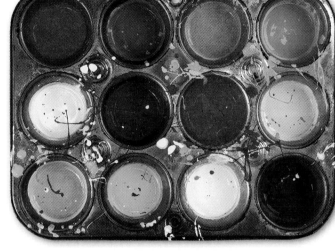

Explorations A and C in Lesson 6-6 continue this exposure: Children make arrays on geoboards, record these arrays, and sort different arrays for the same number. Then they determine how many groups of n objects can be made from a specified number of objects.

Extending these activities in Lessons 6-7–6-10, children act out problems with counters. They solve problems about equal groups, some of which involve objects that form arrays in real life. They make arrays consisting of a certain number of rows with the same number of objects in each row, and they write number models to represent those arrays.

Arrays will become increasingly important in building an understanding of the link between multiplication and division and in learning multiplication and division facts.

The diagram introduced for multiplication serves two purposes: It specifies the unit associated with each quantity, and it identifies the known and unknown quantities in the problem. While it is recommended that you ask children to help you complete such diagrams when discussing a problem, do not expect them to come up with such diagrams on their own. Repeated exposure to such diagrams will help children understand the meanings of multiplication and division.

rows	eggs per row	eggs in all
2	6	?

Because few children have difficulty with equal-sharing problems that involve "leftovers," you need not avoid problems with remainders, even at this early stage in the development of division. But because number models for division with remainders are somewhat more complex than those for other operations, the introduction of division number models will be postponed until a later unit.

 PROFESSIONAL DEVELOPMENT You can read more about multiplication and division in Section of 10.2.2 of the *Teacher's Reference Manual*.

6·1

Addition of Three or More Numbers

 Objective To review strategies for solving addition problems, with emphasis on problems having three addends.

---

1 Teaching the Lesson

materials

Key Activities

Children review strategies for solving addition problems. They identify the easiest order in which to add three numbers, write number models, and practice adding three or more 1-digit and 2-digit numbers.

Key Concepts and Skills

- Use and explain strategies for adding three or more numbers.
[Operations and Computation Goal 2]

- Write number models with three or more numbers.
[Patterns, Functions, and Algebra Goal 2]

- Describe and apply the associative property of addition.
[Patterns, Functions and Algebra Goal 3]

✔ **Ongoing Assessment: Recognizing Student Achievement** Use journal page 131.
[Operations and Computation Goal 2]

- ☐ *Math Journal 1*, p. 131
- ☐ Game Master (*Math Masters*, p. 473; optional)
- ☐ per partnership: number cards 0–20 (1 of each; from the Everything Math Deck, if available)
- ☐ calculator (optional)
- ☐ number grid; counters (optional)

---

2 Ongoing Learning & Practice

materials

Children estimate sums and use the partial-sums algorithm.

Children practice and maintain skills through Math Boxes and Home Link activities.

- ☐ *Math Journal 1*, pp. 132 and 133
- ☐ Home Link Masters (*Math Masters*, pp. 156 and 157)

---

3 Differentiation Options

materials

READINESS

Children use ten frames to practice with sums to ten.

ENRICHMENT

Children solve addition problems with four or more addends.

- ☐ Teaching Master (*Math Masters*, p. 158)
- ☐ Teaching Aid Master (*Math Masters*, p. 422)
- ☐ 10 blue counters; 10 red counters
- ☐ number cards 1–10 (1 of each; from the Everything Math Deck, if available)
- ☐ one half-sheet of paper per child
- ☐ blue and red crayons

Technology

Assessment Management System
Journal page 131
See the iTLG.

Getting Started

Mental Math and Reflexes

Pose addition and subtraction problems that feature multiples of 10.
Suggestions:

○○○ 70 + 20 = ? 90 ○○○ 80 + 15 = ? 95 ○○○ 89 − 49 = ? 40
　　? = 20 + 8 28 　　65 − 5 = ? 60 　　? = 69 + 11 80
　　70 − 20 = ? 50 　　? = 70 + 13 83 　　75 − 15 = ? 60

Math Message

(Use names of children in your class.)

Lia has 13 pencils. Thomas has 6 pencils. Nate has 7. How many pencils do they have in all? 26 pencils

---

① Teaching the Lesson

▶ Math Message Follow-Up

WHOLE-CLASS ACTIVITY

Review strategies for solving addition problems.

Draw a unit box on the board. Ask: *What is the Math Message story about?* Sample answer: Finding the total number of pencils three children have *What label should go in the unit box?* pencils

Invite children to share strategies for solving the Math Message problem. Encourage them to doodle or calculate with a pencil and paper if they need to. *Suggestions:*

▷ Use counters, fingers, or the number grid as an aid for counting up.

▷ Draw pictures or use tally marks. (*See margin.*)

▷ Use a parts-and-total diagram. (*See margin.*)

▷ Solve by mental arithmetic.

▷ Use the partial-sums method. (*See margin.*)

▶ Adding Three Numbers in Any Order

WHOLE-CLASS ACTIVITY

Write number models for the Math Message problem in horizontal format. Then ask:

● Does it make a difference in what order the sums are added? no

● Which order makes it easiest to find the sum?

Unit

pencils

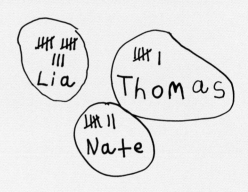

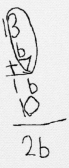

Option 1

Add 13 and 6 first to make 19;

then add 7.

$$13 + 6 + 7 =$$
$$\vee$$
$$19 + 7 = 26$$

Option 2

Add 13 and 7 first to make 20;

then add 6.

$$13 + 7 + 6 =$$
$$\vee$$
$$20 + 6 = 26$$

Option 3

Add 6 and 7 first to make 13;

then double 13.

$$6 + 7 + 13 =$$
$$\vee$$
$$13 + 13 = 26$$

Write other number triplets on the board and ask children to decide which order makes it easiest for them to find the sum. *See the following suggestions.*

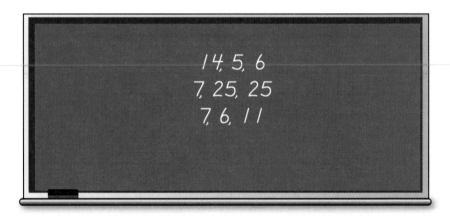

Encourage children to make up similar problems for the class to solve. Some number triplets (for example, 7, 9, and 17) do not have an easiest order for addition.

Summary: Three or more numbers can be added in any order. Also, they can often be ordered in a way that makes it easier to find the sum.

▶ **Playing** *Three Addends*

 PARTNER ACTIVITY

(*Math Journal 1*, p. 131; *Math Masters*, p. 473)

Three Addends gives partners the opportunity to add three numbers in different orders. Instructions are found on journal page 131.

Student Page

Date _____ Time _____

LESSON 6·1 *Three Addends* **Directions** ★

Materials ☐ number cards 0–20 **Skill** Add three numbers.

Players 2

Directions

Object of the Game
To find easy combinations when adding three numbers.

♦ Shuffle the cards. Place the deck number-side down.

♦ Turn over the top 3 cards. Each partner writes the 3 numbers.

♦ Add the numbers. Write a number model to show the order in which you added.

Unit

♦ Compare your answers with your partner's.

Example: Numbers and number models vary in Problems 1–6.

The cards 6, 5, and 14 are turned over. Gillian records the numbers. She adds 14 and 6 first and then adds 5. She records her number model and compares her answer with her partner's.

Numbers: _6_, _5_, _14_ Number model: _14_ + _6_ + _5_ = _25_

1. Numbers: ___, ___, ___
   Number model:
   ___ + ___ + ___ = ___

2. Numbers: ___, ___, ___
   Number model:
   ___ + ___ + ___ = ___

3. Numbers: ___, ___, ___
   Number model:
   ___ = ___ + ___ + ___

4. Numbers: ___, ___, ___
   Number model:
   ___ = ___ + ___ + ___

5. Numbers: ___, ___, ___
   Number model:
   ___ + ___ + ___ = ___

6. Numbers: ___, ___, ___
   Number model:
   ___ + ___ + ___ = ___

Math Journal 1, p. 131

Date   Time

6·1 Ballpark Estimates

Fill in the unit box. Then, for each problem:

◆ Make a ballpark estimate.

◆ Write a number model for your estimate. Then solve the
   problem. For Problems 1, 2, and 3 use the Partial-Sums
   Algorithm. For Problems 4–6, use any strategy you choose.

◆ Compare your estimate to your answer.

 Unit

1. Ballpark estimate:	2. Ballpark estimate:	3. Ballpark estimate:
$30 + 10 = 40$	$90 + 10 = 100$	$40 + 40 = 80$
$29 + 7 = \underline{36}$	$87 + 9 = \underline{96}$	$37 + 42 = \underline{79}$
4. Ballpark estimate:	5. Ballpark estimate:	6. Ballpark estimate:
$30 + 10 = 40$	$40 + 50 = 90$	$40 + 30 = 70$
$27 + 13 = \underline{40}$	$38 + 46 = \underline{84}$	$42 + 28 = \underline{70}$

Math Journal 1, p. 132

Adjusting the Activity

Variations on the *Three Addends* game:

▷ Children use triplets with 2- or 3-digit numbers. For example,
   140 + 150 + 60 350

▷ Children draw 4 cards at each turn and solve problems with 4 addends.

▷ Children use a calculator to solve the problems.

A U D I T O R Y ◆ K I N E S T H E T I C ◆ T A C T I L E ◆ V I S U A L

NOTE *Math Masters,* page 473 is available if children need more space to
record numbers and number models.

 Ongoing Assessment:
Recognizing Student Achievement

Journal
Page 131 ★

Use **journal page 131** to assess children's ability to add three numbers. Children
are making adequate progress if they can correctly add the three numbers using
manipulatives. Some children may be able to add the numbers mentally while
others may be able to order the numbers in a way that makes it easier to find
the sum.

[Operations and Computation Goal 2]

---

2 Ongoing Learning & Practice

▶ Practicing Estimation and the Partial-Sums Algorithm

🗒 **INDEPENDENT ACTIVITY**

(*Math Journal 1,* p. 132)

Review the instructions for the journal page with children. Have
them begin by making a ballpark estimate for each sum. Children
then use the partial-sums algorithm in Problems 1–3 to find
the exact sum. Children use any strategy they choose for
Problems 4–6.

▶ Math Boxes 6·1

🗒 **INDEPENDENT ACTIVITY**

(*Math Journal 1,* p. 133)

 Mixed Practice Math Boxes in this lesson are linked with
Math Boxes in Lessons 6-3 and 6-5. The skills in
Problems 5 and 6 preview Unit 7 content.

Date   Time

6·1 Math Boxes

1. Which is least likely to happen?
   Choose the best answer.

   ⬭ A dog will have puppies today.

   ⬭ You will go to sleep tonight.

   ⬬ Chocolate milk will come out of
      the water fountain.

   ⬭ Someone will read you a book.

2. How long is this line segment?
   _____
   about __7__ cm

3. Arlie harvested 12 bushels of
   corn and 19 bushels of
   tomatoes. How many bushels in
   all? __31__ bushels

   Fill in the diagram and write a number model.

Total	
31	
Part	Part
12	19

   $12 + 19 = 31$

4. How many dots in this 2-by-8
   array?

   • • • • • • • •
   • • • • • • • •

   16

5. Put these numbers in order
   from least to greatest and
   circle the middle number
   (the median).

   109, 99, 129

   99 ⑩⑨ 129

6. Use your calculator. Start at 92.
   Count by 5s.

   92, 97, _102_, _107_, _112_,

   _117_, _122_, _127_, _132_

Math Journal 1, p. 133

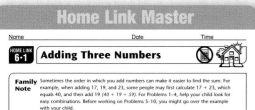

Home Link Master

Name _____ Date _____ Time _____

HOME LINK 6·1 Adding Three Numbers

Family Note Sometimes the order in which you add numbers can make it easier to find the sum. For example, when adding 17, 19, and 23, some people may first calculate 17 + 23, which equals 40, and then add 19 (40 + 19 = 59). For Problems 1–4, help your child look for easy combinations. Before working on Problems 5–10, you might go over the example with your child.

Please return this Home Link to school tomorrow.

For each problem: Sample number models shown.

◆ Think about an easy way to add the numbers.

◆ Write a number model to show the order in which you are adding the numbers.

◆ Find each sum. Tell someone at home why you added the numbers in that order.

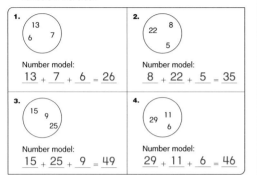

1.   13   6   7

Number model:
13 + 7 + 6 = 26

2.   22   8   5

Number model:
8 + 22 + 5 = 35

3.   15   9   25

Number model:
15 + 25 + 9 = 49

4.   29   11   6

Number model:
29 + 11 + 6 = 46

Math Masters, p. 156

Home Link Master

Name _____ Date _____ Time _____

HOME LINK 6·1 Adding Three Numbers *continued*

Add. Use the partial-sums method.

Example:

			33
			42
			+ 11
Add the tens.	→ (30 + 40 + 10)	→	80
Add the ones.	→ (3 + 2 + 1)	→	6
Add the partial sums.	→ (80 + 6)	→	86

Practice

5. 23   32   + 14   — 60   9   69

6. 14   29   + 27   — 50   20   70

7.   8   19   + 35   — 40   22   62

8. 46   25   + 12   — 70   13   83

9. 40   45   + 63   — 140   8   148

10.   9   85   + 96   — 170   20   190

Math Masters, p. 157

▶ **Home Link 6·1**

(*Math Masters*, pp. 156 and 157)

INDEPENDENT ACTIVITY

Home Connection Children practice adding three numbers in the easiest order. Children also practice using the partial-sums method for adding three numbers.

③ Differentiation Options

READINESS

▶ **Finding Sums of 10 Using a Ten Frame Card**

(*Math Masters*, p. 422)

SMALL-GROUP ACTIVITY

5–15 Min

To provide experience with sums of 10, have children solve addition problems using a ten frame card. Children mix up the number cards and put them facedown on the table. They draw a number card and put that many blue counters on their ten-frame card. They predict how many counters they need to fill the ten-frame card. They check their predictions by placing red counters in the remaining squares. On a half-sheet of paper, they record the dot pattern in their ten-frame card using blue and red crayons, and they write the number sentence for how they got to ten. Have children explain their number sentences; for example, "I started with 6 blue counters and added 4 red counters to get 10 counters total."

Teaching Aid Master

Name _____ Date _____ Time _____

Ten-Frame Card

Math Masters, p. 422

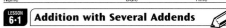

► Adding with Four or More Addends

(Math Masters, p. 158)

INDEPENDENT ACTIVITY

15–30 Min

To further explore children's knowledge of number facts, number sense, and problem solving, have children create number sentences using four or more addends with *Math Masters,* page 158. Within each number sentence, they must include a double and at least one pair of addends whose sum is ten; for example, $37 = \mathbf{10} + \mathbf{10} + 7 + \mathbf{6} + \mathbf{4}$. Have children explain the strategies they use to add the numbers.

Teaching Master

Name   Date   Time

LESSON 6·1 | **Addition with Several Addends**

For each sum, write a number sentence using four or more addends. Each number sentence must include a double and at least one pair of addends that equal ten.

43	62
Sample answer: $6 + 4 + 15 + 15 + 3$ $= 43$	Sample answer: $8 + 2 + 26 + 26$ $= 62$
79	**112**
Sample answer: $7 + 3 + 33 + 33 + 3$ $= 79$	Sample answer: $9 + 1 + 51 + 51$ $= 112$

Math Masters, p. 158

6·2 Comparison Number Stories

 Objective To introduce comparison number stories by using comparison diagrams.

---

1 Teaching the Lesson

materials

Key Activities
Children are introduced to the comparison diagram as a tool for recording known and missing information in a comparison number story. Children then solve comparison number stories by using comparison diagrams and writing number models.

Key Concepts and Skills
• Share number story solution strategies. [Operations and Computation Goal 2]
• Describe and solve comparison number stories. [Operations and Computation Goal 4]
• Write number models to summarize addition and subtraction number stories.
[Patterns, Functions, and Algebra Goal 2]

Key Vocabulary
comparison number story • difference • comparison diagram

☑ **Ongoing Assessment:** Informing Instruction See page 387.

☑ **Ongoing Assessment:** Recognizing Student Achievement Use journal page 134.
[Operations and Computation Goal 4]

☐ *Math Journal 1,* pp. 134 and 135
☐ *My Reference Book,* pp. 110 and 111
☐ Home Link 6·1
☐ Transparency (*Math Masters,* p. 436; optional)
☐ semipermanent chalk (optional)
☐ number line; number grid (optional)

***See* Advance Preparation**

---

2 Ongoing Learning & Practice

materials

Children practice adding three or four numbers by playing another version of *Addition Top-It.*

Children practice and maintain skills through Math Boxes and Home Link activities.

☐ *Math Journal 1,* p. 136
☐ *My Reference Book,* pp. 122 and 123
☐ Home Link Masters (*Math Masters,* pp. 159 and 160)

☐ Game Masters (*Math Masters,* pp. 449 and 473; optional)
☐ per partnership: number cards 0–20 (1 of each; from the Everything Math Deck, if available)

---

3 Differentiation Options

materials

READINESS
Children do a Penny Grab activity to practice comparing numbers.

ENRICHMENT
Children compare two number stories.

☐ Teaching Master (*Math Masters,* p. 161)
☐ 30 pennies or other small counters

Additional Information

Advance Preparation For the Solving Comparison Number Stories activity in Part 1, decide how you will display a comparison diagram. Some possibilities:
• Make an overhead transparency of *Math Masters,* page 436.
• Draw one on the board with semipermanent chalk.
• Draw and erase comparison diagrams on the board as needed.

Technology
Assessment Management System
Journal page 134, Problems 1 and 2
See the **iTLG.**

Getting Started

Mental Math and Reflexes

Write multiple-addend problems like the following on the board. Encourage children to look for combinations that will make the addition easier.

○○○ 3 + 9 + 7 = ? 19
     14 + 8 + 6 = ? 28
     6 + 8 + 4 = ? 18
○○○ ? = 21 + 5 + 9 35
     34 + 6 + 7 = ? 47
     57 + 10 + 5 = ? 72
○○○ ? = 8 + 5 + 12 + 5 30
     22 + 28 + 7 = ? 57
     63 + 27 + 9 = ? 99

Math Message

Silva has 17 CDs. Mark has 8 CDs.

How many more CDs does Silva have than Mark?

9 more CDs

Home Link 6·1 Follow-Up

Ask volunteers to share how they found the answer to each problem and why they chose the order in which they added the three numbers.

---

1 Teaching the Lesson

▶ Math Message Follow-Up

WHOLE-CLASS ACTIVITY

(*Math Masters,* p. 436)

Use the Math Message problem to start a discussion of **comparison number stories.** Comparison stories involve the difference between two quantities.

You can compare things that are counted.

Example:

▷ Beth scored 14 points. Ivy scored 8 points. So Beth scored 6 more points than Ivy. (Alternately, Ivy scored 6 fewer points than Beth.) The difference in points scored is 6 points.

You can also compare things that are measured.

Example:

▷ The big fish is 14 inches long. The small fish is 8 inches long. So the small fish is 6 inches shorter. (Alternately, the big fish is 6 inches longer.) The difference in length is 6 inches.

Draw a picture on the board (*See margin.*) and show how children can solve the Math Message problem by matching the two quantities one to one. Discuss the meaning of the word *quantity* in the diagram. The quantity that is left unmatched is the difference. In the Math Message problem, the **difference** tells how many more CDs Silva has than Mark.

Display a transparency of a **comparison diagram** (*Math Masters,* page 436) or draw on the board. In it, write the numbers 17, 8, and 9 (*See margin.*) Say that the diagram is a convenient way to represent the CD comparison story. The longer Quantity cell shows the larger number of CDs that Silva has. The shorter Quantity cell shows the smaller number of CDs that Mark has. The Difference cell shows how many more CDs Silva has.

> **NOTE** Point out that the quantity box on the top is as long as the quantity and difference boxes on the bottom. This often provides a good visual for children.

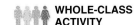

8 matched   9 more unmatched

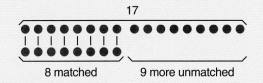

Quantity
Silva 17 CDs

Quantity	
Mark 8 CDs	9

Difference

Adjusting the Activity

Whenever a comparison diagram is provided, children should always write the known and missing information (shown with a question mark) on the diagram. Have children write words or short phrases on the diagram as a reminder of what the numbers mean. For the Math Message problem, the names of the children might be written as reminders.

AUDITORY ◆ KINESTHETIC ◆ TACTILE ◆ VISUAL

Quantity
30 Joey

Quantity	
10 Max	?
	Difference

Quantity
$47 radio

Quantity	
$20 watch	?
	Difference

Quantity
$47 radio

Quantity	
? calculator	$12
	Difference

Ask children to write a number model for this problem. Any one of the number models $8 + 9 = 17$, $9 + 8 = 17$, $17 - 8 = 9$, or $17 - 9 = 8$ summarizes the problem. The choice of a number model depends on how a child thinks about the problem.

Beneath the filled-in comparison diagram, list the four number models named above. Add a title: "Four Possible Number Models."

▶ ## Solving Comparison Number Stories

 **WHOLE-CLASS ACTIVITY**

(*My Reference Book*, pp. 110 and 111)

You may wish to read about comparison diagrams in *My Reference Book*, pages 110 and 111 with your class. Display a comparison diagram. Work with the children to solve several comparison stories.

Example 1

Joey scored 30 points. Max scored 10 points. How many more points did Joey score than Max? 20 points

Fill in the comparison diagram as shown in the margin. Write ? for the difference, which is the number to be found. Invite children to share mental-arithmetic strategies for finding the difference between 30 and 10.

Sample strategy: Count up from 10 to 30.

▷ Think, "What must I add to 10 to get 30?"

▷ Think of the comparison diagram as a Fact Triangle. Think, "$30 - 10$ is the difference I want."

Write the difference in the Difference cell. 20 Ask volunteers to come to the board and write a number model that summarizes the problem.

▷ A child who counted up from 10 to 30 might write $10 + 20 = 30$.

▷ A child who found the difference by subtracting would likely write $30 - 10 = 20$.

Example 2

A radio costs $47. A watch costs $20. How much more does the radio cost? $27

This problem is similar to the previous example. Fill in the comparison diagram as shown in the margin. Once children find the difference 27, write 27 in the Difference space. Then have children write a number model for the story. $27 + 20 = 47$, $20 + 27 = 47$, $47 - 20 = 27$, or $47 - 27 = 20$

Example 3

A radio costs $47. A calculator costs $12 less than the radio. How much does the calculator cost? $35 Fill in the diagram as shown in the margin.

This example differs from the previous ones—this time, the smaller quantity is not known, but the difference is known. Make sure that children understand this. The strategies for solving this problem are the same as before, except that counting up is replaced by counting back (*start at 47, count back 12*). When children find the cost of the calculator 35, write 35 in the short Quantity cell. Then have children write a number model for the story. $47 - 12 = 35$, $12 + 35 = 47$, $47 - 35 = 12$, or $35 + 12 = 47$

Solving Comparison Number Stories

 PARTNER ACTIVITY

(*Math Journal 1*, pp. 134 and 135)

Partners complete the problems on the journal pages. Check that children are recording the known information in the comparison diagram and that they are writing a question mark to represent the unknown number. For most problems, the difference will be the unknown number. For some problems, however, the difference will be known, and one of the two quantities will be unknown.

 Ongoing Assessment: **Journal page 134**
Recognizing Student Achievement **Problems 1 and 2**

Use **journal page 134, Problems 1 and 2** to assess children's ability to solve comparison number stories. Children are making adequate progress if they can solve the problems using the number grid, number line, drawings, or manipulatives. Some children may be able to write a number model that summarizes the problem. Others may be able to do Problems 5, 6, and 7 with an unknown quantity.

[Operations and Computation Goal 4]

Ongoing Assessment: Informing Instruction

Watch for children who have difficulty writing a number model; have them think of 17, 8, and 9 as the numbers on a Fact Triangle. Ask them what addition and subtraction sentences they can make using the three numbers.

Children may use number lines, number grids, or any other learning tool. It is fine for children to draw pictures and doodles.

2 Ongoing Learning & Practice

Playing *Addition Top-It*

 PARTNER ACTIVITY

(*My Reference Book*, pp. 122 and 123; *Math Masters*, p. 449)

Addition Top-It was introduced in Lesson 1-4 to practice facts and compare sums. A domino version was played in Lesson 2-5. An optional record sheet can be found on *Math Masters*, page 449.

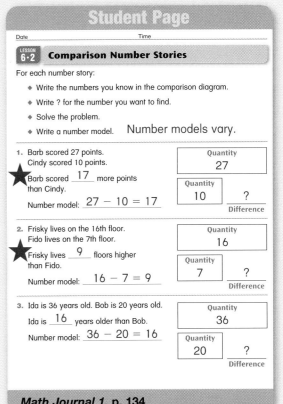

Math Journal 1, p. 134

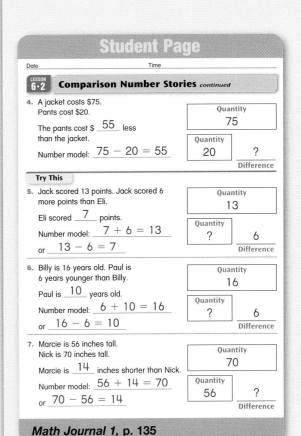

Math Journal 1, p. 135

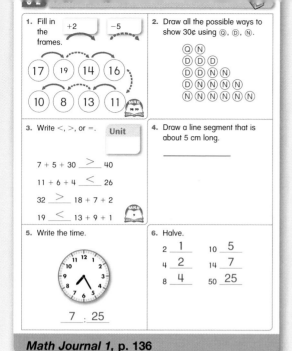

Math Journal 1, p. 136

---

20. They draw 3 or 4 cards at each turn to practice addition with 3 or 4 numbers.

NOTE Some children may prefer to play *Three Addends* from Lesson 6-1 again. *Math Masters,* page 473 is available for children to record their numbers and number models.

▶ # Math Boxes 6·2

(*Math Journal 1,* p. 136)

INDEPENDENT ACTIVITY

Mixed Practice Math Boxes in this lesson are paired with Math Boxes in Lesson 6-4. The skill in Problem 6 previews Unit 7 content.

Writing/Reasoning Have children draw, write, or verbalize their answers to the following: *Explain how you know you have written all the possible coin combinations for 30¢ in Problem 2.* Sample answer: I started with a quarter and a nickel. I then used 3 dimes to make 30¢ and then I kept breaking the dimes into 2 nickels until I used all nickels. This is the smallest coin I could use.

▶ # Home Link 6·2

(*Math Masters,* pp. 159 and 160)

INDEPENDENT ACTIVITY

Home Connection Children solve comparison number stories. They fill in a comparison diagram and write a number model for each problem. The explanation in the Family Note will help parents and guardians feel comfortable when participating in these activities with their children.

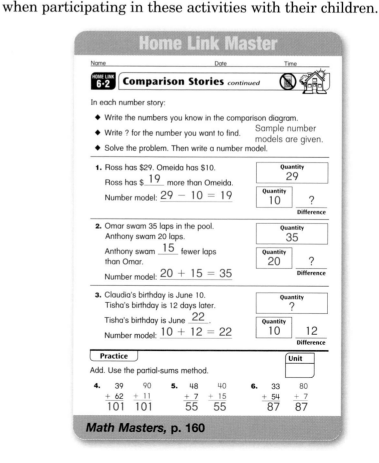

Math Masters, p. 159

Math Masters, p. 160

READINESS

👫 **PARTNER ACTIVITY**

▶ **Doing a Penny Grab Activity**

🕐 **5–15 Min**

To provide experience with comparing numbers using a concrete model, have children do the following Penny Grab activity.

1. Place a pile of pennies or other counters on a table between two children.

2. Each child grabs a handful of pennies, counts them, and records the amount.

3. Partners compare their amounts by lining up the pennies side-by-side and finding the difference.

4. Partners work together to record number models that describe the lined-up pennies. For example, $9 - 6 = 3$.

Encourage such remarks as, "I have 3 more than you. You have 3 less than I do."

The difference between 9 and 6 is 3.

ENRICHMENT

🧍 **INDEPENDENT ACTIVITY**

▶ **Comparing Number Stories**

🕐 **5–15 Min**

(*Math Masters*, p. 161)

To further explore comparison number stories, have children complete *Math Masters*, page 161. Children compare number stories by writing number models and answering related questions.

Teaching Master

Name   Date   Time

LESSON 6·2   **Comparing Number Stories**

Solve each number story. Be sure to write a number model. Then answer the questions at the bottom of the page.

1. There were 23 children in the classroom. 17 went to the computer lab. How many were left in the classroom?

Number Model: $23 - 17 = 6$

2. There were 6 children in the classroom. 17 came back from the computer lab. How many children are in the classroom now?

Number Model: $6 + 17 = 23$

How are the problems alike?
Sample answer: They use the same
3 numbers.

How might solving Problem 1 help you solve Problem 2? Explain your thinking.
Sample answer: If you know that the
three numbers go together in a subtraction
problem, then they are a fact family and
will go together in an addition problem.

Math Masters, p. 161

6·3

Data Day: The Four Food Groups

⊚ **Objective** To provide experiences with collecting, sorting, tallying, and graphing data.

① Teaching the Lesson

materials

Key Activities

Children are introduced to the basic food groups and the Food Guide Pyramid. Then they make a data-table tally of favorite class foods, analyze the data table, and make a bar graph of the favorite-food data.

Key Concepts and Skills

• Generate whole numbers from sets of tally marks.
  [Number and Numeration Goal 5]

• Collect data and tabulate it in a tally chart.
  [Data and Chance Goal 1]

• Use data in a tally chart to draw and interpret a bar graph.
  [Data and Chance Goal 1]

• Draw conclusions and answer questions from tally-chart and bar-graph data.
  [Data and Chance Goal 2]

Key Vocabulary

basic food groups • data table • bar graph

☑ **Ongoing Assessment: Informing Instruction** See page 393.

☑ **Ongoing Assessment: Recognizing Student Achievement** Use an Exit Slip.
  [Data and Chance Goal 2]

☐ *Math Journal 1*, p. 137
☐ Home Link 6·2
☐ Teaching Master (*Math Masters*, p. 162)
☐ Teaching Aid Master (*Math Masters*, p. 415)
☐ Transparencies (*Math Masters*, pp. 162 and 163; optional; and p. 164)
☐ Class Data Pad (optional)
☐ Crayons or color pencils

***See* Advance Preparation**

② Ongoing Learning & Practice

materials

Children solve comparison number stories about lengths of fish on the Fish Poster.

Children practice and maintain skills through Math Boxes and Home Link activities.

☐ *Math Journal 1*, p. 80, optional; and pp. 138–140
☐ Home Link Master (*Math Masters*, p. 165)

③ Differentiation Options

materials

ENRICHMENT

Children survey adults about favorite foods, make a bar graph of the results, and compare this set of data to the children's data collected in Part 1.

EXTRA PRACTICE

Children use tally marks to keep track of the number of pennies dropped into a can one at a time.

☐ Teaching Master (*Math Masters*, p. 166)
☐ pennies
☐ can or other container
☐ slate
☐ crayons

Additional Information

Advance Preparation For the teaching activities in Part 1, you might want to make overhead transparencies for *Math Masters*, pages 162–164.

Technology

Assessment Management System
Exit Slip
See the **iTLG**.

Getting Started

Mental Math and Reflexes

Pose comparison number stories like the following. Have children share their strategies:

○○○ It takes Maurice about 14 minutes to get to school in the morning. It takes Eva about 7 minutes. About how much longer does it take Maurice to get to school? *About 7 minutes longer*

○○○ Josh read 25 pages. Steven read 15 pages. How many fewer pages did Steven read than Josh? *10 fewer pages*

○○○ Mike collected 54 cans. Marti collected 30 more than Mike. How many cans did Marti collect? *84 cans*

Math Message

What is your favorite food?
(Candy, soda, and pizza don't count!)

Home Link 6·2 Follow-Up

Review answers as necessary. As time permits, have children share the strategies they used to do the computation.

---

① Teaching the Lesson

▶ Math Message Follow-Up

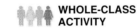 **WHOLE-CLASS ACTIVITY**

(*Math Masters*, p. 162)

Before talking about favorite foods, talk with children about good nutrition.

People need to eat balanced diets to stay healthy. There are **5 basic food groups:**

1. Fruits

2. Vegetables

3. Grains

4. Meat & Beans

5. Milk

NOTE Recent recommendations from the U.S. Department of Agriculture have split the old Fruits and Vegetables food group into two separate groups, making five food groups instead of four. One reason for this was to emphasize the importance of fruits and vegetables in a healthy diet.

The Dietary Guidelines for Second Graders (*Math Masters*, page 162) shows the recommended number of servings per day from each of the basic food groups. The guidelines are based on a 1,600 calorie/day diet, which is recommended for moderately active 4–8 year old boys and girls. More active children should eat more.

Discuss the foods that a person should eat the most of: fruits, vegetables, and grains. Discuss the foods that a person should eat less of: dairy products, meat, poultry, fish, beans, eggs, and nuts. Discuss things to be eaten sparingly: fats, oils, and sweets.

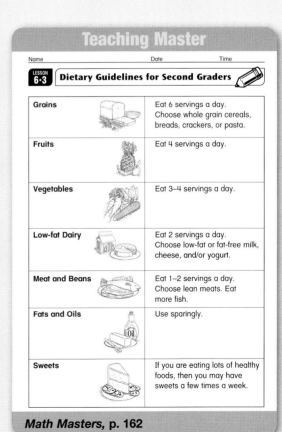

Math Masters, p. 162

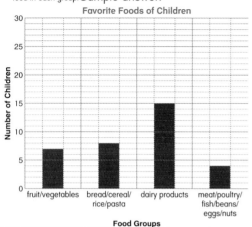

Student Page

Date _____ Time _____

LESSON 6·3   What Is Your Favorite Food?

1. Make tally marks to show the number of children who chose
   a favorite food in each group. Sample answer:

fruit/ vegetables	bread/cereal/ rice/pasta	dairy products	meat/poultry/fish/ beans/eggs/nuts
HHT //	HHT ///	HHT HHT HHT	////

2. Make a graph that shows how many children chose a favorite
   food in each group. Sample answer:

Favorite Foods of Children

(bar graph: Number of Children vs. Food Groups)

Food Groups

Math Journal 1, p. 137

NOTE Some teachers have reported that assigning a favorite food to a single group can be confusing and time-consuming. For example, are beef enchiladas in the bread, dairy, or meat groups? Other teachers have said that this activity has not been problematic and that children have come to a consensus about the primary ingredient in a food item and then assigned that favorite food to a food group based on that criterion.

If you foresee having problems in your classroom, consider the following option: Display an overhead transparency of *Math Masters,* page 163. This master lists foods that belong in each of the food groups. Ask children to pick the group that they like best. The foods listed as belonging in that group may not be their favorite foods, but they do represent types of foods that children like.

There is room on *Math Masters,* page 163 to tailor the list to include special foods that may be popular in your region or with children in your school.

► **Collecting Data on Favorite Foods**

(*Math Journal 1,* p. 137; *Math Masters,* pp. 162 and 164)

On the Class Data Pad, draw a table like the one shown in Problem 1 on the journal page or use an overhead transparency of *Math Masters,* page 164. Ask each child to name his or her favorite food. As a class, assign each food named to the most appropriate food group. Make a tally mark in the table on the Class Data Pad as children do the same on the journal page.

Use the Dietary Guidelines for Second Graders on *Math Masters,* page 162 as a reference. (You might want to use an overhead transparency of this page during your discussion.) For the more problematic foods, you can make suggestions or act as the final authority. Continue until each child has named a favorite food and each food named has been assigned to one of the food groups.

► **Discussing the Favorite-Food Data Table**

(*Math Journal 1,* p. 137)

Discuss the resulting **data table** with children. Ask:

● Which is the most popular food group among children in the class?

● Which is the least popular?

● Why do you think children prefer one food group over another?

● Do you think children in other parts of the world would have similar results on their data tables?

● Do you think adults prefer the same foods as children?

Adjusting the Activity

If there are other second-grade classrooms in your school, share data-table results and make comparisons between the classrooms. For example, ask: *Which is the most popular food group in Mr. Mazzuca's classroom? Is it the same food group as in our classroom? Do you think all children have similar tastes in food?*

AUDITORY ♦ KINESTHETIC ♦ TACTILE ♦ VISUAL

► Making a Bar Graph of the Favorite-Food Data

WHOLE-CLASS ACTIVITY

(Math Journal 1, p. 137; Math Masters, p. 164)

Display an overhead transparency of *Math Masters*, page 164 as children follow along in their journals. Remind children how a **bar graph** is drawn using vertical or horizontal bars to represent data. Ask questions such as the following about the bar graph in their journals:

NOTE You might want to show children how the graph would look if it were created with graphing software.

- What do the labels at the bottom of the graph refer to? The food groups What do the numbers on the left side of the graph refer to? The number of children

- Suppose 15 children chose a dairy product as their favorite food. How would you show this on the graph? Color the dairy products column up to the line for 15

- How would you show on the graph that 7 children had chosen a fruit or vegetable as their favorite food? Color the fruit/vegetables column up to the line for 7

Show children how to graph the data for the fruit/vegetables group on the overhead transparency of *Math Masters*, page 164 or a Class Data Pad.

Children can use crayons or color pencils to color the bars of the graphs in their journals.

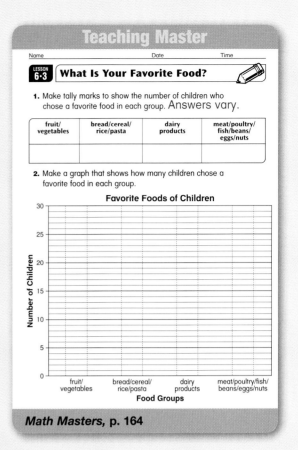

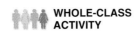

Teaching Master

Name _____ Date _____ Time _____

LESSON 6·3 What Is Your Favorite Food?

1. Make tally marks to show the number of children who chose a favorite food in each group. Answers vary.

fruit/ vegetables	bread/cereal/ rice/pasta	dairy products	meat/poultry/ fish/beans/ eggs/nuts

2. Make a graph that shows how many children chose a favorite food in each group.

Favorite Foods of Children

Math Masters, p. 164

NOTE Graphing the data on a Class Data Pad will allow you to keep the graph posted to refer to later, if needed.

★ Ongoing Assessment: Informing Instruction

Watch for children who find it difficult to fill in the bar graph. It may be helpful to lay a straightedge or piece of paper across the vertical axis to help them determine how far up they should color each bar. This will be especially helpful for the bars that are farthest from the numbers.

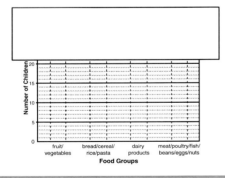

Partners should work together to complete the bar graph. Children who used *Everyday Mathematics* in first grade should be familiar with bar graphs. You might want to complete the graph as a whole-class activity.

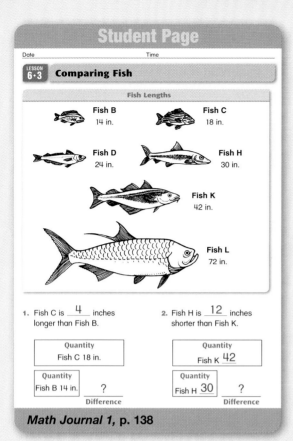
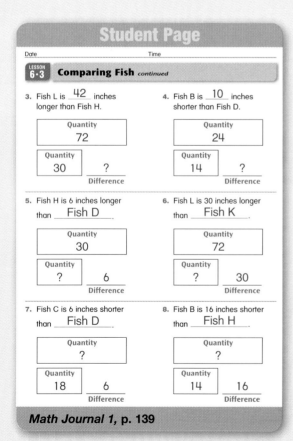
 Ongoing Assessment:
Recognizing Student Achievement   Exit Slip

Use an **Exit Slip** (*Math Masters*, page 415) to assess children's progress in reading graphs. Ask children to interpret the bar graph of favorite-food data. Children are making adequate progress if they can write one thing they learned from reading the graph. Some children may be able to write more than one thing.

[Data and Chance Goal 2]

2 Ongoing Learning & Practice

▶ Comparing Lengths of Fish on the Fish Poster
INDEPENDENT ACTIVITY

(*Math Journal 1*, pp. 138 and 139)

Guide children through Problem 1.

Adjusting the Activity

Have children use counters to match the quantities (See page 385). For larger numbers, have children use the numbers on 2 tape measures to represent the quantities.

AUDITORY ◆ KINESTHETIC ◆ TACTILE ◆ VISUAL

▶ Math Boxes 6·3
INDEPENDENT ACTIVITY

(*Math Journal 1*, p. 140)

Mixed Practice Math Boxes in this lesson are linked with Math Boxes in Lessons 6-1 and 6-5. The skills in Problems 5 and 6 preview Unit 7 content.

Writing/Reasoning Have children draw, write, or verbalize their answers to the following: *In Problem 2, how many more inches would you need to add to the line segment to make it 10 inches long? Write a number model.* Sample answer: 7 inches; $10 - 3 = 7$

▶ Home Link 6·3
INDEPENDENT ACTIVITY

(*Math Masters*, p. 165)

 Home Connection Children use survey data about favorite fruit to make a bar graph. They then use the information to draw conclusions about fruit preferences.

3 Differentiation Options

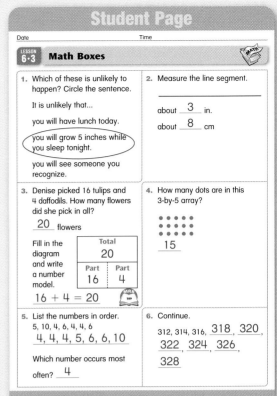

ENRICHMENT

INDEPENDENT ACTIVITY

▶ **Collecting Favorite-Food Data**

30+ Min

(*Math Masters*, p. 166)

To further explore collecting data, have children survey adults around school or at home, asking adults to name their favorite food.

Children tally their data as they collect it, using the table at the top of *Math Masters,* page 166. They use their tallied data to make a bar graph, compare the adult data and the class data collected in this lesson, and report their findings to the class.

EXTRA PRACTICE

SMALL-GROUP ACTIVITY

▶ **Making a Listening Tally**

5–15 Min

To give children practice making and counting tally marks, drop a selected number of pennies into a container, one at a time. Make sure you do this out of the children's view. Tell them to make a tally mark on their slates each time they hear a penny drop. Then have them count the tally marks and write a total number of pennies on their slates. Check that children have grouped their tally marks by 5s. Repeat as time allows.

Math Journal 1, p. 140

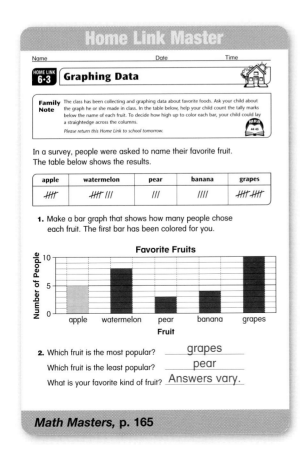

Math Masters, p. 165

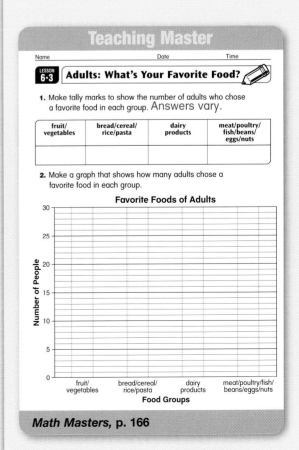

Math Masters, p. 166

6·4 Mixed Addition and Subtraction Stories

 Objective To guide children in selecting and completing an appropriate diagram to help solve an addition or subtraction problem.

---

1 Teaching the Lesson

materials

Key Activities

Children categorize number stories as change, parts-and-total, or comparison problems; fill in an appropriate diagram to record known and missing information; and write number models to summarize their solutions.

Key Concepts and Skills

- Explain solution strategies.
  [Operations and Computation Goal 2]
- Solve 2-digit addition and subtraction problems within number stories.
  [Operations and Computation Goal 2]
- Identify change, parts-and-total, and comparison number stories.
  [Operations and Computation Goal 4]

☑ **Ongoing Assessment: Informing Instruction** See page 398.

☑ **Ongoing Assessment: Recognizing Student Achievement** Use journal page 141.
  [Operations and Computation Goal 2]

- ☐ *Math Journal 1*, p. 141
- ☐ Home Link 6·3
- ☐ Teaching Aid Master (*Math Masters*, p. 437); 2 copies per child
- ☐ Transparency (*Math Masters*, p. 437; optional)
- ☐ slate
- ☐ number grid; number line (optional)

***See* Advance Preparation**

---

2 Ongoing Learning & Practice

materials

Children practice ballpark estimation.

Children practice and maintain skills through Math Boxes and Home Link activities.

- ☐ *Math Journal 1*, pp. 142 and 143
- ☐ Home Link Masters (*Math Masters*, pp. 167 and 168)
- ☐ calculator

---

3 Differentiation Options

materials

READINESS

Children use counters to solve a number story told by a partner.

ENRICHMENT

Children make up parts-and-total, comparison, and change number stories.

EXTRA PRACTICE

Children make up addition number stories.

- ☐ Teaching Aid Masters (*Math Masters*, pp. 419 and 437)
- ☐ *Minute Math*®+, p. 16
- ☐ counters or tool-kit coins

Additional Information

Advance Preparation For the second activity in Part 1, you might want to make an overhead transparency of *Math Masters*, page 437.

Technology

Assessment Management System
Journal page 141, Problems 1 and 2
See the **iTLG.**

Getting Started

Mental Math and Reflexes

Write multiple-addend problems on the board. Encourage children to look for combinations that will make the addition easier.

○○○ ? = 43 + 5 + 7 55

●○○ 6 + 8 + 9 = ? 23; no particularly easy way to add these numbers

○○○ ? = 1 + 15 + 29 + 5 50

Math Message

Make a list of some things you like to collect.

Home Link 6·3 Follow-Up

Ask comparison questions about the survey data such as the following:

• How many more people like watermelon than like grapes?

Ask parts-and-total questions, such as the following:

• What is the total number of people who like apples and pears?

---

1 Teaching the Lesson

▶ Math Message Follow-Up

INDEPENDENT ACTIVITY

(Math Journal 1, p. 141)

Ask children to describe some of the things they like to collect. Record their responses on the board. Sample answers: coins, shells, sports cards, dolls, stuffed animals

Have each child select two items to use as topics for number stories on the journal page. Different children might select different things.

Problems 1 and 2 on the journal page have answer blanks within their number stories. Ask children to select one item for each problem and to write that item in all the empty boxes. For example, suppose "coins" is one of the selected items. Problem 1 would be completed as follows: Colin has 20 coins. Fiona has 30 coins. How many coins do they have in all?

▶ Selecting Diagrams and Solving Number Stories

INDEPENDENT ACTIVITY

(Math Journal 1, p. 141; Math Masters, p. 437)

Until now, lessons have focused on one type of number story at a time. For example, all the problems in Lesson 6-2 were based on comparison stories, and the comparison diagram was the only diagram used. In this lesson, children are asked to categorize addition and subtraction stories: They must decide which type of story (change, parts-and-total, or comparison) best matches the problem at hand and then use the appropriate diagram to find a solution.

The journal page contains four number stories, and the master has two sets of diagrams. Each set includes a change diagram, a parts-and-total diagram, and a comparison diagram.

Student Page

Date _____ Time _____

LESSON 6·4 Addition and Subtraction Number Stories

Do the following for each problem:

♦ Choose one diagram from Math Masters, page 437.

♦ Fill in the numbers in the diagram. Write ? for the number you want to find. Find the answer. Write a number model.

♦ In Problems 1 and 2, write your own unit.

1. Colin has 20 Answers vary.

Fiona has 30 _____.

How many _____ do they have in all?

Colin and Fiona have 50

_____ in all.
　　　(unit)

Number model:
　　20 + 30 = 50

2. Alexi had 34 Answers vary.

He gave 12 _____ to Theo. How many _____ does Alexi have now?

Alexi has 22

_____ now.
　　　(unit)

Number model:
　　34 − 12 = 22

3. Rushing Waters has 26 water slides. Last year, there were only 16 water slides. How many new slides are there this year?

There are 10 new water slides.

Number model:
26 − 16 = 10 or 16 + 10 = 26

4. The Loop Slide is 65 feet high. The Tower Slide is 45 feet high. How much shorter is the Tower Slide?

It is 20 feet shorter.

Number model:
65 − 45 = 20 or 45 + 20 = 65

Math Journal 1, p. 141

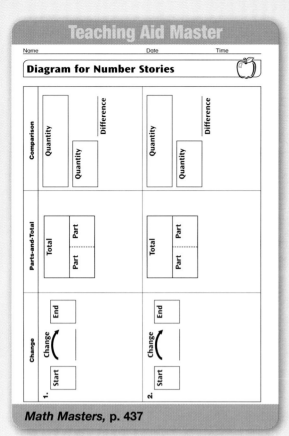

Name _____ Date _____ Time _____

Diagram for Number Stories

Math Masters, p. 437

NOTE Do not expect children to always select the same diagram. Different children might think of a problem in different ways and select the diagrams that match their thinking.

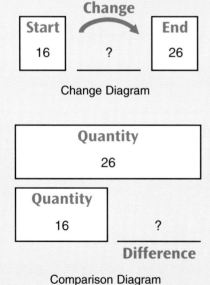

Change

Start		End
16	?	26

Change Diagram

Quantity
26

Quantity	
16	?
	Difference

Comparison Diagram

Total	
26	
Part	**Part**
16	?

Parts-and-total Diagram

Ongoing Assessment: Recognizing Student Achievement

Journal page 141 Problems 1 and 2 ★

Use **journal page 141, Problems 1 and 2** to assess children's progress solving number stories. Children are making adequate progress if they can solve the problem using the number grid, number line, or any other manipulative. Some children may be able to solve the problem using mental math and then write a number model that summarizes the problem.

[Operations and Computation Goal 2]

Ongoing Assessment: Informing Instruction

Watch for children who are having difficulty choosing a diagram. Ask them first to explain how they view the problem. Then direct them toward the diagram that best matches their way of thinking. Alternatively, pick a diagram and ask children if they are able to explain how to solve the problem using that diagram.

For each number story, children do the following:

1. Choose one diagram they think is appropriate.

2. Fill in the diagram by writing known numbers in the appropriate places and by writing a question mark to represent the unknown number.

3. Calculate the sum or difference and solve the problem.

4. Write a number model to summarize the problem.

Solve Problems 3 and 4 with the class. Display an overhead transparency of *Math Masters,* page 437 or draw the three kinds of diagrams on the board. Ask a volunteer to select one of the diagrams, explain his or her choice, and model the solution at the board. When the problem has been solved in one way, ask if anyone selected one of the other diagrams and solved it in a different way.

Do not force any number story into a particular mold or say that there is a best diagram for the problem. As the following examples show, there may be several ways to view a problem—and to select a diagram:

Example 1: *Problem 3 viewed as a change problem*

Think: Last year there were 16 slides (the Start number). New slides were added (the Change number). Now, this year, there are 26 slides (the End number). I want to find the Change number.

Example 2: *Problem 3 viewed as a comparison problem*

Think: I'm comparing the number of slides this year (the larger Quantity, 26) to the number of slides last year (the smaller Quantity, 16). I want to find how many more slides there are this year (the Difference).

Example 3: *Problem 3 viewed as a parts-and-total problem*

Think: I know there are 26 slides in all (the Total). 16 of them (the first Part) were there last year, and some new slides (the second Part) were added this year. I want to find the second Part.

Summary: The purpose of diagrams is to help children organize the information in a number story, identify the missing information, and determine whether to add or subtract to solve the problem. Children should be encouraged to select the diagram that best matches the way they see the problem. There is no right or wrong diagram for any given problem; what matters is that the chosen diagram matches the child's thinking and is used as a tool for finding the correct answer.

2 Ongoing Learning & Practice

▶ Reviewing Ballpark Estimation

INDEPENDENT ACTIVITY

(*Math Journal 1,* p. 142)

Children complete this journal page by finding a ballpark estimate for each problem. They then solve the problem using a calculator. When most children have completed this journal page, have them compare their estimates to the exact answer to see if the exact answer is in the ballpark of their estimate. Discuss.

▶ Math Boxes 6·4

INDEPENDENT ACTIVITY

(*Math Journal 1,* p. 143)

Mixed Practice Math Boxes in this lesson are paired with Math Boxes in Lesson 6-2. The skill in Problem 6 previews Unit 7 content.

▶ Home Link 6·4

INDEPENDENT ACTIVITY

(*Math Masters,* pp. 167 and 168)

Home Connection Children make up number stories to match diagrams. Then they solve their number stories and complete a number model.

3 Differentiation Options

READINESS

▶ Solving a Partner's Number Story

PARTNER ACTIVITY

5–15 Min

To provide experience with number stories, have children tell a partner a number story. Encourage them to tell change stories and parts-and-total stories. Children can use counters or coins to model their stories. They use the laminated diagrams and act out

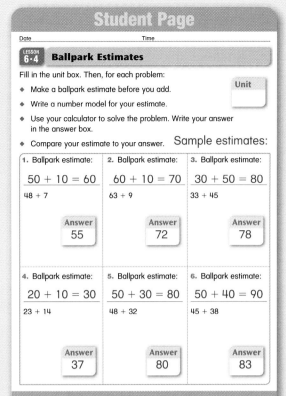
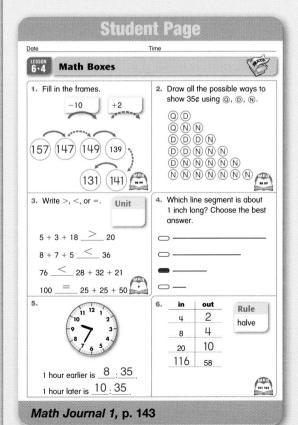

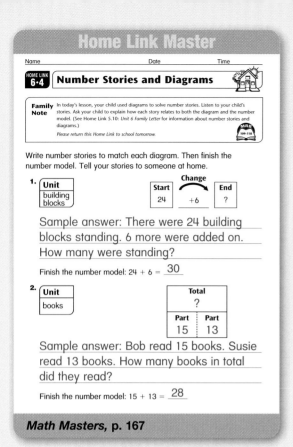

Math Masters, p. 167

the story with counters and coins. For example, *Julia had 48 cents, and Marcus had 35 cents. If Marcus gives his money to Julia, how much money will she have?* Children can place the coins in a change diagram and figure out the total. *How much did Julia and Marcus have all together?* Children can place the coins in the parts-and-total diagram and figure out the total.

ENRICHMENT

INDEPENDENT ACTIVITY

15–30 Min

▶ **Using Different Diagrams to Write Number Stories**

(*Math Masters,* pp. 437 and 419)

To further explore addition and subtraction number stories, have children solve a number story using all three diagrams. Tell children a number story. For example say: *Francis wanted to buy a toy turtle from the store. He had 67 cents. The turtle cost 83 cents.* Have them fill in all three diagrams (with a question mark for the missing number) to show how all three diagrams could be used to solve the problem correctly. When they have finished, have them explain their thinking.

EXTRA PRACTICE

SMALL-GROUP ACTIVITY

5–15 Min

▶ *Minute Math+*

To offer children more experience with making up number stories, see the following page in *Minute Math+*: p. 16.

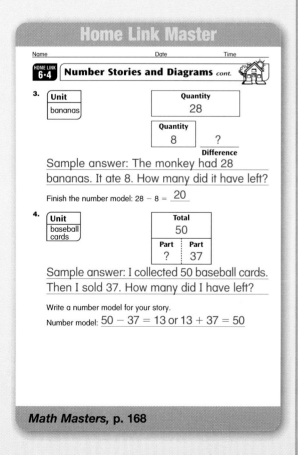

Math Masters, p. 168

Teaching Aid Master

Name   Date   Time

A Number Story

Unit

Math Masters, p. 419

6·5 Subtraction Strategies

 Objective To review solution strategies for subtraction of 2-digit numbers.

1 Teaching the Lesson

Key Activities
Children solve 2-digit subtraction problems using a variety of strategies.

Key Concepts and Skills
• Count up and back by 1s and 10s. [Number and Numeration Goal 1]
• Model 2-digit numbers using base-10 blocks. [Number and Numeration Goal 2]
• Develop counting up and back strategies for subtraction.
  [Operations and Computation Goal 2]
• Use and explain strategies for solving 2-digit-by-2-digit subtraction problems.
  [Operations and Computation Goal 2]

Key Vocabulary
trade (a base-10 long for 10 cubes)

✔ **Ongoing Assessment: Informing Instruction** See page 402.

materials
☐ *Math Journal 1,* p. 144
☐ Home Link 6·4
☐ base-10 blocks per partnership: 6 longs, 30 cubes
☐ overhead base-10 blocks (optional): 6 longs and 18 cubes
☐ number grid
☐ pennies or other counters (optional)
☐ play money (optional)

2 Ongoing Learning & Practice

Children practice 2-digit subtraction by playing the *Number-Grid Difference Game.*

Children practice and maintain skills through Math Boxes and Home Link activities.

✔ **Ongoing Assessment: Recognizing Student Achievement**
Use journal page 145.
[Data and Chance Goal 3]

materials
☐ *Math Journal 1,* p. 145
☐ *My Reference Book,* pp. 140 and 141
☐ Home Link Master (*Math Masters,* pp. 169 and 170)
☐ Teaching Aid Master (*Math Masters,* p. 418)
☐ Game Master (*Math Masters,* p. 463)
☐ two pennies or counters
☐ calculator
☐ number cards 0–9 (4 of each; from the Everything Math Deck, if available)

3 Differentiation Options

READINESS

Children play the *Base-10 Trading Game* to practice place-value exchanges.

ENRICHMENT

Children analyze subtraction strategies.

materials
☐ Teaching Master (*Math Masters,* p. 171)
☐ Teaching Aid Master (*Math Masters,* p. 427; one per player)
☐ base-10 blocks (2 flats, 20 longs, 40 cubes)
☐ two dice

Technology
Assessment Management System
Math Boxes, Problem 1
See the **iTLG.**

Getting Started

Mental Math and Reflexes

Pose subtraction problems that feature multiples of 10.
Suggestions:

●○○ 48 − 10 = ? 38   ●●○ 63 − 30 = ? 33   ●●● 195 − 80 = ? 115
    72 − 10 = ? 62   72 − 50 = ? 22   152 − 20 = ? 132
    ? = 48 − 20 28   ? = 72 − 20 52   ? = 295 − 60 235

Math Message

Solve the problem. Try to find the answer in two different ways.
Be ready to explain how you found the answer.   56 − 24 = ? 32

Home Link 6·4 Follow-Up

Invite several children to share their
stories with the class. Collect children's
stories to use when you need a quick "sponge" or filler
activity or for use during future Mental Math and
Reflexes sessions.

---

1 Teaching the Lesson

▶ Math Message Follow-Up

 WHOLE-CLASS ACTIVITY

Have children share their solution strategies. For each problem,
record on the board any strategies that result in the correct
answer. Emphasize that there are many good ways to get correct
answers to problems.

You or the children might suggest the following strategies:

Strategy 1

Counting Up: Start with the smaller number, 24. Model on a
number grid. Count up by ones, or 10s and ones. 34, 44, 54, 55,
56; 56 − 24 = 32

✓ Ongoing Assessment: Informing Instruction

Watch for children who use the counting up strategy but include the 24 in their
counts. For example, 24 (1), 25 (2), 26 (3), 27 (4)... + 56 (33). This will yield an
almost correct answer. This situation might be used to spark a discussion: "Mahli
has 33, but Harry has 32. Who's right? How did Mahli get 33? How did Harry get
32?" You might also provide a penny for the children to count each move or jump.

Strategy 2

Counting Back: Start with the bigger number, 56. Model on a
number grid. Count back to 24 by ones, or 10s and 1s. 46, 36, 26,
25, 24

Strategy 3

Money: Think of $56 dollars. Subtract $20 and then subtract $4.

Strategy 4

Manipulatives: Use manipulatives to act out the problem. Start
with 56 pennies and take away 24 pennies.

If no one suggests it, point out that they may use base-10 blocks to solve 2-digit subtraction problems as well.

Adjusting the Activity

Use play money to illustrate *Strategy 3*. Put five $10 bills and six $1 bills in one stack. Take out two $10 bills and four $1 bills.

AUDITORY ◆ KINESTHETIC ◆ TACTILE ◆ VISUAL

NOTE *Everyday Mathematics* students solve subtraction problems using many different strategies even though they have not been introduced to a standard algorithm. These experiences help children understand the concept and prepare them for more formal work with subtraction algorithms in Unit 11. If children suggest a standard paper-and-pencil algorithm, record it on the board, but do not take the time to teach it. Formal subtraction methods are addressed in Unit 11.

▶ Using Base-10 Blocks to Model Subtraction

WHOLE-CLASS ACTIVITY

Write the following problem on the board:

$$\begin{array}{r} 36 \\ -14 \end{array}$$

Ask partners to represent the top number (the minuend) with the least number of blocks. Then ask them to subtract the bottom number (the subtrahend) by removing the correct combination of blocks.

Invite children to demonstrate and explain what they did. Have the class gather around a table as children demonstrate with actual blocks. You might want to use base-10 blocks for the overhead if you have them. Refer to the longs alternately as longs and as 10s; refer to the cubes alternately as cubes and as 1s.

Example: Model $36 - 14 = ?$ as follows:

1. Count out three longs and six cubes to represent 36. Lay these on the table, with the longs to the left of the cubes.

2. Ask: *Are there enough longs and cubes on the table so I can remove 14 (1 long and 4 cubes)?* yes

3. Remove 1 long and 4 cubes.

4. Count the remaining blocks and record the answer (the difference) on the board. 22

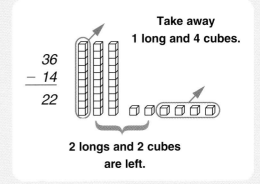

$$\begin{array}{r} 36 \\ -14 \\ \hline 22 \end{array}$$

Take away
1 long and 4 cubes.

2 longs and 2 cubes
are left.

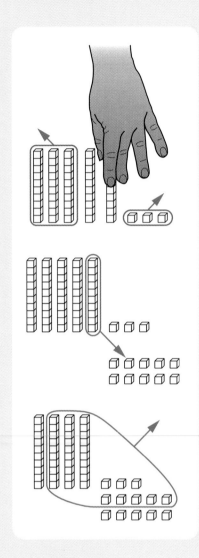

Write the following problem on the board:

$$\begin{array}{r} 53 \\ -\ 38 \\ \hline \end{array}$$

Ask partners to represent the top number (the minuend) with the fewest blocks. Then ask them to subtract the bottom number (the subtrahend) in any way they can.

Children cannot solve these problems by simply removing some of the blocks shown. Invite them to come up with strategies. *For example:*

▷ Subtract 38 in two stages. First, remove 3 longs and 3 cubes, leaving 2 longs. Then cover up 5 cubes on one of the longs. That leaves one long (10 cubes), plus 5 cubes showing on the second long, for a total of 15.

▷ **Trade** one of the longs for 10 separate cubes so 53 is represented by 4 longs and 13 cubes. Then remove 8 cubes and 3 longs, leaving 1 long and 5 cubes, or 15. To support English language learners, discuss the everyday meaning of *trade* as well as its meaning in this context.

Have the class gather around a table as children demonstrate with actual blocks. You might want to use base-10 blocks for the overhead if you have them.

Show 53

Trade a long for 10 cubes.

Take 38 away.

Example: Model $53 - 38 = ?$ as follows:

1. Count out five 10s and three 1s to represent 53. Lay these on the table, with longs to the left of the cubes.

2. Ask: *Are there enough longs and cubes on the table so I can remove exactly 38 (3 longs and 8 cubes)?* No. There are only 3 cubes on the table, so it's not possible to remove 8 cubes.

3. Trade a long for cubes: Remove one of the longs that is used to represent 53 and replace it with 10 cubes. 53 is now represented by 4 longs and 13 cubes.

4. Remove 38 (3 longs and 8 cubes) from the table.

5. Record the answer (difference) on the board. 15

▶ **Solving Subtraction Problems**   PARTNER ACTIVITY

(*Math Journal 1*, p. 144)

Partners work together to solve the subtraction problems.

For Problems 1–4, children are expected to continue using base-10 blocks; many will actually trade 1 long for 10 cubes. Some children might simply move one of the longs next to the pile of cubes and answer the problem without actually exchanging the long for cubes.

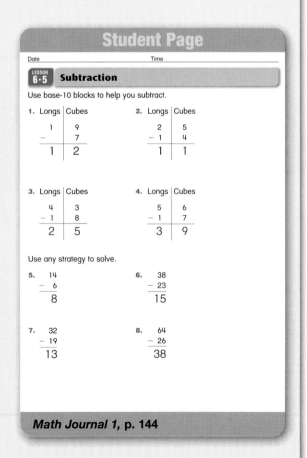

Student Page

Date _____ Time _____

LESSON 6·5   **Subtraction**

Use base-10 blocks to help you subtract.

1. Longs	Cubes
1	9
−	7
1	2

2. Longs	Cubes
2	5
− 1	4
1	1

3. Longs	Cubes
4	3
− 1	8
2	5

4. Longs	Cubes
5	6
− 1	7
3	9

Use any strategy to solve.

5. $\begin{array}{r} 14 \\ -\ 6 \\ \hline 8 \end{array}$ 6. $\begin{array}{r} 38 \\ -\ 23 \\ \hline 15 \end{array}$

7. $\begin{array}{r} 32 \\ -\ 19 \\ \hline 13 \end{array}$ 8. $\begin{array}{r} 64 \\ -\ 26 \\ \hline 38 \end{array}$

Math Journal 1, p. 144

2 Ongoing Learning & Practice

▶ Playing the *Number-Grid Difference Game*

PARTNER ACTIVITY

(*Math Masters*, pp. 418 and 463; *My Reference Book*, pp. 140 and 141)

Children practice subtraction skills by playing the *Number-Grid Difference Game*. Children will find directions on page 140 of *My Reference Book*.

▶ Math Boxes 6·5

INDEPENDENT ACTIVITY

(*Math Journal 1*, p. 145)

Mixed Practice Math Boxes in this lesson are linked with Math Boxes in Lessons 6-1 and 6-3. The skills in Problems 5 and 6 preview Unit 7 content.

▶ Home Link 6·5

INDEPENDENT ACTIVITY

(*Math Masters*, pp. 169 and 170)

Home Connection Children subtract by crossing out cubes. Before sending this Home Link with the children, go over the example and make sure they understand that each long shows 10 connected cubes.

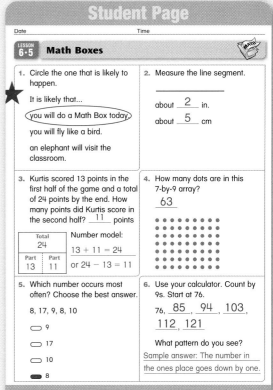

Student Page

Date   Time

LESSON 6·5   Math Boxes

1. Circle the one that is likely to happen.

It is likely that...

(you will do a Math Box today.)

you will fly like a bird.

an elephant will visit the classroom.

2. Measure the line segment.

_____

about __2__ in.

about __5__ cm

3. Kurtis scored 13 points in the first half of the game and a total of 24 points by the end. How many points did Kurtis score in the second half? __11__ points

Total	Number model:
24	$13 + 11 = 24$
Part	Part	or $24 - 13 = 11$
13	11	

4. How many dots are in this 7-by-9 array? __63__

5. Which number occurs most often? Choose the best answer.

8, 17, 9, 8, 10

○ 9

○ 17

○ 10

● 8

6. Use your calculator. Count by 9s. Start at 76.

76, __85__, __94__, __103__, __112__, __121__

What pattern do you see?

Sample answer: The number in the ones place goes down by one.

Math Journal 1, p. 145

★ Ongoing Assessment: Recognizing Student Achievement

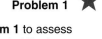

Math Boxes Problem 1 ★

Use **Math Boxes, Problem 1** to assess children's knowledge of probability language. Children are making adequate progress if they circle the correct answer.

[Data and Chance Goal 3]

Home Link Master

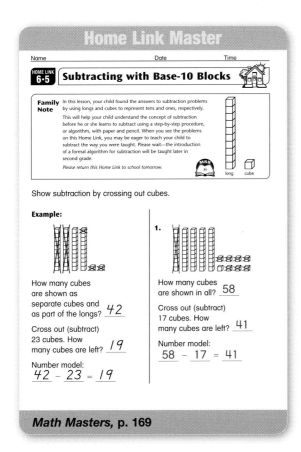

Name   Date   Time

HOME LINK 6·5   Subtracting with Base-10 Blocks

Family Note In this lesson, your child found the answers to subtraction problems by using longs and cubes to represent tens and ones, respectively.

This will help your child understand the concept of subtraction before he or she learns to subtract using a step-by-step procedure, or algorithm, with paper and pencil. When you see the problems on this Home Link, you may be eager to teach your child to subtract the way you were taught. Please wait—the introduction of a formal algorithm for subtraction will be taught later in second grade.

Please return this Home Link to school tomorrow.

long   cube

Show subtraction by crossing out cubes.

Example:

How many cubes are shown as separate cubes and as part of the longs? **42**

Cross out (subtract) 23 cubes. How many cubes are left? **19**

Number model: $42 - 23 = 19$

1.

How many cubes are shown in all? **58**

Cross out (subtract) 17 cubes. How many cubes are left? **41**

Number model: $58 - 17 = 41$

Math Masters, p. 169

Home Link Master

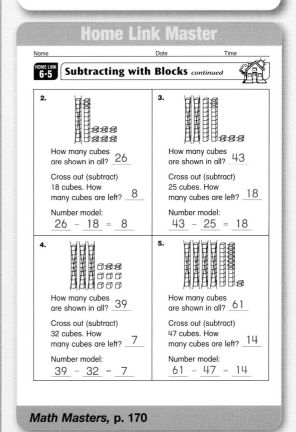

Name   Date   Time

HOME LINK 6·5   Subtracting with Blocks *continued*

2.

How many cubes are shown in all? **26**

Cross out (subtract) 18 cubes. How many cubes are left? **8**

Number model: $26 - 18 = 8$

3.

How many cubes are shown in all? **43**

Cross out (subtract) 25 cubes. How many cubes are left? **18**

Number model: $43 - 25 = 18$

4.

How many cubes are shown in all? **39**

Cross out (subtract) 32 cubes. How many cubes are left? **7**

Number model: $39 - 32 = 7$

5.

How many cubes are shown in all? **61**

Cross out (subtract) 47 cubes. How many cubes are left? **14**

Number model: $61 - 47 = 14$

Math Masters, p. 170

Teaching Aid Master

Name Date Time

Place-Value Mat

ones	
tens	
hundreds	

Math Masters, p. 427

Teaching Master

Name Date Time

LESSON 6•5 **A Subtraction Strategy**

Meredith uses an interesting strategy for solving subtraction problems when you have to trade. Try to figure out how it works.

42 − 27

On my first step, I get 12.

On my second step I get 15.

15 is my final answer.

34 − 19

On my first step, I get 14.

On my second step I get 15.

15 is my final answer.

71 − 36

First Step: 31

Second Step: 35

Final Answer: 35

Try This

93 − 48

First Step: 43

Second Step: 45

Final Step: 45

Math Masters, p. 171

3 Differentiation Options

READINESS

PARTNER ACTIVITY

15–30 Min

▶ Playing the *Base-10 Trading Game*

(*Math Masters,* p. 427)

To provide experience with subtraction using a concrete model, have children play the *Base-10 Trading Game.*

Begin with a bank that has 20 longs and 40 cubes. Each partner begins with 1 flat on their Place-Value Mat.

Rules:

Take turns. On each turn, a player does the following:

1. Roll the dice and find the sum of the dice.
2. Return that number of cubes to the bank. (When there are not enough individual cubes, make exchanges.)
3. The player not rolling the dice checks on the accuracy of the transactions.
4. The first player to clear their Place-Value Mat wins the game.

ENRICHMENT

SMALL-GROUP ACTIVITY

15–30 Min

▶ Analyzing a Subtraction Strategy

(*Math Masters,* p. 171)

To apply children's understanding of subtraction, have them analyze a subtraction strategy. When children have figured out the strategy and applied it to solving a new problem, have volunteers share explanations of the strategy and how they figured it out. Sample answer: "I noticed a pattern—that in the first step, only the tens place changed. Then I figured out you add back the difference between your second number and a multiple of ten."

Ask: *What is easy about Meredith's strategy?* Sample answer: You always subtract a multiple of 10 and then add some back on.

Ask: *What is hard about Meredith's strategy?* Sample answer: Sometimes it's hard to remember what to add back on.

6·6

Exploring Arrays, Coins, and Division

 Objectives To develop readiness for multiplication; to guide children in finding coin combinations equivalent to $1.00; and to explore one meaning of division.

---

1 Teaching the Lesson

Key Activities

Exploration A: Children make arrays on geoboards, record these arrays on dot paper, and sort arrays having the same number of dots into groups.

Exploration B: Children make and record different combinations of nickels, dimes, and quarters that are equivalent to $1.00.

Exploration C: Children determine how many groups of *n* objects can be made from a specified number of objects and how many objects are left over.

Key Concepts and Skills

• Count dots in an array. [Number and Numeration Goal 1]

• Create equal-size groupings. [Operations and Computation Goal 4]

• Use geoboards to create arrays. [Operations and Computation Goal 4]

• Create complements of $1.00 using nickels, dimes, and quarters. [Measurement and Reference Frames Goal 4]

✔ **Ongoing Assessment: Recognizing Student Achievement** Use an Exit Slip. [Measurement and Reference Frames Goal 4]

materials

☐ Home Link 6·5
☐ slate
Exploration A: Per child (except per group where noted):
☐ Teaching Masters (*Math Masters*, p. 172; and p. 173 or 174)
☐ geoboard and rubber band
☐ overhead geoboard (optional)
☐ scissors per group
☐ large sheet of paper and glue or paste per group (optional)
Exploration B: Per child:
☐ Teaching Master (*Math Masters*, p. 175)

☐ Teaching Aid Master (*Math Masters*, p. 415)
☐ 20 nickels, 10 dimes, 4 quarters; 2 half-dollars (optional)
☐ paper
Exploration C: Per child (except per group where noted):
☐ *Math Journal 1*, p. 146
☐ Teaching Master (*Math Masters*, p. 176)
☐ about 50 pennies or other counters per group
☐ 1 six-sided die per group

See **Advance Preparation**

---

2 Ongoing Learning & Practice

Children look for combinations of numbers that make those numbers easier to add by playing *Three Addends*.

Children practice and maintain skills through Math Boxes and Home Link activities.

materials

☐ *Math Journal 1*, pp. 131 and 147
☐ Home Link Master (*Math Masters*, p. 177)
☐ Game Master (*Math Masters*, p. 473)
☐ per partnership: number cards 0–20 (from the Everything Math Deck, if available)

---

3 Differentiation Options

ENRICHMENT

Children solve dollar riddles to apply their understanding of coins and coin combinations.

EXTRA PRACTICE

Children solve problems including money.

materials

☐ *Math Masters*, p. 178
☐ tool-kit coins
☐ *Minute Math*®+, pp. 64–67

Additional Information

Advance Preparation Plan to spend most of your time working on Exploration A with children. *Math Masters*, pages 172, 175, and 176 give directions for the Explorations.

Technology
Assessment Management System
Exit Slip
See the **iTLG**.

Getting Started

Mental Math and Reflexes

Write subtraction problems like the following on the board. Have children write ballpark estimates and the number models they used to make them on their slates.

○○○ 98 − 42   100 − 40 = 60

○○● 45 − 22   45 − 20 = 25; or 40 − 20 = 20

○○○ 173 − 39   170 − 40 = 130

Math Message

How many dots?

Home Link 6·5 Follow-Up

As children share their answers, circulate and note how they crossed out (subtracted) cubes.

Some children will not cross out the cubes they are subtracting in the simplest way. For example, in Problem 3, a child may cross out 25 cubes by crossing out 5 from each of the first 3 longs and 10 from the final long–leaving 5, 5, 5, 0, and 3 cubes.

Because 25 is 2 tens and 5 ones, it can be represented by 2 longs and 5 cubes. The simplest approach is to cross out 2 longs, then the 3 cubes, and finally 2 more cubes on a remaining long.

	How many rows?	How many dots in each row?	How many dots in all?
1.			
2.			
3.			
4.			

In Exploration A, children use either a 5 × 5 geoboard (*Math Masters,* page 173), or a 7 × 7 geoboard (*Math Masters,* page 174.)

Teaching Master

Name _____ Date _____ Time _____

LESSON 6·6   Geoboard Arrays

Materials ☐ geoboard dot paper for each person
  ☐ geoboard for each person
  ☐ rubber band for each person
  ☐ scissors for the group
  ☐ glue or paste for the group (optional)
  ☐ large sheet of paper for the group (optional)

Work by yourself to complete Steps 1–5.

1. Use one rubber band to make a rectangle on your geoboard. The pegs inside and the pegs that touch the rubber band make an array.

2. Draw your array on the geoboard dot paper.

3. Write about your array at the bottom of the geoboard dot paper. Tell how many rows are in your rectangle, how many dots are in each row, and how many dots in all are in your rectangle.

There are 2 rows of 5 pegs. 10 pegs are in the array.

4. Make 3 more arrays—all different. Follow steps two and three.

5. Cut apart the dot-paper records of your 4 arrays.

Work with your group to complete Step 6.

6. Sort your group's arrays into piles that have the same number of dots. You might want to use the arrays in each pile to make a display about that number.

Math Masters, p. 172

---

① Teaching the Lesson

▶ Math Message Follow-Up

WHOLE-CLASS ACTIVITY

Ask:

● How many rows of dots are there? 2

● How many dots are in each row? 5

● How many dots are there in all? 10

Use an overhead geoboard to show children how to use a rubber band to enclose 10 pegs in a 2 × 5 rectangle or demonstrate this on a regular geoboard and pass it around the classroom. Explain that in one of the Explorations in this lesson, children will use rubber bands to form rectangles and then count the number of pegs in the enclosed array including the ones touching the rubber bands.

▶ Exploration A: Making Geoboard Arrays

PARTNER ACTIVITY

(*Math Masters,* p. 172; and p. 173 or 174)

Directions for making rectangles on a geoboard are found on *Math Masters,* page 172. Before proceeding, check the size of your class's geoboards. If the geoboards in your classroom are 5 × 5, use *Math Masters,* page 173. If the geoboards are 7 × 7, use *Math Masters,* page 174.

▶ Exploration B: Making a Dollar

 SMALL-GROUP ACTIVITY

(*Math Masters*, p. 175)

 Before children begin, ask them to think about an organized way to determine the different groups of coins equivalent to $1.00. Children are given a hint: Find ways of using 3 quarters and other coins.

Children plan how to find the coin combinations and then record the groups of coins using , , and .

Coin combinations

⬆ Adjusting the Activity

Add two half-dollars to the set of coins.

AUDITORY ◆ KINESTHETIC ◆ TACTILE ◆ VISUAL

★ Ongoing Assessment: Recognizing Student Achievement

Exit Slip

Use an **Exit Slip** (*Math Masters*, page 415) to assess children's ability to make bill and coin exchanges. Have children record as many combinations for $1.00 as they can. Children are making adequate progress if they can draw four or more combinations. Some children may be able to find all possible combinations.

[Measurement and Reference Frames Goal 4]

▶ Exploration C: Finding How Many Children Get *n* Things

 **SMALL-GROUP ACTIVITY**

(*Math Journal 1*, p. 146; *Math Masters*, p. 176)

Using instructions from *Math Masters*, page 176, children make as many equal piles as possible. Then, on journal page 146, they record the total number of counters, the number of counters in each group, and the total number of groups. They also record how many counters are left over; that is, how many are not in a full group.

Name _____ Date _____ Time _____

LESSON 6·6 | **Making a Dollar** ✏

Work together in a small group.

Materials ☐ 20 nickels
☐ 10 dimes
☐ 4 quarters
☐ paper and pencil

Directions

1. Use the coins to find as many different ways as you can to make $1.00.

2. Before you begin, THINK about how to do this. *Hint:* First, make a dollar using 3 quarters and some other coins.

3. Plan how you will record the different ways to make $1.00.

4. On a sheet of paper, record the different ways you find to make $1.00. Use ⓝ, ⓓ, and ⓠ to show the coins.

Follow-Up

◆ How many ways did you find to make $1.00? Check with other groups to see if they thought of any ways that your group didn't find.

◆ Did you have a plan to find all the combinations? Compare your plan with the plan used by another group.

Math Masters, p. 175

Date _____ Time _____

LESSON 6·6 | **How Many Children Get *n* Things?**

Follow the directions on *Math Masters*, page 177 to fill in the table.

What is the total number of counters?	How many counters are in each group? (Roll a die to find out.)	How many groups are there?	How many counters are left over?

Children record totals in Exploration C on *Math Journal*, page 146.

Name _____ Date _____ Time _____

LESSON 6·6 | **How Many Children Get *n* Things?** ✏

Materials ☐ *Math Journal 1*, p. 146 (per person)
☐ one container with about 50 pennies or other counters (per group)
☐ 1 six-sided die (per group)

Use counters to make up and solve problems like this one:
Your group has been given 32 crayons.
Each person is to get 8 crayons.
How many of you will get 8 crayons?
Are there any crayons left over?

Now make up your own problems. Follow these steps:

1. Each person takes a handful of counters. Put all the counters together in a pile.

   How many counters are in the pile? Count them and record the number on the journal page.

2. Make equal-size groups of counters. One person rolls the die. The number that lands faceup tells how many counters to put in each group.

   Record this number on the journal page.

3. Make as many groups as you can with the counters in the pile.

4. Record on the journal page how many groups you made. If any counters are left over, record that number, too.

5. Put the counters back in the container. Repeat Steps 1–4.

Math Masters, p. 176

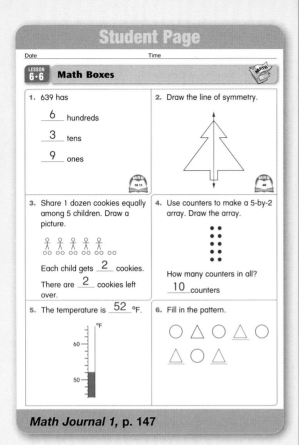
In Lesson 5-1, children had experience with equal-sharing division situations. In this activity, children work with equal-grouping division situations. It isn't important that children be able to distinguish between the two meanings of division at this point. However, it is important that they have had informal experience with both meanings. In Lesson 6-10, children will begin to formalize their understanding of equal-sharing and equal-grouping. This is an early exposure to the concept of division. Knowing and applying multiplication facts and generating related division facts are Grade 4 Goals.

② Ongoing Learning & Practice

▶ Playing *Three Addends*

PARTNER ACTIVITY

(*Math Journal 1*, p. 131; *Math Masters*, p. 473)

Children practice addition skills by playing *Three Addends*. For detailed instructions, see Lesson 6-1.

▶ Math Boxes 6·6

INDEPENDENT ACTIVITY

(*Math Journal 1*, p. 147)

Mixed Practice Math Boxes in this lesson are linked with Math Boxes in Lessons 6-8 and 6-10. The skill in Problem 6 previews Unit 7 content.

Writing/Reasoning Have children draw their answers to the following to extend Problem 2: *Draw a shape that has one line of symmetry. Next, draw another shape that has more than one line of symmetry.* Sample answers: an isosceles trapezoid; a circle or square

▶ Home Link 6·6

INDEPENDENT ACTIVITY

(*Math Masters*, p. 177)

Home Connection Children draw arrays with specified numbers of Xs. For each array, children give the number of rows and the number of Xs in each row.

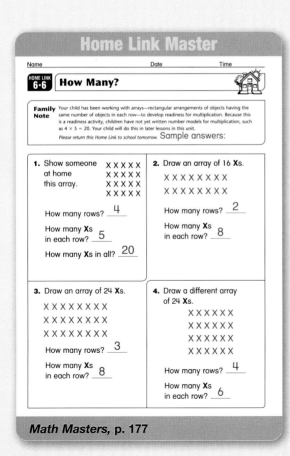

3 Differentiation Options

ENRICHMENT

 PARTNER ACTIVITY

15–30 Min

▶ **Solving Dollar Riddles**

(*Math Masters*, p. 178)

To apply children's understanding of coins and coin combinations, have them solve dollar riddles. Have children share strategies for solving some of the more difficult problems.

EXTRA PRACTICE

 SMALL-GROUP ACTIVITY

 5–15 Min

▶ *Minute Math+*

To offer children more experience with problems including money, see the following pages in *Minute Math+*: p. 64–67.

Teaching Master

Name ____ Date ____ Time ____

LESSON 6·6 Solving Dollar Riddles

1. To make a dollar, use all four types of coins and create a coin combination where there are two times as many of one type of coin as another.
   Sample answers: 10 pennies, 5 dimes, 1 quarter, 3 nickels; 10 nickels, 5 pennies, 1 quarter, 2 dimes

2. To make a dollar, use all four types of coins. Use half as many of one type of coin.
   Sample answers: 4 nickels, 2 quarters, 2 dimes, 10 pennies; 2 quarters, 1 dime, 7 nickels, 5 pennies

3. To make a dollar, use only nickels and dimes and create a coin combination where one type of coin is used twice as much as the other type. Ten nickels and five dimes

4. Using only three types of coins, make a dollar with the least number of coins you could use. 3 quarters, 2 dimes, 1 nickel
   Using only three types of coins, make a dollar with the greatest number of coins you could use. 85 pennies, 1 dime, 1 nickel

Try This

Use pennies, nickels, dimes, and quarters. Make a combination that is worth one dollar where you have one of some kind of coin, double of another, double that of another, and some number of the last coin.
Sample answers: 4 dimes, 2 quarters, 1 nickel, 5 pennies; 4 nickels, 2 quarters, 1 dime, 20 pennies

Math Masters, p. 178

Multiples of Equal Groups

Objective To introduce multiplication as a way to find the total number of things in several equal groups.

---

1 Teaching the Lesson

materials

Key Activities

Children are introduced to diagrams to identify the known and unknown quantities in multiplication problems and to complete number models to summarize the solutions. Children also solve number stories about equal groups of things.

Key Concepts and Skills

- Count the total number of objects in several groups.
  [Number and Numeration Goal 1]
- Make arrays to represent equal groups.
  [Operations and Computation Goal 4]
- Use various strategies to solve equal-groups number stories.
  [Operations and Computation Goal 4]

Key Vocabulary

equal groups • multiplication • times • multiplied by

✔ **Ongoing Assessment: Recognizing Student Achievement** Use the Math Message.
[Operations and Computation Goal 4]

☐ *Math Journal 1*, p. 148
☐ *My Reference Book*, pp. 112 and 113
☐ Home Link 6•6
☐ Teaching Aid Master (*Math Masters*, p. 415)
☐ 40 pennies or other counters per group of 4 to 5 children
☐ 6 boxes or bags to hold pennies or other counters

---

2 Ongoing Learning & Practice

materials

Children use Fact Triangles to practice addition and subtraction facts.

Children practice and maintain skills through Math Boxes and Home Link activities.

☐ *Math Journal 1*, p. 149
☐ Home Link Master (*Math Masters*, p. 179)
☐ addition/subtraction Fact Triangles in an envelope

---

3 Differentiation Options

materials

READINESS
Children solve equal-groups problems.

ENRICHMENT
Children solve equal-groups number riddles.

EXTRA PRACTICE
Children identify and solve multiplication problems found in literature.

ELL SUPPORT
Children enter *multiplication* in their Math Word Banks.

☐ Teaching Masters (*Math Masters*, pp. 180 and 181)
☐ *Differentiation Handbook*
☐ calculator
☐ *Each Orange Had Eight Slices: A Counting Book*

See Advanced Preparation

Additional Information

For the optional Extra Practice activity in Part 3, obtain the book *Each Orange Had Eight Slices: A Counting Book,* by Paul Giganti, Jr. (Greenwillow Books, 1992).

Technology

Assessment Management System
Math Message
See the **iTLG.**

Getting Started

Mental Math and Reflexes

Have children share strategies for solving comparison number stories like the following:

- ○○○ Dave is $2\frac{1}{2}$ years old and weighs 30 pounds. Elen is 10 months old and weighs 20 pounds. *How much more does Dave weigh than Elen?* 10 pounds more
- ○○○ Amos learned 26 new spelling words this week. Trung learned 6 fewer words than Amos. *How many new spelling words did Trung learn?* 20 new words
- ○○○ Marque ran around the track for 15 minutes. Liz ran for 7 minutes more than Marque. *How many minutes did Liz run?* 22 minutes

Math Message ★

Jane bought 3 packs of gum. There are 5 sticks of gum per pack. How many sticks of gum did she buy? Show how you found your answer on an Exit Slip (Math Masters, page 415).

Home Link 6·6 Follow-Up

Children draw the different arrays they made with 24 Xs. Be sure to include the following arrays: 1 row of 24 Xs and 24 rows of 1 X each. Show children any other possible arrays that they do not suggest.

1 Teaching the Lesson

▶ Math Message Follow-Up

 WHOLE-CLASS DISCUSSION

✔ Ongoing Assessment: Recognizing Student Achievement

Math Message ★

Use the **Math Message** to assess children's understanding of combining equal groups to find the total. Children are making adequate progress if they can find the answer by counting by 1s, 5s, drawing a picture, creating tally marks, or adding the equal groups. Some children may be able to write a multiplication number model for the problem.

[Operations and Computation Goal 4]

Ask children to share their solution strategies. Expect a variety of strategies: count by 1s; count by 5s; add 5s; double 5, and then add 5. Some children might draw pictures or use tallies. (*See margin.*)

Use the Math Message problem to lead into a discussion about **equal groups.** Write *equal groups* on the board. Ask children to name things that come in equal groups and write their responses on the board. To support English language learners, draw pictures of any unfamiliar contexts. In the Math Message problem, the packs of gum are equal groups, because each pack has five sticks of gum in it. Six-packs of soft drinks are another familiar example of equal groups, because each six-pack has six cans or bottles in it. Ask children to name things that do not come in equal groups.
Sample answers: Families, classroom sizes

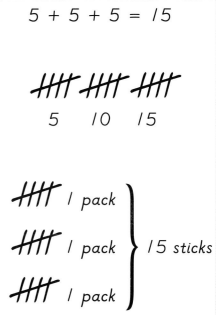

Some solution strategies for the Math Message problem

Tell children that they can find the total number of things in several equal groups by **multiplication.** Emphasize that in a multiplication situation, each group must have the same number of things.

Show children what a number model for the number story looks like: $3 \times 5 = 15$. Mention that 3×5 is read "3 **times** 5" or "3 **multiplied by** 5." To support English language learners, review the meaning of *times* in this context.

▶ Solving Number Stories about Equal Groups

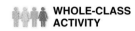

Divide the class into groups of 4 or 5. Display several boxes of an item, such as pennies, paper clips, dominoes, or crayons. Each box should contain the same number of the item selected.

Example: Display five boxes and put four pennies in each one. Tell the class that there are four pennies per box. Ask children to find the total number of pennies in all the boxes by using counters to act out a solution.

Suggested questions:

● How many groups of pennies are there? 5, because there are 5 boxes

● How many pennies are in each group? 4 Are they equal groups? Yes, because there is an equal number of pennies in each box.

● How many pennies are there in all? 20

Draw a diagram on the board that identifies the known and unknown quantities. Point out that the numbers in the diagram tell the quantities we know and that the question mark indicates the quantity we are trying to find. Once children have found the answer, erase the question mark, write in the answer 20, and circle it. (*See below.*)

boxes	pennies per box	pennies in all
5	4	⑳

$$5 \times 4 = 20$$

Make up other stories by changing the number of boxes and the number of items per box. Emphasize the language of equal groups: for example, three boxes with seven marbles *per* box and three boxes with seven crayons *in each* box.

Children should continue using counters, pictures, doodles, or anything else that might help them find the total number of items. As they share solution strategies, write number models on the board and read the models aloud. *For example:*

▷ $3 \times 7 = 21$ 3 times 7 is 21.

▷ $4 \times 6 = 24$ 6 multiplied by 4 equals 24.

Continue to fill in a diagram for each of the problems on the board. Write in the known quantities, and write a question mark for the unknown quantity. Ask children to help you complete the diagrams as you discuss problems, but do not expect children to come up with diagrams on their own. Repeated exposure to such diagrams will help children understand the meanings of multiplication and division.

Next, make up several number stories that do not require boxes of items as props. Fill in diagrams as before. As children share solutions, write number models on the board. *Suggestions:*

6 children have wet shoes, 2 shoes per child. How many wet shoes? 12

3 children took 4 crackers each. How many crackers? 12

4 packs of juice, 6 cans per pack. How many cans? 24

2 weeks, 7 days per week. How many days? 14

Adjusting the Activity

Pose problems using larger numbers. *For example:*

• 3 hours, 50 miles per hour. How many miles? 150

• 5 toys, 99 cents per toy. Total cost? $4.95

AUDITORY ◆ KINESTHETIC ◆ TACTILE ◆ VISUAL

▶ Solving Number Stories about Equal Groups

♙♙ PARTNER ACTIVITY

(*Math Journal 1*, p. 148; *My Reference Book,* pp. 112 and 113)

You may wish to read about number stories with equal groups in *My Reference Book,* pages 112 and 113 with your class. Partners act out and solve the multiplication stories on the journal page. Ask them to show how they solved the problems. Children might draw pictures or use counters.

Math Journal 1, p. 149 content

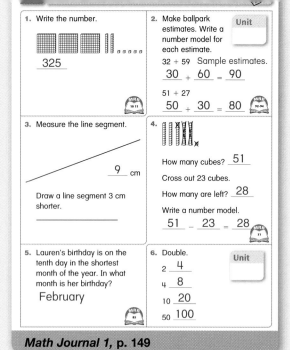

1. Write the number.

325

2. Make ballpark estimates. Write a number model for each estimate.

32 + 59 Sample estimates.

30 + 60 = 90

51 + 27

50 + 30 = 80

3. Measure the line segment.

9 cm

Draw a line segment 3 cm shorter.

_____

4.

How many cubes? 51

Cross out 23 cubes.

How many are left? 28

Write a number model.

51 − 23 = 28

5. Lauren's birthday is on the tenth day in the shortest month of the year. In what month is her birthday?

February

6. Double.

2   4
4   8
10 20
50 100

Math Journal 1, p. 149

▶ **Practicing with Addition/Subtraction Fact Triangles**

PARTNER ACTIVITY

Have children work with a partner to use the Fact Triangles as flash cards.

▶ **Math Boxes 6·7**

INDEPENDENT ACTIVITY

(*Math Journal 1*, p. 149)

Mixed Practice Math Boxes in this lesson are paired with Math Boxes in Lesson 6-9. The skill in Problem 6 previews Unit 7 content.

Writing/Reasoning Have children draw, write, or verbalize their answers to the following: *In Problem 5, if Lauren was born the same year as you, is she older or younger? What strategy did you use to solve the problem?* Sample answer: She is older than me; I was born in June, so she would turn 8 years old first. She is younger than me, I was born in January, so I would turn 8 years old first.

▶ **Home Link 6·7**

INDEPENDENT ACTIVITY

(*Math Masters*, p. 179)

Home Connection Children can use objects, draw pictures, count, or use any other helpful device to solve problems about equal groups.

Home Link Master

Name   Date   Time

HOME LINK 6·7 **How Many?**

Family Note In today's lesson, your child learned that multiplication is an operation used to find the total number of things in several equal groups. As you help your child solve the following problems, emphasize that each group has the same number of things. Your child can use objects, draw pictures, count, or use any other helpful devices to find the answers.
Please return this Home Link to school tomorrow.

Example:

How many apples in 4 packages?

HHT HHT HHT HHT

5 + 5 + 5 + 5 = 20

There are 20 apples in 4 packages.

1. △ △ △ △ △ △

How many sides on each triangle? 3 sides

How many sides in all? 18 sides

2.

How many wheels on each bike? 2 wheels

How many wheels in all? 8 wheels

3.

How many fingers for each person? 10 fingers

How many fingers in all? 80 fingers

Math Masters, p. 179

---

③ **Differentiation Options**

READINESS

INDEPENDENT ACTIVITY

▶ **Finding Totals for Equal Groups**

 5–15 Min

(*Math Masters*, p. 180)

To provide experience with solving equal-groups problems, have children use their calculators and repeated addition. Some children may want to program the calculator to skip count, while others may want to enter ⊞ repeatedly. When they have finished solving the problems, have them compare their answers. They should rework problems on which they don't agree. Have volunteers share their strategies for solving the problems. Consider having children record addition number sentences to show how they solved problems.

▶ Solving Equal-Groups Riddles

(*Math Masters*, p. 181)

 **SMALL-GROUP
ACTIVITY**

15–30 Min

To further explore the concept of equal groups, have children use *Math Masters,* page 181 to create and solve equal-groups riddles.

▶ Equal Groups in Literature

**SMALL-GROUP
ACTIVITY**

15–30 Min

 Read the following book to groups of children, or have children read the book themselves.

Each Orange Had Eight Slices: A Counting Book by Paul Giganti, Jr. (Greenwillow Books, 1992) *Summary:* Multiplication concepts are explored in the full-color book. In the first presentation, 3 red flowers are seen; each flower has 6 petals, and each petal has 2 black bugs. Questions are posed about the number of flowers, the number of petals, and the number of bugs. Have children answer the questions posed in the book.

▶ Building a Math Word Bank

(*Differentiation Handbook*)

**SMALL-GROUP
ACTIVITY**

5–15 Min

To provide language support for multiplication, have children use the Word Bank template found in the *Differentiation Handbook.* Ask children to write the term, *multiplication,* draw a picture representing the term, and write other related words. See the *Differentiation Handbook* for more information.

Name   Date   Time

LESSON 6·7 | **Finding Totals for Equal Groups**

You may use your calculator to help you solve the problems.
Answers vary.

1. How many people are in my group? _____

   How many hands do the people in my group have all together? _____

   How many fingers do the people in my group have all together? _____

2. How many tables are in the classroom? _____

   How many legs do the tables have? _____

3. One flower has 5 petals.

   How many petals do 6 flowers have? _____

4. Make up your own problem like the ones above. Draw a picture to help someone solve your problem.

   _____
   _____
   _____

Math Masters, p. 180

Name   Date   Time

LESSON 6·7 | **Equal-Groups Riddles**

What Number Am I?

1. If you put me into 7 equal groups with 3 in each group and 5 are left over, what number am I?
   26

   Draw a picture of what you did.
   Sample answer:

2. I am a number between 20 and 30. When you put me into 6 equal groups, there is an even number in each group and 1 is left over.

   What number am I? **25**

   Draw a picture of what you did.
   Sample answer:

3. Try writing your own equal-groups riddle.
   Answers vary.
   _____
   _____

Math Masters, p. 181

Multiplication-Array Number Stories

 Objectives To introduce everyday examples of rectangular arrays; and to provide experiences with solving multiplication problems using multiplication diagrams and array models.

1 Teaching the Lesson

materials

Key Activities
Children identify and describe familiar arrays, create and solve number stories about arrays using multiplication diagrams and array models, and complete number models to summarize solutions.

Key Concepts and Skills
• Solve multiplication number stories using rectangular arrays.
[Operations and Computation Goal 4]
• Create multiplication number stories using rectangular arrays.
[Operations and Computation Goal 4]
• Write a number model that represents a rectangular array.
[Patterns, Functions, and Algebra Goal 2]

Key Vocabulary
multiplication diagram • *x*-by-*y* array

✔ **Ongoing Assessment: Recognizing Student Achievement** Use journal page 151.
[Operations and Computation Goal 4]

☐ *Math Journal 1,* pp. 150 and 151
☐ Home Link 6·7
☐ Teaching Masters (*Math Masters,* p. 182; optional; and p. 183)
☐ Teaching Aid Master (*Math Masters,* p. 438)
☐ Transparency (*Math Masters,* p. 438; optional)
☐ 50 pennies or other counters per partnership (optional)
☐ calculator

***See* Advance Preparation**

2 Ongoing Learning & Practice

materials

Children practice fact extensions by playing the *Fact Extension Game.*

Children practice and maintain skills through Math Boxes and Home Link activities.

☐ *Math Journal 1,* p. 152
☐ *My Reference Book,* pp. 134 and 135
☐ Home Link Master (*Math Masters,* p. 183)

3 Differentiation Options

materials

READINESS
Children play *Simon Says* to practice making equal rows.

ENRICHMENT
Children create array number stories.

ELL SUPPORT
Children enter *array* in their Math Word Bank.

☐ Teaching Aid Master (*Math Masters,* p. 419)
☐ *Differentiation Handbook*
☐ 24 counters per child

Additional Information

Advance Preparation In Part 1, choose one of the following to display a multiplication diagram and associated array:

• Make an overhead transparency of *Math Masters,* page 438.

• Draw and erase multiplication diagrams, arrays, and number models on the board as needed. You may use semipermanent chalk for the multiplication diagram.

Technology
Assessment Management System
Journal page 151, Problems 1 and 2
See the **iTLG.**

Getting Started

Mental Math and Reflexes

Pose number stories about multiples of equal groups.

Suggestions:

○○○ Yuko has 2 boxes of crayons. There are 8 crayons in each box. How many crayons in all? 16

○○○ Arlie can walk about 3 miles per hour. About how many miles can he walk in 4 hours? About 12 miles

○○○ Each apple costs 25 cents. Jenna bought 5. How much did she pay? $1.25

Math Message

Egg carton: 2 rows of 6 eggs. Use your calculator to find how many eggs in all. 12 eggs

Home Link 6·7 Follow-Up

Review answers. Ask children to write number models for each problem and to read them aloud.
6 × 3 = 18, 2 × 4 = 8, 8 × 10 = 80

---

1 Teaching the Lesson

▶ **Math Message Follow-Up**   👪👪 **WHOLE-CLASS ACTIVITY**

(*Math Masters*, p. 438)

Have children share how they solved the problem on their calculator.

For example:

▷ I entered 6 ⊞ 6 on my calculator. (all calculators)

▷ I entered 6 ⊠ 2 ⊟. (all calculators)

▷ I entered 2 ⊞, ⊟, ⊟, ⊟, ⊟, ⊟, ⊟. (on the TI-108)

▷ I entered 2 ⊕ ⊕ ⊜, ⊜, ⊜, ⊜, ⊜. (on the Casio SL-450)

If children do not mention the 6 ⊠ 2 option, be sure to point it out and have children solve the Math Message by entering

6 ⊠ 2 ⊟.

Explain that this key is the standard multiplication key and that they will have an opportunity to use this key in later lessons.

Next, ask someone to draw the egg carton on the board. Remind children that an array is a rectangular arrangement of objects in rows and columns and point out that the eggs form an array. There are 2 rows of eggs with 6 eggs in each row, so there are 12 eggs in all.

Display a **multiplication diagram.** (*See Advance Preparation.*) Fill it in. Mark or draw a 2-by-6 array and write a number model as shown in the margin.

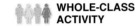

rows	*eggs* per row	*eggs* in all
2	6	? ⑫

Number model: _2_ × _6_ = _12_

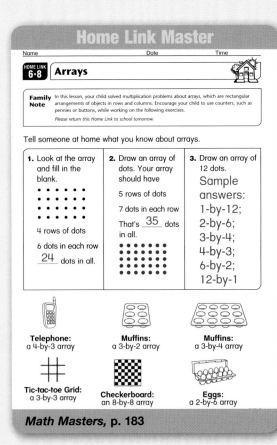
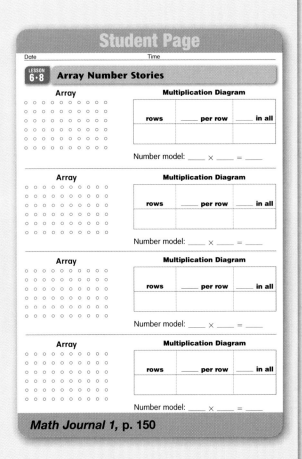

Math Journal 1, p. 150

▶ Identifying Familiar Arrays

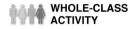 **WHOLE-CLASS ACTIVITY**

(*Math Masters*, p. 183)

Distribute Home Link 6-8. At the bottom it includes pictures of six familiar arrays. For each array, ask children how many rows there are and how many items there are in each row. Encourage them to talk about **x-by-y arrays.** *For example:*

▷ Telephone: 4 rows of keys, 3 keys in each row; a 4-by-3 array

▷ Checkerboard: 8 rows of squares, 8 squares per row; an 8-by-8 array

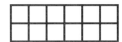

2-by-6 arrays: 2 rows, 6 per row

▶ Creating and Solving Number Stories about Arrays

 **WHOLE-CLASS ACTIVITY**

(*Math Journal 1*, p. 150; *Math Masters*, p. 182)

Display a multiplication diagram.

You or the children make up number stories involving arrays of objects. (See the number-story suggestions on page 421.) For each story, children work alone or with a partner to do the following:

Solving Number Stories

1. Fill in the headings on the multiplication diagram on the journal page. For example, if the story is about rows of keys, fill in "keys" on the first line of the multiplication diagram.

2. Fill in the known numbers and write a question mark for the number to be found.

3. Make an array with counters to model the story.

4. Show the array next to the multiplication diagram by coloring the circles, drawing a ring around the circles, or marking the circles with Xs.

5. Write the answer on the diagram and circle it.

6. Write a number model.

As children solve each problem, fill in the displayed diagram, mark or draw an array picture, and ask for the answer. Help children to summarize by writing a number model. A sample solution is shown below.

▷ Telephone: 4 rows of keys, 3 keys in each row. How many keys?

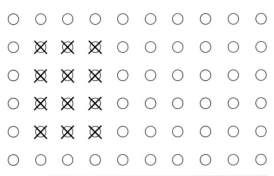

rows	_keys_ per row	_keys_ in all
4	3	? ⑫

Number model: 4 × 3 = 12

Number-story suggestions:

▷ Carton of soup cans: 4 rows of cans, 6 cans per row. How many cans? 24

▷ Floor tiles: 5 rows of tiles, 9 tiles in each row. How many tiles? 45

▷ Tic-tac-toe: 3 rows of squares, 3 squares per row. How many squares? 9

▷ Math Boxes: 3 rows of problems, 2 problems in each row. How many problems? 6

▷ Calendar: 3 weeks, 7 days in each week. How many days? 21

Summary: Arrays are examples of equal groups of objects. The total number of objects in an array can be found by using multiplication.

Adjusting the Activity

ELL

Pose problems like these:

Theater seats: 15 rows of seats, 10 seats per row. How many seats? 150

Cases of soda: 10 cases of soda, 24 cans per case. How many cans? 240

Imagine a 20-by-30 array of dots. How many dots in all? Use your calculator to solve. 600

A U D I T O R Y   ◆   K I N E S T H E T I C   ◆   T A C T I L E   ◆   V I S U A L

Adjusting the Activity

ELL

First, children make the arrays with counters. Then they record their arrays on the journal page.

A U D I T O R Y   ◆   K I N E S T H E T I C   ◆   T A C T I L E   ◆   V I S U A L

Teaching Master

Name _____ Date _____ Time _____

LESSON 6·8 **Array Number Stories**

Array	Multiplication Diagram

| rows ___ | per row ___ | in all ___ |

Number model: ___ × ___ = ___

Array	Multiplication Diagram

| rows ___ | per row ___ | in all ___ |

Number model: ___ × ___ = ___

Array	Multiplication Diagram

| rows ___ | per row ___ | in all ___ |

Number model: ___ × ___ = ___

Array	Multiplication Diagram

| rows ___ | per row ___ | in all ___ |

Number model: ___ × ___ = ___

Math Masters, p. 182

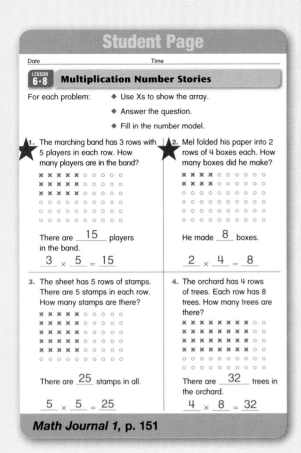
▶ Solving Array Multiplication Problems

PARTNER ACTIVITY

(*Math Journal 1*, p. 151)

Partners work together to draw arrays, solve problems, and write number models.

✓ Ongoing Assessment: Recognizing Student Achievement

Journal page 151 Problems ★ 1 and 2

Use **journal page 151, Problems 1 and 2** to assess children's ability to show an array. Children are making adequate progress if they can make the array and count the total. Some children may be able to complete the number model.

[Operations and Computation Goal 4]

---

(2) Ongoing Learning & Practice

▶ Playing the *Fact Extension Game*

PARTNER ACTIVITY

(*My Reference Book*, pp. 134 and 135)

Children practice fact extensions through the *Fact Extension Game* first introduced on page 292 in Lesson 4-8. Directions for the game can be found on pages 134 and 135 in *My Reference Book*.

▶ Math Boxes 6·8

INDEPENDENT ACTIVITY

(*Math Journal 1*, p. 152)

Mixed Practice Math Boxes in this lesson are linked with Math Boxes in Lessons 6-6 and 6-10. The skill in Problem 6 previews Unit 7 content.

▶ Home Link 6·8

INDEPENDENT ACTIVITY

(*Math Masters*, p. 183)

Home Connection Children describe arrays and solve array problems.

③ Differentiation Options

READINESS

▶ Playing Simon Says

SMALL-GROUP ACTIVITY

5–15 Min

To provide experience with making equal rows using a concrete model, have children play Simon Says where the directions are about modeling numbers in rows. Distribute 24 counters to each child. Give directions like the following:

- Simon says, "Put your counters in 4 equal rows."
- How many counters are in each row? 6 counters
- Simon says, "Put your counters in rows with 3 in each row."
- How many rows of counters are there? 8 rows

Be sure to discuss instances where children cannot make equal rows.

HOME LINK 6·8   **Arrays**

Family Note In this lesson, your child solved multiplication problems about arrays, which are rectangular arrangements of objects in rows and columns. Encourage your child to use counters, such as pennies or buttons, while working on the following exercises.

Please return this Home Link to school tomorrow.

Tell someone at home what you know about arrays.

1. Look at the array and fill in the blank.

4 rows of dots
6 dots in each row
__24__ dots in all.

2. Draw an array of dots. Your array should have

5 rows of dots
7 dots in each row
That's __35__ dots in all.

3. Draw an array of 12 dots.

Sample answers:
1-by-12;
2-by-6;
3-by-4;
4-by-3;
6-by-2;
12-by-1

Telephone: a 4-by-3 array
Muffins: a 3-by-2 array
Muffins: a 3-by-4 array
Tic-tac-toe Grid: a 3-by-3 array
Checkerboard: an 8-by-8 array
Eggs: a 2-by-6 array

Math Masters, p. 183

ENRICHMENT

▶ Creating Array Number Stories

INDEPENDENT ACTIVITY

15–30 Min

(*Math Masters*, p. 419)

To apply children's understanding of array multiplication, have them write multiplication-array number stories on *Math Masters*, page 419. Children write the number stories in words, draw an array for the number story, and write a number model to represent the story.

Example:

Farmer Hannah planted 3 rows of corn. Each row had 9 corn stalks in it. How many corn stalks were there in all?

$3 \times 9 = 27$ corn stalks

When children are finished writing their number stories, encourage them to trade with a partner and solve.

A Number Story

Unit

ELL SUPPORT

▶ Building a Math Word Bank

SMALL-GROUP ACTIVITY

5–15 Min

(*Differentiation Handbook*)

To provide language support for multiplication, have children use the Word Bank template found in the *Differentiation Handbook*. Ask children to write the term, *array*, draw a picture representing the term, and write other related words. See the *Differentiation Handbook* for more information.

Math Masters, p. 419

Multiplication with Arrays

 Objectives To introduce everyday examples of arrays; and to provide experiences with solving multiplication problems using multiplication diagrams and array models.

1 Teaching the Lesson

materials

Key Activities
Children draw and name *x*-by-*y* arrays and practice finding the total number of items in an array by playing *Array Bingo*.

Key Concepts and Skills
• Count objects in an array.
[Number and Numeration Goal 1]
• Create rectangular arrays using concrete objects.
[Operations and Computation Goal 4]

☐ *Math Journal 1*, pp. 154 and 155
☐ Home Link 6·8
☐ Game Master (*Math Masters*, p. 450)
☐ 2 six-sided dice, 1 twelve-sided die, or an egg-carton number generator per partnership or group
☐ per partnership or group: 1 twenty-sided die or 1 each of number cards 1–20 (from the Everything Math Deck, if available); optional
☐ 40 counters per partnership or group
☐ 40 overhead counters (optional)
☐ paper clip; envelope; scissors

See **Advance Preparation**

2 Ongoing Learning & Practice

materials

Children continue playing *Array Bingo*.

Children practice and maintain skills through Math Boxes and Home Link activities.

✓ **Ongoing Assessment: Recognizing Student Achievement** Use journal page 153.
[Measurement and Reference Frames Goal 1]

☐ *Math Journal 1*, pp. 153–155
☐ Home Link Masters (*Math Masters*, pp. 184 and 185)
☐ Game Master (*Math Masters*, p. 450)

3 Differentiation Options

materials

READINESS
Children build rectangular arrays with pattern blocks.

ENRICHMENT
Children build all possible rectangular arrays for a given number.

☐ Teaching Masters (*Math Masters*, pp. 186 and 187)
☐ Teaching Aid Master (*Math Masters*, p. 420)
☐ pattern blocks
☐ cm cubes
☐ dice
☐ Pattern-Block Template

Additional Information

Advance Preparation Before children play *Array Bingo* in Part 1, you might want to have them cut out the cards on *Math Masters,* page 450.

Technology

Assessment Management System
Math Boxes, Problem 3
See the **iTLG.**

Getting Started

Mental Math and Reflexes

Pose subtraction problems that feature multiples of 10.
Suggestions:

◉○○ 54 − 10 = ? 44   ◉◉○ 58 ? = 68 − 10   ◉◉◉ 179 − 60 = ? 119

    54 − 20 = ? 34   48 ? = 68 − 20   192 − 50 = ? 142

    54 − 30 = ? 24   18 ? = 68 − 50   124 − 30 = ? 94

Math Message

3 rows of window panes. 5 panes in each row. Draw the array. How many panes in all?

Home Link 6·8 Follow-Up

Call on volunteers to draw their arrays of 12 dots on the board. For each array ask: *How many rows? How many dots in each row?* Then write a number model under the array.

Continue until all possible arrays have been drawn. Be sure to include the 1-by-12 and 12-by-1 arrays.

---

① Teaching the Lesson

▶ Math Message Follow-Up

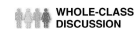 **WHOLE-CLASS DISCUSSION**

Briefly discuss the problem using the approach described in Lesson 6-8. Review the language of arrays: *3 rows of 5 panes each* or a *3-by-5 array of window panes.* Display and fill in a multiplication diagram and write a number model.

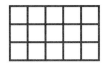

rows	panes per row	panes in all
3	5	? ⑮

$3 \times 5 = 15$

Solution for Math Message

If you think children need more practice with array multiplication, pose some array number stories like those on journal page 151.

▶ Making *x*-by-*y* Arrays

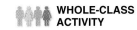 **WHOLE-CLASS ACTIVITY**

Ask children to make a 5-by-2 array with counters to represent an arrangement of desks. Ask how many desks there are in all. As you discuss the solution, write a number model: $5 \times 2 = 10$.

Repeat with other *x*-by-*y* array problems as needed. Be sure to include some 1-by-*y* and *x*-by-1 arrays. You might want to use overhead counters to model the arrays.

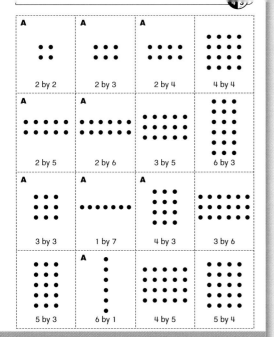

Math Masters, p. 450

(*Math Masters,* p. 450; *Math Journal 1,* pp. 154 and 155)

Read through the rules of *Array Bingo* with the class. Then show children *Math Masters,* page 450 and say that these are the cards that are used to play the game.

Be sure to explain that arranging the cards at random means to arrange them "in no pattern or order."

NOTE Some teachers suggest that children glue their *Array Bingo* cards in a random arrangement (3-by-3 or 4-by-4) on card stock paper. In this way, cards will not be lost. Instead of turning cards facedown while playing, children place counters on cards. The first player to cover a row, column, or diagonal with counters calls "Bingo!"

▶ Playing *Array Bingo*

(*Math Masters,* p. 450; *Math Journal 1,* pp. 154 and 155)

Divide the class into partnerships. After children have learned how to play the game, they might choose to play in small groups. The rules are on *Math Journal 1,* page 154.

Before the start of the game, each child should cut out the A cards from *Math Masters,* page 450.

After children finish playing, they should fasten their array cards with a paper clip and store them in an envelope in their tool kits so they can play the game again later.

NOTE To include the ideas of chance and the likelihood of events in this game, ask questions such as:

● How likely is it that you will get a 14 when you throw the dice? Why?

● How likely is it that you will get a number less than 9 when you throw the dice?

● How likely is it that you will get a number greater than or equal to 6?

Adjusting the Activity

Players cut out and use all 16 array cards on *Math Masters,* page 450. The rules for playing with all 16 cards are on *Math Journal 1,* page 155.

AUDITORY ◆ KINESTHETIC ◆ TACTILE ◆ VISUAL

2 Ongoing Learning & Practice

▶ Playing *Array Bingo*

(*Math Masters,* p. 450; *Math Journal 1,* pp. 154 and 155)

Children continue to practice finding the total number of items in an array by playing *Array Bingo.*

Student Page

Date   Time

6·9 *Array Bingo* **Directions**

Materials ☐ 2 six-sided dice, 1 twelve-sided die, or an egg-carton number generator

☐ 9 cards labeled "A" cut from *Math Masters,* p. 450 for each player

Players   2–5

Skill   Recognize an array for a given number.

Object of the Game Turn over a row, column, or diagonal of cards.

Directions

1. Each player arranges the 9 cards at random in a 3-by-3 array.

2. Players take turns. When it is your turn:

   Generate a number from 1 to 12, using the dice, die, or number generator. This number represents the total number of dots in an array.

   Look for the array card with that number of dots. Turn that card facedown.

3. The first player to have a row, column, or diagonal of facedown cards calls "Bingo!" and wins the game.

Math Journal 1, p. 154

▶ Math Boxes 6∙9

(*Math Journal 1*, p. 153)

Mixed Practice Math Boxes in this lesson are paired
with Math Boxes in Lesson 6-7. The skill in Problem 6
previews Unit 7 content.

**INDEPENDENT
ACTIVITY**

Ongoing Assessment:
Recognizing Student Achievement

**Math Boxes
Problem 3** ★

Use **Math Boxes, Problem 3** to assess children's progress with drawing and
measuring a 3-inch line segment. Children are making adequate progress if they
are able to draw a line about three inches long. Some children may be able to
complete the Math Box.

[Measurement and Reference Frames Goal 1]

▶ Home Link 6∙9

(*Math Masters*, pp. 184 and 185)

**INDEPENDENT
ACTIVITY**

Home Connection Children draw arrays, complete number
models, and answer questions about given arrays.

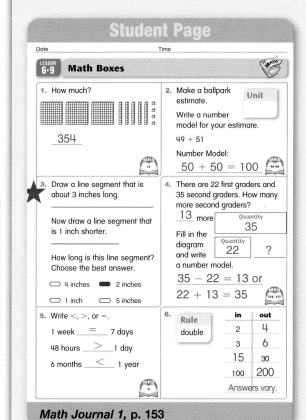

Math Journal 1, p. 153

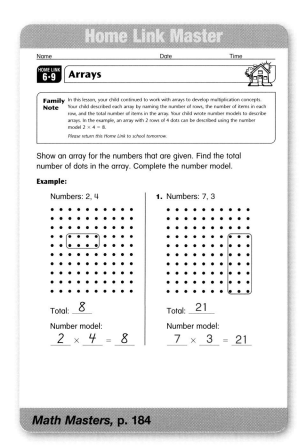

Math Masters, p. 184

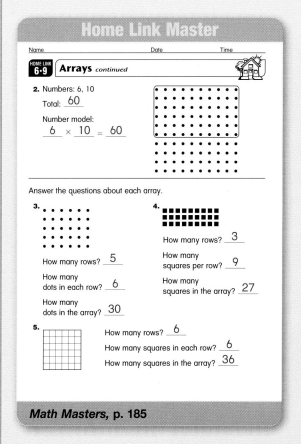

Math Masters, p. 185

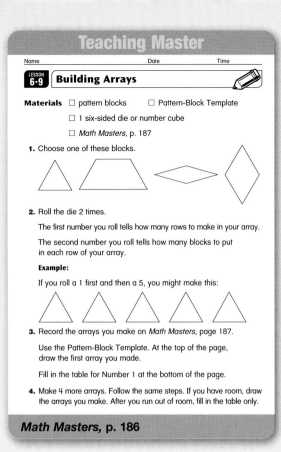

Teaching Master

Name   Date   Time

LESSON 6·9 | **Building Arrays**

Materials ☐ pattern blocks   ☐ Pattern-Block Template

☐ 1 six-sided die or number cube

☐ *Math Masters*, p. 187

1. Choose one of these blocks.

2. Roll the die 2 times.

The first number you roll tells how many rows to make in your array.

The second number you roll tells how many blocks to put in each row of your array.

Example:

If you roll a 1 first and then a 5, you might make this:

3. Record the arrays you make on *Math Masters*, page 187.

Use the Pattern-Block Template. At the top of the page, draw the first array you made.

Fill in the table for Number 1 at the bottom of the page.

4. Make 4 more arrays. Follow the same steps. If you have room, draw the arrays you make. After you run out of room, fill in the table only.

Math Masters, p. 186

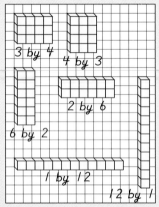

Example arrays on grid paper

Teaching Master

Name   Date   Time

LESSON 6·9 | **Building Arrays** *continued*

Use your Pattern-Block Template. Show one or more of your arrays.

Record the arrays you made.

	How many rows?	How many shapes in each row?	How many shapes in all?
1.			
2.			
3.			
4.			
5.			

Math Masters, p. 187

3 Differentiation Options

INDEPENDENT ACTIVITY

▶ Building Arrays

15–30 Min

(*Math Masters*, pp. 186 and 187)

To provide experience with connections between arrays and number models, have children build pattern block arrays and write matching number models. They determine the number of rows and the number of blocks in each row by rolling dice. They draw each array by using the Pattern-Block Template. Then children record the number of rows, the number of shapes in each row, and the total number of shapes in the array. Ask children to describe their arrays. For example, "My array has 3 rows;" "There are 4 counters in each row;" "My array has 4 columns;" and so on.

ENRICHMENT

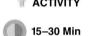
INDEPENDENT ACTIVITY

▶ Finding Arrays

15–30 Min

(*Math Masters*, p. 420)

To apply children's understanding of arrays, have them build all possible arrays for a given number. Assign each child a different number to represent. Assign numbers that have several factors; for example, 12, 18, 24, 30, or 36. Have children build and then record all possible arrays for their assigned number. They should label each array with the correct *x*-by-*y* statement. When children have found all of the arrays for their number, have them explain how they know they have found them all.

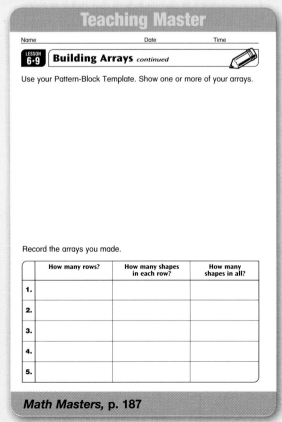

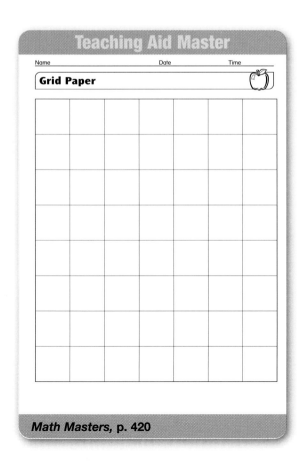

Teaching Aid Master

Name   Date   Time

Grid Paper

Math Masters, p. 420

6·10 Division Stories

 Objective To guide children as they explore situations that require equal sharing or making equal groups of things.

---

1 Teaching the Lesson

materials

Key Activities
Children use drawings or counters to find how a total number of items can be separated into an equal number of groups, or into groups of equal size. They also solve division number stories.

Key Concepts and Skills
• Explore the concept of equal sharing and equal grouping. [Operations and Computation Goal 4]
• Create rectangular arrays. [Operations and Computation Goal 4]
• Solve division number stories using concrete objects. [Operations and Computation Goal 4]

Key Vocabulary division • equal sharing • remainder • equal grouping

☑ **Ongoing Assessment: Recognizing Student Achievement** Use an Exit Slip.
[Operations and Computation Goal 4]

☐ *Math Journal 1*, p. 156
☐ Home Link 6·9
☐ Teaching Aid Master (*Math Masters*, p. 415)
☐ slate
☐ 30 pennies or counters for each group of 3 children
☐ calculator

---

2 Ongoing Learning & Practice

materials

Children practice 2-digit subtraction playing the *Number-Grid Difference Game*.

Children practice and maintain skills through Math Boxes and Home Link activities.

☐ *Math Journal 1*, p. 157
☐ *My Reference Book*, pp. 140 and 141
☐ Home Link Master (*Math Masters*, p. 188)
☐ Teaching Aid Master (*Math Masters*, p. 418)
☐ Game Master (*Math Masters*, p. 463)
☐ two pennies or counters
☐ calculator
☐ number cards 0–9 (4 of each; from the Everything Math Deck, if available)

---

3 Differentiation Options

materials

READINESS
Children solve repeated subtraction problems.

ENRICHMENT
Children explore the relationship between multiplication and division.

ELL SUPPORT
Children identify phrases associated with multiplication and division.

☐ Teaching Masters (*Math Masters*, pp. 189 and 190)
☐ counters
☐ calculator

Technology
Assessment Management System
Exit Slip
See the **iTLG.**

Getting Started

Write multiple-addend problems like the following on the board. Have children answer aloud or on their slates. Encourage them to look for combinations that will make the addition easier. *Suggestions:*

○○○ 89 ? = 72 + 9 + 8

○●○ 43 + 7 + 15 = ? 65

○○● 90 ? = 4 + 25 + 36 + 25

○○○ 11 + 4 + 7 = ? 22; There isn't a particularly easy way to add these numbers.

Math Message

How would you use your calculator to solve this problem?

3 children share 12 pennies equally. How many pennies does each child get?

Home Link 6·9 Follow-Up

Review answers as necessary.

Before children turn in Home Link 6-9, consider asking them to respond to one of the following on the back of the Home Link:

- I think arrays are...
- Arrays are easy if...
- When solving array problems, I still don't understand...

1 Teaching the Lesson

▶ **Math Message Follow-Up**    SMALL-GROUP ACTIVITY

Have children share how they solved the problem on their calculator.

If children do not mention the 12 ÷ 3 option, be sure to point it out and have children solve the Math Message by entering 12 ÷ 3 =. Explain that this key is the standard division key and that they will have an opportunity to use this key in later lessons. To support English language learners, write *12 divided by 3 = 4* on the board. Then write *12 ÷ 3 = 4* under it. Also, write the word **division** on the board.

Next, divide the class into groups of 3. Start by having children act out the Math Message problem with pennies or other counters. As children share their solution strategies, draw a picture on the board to illustrate the problem.

Repeat the activity using 10 pennies. Elicit that when pennies are shared equally, it is not always possible to share all of them. Some pennies may be left over. Ask the following questions and write them on the board:

- If 10 pennies are shared equally by 2 people, will any pennies be left over? No; each person will get 5 pennies.

- What if 10 pennies are shared equally by 4 people? Each person will get 2 pennies, with 2 pennies left over.

- What if 10 pennies are shared equally by 5 people? Each person will get 2 pennies, with none left over.

Ask children to make up other **equal-sharing** stories for one another to solve. Be sure they vary the numbers of pennies and children from story to story. They should act out the stories with pennies. Ask volunteers to share some of their stories.

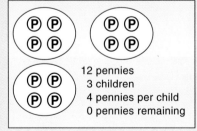

12 pennies
3 children
4 pennies per child
0 pennies remaining

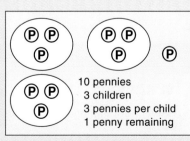

10 pennies
3 children
3 pennies per child
1 penny remaining

Say that the operation called division can be used to solve equal-sharing problems. The number of things that are left over or remaining is called the **remainder.** Use these terms frequently, but do not expect children to use them.

▶ Modeling Equal-Sharing Number Stories

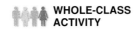 **WHOLE-CLASS ACTIVITY**

Pose the following problem:

- 5 children share 12 books equally. How many books does each child get? 2 How many books are remaining? 2

Ask children to solve the problem. Children can illustrate the story with a drawing or act it out with counters.

Discuss their methods and answers, and ensure that both strategies—drawings and counters—are presented. (See the sample solutions in the margin.)

Repeat this procedure with a few more division stories about equal sharing. *For example:*

- 18 chairs in 3 equal rows. How many chairs in each row? 6 with none left over

- 4 friends share 14 marbles equally. How many marbles does each friend get? 3 How many marbles are remaining? 2

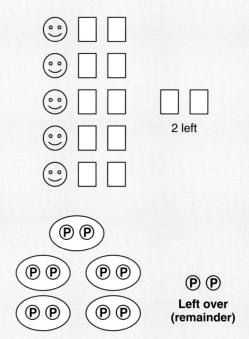

▶ Modeling Equal-Grouping Number Stories

 **WHOLE-CLASS ACTIVITY**

Some division number stories involve making equal groups of things. It is not important that children distinguish these kinds of stories from equal-sharing stories, because they can solve either of them using pictures or counters.

NOTE Children have participated in several informal activities to explore the meanings of division.

For example, in Lesson 5-1, children worked with equal-grouping situations by sharing eggs equally among nests. In Lesson 6-6, children worked with equal-sharing situations by determining how many children get *n* things.

Work together with children to solve an **equal-grouping** story. Then have them try several on their own. *For Example:*

▷ There are 13 cans of soda. How many six-packs is that? Two six-packs, with 1 can remaining

Begin by drawing a picture of a single six-pack or by putting down six counters to represent a single six-pack. Continue making additional six-packs until the 13 cans are accounted for.

Other possible story ideas:

▷ A building has 30 windows. There are 6 windows on each floor. How many floors does the building have? 5 floors

NOTE Think about equal groupings as How many groups? and equal sharing as How many in each group?

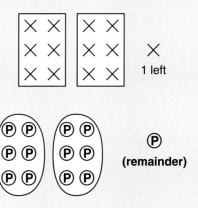

Student Page

Date _____ Time _____

LESSON 6·10 Division Problems

Use counters or simple drawings to find the answers. Fill in the blanks.

1. 16 cents shared equally

by 2 people
__8__ ¢ per person
__0__ ¢ remaining

by 3 people
__5__ ¢ per person
__1__ ¢ remaining

by 4 people
__4__ ¢ per person
__0__ ¢ remaining

by 5 people
__3__ ¢ per person
__1__ ¢ remaining

2. 25 cents shared equally

by 3 people
__8__ ¢ per person
__1__ ¢ remaining

by 4 people
__6__ ¢ per person
__1__ ¢ remaining

by 5 people
__5__ ¢ per person
__0__ ¢ remaining

by 6 people
__4__ ¢ per person
__1__ ¢ remaining

3. 16 crayons, 6 crayons per box

How many boxes? __2__   How many crayons remaining? __4__

4. 24 eggs, 6 eggs in each cake

How many cakes? __4__   How many eggs remaining? __0__

Math Journal 1, p. 156

Links to the Future

The equal-grouping and equal sharing activities in this lesson are an early exposure to division concepts. These concepts will be revisited in third grade. Using and explaining strategies to divide a multidigit whole number by a 1-digit whole number is a Grade 4 Goal.

Student Page

Date _____ Time _____

LESSON 6·10 Math Boxes

1. Use the digits 3, 1, and 5.

Write the smallest possible number.
135

Write the largest possible number.
531

2. Do these objects have at least one line of symmetry?

Yes or No?

yes   no

3. 18 cans of juice are shared by 5 people. Draw a picture.

__3__ cans per person

__3__ cans left over

4. 4 rows of 4 chairs. How many chairs in all? __16__ chairs

Draw an array to solve. Fill in the multiplication diagram.

rows	chairs per row	chairs in all
4	4	16

5. Find the differences.

32°F and 53°F __21__

37°C and 19°C __18__

75°F and 93°F __18__

6. Which figure does not belong? Choose the best answer.

- ⬡ circle with diagonal lines
- ⬤ empty circle
- ⬡ circle with vertical lines
- ⬡ circle with horizontal lines

Math Journal 1, p. 157

▷ 24 children want to play ball. How many teams can you make with 5 children on each team? 4 teams, with 4 children remaining and not on a team

Summary: The operation called division can be used to solve equal-sharing and equal-grouping problems. The number of things left over is called the remainder.

▶ Solving Division Number Stories

 PARTNER ACTIVITY

(*Math Journal 1*, p. 156)

Partners model each story with drawings or counters. Problems 1 and 2 are equal-sharing problems. Problems 3 and 4 are equal-grouping problems.

✓ Ongoing Assessment: Recognizing Student Achievement

Exit Slip

Portfolio Ideas — Use an **Exit Slip** to assess children's understanding of the equal-sharing concept. Have children show their work for solving the following equal-sharing problem: *14 candies shared by 2 people.* Children are making adequate progress if they use counters and drawings to solve the problem. Some children may be able to write a number model to show their work.

[Operations and Computation Goal 4]

② Ongoing Learning & Practice

▶ Playing the *Number-Grid Difference Game*

 PARTNER ACTIVITY

(*Math Masters,* pp. 418 and 463; *My Reference Book,* pp. 140 and 141)

Children practice finding differences on the number grid by playing the *Number-Grid Difference Game.* For detailed instructions, see Lesson 6-5 and *My Reference Book,* pages 140 and 141.

▶ Math Boxes 6·10

INDEPENDENT ACTIVITY

(*Math Journal 1*, p. 157)

Mixed Practice Math Boxes in this lesson are linked with Math Boxes in Lessons 6-6 and 6-8. The skill in Problem 6 previews Unit 7 content.

▶ Home Link 6·10

INDEPENDENT ACTIVITY

(*Math Masters,* p. 188)

Home Connection Using a handful of items, children solve equal-sharing problems by acting them out.

3 Differentiation Options

READINESS

▶ Sharing Cookies Equally

(*Math Masters*, p. 189)

SMALL-GROUP ACTIVITY

5–15 Min

To explore division in the context of repeated subtraction, have children solve the problems on *Math Masters*, page 189 and share their solution strategies. Ask if anyone can think of a way to use the calculator to solve the problems. Ask: *What if she had baked 100 cookies?* Sample answers: Subtract 3 over and over and keep track of how many times you subtracted. Count backwards by 3s, and keep track of how many times you pressed the [ ] button on the calculator.

ENRICHMENT

▶ Using a Multiplication Diagram for Division

(*Math Masters*, p. 190)

SMALL-GROUP ACTIVITY

5–15 Min

To further explore the relationship between multiplication and division, have children complete multiplication diagrams for the problems they solved on journal page 156. You may want to have them write a multiplication number sentence using a ? for the missing number.

ELL SUPPORT

▶ Writing Multiplication and Division Phrases

SMALL-GROUP ACTIVITY

5–15 Min

To provide language support for understanding multiplication and division phrases, have children draw and label a table with three columns on chart paper as shown below. Ask children to identify words or phrases associated with multiplication and division. Write their responses in the table.

Multiplication	Both Multiplication and Division	Division
Addition	Equal Groups	Subtraction
Packages of objects	Arrays	Share
Multiples	Fact Families	How many groups are there?
Skip Counting	Fact Triangles	How many in each group?
All Together		Remaining

Name   Date   Time

HOME LINK 6·10 Division

Family Note In this lesson, your child worked on the concept of division by putting objects into equal groups and sharing objects equally among several people. Objects that are left over are called the *remainder*. If 9 books are shared equally among 4 people, each person gets 2 books, and the 1 book that is left over is the remainder.

Watch as your child divides things equally among family members. Try to use groups of objects that can be divided with no remainder as well as groups that have remainders.

Please return this Home Link to school tomorrow.

1. Have someone at home give you a group or handful of small items, such as raisins, buttons, or popcorn. Show how you can divide the items equally among your family members. Are any items left over?  Answers vary.

   Make a record of what you did. Be ready to tell about it in class.

   I shared _____ (how many?) items equally among _____ people.

   Each person got _____. There were _____ left over.

2. Do this again with some other kind of item. Answers vary.

   I shared _____ items equally among _____ people.

   Each person got _____. There were _____ left over.

3. 19 cents shared equally

by 2 people	by 3 people	by 4 people
9 ¢ per person	**6** ¢ per person	**4** ¢ per person
1 ¢ remaining	**1** ¢ remaining	**3** ¢ remaining

Math Masters, p. 188

---

rows	_____ per row	_____ in all
?	2	16

$$? \times 2 = 16$$

On *Math Masters*, page 190, children use a ? to indicate unknown numbers in the multiplication diagram.

Name   Date   Time

LESSON 6·10 Sharing Cookies Equally

Use counters to help you solve the problems.

1. Ruth's grandma had just baked a fresh tray of 12 cookies.

   When Ruth came into the kitchen, her grandma gave her 3 warm cookies.

   Write a number model to show how many cookies were still on the tray. Sample answer: $12 - 3 = 9$

   When Ruth's sister came into the kitchen, Grandma gave her 3 cookies.

   Write a number model to show how many cookies were still on the tray. Sample answer: $9 - 3 = 6$

   How many more people can Grandma give cookies to if she gives each person three cookies?

   Show your work. 2 people

2. The next time grandma baked cookies, she used a larger tray. She made 15 cookies.

   How many people can have cookies this time if everyone gets 3?

   Show your work. 5 people

Math Masters, p. 189

Progress Check 6

 Objective To assess children's progress on mathematical content through the end of Unit 6.

1 Assessing Progress   materials

Progress Check 6 is a cumulative assessment of concepts and skills taught in Unit 6 and in previous units.

See the Appendix for a complete list of Grade 2 Goals.

☐ Home Link 6·10

☐ Assessment Masters (*Assessment Handbook,* pp. 178–181 and 223–226)

☐ slate

☐ counters

CONTENT ASSESSED	LESSON(S)	ASSESSMENT ITEMS			
		SELF	ORAL/SLATE	WRITTEN PART A	WRITTEN PART B
Use manipulatives, mental arithmetic, paper and pencil algorithms, and calculators to solve 2-digit addition and subtraction problems. [Operations and Computation Goal 2]	6·1–6·6, 6·8–6·10	6	3–6		8–10
Make reasonable estimates. [Operations and Computation Goal 3]	6·1, 6·4, 6·6 6·7, 6·9	2			5
Use arrays to model multiplication; identify and describe parts-and-total and comparison situations. [Operations and Computation Goal 4]	6·1–6·10	4	1, 2	2	6, 7
Tell and show time. [Measurement and Reference Frames Goal 6]	6·2, 6·4	1		1	
Extend, describe, and create numeric patterns; describe rules for patterns and use them to solve problems. Complete the "What's My Rule?" table. [Patterns, Functions, and Algebra Goal 1]	6·4, 6·9	3		3	
Use the $<$, $>$, and $=$ symbols. [Patterns, Functions, and Algebra Goal 2]	6·2, 6·4, 6·9	5		4	

2 Building Background for Unit 7   materials

Math Boxes 6·11 previews and practices skills for Unit 7.

The **Unit 6 Family Letter** introduces families to Unit 7 topics and terms.

☐ *Math Journal 1,* p. 158

☐ Home Link Masters (*Math Masters,* pp. 191–194)

Additional Information

See Assessment Handbook, pages 92–99 for additional assessment information. For assessment checklists, see pages 256–259.

Technology

Assessment Management System
Progress Check 6
See the **iTLG.**

Getting Started

Math Message •
Self Assessment

Complete the Self Assessment (Assessment Handbook, page 178).

Home Link 6·10 Follow-Up

Have children tell what they shared and how they divided the items among family members. Review answers for Problem 3.

---

1 Assessing Progress

▶ Math Message Follow-Up

INDEPENDENT ACTIVITY

(Self Assessment, *Assessment Handbook*, p. 178)

The Self Assessment offers children the opportunity to reflect upon their progress.

▶ Oral and Slate Assessment

WHOLE-CLASS ACTIVITY

Problems 3 through 6 provide summative information and can be used for grading purposes. Problems 1 and 2 provide formative information that can be useful in planning future instruction.

Oral Assessment

1. 3 shelves with books, 5 books per shelf. How many books? 15 books

2. 4 packages of pencils, 3 pencils in each package. How many pencils? 12 pencils

Slate Assessment

3. $40 + 30 = ?$ 70

4. $50 + 9 = ?$ 59

5. $80 - 20 = ?$ 60

6. $47 - 7 = ?$ 40

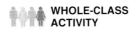

Assessment Master

Name		Date		Time

LESSON 6·11 **Self Assessment** Progress Check 6

Check one box for each skill.

Skills	I can do this by myself. I can explain how to do this.	I can do this by myself.	I can do this with help.
1. Tell time.			
2. Make a ballpark estimate.			
3. Solve "What's My Rule?" problems.			
4. Solve number stories.			
5. Compare numbers.			
6. Solve subtraction problems.			

Assessment Handbook, p. 178

Assessment Master

Name   Date   Time

LESSON 6·11 Written Assessment   Progress Check 6

Part A

1. Write the time.

7 : 15

2. Fish K weighs 35 pounds. Fish G weighs 10 pounds. How much do they weigh together?

45 pounds

Total
45

Part	Part
35	10

3. Solve.

in	out
0	6
4	10
14	20
6	12

Rule +6

4. Write <, > or =.

64 > 46

210 > 201

437 < 447

Part B

5. Make ballpark estimates. Write a number model for each estimate. Sample answers

42 + 39
40 + 40 = 80

31 + 27
30 + 30 = 60

Assessment Handbook, p. 179

▶ Written Assessment

(*Assessment Handbook*, pp. 179 and 180)

 INDEPENDENT ACTIVITY

Part A   Recognizing Student Achievement

Problems 1 through 4 provide summative information and may be used for grading purposes.

Problem(s)	Description
1	Write the time.
2	Solve a parts-and-total situation.
3	Complete the "What's My Rule?" table.
4	Use the >, <, and = symbols.

Part B   Informing Instruction

Problems 5 through 10 provide formative information that can be used in planning future instruction.

Problem(s)	Description
5	Make ballpark estimates.
6	Use arrays to model multiplication.
7	Solve a comparison situation.
8–10	Solve 2-digit subtraction problems.

Assessment Master

Name   Date   Time

LESSON 6·11 Written Assessment *continued*

6. Draw an array with 3 rows and 5 dots in each row.

• • • • •
• • • • •
• • • • •

How many dots in all? 15

Number model: Sample answer:
3 × 5 = 15

7. Fish J weighs 24 pounds. Fish H weighs 14 pounds. How much more does Fish J weigh?

10 pounds more

Quantity
24

Quantity	
14	10
	Difference

8.	78	9.	64	10.	83
	− 52		− 29		− 59
	26		35		24

Assessment Handbook, p. 180

Assessment Master

Name   Date   Time

LESSON 6·11 Open Response   Progress Check 6

Counting Cookies

There are a total of 52 cookies on 3 plates in my kitchen.
When I take away 14 cookies from the first plate, there are still 7 cookies left on the first plate.
There are 12 cookies on the second plate.
Write your own problem using the cookie information.

Solve your problem. Use counters or draw pictures.
Show your work and explain how you solved your problem.

Assessment Handbook, p. 181

▶ Open Response

(*Assessment Handbook*, pp. 95–99 and 181)

INDEPENDENT
ACTIVITY

Counting Cookies

The open response item requires children to apply skills and concepts from Unit 6 to solve a multistep problem. See the *Assessment Handbook*, pages 95–99 for rubrics and children's work samples for this problem.

▶ Midyear Assessment

INDEPENDENT
ACTIVITY

(*Assessment Handbook*, pp. 100, 101, and 223–226)

The Midyear Assessment (*Assessment Handbook*, pages 223–226) provides an additional assessment opportunity that you may use as part of your balanced assessment plan. This assessment covers some of the important concepts and skills presented in *Second Grade Everyday Mathematics*. It should be used to complement the ongoing and periodic assessments that appear within the lessons and at the end of the units. Please see pages 100 and 101 in the *Assessment Handbook* for further information.

---

② Building Background for Grade 7

▶ Math Boxes 6•11

INDEPENDENT
ACTIVITY

(*Math Journal 1*, p. 158)

Mixed Practice This Math Boxes page previews Unit 7 content.

▶ Home Link 6•11: Unit 7 Family Letter

INDEPENDENT
ACTIVITY

(*Math Masters*, pp. 191–194)

Home Connection The Unit 7 Family Letter provides parents and guardians with information and activities related to Unit 6 topics.

Student Page

Date   Time

LESSON 6•11 Math Boxes

1. Find the rule. Complete the table.

   Rule: **halve**

in	out
10	5
16	8
20	10
40	20

2. How much did Kristle weigh when she was 7 years old?

   55 pounds

   Kristle's Weight Chart

3. Which number from this list occurs most often?

   9

   3, 13, 23, 9, 14, 9

4. Double.

   25¢ **50¢**
   50¢ **$1.00**
   15¢ **30¢**
   75¢ **$1.50**

5. Draw the shapes that come next.

   △ □ ○ ○ △

   □ ○ ○

6. Count back by 10s.

   220, 210, **200**, **190**,
   180, **170**, **160**,
   150, **140**, **130**,
   120, **110**, **100**

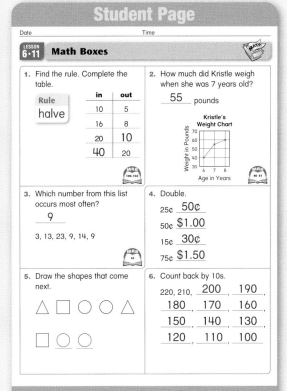

Math Journal 1, p. 158

Home Link Masters

Name   Date   Time

HOME LINK 6•11 Unit 7: Family Letter

Patterns and Rules

In Unit 7, children will concentrate on number patterns, computational skills, and the application of mathematics through the use of data. They will continue to use the 100-grid to support their numeration skills. Children will also explore the patterns of doubling and halving numbers, which will help prepare them for multiplication and division.

Computational work will be extended to several 2-digit numbers and to the subtraction of 1- and 2-digit numbers from multiples of 10.

Children will learn to find complements of tens; that is, they will answer such questions as "What must I add to 4 to get to 10? What must I add to 47 to get to 50?" or "How many tens are needed to get from 320 to 400?"

Children will also collect and work with real-life data about animals, adults, and themselves. For example, they will collect data by measuring the lengths of their standing long jumps and then find the median jump length for the class.

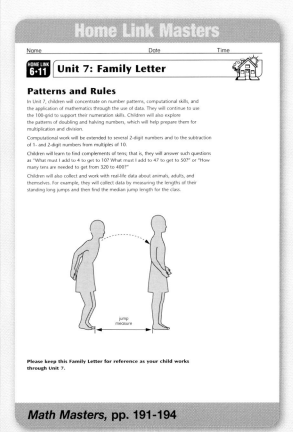

jump measure

Please keep this Family Letter for reference as your child works through Unit 7.

Math Masters, pp. 191-194

Appendices

Contents

Boxes, Boxes, Beautiful Boxes

 Objective To guide children as they name fractional parts, practice following directions, and use paper-folding techniques to make useful, open paper boxes.

1 Doing the Project

materials

Recommended Use During Unit 2 or Unit 7

Key Activities

Children fold a piece of paper into two, four, eight, and sixteen equal parts. Children then make various folds and "cuffs" to complete their paper box.

Key Concepts and Skills

• Model fractions as equal parts of a region.
  [Number and Numeration Goal 3]

• Create 2-dimensional symmetric shapes.
  [Geometry Goal 3]

☐ several sheets of rectangular and square pieces of colorful paper (magazine covers, catalog pages, wallpaper samples, construction paper, and so on) per child

☐ large rectangular piece of paper for demonstration

2 Extending the Project

materials

Children make boxes of various sizes and other origami figures.

Children practice skills through Home Link activities.

☐ *Fun with Easy Origami: 32 Projects and 24 Sheets of Origami Paper* by John Montroll

☐ *Complete Origami: An A–Z of Facts and Folds, with Step-by-Step Instructions for Over 100 Projects* by Eric Kenneway

***See* Advance Preparation**

Additional Information

Background Information See the discussion of Projects in the Management Guide section of the *Teacher's Reference Manual*.

Advance Preparation You may want to obtain the following books for the Extension Suggestions in Part 2:

▷ *Fun with Easy Origami: 32 Projects and 24 Sheets of Origami Paper* by John Montroll (Dover, 1993)

▷ *Complete Origami: An A–Z of Facts and Folds, with Step-by-Step Instructions for Over 100 Projects* by Eric Kenneway (St. Martin's, 1987)

Technology

Assessment Management System
Project 1
See the **iTLG.**

▶ Making Boxes

An *Everyday Mathematics* teacher, Mary Lewis, shared these directions for making an open paper box. She has used them successfully with her students. Model each step with a large rectangular piece of paper. After you complete a step, children do the step with their papers.

1. Fold the paper in half lengthwise. Make sure all corners are even. Unfold the paper.

   Ask: *How many parts are there?* two *Each part is what fraction of the whole paper?* Half, or one-half

2. Fold each long side so the outside edge comes exactly to the middle line, as shown below. Unfold the paper.

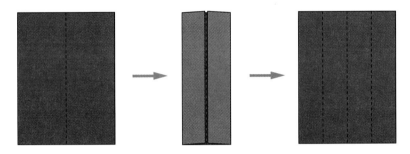

   Ask: *How many parts are there now?* four *Each part is what fraction of the whole paper?* one-fourth

3. Fold the paper in half across the width. Unfold it.

   Ask: *How many parts are there now?* eight *Each part is what fraction of the whole paper?* one-eighth

4. Fold the short edges of the paper exactly to the middle, width line, as shown below. Unfold the paper.

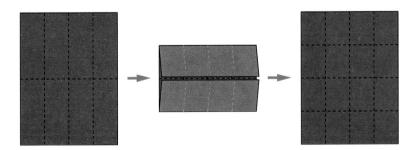

   Ask: *How many parts are there now?* sixteen *Each part is what fraction of the whole paper?* one-sixteenth

5. Fold the short edges back to the middle again. Crease the folds hard.

6. Fold a triangle at a corner. One side of the triangle should match up to the fold nearest the corner. Fold a triangle at the other corners. Crease the folds hard.

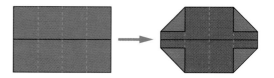

7. Fold back the long edges at the center, over the corner folds, to form two cuffs, as shown below. Crease hard.

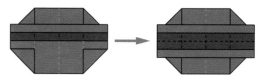

8. Gently open the box by pulling apart the center of the cuffs. Crease the four corners of the box again.

A completed box

② Extending the Project

▶ Extension Suggestions

1. Have children make a second box, slightly larger than the first, to use as a cover for the first box.

2. Have children make boxes from different-size rectangles or squares. They can use almost any kind of sturdy paper.

3. ⟳ Literature Link Obtain a book on origami, such as *Fun with Easy Origami: 32 Projects and 24 Sheets of Origami Paper* by John Montroll (Dover, 1993) or *Complete Origami: An A–Z of Facts and Folds, with Step-by-Step Instructions for Over 100 Projects* by Eric Kenneway (St. Martin's, 1987), and have children make some of the figures.

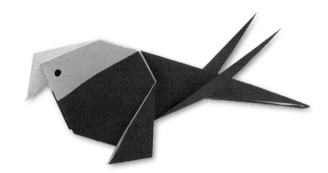

Origami bird

Origami butterfly

▶ Home Link Suggestions

Home Connection Children tell the box-making steps in order to a family member. Then they list the steps in order for making (or doing) something else with which they are familiar, such as making a sandwich, getting dressed, or using a computer program.

PROJECT 2

Weather Station

 Objective To guide children as they read thermometers using the Fahrenheit and Celsius scales and as they observe and collect data on outdoor weather conditions and temperatures for a week.

1 Doing the Project

materials

Recommended Use During Unit 2 or Unit 8

Key Activities

Children assemble thermometers and practice reading various temperatures. Children also collect weather data and record it on a weather observation chart.

Key Concepts and Skills

• Organize data on a chart.
  [Data and Chance Goal 1]

• Collect weather data from a chart.
  [Data and Chance Goal 1]

• Read temperatures on the Fahrenheit and Celsius scales.
  [Measurement and Reference Frames Goal 5]

☐ Project Masters (*Math Masters*, pp. 408 and 409)
☐ class outdoor thermometer
☐ scissors
☐ tape or glue
☐ red crayon or marker
☐ clear, self-adhesive vinyl sheets (optional)

2 Extending the Project

materials

Children find and read about weather in other parts of the country. Children read, watch, or listen to weather reports.

Children practice skills through Home Link activities.

☐ weather reports from different parts of the country
☐ encyclopedia
☐ literature selections
☐ barometer (optional)

***See* Advance Preparation**

Additional Information

Background Information See the discussion of Projects in the Management Guide section of the *Teacher's Reference Manual.*

Advance Preparation You may want to obtain the following books for the Extension Suggestions in Part 2:

▷ *Weather* by Tom Kierein (National Geographic Society, 1994)

▷ *The Magic School Bus Wet All Over: A Book about the Water Cycle* by Pat Relf (Scholastic, 1996)

▷ *Weather Forecasting* by Gail Gibbons (Aladdin, 1993)

▷ *Weather: Poems for All Seasons* by Lee Bennett Hopkins (HarperTrophy, 1995)

Technology

Assessment Management System
Project 2
See the **iTLG.**

① Doing the Project

▶ Assembling Paper Thermometers

(*Math Masters*, p. 408)

Science Link Guide children through the following steps to assemble their paper thermometers from *Math Masters*, page 408.

1. Color the bulb at the bottom of the thermometer red.

2. Color the strip marked "Color this red."

3. Cut out both strips and the thermometer.

4. Tape or glue the strips together on the space marked to make a single indicator strip.

   Optional: At this point, laminate the thermometers or cover them with clear, self-adhesive vinyl sheets to make them more durable.

5. Cut slits along the dashed lines at the top and bottom of the thermometer.

6. Insert the indicator strip (with the red part at the bottom) through the slits so it slides down the face of the thermometer, as shown in the margin below.

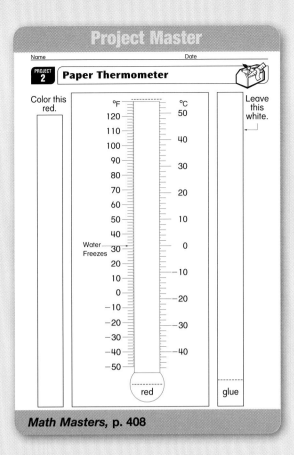

Math Masters, p. 408

▶ Reviewing Thermometers and Temperature Readings

Have available the class outdoor thermometer and the paper thermometers. The scales on the class outdoor thermometer and the paper thermometers may not be exactly alike. If they differ somewhat, focus on the paper thermometers.

Ask: *What unit are temperatures reported in?* degrees

Point out the two scales—°F and °C. Ask: *What are the names of the two scales? What do F and C stand for?* Fahrenheit and Celsius *What does the small raised circle mean?* degrees

Ask a volunteer to tell why many thermometers have two different scales. The Celsius scale is used in most of the world; the Fahrenheit and Celsius scales are used in the United States.

Ask such questions as the following:

- Are the two scales the same? No; on the Fahrenheit scale, water freezes at 32°. On the Celsius scale, water freezes at 0°.

- On each scale, there are three different-size marks. How many degrees are shown between a long mark and the next long mark? 10 degrees How many degrees are shown between one shortest mark and the next shortest mark? 2 degrees How many degrees are shown between a mark and the next mark? 1 degree

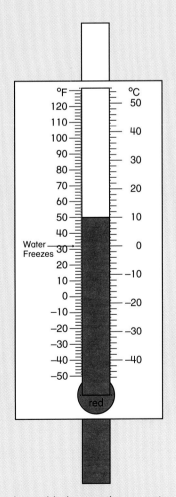

Assembled paper thermometer

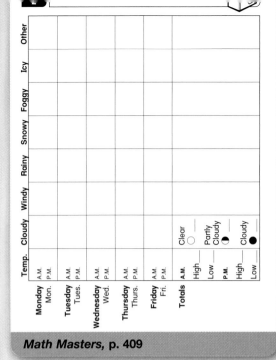

Math Masters, p. 409

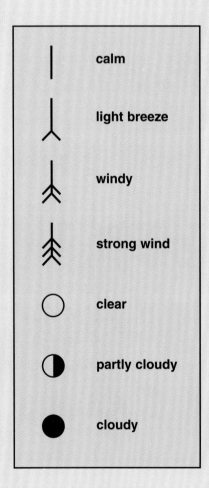

	calm
	light breeze
	windy
	strong wind
	clear
	partly cloudy
	cloudy

- Which scale is more likely to record negative temperatures? Celsius Why? Because all temperatures below freezing are negative Which scale is more likely to record 3-digit temperatures? Fahrenheit Why? Because 3-digit Fahrenheit temperatures begin a little below 38 degrees Celsius

Say several temperatures. Have children display these temperatures on their paper thermometers as you circulate and check. Include some negative temperatures. Compare pairs of temperatures: Which is warmer? Colder? Repeat this activity often over the next few days.

Give children two different temperatures in the same scale to compare. For example, ask: *How much warmer is 50 degrees Fahrenheit than 30 degrees Fahrenheit?* 20 degrees Fahrenheit *How much colder is 5 degrees Celsius than 15 degrees Celsius?* 10 degrees Celsius Encourage children to share their solution strategies; record them on the board. Repeat this activity often as a review, especially during the week of this project.

▶ Collecting Weather Data

(*Math Masters,* p. 409)

Examine *Math Masters,* page 409 with the class. Point out the following:

▷ The rows are labeled at the left with the five days of the school week.

▷ The columns are labeled at the top with various weather conditions.

▷ The large row at the bottom is used to record information or summaries for the week.

Discuss how to fill in the chart for the current day. Help the class reach a consensus about how to describe the day—sunny, cloudy, windy, or something else. Design and record symbols as needed, such as those for wind and cloud cover shown in the margin.

Have a volunteer read and report the current outside temperature. Note that the temperature column has spaces for A.M. and P.M. readings. Recording morning and afternoon temperatures will probably show temperature changes during the day and provide real data for temperature-difference problems.

Each day for a week, allow a few minutes for the children to fill in their weather observation chart for the day. Assign a pair of students to create a report for the class.

At the end of the week, children fill in the bottom row with the week's high and low morning and afternoon temperatures: the number of clear, partly cloudy, and cloudy days, and other comments or data.

② Extending the Project

▶ Extension Suggestions

1. Repeat this activity during different seasons of the year.

2. Find out the temperatures in other parts of the country and compare them with the class readings.

3. ◯ **Literature Link** Read about weather and weather forecasting in an encyclopedia or books such as *Weather* by Tom Kierein (National Geographic Society, 1994), *The Magic School Bus Wet All Over: A Book about the Water Cycle* by Pat Relf (Scholastic, 1996), or *Weather Forecasting* by Gail Gibbons (Aladdin, 1993). *Weather: Poems for All Seasons* by Lee Bennett Hopkins (HarperTrophy, 1995) is a collection of poems about weather.

4. Have children read, watch, or listen to weather reports to find out amounts of rain or snow, wind speeds, and so on, for the previous day. They then incorporate this information into their charts.

5. Have children read, watch, or listen to weather forecasts and compare them with the actual weather.

6. Introduce the barometer and its role in weather forecasting. Barometric pressure readings are part of many weather reports.

▶ Home Link Suggestions

Home Connection Children and family members take turns making up and solving temperature-comparison number stories. These stories can be generated while the family watches a televised weather report for your local area or for the entire country.

PROJECT 3

Chinese Calendar

 Objectives To provide experiences counting up and back by 12s using 4-digit numbers; and to guide children as they become familiar with the 12-year animal cycle of the Chinese calendar.

1 Doing the Project

materials

Recommended Use During Unit 6

Key Activities

Children explore the cycle of the Chinese calendar. Children also fill in their own Chinese calendar based on their assigned animals.

Key Concepts and Skills

• Count on and back by various numbers.
  [Number and Numeration Goal 1]

• Subtract years on a calendar.
  [Operations and Computation Goal 2]

• Add years on a calendar.
  [Operations and Computation Goal 2]

• Collect and organize data on a chart.
  [Data and Chance Goal 1]

☐ Project Masters (*Math Masters,* pp. 410 and 411)

☐ crayons or markers

☐ glue or tape (optional)

2 Extending the Project

materials

Children investigate Chinese New Year and read about calendars. Children read about calendars and timekeeping.

Children practice skills through Home Link activities.

☐ *The Greenwich Guide to Time and the Millennium* by Graham Dolan

***See** Advance Preparation*

Additional Information

Background Information See the discussion of Projects in the Management Guide section of the *Teacher's Reference Manual.*

Advance Preparation You may want to obtain the following book for the Extension Suggestions in Part 2:

▷ *The Greenwich Guide to Time and the Millennium* by Graham Dolan (Heinemann Library, 1999)

Technology

Assessment Management System
Project 3
See the **iTLG.**
See Web site on page 451.

① Doing the Project

▶ Discussing the Chinese Calendar's 12-Year Animal Cycle

(*Math Masters,* p. 410)

The ancient Chinese developed an accurate calendar based on the motion of the sun and moon. Beginning in the Zhou dynasty (1045 B.C.), the Chinese numbered years in a 12-year cycle. Each year was named for one of twelve animals (six wild and six domesticated), as shown below:

Number	Name	Animal
1	Zi	Rat
2	Chou	Ox
3	Yin	Tiger
4	Mao	Rabbit
5	Chen	Dragon
6	Si	Snake
7	Wu	Horse
8	Wei	Sheep
9	Shen	Monkey
10	You	Rooster
11	Xu	Dog
12	Hai	Pig

Source: E. G. Richards, *Mapping Time: The Calendar and Its History* (Oxford University, 1999)

The animals repeat in this order every twelve years. (According to legend, the Buddha called all the animals to him before he left Earth. Only twelve came. He named a year after each in the order in which they arrived.) In addition to the 12-year cycle, there is a 60-year cycle (five 12-year cycles).

The first circle on *Math Masters,* page 410 shows the animals for twelve years going backward from 2006 on the Western calendar; the second circle shows animals for twelve years going forward from 2006.

Suggestions for discussion based on *Math Masters,* page 410:

● On our calendar, which Chinese year is it? Use the current year; for example, 2007 The Chinese call it the year of the ____. For 2007, the pig

● What will be the next year of this animal? For the pig, 2019 Besides using the Project Master, is there another way to figure out the next year of this animal? Add 12 to the current year.

● What was the last year of this animal? For the pig, 1995 How can you figure this out mathematically? Subtract 12 from the current year.

Have children share their strategies for adding and subtracting 12 mentally. For example, count up or back by 1s; count up or back by

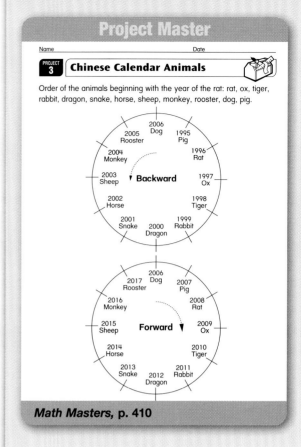

PROJECT 3 Chinese Calendar Animals

Order of the animals beginning with the year of the rat: rat, ox, tiger, rabbit, dragon, snake, horse, sheep, monkey, rooster, dog, pig.

Math Masters, **p. 410**

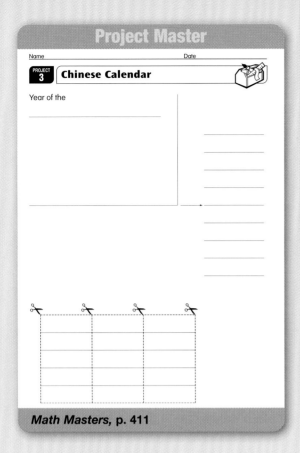
10s, and then add or subtract 2; count up or back by 6s; and so on. The years in the cycle can also be determined by counting up or back by 12s on the calculator.

Artist rendition of the Chinese Horoscope

Determine the birth years of different members of the class. Then have children find the animals that represent the years of those births. When will the years of those particular animals come again?

▶ Listing Past and Future Animal Years

(*Math Masters,* pp. 410 and 411)

If possible, assign two children to each of the animals represented in the cycle. Have them fill in the name of their animal and draw a picture of it in the blank space on *Math Masters,* page 411.

Children find their animal on one of the circles on *Math Masters,* page 410 and write the corresponding year on the line next to the arrow on *Math Masters,* page 411. Then they fill in the four years before (above) and four years after (below) their initial year by adding and subtracting 12 years from that line. That is, they will count by 12 forward and backward, using whichever method they choose. Encourage them to use scratch paper if they need to.

As you circulate, check on the mathematics and talk about the methods children are using to determine the years into the future and the past.

If children are interested in making a scroll by extending their counts in either direction, have them cut out the columns on *Math Masters,* page 411 and glue or tape them to the bottom and/or top of their initial column.

You can post the completed lists on a bulletin board so the entire animal cycle can be seen.

GONG XI FA CAI!

(Happy and Prosperous New Year)

② Extending the Project

▶ Extension Suggestions

1. The date of the Chinese New Year varies from late January to the middle of February—January 29 in 2006, February 18 in 2007, and so on. Children can investigate the Chinese New Year and how it is celebrated on the following Web site: http://dir.yahoo.com/Society_and_Culture/Cultures_and_ Groups/Cultures/Chinese/Holidays_and_Observances/Chinese_ New_Year/

2. Help children read about calendars and timekeeping in books such as *The Greenwich Guide to Time and the Millennium* by Graham Dolan (Heinemann Library, 1999).

▶ Home Link Suggestions

Home Connection Children take home copies of *Math Masters,* page 410. With the help of family members, they find the animal that represents their birth year. They then list the next three years represented by that particular animal.

PROJECT 4

Dates on Pennies

 Objectives To provide experience with writing 4-digit numbers in the form of notation for years (2005, 2006, and so on); and to guide children to tally, graph, and compare data.

1 Doing the Project

materials

Recommended Use During or after Unit 3

Key Activities

Children collect and tally pennies based on the year of the penny. Children also construct a bar graph showing the years in the class penny collection.

Key Concepts and Skills

- Write 4-digit numbers to indicate specific years.
  [Number and Numeration Goal 2]
- Collect and organize data.
  [Data and Chance Goal 1]
- Create a tally chart using organized data.
  [Data and Chance Goal 1]
- Use a graph to answer questions.
  [Data and Chance Goal 2]

☐ about 1,000 pennies

☐ small magnifying lenses (optional)

☐ Class Data Pad (optional)

2 Extending the Project

materials

Children view coin catalogs to price coins and read about money.

Children practice skills through Home Link activities.

☐ coin collector's catalog

☐ *Let's Find Out about Money* by Kathy Barabas

☐ *Money* by Joe Cribb

***See* Advance Preparation**

Additional Information

Background Information See the discussion of Projects in the Management Guide section of the *Teacher's Reference Manual*.

Advance Preparation You may want to obtain the following books for the Extension Suggestions in Part 2:

▷ *Let's Find Out about Money* by Kathy Barabas (Scholastic, 1997)

▷ *Money* by Joe Cribb (DK Publishing, 2005)

Technology

Assessment Management System
Project 4
See the **iTLG.**

1 Doing the Project

▶ Observing Dates on Pennies

Each child examines two or three pennies to find the years they were made (minted). Some dates have a D under the year, indicating that they were minted at the Denver Mint. Make sure most children can find the dates easily. Small magnifying lenses may help.

Have children call out some of their pennies' years as you record them on the board in a systematic way. Continue until you have a range of years. Use a tally mark to record each reoccurrence. Ask: *In which year were the oldest pennies minted? The newest pennies?*

▶ Tallying Dates for a Large (Diverse) Collection of Pennies

In roughly equal batches, distribute a collection of pennies among pairs of children. Have partners record the year and make a tally mark for each penny in their collection. They can use the method you modeled on the board or devise their own scheme.

After all or most of the pennies have been recorded, bring the class together and record on the board or Class Data Pad the total number for each year found. Compare the range of years and the various totals by asking questions about the data. *Suggestions:*

- What is the range of years?

- In which year were the fewest pennies minted? How many pennies were minted in that year? What is the difference between the fewest number of pennies minted and the most?

- Why are there fewer older pennies?

- Are there pennies older than class members? How much older?

- How much older is the oldest penny than the newest one?

▶ Graphing the Data

Work with children to construct a bar graph showing the years in the class penny collection. After the class starts building the graph, assign each partnership one or two years to add to the graph by using the information on the board or the Class Data

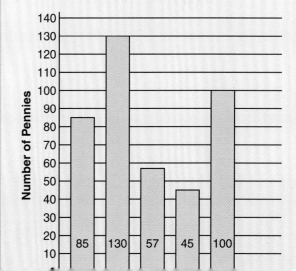

Class Penny Collection

Number of Pennies

140 130 120 110 100 90 80 70 60 50 40 30 20 10

| 85 | 130 | 57 | 45 | 100 |

② Extending the Project

▶ Extension Suggestions

1. Obtain a catalog of U.S. coins that features illustrations of pennies and other coins over the years and gives prices for them.

2. **Literature Link** Suggest that children read about money in books such as *Let's Find Out about Money* by Kathy Barabas (Scholastic, 1997) and *Money* by Joe Cribb (DK Publishing, 2005).

▶ Home Link Suggestions

Home Connection Children tally the dates found on pennies at home. They explain to family members how to compare the data represented by these pennies. Children may also tally the dates found on nickels, dimes, and quarters at home.

Snowflakes

Objective To guide children as they experiment with paper folding and creating paper snowflakes that represent six-sided water crystals.

1 Doing the Project

materials

Recommended Use During Unit 4, Unit 6, or Unit 8

Key Activities
Children fold and cut paper as marked to make various shapes of snowflakes.

Key Concepts and Skills
• Model fractions as equal parts.
  [Number and Numeration Goal 3]
• Create and complete 2-dimensional symmetric designs.
  [Geometry Goal 3]

☐ lightweight, white paper of various sizes
☐ scissors
See **Advance Preparation**

2 Extending the Project

materials

Children discuss the symmetry of their snowflakes. Children read stories about snow.

Children practice skills through Home Link activities.

☐ magnifying lens
☐ literature selections
See **Advance Preparation**

Additional Information

Background Information See the discussion of Projects in the Management Guide section of the *Teacher's Reference Manual*.

Advance Preparation If possible, ask at least two adults to help children with the initial paper folding; or, if your school has a program in which your class is paired with an older class for certain activities, this is a good activity to involve older children. It is helpful if helpers know the folding routine in advance.

Children use lightweight paper in this project because it is easy to fold and cut; $8\frac{1}{2}$" by 11" is a good size to begin with. The paper needs to be square. You could cut square pieces yourself, or you can have children cut square pieces as the first step. (See the activity Making Paper Snowflakes.)

You may want to obtain the following books for the Extension Suggestions in Part 2:

▷ *Snow Crystals* by W. A. Bentley and W. J. Humphreys (Dover, 1962)

▷ *Snowflake Bentley* by Jacqueline Briggs Martin (Houghton Mifflin, 1998)

▷ *Snow* by Uri Shulevitz (Farrar, Straus and Giroux, 1998)

▷ *The Snowy Day* by Ezra Jack Keats (Viking, 1996)

Technology
Assessment Management System
Project 5
See the **iTLG**.

① Doing the Project

▶ Talking about Snowflakes

Snowflakes are hexagonal (six-sided) crystals of water that form in clouds. Snowflakes come in many forms, from six-sided clumps to lacey, six-pointed stars. The type that forms depends on the temperature and the amount of moisture in the air. It was once thought that no two snowflakes are alike, but identical snowflakes have been found. However, these are rare. Like the paper snowflakes children will make, most real snowflakes are unique.

▶ Making Paper Snowflakes

Follow these directions or use other directions you are familiar with.

1. If the paper is not already square, make it square by first folding it and then cutting it.

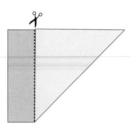

2. Fold a square sheet of paper in half along a diagonal to make a triangle. Place the fold at the bottom.

3. Fold the triangle into thirds. *Hint:* To fold into thirds, first find the center of the bottom edge. This will be the point of the triangular-shape folded paper. Put the tip of an index finger here while folding. Be careful to fold exactly into thirds. The edge of one side must match the fold on the other side.

4. Fold in half again. *Hint:* Fold back so an "ear" is on the outside top of the folded paper.

5. Cut off the "ears" along the straight edge on top. This makes each arm of the snowflake identical.

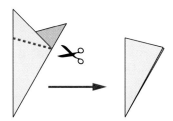

6. Draw a curve or jagged line to indicate the shape you would like the snowflake to be. Begin near the bottom point of the double-folded edge; end near the top of the single-folded edge. *Hint:* Do not draw too close to the bottom point, or the snowflake will fall apart when it is cut out.

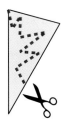

7. Cut along the curve or line drawn.

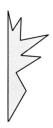

8. Carefully unfold the snowflake. The dark part of the snowflake in the picture is the part that was originally drawn.

Children cut out additional snowflakes as time permits. The beauty of making snowflakes is that it gets easier each time children do it. Encourage them to experiment with different shapes and to make small cutouts along the single fold or the spine of the points of the snowflake.

② Extending the Project

▶ Extension Suggestions

1. Discuss features of children's snowflakes. For example, each is *symmetric*—it can be folded in half so the two halves match. Ask: *In how many ways can a snowflake be folded so the two halves match?* 6 The six arms are *congruent*—they are all the same shape and size.

2. Children go outside to observe actual snowflakes with a magnifying lens, weather permitting.

3. 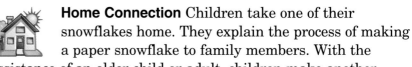 Science Link Read about snow in books such as *Snow Crystals* by W. A. Bentley and W. J. Humphreys (Dover, 1962), which contains more than 2,000 illustrations of snowflakes. W. A. Bentley, who devoted his life to studying snow, is the subject of the biography *Snowflake Bentley,* written for children by Jacqueline Briggs Martin (Houghton Mifflin, 1998). The book includes sidebars describing Bentley's experiments and techniques for photographing snowflakes.

4. Literature Link Read stories about snow, such as *Snow* by Uri Shulevitz (Farrar, Straus and Giroux, 1998). *The Snowy Day* by Ezra Jack Keats (Viking, 1996) is a beautiful, classic book for younger children.

▶ Home Link Suggestions

Home Connection Children take one of their snowflakes home. They explain the process of making a paper snowflake to family members. With the assistance of an older child or adult, children make another snowflake or a different item (such as a boat or a hat) out of paper.

Time Capsule

 Objective To guide children as they agree on, collect, and display information to be included in a time capsule, and as they make predictions about life four years from now.

1 Doing the Project

materials

Recommended Use During or after Unit 7; possibly at the end of the year

Key Activities

Children gather information about themselves and make predictions that are sealed in a time capsule. Children leave the time capsule with the principal to be opened in sixth grade (or another appropriate grade) when children are about to leave the school.

Key Concepts and Skills

• Use addition and subtraction to calculate elapsed time.
  [Operations and Computation Goal 2]

• Collect and organize data.
  [Data and Chance Goal 1]

☐ shoe box or other time capsule container

☐ calculator

See Advance Preparation

2 Extending the Project

materials

Children research and investigate time capsules.

Children practice skills through Home Link activities.

☐ none

Additional Information

Background Information See the discussion of Projects in the Management Guide section of the *Teacher's Reference Manual*.

Advance Preparation Arrange an appointment with the principal for delivery of the capsule to his or her care (preferably in front of the class).

Technology

Assessment Management System
Project 6
See the **iTLG**.
See Web sites on page 462.

1 Doing the Project

▶ Explaining the Purpose of the Time Capsule

Discuss the idea of a time capsule with the class. Explain that a time capsule is a container holding items that represent a group, such as the residents of a town, at a particular moment in history. The items might be handicrafts, commercial products, newspapers, books, photographs, audiotapes, videotapes, and so on. The time capsule is buried or otherwise preserved for the future. Time capsules are often placed in the cornerstones of new buildings, to be opened after a certain time or when the buildings are remodeled or torn down.

The object shown in the margin was sent as a time capsule on two Voyager space probes, which have left the solar system. It is a 12-inch gold-plated copper disk containing sounds and images selected to portray the diversity of life and culture on Earth. There are images, recorded sounds, musical selections from different cultures and eras, spoken greetings in fifty-five languages, and printed messages. The contents were chosen to represent civilization on Earth in a way that might be understood by a distant civilization.

Time capsule for the Voyager space probes

The idea of a second-grade time capsule is to have children seal information about themselves in a box, and instead of leaving it for a far distant age, they leave it with the principal of the school until they are in sixth grade. When they open the time capsule, they will find instructions to help them determine which things have changed about the class and how accurate (or inaccurate) some of their predictions were.

▶ Deciding upon the Contents of the Time Capsule

Have children suggest items to go into the time capsule. List their suggestions on the board. *For example:*

▷ a class photograph with each person identified

▷ median height and weight of the class

▷ surveys of favorite activities, sports teams, food, books, television shows, musical groups, school subjects, topics in mathematics, and so on

▷ the distance some of us can run in 10 seconds (Project 8); distance some of us can throw a ball

▷ a list of important current world, national, and local events

Have the class choose about six topics around which to gather data for the time capsule. Each child might write a brief description of herself or himself—likes, dislikes, height, weight, and so on—and seal it in an envelope to be put into the time capsule. Invite children to add pictures and recordings to the time capsule.

▶ Preparing Information for the Time Capsule

Divide the class into small groups. Assign one or more data-gathering tasks to each group. Within the groups, let children decide how they are going to collect and display the information assigned to them.

Bring the class together and have each group present its plan. Work with the class as a whole to fine-tune plans; children from other groups might have suggestions for improving or adding to some of the plans. Ask children for suggestions as to what to tell the future sixth-grade class (themselves) about comparing the data from second grade with the data from sixth grade.

Develop a schedule for carrying out each group's plans over the next few days. For example, if a survey of favorite foods is needed, the group takes a poll and carries out its plan for displaying that information. If predictions are made, these are written with space allowed for the future sixth graders to compare predictions to reality to see how accurate those predictions were.

Encourage children to look ahead four years and make predictions to include in the time capsule. *For example:*

- How many members of the current class will be in the same classroom or in the same school in sixth grade?

- About how much will class members have grown—that is, what will be the median number of inches grown or pounds gained?

- Will their favorite television shows still be on the air? Will their favorite musical groups still be together?

- What will computers and the Internet be like?

- Who will be president of the United States?

▶ Preparing the Time Capsule

After all the information has been gathered, each group takes a few minutes to share its data with the rest of the class. Then seal all the information and other items in a shoe box or other appropriate container. Be sure to label the time capsule with instructions for opening at the appropriate time. Deliver the time capsule to the principal.

▶ Asking Time-Capsule Questions

Ask the class questions such as the following: If the time capsule is opened the same day of the year in sixth grade ...

- How many years will have gone by since second grade?
- Will that day be a school day?
- How old will you be then?
- How many months are there until then? (Use a calculator to help.)
- Will there be a leap year between now and then?

② Extending the Project

▶ Extension Suggestions

1. Have children research time capsules at these Web sites:

   http://www.iuinfo.indiana.edu/HomePages/120498/text/cosmic.htm

   http://www.jpl.nasa.gov/news/features.cfm?feature=555

   http://www.oglethorpe.edu/about_us/crypt_of_civilization/most_wanted_time_capsules.asp

2. Suggest that children investigate time capsules that have been placed in cornerstones of buildings in your community.

▶ Home Link Suggestions

 Home Connection Children plan and create a time capsule with members of their family. They devise a plan, gather information, and prepare the time capsule. Encourage children to write a short paragraph describing their family time capsules.

Collections

 Objective To provide opportunities to describe a collection in terms of number, size, age, and other attributes.

1 Doing the Project

materials

Recommended Use During Unit 7 or Unit 11

Key Activities

Children prepare an information sheet about a collection of their own, someone in their family, or someone they know well. They bring a selection from the collection to display. If the collection is too fragile or valuable for classroom display, they represent it in some other way.

Key Concepts and Skills

• Collect and organize data.
  [Data and Chance Goal 1]

• Describe patterns found in a collection.
  [Patterns, Functions, and Algebra Goal 1]

☐ writing paper

See **Advance Preparation**

2 Extending the Project

materials

Children discuss, view, and read about collections of diverse things. Children go to a museum to review a collection.

Children practice skills through Home Link activities.

☐ *A Kid's Guide to the Smithsonian* by Ann Phillips Bay

See **Advance Preparation**

Additional Information

Background Information See the discussion of Projects in the Management Guide section of the *Teacher's Reference Manual.*

Advance Preparation You might want to check out the feasibility of this project in advance by surveying the class to find out whether children have collections of any particular objects or know someone who has.

Send a note home explaining the project. If possible, children bring in a collection or a selection from a collection; alternatively, they bring in a representation of the collection (photos, drawings, lists, catalog pictures, and so on).

You may want to obtain the following book for the Extension Suggestions in Part 2:

▷ *A Kid's Guide to the Smithsonian* by Ann Phillips Bay (Smithsonian Institution, 1996)

Technology

Assessment Management System
Project 7
See the **iTLG.**

1 Doing the Project

▶ Talking about Collections

Many children have collections of different types of toys, rocks, hats, tropical fish, seashells, stamps, books, sports cards, and so on. Encourage them to talk about their collections as you list the different kinds on the board. Some children may think they have no collections. Ask whether they have several of one kind of toy (such as cars, dolls, or stuffed animals). They may have collections and not realize it.

Children who have no collections can talk about a collection they know about, maybe a friend's or a family member's. Or they can work with a classroom partner who has a collection.

The start of a collection

▶ Gathering Data about the Collections

Discuss what kinds of data or information about collections might be of interest to other people. List responses on the board. *For example:*

▷ the size of the collection

▷ categories or organization within the collection, such as stamps by country, year, intended use, denomination

▷ the approximate length of time since the collection began

▷ the smallest or largest item in the collection

▷ the source(s) of items in the collection

▷ items most prized (and why)

▷ reasons the collection was begun

▶ Preparing Information Sheets

Using the list on the chalkboard, children decide which facts are appropriate for their collections. Then they prepare an information sheet to remind them of the data they have chosen to report on.

Children take the information sheets home to complete. You may want to send them as Home Links. (*See next page.*) Children bring the information sheets back to school in two or three days. They also bring to class a few representative items from the collections they described, or a representation of several items—photos, drawings, lists, videotapes, catalog pictures, and so on.

▶ Reporting on the Collections

Over the course of the next few days, allow time for children to report on and display selections from their collections.

② Extending the Project

▶ Extension Suggestions

1. Invite a parent, friend, or local expert (for example, a baseball card collector) to class to display and describe a collection.

2. Go on a field trip to a museum or art gallery featuring a particular collection.

3. Have children read about a collection of diverse things, from dinosaurs to Dorothy's red shoes to the Apollo 11 command module that returned from the moon, in *A Kid's Guide to the Smithsonian* by Ann Phillips Bay (Smithsonian Institution, 1996).

▶ Home Link Suggestions

 Home Connection Children complete their information sheets. They discuss with family members which items, if any, they will take to school. Children take photos, draw pictures, or make a list of items in their collections.

PROJECT 8

How Far Can I Run in 10 Seconds?

 Objective To guide children as they measure the distances they can run in 10 seconds.

1 Doing the Project

Recommended Use During Units 10, 11, or 12

Key Activities

Children mark how far they can run in 10 seconds. They measure the distance in feet and report the data. Children make a bar graph and find the range and median using their data.

Key Concepts and Skills

• Collect and organize running times data.
[Data and Chance Goal 1]

• Create a bar graph.
[Data and Chance Goal 1]

• Find the range and median of a set of data.
[Data and Chance Goal 2]

• Measure length in feet.
[Measurement and Reference Frames Goal 1]

materials

☐ Project Master (*Math Masters,* p. 412)

Per group of 3:

☐ string or yarn

☐ masking tape, chalk, colored blocks, or other marker

☐ stopwatch or watch with a second hand (optional)

☐ slip of paper or stick-on note

***See* Advance Preparation**

2 Extending the Project

Children make predictions about distances and compare results.

Children practice skills through Home Link activities.

materials

Per group of 3:

☐ string or yarn

☐ masking tape, chalk, colored blocks, or other marker

☐ stopwatch or watch with a second hand (optional)

Additional Information

Background Information See the discussion of Projects in the Management Guide section of the *Teacher's Reference Manual.*

Advance Preparation You may want to enlist the help of the physical education teacher in collecting the data.

Each group of three children will need a 10-foot length of string or yarn marked off at 1-foot intervals. You may want to have several children help you prepare these. In addition, children will need some way of timing 10-second intervals. Using a clock, a stopwatch, or a watch that shows seconds will give more accurate results than by counting aloud.

Technology

Assessment Management System
Project 8
See the **iTLG.**

1 Doing the Project

▶ Finding Out How Far Children Can Run in 10 Seconds

(*Math Masters*, p. 412)

Plan for the actual data collection to take place outside, on the playground or other large, open space.

Children will collect the data in groups of 3; they will take turns being "runner," "timer," and "spotter." Before you leave the classroom, explain the steps for collecting the data:

Data-Collecting Steps

1. The timer gives the runner the signal to start and begins timing.

2. The spotter follows the runner.

3. When 10 seconds are up, the timer says "Stop!" and drops a raised arm or gives some other prearranged signal.

4. The spotter marks the spot reached by the runner with masking tape, chalk, a colored block, or other marker.

5. The group cooperatively uses a 10-foot string to measure the distance covered.

6. The runner records the distance he or she ran in 10 seconds on a slip of paper or stick-on note.

Once the class gets to the running location, have each group mark a starting line with chalk, masking tape, or other marker. Be sure there is enough room between starting lines so that groups will not get in one another's way.

Before groups start running, have a volunteer demonstrate how to measure distances greater than 10 feet by laying a 10-foot length of string end-to-end.

Also demonstrate how to time the runners. If children count to time the runners, remind them to count aloud: 1,001; 1,002; 1,003 ....

If children record their distances on stick-on notes, collect the notes and make a bar graph of the data on the wall. (*See margin.*) Discuss the graph.

Have children find the range of 10-second distances, as well as a middle 10-second distance.

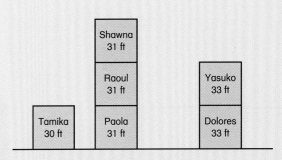

Bar graph made of stick-on notes

② Extending the Project

▶ Extension Suggestion

Have children make predictions about the distance they would run in 20 seconds and/or 30 seconds. Children may test their predictions. Children then compare and discuss the results.

▶ Home Link Suggestions

 Home Connection Children discuss with family members what they have learned about the speed at which children run. They investigate the speed at which adults run by conducting an activity similar to the one in the project with adult volunteers.

For a more comprehensive glossary that includes additional entries and illustrations, please refer to the *Teacher's Reference Manual.*

NOTE: In a definition, terms in italics are defined elsewhere in the glossary.

addend   Any one of a *set* of numbers that are added. For example, in 5 + 3 + 1, the addends are 5, 3, and 1.

addition fact   Two 1-digit numbers and their *sum*, such as 9 + 7 = 16.

algorithm   A set of step-by-step instructions for doing something, such as carrying out a computation or solving a problem. The most common algorithms are those for basic arithmetic computation, but there are many others. Some mathematicians and many computer scientists spend a great deal of time trying to find more efficient algorithms for solving problems.

A.M.   The abbreviation for *ante meridiem,* meaning "before the middle of the day" in Latin. From midnight to noon.

analog clock   (1) A clock that shows the time by the positions of the hour and minute hands. (2) Any device that shows time passing in a continuous manner, such as a sundial. Compare to *digital clock.*

angle   A figure formed by two rays or two *line segments* with a common *endpoint* called the *vertex* of the angle. The rays or segments are called the *sides* of the angle. An angle is measured in *degrees* between 0 and 360. One side of an angle is the rotation image of the other side through a number of *degrees*. Angles are named after their vertex point alone as in ∠A below; or

by three *points,* one on each side and the *vertex* in the middle as in ∠BCD below.

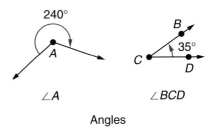

∠A   ∠BCD

Angles

apex   In a *pyramid* or *cone,* the *vertex* opposite the *base.* In a pyramid, all the non-base *faces* meet at the apex.

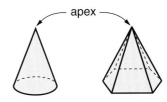

area   The amount of *surface* inside a *2-dimensional figure.* The figure might be a *triangle* or *rectangle* in a *plane,* the curved surface of a *cylinder,* or a state or country on Earth's surface. Commonly, area is measured in *square units* such as square *miles,* square *inches,* or square *centimeters.*

A triangle with area   A rectangle with area
21 square units   1.2 cm × 2 cm = 2.4 cm²

The area of the United States is about 3,800,000 square miles.

array   (1) An arrangement of objects in a regular *pattern,* usually rows and *columns.* (2) A rectangular array. In *Everyday Mathematics,* an array is a rectangular array unless specified otherwise.

arrow rule In *Everyday Mathematics,* an operation that determines the number that goes into the next frame in a *Frames-and-Arrows* diagram. There may be more than one arrow rule per diagram.

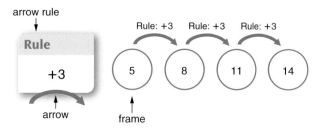

arrows In *Everyday Mathematics,* the links representing the *arrow rule(s)* in a *Frames-and-Arrows* diagram.

Associative Property of Addition A *property* of addition that three numbers can be added in any order without changing the *sum.* For example, $(4 + 3) + 7 = 4 + (3 + 7)$ because $7 + 7 = 4 + 10.$ In symbols:

For any numbers *a, b,* and *c,*
$(a + b) + c = a + (b + c).$

Subtraction is not associative. For example, $(4 - 3) + 7 \neq 4 - (3 + 7)$ because $8 \neq -6.$

Associative Property of Multiplication A *property* of multiplication that three numbers can be multiplied in any order without changing the *product.* For example, $(4 \times 3) \times 7 = 4 \times (3 \times 7)$ because $12 \times 7 = 4 \times 21.$ In symbols:

For any numbers *a, b,* and *c,*
$(a \times b) \times c = a \times (b \times c).$

Division is not associative. For example, $(8 \div 2) \div 4 \neq 8 \div (2 \div 4)$ because $1 \neq 16.$

attribute A feature of an object or common feature of a *set* of objects. Examples of attributes include size, shape, color, and number of sides. Same as *property.*

attribute blocks A *set* of blocks in which each block has one each of four *attributes* including color, size, thickness, and shape. The blocks are used for attribute identification and sorting activities. (Compare to *pattern blocks.*)

ballpark estimate A rough *estimate;* "in the ballpark." A ballpark estimate can serve as a check of the reasonableness of an answer obtained through some other procedure, or it can be made when an exact value is unnecessary or is impossible to obtain.

bar graph A graph with horizontal or vertical bars that represent *data.*

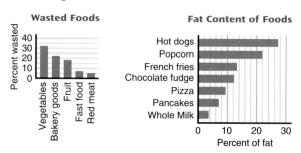

Source: The Garbage Product   *Source:* The New York Public Library Desk Reference

base of a prism or a cylinder Either of the two *parallel* and congruent *faces* that define the shape of a *prism* or a *cylinder.* In a cylinder, the base is a *circle.*

base of a pyramid or cone The *face* of a *pyramid* or *cone* that is oppposite its *apex.* The *base* of a cone is a *circle.*

base 10 Our system for writing numbers that uses only the 10 symbols 0, 1, 2, 3, 4, 5, 6, 7, 8, and 9, called *digits.* You can write any number using one or more of these 10 digits, and each digit has a value that depends on its place in the number (its *place value*). In the base-10 system, each place has a value 10 times that of the place to its right, and 1 tenth the value of the place to its left.

base-10 blocks A set of blocks to represent ones, tens, hundreds, and thousands in the *base-10 place value* system. In *Everyday Mathematics,* the unit block, or *cube,* has 1-cm *edges;* the ten block, or *long,* is 10 unit blocks in length; the hundred block, or *flat,* is 10 longs in width; and the thousand block, or *big cube,* is 10 flats high. See *cube, long, flat,* and *big cube* for illustrations of the blocks.

base-10 shorthand In *Everyday Mathematics,* a written notation for *base-10 blocks.*

Name	Base-10 block	Base-10 shorthand
cube		.
long		|
flat		☐
big cube		

big cube In *Everyday Mathematics,* a *base-10* block cube that measures 10 cm by 10 cm by 10 cm. A big cube is worth 1,000 1-cm cubes.

C

capacity (1) The amount of space occupied by a *3-dimensional figure.* Same as *volume.* (2) Less formally, the amount a container can hold. Capacity is often measured in *units* such as *quarts, gallons, cups,* or *liters.* (3) The *maximum weight* a *scale* can measure.

Celsius A *temperature scale* on which pure water at sea level freezes at 0° and boils at 100°. The Celsius scale is used in the *metric system.* A less common name for this scale is centigrade, because there are 100 *units* between the freezing and boiling points of water. Compare to *Fahrenheit.*

centimeter (cm) A metric *unit* of *length* equivalent to 10 *millimeters,* $\frac{1}{10}$ of a *decimeter,* and $\frac{1}{100}$ of a *meter.*

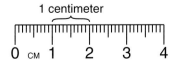

century One hundred years.

change diagram A diagram used in *Everyday Mathematics* to model situations in which quantities are either increased or decreased by addition or subtraction. The diagram includes a starting quantity, an ending quantity, and an amount of change.

A change diagram for 14 − 5 = 9

circle The *set* of all *points* in a *plane* that are equally distant from a fixed point in the plane called the center of the circle. The distance from the center to the circle is the radius of the circle. The diameter of a circle is twice its radius. Points inside a circle are not part of the circle. A circle together with its interior is called a disk or a circular region.

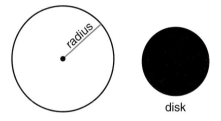

Class Data Pad In *Everyday Mathematics,* a large pad of paper used to store and recall *data* collected throughout the year. The data can be used for analysis, graphing, and generating *number stories.*

column (1) A vertical arrangement of objects or numbers in an *array* or a table.

(2) A vertical *set* of cells in a spreadsheet.

Commutative Property of Addition A *property* of addition that two numbers can be added in either order without changing the *sum.* For example, 5 + 10 = 10 + 5. In *Everyday Mathematics,* this is called a *turn-around fact,* and the two Commutative Properties are called turn-around rules. In symbols:

For any numbers a and b, $a + b = b + a$.

Subtraction is not commutative. For example, $8 - 5 \neq 5 - 8$ because $3 \neq -3$.

Commutative Property of Multiplication A *property* of multiplication that two numbers can be multiplied in either order without changing the *product*. For example, $5 \times 10 = 10 \times 5$. In *Everyday Mathematics,* this is called a *turn-around fact,* and the two Commutative Properties are called turn-around rules. In symbols:

For any numbers a and b, $a \times b = b \times a$.

Division is not commutative. For example, $10 \div 5 \neq 5 \div 10$ because $2 \neq \frac{1}{2}$.

comparison diagram A diagram used in *Everyday Mathematics* to model situations in which two quantities are compared by addition or subtraction. The diagram contains two quantities and their difference.

A comparison diagram for $12 = 9 + ?$

cone A *geometric solid* with a circular *base,* a *vertex (apex)* not in the *plane* of the base, and all of the *line segments* with one *endpoint* at the apex and the other endpoint on the circumference of the base.

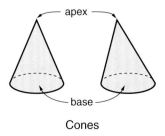

Cones

consecutive Following one after another in an uninterrupted order. For example, A, B, C, and D are four consecutive letters of the alphabet; 6, 7, 8, 9, and 10 are five consecutive whole numbers.

corner Same as *vertex.*

counting numbers The numbers used to count things. The *set* of counting numbers is {1, 2, 3, 4, ...}. Sometimes 0 is included, but not in *Everyday Mathematics.* Counting numbers are in the sets of whole numbers, integers, rational numbers, and real numbers, but each of these

sets include numbers that are not counting numbers.

cube (1) A *regular polyhedron* with 6 square *faces.* A cube has 8 *vertices* and 12 *edges.*

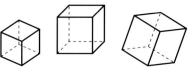

Cubes

(2) In *Everyday Mathematics,* the smaller cube of the *base-10 blocks,* measuring 1 cm on each edge.

cubit An ancient unit of *length,* measured from the point of the elbow to the end of the middle finger. The cubit has been standardized at various times between 18 and 22 *inches.* The Latin word *cubitum* means elbow.

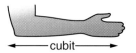

cup (c) A U.S. customary *unit* of *volume* or *capacity* equal to 8 fluid *ounces* or $\frac{1}{2}$ *pint.*

curved surface A *2-dimensional* surface that does not lie in a *plane. Spheres, cylinders,* and *cones* each have one curved surface.

cylinder A *geometric solid* with two congruent, parallel circular regions for bases and a curved *face* formed by all the segments with an *endpoint* on each *circle* that are parallel to a segment with endpoints at the centers of the circles. Also called a circular cylinder.

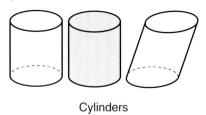

Cylinders

data Information that is gathered by counting, measuring, questioning, or observing. Strictly, data is the plural of datum, but data is often used as a singular word.

decade Ten years.

deci- A prefix meaning 1 tenth.

decimal point   A mark used to separate the ones and tenths places in decimals. A decimal point separates dollars from cents in *dollars-and-cents notation*. The mark is a dot in the *U.S. customary system* and a comma in Europe and some other countries.

decimeter (dm)   A metric *unit* of *length* equivalent to $\frac{1}{10}$ *meter* or 10 *centimeters*.

degree (°)   (1) A *unit* of measure for *angles* based on dividing a *circle* into 360 equal parts. Lines of latitude and longitude are measured in degrees, and these degrees are based on angle measures. (2) A unit for measuring *temperature*. See *Celsius* and *Fahrenheit*. The symbol ° means degrees of any type.

denominator   The nonzero divisor b in a *fraction* $\frac{a}{b}$ and a/b. In a part-whole fraction, the denominator is the number of equal parts into which the *whole,* or *ONE,* has been divided. Compare to *numerator*.

diagonal   (1) A *line segment* joining two nonconsecutive *vertices* of a *polygon*. (2) A segment joining two nonconsecutive vertices on different *faces* of a *polyhedron*.

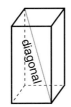

(3) A line of objects or numbers from upper left to lower right or from lower left to upper right, in an *array* or a table.

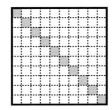

A diagonal of an array

difference   The result of subtracting one number from another. For example, the difference of 12 and 5 is $12 - 5 = 7$.

digit   (1) Any one of the symbols 0, 1, 2, 3, 4, 5, 6, 7, 8, and 9 in the *base-10* numeration system. For example, the numeral 145 is made up of the digits 1, 4, and 5. (2) Any one of the symbols in any number system. For example, A, B, C, D, E, and F are digits along with 0 through 9 in the base-16 notation used in some computer programming.

digital clock   A clock that shows the time with numbers of hours and minutes, usually separated by a colon. This display is discrete, not continuous, meaning that the display jumps to a new time after a minute delay. Compare to *analog clock*.

Digital clock

dollars-and-cents notation   The U.S. customary notation for writing amounts of money as a number of dollars and hundredths of dollars (*cents*). The decimal is preceded by the $ symbol, as in $8.98, meaning "eight dollars and 98 cents".

doubles fact   The *sum* (or *product*) of a 1-digit number added to or multiplied by itself, such as $4 + 4 = 8$ or $3 \times 3 = 9$. A doubles fact does not have a *turn-around fact* partner.

edge   (1) Any *side* of a *polyhedron's* faces. (2) A *line segment* or curve where two *surfaces* of a *geometric solid* meet.

edges

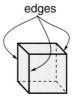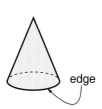

edge

endpoint   A point at the end of a *line segment,* ray, or arc. These shapes are usually named using their endpoints. For example, the segment below is "segment *TL*" or "segment *LT*."

endpoints

T   *L*

equal   Same as *equivalent*.

equal-grouping story   A *number story* in which a quantity is divided into equal groups. The total and size of each group are known. For example, *How many tables seating 4 people each are needed to seat 52 people?* is an equal-grouping story. Often division can be used to solve equal-grouping stories. Compare to *equal-sharing story*.

equal groups   *Sets* with the same number of elements, such as cars with 5 passengers each, rows with 6 chairs each, and boxes containing 100 paper clips each.

equal-sharing story   A *number story* in which a quantity is shared equally. The total quantity and the number of groups are known. For example, *There are 10 toys to share equally among 4 children; how many toys will each child get?* is an equal-sharing story. Often division can be used to solve equal-sharing stories. Compare to *equal-grouping story*.

equivalent   Equal in value but possibly in a different form. For example, $\frac{1}{2}$, 0.5, and 50% are all equivalent.

equivalent names   Different ways of naming the same number. For example, 2 + 6, 4 + 4, 12 − 4, 18 − 10, 100 − 92, 5 + 1 + 2, eight, VIII, and ~~HH~~ /// are all equivalent names for 8. See *name-collection box*.

estimate   (1) An answer close to, or approximating, an exact answer. (2) To make an estimate.

even number   (1) A *counting number* that is divisible by 2. (2) An integer that is divisible by 2. Compare to *odd number*.

Explorations   In *First* through *Third Grade Everyday Mathematics,* independent or small-group activities that focus on one or more of the following: concept development, manipulatives, data collection, problem solving, games, and skill reviews.

expression   (1) A mathematical phrase made up of numbers, variables, operation symbols, and/or grouping symbols. An expression does not contain *relation symbols* such as =, >, and ≤. (2) Either side of an equation or inequality.

extended facts   Variations of basic arithmetic facts involving multiples of 10, 100, and so on. For example, 30 + 70 = 100, 40 × 5 = 200, and 560 ÷ 7 = 80 are extended facts. See *fact extensions*.

face   (1) In *Everyday Mathematics,* a flat *surface* on a *3-dimensional* figure. Some special faces are called *bases.* (2) More generally, any *2-dimensional surface* on a 3-dimensional figure.

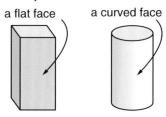

a flat face   a curved face

fact extensions   Calculations with larger numbers using knowledge of basic arithmetic facts. For example, knowing the addition fact 5 + 8 = 13 makes it easier to solve problems such as 50 + 80 = ? and 65 + ? = 73. Fact extensions apply to all four basic arithmetic operations. See *extended facts*.

fact family   A *set* of related arithmetic facts linking two inverse operations. For example,

5 + 6 = 11,   6 + 5 = 11,   11 − 5 = 6,   and   11 − 6 = 5

are an addition / subtraction fact family. Similarly,

5 × 7 = 35,   7 × 5 = 35,   35 ÷ 7 = 5,   and   35 ÷ 5 = 7

are a multiplication / division fact family. Same as *number family*.

fact power   In *Everyday Mathematics,* the ability to automatically recall basic arithmetic facts. Knowing the facts automatically is as important to arithmetic as knowing words by sight is to reading.

Fact Triangle   In *Everyday Mathematics,* a triangular flash card labeled with the numbers of a *fact family* that students can use to practice addition / subtraction and multiplication / division facts. The two 1-digit numbers and their *sum* or *product* (marked with a dot) appear in the corners of each *triangle*.

facts table A chart showing arithmetic facts. An addition/subtraction facts table shows addition and subtraction facts. A multiplication/division facts table shows multiplication and division facts.

factor (1) Each of the two or more numbers in a *product*. For example, in 6×0.5, 6 and 0.5 are factors. (Compare to factor of a counting number n.) (2) To represent a number as a product of factors. For example, factor 21 by rewriting as 7×3.

Fahrenheit A *temperature scale* on which pure water at sea level freezes at $32°$ and boils at $212°$. The Fahrenheit scale is widely used in the U.S. but in few other places. Compare to *Celsius*.

flat In *Everyday Mathematics,* the *base-10 block* consisting of one hundred 1-cm cubes.

A flat

flat surface A *surface* contained entirely in one *plane*.

foot (ft) A U.S. customary *unit* of *length* equivalent to 12 *inches* or $\frac{1}{3}$ of a *yard*.

fraction (primary definition) A number in the form $\frac{a}{b}$ or a/b, where a and b are whole numbers and b is not 0. A fraction may be used to name part of an object or part of a collection of objects, to compare two quantities, or to represent division. For example, $\frac{12}{6}$ might mean 12 eggs divided into 6 groups of 2 eggs each, a ratio of 12 to 6, or 12 divided by 6.

fraction (other definitions) (1) A fraction that satisfies the previous definition and includes a unit in both the *numerator* and *denominator*. For example, the rates $\frac{50 \text{ miles}}{1 \text{ gallon}}$ and $\frac{40 \text{ pages}}{10 \text{ minutes}}$ are fractions. (2) A number written using a fraction bar, where the fraction bar is used to indicate division. For example, $\frac{2.3}{6.5}$, $\frac{1\frac{4}{5}}{12}$, and $\frac{3}{4}{8}$.

Frames and Arrows In *Everyday Mathematics,* diagrams consisting of frames connected by arrows used to represent *number sequences*. Each frame contains a number, and each arrow represents a rule that determines which number goes in the next frame. There may be more than

one rule, represented by different-color arrows. Frames-and-Arrows diagrams are also called chains.

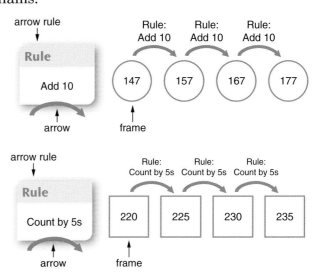

frequency (1) The number of times a value occurs in a *set* of *data*. (2) A number of repetitions per *unit* of time. For example, the vibrations per second in a sound wave.

frequency graph A graph showing how often each value occurs in a *data set*.

Colors in a Bag of Gumdrops

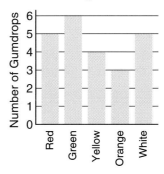

frequency table A table in which *data* are *tallied* and organized, often as a first step toward making a *frequency graph*.

Color	Number of Gumdrops
red	ЖЖ
green	ЖЖ l
yellow	////
orange	///
white	ЖЖ

function machine In *Everyday Mathematics,* an imaginary device that receives *inputs* and pairs them with *outputs.* For example, the function machine below pairs an input number with its double.

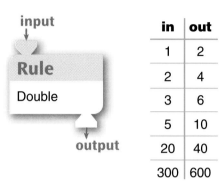

in	out
1	2
2	4
3	6
5	10
20	40
300	600

A function machine and function table

gallon (gal) A U.S. customary *unit* of *volume* or *capacity* equal to 4 *quarts.*

geometric solid The *surface* or surfaces that make up a *3-dimensional figure* such as a *prism, pyramid, cylinder, cone,* or *sphere.* Despite its name, a geometric solid is hollow, that is, it does not include the points in its interior. Informally, and in some dictionaries, a solid is defined as both the surface and its interior.

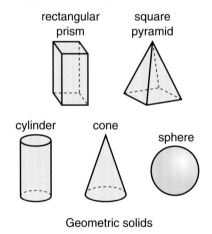

Geometric solids

gram (g) A metric *unit* of mass equal to $\frac{1}{1,000}$ of a *kilogram.*

height (1) In *Everyday Mathematics,* same as *height* of a figure. (2) Distance above sea level.

heptagon A 7-sided *polygon.*

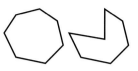

Heptagons

hexagon A 6-sided *polygon.*

A hexagon

Home Link In *First* through *Third Grade Everyday Mathematics,* a suggested follow-up or enrichment activity to be done at home.

inch (in.) A U.S. customary *unit* of *length* equal to $\frac{1}{12}$ of a *foot* and 2.54 *centimeters.*

input (1) A number inserted into an imaginary *function machine,* which applies a rule to pair the input with an *output.* (2) The values for *x* in a function consisting of ordered pairs (*x,y*). (3) Numbers or other information entered into a calculator or computer.

kilogram A metric *unit* of mass equal to 1,000 *grams.* The international standard kilogram is a 39 mm diameter, 39 mm high *cylinder* of platinum and iridium kept in the International Bureau of Weights and Measures in Sévres, France. A kilogram is about 2.2 *pounds.*

kilometer A metric *unit* of *length* equal to 1,000 *meters.* A kilometer is about 0.62 *mile.*

kite A *quadrilateral* with two distinct pairs of adjacent *sides* of *equal length.* In *Everyday Mathematics,* the four sides cannot all have equal length; that is, a *rhombus* is not a kite. The diagonals of a kite are perpendicular.

A kite

label (1) A descriptive word or phrase used to put a number or numbers in context. Labels encourage children to associate numbers with real

objects. Flags, snowballs, and scary monsters are examples of labels. (2) In a spreadsheet or graph, words or numbers providing information such as the title of the spreadsheet, the heading for a row or *column,* or the variable on an axis.

length   The distance between two *points* on a 1-dimensional figure. For example, the figure might be a *line segment,* arc, or a hiking path. Length is measured in units such as *inches, kilometers,* and *miles.*

line   In *Everyday Mathematics,* a 1-dimensional straight path that extends forever in opposite directions. A line is named using two *points* on it or with a single, italicized lower-case letter such as *l.* In formal Euclidean geometry, a line is an undefined geometric term.

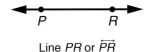

Line *PR* or $\overleftrightarrow{PR}$

line segment   A part of a *line* between and including two *points,* called *endpoints* of the segment. Same as segment. A line segment is often named by its endpoints.

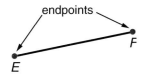

Segment *EF* or $\overline{EF}$

line of symmetry   A *line* that divides a figure into two parts that are reflection images of each other. A figure may have zero, one, or more lines of symmetry. For example, the numeral 2 has no lines of symmetry, a *square* has four lines of symmetry, and a *circle* has infinitely many lines of symmetry. Also called a symmetry line.

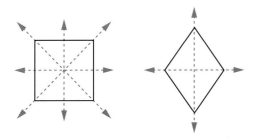

Lines of symmetry are shown in blue.

line plot   A sketch of *data* in which check marks, Xs, or other symbols above a labeled line show the *frequency* of each value.

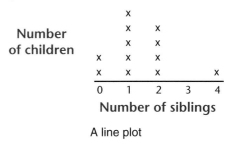

A line plot

liter (L)   A metric *unit* of *volume* or *capacity* equal to the volume of a *cube* with 10-cm-long *edges.* 1 L = 1,000 mL = 1,000 cm³. A liter is a little larger than a *quart.*

long   In *Everyday Mathematics,* the *base-10 block* consisting of ten 1-cm *cubes.* Sometimes called a rod.

Math Boxes   In *Everyday Mathematics,* a collection of problems to practice skills. Math Boxes for each lesson are in the *Math Journal.*

Math Journal   In *Everyday Mathematics,* a place for students to record their mathematical discoveries and experiences. Journal pages give models for conceptual understanding, problems to solve, and directions for individual and small-group activities.

Math Master   In *Everyday Mathematics,* a page ready for duplicating. Most masters support children in carrying out suggested activities. Some masters are used more than once during the school year.

Math Message   In *Everyday Mathematics,* an introductory activity to the day's lesson that children complete before the lesson starts. Messages may include problems to solve, directions to follow, sentences to complete or correct, review exercises, or reading assignments.

maximum   The largest amount; the greatest number in a *set* of *data.* Compare to *minimum.*

measurement unit The reference unit used when measuring. Basic units include *inches* for *length*, *grams* for mass or *weight*, cubic inches for *volume* or *capacity*, seconds for elapsed time, and *degrees Celsius* for change of *temperature*. Compound units include square *centimeters* for *area* and *miles* per hour for speed.

median The middle value in a *set* of *data* when the data are listed in order from smallest to largest or vice versa. If there is an *even number* of data *points*, the median is the mean of the two middle values. Compare to other data landmarks mean and *mode*.

mental arithmetic Computation done by people "in their heads," either in whole or in part. In *Everyday Mathematics*, students learn a variety of mental-calculation strategies to develop automatic recall of basic facts and *fact power*.

Mental Math and Reflexes In *Everyday Mathematics*, exercises at three levels of difficulty at the beginning of lessons for students to get ready to think about math, warm up skills they need for the lesson, continually build mental-arithmetic skills, and help you assess individual strengths and weaknesses.

meter (m) The basic metric *unit* of *length* from which other metric units of length are derived. Originally, the meter was defined as $\frac{1}{10,000,000}$ of the distance from the North Pole to the equator along a meridian passing through Paris. From 1960 to 1983, the meter was redefined as 1,630,763.73 wavelengths of orange-red light from the element krypton. Today, the meter is defined as the distance light travels in a vacuum in $\frac{1}{299,792,458}$ second. One meter is equal to 10 *decimeters,* 100 *centimeters,* or 1,000 *millimeters.*

metric system A measurement system based on the *base-10* (decimal) numeration system and used in most countries and by virtually all scientists around the world. *Units* for *length* include *millimeter, centimeter, meter,* and *kilometer;* units for mass and *weight* include *gram* and *kilogram;* units for *volume* and *capacity* include *milliliter* and *liter;* and the unit for *temperature* change is *degrees Celsius.*

middle value Same as *median*.

mile (mi) A U.S. customary *unit* of *length* equal to 5,280 *feet,* or 1,760 *yards.* A *mile* is about 1,609 *meters.*

milliliter (mL) A metric *unit* of *volume* or *capacity* equal to $\frac{1}{1,000}$ of a *liter,* or 1 cubic *centimeter.*

millimeter (mm) A metric *unit* of *length* equal to $\frac{1}{10}$ of a *centimeter,* or $\frac{1}{1,000}$ of a *meter.*

minimum The smallest amount; the smallest number in a *set* of *data.* Compare to *maximum.*

mode The value or values that occur most often in a *set* of *data.* Compare to other landmarks *median* and mean.

multiple of a number *n* (1) A *product* of *n* and a *counting number.* For example, the multiples of 7 are 7, 14, 21, 28, ... (2) A product of *n* and an integer. For example, the multiples of 7 are ..., −21, −14, −7, 0, 7, 14, 21, ...

multiplication/division diagram A diagram used in *Everyday Mathematics* to model situations in which a total number is made up of equal-size groups. The diagram contains a number of groups, a number in each group, and a total number. Also called a "multiplication diagram" for short.

rows	chairs per row	chairs in all
15	25	?

A multiplication/division diagram

multiplication fact The *product* of two 1-digit numbers, such as $6 \times 7 = 42$.

name-collection box In *Everyday Mathematics,* a diagram that is used for collecting *equivalent names* for a number.

number family Same as *fact family*.

number grid   In *Everyday Mathematics,* a table in which *consecutive* numbers are arranged in rows, usually 10 columns per row. A move from one number to the next within a row is a change of 1; a move from one number to the next within a column is a change of 10.

−9	−8	−7	−6	−5	−4	−3	−2	−1	0
1	2	3	4	5	6	7	8	9	10
11	12	13	14	15	16	17	18	19	20
21	22	23	24	25	26	27	28	29	30
31	32	33	34	35	36	37	38	39	40
41	42	43	44	45	46	47	48	49	50
51	52	53	54	55	56	57	58	59	60
61	62	63	64	65	66	67	68	69	70
71	72	73	74	75	76	77	78	79	80
81	82	83	84	85	86	87	88	89	90
91	92	93	94	95	96	97	98	99	100
101	102	103	104	105	106	107	108	109	110

A number grid

number-grid puzzle   In *Everyday Mathematics,* a piece of a *number grid* in which some, but not all, of the numbers are missing. Students use number-grid puzzles to practice *place-value* concepts.

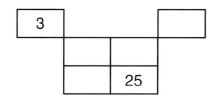

A number-grid puzzle

number line   A *line* on which *points* are indicated by tick marks that are usually at regularly spaced intervals from a starting point called the origin, the zero point, or simply 0. Numbers are associated with the tick marks on a *scale* defined by the unit interval from 0 to 1. Every real number locates a point on the line, and every point corresponds to a real number.

number model   A *number sentence, expression,* or other representation that models a *number story* or situation. For example, the story *Sally had \$5, and then she earned \$8* can be modeled as the number sentence 5 + 8 = 13, as the expression 5 + 8, or by

$$\begin{array}{r} 5 \\ +\ 8 \\ \hline 13 \end{array}$$

number scroll   In *Everyday Mathematics,* a series of *number grids* taped together.

A number scroll

number sentence   Two *expressions* with a *relation symbol.* For example,

$$5 + 5 = 10$$
$$2 - ? = 8$$
$$16 \le a \times b$$
$$a^2 + b^2 = c^2$$

Number sentences

number sequence   A list of numbers, often generated by a rule. In *Everyday Mathematics,* students explore number sequences using *Frames-and-Arrows* diagrams.

$$1, 2, 3, 4, 5, \dots \qquad 1, 4, 9, 16, 25, \dots$$
$$1, 2, 1, 2, 1, \dots \qquad 1, 3, 5, 7, 9, \dots$$

Number sequences

number story   A story that involves numbers and one or more explicit or implicit questions. For example, *I have 7 crayons in my desk. Carrie gave me 8 more crayons. Now I have 15 crayons in all* is a number story.

numerator   The dividend a in a *fraction* $\frac{a}{b}$ or a/b.

O

octagon   An 8-sided *polygon*.

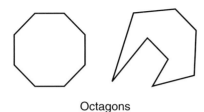

Octagons

odd number   A *counting number* that is not divisible by 2. Compare to *even number*.

ONE   In *Everyday Mathematics,* same as *whole* or *unit whole.*

operation   A rule performed on one or more mathematical objects such as numbers, variables, or *expressions,* to produce another mathematical object. Addition, subtraction, multiplication, and division are the four basic arithmetic operations. Taking a square root, squaring a number, and multiplying both sides of an equation by the same number are also operations. In *Everyday Mathematics,* students learn about many operations along with several procedures, or *algorithms,* for carrying them out.

ordinal number   The position or order of something in a sequence, such as first, third, or tenth. Ordinal numbers are commonly used in dates, as in "May fifth" instead of "May five."

ounce (oz)   A U.S. customary *unit* of *weight* equal to $\frac{1}{16}$ of a *pound* or about 28.35 *grams.*

outcome   A possible result of a chance experiment or situation. For example, HEADS and TAILS are the two possible outcomes of flipping a coin.

output   (1) A number paired to an *input* by an imaginary *function machine* applying a rule. (2) The values for y in a function consisting of ordered pairs (x,y). (3) Numbers or other information displayed by calculator or computer.

P

pan balance   A device used to weigh objects or compare their *weights.*

parallel lines   *Lines* in a *plane* that never meet. Two parallel lines are always the same distance apart. *Line segments* or rays on parallel lines are parallel to each other.

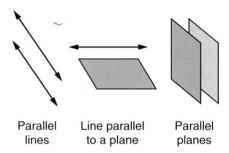

| Parallel lines | Line parallel to a plane | Parallel planes |

parallelogram   A *quadrilateral* with two pairs of parallel sides. Opposite sides of a parallelogram have the same *length* and opposite angles have the same measure. All *rectangles* are parallelograms, but not all parallelograms are rectangles because parallelograms do not necessarily have right angles.

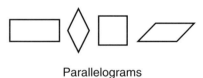

Parallelograms

partial-sums addition   An addition *algorithm* in which separate *sums* are computed for each *place value* of the numbers and then added to get a final sum.

parts-and-total diagram   In *Everyday Mathematics,* a diagram used to model problems in which two or more quantities (parts) are combined to get a total quantity.

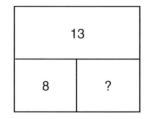

Parts-and-total diagrams for 13 = 8 + ?

pattern   A repetitive order or arrangement. In *Everyday Mathematics,* students mainly explore visual and number patterns in which elements are arranged so that what comes next can be predicted.

pattern blocks   A set of *polygon*-shaped blocks of varying sizes in which smaller blocks can be placed on larger blocks to show fractional parts. The blocks are used for geometric shape identification and fraction activities. Compare to *attribute blocks*.

Pattern-Block Template   In *First* through *Third Grade Everyday Mathematics,* a sheet of plastic with geometric shapes cut out, used to draw *patterns* and designs.

pentagon   A 5-sided *polygon*.

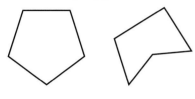

Pentagons

per   For each, as in *ten chairs per row* or *six tickets per family.*

perimeter   The distance around the boundary of a *2-dimensional figure*. The perimeter of a *circle* is called its circumference. A formula for the perimeter *P* of a *rectangle* with *length l* and *width w* is $P = 2 \times (l + w)$. Perimeter comes from the Greek words for "around measure."

pint (pt)   A U.S. customary *unit* of *volume* or *capacity* equal to 2 *cups* or 16 fluid *ounces*. A handy saying to remember is *A pint's a pound the world around,* meaning that a pint of water weighs about 1 pound.

place value   A system that gives a *digit* a value according to its position, or place, in a number. In our standard, *base-10* (decimal) system for writing numbers, each place has a value 10 times that of the place to its right and 1 tenth the value of the place to its left.

thousands	hundreds	tens	ones	tenths	hundredths

A place-value chart

plane   In *Everyday Mathematics,* a *2-dimensional* flat *surface* that extends forever in all directions. In formal Euclidean geometry, a plane is an undefined geometric term.

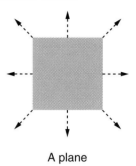

A plane

point   In *Everyday Mathematics,* an exact location in space. Points are usually labeled with capital letters. In formal Euclidean geometry, a point is an undefined geometric term.

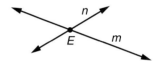

Lines *m* and *n* intersect at point *E.*

polygon   A *2-dimensional figure* formed by three or more *line segments* (*sides*) that meet only at their *endpoints* (*vertices*) to make a closed path. The *sides* may not cross one another.

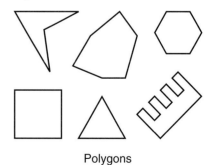

Polygons

polyhedron   A *3-dimensional figure* formed by *polygons* with their interiors (*faces*) and having no holes. Plural is polyhedrons or polyhedra.

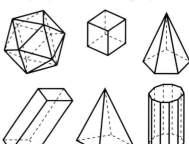

poster In *Everyday Mathematics,* a page displaying a collection of illustrated numerical *data.* A poster may be used as a source of data for developing *number stories.*

pound (lb) A U.S. customary *unit* of *weight* equal to 16 *ounces* and defined as 0.45359237 *kilograms.*

prism A *polyhedron* with two parallel and congruent polygonal regions for *bases* and lateral *faces* formed by all the *line segments* with *endpoints* on corresponding *edges* of the bases. The lateral faces are all *parallelograms.* Lateral faces intersect at lateral edges. In a right prism, the lateral faces are rectangular. Prisms get their names from the shape of their bases.

| A triangular prism | A rectangular prism | A hexagonal prism |

probability A number from 0 through 1 giving the likelihood that an event will happen. The closer a probability is to 1, the more likely the event is to happen. The closer a probability is to 0, the less likely the event is to happen. For example, the probability that a fair coin will show heads is $\frac{1}{2}$.

product The result of multiplying two numbers, called *factors.* For example, in $4 \times 3 = 12$, the product is 12.

Project In *Everyday Mathematics,* a thematic activity to be completed in one or more days by small groups or by a whole class. Projects often involve collecting and analyzing data and are usually cross-curricular in nature.

property (1) A generalized statement about a mathematical relationship such as the Distributive Property of Multiplication over Addition. (2) Same as *attribute.*

pyramid A *polyhedron* made up of any polygonal region for a *base,* a *point (apex)* not in the *plane* of the base, and all of the *line segments* with one *endpoint* at the apex and the other on an *edge* of

the base. All faces except the base are triangular. Pyramids get their name from the shape of their base.

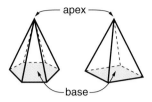

A hexagonal   A square
pyramid   pyramid

Q

quadrangle Same as *quadrilateral.*

quadrilateral A 4-sided *polygon.* See *square, rectangle, parallelogram, rhombus, kite,* and *trapezoid.*

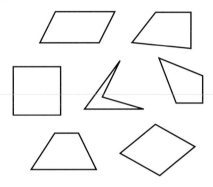

Quadrilaterals

quart A U.S. customary *unit* of *volume* or *capacity* equal to 32 fluid *ounces,* 2 *pints,* or 4 *cups.*

quotient The result of dividing one number by another number. For example, in $10 \div 5 = 2$, the quotient is 2.

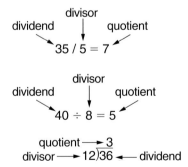

R

range The *difference* between the *maximum* and the *minimum* in a *set* of *data*. Used as a measure of the spread of the data.

rate-multiplication story A *number story* in which one quantity is a rate times another quantity. A typical rate is speed, which multiplied by a time traveled gives distance traveled. There are many other rates such as price *per pound* or hours per person. For example, *8 people work a total of 20 hours. What is the average number of work hours per person?* is a rate-multiplication story.

rectangle A *parallelogram* with all *right angles*.

rectangular prism A *prism* with rectangular *bases*. The four *faces* that are not bases are either *rectangles* or *parallelograms*. For example, a shoe box models a rectangular prism in which all *sides* are rectangles.

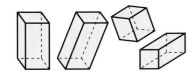

Rectangular prisms

rectangular pyramid A *pyramid* with a rectangular base.

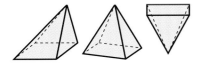

Rectangular pyramids

regular polygon A *polygon* in which all *sides* are the same *length* and all *angles* have the same measure.

Regular polygons

regular polyhedron A *polyhedron* whose *faces* are all congruent *regular polygons* and in which the same number of faces meet at each *vertex*. The five regular *polyhedrons,* known as the Platonic solids, are shown below.

Tetrahedron	Cube	Octahedron
(4 equilateral triangles)	(6 squares)	(8 equilateral triangles)

Dodecahedron	Icosahedron
(12 regular pentagons)	(20 equilateral triangles)

relation symbol A symbol used to express a relationship between two quantities.

Relation	Meaning
$=$	is equal to
$\neq$	is not equal to
$<$	is less than
$>$	is greater than
$\leq$	is less than or equal to
$\geq$	is greater than or equal to
$\approx$	is approximately equal to

remainder An amount left over when one number is divided by another number. For example, in $16 \div 3 \rightarrow 5$ R1, the *quotient* is 5 and the remainder R is 1.

rhombus A *parallelogram* with all *sides* the same *length*. All rhombuses are parallelograms. Every *square* is a rhombus, but not all rhombuses are squares. Also called a diamond. Plural is rhombuses or rhombi.

Rhombuses

right angle   A 90° *angle*.

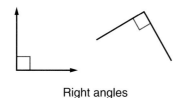

Right angles

round   (1) To approximate a number to make it easier to work with, or to make it better reflect the precision of the *data*. Rounding up means to approximate larger than the actual value. Rounding down means to approximate smaller than the actual value. (2) Circular in shape.

scale   (1) The relative size of something. (2) Same as scale factor. (3) A tool for measuring *weight*.

set   A collection or group of objects, numbers, or other items.

side   (1) One of the *line segments* that make up a *polygon*. (2) One of the rays or segments that form an *angle*. (3) One of the *faces* of a *polyhedron*.

slate   A lap-size (about 8-inch-by-11-inch) chalkboard or whiteboard that children use in *Everyday Mathematics* for recording responses during group exercises and informal group assessments.

sphere   The *set* of all *points* in space that are an equal distance from a fixed point called the center of the sphere. The distance from the center to the sphere is the radius of the sphere. The diameter of a sphere is twice its radius. Points inside a sphere are not part of the sphere.

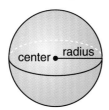

A sphere

square   A *rectangle* with all *sides* of equal *length*. All *angles* in a square are *right angles*.

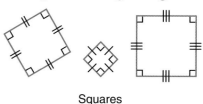

Squares

square corner   Same as a *right angle*.

square numbers   Figurate numbers that are the *product* of a *counting number* and itself. For example, 25 is a square number because $25 = 5 \times 5$. A square number can be represented by a square *array* and as a number squared, such as $25 = 5^2$.

square of a number *n*   The *product* of *n* and itself, commonly written n^2. For example, $81 = 9 \times 9 = 9^2$ and $3.5^2 = 3.5 \times 3.5 = 12.25$.

square pyramid   A *pyramid* with a square base.

square unit   A *unit* to measure *area*. A model of a square unit is a *square* with each *side* a related unit of *length*. For example, a square *inch* is the area of a square with 1-inch sides. Square units are often labeled as the length unit squared. For example, 1 cm² is read "1 square centimeter" or "1 centimeter squared."

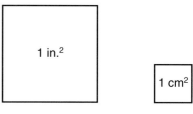

Square units

straightedge   A tool used to draw *line segments*. Strictly speaking, a straightedge does not have a measuring *scale* on it, so ignore the marks if you use a ruler as a straightedge. Together, a compass and straightedge are used to construct geometric figures.

sum   The result of adding two or more numbers. For example, in $5 + 3 = 8$, the sum is 8. Same as *total*.

surface   (1) The boundary of a *3-dimensional* object. The part of an object that is next to the air. Common surfaces include the top of a body of

water, the outermost part of a ball, and the topmost layer of ground that covers the Earth. (2) Any *2-dimensional* layer, such as a *plane* or a *face* of a *polyhedron.*

survey   A study that collects *data.* Surveys are commonly used to study demographics such as people's characteristics, behaviors, interests, and opinions.

symmetry   The balanced distribution of *points* over a *line* or around a point in a symmetric figure.

A figure with line symmetry   A figure with rotation symmetry

tally   (1) To keep a record of a count, commonly by making a mark for each item as it is counted. (2) The mark used in a count. Also called "tally mark" and "tick mark."

temperature   How hot or cold something is relative to another object or as measured on a standardized *scale* such as degrees *Celsius* or degrees *Fahrenheit.*

tetrahedron   A *polyhedron* with 4 *faces.* A tetrahedron is a *triangular pyramid.*

thermometer   A tool to measure *temperature* in *degrees* according to a fixed *scale.* The most common scales are *Celsius* and *Fahrenheit.*

3-dimensional (3-D) figure   A figure whose *points* are not all in a single *plane.* Examples include *prisms, pyramids,* and *spheres,* all of which have *length,* width, and *height.*

tiling   A *pattern* of shapes that covers a *surface* completely without overlaps or gaps.

timeline   A *number line* showing when events took place. In some timelines the origin is based on the context of the events being graphed, such as the birth date of the child's life graphed below. The origin can also come from another reference system, such as the year A.D. in which case the *scale* below might cover the years 2000 through 2005.

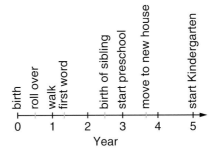

A timeline of a child's milestones

tool kit   In *First* through *Third Grade Everyday Mathematics,* a bag or a box containing a calculator, measuring tools, and manipulatives often used by children in the program.

total   Same as *sum.*

trade-first subtraction   A subtraction *algorithm* in which all necessary trades between places in the numbers are done before any subtractions are carried out. Some people favor this algorithm because they can concentrate on one thing at a time.

trapezoid   A *quadrilateral* that has exactly one pair of *parallel* sides. In *Everyday Mathematics,* both pairs of *sides* cannot be parallel; that is, a *parallelogram* is not a trapezoid.

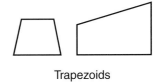

Trapezoids

triangle   A 3-sided *polygon.*

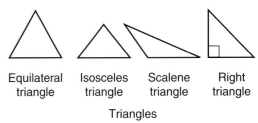

Equilateral   Isosceles   Scalene   Right
triangle   triangle   triangle   triangle

Triangles

Triangular prisms

triangular pyramid A *pyramid* in which all *faces* are *triangles,* any one of which is the *base.* A regular tetrahedron has four equilateral *triangles* for faces and is one of the five regular *polyhedrons.*

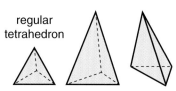

regular tetrahedron

Triangular pyramids

turn-around facts A pair of multiplication (or addition) facts in which the order of the *factors* (or *addends*) is reversed. For example, $3 \times 9 = 27$ and $9 \times 3 = 27$ are turn-around multiplication facts, and $4 + 5 = 9$ and $5 + 4 = 9$ are turn-around addition facts. There are no turn-around facts for subtraction or division. Turn-around facts are instances of the *Commutative Properties of Addition* and *Multiplication.*

2-dimensional (2-D) figure A figure whose points are all in one *plane* but not all on one *line.* Examples include *polygons* and *circles,* all of which have *length* and width but no *height.*

unit A label used to put a number in context. In measuring *length,* for example, *inches* and *centimeters* are units. In a problem about 5 apples, apple is the unit. In *Everyday Mathematics,* students keep track of units in *unit boxes.*

unit box In *Everyday Mathematics,* a box displaying the *unit* for the numbers in the problems at hand.

Unit
Days

A unit box

among units within measurement systems. For example, because 1 *foot* = 12 *inches* you can multiply a number of inches by $\frac{1}{12}$ to convert to feet.

unit whole Same as *whole* or *ONE.*

U.S. customary system The measuring system used most often in the United States. *Units* for *length* include *inch, foot, yard,* and *mile;* units for *weight* include *ounce* and *pound;* units for *volume* or *capacity* include *cup, pint, quart, gallon* and cubic units; and the main unit for *temperature* change is *degrees Fahrenheit.*

vertex The point at which the rays of an *angle,* the *sides* of a *polygon,* or the *edges* of a *polyhedron* meet. Plural is vertexes or vertices. In *Everyday Mathematics,* same as *corner.*

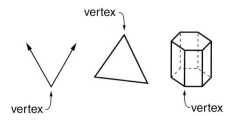

vertex

vertex

vertex

volume (1) The amount of space occupied by a *3-dimensional* figure. Same as *capacity.* (2) The amount a container can hold. Volume is often measure in cubic units, such as cm^3, cubic inches, or cubic feet.

weight A measure of how heavy something is; the force of gravity on an object. An object's mass is constant, but it weighs less in weak gravity than in strong gravity. For example, a person who weighs 150 *pounds* in San Diego weighs about 23 pounds on the moon.

"What's My Rule?" problem In *Everyday Mathematics,* a problem in which two of the three parts of a function (*input, output,* and rule) are known, and the third is to be found out.

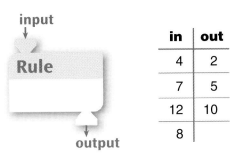

in	out
4	2
7	5
12	10
8	

A "What's My Rule?" problem

whole An entire object, collection of objects, or quantity being considered in a problem situation; 100%. Same as *ONE* and *unit whole.*

width of a rectangle The *length* of one *side* of a *rectangle* or rectangular object, typically the shorter side.

yard (yd) A U.S. customary *unit* of *length* equal to 3 *feet* or 36 *inches.* To Henry I of England, a yard was the distance from the tip of the nose to the tip of the middle finger. In *Everyday Mathematics,* it is from the center of the chest to the tip of the middle finger.

zero fact In *Everyday Mathematics:* (1) The *sum* of two 1-digit numbers when one of the *addends* is 0, as in $0 + 5 = 5$. If 0 is added to any number, there is no change in the number. (Same as the additive identity.) (2) The *product* of two 1-digit numbers when one of the *factors* is 0, as in $4 \times 0 = 0$. The product of a number and 0 is always 0.

Grade-Level Goals

Everyday Mathematics organizes content through Program Goals and Grade-Level Goals. The Grade-Level Goals Chart shows the units in which goal content is taught and then practiced. For more information, see the *Assessment Handbook*.

The Grade-Level Goals are divided according to the content strands below.

Content Strands   Pages

How to Read the Grade-Level Goals Chart

Each section of the chart includes Grade-Level Goals organized by content strand. The three grade-level columns divided into units indicate in which units the goals are addressed.

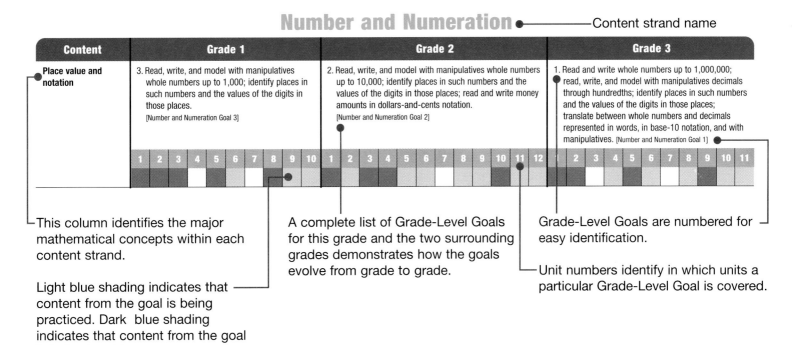

Number and Numeration ● —— Content strand name

Content	Grade 1	Grade 2	Grade 3
Place value and notation	3. Read, write, and model with manipulatives whole numbers up to 1,000; identify places in such numbers and the values of the digits in those places. [Number and Numeration Goal 3]	2. Read, write, and model with manipulatives whole numbers up to 10,000; identify places in such numbers and the values of the digits in those places; read and write money amounts in dollars-and-cents notation. [Number and Numeration Goal 2]	1. Read and write whole numbers up to 1,000,000; read, write, and model with manipulatives decimals through hundredths; identify places in such numbers and the values of the digits in those places; translate between whole numbers and decimals represented in words, in base-10 notation, and with manipulatives. [Number and Numeration Goal 1] ●

This column identifies the major mathematical concepts within each content strand.

Light blue shading indicates that content from the goal is being practiced. Dark blue shading indicates that content from the goal is being taught.

A complete list of Grade-Level Goals for this grade and the two surrounding grades demonstrates how the goals evolve from grade to grade.

Grade-Level Goals are numbered for easy identification.

Unit numbers identify in which units a particular Grade-Level Goal is covered.

Number and Numeration

Content	Grade 1	Grade 2	Grade 3
Rote counting	1. Count on by 1s, 2s, 5s, and 10s past 100 and back by 1s from any number less than 100 with and without number grids, number lines, and calculators. [Number and Numeration Goal 1] 1 2 3 4 5 6 7 8 9 10	1. Count on by 1s, 2s, 5s, 10s, 25s, and 100s past 1,000 and back by 1s from any number less than 1,000 with and without number grids, number lines, and calculators. [Number and Numeration Goal 1] 1 2 3 4 5 6 7 8 9 10 11 12	 1 2 3 4 5 6 7 8 9 10 11
Rational counting	2. Count collections of objects accurately and reliably; estimate the number of objects in a collection. [Number and Numeration Goal 2] 1 2 3 4 5 6 7 8 9 10	 1 2 3 4 5 6 7 8 9 10 11 12	 1 2 3 4 5 6 7 8 9 10 11
Place value and notation	3. Read, write, and model with manipulatives whole numbers up to 1,000; identify places in such numbers and the values of the digits in those places. [Number and Numeration Goal 3] 1 2 3 4 5 6 7 8 9 10	2. Read, write, and model with manipulatives whole numbers up to 10,000; identify places in such numbers and the values of the digits in those places; read and write money amounts in dollars-and-cents notation. [Number and Numeration Goal 2] 1 2 3 4 5 6 7 8 9 10 11 12	1. Read and write whole numbers up to 1,000,000; read, write, and model with manipulatives decimals through hundredths; identify places in such numbers and the values of the digits in those places; translate between whole numbers and decimals represented in words, in base-10 notation, and with manipulatives. [Number and Numeration Goal 1] 1 2 3 4 5 6 7 8 9 10 11
Meanings and uses of fractions	4. Use manipulatives and drawings to model halves, thirds, and fourths as equal parts of a region or a collection; describe the model. [Number and Numeration Goal 4] 1 2 3 4 5 6 7 8 9 10	3. Use manipulatives and drawings to model fractions as equal parts of a region or a collection; describe the models and name the fractions. [Number and Numeration Goal 3] 1 2 3 4 5 6 7 8 9 10 11 12	2. Read, write, and model fractions; solve problems involving fractional parts of a region or a collection; describe strategies used. [Number and Numeration Goal 2] 1 2 3 4 5 6 7 8 9 10 11

Content	Grade 1	Grade 2	Grade 3
number theory	5. Use manipulatives to identify and model odd and even numbers. [Number and Numeration Goal 5]	4. Recognize numbers as odd or even. [Number and Numeration Goal 4]	3. Find multiples of 2, 5, and 10. [Number and Numeration Goal 3]
equivalent names for whole numbers	6. Use manipulatives, drawings, tally marks, and numerical expressions involving addition and subtraction of 1- or 2-digit numbers to give equivalent names for whole numbers up to 100. [Number and Numeration Goal 6]	5. Use tally marks, arrays, and numerical expressions involving addition and subtraction to give equivalent names for whole numbers. [Number and Numeration Goal 5]	4. Use numerical expressions involving one or more of the basic four arithmetic operations to give equivalent names for whole numbers. [Number and Numeration Goal 4]
equivalent names for fractions, decimals, and percents		6. Use manipulatives and drawings to model equivalent names for $\frac{1}{2}$. [Number and Numeration Goal 6]	5. Use manipulatives and drawings to find and represent equivalent names for fractions; use manipulatives to generate equivalent fractions. [Number and Numeration Goal 5]
comparing and ordering numbers	7. Compare and order whole numbers up to 1,000. [Number and Numeration Goal 7]	7. Compare and order whole numbers up to 10,000; use area models to compare fractions. [Number and Numeration Goal 7]	6. Compare and order whole numbers up to 1,000,000; use manipulatives to order decimals through hundredths; use area models and benchmark fractions to compare and order fractions. [Number and Numeration Goal 6]

Operations and Computation

Content	Grade 1	Grade 2	Grade 3
Addition and subtraction facts	1. Demonstrate proficiency with +/− 0, +/− 1, doubles, and sum-equals-ten addition and subtraction facts such as 6 + 4 = 10 and 10 − 7 = 3. [Operations and Computation Goal 1]	1. Demonstrate automaticity with +/− 0, +/− 1, doubles, and sum-equals-ten facts, and proficiency with all addition and subtraction facts through 10 + 10.* [Operations and Computation Goal 1]	1. Demonstrate automaticity with all addition and subtraction facts through 10 + 10; use basic facts to compute fact extensions such as 80 + 70. [Operations and Computation Goal 1]
Addition and subtraction procedures	2. Use manipulatives, number grids, tally marks, mental arithmetic, and calculators to solve problems involving the addition and subtraction of 1-digit whole numbers with 1- or 2-digit whole numbers; calculate and compare the values of combinations of coins. [Operations and Computation Goal 2]	2. Use manipulatives, number grids, tally marks, mental arithmetic, paper & pencil, and calculators to solve problems involving the addition and subtraction of 2-digit whole numbers; describe the strategies used; calculate and compare values of coin and bill combinations. [Operations and Computation Goal 2]	2. Use manipulatives, mental arithmetic, paper-and-pencil algorithms, and calculators to solve problems involving the addition and subtraction of whole numbers and decimals in a money context; describe the strategies used and explain how they work. [Operations and Computation Goal 2]
Multiplication and division facts			3. Demonstrate automaticity with × 0, × 1, × 2, × 5, and × 10 multiplication facts; use strategies to compute remaining facts up to 10 × 10. [Operations and Computation Goal 3]
Multiplication and division procedures			4. Use arrays, mental arithmetic, paper-and-pencil algorithms, and calculators to solve problems involving the multiplication of 2- and 3-digit whole numbers by 1-digit whole numbers; describe the strategies used. [Operations and Computation Goal 4]

* Children practice fact triangles and record the ones they know at least once per unit.

Content	Grade 1	Grade 2	Grade 3
Computational estimation	3. Estimate reasonableness of answers to basic fact problems (e.g., Will 7 + 8 be more or less than 10?). [Operations and Computation Goal 3] 1 2 3 4 5 6 7 8 9 10	3. Make reasonable estimates for whole number addition and subtraction problems; explain how the estimates were obtained. [Operations and Computation Goal 4] 1 2 3 4 5 6 7 8 9 10 11 12	5. Make reasonable estimates for whole number addition and subtraction problems; explain how the estimates were obtained. [Operations and Computation Goal 5] 1 2 3 4 5 6 7 8 9 10 11
Models for the operations	4. Identify change-to-more, change-to-less, comparison, and parts-and-total situations. [Operations and Computation Goal 4] 1 2 3 4 5 6 7 8 9 10	4. Identify and describe change, comparison, and parts-and-total situations; use repeated addition, arrays, and skip counting to model multiplication; use equal sharing and equal grouping to model division. [Operations and Computation Goal 4] 1 2 3 4 5 6 7 8 9 10 11 12	6. Recognize and describe change, comparison, and parts-and-total situations; use repeated addition, arrays, and skip counting to model multiplication; use equal sharing and equal grouping to model division. [Operations and Computation Goal 6] 1 2 3 4 5 6 7 8 9 10 11

Data and Chance

Content	Grade 1	Grade 2	Grade 3
Data collection and representation	1. Collect and organize data to create tally charts, tables, bar graphs, and line plots. [Data and Chance Goal 1] 1 2 3 4 5 6 7 8 9 10	1. Collect and organize data or use given data to create tally charts, tables, bar graphs, and line plots. [Data and Chance Goal 1] 1 2 3 4 5 6 7 8 9 10 11 12	1. Collect and organize data or use given data to create charts, tables, bar graphs, and line plots. [Data and Chance Goal 1] 1 2 3 4 5 6 7 8 9 10 11
Data analysis	2. Use graphs to answer simple questions and draw conclusions; find the maximum and minimum of a data set. [Data and Chance Goal 2] 1 2 3 4 5 6 7 8 9 10	2. Use graphs to ask and answer simple questions and draw conclusions; find the maximum, minimum, mode, and median of a data set. [Data and Chance Goal 2] 1 2 3 4 5 6 7 8 9 10 11 12	2. Use graphs to ask and answer simple questions and draw conclusions; find the maximum, minimum, range, mode, and median of a data set. [Data and Chance Goal 2] 1 2 3 4 5 6 7 8 9 10 11

Data and Chance (cont.)

Qualitative probability

Grade 1
3. Describe events using *certain*, *likely*, *unlikely*, *impossible* and other basic probability terms. [Data and Chance Goal 3]
(grid 1–10)

Grade 2
3. Describe events using *certain*, *likely*, *unlikely*, *impossible* and other basic probability terms; explain the choice of language. [Data and Chance Goal 3]
(grid 1–12)

Grade 3
3. Describe events using *certain*, *very likely*, *likely*, *unlikely*, *very unlikely*, *impossible*, and other basic probability terms; explain the choice of language. [Data and Chance Goal 3]
(grid 1–11)

Quantitative probability

Grade 1 (grid 1–10)

Grade 2 (grid 1–12)

Grade 3
4. Predict the outcomes of simple experiments and test the predictions using manipulatives; express the probability of an event by using "_____ out of _____" language. [Data and Chance Goal 4]
(grid 1–11)

Measurement and Reference Frames

Length, weight, and angles

Grade 1
1. Use nonstandard tools and techniques to estimate and compare weight and length; measure length with standard measuring tools. [Measurement and Reference Frames Goal 1]
(grid 1–10)

Grade 2
1. Estimate length with and without tools; measure length to the nearest inch and centimeter; use standard and nonstandard tools to measure and estimate weight. [Measurement and Reference Frames Goal 1]
(grid 1–12)

Grade 3
1. Estimate length with and without tools; measure length to the nearest $\frac{1}{2}$ inch and $\frac{1}{2}$ centimeter; draw and describe angles as records of rotations. [Measurement and Reference Frames Goal 1]
(grid 1–11)

Area, perimeter, volume, and capacity

Grade 1 (grid 1–10)

Grade 2
2. Count unit squares to find the area of rectangles. [Measurement and Reference Frames Goal 2]
(grid 1–12)

Grade 3
2. Describe and use strategies to measure the perimeter of polygons; count unit squares to find the areas of rectangles. [Measurement and Reference Frames Goal 2]
(grid 1–11)

Units and systems of measurement

Grade 2: 3. Describe relationships between days in a week and hours in a day. [Measurement and Reference Frames Goal 3]

1	2	3	4	5	6	7	8	9	10	11	12

Grade 3: 3. Describe relationships among inches, feet, and yards; describe relationships between minutes in an hour, hours in a day, days in a week. [Measurement and Reference Frames Goal 3]

1	2	3	4	5	6	7	8	9	10	11

Money

Grade 1: 2. Know and compare the value of pennies, nickels, dimes, quarters, and dollar bills; make exchanges between coins. [Measurement and Reference Frames Goal 2]

1	2	3	4	5	6	7	8	9	10

Grade 2: 4. Make exchanges between coins and bills. [Measurement and Reference Frames Goal 4]

1	2	3	4	5	6	7	8	9	10	11	12

Temperature

Grade 1: 3. Identify a thermometer as a tool for measuring temperature; read temperatures on Fahrenheit and Celsius thermometers to the nearest 10°. [Measurement and Reference Frames Goal 3]

1	2	3	4	5	6	7	8	9	10

Grade 2: 5. Read temperature on both the Fahrenheit and Celsius scales. [Measurement and Reference Frames Goal 5]

1	2	3	4	5	6	7	8	9	10	11	12

Time

Grade 1: 4. Use a calendar to identify days, weeks, months, and dates; tell and show time to the nearest half and quarter hour on an analog clock. [Measurement and Reference Frames Goal 4]

1	2	3	4	5	6	7	8	9	10

Grade 2: 6. Tell and show time to the nearest five minutes on an analog clock; tell and write time in digital notation.* [Measurement and Reference Frames Goal 6]

1	2	3	4	5	6	7	8	9	10	11	12

Grade 3: 4. Tell and show time to the nearest minute on an analog clock; tell and write time in digital notation.* [Measurement and Reference Frames Goal 4]

1	2	3	4	5	6	7	8	9	10	11

*dren record their start time at the top of journal pages on a daily basis.

Geometry

Content	Grade 1	Grade 2	Grade 3
Lines and angles		1. Draw line segments and identify parallel line segments. [Geometry Goal 1]	1. Identify and draw points, intersecting and parallel line segments and lines, rays, and right angles. [Geometry Goal 1]
Plane and solid figures	1. Identify and describe plane and solid figures including circles, triangles, squares, rectangles, spheres, cylinders, rectangular prisms, pyramids, cones, and cubes. [Geometry Goal 1]	2. Identify, describe, and model plane and solid figures including circles, triangles, squares, rectangles, hexagons, trapezoids, rhombuses, spheres, cylinders, rectangular prisms, pyramids, cones, and cubes. [Geometry Goal 2]	2. Identify, describe, model, and compare plane and solid figures including circles, polygons, spheres, cylinders, rectangular prisms, pyramids, cones, and cubes using appropriate geometric terms including the terms *face, edge, vertex,* and *base.* [Geometry Goal 2]
Transformations and symmetry	2. Identify shapes having line symmetry; complete line-symmetric shapes or designs. [Geometry Goal 2]	3. Create and complete two-dimensional symmetric shapes or designs. [Geometry Goal 3]	3. Create and complete two-dimensional symmetric shapes or designs; locate multiple lines of symmetry in a two-dimensional shape. [Geometry Goal 3]

Patterns, Functions, and Algebra

Content	Grade 1	Grade 2	Grade 3
Patterns and functions	1. Extend, describe, and create numeric, visual, and concrete patterns; solve problems involving function machines, "What's My Rule?" tables, and Frames-and-Arrows diagrams. [Patterns, Functions, and Algebra Goal 1]	1. Extend, describe, and create numeric, visual, and concrete patterns; describe rules for patterns and use them to solve problems; use words and symbols to describe and write rules for functions involving addition and subtraction and use those rules to solve problems. [Patterns, Functions, and Algebra Goal 1]	1. Extend, describe, and create numeric patterns; describe rules for patterns and use them to solve problems; use words and symbols to describe and write rules for functions involving addition, subtraction, and multiplication and use those rules to solve problems. [Patterns, Functions, and Algebra Goal 1]

Content	Grade 1	Grade 2	Grade 3
Algebraic notation and solving number sentences	2. Read, write, and explain expressions and number sentences using the symbols +, −, and = and the symbols > and < with cues; solve equations involving addition and subtraction. [Patterns, Functions, and Algebra Goal 2] 1 2 3 4 5 6 7 8 9 10	2. Read, write, and explain expressions and number sentences using the symbols +, −, =, >, and <; solve number sentences involving addition and subtraction; write expressions and number sentences to model number stories. [Patterns, Functions, and Algebra Goal 2] 1 2 3 4 5 6 7 8 9 10 11 12	2. Read, write, and explain number sentences using the symbols +, −, ×, ÷, =, >, and <; solve number sentences; write expressions and number sentences to model number stories. [Patterns, Functions, and Algebra Goal 2] 1 2 3 4 5 6 7 8 9 10 11
Order of operations			3. Recognize that numeric expressions can have different values depending on the order in which operations are carried out; understand that grouping symbols can be used to affect the order in which operations are carried out. [Patterns, Functions, and Algebra Goal 3] 1 2 3 4 5 6 7 8 9 10 11
Properties of the arithmetic operations	3. Apply the Commutative Property of Addition and the Additive Identity to basic addition fact problems. [Patterns, Functions, and Algebra Goal 3] 1 2 3 4 5 6 7 8 9 10	3. Describe the Commutative and Associative Properties of Addition and apply them to mental arithmetic problems. [Patterns, Functions, and Algebra Goal 3] 1 2 3 4 5 6 7 8 9 10 11 12	4. Describe and apply the Commutative and Associative Properties of Addition, the Commutative Property of Multiplication, and the Multiplicative Identity. [Patterns, Functions, and Algebra Goal 4] 1 2 3 4 5 6 7 8 9 10 11

Throughout *Everyday Mathematics*, children repeatedly encounter skills in each of the content strands. Each exposure builds on and extends children's understanding. They study important concepts over consecutive years through a variety of formats. The Scope and Sequence Chart shows the units in which these exposures occur. The symbol ● indicates that the skill is introduced or taught. The symbol ■ indicates that the skill is revisited, practiced, or extended. These levels refer to unit content within the K–6 *Everyday Mathematics* curriculum.

The skills are divided according to the content strands below.

How to Read the Scope and Sequence Chart

Each section of the chart includes a content strand title, three grade-level columns divided by units or sections, and a list of specific skills grouped by major concepts.

Number and Numeration ●——— Content Strand

Place Value and Notation	Grade 1 Units										Grade 2 Units												Grade 3 Units										
	1	2	3	4	5	6	7	8	9	10	1	2	3	4	5	6	7	8	9	10	11	12	1	2	3	4	5	6	7	8	9	10	11
Read and write numbers to 20	●	●	●	●	●	●	●				●	●	■										●	●		●	●		●				
Read and write 2-digit numbers				●	■	●	●				●	●	●	●		●				●	●		●	●			●		●		●		
Read and write 3-digit numbers				●		●	●	■	●	●	●		●	■	■	■				●			●	●		●			●		●		
Read and write 4- and 5-digit numbers								●	●		●	●		●	●					●	●		●				●	■					

This row identifies the major mathematical concepts within each content strand. A list of related skills appear below this head.

Find specific skills in this list and then follow across the row to find where they appear in Kindergarten or at each grade level.

The colored circle indicates where the skill is introduced or taught.

The colored square indicates where the skill is primarily revisited, practiced, or extended.

Number and Numeration

	Grade 1 Units										Grade 2 Units												Grade 3 Units										
	1	2	3	4	5	6	7	8	9	10	1	2	3	4	5	6	7	8	9	10	11	12	1	2	3	4	5	6	7	8	9	10	11
Rote Counting																																	
Perform rote counting	●	●	●	●	●	●	●	●		■	●	●	●	●		●	●	●	●	●	●					●	■				●	●	
Count by 2s, 5s, and 10s forward and backward (may include the use of concrete objects)	●	●	●	●	●	●	●	●	●	●	●	●	●	●	■	●	●	●	●	●	●	■	●	■	■	●	●	■	●	●	●	●	●
Count by numbers greater than 10				●		●		●	●	●	●	●	●	●	■				●	●			●	■							●		
Count by 25s					●	●			●	●	●												●				●			■			
Count by 100s					●		●	■	●	●	●			■		●		●		●	●					■	●	■	■	■	●		■
Count up and back on a number grid	■	■		●	●		■		●	■	●	■	■			■			■	■		■	●			■		■					
Locate numbers on a number line; count up and back on a number line; complete a number line	●		●	●							●		●			●	●		●			●	●			●	●						
Count using a calculator or calculator repeat key			●		●	●	●	●	●	●	●						●			●	●		●	●	●	●	●						
Count back past zero																				●	●	●	●	●	●	●	●	■	●		●		
Count by tenths																							●				●	■					
Count by thousandths																						■	■					■					
Rational Counting																																	
Perform rational counting	●	●	●	●	●	●	●	●	●	●	●	●	●	●	●	●	●	■	●	●	●		■	●	●	●	●	●	●	●	●	●	●
Estimate quantities of objects			■	■				■		■						■		●				■		●		●			■		●	■	■
Place Value and Notation																																	
Read and write numbers to 20	●	●	●	●	●	●	●	●			●	●				●	●	●	●	●			●	●		●			●				
Read and write 2-digit numbers						■					●	●	■										●	●	●				●				
Read and write 3-digit numbers					●	●	●	●	●	●	●		●	●	■	●			■	●			●	●	●	●			●	●			●
Read and write 4- and 5-digit numbers										●	●			●						●	●		●	●	●	●	●						
Read and write 6- and 7-digit numbers											●	■				■				●								●		■			
Display and read numbers on a calculator			●		●	●		●			●		■		●	■				●	●		●	●	●	●	●	■	●	●		●	
Read, write, or use ordinal numbers		●			●	●					●									●			●										
Explore place value using a number grid					●				●		●	■								●			●				●						
Identify place value in 2-digit numbers		●	●			■		■		■	●					●		■		●	●		●			●	●			●			■

Place Value and Notation (cont.)

	1	2	3	4	5	6	7	8	9	10		1	2	3	4	5	6	7	8	9	10	11	12		1	2	3	4	5	6	7	8	9	10	11
Identify place value in 3-digit numbers		●	●					●	●	●		■	■	●	●	■	■		■		●				■				●		■	●	●	■	■
Identify place value in 4-digit numbers		●	●					●	●			■		●	●	■			■		●	■			■			●	●		●	●	●	■	■
Identify place value in larger numbers					■			●				■	■	●	●	■			■	■	■				■		■	●	●		■	●	●	■	■
Make exchanges among place values					●			●													●														
Make least and greatest numbers with randomly selected digits									■																										
Write numbers in expanded notation																						■			■			■	■				●	●	●
Use cents notation		●	●		■	■		■	■	●		●		●	■		●		■	■	●			●				■	■		●	●	●	■	■
Use dollars-and-cents notation		●	●		■		●	●	●	●	●			●	●	●	●		■	■	●	●		●			■	●	●	■	●	●	●	■	■
Use calculator to count/compute money amounts								■					■								●						■		●						
Explore uses for decimals								●																●				■		●					
Model decimals with base-10 materials																					●									●	●	●	■		
Read and write 1- and 2-digit decimals																					●			●					●	●	●	●	●	●	●
Read and write 3-digit decimals																													●			●			
Read and write decimals beyond thousandths																																			
Identify place value in decimals through thousandths																					●							■	●		●	●	●	●	●
Write decimals with expanded notation																								●					■				●	●	■

Meanings and Uses of Fractions

	1	2	3	4	5	6	7	8	9	10		1	2	3	4	5	6	7	8	9	10	11	12		1	2	3	4	5	6	7	8	9	10	11
Understand the meaning or uses of fractions								●	●	■									●	●	■	■							●	●	●	●	●	●	■
Construct concrete models of fractions and equivalent fractions; identify fractions on a number line								●	●										●	●	●	■						●	●	●	●	●	●	●	■
Identify pennies and dimes as fractional parts of a dollar																	●		●		●		■							■	●				
Identify numerator and denominator								●	●										●		●	■							●	●	●	●	●	●	●
Shade and identify fractional parts of a region								●	●									■	●	●	■								●	●	●	●	●	●	●
Shade and identify fractional parts of a set								●										■	●	●	●		■				■		●	●	●	●	●	●	●
Understand that the amount represented by a fraction depends on the size of the whole (ONE)								■											●										■				●	●	●
Identify and name mixed numbers																															●	●	●	●	■

Topic	Grade 1 Units										Grade 2 Units												Grade 3 Units										
	1	2	3	4	5	6	7	8	9	10	1	2	3	4	5	6	7	8	9	10	11	12	1	2	3	4	5	6	7	8	9	10	11
Meanings and Uses of Fractions (cont.)																																	
Write fraction words																														●	●	●	
Use fractions in number stories									■									●	■											●	●	●	■
Demonstrate the concept of percent																			■												■		
Number Theory																																	
Explore or identify even and odd numbers			●								●			●			●						●	●									
Equivalent Names for Whole Numbers																																	
Find equivalent names for numbers	●				●	●						●	●	●		●			●	●	●								●	●			
Use Roman numerals											■																						
Equivalent Names for Fractions, Decimals, and Percents																																	
Find equivalent fractions									●								■	●	●	●	●	■	●							●			
Convert between mixed numbers and fractions																		●												●			
Comparing and Ordering Numbers																																	
Compare and order numbers to 20			●		●	●					●						●	●	●				●				●						
Compare and order 2-digit numbers				●	●	●			●	●	●				●	●	●	●				●	●			●	●						
Compare and order 3-digit numbers				●					●	●													●				●						
Compare and order 4- or 5-digit numbers											●								●	●	●			■	■	■	●						
Compare and order larger numbers																				●		●				●			■				
Compare numbers using the symbols <, >, and =					●				●														●										
Explore magnitude of numbers																											●						
Compare and order fractions; use manipulatives to identify/compare fractions									■									●	●	●													
Compare fractions less than one																		●												●			
Compare and order decimals																						■	●					■		■		■	
Explore uses for positive and negative numbers (integers)																															●		
Explore zero as a reference point																															●		

Operations and Computation

Addition and Subtraction Facts	Grade 1 Units												Grade 2 Units												Grade 3 Units										
	1	2	3	4	5	6	7	8	9	10	11	12	1	2	3	4	5	6	7	8	9	10	11	12	1	2	3	4	5	6	7	8	9	10	11
Find/use complements of 10	●	●	■	■	■	■		●	●											●													●		
Practice basic facts; know +/− fact families	●	●	●	●	●	●	●		■	■	■	■	■	●	■	●	■	●	●	■	●	●	●	●	●	●	●	■	■	■			●	●	●
Practice extensions of basic facts									■					■									●	■	■	●	■	●	■	■	■				●
Make and solve number-grid puzzles				●					●	●				●											■	■		■		■	■				
Addition and Subtraction Procedures	1	2	3	4	5	6	7	8	9	10	11	12	1	2	3	4	5	6	7	8	9	10	11	12	1	2	3	4	5	6	7	8	9	10	11
Understand meaning of addition/subtraction; model addition/subtraction using concrete objects	●	●	●	●	●	●		●	●				●	●	●	●	●	●	●						●	●			●		●	■			
Investigate the inverse relationships between addition and subtraction					●	●							●	●												●									
Use mental arithmetic or fact strategies to add/subtract			●		●	●			●				●	●	●	●	●	●	●		■	■	●		●	●			■		●	■	■	■	●
Use addition/subtraction algorithms																		●	●				●		■	●			■		●	■			
Explore calculator functions					●	●			■				●	●			●	●							■	●					●		●	●	
Make up and/or solve addition/subtraction number stories; determine operation needed to solve a problem	●	●	●	●	●	●	●	●	●	●	●	●	●	●	●	●	●	●	●	●	●	●	●	●	●	●	■	●	■	■	●	●	■	■	●
Use an Addition/Subtraction Facts Table	●		■		●	●								●												●									
Add/subtract using a number grid	●				●					●			●					●					■			●									
Add/subtract using a number line	●				■													●							■	■									
Add/subtract using a calculator					●	●			●				●	●			●	■	●			■			●	●				■	●		●		
Add/subtract multiples of 10										●	●	●	●	●										●	●										
Add 3 or more 1-digit numbers					●	●			●	●	●		●				●	●	●												■				
Add/subtract 2-digit numbers						●							●	■							■							■		■	■				
Add 3 or more 2-digit numbers														■		●		■		■								■			●				
Add/subtract 3- and 4-digit numbers						●		●	●	●			●	●		●	●	●	●		●	●	●	●	●	●	■	●	■		●		■		■
Add/subtract money amounts/decimals; make change						●		●	●	●						■		■				●	●	●		●		●			●		■		■
Solve money number stories					●				●	●									●						●	●							■		■
Make change																		■							●	●							■		■

Operations and Computation (cont.)

	Grade 1 Units										Grade 2 Units												Grade 3 Units										
	1	2	3	4	5	6	7	8	9	10	1	2	3	4	5	6	7	8	9	10	11	12	1	2	3	4	5	6	7	8	9	10	11
Addition and Subtraction Procedures (cont.)																																	
Use positive and negative numbers (integers) in number stories																															●		
Multiplication and Division Facts																																	
Practice multiplication/division facts																										●			●	■	●		■
Find complements for multiples of 10																	●										●		■			■	
Recognize and know square products																													■				
Multiplication and Division Procedures																																	
Use manipulatives, drawings/arrays, number sentences, repeated addition, or story problems to explain and demonstrate the meaning of multiplication/division				●				●							■			●			●	●			●	●		■	●	■	●		
Understand meaning of multiplication/division and related vocabulary															●	●										●		■			●		
Make up and/or solve multiplication/division number stories																●	●				●	●			●	●	●		●		●		
Investigate relationships between multiplication and division																●										■		■	●		■		
Multiply/divide using a number line or number grid																■										■			●				■
Explore square numbers																					●							●	●				■
Interpret a remainder in division number stories																													■		●		
Solve multi-step multiplication/division number stories																						■									●		
Make difference and ratio comparisons																											●		●				
Multiply/divide with 2-digit numbers																															■		
Use a calculator to multiply or divide																					●					●			●		●		
Use a Multiplication/Division Facts Table																					●					●			●		●		
Use mental arithmetic to multiply/divide																					●								●		●		
Multiply/divide multiples of 10, 100, and 1,000 by 1-digit numbers																					■			●		●		■	■	■	●		
Use multiplication/division algorithms																					■					●	●				■		
Multiply multidigit numbers by 1- or 2-digit numbers																					■					●					●		■

504   **Scope and Sequence Chart**

Grade-Level Goals — Operations and Computation (continued)

The following chart uses ● to indicate a Program Goal that is a focus in a grade and ■ to indicate a Program Goal that is developed, maintained, or applied.

Multiplication and Division Procedures (cont.)

Goal	1	2	3	4	5	6	7	8	9	10	11		1	2	3	4	5	6	7	8	9	10	11	12		1	2	3	4	5	6	7	8	9	10
Multiply/divide money amounts	■			■	●	■	●	■	●	●	■																								
Identify factors of a number				●	●	■		●	●		■													■											

Procedures for Addition and Subtraction of Fractions

Goal	1	2	3	4	5	6	7	8	9	10	11		1	2	3	4	5	6	7	8	9	10	11	12		1	2	3	4	5	6	7	8	9	10
Add/subtract positive and negative numbers, fractions, and decimals	■	●						●	●																										

Computational Estimation

Goal	1	2	3	4	5	6	7	8	9	10	11		1	2	3	4	5	6	7	8	9	10	11	12		1	2	3	4	5	6	7	8	9	10
Estimate reasonableness of answers to basic facts	■	●		■	■	■		■	●	■																		●	■	■		■	●	■
Use estimation strategies to add/subtract; make ballpark estimates	●	●	■	●	●	■	■			●											●		●			●								
Round whole numbers to the nearest ten																						■				●								
Use estimation to multiply/divide				●			●		●	●									●	●		●		●										
Estimate costs			●		●	■		■								●					●	●		●							■			

Models for Operations

Goal	1	2	3	4	5	6	7	8	9	10	11	12		1	2	3	4	5	6	7	8	9	10		1	2	3	4	5	6	7	8	9	10
Solve change-to-more and change-to-less number stories/diagrams	●	●	●						●		●			●					●					●				●			■			
Solve parts-and-total number stories/diagrams	●	●	■	●	●	●		●	●	■	●			●	●			●	●			●						●	■	■		●	●	
Solve comparison number stories/diagrams		●	■	■	■	●	■	■	■	●	●			●				●				●												
Solve missing factor number models							■		■	●		■										●								●	■	●	●	●
Solve equal-grouping and equal-sharing division problems					■					■						●		●			●	●							●	●			●	●

Data and Chance

Data Collection and Representation

	Grade 1 Units										Grade 2 Units												Grade 3 Units										
	1	2	3	4	5	6	7	8	9	10	1	2	3	4	5	6	7	8	9	10	11	12	1	2	3	4	5	6	7	8	9	10	11
Collect data by counting	■															●	●					●			●	●					●		
Collect data by interviewing	●															■							●										
Collect data from print sources and/or posters																			■			●					●		■			●	●
Collect data from a map																			●								●					●	
Use a weather map										●												●					●						●
Conduct a survey					●	●										●																	●
Make a tally chart					●	■					■		●			●								●	■								
Record data in a table/chart	●			●		●							●			●	●					●	●		■	●				■		●	●
Record days/events on a timeline																			■						■			■					
Create/interpret a bar graph, pictograph, or Venn diagram				●	●	●		■	■	●			●			●	●					●	■			●	■			■			
Create/interpret a line plot			●			■											●					●	■							■			
Explore graphing software to make a bar graph or line plot				●		●				●						■						●	■				■	■					●

Data Analysis

	Grade 1 Units										Grade 2 Units												Grade 3 Units										
	1	2	3	4	5	6	7	8	9	10	1	2	3	4	5	6	7	8	9	10	11	12	1	2	3	4	5	6	7	8	9	10	11
Read tables, graphs, and maps (including map scale, scale drawing)	●	●	●	●		●				●	●	●	●						●			●				●	●						●
Use a scale drawing																											●						
Summarize and interpret data	●	●	●	●		●				■						●						●				●						●	●
Compare two sets of data; use calculator to compare data						■			■			■				■													■	■			■
Make predictions about data		●				●							●			●							■							●			
Make a frequency table						●											●					●	■				●						
Compare quantities from a bar graph			●		■	●									■	■								■	■								
Find the minimum/maximum of a data set						●				●			●				●					●	●			■	●				■	●	●
Find the range				●						■			●							■		●				●					■	●	●
Find the median				●						●			●				●					●				■					■	●	●
Find the mode										●												●				■					●		■

506   Scope and Sequence Chart

Data Analysis (cont.)																																	
	1	2	3	4	5	6	7	8	9	10	1	2	3	4	5	6	7	8	9	10	11	12	1	2	3	4	5	6	7	8	9	10	11
Find the mean																									●	■	■				■	●	■	●
Use data in problem solving	●	●	●	●		●	●										●		■	■	■	●		●							●	●	●	●

Qualitative and Quantitative Probability																																		
	1	2	3	4	5	6	7	8	9	10	11	1	2	3	4	5	6	7	8	9	10	11	12	1	2	3	4	5	6	7	8	9	10	11
Understand and use the language of probability to discuss likelihood of a given situation (using words such as *certain, likely, unlikely, always, maybe, sometimes, never, possible, impossible*)	■		■	■	●	■	■	■	■	■		■	■	■	■	■	■	■	■					●		●	■				■	■	■	●
Explore equal-chance events					●	●		■																			■				●	■	■	
Explore fair and unfair games																											●					■		●
Classify events																								●								■		●
Predict outcomes; solve problems involving chance outcomes	●	●	■	■	■	■							●					■						●		●	●			●	●	■	●	●
Conduct experiments; test predictions using concrete objects		●																								●	●			●	●	■	●	●
Use fractions to record probabilities of events																															●			●
Find combinations (Cartesian products)								■										■	■											●		■		
Understand area model of probability and solve simple spinner problems																														●	●	■	●	●
Explore random sampling																										●					●	■	■	●

Measurement and Reference Frames

Length, Weight, and Angles	Grade 1 Units										Grade 2 Units												Grade 3 Units										
	1	2	3	4	5	6	7	8	9	10	1	2	3	4	5	6	7	8	9	10	11	12	1	2	3	4	5	6	7	8	9	10	11
Name tools used to measure length	●																■		●					■	●						■	■	
Estimate, compare, and order lengths/heights of objects	●		■	●		●			●	●				■		■			●	■				■	●	■						■	
Measure lengths with nonstandard units				●															●	■					●								
Measure to the nearest foot				●															●						●								
Measure to the nearest inch				●					●					●					●						●						■		
Measure to the nearest $\frac{1}{2}$ inch				●													●		●						●						●	●	
Measure to the nearest $\frac{1}{4}$ inch					■													■												●	●		
Measure to the nearest $\frac{1}{8}$ inch																										■					■		
Investigate the yard																			●						●								
Measure to the nearest yard																			●						●								
Measure to the nearest centimeter						●								●					●				●		●								
Measure to the nearest $\frac{1}{2}$ centimeter															■					■	■				●	■	■				●	●	
Measure to the nearest millimeter																			●						●								
Investigate the meter						●													●						■								
Measure to the nearest meter and/or decimeter																			●						●							●	
Relate decimals to metric measurement																			●								■					●	
Solve length/height number stories																		■			■											■	
Investigate the mile and/or kilometer																		■	●	■											■	●	
Estimate and compare distances																		■	●													●	
Read measurement to the nearest mile																																	
Solve distance number stories																				■							■						
Estimate, compare, and order weights									■			■						■	●	■						●						●	
Name tools used to measure weight																			●													●	
Order objects by weight					●	●																										●	
Use a pan balance					●	●					●	●																				●	

Length, Weight, and Angles (cont.)

- Use a bath scale
- Use a spring scale
- Choose the appropriate scale
- Solve weight number stories
- Measure angles with nonstandard units
- Draw angles to record rotations

Area, Perimeter, Volume, and Capacity

- Investigate area
- Find the area of regular shapes concretely
- Find the perimeter of regular shapes concretely, graphically, or with pictorial models
- Find the area of a rectangular region divided into square units
- Find the area of irregular shapes concretely
- Find the perimeter of irregular shapes concretely, graphically, or with pictorial models
- Estimate area
- Estimate perimeter
- Compare perimeter and area
- Name tools used to measure area
- Estimate volume/capacity
- Name tools used to measure volume and/or capacity
- Find volume
- Measure capacities of irregular containers
- Compare and order the capacities of containers
- Order objects by volume
- Investigate the relationship between volume and weight

Measurement and Reference Frames (cont.)

	Grade 1 Units										Grade 2 Units												Grade 3 Units										
	1	2	3	4	5	6	7	8	9	10	1	2	3	4	5	6	7	8	9	10	11	12	1	2	3	4	5	6	7	8	9	10	11
Area, Perimeter, Volume, and Capacity (cont.)																																	
Explore the relationship between diameter and circumference; measure diameter and circumference																									●			●					
Units and Systems of Measurement																																	
Select and use appropriate nonstandard units to measure time																			■							■				■	■	■	■
Estimate the duration of a minute		●																					●			■						■	
Investigate the duration of an hour			●																									●					
Investigate 1-minute intervals											■											■	■										
Identify equivalent customary units of length												●	●						●						●	■	■				●	●	
Identify equivalent metric units of length												●	●						●						●	■	■				●	●	
Identify customary and/or metric units of weight																			●											■	●	●	
Identify equivalent customary units of weight																			●												●	●	
Identify customary and/or metric units of capacity									●										●											■	●	●	
Identify equivalent customary/metric units of capacity																			●												●	●	
Choose the appropriate unit of measure													●						●						●	■	●				●	●	
Money																																	
Recognize pennies and nickels	●		■		■			■				■	■	●	■	■	■	■	■	■	■	■											
Recognize dimes		●	●	●			■	●	●	●	●	■	■	●	■	■	■	■	■	■	■	■											
Recognize quarters						●	●	●			●	■	■	●	■			■	■	■	■	■											
Recognize dollars								●			●			■						■	■	■											
Calculate the value of coin combinations					■	●	●	●	●	●	●			●	●				■	●								●					
Calculate the value of bill combinations											●			■		■	■		■	●													
Calculate the value of coins/bills		●						●			●			●			●	●										●		●			
Compare values of sets of coins or money amounts using <, >, and = symbols			■		●	●	■	■	■	■	■			●	■	■	■	■	■	■			●			■	■		●				●
Identify equivalencies and make coin exchanges	●	●	●			●			●		■			●	●	●		●	●	●							■						

Money (cont.)

Identify equivalencies and make coin/bill exchanges

Temperature

Use a thermometer

Use the Fahrenheit temperature scale

Use the Celsius temperature scale

Solve temperature number stories

Time

Demonstrate an understanding of the concepts of time; estimates and measures the passage of time using words like *before, after, yesterday, today, tomorrow, morning, afternoon, hour, half-hour*

Order or compare events according to duration; calculate elapsed time

Name tools used to measure time

Relates past events to future events

Investigate A.M. and P.M.

Use the calendar; identify today's date

Number and name the months in a year or days of the week

Investigate the second hand; compare the hour and minute hands

Use an analog or digital clock to tell time on the hour

Tell time on the half-hour

Tell time on the quarter-hour

Tell time to the nearest 5 minutes

Use digital notation*

Tell time to the nearest minute*

Read time in different ways and/or identify time equivalencies

Solve time number stories

*In Grades 2 and 3, children record their start time at the top of journal pages on a daily basis.

Coordinate Systems	G1-1	G1-2	G1-3	G1-4	G1-5	G1-6	G1-7	G1-8	G1-9	G1-10	G2-1	G2-2	G2-3	G2-4	G2-5	G2-6	G2-7	G2-8	G2-9	G2-10	G2-11	G2-12	G3-1	G3-2	G3-3	G3-4	G3-5	G3-6	G3-7	G3-8	G3-9	G3-10	G3-11
Find and name locations with simple relationships on a coordinate system									■																							●	
Identify, locate, and plot ordered pairs on a graph																																●	

Geometry

Lines and Angles	G1-1	G1-2	G1-3	G1-4	G1-5	G1-6	G1-7	G1-8	G1-9	G1-10	G2-1	G2-2	G2-3	G2-4	G2-5	G2-6	G2-7	G2-8	G2-9	G2-10	G2-11	G2-12	G3-1	G3-2	G3-3	G3-4	G3-5	G3-6	G3-7	G3-8	G3-9	G3-10	G3-11
Identify and name line segments																					■		●				●	●	■		●		
Draw line segments with a straightedge					●										●		■	■									●	●	■				
Draw line segments to a specified length														■				■	■									●		●			
Draw designs with line segments																■										●					●		
Identify and name points															●													●			●		
Model parallel lines on a geoboard															●																		
Draw parallel lines with a straightedge															●													●	●				
Identify and name lines																												●	■				
Identify, name, and/or model intersecting lines using concrete objects															●				■									●	●				
Identify parallel, nonparallel, and intersecting line segments																												●	■				
Identify and name rays																												●	●				
Draw lines and rays																												●	●				
Identify parts of an angle and name angles																												●				■	
Model line segments, rays, and angles																												●				■	
Measure angles with degree units																												●				■	●
Solve degree problems																																	●

Plane and Solid Figures

Skill	1	2	3	4	5	6	7	8	9	10	11
Explore shape relationships			●			●			▪		
Recognizes open and closed figures						▪			▪		
Identify characteristics of 2-dimensional shapes; sort shapes by attributes						▪	●	●			
Explore 2-dimensional shapes utilizing technology or multimedia resources				●		▪			▪		
Identify characteristics and use appropriate vocabulary to describe properties of 2-dimensional shapes			●			●	▪		●	▪	
Construct models of polygons using manipulatives such as straws, geoboards			●		▪	●					
Draw 2-dimensional shapes (such as triangles and quadrilaterals); draw/describe objects in the environment that depict geometric figures			●		▪	●	▪				
Create/extend designs with 2-dimensional shapes						●			▪		
Combine shapes and take them apart to form other shapes						●	●		●		
Record shapes or designs			▪		▪	●					
Identify and draw congruent or similar shapes					●	●	●				
Classify and name polygons			●		●	●	●				
Compare 2-dimensional shapes							▪				
Compare polygons and non-polygons									▪		
Solve 2-dimensional-shapes problems					▪	●					
Identify/compare 3-dimensional shapes; sort shapes and/or describe attributes of each group			▪		●	●	●			●	
Construct 3-dimensional shapes						●			●		
Identify the number of faces, edges, vertices, and bases of prisms and pyramids					●	●	●	▪		●	
Identify the shapes of faces						●				●	
Explore slanted 3-dimensional shapes						●				▪	

Skill	1	2	3	4	5	6	7	8	9	10	11	12
Explore shape relationships					●				●	▪	▪	▪
Recognizes open and closed figures		▪										▪
Identify characteristics of 2-dimensional shapes; sort shapes by attributes					●							▪
Explore 2-dimensional shapes utilizing technology or multimedia resources												
Identify characteristics and use appropriate vocabulary to describe properties of 2-dimensional shapes	▪			▪	●							
Construct models of polygons using manipulatives such as straws, geoboards	▪			●	●				●			
Draw 2-dimensional shapes (such as triangles and quadrilaterals); draw/describe objects in the environment that depict geometric figures	●				●				●			
Create/extend designs with 2-dimensional shapes	▪			▪	●	●	●		▪			▪
Combine shapes and take them apart to form other shapes			●		●			●	●	●		
Record shapes or designs				●								
Identify and draw congruent or similar shapes			▪				●	●	▪			▪
Classify and name polygons	●	●			●	●		●				▪
Compare 2-dimensional shapes					●		●					
Compare polygons and non-polygons							▪					
Solve 2-dimensional-shapes problems		▪			▪							
Identify/compare 3-dimensional shapes; sort shapes and/or describe attributes of each group	●			▪	●	▪			▪			▪
Construct 3-dimensional shapes					●				●			
Identify the number of faces, edges, vertices, and bases of prisms and pyramids					●							
Identify the shapes of faces												
Explore slanted 3-dimensional shapes												

Skill	1	2	3	4	5	6	7	8	9	10
Explore shape relationships	●	▪							●	
Recognizes open and closed figures				▪						
Identify characteristics of 2-dimensional shapes; sort shapes by attributes		▪				●	●	▪	▪	●
Explore 2-dimensional shapes utilizing technology or multimedia resources							●			
Identify characteristics and use appropriate vocabulary to describe properties of 2-dimensional shapes	●			●	●					
Construct models of polygons using manipulatives such as straws, geoboards	▪		●	●		●		●		●
Draw 2-dimensional shapes (such as triangles and quadrilaterals); draw/describe objects in the environment that depict geometric figures	●		●							
Create/extend designs with 2-dimensional shapes	▪			▪	●	●	●		●	
Combine shapes and take them apart to form other shapes				●	●			●		
Record shapes or designs				●						
Identify and draw congruent or similar shapes					▪		●	▪	▪	
Classify and name polygons	●				●	●		●		
Compare 2-dimensional shapes					●		●			
Compare polygons and non-polygons							▪			
Solve 2-dimensional-shapes problems										
Identify/compare 3-dimensional shapes; sort shapes and/or describe attributes of each group	●			▪	●	▪			▪	●
Construct 3-dimensional shapes										●
Identify the number of faces, edges, vertices, and bases of prisms and pyramids										
Identify the shapes of faces						▪	▪			
Explore slanted 3-dimensional shapes							▪			

Transformations and Symmetry

Skill	1	2	3	4	5	6	7	8	9	10	11
Identify symmetrical figures or symmetry in the environment (Block A)					●	●		●			
Identify symmetrical figures or symmetry in the environment (Block B)				▪	●		●	▪	●		
Identify symmetrical figures or symmetry in the environment (Block C)							●			

Geometry (cont.)

Transformations and Symmetry (cont.)	Grade 1 Units										Grade 2 Units												Grade 3 Units										
	1	2	3	4	5	6	7	8	9	10	1	2	3	4	5	6	7	8	9	10	11	12	1	2	3	4	5	6	7	8	9	10	11
Fold and cut symmetrical shapes							●	■							●													●					
Create/complete a symmetrical design/shape using concrete models, geoboard, and/or technology							●		●						●	■		■										●		■			
Identify lines of symmetry							●		●						●	■	■		■								■	●	■	●			
Use objects to explore slides, flips, and turns; predict the results of changing a shape's position or orientation using slides, flips, and turns			●												■													■					
Model clockwise and counterclockwise turns/rotations																												●					●

Spatial	1	2	3	4	5	6	7	8	9	10	1	2	3	4	5	6	7	8	9	10	11	12	1	2	3	4	5	6	7	8	9	10	11
Recognize that the quantity remains the same when the spatial arrangement changes		●																															
Arrange or describe objects by proximity, position, or direction using words such as over, under, above, below, inside, outside, beside, in front of, behind			●				●		●																			●					
Give or follow directions for finding a place or object						●	■													■								●					
Identify structures from different views or match views of the same structures portrayed from different perspectives														■														●					

Patterns, Functions, and Algebra

Patterns and Functions	Grade 1 Units										Grade 2 Units												Grade 3 Units										
	1	2	3	4	5	6	7	8	9	10	1	2	3	4	5	6	7	8	9	10	11	12	1	2	3	4	5	6	7	8	9	10	11
Explore and extend visual patterns		■	●	■	●	●	●										●							■		■		●	■		●		●
Find patterns and common attributes in objects and people in the real world		■		●	●									●	●	■								●				●					
Create and complete patterns with 2-dimensional shapes	■		●					●		●							●	●		●						●	●	■					
Identify and use patterns on a number grid			■	●	●	■	■		■	●	■			■	■		●			■				■	■	●	●	■					
Add and subtract using a number grid																							●	●									
Investigate even and odd number patterns; create, describe, extend simple number patterns/sequences		●	●	■							■				■								●			■				■		■	
Explore counting patterns using a calculator		●	●					●			●						●						●										
Solve "What's My Rule?" (function machine) problems				●	●	●			■		■	●		●	●		●			●	●			●		●			●	■	●	●	●
Solve Frames-and-Arrows problems with one or two rules			●	■	■	■			■	■	■		●						■		■		■			●							■
Find patterns in addition and subtraction facts			●		●	●	●	●			■					■	●						●	●		●			●				
Explore patterns in doubling or halving numbers					●												●																
Find patterns in multiplication and division facts						●			■	●	■			■	■		■		●	●	●		■	●	■	●		■	●	●		●	●
Find patterns in multiples of 10, 100, and 1,000																				■	●								■				
Investigate square numbers																																	
Find number patterns that describe the relationship between similar figures																									●								
Identify and/or use number patterns in data or to solve problems																						■	●	●			●		●	■	●	■	■

Algebraic Notation and Solving Number Sentences	1	2	3	4	5	6	7	8	9	10	1	2	3	4	5	6	7	8	9	10	11	12	1	2	3	4	5	6	7	8	9	10	11
Use symbols ×, ÷, =			●		●											●	●		●	●	●	●	●			●	●		●	●	●	●	
Use symbols +, −, =; pictures; manipulatives; and models to organize, record, and communicate mathematical ideas	●						●			●	●	■	●	●	■	■	■	●	●	●	●	■	●	●	●	■	■		■	■		■	
Compare numbers using <, > symbols					●						●			■					■	●			●				●						
Write/solve addition and subtraction number sentences	●										●		●	●	●				●	●	●		●	●		●			●	■		■	
Write/solve number sentences with missing addends					●							●									●		●	●									

Algebraic Notation and Solving Number Sentences	Grade 1 Units										Grade 2 Units												Grade 3 Units										
	1	2	3	4	5	6	7	8	9	10	1	2	3	4	5	6	7	8	9	10	11	12	1	2	3	4	5	6	7	8	9	10	11
Write/solve multiplication number sentences																●	●				●	●				●	●	●	●	■	■	■	
Write/solve division number sentences																					●	●				●		■			■		
Write/solve number sentences with missing factors; know that symbols can be used to represent missing or unknown quantities												●									●	●		●		●				■			

Order of Operations	Grade 1 Units										Grade 2 Units												Grade 3 Units										
	1	2	3	4	5	6	7	8	9	10	1	2	3	4	5	6	7	8	9	10	11	12	1	2	3	4	5	6	7	8	9	10	11
Make up and/or solve number sentences involving parentheses																				●									●		■		
Add/subtract 2-digit numbers in number sentences containing parentheses																												■	●	■		■	

Properties of Arithmetic Operations	Grade 1 Units										Grade 2 Units												Grade 3 Units										
	1	2	3	4	5	6	7	8	9	10	1	2	3	4	5	6	7	8	9	10	11	12	1	2	3	4	5	6	7	8	9	10	11
Investigate properties of addition/subtraction					■							●													■		●		●				
Investigate properties of multiplication/division																					●			●		●			●			●	
Explore number properties (commutative, zero, and identity)					■																		■	●		●		■	●				

Index

Liter cube, 699–702
Lost-and-Found Box, 25

Magic squares, completing, 205, 774
Making Change, 227
Making-change problems, 759
Making Shapes out of Triangles and
    Rectangles, 341
Manipulatives, 381, 402. *See also*
    Base-10 blocks
  attribute blocks, 264, 285, 335
  base-10 blocks, 73–75, 185–188,
    206, 295–296, 403–404, 406,
    552, 558, 765–766, 768, 773,
    814, 817
  Everything Math Deck, 35, 189,
    627, 695
  Fact Triangles, 626–630, 632–634,
    697, 891
  pattern blocks, 35, 265, 342, 608,
    611–612, 614, 760
Maps, 684–685, 687
Math Boxes, 16, 43, 49, 54, 59, 63,
    75, 79, 97, 103, etc.
Mathematics, talking about, 19
Mathematics All Around Bulletin
    Board, 19, 22
Math Journal, introducing, 20
Math Message, 14, 18–19, 24, 29, 34,
    39, 43, 47, 52, 56, 62, etc.
Math Word Bank
  building, 50, 110, 115, 160, 195,
    201, 212, 264–265, 287, 293,
    331, 417, 423, 564, 625, 635,
    665, 698, 709, 736, 752, 823,
    829, 839, 895, 907
  template for, 50
Maximum, 208, 905
Maze practice routine, 103
Mean. *See* Average
Measurement
  discussing need for accurate,
    673–674
  of objects, 574, 580
  units of, 687
Measurement fractions, 630
Measures All Around Museum, 664,
    665, 667, 679
Measuring cups, 704
Measuring spoons, 704
Median, 210, 577, 579, 581, 586,
    661,759, 898, 899, 905
  of arm span lengths, 554
  discussing meanings of, 581
  finding, 741
  finding for standing long jumps,
    578–579
  finding of distances, 898–899
Mental Math and Reflexes, 19, 24, 29,
    34, 39, 43, 47, 52, 56, 62, etc.
Meters, 677, 680
  as standard length, 662, 663
Meterstick, 663
Metric system, 663
  units of capacity in, 702

units of length in, 283–284,
    662–663, 668, 677, 680,
    684–685
Middle number, 208–209, 577
Midyear Assessment, 437
Mile, 684
Military time, 877
Milliliter, 702
Millimeters, 675
Minimum, 208, 873
Minuend, 127, 403
Minute hand on analog clocks, 30, 198
  estimating time with, 199
Minute Math®+, 45, 50, 75, 115, 137,
    160, 165, 206, 229, 281, 299,
    321, 348, 400, 411, 569, 587,
    615, 630, 639, 704, 709, 736,
    768, 774,839, 845
Missing-factor number model, 895
Missing-part number stories, 259
Mode, 210, 585, 661, 903, 905
Models. *See also* Base-10 blocks;
    Number models
  for addition number stories, 98
  for equal-sharing number stories,
    431–432
  exploring doubles with, 109
  place value, 188
  for properties of tens, 292–293
Money, 694–698. *See also* Coins;
    specific coins
  addition number stories with,
    802–806
  amounts with calculator, 737–742
  buying items with exact change
    only, 225
  buying items without exact change,
    226
  comparing place value with Base-10
    blocks and, 766
  counting, 39, 729
  decimal notation for, 733
  displaying, on calculator, 742
  estimating costs, 272–276, 748–752
  exploring relationships among
    pennies, dimes, and collars,
    735–736
  finding the cost of two or more
    items, 256
  finding ways to make a dollar, 698
  games with
    Dollar Rummy, 211, 336
    Money Exchange, 40, 766
    Spinning for Money, 193, 729
  making change in, 753–757
    by counting up, 219–223
  making equivalent amounts with
    coins and bills, 728
  making vending machines
    purchases, 227
  problem solving with, 59, 747
  reviewing exchanges, 728, 729
  reviewing values of coins and bills,
    727
  sharing, 567
  shopping activities and, 277–281

subtraction number stories with,
    807–811
  subtraction of, 402
  using calculator to solve problems
    with, 743–747
  using ten frames to estimate
    amounts, 806
Money Exchange Game, 40, 766
Month
  building calendar for, 29–30
  number of, in year, 29
More
  measuring, than one foot, 670
  using a scale to show, 253
More than, 635
Multidigit addition, 278–279, 291,
    293, 320, 389, 686, 806, 876
Multidigit subtraction, 817, 876
Multiple-addend problems, 385, 430,
    803–804
Multiples of 10, 545
  addition of, 292–293, 295, 379
  finding next, 553
  making, 553
  subtraction of, 379
Multiples of equal groups, 818–823
  problems, solving, 823
Multiplication
  analyzing strategies in, 889
  with arrays, 422, 424–428, 889
  doubling in, to multiply by 2, 849
  of equal groups, 413, 545
  with Fact Triangles, 848
  by 5, 832, 844
  games,140
  inverse relationship, 890–895
  products, 835–839
  reviewing ideas and terms, 820
  by 10, 832, 844
  turn-around rule for, 878, 891
  by 2, 832, 844
Multiplication-array number stories,
    418–423
Multiplication diagrams, 419, 819,
    825, 836, 841–842
  for division, 433
Multiplication/division diagrams,
    825–826
Multiplication/division fact families,
    840–845
Multiplication facts, 830–840,
    847–849, 873, 884–889, 903
  discussing meaning of, 831
  doubles, 885
  with Fact Triangles, 869, 887
  listing from 2s to 10s, 832–833
  solving related problems, 893
  times-2, 885
Multiplication Fact Triangle, 844,
    848, 869, 887, 889
Multiplication shortcuts and strategies
  0-shortcut, 886
  1-shortcut, 886
  A times-2 strategy, 887
  A times-5 strategy, 887
  A times-10 strategy, 887
  turn-around rule, 886

x-by-y arrays, 420, 425

Yard, 662
  as standard length, 662–663
Yardsticks, checking estimates by
      measuring distances with, 663
Years, leap, 868, 871

Zero
  numbers below, 19, 58
  as place holder, 744, 766, 777

Notes

Notes

Notes

Notes

Notes